strada lex

Activering van het boek online
Identificatiecode

Indien u abonnee bent van Strada lex **www.stradalex.com**, Strada lex Luxembourg **www.stradalex.lu** of Strada lex Europe **www.stradalex.eu** kunt u gratis, met behulp van bovenstaande identificatiecode, toegang krijgen tot de elektronische versie van voorliggend boek*.

Mocht u moeilijkheden ondervinden bij het activeren gelieve dan contact op te nemen met onze helpdesk: **tel. : +32(0)2 548 07 20** • **fax : +32(0)2 548 07 22** • **info@stradalex.com**. U dient een aankoopbewijs van het boek voor te kunnen leggen.

De identificatiecode kan slechts éénmaal door één enkele gebruiker, geïdentificeerd als abonnee van Strada lex, geactiveerd worden. Eenmaal geactiveerd, kan het boek geraadpleegd worden binnen de modaliteiten van uw abonnement op Strada lex.

U bent nog geen abonnee op één van onze databanken en u wenst hierover meer informatie te ontvangen of een presentatie van één van onze vertegenwoordigers? Neem dan snel contact op via het e-mailadres info@stradalex.com.

Onder voorbehoud van beschikbaarheid in één van de vermelde databanken. Ga naar www.larcier.com om na te gaan in welke databank(en) deze monografie toegankelijk is.

DISCRIMINATION IN ONLINE PLATFORMS

DISCRIMINATION IN ONLINE PLATFORMS

A Comparative Law Approach to Design, Intermediation and Data Challenges

Ana Maria CORRÊA

◭ INTERSENTIA

Cambridge – Antwerp – Chicago

Intersentia Ltd
8 Wellington Mews | Wellington Street
Cambridge | CB1 1HW | United Kingdom
Tel.: +44 1223 736 170
Email: mail@intersentia.co.uk
www.intersentia.com | www.intersentia.co.uk

Distribution for the UK and the rest of the world (incl. Eastern Europe):
NBN International
1 Deltic Avenue, Rooksley
Milton Keynes MK13 8LD
United Kingdom
Tel.: +44 1752 202 301 | Fax: +44 1752 202 331
Email: orders@nbninternational.com

Distribution for Europe:
Lefebvre Sarrut Belgium NV
Hoogstraat 139/6
1000 Brussels
Belgium
Tel.: +32 3 680 15 50 | Fax: +32 3 658 71 21
Email: mail@intersentia.be

Distribution for the USA and Canada:
Independent Publishers Group
Order Department
814 North Franklin Street
Chicago, IL60610
USA
Tel.: +1 800 888 4741 (toll free) | Fax: +1312 337 5985
Email: orders@ipgbook.com

Discrimination in online platforms. A Comparative Law
Approach to Design, Intermediation and Data Challenges
© Ana Maria Corrêa 2022

Cover design: © Steve Johnson / www.pexels.com/photo/art-graffiti-dirty-brush-
7338719/

ISBN 978-1-83970-288-4 (paperback)
ISBN 978-1-83970-289-1 (PDF)
D/2022/7849/124
NUR 820

British Library Cataloguing in Publication Data. A catalogue record for this book is available from the British Library.

ACKNOWLEDGEMENTS

An academic book is never a solitary work but the result of constant interactions between the author and selected expert readers, drafting and redrafting, material support, and a good dose of resilience. This particular book is the outcome of my PhD research, my thesis and updates I was able to provide during my post-doctoral fellowship at CiTiP/KU Leuven. I would like to deeply thank professor Anton Vedder for his mentorship and the CiTiP's board of directors for all the necessary support to have this manuscript published.

I also would like to express my gratitude to my PhD supervisor Isabelle Rorive at the ULB. Along my doctoral path, she has assisted me above and beyond her expected professional duties. When I first arrived in Brussels, still without a permanent place to settle, and with everything getting closed and inaccessible in Belgium because of the terrorist attacks in 2015, she offered me a room at her own house. It is worth mentioning that she had met me in person only a couple of times before that. This very short anecdote is illustrative of her generosity across years of our collaboration. Since then, I have had the great chance to work with her in several interesting projects. I learned so much. I had the opportunity to contribute in the production of her book project, to write an article and book chapter together, to present our research in Brussels, Stockholm, Rio de Janeiro and Nice, to participate in the coordination of the *Equality Law Clinic*, to give classes in the Comparative Law Course, to be introduced to the *Berkeley Comparative Equality & Antidiscrimination Law Study Group*, and to have her closely guide to my thesis research. All these experiences, in addition to the funds provided by her project Human Rights Integration (PAI Belspo) that allowed me to present my research in conferences at the *Queen Mary University*, in London, *Universidade Católica Portuguesa*, in Lisbon, *Science Po*, in Paris, *Law and Society Association (LSA)*, in Mexico City, among several other international conferences, shaped me into the researcher I am today. Isabelle has also read my writings several times, exhaustively commented and discussed them with me until the very end of this journey. All that in a detailed-oriented fashion, which is amazingly impressive for a person as busy as her. Having a dedicated supervisor like professor Isabelle Rorive was my greatest fortune during my PhD years. I vividly thank her for her valuable advice, encouragement and mentorship.

Turning to my evaluation committee, I would like to thank professors Benoît Frydman and Arnaud Van Waeyenberge for their valuable readings and comments on my thesis. They deeply challenged my way of understanding research. They inspired me to dare more and to seek creative responses for several intellectual problems. Still, all errors remain mine.

I also would like to thank Gregory Lewkowicz for the teaching experience I had in Frankfurt, in the Legal Theory L.L.M. program. It was during that intensive week of lectures and work that we discussed new paths of research. That week was decisive for my research journey during the final three years of my PhD.

I am also grateful for all the interesting exchanges I had with Emmanuelle Bribosia, Joséphine Woronoff, David Restrepo, Pauline Bégasse, Louise Fromont, Sarah Ganty, Tilen Cuk, Caroline Lesquene-Roth, Caroline Bricteux, Chloé Leroy, Nathan Genicot, Stefan Goltzberg, Dorothea Staes, Stéphanie Dragojevic, Fréderic Audren, Hania Ouhnaoui and Joseph Damamme. They all supported me by reading my texts, translating legal decisions written in Dutch, sharing their rooms during international conferences, collaborating in the organization of conferences, recommending interesting bibliography or simply, but just as importantly, making my experience as a researcher more joyful.

I thank professors Sophie Robin-Olivier and Sofia Ranchordas for having accepted being part of my jury. I have been following their work for a long time and it is an honour to have my work read and assessed by them.

The sponsorship of my research by the CAPES foundation was also essential for the completion of this book. I sincerely thank CAPES for believing in my project.

Last but not least, I warmly thank my family for their oversea inspiration, vivid discussions and limitless support. I deeply thank John Harcus, who probably knows this book in detail, for having read and commented several of my writings including this one. I thank him for all the support along all these years.

May 2022, Leuven.

ABBREVIATIONS

ACLU	American Civil Liberties Union
ADA	Americans with Disabilities Act of 1990
ADEA	Age Discrimination in Employment Act of 1967
AHTOP	Association pour un Hébergement et un Tourisme Professionnel
CDA	Communications Decency Act of 1996
CDA	Communications Decency Act of 1996
CFAA	Computer Fraud and Abuse Act
CJEU	Court of Justice of the European Union
CNIL	Commission Nationale de l'Informatique et des Libertés
COE	Council of Europe
COM	Communication
COPPA	Children's Online Privacy Protection Act
CWA	Communications Workers of America
DAA	Digital Advertising Alliance
DFEH	Department of Fair Employment and Housing of the State of California
DMCA	Digital Millennium Copyright Act
DPA	Data Protection Authority
DSA	Digital Services Act
EASA	European Advertising Standards Alliance
ECHR	European Convention on Human Rights
ECOA	Equal Credit Opportunity
EDAA	European Interactive Digital Advertising Alliance
EEOC	US Equal Employment Opportunity Commission
ELCPA	Electronic Communications Privacy Act
ENAR	European Network Against Racism
ERA	Academy of European Law
EU	European Union
FAA	Federal Arbitration Act
FCRA	Fair Credit Reporting Act
FEHA	California Fair Employment and Housing Act
FHA	Fair Housing Act
FIPs	Fair Information Practices
FLSA	Fair Labor Standards Act
FRA	Fundamental Rights Agency

FTC	Federal Trade Commission
GDN	Google Display Network
GDPR	General Data Protection Regulation
GLBA	Gramm-Leach-Bliley Act
HIPPA	Health Insurance Portability and Accountability Act
HUD	United States Department of Housing and Urbanism
IAB	Interactive Advertising Bureau
ICCPR	International Covenant on Civil and Political Rights 1996
ICT	Information Communication Technology
ILO	International Labour Organisation
IP	Internet Protocol Address
IPO	Initial Public Offering
ISP	Internet Service Provider
ITU	International Telecommunication Union
LDH	Ligue des Droits Humains
NAI	Network Advertising Initiative
NFHA	National Fair Housing Alliance
NLRA	National Labor Relations Act
NMWA	National Minimum Wage Act 1998
OBA	Online Behavioral Advertisement
OECD	Organisation for Economic Co-Operation and Development
PII	Personally Identifiable Information
STEM	Science, Technology, engineering, and mathematics
TFEU	Treaty on the Functioning of the European Union
TNC	Transportation Network Company
UDHR	Universal Declaration of Human Rights
UK	United Kingdom
US	United States of America
USC	United States Code
VPPA	Video Privacy Protection Act
WP29	Article 29 Working Party
WRC	Work Relation Commission (Ireland)
WRT	Working Time Regulations 1998

FOREWORD

This book is the result of Ana's doctoral thesis, which was conducted at the Perelman Centre of the Université libre de Bruxelles (ULB), and updated in her current position at the Center for IT & IP Law (CiTiP) of the KU Leuven. Her research was initially funded by CAPES to whom I am very grateful for providing me with the opportunity to work with Ana. Multiple twists and turns marked this successful doctoral research which began with a complete lockdown of Brussels, following the November 2015 terrorist attacks in Paris, and ended with several confinements and drastic curfews imposed on the civil population in an attempt to contain the Covid-19 pandemic.

It was in this turbulent political and social context that Ana tackled a major challenge, which, at that point, had been overlooked by the legal academic writing in Europe: Mapping how discrimination against protected classes (including gender, ethnic origin, age and sexual orientation) on online platforms were developing, in particular through the design of these platforms. In a judicious way, Ana correlates real occurrences of discrimination against protected classes to three design aspects of online platforms: (1) their aesthetic choices concerning users' protected markers, (2) the design of matching tools that enables users to exclude others with protected aspects from receiving goods, services and work offers, and (3) the design of evaluation systems that facilitates the permanent exclusion of users of protected classes from the system.

At the time of her research, the issue of discrimination against protected classes in online platforms, due to their design, had mainly attracted the attention of scholars in United States business schools, despite the fact that the transition of entire economic sectors to online platforms had already created several challenges for the respect of fundamental rights and, more particularly, for the principle of equality and non-discrimination in the European Union. To fill this gap, this research covers both European Union law and the federal law of the United States. This comparison with the United States is essential to draw lessons from litigation that did not yet exist in Europe. Moreover, the comparative approach is essential for a better understanding of the windows of opportunity offered by the sources of convergence and divergence of non-discrimination laws, the liability regime of Internet Service Providers, and the data protection legal framework, in both legal systems.

This book relies on a problem-based approach, dear to the École de Bruxelles.[1] In order to consider the stakes of businesses and end-users' discrimination against protected classes, three distinct sectors are investigated in depth: the housing, advertisement and labor markets. These three case studies are structured in the following titles: Online Housing and Accommodation Markets: The Crossroads of Intermediary Liability and Antidiscrimination Law; Online Advertising Markets: Widespread Data Collection and Unequal Access to Employment, Goods and Services; and Online Labor Markets: Performance Evaluation and Discriminatory Termination of Platform Workers.

The research shows the incompleteness and partial inadequacy of existing legislation at the European Union and at the United States federal level. It outlines how the regulatory framework that applies to online intermediaries deepens existing inequalities. Moreover, it calls for a structural approach to the mechanisms of discrimination in online platforms.

Ana offers an innovative comparative law perspective of what is now recognized as a global problem: inequality in the platform economy. She does not stop with this observation. She argues that the fight against discrimination in online platforms requires a novel model of co-regulation, given that self-regulation has proven powerless to address inequality in these online markets. She also identifies specific issues that require regulatory changes. To this end, three regulatory requirements are convincingly presented: transparency (disclosure of processes potentially resulting in discrimination), fairness (fair procedures to tackle discriminatory decisions) and business cooperation (between platforms and national equality bodies). Since then, some of these suggestions have been on the table of the European legislator with the AI package and the proposal for a Digital Services Act. The latter establishes an extensive regulatory framework for the accountability and transparency duties of major online platforms operating in the European Union, including additional obligations to very large online platforms to address systemic risks, such as discrimination. Ana included these important developments in her research and kept up her book with the times that she partly anticipated.

Meanwhile, a few cases relating to the effects of digital governance of platforms on the topic of equal treatment have finally been decided by national courts and data protection authorities of European Union member states.[2]

---

[1] See Frédéric Audren, Benoît Frydman, Nathan Genicot (eds), La Naissance de l'École de Bruxelles (EUB 2022); Benoît Frydman, Gregory Lewkowicz (eds), Le Droit selon l'École de Bruxelles (EUB 2022).

[2] See, for instance, Court of Bologna (1st Instance, Labour Section), Filcams CGIL Bologna & al. c. Deliveroo Italia SRL, 12 December 2020, Case no. 2949/2019; Court of Amsterdam (1st Instance, Private Law Section), Uber BV, 24 February 2021, Case no. C/13/69010 / HA ZA 21–81; Italian Data Protection Authority (Garante per la protezione dei dati personali – GPDP), Injuction Order against Foodinho s.r.l., 10 June 2021, Case no. 9675440; Italian Data Protection Authority (GPDP), Injuction Order against Deliveroo Italy s.r.l., 22 July 2021, Case no. 9685994.

These cases concern restrictions on access to employment due to automated discrimination. The analysis of these cases alongside those of United States cases confirms the many obstacles to effective implementation of European non-discrimination law, significantly when automated decisions are opaque and evidence is unavailable. In this regard, the rules on the sharing of the burden of proof, which imply bringing forward a set of facts establishing a prima facie case of discrimination, are powerless to remove the numerous barriers to accessing evidence (lack of transparency, algorithm black box, business secrecy and intellectual property, scattering of platform workers, etc.). Ultimately, these cases show the extent to which personal data protection law offers valuable resources to challenge discriminatory automated decisions.[3]

Ana's research anticipated these types of jurisprudential developments. Her book is an extremely valuable resource for understanding the origins of these disciplinary shifts and their current challenges.

Brussels, June 2022.

Isabelle RORIVE
Full professor at the Law Faculty of the ULB and president of the Perelman Centre

---

[3]   On these case law developments, see Robin Médard-Inghilterra, "Les droit des données personnelles au secours du droit de la non-discrimination? Stratégies et enjeux du contentieux des plateformes", in *Les droits et libertés face aux transformations technologiques, Actes du colloque organisé par l'Université de Bordeaux* from 8–10 December 2021, in press, to be published in 2022.

CONTENTS

GENERAL INTRODUCTION

1. SETTING THE STAGE

Discrimination is a perennial challenge to societies that hold equality as a collective aim.[1] A snapshot of three dynamic markets – labor, housing, and credit – in which transactions heavily depend on discretionary choices to be concluded, illustrates how equality is still a path to be paved. In this respect, numbers show that throughout Europe ethnic minorities have fewer chances of being contacted by employment recruiters[2]; women are 40% less likely to be an elected board member of a private company[3]; women of color are particularly vulnerable to workplace discrimination and experience higher rates of overqualification[4]; and individuals with Northern African origins (Maghreb) have been reportedly refused by landlords in France, Belgium, the Netherlands, Germany, and Spain.[5] In the United States, white employment applicants receive, on average, 36% more callbacks from recruiters than Black American[6] applicants and 24% more

---

[1]   Sandra Fredman, *Discrimination Law* 2ed (Oxford University Press, 2012), chapter 1.

[2]   European Network Against Racism (ENAR), *Racism & Discrimination in Employment in Europe 2013–2017* (March 2017), European Commission, p 4 and 5.

[3]   European Institute for Gender Equality, *Gender Statistics* Database (January 2019), online: EIGE <https://eige.europa.eu/gender-statistics/dgs>; Also, European Commission, *2018 Report on Equality Between Women and Men in the EU* (March 2018), European Commission, p 9.

[4]   European Network Against Racism (ENAR), *Racism & Discrimination in Employment in Europe 2013–2017, op. cit.*, p 5.

[5]   Kristof Heylen, Katleen Van den Broeck, "Discrimination and Selection in the Belgian Private Rental Market" (2015) 31:2 Housing Studies 223; Joachim Brüb, "Experiences of Discrimination Reported by Turkish, Moroccan and Bangladeshi in Three European Cities" (2008) 34:6 Journal of Ethnic and Migration Studies 875l Maurice Crul, Liesbeth Heering, *The Position of the Turkish and Moroccan Second Generation in Amsterdam and Rotterdam: The TIES Studies in the Netherlands* (Amsterdam: Amsterdam University Press, 2008); Sako Musterd, "Social and Ethnic Segregation in Europe: Levels, Causes and Effects" (2005) 27:3 Journal of Urban Affairs 331.

[6]   There is no consensus on which nomenclature is most appropriated or convenient: Black or African American. On the one hand, African American is reputed to connect to heritage, in the same way other groups are called, Jewish-American, Italian-Americans, for example; on the other hand, some people argue that the continuity between their root in Africa and their existence in America has been broken and they identify themselves as simply Black. I respectfully opted in this thesis for the term Black American. *See* Ben L Martin, "From Negro to Black to African American: The Power of Names and Naming" (1991) 106 Political Science Quarterly 83.

callbacks than Hispanic applicants with similar experience[7]; the callback rate for highly skilled male workers is four times greater than for highly skilled female workers[8]; Black Americans, Hispanics, immigrants, same-sex couples, and, to some extent, individuals with disabilities have faced discrimination when seeking a place to live[9]; and Black Americans and Hispanics applying for credit are denied loans two to three times more often than white individuals.[10]

Over the past 20 years, markets have expanded to the internet where individuals and companies directly provide services, connect supply and demand, or advertise their products.[11] In this context, online platforms have emerged as a driving force in most economies.[12] They have become a ubiquitous tool for all sorts of transactions and interactions. Particularly, online platforms have evolved into spaces through which ordinary citizens shop (Amazon, eBay); apply for jobs (LinkedIn, Sumry); search for housing (Craigslist, Roommates, SpareRoom); advertise employment, services, and goods (Facebook, Google); connect with friends (Facebook, Instagram); seek entertainment (YouTube); search for knowledge (Google, Udemy); book accommodation for their next vacation (Airbnb, Abritel); and apply for credit (Prosper, Peerform).

Social interactions taking place in these online spaces have expectedly mirrored the state of inequality of these markets offline. Media, scholars, and case law have documented the development of discrimination against statutorily protected classes in online platforms.[13] In this regard, individuals with Northern

---

[7]   Lincoln Quillian et al., "Meta-Analysis of Field Experiments Shows No Change in Racial Discrimination in Hiring Over Time" (2017) 114 Proceedings of the National Academy of Sciences 10870, p 10871.

[8]   David S Pedulla, *Pathways the Poverty and Inequality Report – Gender* (November 2018), online: Stanford <https://inequality.stanford.edu/sites/default/files/Pathways_SOTU_2018.pdf>, p 36.

[9]   HUD, *Housing Discrimination Against Racial and Ethnic Minorities* (June 2013), online: US Department of Housing <https://www.huduser.gov/portal/publications/fairhsg/hsg_discrimination_2012.html>; HUD, *An Estimate of Housing Discrimination Against Same-Sex Couple* (June 2013), online: US Department of Housing <https://www.huduser.gov/portal/publications/fairhsg/discrim_samesex.html>; HUD, *Housing Discrimination in the Rental Housing Market Against People Who Are Deaf and People Who Use Wheelchairs: National Study Findings* (June 2015), online: US Department of Housing <https://www.huduser.gov/portal/publications/fairhsg/hds_disability.html>.

[10]   Peter Swire, *Lessons from Fair Lending Law for Fair Marketing and Big Data* (September 2014), online: Federal Trade Commission <https://www.ftc.gov/system/files/documents/public_comments/2014/09/00042–92638.pdf>, p 2.

[11]   Orly Lobel, "The Law of The Platform" (2016) 101 Minnesota Law Review 87.

[12]   *Ibid.*

[13]   *See* Rigel C Oliveri, "Discriminatory Housing Advertisements Online: Lessons from Craigslist" (2010) 43 Indiana Law Review 1125 p 1128; and National Fair Housing Alliance, *2010 Fair Housing Trends Report* (May 2010), online: National Fair Housing <https://nationalfairhousing.org/wp-content/uploads/2017/04/fair_housing_trends_report_2010.pdf>; Andrew Hanson, Zackary Hawley, "Do Landlords Discriminate in the Rental of Housing Market? Evidence from an Internet Field in US Cities (2011) 70:2 Journal of Urban Economics 99; Andrew Hanson, Michael Santas, "Field Experiment Tests for Discrimination Against Hispanics in the US Rental Housing Market" (2014) 81:1 Southern Economic Journal

African names have been unjustifiably refused a rental on Airbnb.[14] Housing owners advertising their property for sale have excluded users belonging to ethnic minorities from their targeted advertisements on a social network.[15] Employment advertisements for the science, technology, engineering, and mathematics (STEM) sector were shown over 20% more times to men than women in 191 countries.[16] Hotel owners have the possibility to target or exclude advertisements concerning lodging to individuals labeled as "homosexual" in Germany, Spain, France, and Italy.[17] Sex and "race" were significantly correlated with negative evaluations and search rankings on TaskRabbit and Fiverr.[18] Women are charged with higher interest rates than men on a peer-to-peer loan

---

135; Olivia Solon, *Airbnb Host Who Canceled Reservation Using Racist Comment Must $5,000* (July 2017), online: The Guardian <https://www.theguardian.com/technology/2017/jul/13/airbnb-california-racist-comment-penalty-asian-american>; Nellie Bowles, *Airbnb Faces Outcry After Transgender Guest Was Denied Stay by a Host* (June 2016), online: The Guardian <https://www.theguardian.com/technology/2016/jun/06/airbnb-criticism-transgender-guest-denied-super-host>; Henri Seckel, *Pour Réserver sur Airbnb, Mieux Vaut S'Appeler Isabelle que Djamila* (August 2018), online: LeMonde <https://www.lemonde.fr/societe/article/2018/08/24/airbnb-abritel-discriminations-en-ligne_5345587_3224.html>; Benjamin G Edelman, Michael Luca, *Digital Discrimination: The Case of Airbnb.com* (January 2014), online: Harvard Business School <https://www.hbs.edu/faculty/Publication%20Files/Airbnb_92dd6086-6e46-4eaf-9cea-60fe5ba3c596.pdf>; Venoo Kakar, Joel Voelz, Julia Wu, Julisa Franco, "The Visible Host: Does Race Guide Airbnb Rental Rates in San Francisco? (2018) 40 Journal of Housing Economics 25; Morgane Laouenan, Roland Rathelot, *Ethnic Discrimination on an Online Martketplace of Vacation Rental* (April 2017), online: HAL Working Paper Series <https://hal.archives-ouvertes.fr/hal-01514713/document>; Ray Fisman, Michael Luca, "Fixing Discrimination in Online Marketplaces" (2016) 94:2 Harvard Business Review 2; Devin G Pope, Justin R Sydnor, "What's in a Picture? Evidence of Discrimination from Prosper.com" (2011) 46:1 Journal of Human Resources 53; Amit Datta, Michael Carl Tschantz and Anupam Datta, "Automated Experiments on Ad Privacy Settings: A Tale of Opacity, Choice and Discrimination" (2015) 1 Proceedings on Privacy Enhancing Technologies 92; Anja Lambrecht and Catherine Tucker, "Algorithmic Bias? An Empirical Study of Apparent Gender-Based Discrimination in the Display of STEM Career Ads" (2019) Management Science 1; Latanya Sweeney, "Discrimination in Online Ad Delivery", (2013) 56 ACM 44; José González Cabañas, Ángel Cuevas and Rubén Cuevas, "Facebook Use of Sensitive Data for Advertising in Europe" (2018) Social and Information Networks Cornell University 1; Ánikó Hannák, Claudia Wagner, David Garcia, Alan Mislove, Markus Strohmaier, Christo Wilson, "Bias in Online Freelance Marketplaces: Evidence from TaskRabbit and Fiverr" (2017) Proceedings of the 2017 ACM Conference on Computer Supported Cooperative Work and Social Computing 1914. For the legal cases, *see* section 1, below.

14   Henri Seckel, *Pour Réserver sur Airbnb, Mieux Vaut S'Appeler Isabelle que Djamila* (August 2018), online: LeMonde <https://www.lemonde.fr/societe/article/2018/08/24/airbnb-abritel-discriminations-en-ligne_5345587_3224.html>.

15   *Onuoha v Facebook, Inc.*, No. 5: 16-cv-06440-EJD (N.D. Cal. Apr. 7, 2017).

16   Anja Lambrecht and Catherine Tucker, "Algorithmic Bias? An Empirical Study of Apparent Gender-Based Discrimination in the Display of STEM Career Ads" (2019) Management Science 1.

17   José González Cabañas, Ángel Cuevas and Rubén Cuevas, "Facebook Use of Sensitive Data for Advertising in Europe" (2018) Social and Information Networks Cornell University 1.

18   Ánikó Hannák, Claudia Wagner, David Garcia, Alan Mislove, Markus Strohmaier, Christo Wilson, "Bias in Online Freelance Marketplaces: Evidence from TaskRabbit and Fiverr"

---

platform.[19] In London, Paris, Milan, and Rome, Airbnb's hosts who have a first name associated with an Arabic or a Sub-Saharan African ethnicity receive 9.4% less for their short-term rental than white hosts with similar properties.[20] Listings on housing platforms frequently include statements such as "prefer white male roommates," "not looking for Black Muslims,"[21] or "no women of color need to apply."[22]

Discrimination in online platforms raises concerns because of their particular structures.[23] Online platforms have replaced traditional forms of production, known as pipeline arrangements, for network arrangements.[24] In pipeline arrangements, businesses create value in linear supply chains with producers at one end and consumers at the other. In network structures, businesses do not generate value by creating the products or goods they are main known for.[25] Alternatively, they create value by fostering networking or, in other words, by connecting a very high number of service providers/producers to consumers. Three main platform businesses illustrate this idea: eBay does not sell any product by itself, Airbnb does not have any property to rent for guests on vacation, and YouTube does not produce any video content.

The network structure is the vital core of online platforms. Without fostering networks between the sides of supply and demand, platform businesses do not generate any value. In this context, scale and design are fundamental for creating value and are the engines for economic growth for platform businesses. First, concerning scale, as more users engage with and provide services or goods through these companies with platform structures, the more profitable these

---

(2017) Proceedings of the 2017 ACM Conference on Computer Supported Cooperative Work and Social Computing 1914.

[19]   Dongyu Chen, Xialin Li, Fujun Lai, "Gender Discrimination in Online Peer-to-Peer Credit Lending: Evidence from a Lending Platform in China" (2017) 17:4 Electronic Commerce Research 553.

[20]   Morgane Laouenan, Roland Rathelot, *Ethnic Discrimination on an Online Martketplace of Vacation Rental* (April 2017), online: HAL Working Paper Series <https://hal.archives-ouvertes.fr/hal-01514713/document>, p 12.

[21]   *Fair Housing Council of San Fernando Valley v Roommates, LLC*, CV 03–9386 PA (RZx) (C.D. Cal. Nov. 7, 2008), p 3472.

[22]   *Chicago Lawyers' v Craigslist Inc*, No. 07–1101 (7th Cir. 2008).

[23]   Benjamin Edelman, Michael Luca, Dan Svirsky, "Racial Discrimination in the Sharing Economy: Evidence from a Field Experiment" (2017) 9 American Economic Journal: Applied Economics 1; Andrew Selbst and Solon Barocas, "Big Data's Disparate Impact" (2016) 104 California Law Review 671; Alex Rosenblat, Karen E C Levy, Solon Barocas, Tim Hwang, "Discriminating Tastes: Uber's Customer Ratings as Vehicles for Workplace Discrimination" (2017) 9:3 Policy & Internet 256; Miriam Kullmann, "Platform Work: Algorithmic Decision-Making, and EU Gender Equality Law (2018) 34:1 International Journal of Comparative Labour Law and Industrial Relations 1.

[24]   Geoffrey G Parker, Marshall W Van Alstyne, Sangeet Paul Choudary, *Platform Revolution: How Networked Markets Are Transforming the Economy and How to Make Them Work for You* (Norton & Company, 2016), p 7.

[25]   Peter C Evans, Annabelle Gawer, "The Rise of the Platform Enterprise: A Global Survey" (2016) The Emerging Platform Economy Series 1.

companies become either by charging their users fees or by being attractive for advertising. Second, the design of online platforms is thoughtfully developed to increase trustworthiness and confidence among users and, therefore, to increase the amount of successful transactions intermediated through these platform businesses. Design is considered to help users within their decision-making process.[26] Design includes (1) the aesthetic choices related to the placement of users' profiles and their personal markers, (2) matching tools, and (3) evaluation systems.

2. CHALLENGES TO THE PRINCIPLE OF EQUALITY

With the above reality in mind, this book examines the challenges the online platform economy presents to the principle of equality that is fundamental to the antidiscrimination laws, which protects certain classes against discrimination in the condition and access to goods, services, and work in both Europe and the United States.[27] I guided my research for this book based on two main questions. On the one hand, what are the structural challenges that online platforms pose to the equal treatment of their users? On the other, are antidiscrimination legal frameworks in the United States and the European Union equipped to address discrimination that occurs in online platforms?

Concerning the structural challenges, I argue that certain forms of entrenched discrimination may scale, to the proportion of the number of users, when platforms foster networking. First, the design of certain platforms enhances users' personal traits by displaying their names, photographs, and other proxies for race, gender, age, sexual orientation before transactions are concluded.[28] Second, the design of matching tools enables users to exclude other users with protected aspects from receiving goods, services, and work offers.[29] Third, the design of apparently neutral evaluation rating systems allows users of protected classes to be permanently excluded from the platform or to be poorly ranked in searching-systems.[30] Fourth, online platforms are primarily designed to intermediate the relationship between users. In general, platform businesses are resistant to moderate this relationship.

Regarding the legal challenges, my research demonstrates that the antidiscrimination legal frameworks in the United States and the European

---

[26] Sofia Ranchordás, "Public Values, Private Regulators: Between Regulation and Reputation in the Sharing Economy" (2019) 13:2 The Law & Ethics of Human Rights 203.

[27] I particularly focus on the goods, services and labor markets. For the reasons, *see* section 3.4 bellow.

[28] *See* title I.

[29] *See* title II.

[30] *See* title III.

Union are only partially equipped to address discrimination that occurs in online platforms. Primarily, I indicate that online platforms, in the United States, commonly lack accountability for the illegal activities of their users given the general set of immunities provided by the Communications Decency Act of 1996 and its extensive meaning construed by district courts and courts of appeals over the past decades.[31] This context generally prevents online platform businesses from being liable for discrimination that occurs through their intermediation. Ultimately, my research highlights that the regime of limited immunity, in the EU, provided by the Directive on Electronic Commerce[32] and its construed meaning settled by the CJEU is more equipped to make platforms liable for third-party discrimination, at least in specific cases in which platforms become aware of the third-party illegal conduct or when they promote the illegal content.[33] The co-regulatory moderation regime enshrined in the Directive on Electronic Commerce imposes on online platform businesses the duty to act expeditiously in cases in which they are notified about their users' wrongdoings. Failing to do so results in corporate liability.[34] This sort of tort vicarious liability has proved to be a legal incentive for companies to properly train their agents against discrimination. Moreover, in some circumstances, vicarious liability is also essential to redress victims of discrimination because corporations often have more financial assets than the agents of misconduct.[35]

Even though the co-regulatory regime of the Directive on Electronic Commerce provides users with more remedies in the fight against third-party discrimination, neither the EU's nor the United States' legal system entirely addresses the structural challenges that platforms present to the principle of equal treatment, at the time this research was conducted. These challenges involve, as mentioned above, platforms' flawed aesthetic choices, including the over-salience of their users' protected markers and the opacity of matching tools and evaluation rating systems that do not provide any clear evidence that users were discriminated against because of their protected grounds.[36]

---

[31] *See* chapter 1, section II, 1.6.

[32] Directive 2000/31/EC of the European Parliament and of the Council of 8 June 2000 on certain legal aspects of information society services, in particular electronic commerce, in the Internal Market (Directive on electronic commerce), OJ L 178, 17.7.2000, p 1–16.

[33] *See* chapter 1, p section II, 2.4.

[34] I adopt the perspective that co-regulatory systems are legal tools developed "to put pressure on the points of control to achieve some regulatory results", *see* Benoit Freedman, Ludovic Hennebel, Gregory Lewkowicz, "Public Strategies for Internet Co-Regulation in the United States, Europe and China" in E. Brousseau, M Marzouki, C. Méadel, *Governance, Regulations and Powers on the Internet* (Cambridge: Cambridge University Press, 2008).

[35] Jessica Reingold Katz, "Finding Fault: Implications of Importing the Title VII Standard for Vicarious Punitive Liability to the Fair Housing Act" (2008), *op. cit.*.

[36] In the EU, the Digital Services Act, once in force, will provide requirements related to transparency duties and accountability for online platforms that might be applicable to certain forms of matching operations, such as targeted advertising, and rating systems.

In view of these structural challenges, this book argues that the fight against discrimination in online platforms might produce better outcomes when guided by a model of regulation that promotes the principle of transparency, fairness, and private-public cooperation.[37] This regulatory model would establish the duty for companies to disclose the criteria used to match supply and demand as well as more detailed explanations about the termination of users based on rating evaluation systems.

3. METHODOLOGY

To answer the question of which structural and legal challenges the platform economy poses to the principle of equality in the concerned markets, I opted for a problem-based approach or inductive method.[38]

I searched instances of lawsuits related to discrimination against protected classes occurring in online platforms in Europe and the United States. My research was guided by the legal instruments against discrimination that bind private relationships. I specifically focused on the set of antidiscrimination rights enshrined in the United States Federal Statutes and the European Equality Directives.[39]

Concerning the United States, I conducted my research of cases based on the Civil Rights Act of 1964 and 1968[40], the Age Discrimination in Employment Act (ADEA) of 1967[41], and the Americans with Disabilities Act (ADA) of 1990.[42] The Titles II (Public Accommodation Act) and VII of the Civil Rights of 1964 specifically prohibit discrimination against protected classes in the access to goods, services, facilities in places of public accommodation and in the access and conditions of employment. In addition, the Title II, concerning public accommodation, protects the aspects of race, color, religion, national origin,

---

[37] Model inspired by Regulation (EU) 2019/1150 of the European Parliament and of the Council of 20 June 2019 on Promoting Fairness and Transparency for Business Users of Online Intermediation Services, OJ L 186, 11.7.2019, p 57–79.

[38] Lisa Webley, "Qualitative Approaches to Empirical Legal Research", in Peter Cane, Herbert Kritzer (eds), *Oxford Handbook of Empirical Legal Research* (OUP, 2010), p 926; Benoît Frydman, "Les Défis du Droit Global", in Caroline Bricteux, Benoit Frydman, *Grands Défis du Droit Global, op. cit.*, pp 11–17.

[39] For contextual development of these rights, *see* David B Oppenheimer, "Sources of United States Equality Law: The View from 10000 Meters" (2010) 10 European Anti-Discrimination Law Review 19; Mark Bell, "The Principle of Equal Treatment, Widening and Deepening", in Paul Craig, Grainne de Búrca (eds) *The Evolution of EU Law* (New York: Oxford University Press, 2011), p 611.

[40] 42 U.S.C. §2000a(a)-(b) (2006) (Title II); 42 U.S.C. §2000e(b) (2006) and §2000e(b) (Title VII).

[41] 29 U.S.C. §§621–634(2006). The Act was enacted to protect workers above 40 years old.

[42] 42 U.S.C. §§12101–12213.

and disability[43], and the Title VII, concerning employment, protects the classes of race, color, religion, national origin, disability, age, and sex.[44] The criterion of age was implemented by the ADEA of 1967. Disability was introduced in the Rehabilitation Act of 1973 and expanded by the Americans with Disabilities Act of 1990.[45] The Title VIII of the Civil Rights Act of 1968 (Fair Housing Act) prohibits discrimination against the classes of race, color, religion, sex, handicap, and familial status in a number of housing transactions.[46]

Regarding the EU, I based my research for cases on the classes and scopes provided by the Race Equality Directive[47], the Employment Equality Directive[48], the Gender Equality Directive[49], and the Gender Equal Access to Goods and Services Directive.[50] The Race Equality Directive provides a legal framework against discrimination on the grounds of race and ethnic origin in many scopes, including employment, social protection, social advantages, and access and supply of goods and services available to the public, including housing.[51] The Employment and Gender Equality Directives provide a framework for protection against discrimination on the grounds of religion, belief, disability, age, sexual orientation, and sex in the context of employment.[52] Finally, the Gender Equal Access to Goods and Services Directive establishes a framework to implement the principle of equality between men and women in the access and supply of goods and services available to the public.[53]

I acknowledge the differences of material scope existent between the American Federal Statutes and the European Union Directives. Whereas the former has direct application to private relationships, in principle, the Directives provide a framework to the member states to combat discrimination. However, the Directives might reflect the state of antidiscrimination laws of the member states since they have been transposed into domestic law by the 27 countries

---

[43]   42 U.S.C. §2000a(a)-(b) (2006) (Title II).

[44]   42 U.S.C. §2000e(b) (2006) and §2000e(b) (Title VII).

[45]   29 U.S.C. §791, Rehabilitation Act of 1973 and 42 U.S.C. §12112 to §12114.

[46]   42 U.S.C. §3604 (2006).

[47]   Council Directive 2000/43/EC of 29 June 2000 implementing the principle of equal treatment between persons irrespective of racial or ethnic origin, OJ L 180, 19.7.2000, p 22–26 (Hereinafter, Race Equality Directive).

[48]   Council Directive 2000/78/EC of 27 November 2000 establishing a general framework for equal treatment in employment and occupation, OJ L 303, 2.12.2000, p 16–22 (Hereinafter, Employment Equality Directive).

[49]   Directive 2006/54/EC of the European Parliament and of the Council of 5 July 2006 on the implementation of the principle of equal opportunities and equal treatment of men and women in matters of employment and occupation (recast) OJ L 204, 26.7.2006, p 23–36 (Hereinafter, Gender Equality Directive).

[50]   Council Directive 2004/113/EC of 13 December 2004 implementing the principle of equal treatment between men and women in the access to and supply of goods and services OJ L 373, 21.12.2004, p 37–43 (Hereinafter, Gender Equal Access to Goods and Services Directive).

[51]   Article 3, Race Equality Directive.

[52]   Article 3, Employment Equality Directive; Article 1, Gender Equality Directive.

[53]   Article 1, Gender Equal Access to Goods and Services Directive.

part of the Union.[54] Moreover, when domestic laws diverge from European law, national courts should set them aside according to the principle of the primacy of EU law.[55] Additionally, the principle of direct effect enables individuals to invoke a European provision directly before national courts, provided that certain conditions are complied with.[56] Finally, the principle of non-discrimination enshrined in the Treaty of Lisbon and the Charter of Fundamental Rights of the European Union has direct effect in member states.[57]

The reasons for developing a comparative research between the United States and European markets is twofold. First, several successful online platforms that were first developed in the United States quickly expanded to the European markets, and this combination has created the largest markets in the world.[58] Second, American antidiscrimination laws, the liability regime of Internet Service Providers, and the data protection legal framework have been sources of convergence and divergence with those in the European context.[59] Europe and the United States might have valuable assets to exchange in these three fields.

---

54   Isabelle Chopin, Carmine Conte, Edith Chambrier, *A Comparative Analysis of Non-Discrimination Law in Europe 2018, European Network of Legal Experts in Gender Equality and Non-Discrimination* (November 2018), online: European Commission Directorate-General for Justice and Consumers <https://www.equalitylaw.eu/downloads/4804-a-comparative-analysis-of-non-discrimination-law-in-europe-2018-pdf-1-02-mb>; Alexandra Timmer, Linda Senden, *A Comparative Analysis of Gender Equality Law in Europe 2018* (January 2019), online: European Commission Directorate-General for Justice and Consumers <https://www.equalitylaw.eu/downloads/4829-a-comparative-analysis-of-gender-equality-law-in-europe-2018-pdf-807-kb>.

55   This principle was firstly developed by the CJEU in the seminal case C-6/64 *Costa v ENEL*, ECLI:EU:C:1964:66.

56   For a detailed analysis of the conditions that EU provisions must fulfill to have direct effect, *see* Catherine Barnard, Steve Peers, *European Union Law* (New York: Oxford University Press, 2017), p 146–155. Also, for the developments of the direct effect theory, *see* Sophie Robin-Olivier, "The Evolution of Direct Effect in the EU: Stocktaking, Problems, Projections" (2014) 12:1 International Journal of Constitutional Law 165.

57   *See* C-555/07 *Seda Kücükdeveci v Swedex GmbH & Co. KG*, ECLI:EU:C:2010:21 and C-276/12 *Jiří Sabou v Finanční ředitelství pro hlavní město Prahu*, ECLI:EU:C:2013:678.

58   By 2016, the EU companies represented only 4% of online platforms operating in Europe. Most platforms in Europe were from the United States and Asia. *See* Brussels, 25.5.2016 COM (2016) 288 final. Communication from the Commission to the European Parliament, the Council, the European Economic and Social Committee and the Committee of the Regions: Online Platforms and the Digital Single Market: Opportunities and Challenges for Europe, §3.

59   About legal transplants between American and European antidiscrimination law, *see* Isabelle Rorive, "Lutter contre les Discriminations", in Caroline Bricteux, Benoit Frydman, *Grands Défis du Droit Global* (Brussels: Bruylant, 2018), p 45–52; Emmanuelle Bribosia, Isabelle Rorive, "Anti-Discrimination Law in the Global Age" (2015) 3 European Journal of Human Rights 3; Gráinne de Búrca, "Evolutions in Antidiscrimination Law in Europe and North America" (2012) 60:1 The American Journal of Comparative Law 1; Gerard Quinn, Eilionóir Flynn, "Transatlantic Borrowings: The Past and Future of EU Non-Discrimination Law and Policy on the Ground of Disability" (2012) 60:1 The American Journal of Comparative Law 23; Bruno de Witte, "News Institutions for Promoting Equality in Europe: Legal Transfers, National Bricolage and European Governance (2012) 60:1 The American Journal of

Concerning the presence of digital platforms, Airbnb, for example, has significant presence in European member states, with France, the United Kingdom (before January 31, 2020)[60], Spain, Italy, and Denmark having the highest number of rental listings.[61] Airbnb has its second most important profits in France, just after the United States.[62] Furthermore, in 2018 Facebook had 78.96% and 50.85% of the market share of social media platforms in Europe and in the United States, respectively.[63] Google (as a search engine) had 92.8% in Europe and 88.07% in the United States.[64] Finally, in 2020 Uber had 65% of the ride-hailing market share in Europe.[65]

Regarding legal convergences, in the United States and in the member states of the European Union, antidiscrimination provisions extend beyond the relationship between the state and individuals and reach private relationships.[66] In this regard, the provisions limit the principle of contractual freedoms, and when individuals choose their contractual parties they are not allowed, under certain circumstances, to discriminate against protected characteristics, such as gender, race, ethnic origin, age, sexual orientation[67], disability, religion, or belief. Furthermore, some key concepts have circulated across the American and EU legal regimes, such as the reverse burden of proof, situation tests as means of proof, and disparate impact that prohibits facially neutral practices that have a disproportionately negative effect on individuals with protected aspects.[68] The disparate impact theory, first developed by the Supreme Court of the United

---

Comparative Law 49; Andrew Geddes, Virginie Guiraudon, "Britain, France, and EU Anti-Discrimination Policy: The Emergence of an EU policy Paradigm" (2004) 27:2 West European Politics 334.

[60] This research was initiated before the UK withdrew from the European Union.

[61] Several platform giants were created in the Silicon Valley. Peter C Evans, Annabelle Gawer, "The Rise of the Platform Enterprise: A Global Survey" (2016) The Emerging Platform Economy Series 1; Also, see Jennifer Luty, *Number of Airbnb Listings in Selected European Cities as of 2019* (August 2019), online: Statista <https://www.statista.com/statistics/815145/airbnb-listings-in-europe-by-city/>.

[62] Airbnb, *La Communauté Airbnb en France en 2016* (November 2016), online: Airbnb <http://hr-infos.fr/wp-content/uploads/2017/04/EIS-France.pdf>.

[63] Social Media Stats Worldwide, *Statcounter* (July 2019), online: GlobalStats <http://gs.statcounter.com/social-media-stats/all/united-states-of-america/2018>.

[64] Search Engines Stats Worldwide, *Statcounter* (July 2019), online: GlobalStats <http://gs.statcounter.com/search-engine-market-share/all/united-states-of-america>.

[65] Uber, *2020 Investor Presentation* (February 2020), online: Uber <https://s23.q4cdn.com/407969754/files/doc_financials/2019/sr/InvestorPresentation_2020_Feb6.pdf>.

[66] Emmanuelle Bribosia, Isabelle Rorive, "Anti-Discrimination Law in the Global Age" (2015) 3 European Journal of Human Rights 3; Isabelle Rorive, "Lutter contre les Discriminations", in Caroline Bricteux, Benoit Frydman, *Grands Défis du Droit Global* (Brussels: Bruylant, 2018), 41.

[67] Sexual orientation is not a protected ground in federal statutory law, in the United States, even though some States law have express provision against discrimination grounded on sexual orientation.

[68] Isabelle Rorive, "Lutter contre les Discriminations", in Caroline Bricteux, Benoit Frydman, *Grands Défis du Droit Global* (Brussels: Bruylant, 2018), p 50.

States[69], was primarily transplanted in the United Kingdom[70], later mobilized by the Court of Justice[71], and ultimately enshrined, with some singularities, in the Equality Directives in the EU as indirect discrimination.

Moreover, I articulate how the concept of indirect and direct discrimination in the EU might provide better responses for discrimination occurring in online platforms, given that neither the identification of the victim nor statistical data are required to prove either type of discrimination.[72] This aspect might be an asset in the fight against discrimination online, considering the frequent hurdles concerning the identification of the victims. In the United States, the configuration of both direct discrimination and disparate impact depends on the identification of the victim and data relating to the disparate impact of a facially neutral policy on a protected class.[73]

Furthermore, the legal protection of personal data has also been a source of divergence between the United States and the member states of the European Union. In the United States, the fragmented legal approach towards the regulation of the use of personal information by online platforms does not provide enough protection for third-parties against discrimination.[74] At the federal level, no statute exists to regulate the use of such data. Over the years, the Federal Trade Commission has provided privacy guidelines for online businesses willing to use third-party personal data in their operations.[75] However, those guidelines are not binding. Therefore, the use of personal data for profiling, matching, and targeting practices is, in the best-case scenario, self-regulated by companies under their terms of services. The lack of protection of personal data enables companies to collect and process sensitive data, such as third-party ethnic affiliation or gender, without further accountability. Alternatively, in the EU the General Data Protection Regulation[76] (and its construed meaning by national courts), the CJEU, and Data Protection authorities offer comprehensive

---

[69]   *Griggs v Duke Power Co.*, 401 U.S. 424, 91 S. Ct. 849, 28 L. Ed. 2d 158 (1971).

[70]   In the Race Relations Act of 1976. *See* Isabelle Rorive, "Lutter contre les Discriminations", in Caroline Bricteux, Benoit Frydman, *Grands Défis du Droit Global* (Brussels: Bruylant, 2018), p 49.

[71]   *Ibid*, p 50. Reffering to the cases C-96/80 *JP Jenkins v Kingsgate*, ECLI:EU:C:1981:80 and C-170/84 *Bilka – Kaufhaus GmbH v Karin Weber von Hartz*, ECLI:EU:C:1986:204.

[72]   Case C-54/07 *Centrum voor gelijkheid van kansen en voor racismebestrijding v Firma Feryn NV*, ECLI:EU:C:2008:397 and C-237/94 *O'Flynn v Adjudication Officer*, ECLI:EU:C:1996:206. Also, *see* Sandra Fredman, *Discrimination Law, op. cit.*, p 187.

[73]   *See* chapter 5, section II, 1.2.2.

[74]   *See* chapter 3 and Shawn Marie Boyne, "Data Protection in the United States" (2018) 66 The American Journal of Comparative Law 299.

[75]   Hayes Hagan, "How to Protect Consumer Data? Leave It to the Consumer Protection Agency: FTC Rulemaking as a Path to Federal Cybersecurity Regulation" (2019) 2019 Columbia Business Law Review 735.

[76]   Regulation (EU) 2016/679 of the European Parliament and of the Council of 27 April 2016 on the protection of natural persons with regard to the processing of personal data on the free movement of such data, and repealing Directive 95/46/EC (General Data Protection Regulation), OJ L 119, 4.5.2016, p 1–88.

rules on the use of personal data by companies in their automated processes, matching capabilities, and targeting operations.[77] This composite of rules makes companies accountable for the misuse of third-party personal data. These rules also explicitly protect personal data from being collected and used in a discriminatory fashion.[78]

Ultimately, the regimes of online intermediary liabilities in the United States and in members of the European Union have diverged in terms of tort accountability for third-party wrongdoings.[79] While in the United States the Communications Decency Act of 1996[80] has been broadly construed by courts to offer comprehensive immunity for Internet Service Providers in the majority of legal disputes, the legal framework provided by the EU Directive on Electronic Commerce[81] has offered a more balanced solution for victims of third-party wrongdoings by holding Internet Service Providers accountable in certain circumstances. Therefore, the European regime has been a source of concern for American online intermediary businesses operating in the EU.

My sources to find cases involving online platforms comprised the American electronic system Pacer Monitor, law journals, the Court of Justice of the European Union's online mechanism for research, and, for national cases, the official reports published by the European Network of Legal Experts in Gender Equality and Non-Discrimination and academic law journals.[82] From this research, I created the main corpus of cases upon which I developed my chapters. This main corpus includes cases in the housing, accommodation, targeted advertising, and labor markets.

3.1. SELECTED LITIGATION ON HOUSING AND ACCOMMODATION

In the United States, the selected litigation includes *Chicago Lawyers' v Craigslist Inc.*[83], *Fair Housing Council of San Fernando Valley v Roommates*[84], *Voluntary*

---

[77] Elena Gil González, Paul de Hert, "Understanding the Legal Provisions that Allow Processing and Profiling of Personal Data – an Analysis of GDPR Provisions and Principles" (2019) 19 ERA Forum 597.
[78] *See* chapter 3, section II, 2.
[79] *See* chapter 1, section II.
[80] 47 U.S.C., §230, (1) (1996), Communications Decency Act (CDA).
[81] Directive 2000/31/EC of the European Parliament and of the Council of 8 June 2000 on certain legal aspects of information society services, in particular electronic commerce, in the Internal Market (Directive on electronic commerce), OJ L 178, 17.7.2000, p 1–16.
[82] European Equality Law Network, *homepage* (January 2020), online: EU <https://www.equalitylaw.eu>; and PacerMonitor, *homepage* (January 2020), online: Pacer Gov <https://www.uscourts.gov/court-records/find-case-pacer>.
[83] *Chicago Lawyers' v Craigslist Inc.*, No. 07–1101 (7th Cir. 2008).
[84] *Fair Housing Council of San Fernando Valley v Roommates, LLC*, 2012 WL 310849 (9th Cir. February 2, 2012).

Agreement – Complainant v Airbnb[85], and *Selden v Airbnb.*[86] In the EU and the member states, it comprises the C-390/18 *Airbnb Ireland*[87]; *Tribunal d'Instance, Paris (Airbnb)*, *Jugement du 6 février* 2018, RG 11–17–000190; and *Irish Human Rights and Equality Commission v Daft.*[88]

I first selected the *Chicago Lawyers' v Craigslist Inc.* case because it was one of the early representative lawsuits seeking tort liability against an online intermediary for third-party housing offers with discriminatory statements and requirements in the United States. The Chicago Lawyers Committee for Civil Rights based its tort claim against Craigslist on the federal statute Fair Housing Act, which prohibits discrimination against housing renters and buyers based on several protected aspects, and it holds publishers of housing advertisements liable for third-party discriminatory against protected classes.[89] Despite the fact that the platform had more than 10,000 advertisements with discriminatory statements concerning racial minorities and families with children, the Court of Appeals held Craigslist, in its capacity as an Internet Service Provider, exempt from any tort liability over its users' discriminatory statements against protected classes. The case drew vast attention given that since the Fair Housing Act was enacted in the 1960s, overt discrimination in advertisement with housing offers has been drastically reduced in the traditional media, including newspapers and magazines.[90]

Not long after Craigslist's liability was challenged and defeated, another housing market platform, Roommates, faced tort liability charges under the terms of the Fair Housing Act. I particularly chose this case because it involved further discussions on the design of matching tools developed by the platform to determine whether Roommates was an Internet Service Provider and therefore exempted from liability for its users' discrimination against home seekers, under the terms of the Communications Decency Act. Roommates has designed and provided for its users a drop-down menu to match individuals looking for shared places to live. The drop-down menu mandatorily allowed users to exclude or include protected aspects, such as sexual orientation, gender, and family status from their housing searches. The Court of Appeals ruled that Roommates was the content provider regarding the design of the drop-down menu, and therefore, it was not exempted when users had to mandatorily exclude or include a protected class from their searches. However, this reasoning was hardly followed by courts in later cases to determine the liability of Internet

---

85   *Voluntary Agreement, Complainant v Airbnb, INC.*, Case Nos. 574743–231889 and 574743–231624 (April 2017) California Department of Fair Employment and Housing.
86   *Selden v Airbnb, Inc.*, No. 16-cv-00933 (CRC) (D.C. Nov. 1, 2016).
87   C-390/18 *Airbnb Ireland* ECLI:EU:C:2019:1112.
88   *Irish Human Rights and Equality Commission v Daft Media Limited t/a Daft/ie*, ADJ-00005960, WRC, August 2019.
89   FHA, 42 U.S.C. 3604, (a) (b).
90   *See* chapter 2, 1.

Service Providers for third-party discrimination.[91] Additionally, the platform was exempted from liability under the terms of the Fair Housing Act because the statute does not apply to shared-places.

More recently, after over a decade of precedents exempting Internet Service Providers from third-party tort liability for their users' wrongdoings, the accommodation sharing-economy platform Airbnb faced charges for discriminating against accommodation seekers when its users/hosts refused potential users/guests based on their racial origin.[92] In an attempt to avoid the Communications Decency Act immunities, plaintiffs opted to label the company that operates the Airbnb platform as a hotel or real estate agency, instead of an Internet Service Provider. This case is relevant to the discussion of whether online intermediaries are liable for their users' discriminatory conducts for three reasons. First, it exposes the limits to seek vicarious liability from platform businesses for their users' wrongdoings when they do not have the power of agency over their users. Second, it shows how aesthetic choices made by the platform about where and when to dispose users' protected markers is not a strong argument to underline a discrimination legal charge. Third, the case highlights how platform businesses have avoided judicial precedents in the past 10 years by implementing arbitration clauses. Contrarily to the Craigslist and Roommates cases, the questions whether Airbnb is an Internet Service Provider or whether Airbnb could hold vicarious liability for discrimination perpetrated by their hosts/users against their guests/users were neither publicly responded by a court nor settled as a precedent. The same happened in litigation against Uber concerning arbitration clauses.[93]

Additionally, the voluntary agreement between Airbnb and the Department of Fair Employment and Housing of the State of California (DFEH) underlines my argument that the collaboration of enforcement agencies or public bodies with businesses might be regarded as a relevant asset in the fight against discrimination in online platforms.[94] In this occasion, Airbnb committed to provide the DFEH with data regarding the acceptance rate for White, Hispanic, Black, and Asian American guests through booking on the platform; data related to the frequency that hosts reject guests based on the justification of unavailability; and data referring to the number of discrimination complaints and the number of users delisted from the platform for discriminatory conduct. The agreement had limited time and geographic scope, but it might serve as a

---

[91]   *See* chapter 2, 2.
[92]   *Selden v Airbnb, Inc.*, No. 16-cv-00933 (CRC) (D.C. Nov. 1, 2016).
[93]   *O'Connor v Uber Technologies, Inc*, 82 F. Supp. 3d 1133 (N.D. Cal. 2015) and *Kendall Reese v Uber Technologies, Inc.* (2:18-cv-03300, United District Court for The Eastern District of Pennsylvania, Aug 2018).
[94]   *Voluntary Agreement, Complainant v Airbnb, INC.*, Case Nos. 574743–231889 and 574743–231624 (April 2017) California Department of Fair Employment and Housing.

model to advance the principle of transparency that such businesses should be engaged in.

In Europe, although cases of ethnic origin discrimination against Airbnb guests have been reported by the press[95], so far[96], no legal case regarding the discriminatory refusal of guests based on one or more of their protected aspects has reached national courts.[97]

Nevertheless, contrarily to American courts, the CJEU was given the opportunity to rule that Airbnb is an Internet Service Provider that enables hosts to connect with prospective guests.[98] Even though national courts did not have the possibility to assess whether the platform would hold liability for their users' discriminatory conduct against guests, the co-regulatory system provided by the Directive on Electronic Commerce offers more tools against discrimination than the Communication Decency Act in the United States. In the European Union, the Directive renders Internet Service Providers liable for their users' wrongdoings once they are notified about it. In this regard, in the case *Tribunal d'Instance, Paris (Airbnb), Jugement du 6 février* 2018, RG 11–17–000190, Airbnb was held liable for allowing users to illegally offer to sublet their apartments through the platform. In France, landlords must provide explicit authorization to allow tenants to sublet their rented property. Airbnb was notified by the apartment owner about the illegal offer, but it did not act to stop or remove it. In the end, Airbnb had to pay the landlord a compensation and pay back all the fees received by the illegal sublet. These cases show that even though Internet Service Providers, in their capacity of hosting services, enjoy certain liability immunities for their users' misconduct, these liability immunities are less stringent than the regime provided by the Communications Decency Act in the United States. In a hypothetical lawsuit against Airbnb for racial discrimination, the victim would be given the possibility to be redressed by the company if Airbnb was notified and did not act to keep its users from discriminating against other users.

Moreover, I selected the *Irish Human Rights and Equality Commission v Daft*[99] case because it demonstrates the blurred line that exists between companies offering internet services and those that offer other services such as accommodation in Europe. *Daft* is an online platform through which real estate owners may publish their advertisements with housing offers. Several of the advertisements had discriminatory requirements against home seekers. The Workplace Relation Commission ultimately decided that *Daft* was not

---

[95]   Henri Seckel, *Pour Réserver sur Airbnb, Mieux Vaut S'Appeler Isabelle que Djamila* (August 2018), online: LeMonde <https://www.lemonde.fr/societe/article/2018/08/24/airbnb-abritel-discriminations-en-ligne_5345587_3224.html>.

[96]   The research of cases was concluded in the end of December 2019.

[97]   *See* chapter 2, 4.

[98]   C-390/18 *Airbnb Ireland* ECLI:EU:C:2019:1112.

[99]   *Irish Human Rights and Equality Commission v Daft Media Limited t/a Daft/ie*, ADJ-00005960, WRC, August 2019.

an Internet Service Provider, but alternatively, it was a real estate company. Therefore, it had the duty to prevent discriminatory ads from being published by third-party users. In other words, *Daft* had the legal obligation to monitor its users' activities.

3.2. SELECTED LITIGATION ON TARGETED ADVERTISING

Regarding the offer of goods, services, and work positions in targeted advertising, from the United States I selected the cases *Onuoha v Facebook*[100], *Bradley v T-Mobile US*[101], *National Fair Housing Alliance v Facebook*[102], *Riddick v Facebook*[103], and *Spees et al. v Facebook.*[104] In the EU, I selected the cases *Autoriteit Persoonsgegevens v Facebook* the Netherlands[105], *Commission Nationale de l'Informatique et des Libertés v Facebook*[106], and *Agencia Española de Datos v Facebook.*[107]

In the United States, the *Onuoha v Facebook*, *Bradley v T-Mobile US*, *National Fair Housing Alliance v Facebook*, *Riddick v Facebook,* and *Spees et al. v Facebook* cases show how matching tools that allow the exclusion of protected classes from receiving advertisements pose risks to the principle of equality in the access to real estate, accommodation, credit offers, and employment positions. In these contexts, companies willing to advertise employment offers, housing opportunities, and credit services to Facebook users could select who would receive such offers according to their demographic aspects as precise as their ethnicity, gender, and age, among hundreds of other characteristics. Civil rights organizations mobilized several Civil Rights Acts[108] on the basis of racial,

---

[100]   *Onuoha v Facebook, Inc*, No. 5: 16-cv-06440-EJD (N.D. Cal. Apr. 7, 2017).

[101]   *Bradley v T-Mobile US, Inc.*, No. 17-cv-07232-BLF (N.D. Cal. June 4, 2019).

[102]   *National Fair Housing Alliance v Facebook*, Inc., No. 1:18-cv-02689-JGK (S.D. N.Y. Aug. 08, 2018).

[103]   *Riddick v Facebook, Inc.*, No. 3:18-cv-04429 (N.D. Cal. Mar. 19, 2019).

[104]   *Spees et al v Facebook,* Inc. (EEOC, September 2018).

[105]   Autoriteit Persoonsgegevens, *Common Statement by the Contact Group of the Data Protection Authorities of the Netherlands, France, Spain, Hamburg and Belgium* (May 2017), online: DPA   <https://autoriteitpersoonsgegevens.nl/sites/default/files/atoms/files/common_statement_16_may_2017.pdf>. *See* also the campaign #stopspyingonus started in the June 2019 in several countries of the European Union: Ligue des Droits Humains, *communiqué de presse* (June 2019), online: LDH <http://2ur2r.r.ca.d.sendibm2.com/mk/mr/UrbaMII0WjtmxReL Sprj_R7V06S93d_CzxiYS6on0Hc0KrHFTpgYjto0M6OpQwMaxuSsWJfJASPqf2Mr aSfdwjBjnYydKivSTy6hgUaq5_rVmvht>.

[106]   Délibération nSAN-2017 du 6 mai 2017 pronançant une sanction pécuniaire à l'encontre de la société Facebook.

[107]   Agencia Española de Datos, *Procedimiento no. PS/00219/2017 – Resolución: R/00259/2018* <https://www.aepd.es/media/resoluciones/PS-00219–2017_Resolucion-de-fecha-02–03–2018_Art-ii-culo-11–6-LOPD.pdf>.

[108]   *See* chapter 4, section II, 2.

gender, and age discrimination to seek liability from Facebook for offering such possibilities by design to companies. Ultimately, Facebook's liability was not assessed, because the cases were privately settled. However, the line of defense stuck to the immunity of Facebook as an Internet Service Provider grounded both on the CDA and precedents.[109]

The proactive posture of civil rights organizations, such as the National Fair Housing Alliance, in addition to the high medialization of the cases was pivotal to force Facebook to change its design, despite the fact that no liability was assessed.[110] Facebook then created a special webpage for companies to offer housing, employment, and credit opportunities for Facebook users. In this special webpage, filters related to protected aspects are no longer available.

In the European Union, antidiscrimination lawyers and scholars have not yet addressed the issue of discrimination through targeted advertising, even though the practice exists throughout online platforms. Litigation and research about targeted advertising is mostly related to privacy rights in the European Union. The cases *Autoriteit Persoonsgegevens v Facebook* the Netherlands, *Commission Nationale de l'Informatique et des Libertés v Facebook,* and *Agencia Española de Datos v Facebook* addressed by national data protection authorities indicate how the issue has been treated through the angle of data protection rights. Through my analysis of these cases, I argue that even though data protection laws increasingly provide rules to protect personal data from being collected, processed, and used in a discriminatory fashion, these overarching rules do not provide a strong definition of discrimination. This lack of strong definition requires data lawyers to work directly with antidiscrimination laws. Furthermore, this lack of strong definition implies practical obstacles to address concrete cases of discrimination. Despite this necessity, the correlation between the two fields has not yet happened in a substantive way, which prevents actions such as the one filed against Facebook for its filters in the United States from occurring in Europe as well. In the European Union, data protection laws alone are not fully equipped to address discrimination as it is defined in the Equality Directives.

3.3. SELECTED LITIGATION ON LABOR MATTERS

Regarding the labor market in the United States, I selected O'Connor v Uber Technologies[111], Kendall Reese v Uber Technologies[112], Mohamed v Uber

---

[109] *Ibid.*
[110] *See* chapter 4, section II, 2.4.
[111] *O'Connor v Uber Technologies, Inc.,* 82 F. Supp. 3d 1133 (N.D. Cal. 2015).
[112] *Kendall Reese v Uber Technologies, Inc.* (2:18-cv-03300, United District Court for The Eastern District of Pennsylvania, Aug 2018).

Technologies[113], and Thomas Liu v Uber.[114] In the EU and the member states, I analyzed *Uber BV v Aslam*[115], *X v Uber*[116], and C-434/15, Asociación Profesional Elite Taxi v Uber.[117]

In the United States and in the UK, *Thomas Liu v Uber* and *X v Uber*, respectively, depict how a scored evaluation system might produce racially and gender biased outcomes by allowing users with protected classes to be permanently excluded from the platform servers only based on customers' preferences.

In *Asociación Profesional Elite Taxi v Uber* case, the CJEU construed that Uber provides transportation services along with information society services, because it organizes the transportation activity by determining the conditions under which the drivers provide their services. The reasoning of the CJEU decision has served as inspiration for employment misclassification rulings in the UK, especially the fact that the platform is not limited to intermediation because it manages and controls the selection of the drivers, the clients available to the them, and the price to be charged for each trip.[118]

In *O'Connor v Uber Technologies* and *Uber BV v Aslam*, the scored evaluation systems were assessed as an instrument used by Uber to control and manage their drivers. While drivers were ruled as workers in the UK, which puts them in the scope of the Equality Act 2010, in the United States their employment status – which would define whether they are under the personal scope of Title VII, the ADEA, and the ADA – could not be assessed by the District Courts because drivers have significantly waived their trial and class action rights by accepting arbitration clauses as a mean of resolution to all employment disputes. *Kendall Reese v Uber Technologies* and *Mohamed v Uber Technologies* confirmed that arbitration clauses are not void even in cases concerning discrimination.

From the analysis of these above-mentioned cases, I argue that the main structural challenges to the principle of equality are posed by online platforms' design choices, which includes aesthetic choices (e.g., as used by Airbnb), matching tools (e.g., as used by Roommates, Facebook, Google), evaluation tools (e.g., as used by Uber), and by the impossibility and undesirability of

---

[113] *Mohamed v Uber Technologies, Inc.*, 848 F.3d 1201 (9th Circuit 2016).

[114] *Thomas Liu v Uber, Inc.*, EEOC. The case was publicized in the attorney's law office webpage. *See* Dan Adams, *Boston-Based Attorney Argues Uber's Star Ratings Are Racially Biased* (October 2016) online: Lichten & Liss-Riordan, P.C. <https://www.llrlaw.com/wp-content/uploads/2015/04/Boston-based-Attorney-Argues-Uber's-Star-Ratings-are-Racially-Biased.pdf>.

[115] *Uber BV v Aslam* [2018] EWCA civ 2748.

[116] The claim was brought by the GMB union, on behalf of the women who wanted to remain anonymous. Some details of the case were published on the plaintiff's law firm website. Leigh Day, *British Female Driver Launches Sex Discrimination Claim Against Uber Over Practices* (September 2017), online: Leigh Day Office <https://www.leighday.co.uk/News/News-2017/September-2017/British-female-driver-launches-sex-discrimination>.

[117] C-434/15 *Asociación Profesional Elite Taxi v Uber*, EU:C:2017:981.

[118] *See Uber BV v Aslam* [2018] EWCA civ 2748.

establishing previous control over users' behavior (e.g., Craigslist and Daft) in the accommodation, housing, and labor sectors. Additionally, from the analyses of these cases, my book argues that antidiscrimination laws in the United States and the European Union are only partially equipped to address discrimination that occurs in online platforms because (1) they do not protect individuals from having their demographic markers revealed by online platforms (i.e., aesthetic choices), and (2) the immunities provided by the Communications Decency Act of 1996 in the United States and the Directive on Electronic Commerce in the European Union restrain online platforms from liability for their users' discrimination in a significant number of cases.

With respect to design choices, first, in the housing and accommodation markets, the salience of users' identities – their names and profile photographs – before transactions are concluded have replicated the challenges discriminated groups have long faced offline. This design is an option, as some platforms opt to disclose guests' photographs and names before the transaction is concluded, while others opt to disclose these aspects afterward.[119] Second, in the targeted advertisement sector when platforms such as Google and Facebook design technology, such as cutting-edge data tracking and processing, to enable advertisers to reach their audiences with specific personal features, including race, ethnic affiliations, gender, age, and religion, they allow advertisers to exclude statutorily protected groups to the access of goods, services, and employment.[120] Third, in the online labor markets, simply-designed evaluation rating systems provided to clients to evaluate platform workers' performance raise concerns about discrimination against protected groups because of implicit or explicit biases.[121]

On the subject of liability immunities, online platforms share the fact that they do not directly provide the services or the products available in their online spaces.[122] Rather, they arguably only sell or provide access to their digital service, their software, their matching, and their evaluation tools.[123] When online platforms in the goods, services, and labor sectors only intermediate – or in their own words, put into contact two sides of the same market – *in principle*, they do not have any power of agency over their users. In legal terms, when companies do not have power of agency over the actors they interact with, they

---

[119] Notably, Airbnb opts to disclose it before, while HomeAway disclose it afterwards. *See* chapter 1 and 2.

[120] *See* chapters 3 and 4.

[121] Michael Luca, "Designing Online Marketplaces: Trust and Reputation Mechanisms" (2017) 17 Innovation Policy and the Economy 77; and Alex Rosenblat, Karen E C Levy, Solon Barocas, Tim Hwang, "Discriminating Tastes: Uber's Customer Ratings as Vehicles for Workplace Discrimination" (2017) 9:3 Policy & Internet 256.

[122] *See* title I.

[123] *Selden v Airbnb, Inc.*, No. 16-cv-00933 (CRC) (D.C. Nov. 1, 2016); Case C-390/18 *Airbnb Ireland* ECLI:EY:C:2019:1112.

do not have liability over their acts either, including acts of discrimination.[124] The liability of companies for the action of their agents has been proved to be important because (1) companies have more economic power to redress the victims for their moral and material damages, and (2) they have the legal incentive to change their operational structures and to instruct their agents to act legally.[125]

3.4. REPRESENTATIVENESS OF THE HOUSING, ACCOMMODATION, TARGETED ADVERTISING, AND LABOR MARKETS IN ONLINE PLATFORMS

The choice to focus this research on the sectors of accommodation and housing, the offer of goods and services through targeted advertisement, and the labor sector is related to both their representativeness amid online platforms and the material scope of antidiscrimination laws in the Unites States and in the EU. Moreover, litigation concerning discrimination against users is more present in these three sectors.

3.4.1. Accommodation and Housing Markets

Online platforms specialized in accommodation transactions and advertising housing have experienced exponential growth since the early 2000s.[126] First, they replaced the role of newspapers to a great degree by allowing users to advertise their long- and short-term real estate offers.[127] In this regard, Craigslist, an online board available in the United States and in several European countries, has published over 20 million advertisements concerning housing offers since the beginning of its operations.[128] In addition, many sorts of online real estate platforms that allow real estate owners to directly advertise their properties without a fee are currently available. Zillow, ForSaleByOwner, Fizber, Immoweb,

---

[124] Gregory C Keating, "The Theory of Enterprise Liability and Common Law Strict Liability" (2001) 54 Vanderbilt Law Review 1285, 1286–1287; Vassilis Hatzopoulos, *The Collaborative Economy and the EU Law*, (Portland: Hart Publishing, 2018), p 22–23; Agnieszka A McPeak, "Sharing Tort Liability in the New Sharing Economy" (2016) 49:1 Connecticut Law Review 171.

[125] Gregory C Keating, "The Theory of Enterprise Liability and Common Law Strict Liability" (2001) 54 Vanderbilt Law Review 1285, 1286–1287.

[126] Jeroen Oskam, Albert Boswijk, "Airbnb: The Future of Networked Hospitality Businesses" (2016) 2:1 Journal of Tourism Futures 22, p 24.

[127] Rigel C Oliveri, "Discriminatory Housing Advertisements Online: Lessons from Craigslist" (2010) 43 Indiana Law Review 1125, p 1130.

[128] Smith, *Craigslist Statistics and Facts* (May 2019), online: Business Statistics <https://expandedramblings.com/index.php/craigslist-statistics/>.

and Leboncoin are leaders in the sector.[129] Roommates, a matching platform for long-term shared houses, has over one million page views per day.[130]

Online platforms have evolved over the past decade to embrace travel accommodation bookings, which often involve short-term property rentals. In 2019, peer-to-peer accommodation platforms were responsible for 10% of the bookings in the tourism sector.[131] Airbnb has served over 150 million guests/ tenants across the cities in which it operations.[132] In 2019, without owning a single property, Airbnb offered more accommodation options than the international hotel chains of Hilton and Marriot combined.[133] Airbnb mainly has offers for short-term single rooms and entire houses. The platform leads the peer-to-peer sharing accommodation trend, but it is not alone in the market. For example, its competitor VRBO offers more long-term stays and entire home listings.[134] In HomeAway and Abitrel, guests across 191 countries can find over two million properties listed in 23 different languages.[135]

3.4.2. Targeted Advertising Market

Advertisements have sponsored content online since the beginning of the commercial internet, and, currently, they are ubiquitous to every user's online experience. The fast-growing transition of advertisements from the traditional mass communication medium to the internet made online platform businesses flourish in the past two decades.[136] Over the years, online platforms have highly invested in resources and cutting-edge technology to tailor and target third-

---

129 Zillow, *Post a For Sale by Owner Listing* (December 2019), online: Zillow <https://www. zillow.com/for-sale-by-owner/>; ForSalebyOwner, *Free Listing* (December 2019), online: ForSalebyOwner <https://www.forsalebyowner.com>; Fizber, *Free Real Estate Listing by Fizber* (December 2019), online: Fizber <https://www.fizber.com/>, Immoweb, *hostpage* (December 2019), online: Immoweb <https://www.immoweb.be/fr>; Leboncoin, *Annonces Location Immobilières* (December 2019), online: leboncoin <https://www.leboncoin.fr/ locations/offres/>.

130 Numbers found in the legal action brought against the platform. *Fair Housing Council of San Fernando Valley v Roommates, LLC*, CV 03–9386 PA (RZx) (C.D. Cal. Nov. 7, 2008).

131 Research and Markets, *Global Online Accommodation Booking Market 2019 Report* (yStats GmbH, 2020).

132 Georgios Zervas, Davide Proserpio, John W Byers, "The Rise of the Sharing Economy: Estimating the Impact of Airbnb on the Hotel Industry" (2017) 54 Journal of Marketing Research 687, p 688.

133 Nicole Gurran, "Global Home-Sharing, Local Communities and the Airbnb Debate: A Planning Research Agenda" (2018) 19:2 Planning Theory & Practice 298.

134 Vrbo, *List Your Property on Vrbo and Open Your Door to Rental Income* (December 2019), online: VRBO <https://www.vrbo.com>.

135 HomeAway, *List Your Property* (December 2019), online: HomeAway <https://homeaway. com>; Abitrel, *Publiz Votre Annonce sur Arbitrel.fr et Dites Bonjour à de Nouveaux Revenues* (December 2019), online: Arbitrel <https://abitrel.fr>.

136 The Interactive Advertising Bureau, *IAB Internet Advertising Revenue Report* (November 2018), online: IAB <https://www.iab.com/wp-content/uploads/2018/11/IAB-WEBINAR- HY18-Internet-Ad-Revenue-Report1.pdf>.

party advertisements to the right consumer.[137] So far, advertisement is the main source of revenue for online platforms that offer their services without charge to the public. Platforms providing (1) search engines, such as Google, Bing, and Yahoo; (2) video streaming, such as YouTube and Dailymotion; and (3) social networking, such as Facebook, make their profits by selling online spaces for third-party advertisements. In this context, numbers matter. In 2018, Facebook made $55 billion in ad revenues, and Google alone had half the online advertising share in the United States[138] and earned $116.3 billion only by selling advertisement placements.[139] Aside from considering these online platforms as high-intensive technology companies, investors value them above all else as part of the advertising industry.[140]

3.4.3. Labor Market

The expansion of online labor platforms and their inevitability as an economic driving force for the years ahead has prompted policy makers in the United States, the European Union, and international organizations to address the challenges of the changing workforce conditions within these new arrangements.[141] The figures are not negligible.

---

[137] Engin Bozdag, "Bias in Algorithmic Filtering and Personalization" (2013) 15 Ethics Information Technology 209, p 209.

[138] David A Vise, Mark Malseed, *The Google Story: Inside the Hottest Business, Media and Technology Success of Our Time, op. cit.*, p xi.

[139] *See* United States Securities and Exchange Commission, *Annual Report Pursuant to Section 13 15 (d) of the Securities Exchange Act* (December 2018), online: Facebook Commission File <https://www.sec.gov/Archives/edgar/data/1326801/000132680119000009/fb-12312018x10k.htm#s7598225E01E95F77950D4736C39C55F1> and United States Securities and Exchange Commission, *Annual Report Pursuant to Section 13 15 (d) of the Securities Exchange Act* (December 2018), online: Alphabet Inc. Commission File <https://www.sec.gov/Archives/edgar/data/1652044/000165204419000004/goog10-kq42018.htm>.

[140] David A Vise, Mark Malseed, *The Google Story: Inside the Hottest Business, Media and Technology Success of Our Time, op. cit.*, p 139.

[141] The European Commission has published several studies and trends on the impact of new technologies including online platforms on the working practices and workers. European Group on Ethics in Science and New Technologies, *Future of Work, Future of Society* (December 2018), online: European Commission Directorate-General for Research and Innovation <https://ec.europa.eu/info/sites/info/files/research_and_innovation/ege/ege_future-of-work_opinion_122018.pdf>; Chris Warhusrt, Wil Hunt, "The Digitalisation of Future Work and Employment: Possible Impact and Policy Responses (2019) European Commission JRC117404 1; United Kingdom Government, *Good Work: A Response to the Taylor Review of Modern Working Practices* (February, 2018) online: Government UK <assets.publishing.service.gov.uk/government/uploads/system/uploads/attachment_data/file/679767/ 180206_BEIS_Good_Work_Report Accessible_A4_pdf >; OECD, *Policy Responses to New Forms of Work* (Paris: OECD Publishing, 2019); In August 2019, California created the Future of Work Commission to address, among other things, the impact of technology on work, workers, employers, jobs and society: Future of Work Commission, *Future of Work* (August 2019), online: Labor & Workforce Development Agency <https://labor.ca.gov/fowc/>; In 2017, the ILO launched a commission on the future of work focused

In Europe, the UK has the most significant proportion of individuals amongst its entire active labor force providing work exclusively through platforms (3.6%), followed by the Netherlands (2.8%), Spain (2.7%), Germany (2.6%), Lithuania (2.4%), and Italy (2.4%).[142] Furthermore, in Portugal, 11.5% of the active labor force has worked for online platforms at least once, while this number reaches 12.5% in Spain, 7.9% in Croatia, 7.6% in France, 7.6% in Sweden, 6.9% in Slovakia, 6.9% in Hungary, and 6.5% in Finland.[143]

In the United States, 45.3 million workers or 22% of the active workforce have provided work through an online labor platform.[144] Amid this sample, workers primarily offered services related to home repair and moving (11%), ride-sharing transportation (10%), and food delivery (7%). These workers have been working for multiple platforms throughout their careers.[145] This same survey identified that the share of racial and ethnic minorities and young people is higher in the platform economy, with about 67% of the workers belonging to a racial minority group and 57% born after the 1980s.[146]

Online labor platforms are mostly focused on the service sector. In the past few years, many companies focused on matching service providers with potential clients were created. Some notable examples of these platforms include Amazon Mechanical Turk, Clickworker, Foodora, Etece.es, TaskRunner, Helpling, TaskRabbit, Deliveroo, Uber, and Lyft. The users of these platforms provide a vast range of services, such as errands, handyman services, cleaning, furniture assembly, packing, coding, food delivery, and private transportation. Thus far, the specialized literature has categorized these platforms into different labels, including online labor platforms, professional crowdsourcing platforms, and on-demand work platforms.[147]

---

on a human-centered agenda. The outcome of their work can be consulted in the report: Global Commission on the Future of Work, *Work for a Brighter Future* (January 2019), online: ILO <https://www.ilo.org/global/publications/books/WCMS_662410/lang--en/index.htm>.

142 Cesira Urzi Brancati, Annarosa Pesole, Enrique Fernandez-Macías, *Digital Labour Platforms in Europe: Numbers, Profiles, and Employment Status of Platform Workers* (January 2019), online: Publications Office of the European Union <https://publications.jrc.ec.europa.eu/ repository/bitstream/JRC117330/jrc117330_jrc117330_dlp_counting_profiling.pdf> p 9.

143 *Ibid*, p 9.

144 Burson-Marsteller, *The On-Demand Economy Survey* (2015), online: The Aspen Institute <https://www.aspeninstitute.org/publications/demand-economy-survey/>.

145 *Ibid*.

146 *Ibid*.

147 A detailed typology of online labor platforms is elaborated by Cristiano Codagnone, Federico Biagi, Fabienne Abadie, *The Passions and the Interests: Unpacking the 'Sharing Economy'* (October, 2016) online: European Commission <https://publications.jrc.ec.europa.eu/ repository/bitstream/JRC101279/jrc101279.pdf>; Wilma B Liebman, Andrew Lyubarsky, "Crowdwork, the Law, and the Future of Work" (2016) 1 Perspectives on Work 22; OECD, *New Forms of Work in the Digital Economy* (June 2016) online: OECD Digital Economy Papers <https://www.oecd-ilibrary.org/science-and-technology/new-forms-of-work-in-the-digital-economy_5jlwnklt820x-en>; Jon Messenger, Oscar Vargas Llave, Lutz Gschwind, Simon Boehmer, Greet Vermeylen, Mathijn Wilkens, *Working Anytime, Anywhere: the Effects*

4. DEFINING ONLINE PLATFORMS

The foundations of platform structures are connectivity, intermediation, and interactivity. These three values also represent the core and purpose of the internet. Almost two decades ago, Tim Berners-Lee, the developer of the world-wide web, publicly acknowledged that his initial purpose was to create a place to "collaborate, communicate and share information."[148] History reveals that Berners-Lee's aspirations have become a reality. In the past two decades, technological companies have heavily invested in enabling the exchange of any valued or non-economic valued assets online. From the 2000s to the 2020s, markets have been transformed by connectivity and interactivity as they have been transposed online.[149] Connectivity and interactivity have allowed platform companies to scale the synergy between supply and demand in an unprecedented fashion by eliminating physical barriers. So far, online platforms have become a relevant driver of economic activity and growth in Europe and the United States.[150]

4.1. THE RISE OF THE DIGITAL INFORMATION SOCIETY: FROM "READ ONLY" TO "READ-WRITE-EXECUTE"

In the first generation of the internet, Web 1.0 users were limited to reading the information presented online on static websites.[151] Content was mainly "read only." At that time, companies developed search engines that enabled internet users to find these static websites and be connected to information and knowledge. This period marked the rise of the digital information society as it is currently understood.

The second-generation of the internet, Web 2.0, is distinguished by the beginning of a "read-write-publish" flow.[152] In addition to searching for

---

on the World of Work (February, 2017) online: Eurofond <https://www.eurofound.europa.eu/publications/report/2017/working-anytime-anywhere-the-effects-on-the-world-of-work>.

[148] Orly Lobel, "The Law of The Platform" (2016) 101 Minnesota Law Review 87, p 96.

[149] Karine Perset, "The Economic and Social Role of Internet Intermediaries" (2010) 171 OECD Digital Economy Papers 1.

[150] Annabelle Gawer, *Online Platforms: Contrasting Perceptions of European Stakeholders. A Qualitative Analysis of the European Commission's Public Consultation on the Regulatory Environment for Platforms. A Study Prepared for the European Commission DG Communications Networks, Content & Technology* (May 2016), online: European Commission <https://ec.europa.eu/newsroom/dae/document.cfm?doc_id=15932>, p 3.

[151] Keshab Nath, Sourish Dhar, Subhash Basishtha, "Web 1.0 to Web 3.0: The Evolution of the Web and Its Various Challenges" (2014) International Conference on Reliability Optimization and Information Technology 86.

[152] Tim O'Reilly, "What is Web 2.0? Design Patterns and Business Models for the Next Generation of Software", in Helen Margaret Donelan, Karen Lesley Kear, Magnus Ramage, *Online Communication and Collaboration* (New York: Routledge, 2010), p 225.

information, users could communicate and exchange in newly created spaces. Online marketplaces such as Craigslist, Facebook, eBay, and Amazon were introduced. Individuals were also given a public voice in web spaces, such as through blogs, social media, and video streaming. These new marketplaces disrupted the publishing and retail industry, among others.

The third generation of the internet, Web 3.0, was transformed into a place of "read-write-execute."[153] According to Tim Berners-Lee, this internet is permeated by tailored content and products.[154] In the previous versions of the web, one of the challenges of presenting information was the impossibility of providing context to data. For instance, a keyword research in Web 2.0 search engine systems resulted in an information overload not necessarily related to the user's intentions. The same situation happened regarding online advertisements. They were more generic and not tailored to users. In Web 3.0, matching platforms have been developed and have transformed the service economy.[155]

In Web 3.0, platform companies often have a few physical assets. Their values are based on leading technology, users' connections, and branding.[156] In addition, platform companies offer a myriad of services and ways to monetize their products. Platforms such as Google, Facebook, Uber, and Airbnb illustrate this diversity. Google has considerably evolved from its original mission to organize and list all the digital world's information through a search engine; currently, it has become a company highly-invested in online advertising technologies, cloud computing, digitization of entire libraries, and disruptive future-oriented businesses, such as the one related to the creation of the online researchable maps of the human genome.[157] In the same vein, Facebook has switched from a closed network for Harvard students to an international social

---

[153]   Tobias Kollmann, Carina Lomberg, Anika Peschl, "Web 1.0, Web 2.0 and Web 3.0: The Development of E-Business", in *Encyclopedia of E-Commerce Development, Implementation and Management* (IGI Global, 2010), p 1203.

[154]   Nupur Choudhury, "World Wide Web and Its Journey from Web 1.0 to Web 4.0" (2014) 5:6 International Journal of Computer Science and Information Technologies 8096.

[155]   Orly Lobel, "The Law of The Platform" (2016) 101 Minnesota Law Review 87, p 97.

[156]   For sharing economy in general, *see* Sofia Ranchordas, "Does Sharing Mean Caring? Regulating Innovation in the Sharing Economy" (2015) 16 Minnesota Journal of Law, Science & Technology 1; Vanessa Katz, "Regulating the Sharing Economy" (2015) 30:4 Berkeley Technology Law Journal 1067; Daniel E Rauch, David Schleicher, "Like Uber, But for Local Government Law: The Future of Local Regulation of The Sharing Economy (2015) 76 Ohio St Law Journal 901; Arun Sundararajan, *The Sharing Economy: The End of Employment and The Rise of Crowd-Based Capitalism* (Cambridge: MIT Press, 2017); Vassilis Hatzopoulos, Sofia Roma, "Caring for Sharing? The Collaborative Economy under EU law (2017) 54:1 Common Market Law Review 81; Vassilis Hatzopoulos, *The Collaborative Economy and the EU Law* (2018), *op. cit.*.

[157]   David A Vise, Mark Malseed, *The Google Story: Inside the Hottest Business, Media and Technology Success of Our Time* (New York: Bantam Books, 2018), p 24. Also, chapter 4, section I.

network, encompassing not only individual profiles but also professional ones.[158] In the recent past, Uber has diversified its products from private transportation to food delivery, bike rental, and, recently, to a platform that matches job seekers with employers looking for temporary staff.[159] Uber has also heavily invested in driverless car technologies. Given these changes, these businesses may be described as "everything platforms" or an "everything economy."[160] After all, what do these platforms have in common?

4.2. A BROAD APPROACH OF ONLINE PLATFORMS

The concept of online platforms is a moving target. So far, the term has been used to designate companies that have different purposes and organizational patterns on the internet.[161] The reality shows that the platform economy is much broader than the sharing economy and social networking platforms.[162] Furthermore, the definition of online platforms seems to oscillate according to the speaker or actor. The previous Vice President of the European Commission once stated, "We do not even have a single definition of platforms accepted by everyone. We have hundreds of good definitions (...) when different people are talking about platforms, they have a totally different understanding."[163] References to online platforms often encompass general internet search engines (e.g., Google, Bing); specialized advertisement boards (e.g., Craigslist, OfferUp); online marketplaces (e.g., Amazon, eBay), social networks (e.g., Facebook, LinkedIn, Twitter), video sharing platforms (e.g., YouTube, Dailymotion), and the sharing economy (e.g., Airbnb, Uber, BlablaCar, TaskRabbit).

In an attempt to embrace as many business models as possible and to create policy strategies regarding online platforms, the European Commission and the OECD similarly define platforms as digital services that facilitate the interaction between two or more distinct, independent sets of users in a particular digital

---

[158] David Kirkpatrick, *The Facebook Effect: The Real Inside Story of Mark Zuckerberg and the World's Fastest Growing Company* (Croydon: Ebury Publishing, 2011).

[159] Uber, *Country List* (October 2019) online: Uber <https://www.uber.com/en-BE/country-list/>; and Uber, *Uber Works* (October 2019) online: Uber <https://www.works.co>.

[160] Orly Lobel, "The Law of The Platform" (2016) 101 Minnesota Law Review 87, p 101.

[161] Julie E Cohen, "Law for the Platform Economy" (2017) 51 UCDL Rev. 133, pp 136–153.

[162] Vassilis Hatzopoulos, "Vers un Cadre de la Régulation des Plateformes? (2019) 3 Revue Internationale de Droit Économique 399, p 400.

[163] House of Lords, *Revised Transcript of Evidence Taken Before the Select Committee on the European Union Inquiry on Online Platforms and the EU Digital Single Market Session 15* (December 2015), online: UK Parliament <http://data.parliament.uk/writtenevidence/committeeevidence.svc/evidencedocument/eu-internal-market-subcommittee/online-platforms-and-the-eu-digital-single-market/oral/25770.html>.

space to generate value for at least one of the users.[164] This definition has as a common grounds the internet, connectivity, and the generation of economic or non-economic value. In this book, I embrace such a definition because it facilitates the analysis of companies with different purposes, structures, economic models, and designs. Moreover, this definition is not in conflict with the one suggested in the Digital Services Act proposal, which states that the term "online platforms" refers to providers of hosting services that store and disseminate information to the public at the request of the users of the hosting services.[165]

In this regard, even if businesses such as Airbnb, Facebook, Google, and Uber seem to have different purposes at a first glance, economic models and designs, they are online platforms under the OECD definition because they create economic and non-economic value by offering digital services that intermediate the interaction between individuals in a particular digital space. For instance, Airbnb generates profits by charging a percentage of every accommodation transaction it intermediates. The platform provides digital services that facilitate those transactions to take place. Among these digital services, it is included a thoughtfully planned digital space where hosts and guests may present themselves and their products. Moreover, matching and evaluation tools are supplied to increase the chances that such transaction will happen. On the same token, Google search engine makes profits by connecting advertisers with users who use its digital search services. Google provides numerous services to make sure that the intermediation between advertisers and consumers will succeed. The platform extensively collects data about its users to enable advertisers to reach consumers/users with the most suitable personal aspects. Google offers matching algorithms that allow businesses to target their consumers. These patterns involving the creation of economic and non-economic value, the offer of digital services, and the intermediation between individuals in a particular digital space are present in online platforms businesses analyzed in this book.

---

[164]   The European Commission provided such definition in a public consultation about online platforms: European Commission, *Public Consultation on the Regulatory Environment for Platforms, Online Intermediaries, Data and Cloud Computing and the Collaborative Economy* (September 2015), online: European Commission <https://ec.europa.eu/information_society/newsroom/image/document/2016-7/efads_13917.pdf>, p 5; OECD, *An Introduction to Online Platforms and their Role in the Digital Transformation* (Paris: OECD Publishing, 2019), p 20; The European Commission and OECD's concept of online platforms is found on the economic theory of multi-sided firms and platforms developed in the work of David S Evans, Richard Schmalensee, The Antitrust Analysis of Multi-Sided Platform Businesses, in: Roger Blair, Daniel Sokol (eds), *Oxford Handbook on International Antitrust Economics* (New York: Oxford University Press, 2014), p 404.
[165]   Article 2, (h), Proposal for a Regulation of the European Parliament and of the Council on a Single Market for Digital Services (Digital Services Act) and amending Directive 2000/31/EC. COM/2020/825 final.

5. BOOK OUTLINE

This book is divided into three titles and six chapters. Each title focuses on one market segment. In Title I, I develop the facts and legal aspects related to the housing and accommodation markets. In Title II, I address the targeted advertising segment. In Title III, I examine the stakes of labor relations occurring on online platforms. In each title, I address the structural challenges online platforms pose to the equal treatment of their users and the existent legal limitations to respond to such challenges.

More specifically, in Title I, I demonstrate how platforms dedicated to housing and accommodation markets have mobilized the immunity of online intermediaries' liability, provided by federal statutory law in the United States[166], to avoid liability for race, ethnic origin, sex, and sexual orientation discrimination against housing and accommodation seekers.[167] I also introduce how online platforms might amplify discrimination against protected classes when their aesthetic design choices accentuate users' protected markers before prospective transactions are concluded.[168] In the EU, despite the extensive presence of platforms focused on accommodation and housing, members of the European Network of Legal Experts in Non-Discrimination have reported no specific lawsuit at the national court level regarding the discriminatory refusal of guests or home seekers because of their protected aspect, such as race, ethnic origin, or sex[169]; however, cases of ethnic origin discrimination against guests have been reported by the press.[170] Nevertheless, the question of whether a platform focused on the accommodation market is liable for its hosts' discriminatory refusal to rent their property can be reflected upon through a CJEU ruling concerning Airbnb.[171] Moreover, liability for illegal third-party

---

[166]   Communication Decency Act (CDA), 47 U.S.C., §230, (1) (1996).

[167]   Chicago Lawyers' v Craigslist Inc, No. 07–1101 (7th Cir. 2008); Fair Housing Council of San Fernando Valley v Roommates, LLC, CV 03–9386 PA (RZx) (C.D. Cal. Nov. 7, 2008); *Selden v Airbnb*, INC., No. 16-cv-00933 (CRC) (D.C. Nov. 1, 2016).

[168]   *See* chapter 1 and 2. Particularly, *Airbnb*.

[169]   Eugenia Caracciolo di Torella, Bridgette McLellan, *Gender Equality and the Collaborative Economy* (March 2018), online: European Commission <https://www.equalitylaw.eu/downloads/4573-gender-equality-and-the-collaborative-economy-pdf-721-kb>. Also, Isabelle Chopin, Carmine Conte, Edith Chambrier, *A Comparative Analysis of Non-Discrimination Law in Europe 2018, European Network of Legal Experts in Gender Equality and Non-Discrimination* (November 2018), online: European Commission Directorate-General for Justice and Consumers <https://www.equalitylaw.eu/downloads/4804-a-comparative-analysis-of-non-discrimination-law-in-europe-2018-pdf-1-02-mb>.

[170]   Henri Seckel, *Pour Réserver sur Airbnb, Mieux Vaut S'Appeler Isabelle que Djamila* (August 2018), online: LeMonde <https://www.lemonde.fr/societe/article/2018/08/24/airbnb-abritel-discriminations-en-ligne_5345587_3224.html>.

[171]   Case C-390/18, *Airbnb Ireland*, ECLI:EY:C:2019:1112.

discriminatory housing advertisement has been imposed on platforms dedicated to real estate transactions.[172]

In Title II, I highlight the design of cutting-edge matching technological tools that allow users to exclude protected classes from receiving goods, services, and work offers. I develop how platforms such as Facebook and Google have disrupted the advertising industry by granularly profiling and targeting consumers based on their personal demographic information and online behavioral patterns in the past two decades in the United States and across European countries.[173] Online platforms have become the main gatekeepers for third-party advertisement because they collect a significant amount of data about their users, including location, gender, age, and ethnic origin. This data is either provided by internet users or inferred by the users' online behavior. For instance, Google utilizes personal and non-personal data, such as location and previously used search words, to deliver tailored third-party advertisements to its users.[174] Aside from the data spontaneously provided by its users, Facebook also registers how users interact with content and other users through the available social gestures available, such as likes, shares, and comments.[175]

Lawsuits indicated that Facebook has alleged immunity liability when targeting protected classes such as women and Black Americans to not receive housing, credit, and employment advertisements, because the advertiser chose to not target these categories.[176] In Europe, despite the fact that Facebook allows the same targeting practices, to my knowledge, no case has been brought to national courts specifically mobilizing antidiscrimination laws applied to the access to goods, services, and employment. Alternatively, Facebook was investigated and condemned by national data protection authorities for processing users' personal data for advertising purposes without a proper legal basis[177], even though the cases concerned data related to protected classes in the European antidiscrimination laws.

---

[172] *Irish Human Rights and Equality Commission v Daft Media Limited t/a Daft/ie*, ADJ-00005960, WRC, August 2019.

[173] *See* chapter 3.

[174] Gloria Boone, Jane Secci, Linda Gallant, "Emerging Trends in Online Advertising" (2010) 5 Doxa Communicación 244, p 246.

[175] Engin Bozdag, *op. cit.*, p 211.

[176] *Onuoha v. Facebook, Inc.*, No. 5: 16-cv-06440-EJD (N.D. Cal. Apr. 7, 2017); *Bradley v T-Mobile US, INC.*, No. 17-cv-07232-BLF (N.D. Cal. June 4, 2019); *National Fair Housing Alliance v Facebook, Inc.*, No. 1:18-cv-02689-JGK (S.D. N.Y. Aug. 08, 2018).

[177] Autoriteit Persoonsgegevens, *Informal English Translation of the Conclusions of the Dutch Data Protection Authority in its Final Report of Findings About Its Investigation Into the Processing of Personal Data by Facebook Group* (February 2017), online: DPA <https://autoriteitpersoonsgegevens.nl/sites/default/files/atoms/files/conclusions_facebook_february_23_2017.pdf>; Agencia Española de Datos, *Procedimiento no. PS/00219/2017 - Resolución: R/00259/2018* <https://www.aepd.es/media/resoluciones/PS-00219-2017_Resolucion-de-fecha-02-03-2018_Art-ii-culo-11-6-LOPD.pdf>.

In Title III, I underline the development of facially objective evaluation systems that let protected classes to be permanently excluded from the platform or to be poorly ranked in searching-systems. I indicate how online labor platforms offering sectorial and non-sectorial services have reshaped some sectors in the labor market by providing new forms of coordinating work in the United States and Europe.[178] These platforms have been defined as "digital networks that coordinate labor service transactions in an algorithmic way."[179] Definitions highlight that they act as intermediaries and not as conventional employers. In this context, workers' management is undertaken by algorithms and rating systems. The main documented consequence of low ratings for workers is the unilateral termination of their contract with the platform.[180] In Chapter 6, I analyze cases in which the rating-scored systems of online labor platforms are legally challenged due to potential discriminatory bias. One case concerns an Asian American driver who had his contract terminated unilaterally by Uber based on his low ratings; the other case is related to a woman driver, in the UK, who claimed before the London Employment Tribunal that the Uber rating system put women in a disadvantaged position.

---

[178] Janine Berg, Marianne Furrer, Ellie Harmon, Uma Rani, Six Silberman, *Digital Labour Platforms and the Future of Work Towards Decent Work in the Online World* (September 2018), online: International Labour Organisation <https://www.ilo.org/wcmsp5/groups/public/---dgreports/---dcomm/---publ/documents/publication/wcms_645337.pdf >, p xv.

[179] Annarosa Pesole, Enrique Fenández-Marcías, Cesira Urzí Brancati, Ignacio González Vázquez; Frederico Biagi, *Platform Workers in Europe* (June 2018), online: Joint Research Centre European Commission <https://op.europa.eu/en/publication-detail/-/publication/fe8c6fdf-79b8-11e8-ac6a-01aa75ed71a1/language-en>; Willem Pieter De Groen, Ilaria Maselli, Brian Fabo, *The Digital Market for Local Services: A One-Night Stand for Workers?* (April 2016), online: CEPS European Commission <https://publications.jrc.ec.europa.eu/repository/handle/JRC100678>; and Willem Pieter De Groen, Ilaria Maselli, *The Impact of the Collaborative Economy on the Labour Market* (June 2016), online CEPS European Commission <https://www.ceps.eu/system/files/SR138CollaborativeEconomy_0.pdf>.

[180] *Ibid.*

TITLE I

ONLINE HOUSING AND ACCOMMODATION MARKETS: THE CROSSROADS OF INTERMEDIARY LIABILITY AND ANTIDISCRIMINATION LAW

INTRODUCTION

Online platforms focused on housing and accommodation services have increasingly encroached on spaces traditionally occupied by newspapers, travel agencies, hotels, and real estate brokers. For example, since Airbnb was founded in 2008 as a short-term accommodation marketplace, it has served over 40 million guests.[181] At its peak, Craigslist, a virtual billboard space focused on classifieds, had 50 million users and 30 million advertisements posted monthly.[182] Roommates, specialized on matching individuals seeking shared places to live, boasts 50,000 visitors daily[183], and Daft, centered on housing advertising and matching property seekers with homeowners, has 1,000 property searches every minute.[184]

The sectors in which the above platforms operate have reportedly encountered issues related to racial or ethnic origin discrimination.[185] In this

---

[181] Georgios Zervas, Davide Proserpio, John W Byers, "The Rise of the Sharing Economy: Estimating the Impact of Airbnb on the Hotel Industry" (2017) 54 Journal of Marketing Research 687, p 688.

[182] Craig Smith, *Craigslist Statistics and Facts* (May 2019), online: Business Statistics <https://expandedramblings.com/index.php/craigslist-statistics/>.

[183] Numbers available in the legal action: *Fair Housing Council of San Fernando Valley v Roommates, LLC*, CV 03–9386 PA (RZx) (C.D. Cal. Nov. 7, 2008), p 3450.

[184] Daft.ie, *About Us* (December 2019), online <https://www.daft.ie/about/>.

[185] In Europe: Julie Ringelheim, Nicolas Bernard, *Discrimination in Housing: Thematic Report of the European Network of Legal Experts in the Non-Discrimination Field* (February 2013), online: European Commission Directorate General for Justice and Consumers <https://op.europa.eu/en/publication-detail/-/publication/c8cf0ff7–8676–4751–8d36–59eeffe379ee/language-en>; Natalie Boccadoro, "Housing Rights and Racial Discrimination" (2009) 9 European Anti-Discrimination Law Review 21; Malcolm Harrison, Ian Law, Deborah Phillips, *Migrants, Minorities and Housing: Exclusion, Discrimination and Anti-Discrimination in 15 Member States of the European Union* (December 2005), online: European Monitoring Center on Racism and Xenophobia <https://fra.europa.eu/sites/default/files/fra_uploads/188-CS-Housing-en.pdf>; Bill Edgar, *Policy Measures to Ensure Access to Decent Housing for Migrants and Ethnic Minorities* (December 2004), online: European Commission <https://ec.europa.eu/employment_social/social_inclusion/docs/decenthousing_en.pdf>; (Gender Discrimination – Belgium) Nicolas Bernard, "Les Femmes, la Précarité et le Mal-Logement: un Lien Fatal à Dénouer" (2007) 1970 Courrier Hebdomadaire du Crisp 5; Nicolas Bernard, "Les Lois Anti-Discrimination et le Secteur du Logement (Privé et Social)" in: Sébastien Van Drooghenbroeck et al, *De Nieuwe Federale Antidiscriminatiewetten – Les Nouvelles Lois Luttant Contre la Discrimination* (Bruxelles: La Charte, 2008), 797; Equality and Human Rights Commission, *How Fair is Britain? Equality, Human Rights and Good Relations in 2010* (October 2010) online: Equality Human Rights <https://www.equalityhumanrights.com/sites/default/files/how-fair-is-britain.pdf>; Koen Van der Bracht, "The Not-in-My-Property Syndrome: The Occurrence of Ethnic

---

respect, studies have demonstrated that urban areas are frequently divided not only by social classes but also by ethnic affiliation and national origins in the United States and in the European Union member states.[186]

In Europe, the phenomenon of discrimination in housing transactions has resulted in a sort of ethnic spatial concentration that can be observed, for example, in Paris with Northern Africans, in Barcelona or Genoa with Moroccans and Pakistanis, or in Lisbon with Cape Verdeans.[187] Discrimination is particularly sensitive in the rental market, in which race, ethnic origin, and nationality have imposed barriers to prospective tenants. In this regard, evidence of direct and indirect discrimination is documented in advertisements with statements such as "only national people" or "we do not lease to non-EU foreigners"[188] in Spain; with requirements such as "only German speaking tenants with a regular income"[189] in Berlin, "no colored need apply"[190] in Ireland, or "no Roma" in Hungary[191]; or over a hundred housing advertisements in newspapers and online media requiring "Austrians only," "no foreigners," or "native German-speakers only" in Austria.[192] In

---

Discrimination in the Rental Housing Market in Belgium" (2015) 41:1 Journal of Ethnic and Migration Studies 158; Magnus Carlsson, Stefan Eriksson, "Discrimination in the Rental Market for Apartments" (2014) 23 Journal of Housing Economics 41. In the United States, In the United States: Margery Austin Turner, Rob Santos, Diane K Levy, Doug Wissoker, Claudia Aranda, Rob Pitingolo, *Housing Discrimination Against Racial and Ethnic Minorities 2012* (June 2013) online: US Department of Housing and Urban Development <www.huduser. gov/portal/Publications/pdf/HUD-514_HDS2012.pdf>.

[186]   In Europe, *see*: Sonia Arbaci, "(Re)Viewing Ethnic Residential Segregation in Southern European Cities: Housing and Urban Regimes as Mechanisms of Marginalisation (2008) 23 Housing Studies 589; Julie Ringelheim, Nicolas Bernard, *Discrimination in Housing: Thematic Report of the European Network of Legal Experts in the Non-Discrimination Field* (February 2013), online: European Commission Directorate General for Justice and Consumers <https://op.europa.eu/en/publication-detail/-/publication/c8cf0ff7-8676-4751-8d36-59eeff e379ee/language-en>; In the US, *see*: James A Kushner, "Fair Housing Amendments Act of 1988: The Ssecond Generation of Fair Housing" (1989) 42 Venderbilt Law Review 1049; Joe R Feagin, "Excluding Blacks and Others from Housing: The Foundation of White Racism" (1999) 4:3 Cityscape 79 pp 80–85; Jan Ondrich, Stephen Ross, Jon Yinger, "Geography of Housing Discrimination" (2001) 12 Journal of Housing Research 217.

[187]   Sonia Arbaci, "(Re)Viewing Ethnic Residential Segregation in Southern European Cities: Housing and Urban Regimes as Mechanisms of Marginalisation", p 590.

[188]   Malcon Harrison, Ian Law, Deborah Phillips, "Migrants, Minorities and Housing: Exclusion, Discrimination and Anti-Discrimination in 15 Member States of the European Union" (December 2005), online: FRA <https://fra.europa.eu/sites/default/files/fra_uploads/188-CS-Housing-en.pdf> p 68.

[189]   *Ibid*, p 68.

[190]   *Ibid*, p 69.

[191]   Andras Kadar, *Transposition and Implementation at National Level of Council Directives 2000/43 and 2000/78 Country Report Hungary* (January 2019), online: European Commission Directorate for Justice and Consumers <https://www.equalitylaw.eu/downloads/5001-hungary-country-report-non-discrimination-2019-pdf-1-80-mb>, p 62.

[192]   Julie Ringelheim, Nicolas Bernard, *Discrimination in Housing: Thematic Report of the European Network of Legal Experts in the Non-Discrimination Field* (February 2013), *op. cit.*, p 47.

France, for instance, cases involving landlords' refusal to rent their property to non-national tenants, real estate agents who agree to comply with landlords' discriminatory requirements, and rental offers specifying "no immigrants" have reached the courts.[193] In particular, empirical studies have stressed that discrimination against people with Northern-African origins is high and is not only related to a supposed financial vulnerability.[194] Individuals with Northern-African origins are one-third less likely to receive a favorable outcome to an apartment visit request.[195]

In the United States, racial segregation in housing transactions and places of public accommodation was legal in several cities in the South until the middle of the last century.[196] Regarding the housing market, land-use planning was developed to spatially separate Black Americans from white neighborhoods.[197] Racist policies were explicitly fixed, such as "Black persons are not allowed in this apartment complex,"[198] and written in private contracts, such as "no part of said land shall be transacted to any negro or person of African descent or with negro of African blood in their veins."[199] Although this sort of discrimination has become unaccepted and illegal in the present day, more subtle forms of discrimination have occurred, and several cities across the country still present

---

193 *Cour d'Appel Grenoble* [Grenoble Court of Appeal], no 06/0053, 08/11/2006, Dezempt, Boyer c. Ghezzal; Tribunal de Grande Instance de Paris [Paris Regional Court], no 0527808779, 16/11/2006, MRAP, ADIB c. TESSIAU; *Tribunal de Grande Instance de Paris* [Paris Regional Court], 16 Nov. 2006, n. 0527808770; *Cour d'Appel de Toulouse* [Toulouse Court of Appeal], 3rd Criminal Chamber, 5 Oct. 2004, decision n. 03/00593, Juris-Data, no 2004–254288, confirmed by the *Cour de Cassation* [Supreme Court of Appeal], Criminal Chamber, 7 June 2005, n 04–87354; *Tribunal Correctionnel de Paris* [Paris Regional Criminal Court], 20 Sept. 2007, no 0308500058.

194 Julie Le Gallo, Yannick l'Horty, Loic Du Parquet, Pasquale Petit, *Les Discriminations dans L'Accès au Logement en France: un Testing de Couverture Nationale* (September 2018) online: HAL <https://halshs.archives-ouvertes.fr/halshs-01878188/document>; Mathieu Brunel, Yannick l'Horty, Loic du Parquet, Pascale Petit, *Les Discriminations dans l'Accès au Logement à Paris: Une Expérience Contrôlée* (March 2017) online: HAL <https://ideas.repec.org/p/tep/tepprr/rr17–01.html>.

195 *Ibid.* Also, a controlled survey has demonstrated that around 80% of French people recognize that discrimination guide rental decisions. *See* Les Défenseur des Droits, *Enquête sur les Discriminations dans L'Accès au Logement* (October 2012) online: le Défenseur des Droits <https://juridique.defenseurdesdroits.fr/doc_num.php?explnum_id=10627>.

196 In the last century, the *Green Books* listed places where Black Americans were allowed to stay, shop and eat. Myra B Young Armstead, "Revisiting Hotels and Other Lodgings: American Tourist Spaces Through the Lens of Black Pleasure Travelers 1850,1950" (2005) 25 The Journal of Decorative and Propaganda 136. James W Fox Jr, "Intimations of Citizenship: Repressions and Expressions of Equal Citizenship in the Era of Jim Crow" (2006) Howard Law Journal 113; Barbara Y Welke, "Beyond Plessy: Space, Status, and Race in the Era of Jim Crow" (2000) Utah Law Review 267.

197 Richard Rothstein, *The Color of Law: A Forgotten History of How Our Government Segregated America* (New York: Liveright Publishing, 2017), p 70.

198 *United States v L & H Land Corp., Inc.* 407 F. Supp. 576 (S.D. Fla. 1976). Also, Michael J Klarman, "The Plessy Era" (1998) The Supreme Court Review 303.

199 *Mayers v Ridley* 465 F.2d 630 (D.C. Circ. 1972), 631.

---

ethnic concentration.[200] Even if discrimination against Black Americans is the most widely discussed in the context of housing transactions, other protected classes have also reported an inequality of treatment in this sector.[201] Hispanics, immigrants, same-sex couples, and individuals with disabilities still face difficulties to rent and buy a place to live.[202]

Platforms focused on the housing and accommodation sectors currently present two distinctive structural challenges to the above-developed state of inequality. The first one concerns scale. The number of landlords offering housing opportunities online are neither limited by physical space, such as in the case of printed media; by costs, considering some online billboards are free or considerably inexpensive; nor by a central editorial control, as the purpose of these online spaces is to connect demand and supply rather than publish or monitor content.[203] These combined characteristics have

---

[200]   Frances L Edwards, Grayson Bennet Thomson, "The Legal Creation of Raced Space: The Subtle and Ongoing Discrimination Created Through Jim Crow Laws" (2010) 12 Berkeley Journal of African-American Law & Policy 145; HUD, *Housing Discrimination Against Racial and Ethnic Minorities 2012* (June 2013), online: US Department of Housing <https://www. huduser.gov/portal/publications/fairhsg/hsg_discrimination_2012.html>; Stephen L Ross, Margery Austin Turner, "Housing Discrimination in Metropolitan America: Explaining Changes Between 1989 and 2000" (2005) 52:2 Social Problems 152; George Galster, Erin Godfrey, "By Words and Deeds: Racial Steering by Real Estate Agents in the US in 2000" (2005) 71:3 Journal of the American Planning Association 251; Jan Ondrich, Stephen Ross, Jon Yinger, "Geography of Housing Discrimination" (2001) 12 Journal of Housing Research 217; Stacy Seicshnaydre, Robert Collins Cashuana Hill, Maxwell Ciardullo, Rigging the Real Estate Market: Segregation, Inequality, and Disaster Risk (April 2018) online: The New Orleans Prosperity Index: Tricentennial Collection <https://s3.amazonaws.com/gnocdc/ reports/TDC-prosperity-brief-stacy-seicshnaydre-et-al-FINAL.pdf>.

[201]   Adrian G Carpusor, Willian E Loges, "Rental Discrimination and Ethnicity in Names" (2006) 36 Journal of Applied Social Psychology 934; Michael Ewens, Bryan Tomlin, Liang Choon Wang, "Statistical Discrimination or Prejudice? A Large Sample Field Experiment" (2014) 96 The Review of Economics and Statistics 119; Veronica M Reed, "Civil Rights Legislation and the Housing Status of Black Americans: Evidence from Fair Housing Audits and Segregation Indices" (1991) 19 The Review of Black Political Economy 29, p 38.

[202]   Mattew Desmond, Monica Bell, "Housing, Poverty and the Law" (2015) 11 Annual Review of Law and Social Science 15; HUD, *Housing Discrimination Against Racial and Ethnic Minorities* (June 2013), online: US Department of Housing <https://www.huduser.gov/ portal/publications/fairhsg/hsg_discrimination_2012.html>; HUD, *An Estimate of Housing Discrimination Against Same-Sex Couple* (June 2013), online: US Department of Housing <https://www.huduser.gov/portal/publications/fairhsg/discrim_samesex.html>; HUD, *Housing Discrimination in the Rental Housing Market Against People Who Are Deaf and People Who Use Wheelchairs: National Study Findings* (June 2015), online: US Department of Housing <https://www.huduser.gov/portal/publications/fairhsg/hds_disability.html>. Also, Andrew Hanson, Michael Santas, "Field Experiment Tests for Discrimination Against Hispanics in the US Rental Housing Market" (2014) 81:1 Southern Economic Journal 135; Andrew Hanson, Zackary Hawley, "Do Landlords Discriminate in the Rental of Housing Market? Evidence from an Internet Field in US Cities (2011) 70:2 Journal of Urban Economics 99.

[203]   Jeff Kosseff, "The Gradual Erosion of the Law that Shaped the Internet: Section 230's Evolution Over the Two Decades" (2016) 18:1 The Columbia Science & Technology Law Review 1. In general: Karine Perset, *The Economic and Social Role of Internet Intermediaries* (April 2010),

increased the proliferation of publicly visible housing advertisements that contain discriminatory preferences and statements against protected classes.[204] Moreover, some online platforms have scaled up the number of landlords renting a fraction of their properties for short-term periods. These contractual relationships are not generally covered by antidiscrimination laws.[205] The second structural challenge to the principle of equality regards the design of some of these marketplaces. On the one hand, platforms offering matching tools to connect landlords with prospective tenants have given individuals the possibility to include or exclude from their search protected aspects, such as sexual orientation or rental allowances.[206] On the other hand, the salience of protected markers, such as ethnic origin and sex, displayed before the transaction is concluded coupled with total discretion landlords have over the choice of their tenants might enhance the refusal of protected classes in certain housing transactions, particularly in short-term rental offers.[207]

Currently, the European Union and the United States have comprehensive legislation to address discrimination against protected classes in housing transactions and in the access of public accommodations. More specifically, in the EU the Race Equality Directive and the Gender Equal Access to Goods and Services Directive provide a legal framework that prohibits direct and indirect discrimination on the grounds of race, ethnic origin, and sex in the provision of services available to the public.[208] In the United States, federal statutes prohibit discrimination on the grounds race, color, religion, national origin, and disability in the provision of services and access to places of public accommodation.[209] Moreover, federal fair housing statutes protect the grounds of sex and family status in addition to race, color, religion, national origin, and disability in the specific context of housing transactions.[210] Finally, several European member states and U.S. states have laws with broader personal scope.[211]

In this title, I argue that this set of laws is only partially equipped to address housing- and accommodation-related discrimination in online platforms. In the United States, the Communications Decency Act of 1996 (CDA) provides full immunity to liability for Internet Service Providers on illegal third-party content,

---

online: OECD <https://www.oecd.org/internet/ieconomy/44949023.pdf >, p 9–11; Sophie Stalla-Bourdillon, "Chilling ISPs… When Private Regulators Act Without Adequate Public Framework" (2010) 26:3 Computer Law & Security Review 290, p 291; Jaani Riordan, *The Liability of Internet Intermediaries* (Oxford: OUP 2016).

[204] *See* chapter 1.
[205] In Europe, right to private life and in the United States, freedom of association.
[206] Notably Roommates and Daft, *see* chapter 2.
[207] *See* Airbnb, chapter 2.
[208] Article 3, Race Equality Directive; Article 1, Gender Equal Access to Goods and Services Directive.
[209] 42 U.S.C. §2000a (a), (b) and (c), title II of the Civil Rights Act (Public Accommodations) and 42 U.S.C. §12181. (ADA).
[210] FHA, 42 U.S.C. §3605 (a)(b).
[211] *See* chapter 1.

including discriminatory advertisements.[212] A few exceptions to these rules are developed in Chapter 1, but they do not concern discriminatory content. Over the years, online platforms have invested in self-regulatory measures to address illegal third-party content. They have implemented flagging tools as well as automated filters that take down illegal material.[213] However, in cases in which Internet Service Providers fail to take down illegal content due to either a lack of staff capability or negligence, they have no duty to redress the infringed party. In cases of discriminatory housing ads, if the victims of discrimination do not find the author of the content, they remain without redressing possibilities.

In the European Union, the legal framework set by the Directive on Electronic Commerce has a more balanced approach concerning the liability of online intermediaries over third-party illegal content.[214] First, similar to the CDA, it does not oblige online intermediaries to filter or monitor illegal third-party content in cases in which the platform passively hosts the content.[215] Second, contrarily to the CDA, the immunity of liability for third-party content ends once the platform becomes aware of illegal content and fails to take it down. This balanced approach offers more possibilities to redress victims in cases of discriminatory advertisements. These liberal (United States) and more balanced (EU) approaches to the liability of intermediaries provide different ways of redressing infringed parties, but they cannot intrinsically avoid the aspect of the scale of illegal content online and the lack of editorial control online platforms have over their users' publications.

Moreover, antidiscrimination laws offer limited tools to address cases in which hosts using a platform focused on accommodation refuse to accept a guest because of one of their protected grounds, including their gender or race, either in countries of the European Union or in the United States. First, in the United States, the Fair Housing Act does not apply to cases of single-family, privately owned homes or to multifamily properties of four units or less where the landlord (named "host" in online platforms dedicated to accommodation) lives in one of the units[216] because of the principle of freedom of association. In these cases, hosts may discretionarily exclude prospective guests because of their protected classes under their constitutional right of freedom of association. In this regard, all the listed properties falling under this condition are outside the scope of the principle of equal treatment.

---

[212]   §230, c, 47 U.S.C. Communications Decency Act of 1996 (CDA) (Title V, Telecommunications Act of 1996).

[213]   *See* chapter 1.

[214]   Article 14, Directive on Electronic Commerce. This balanced approached has been maintained in the proposal for the Digital Services Act.

[215]   The regime has changed with regards to copyrights. *See* Directive (EU) 2019/790 of the European Parliament and of the Council of 17 April 2019 on Copyright and Related Rights in the Digital Single Market and Amending Directives 96/9/EC and 2001/29/EC, OJ L 130, 157.5.2019.

[216]   FHA, 42 U.S.C. §3603 (b) (1).

In the European Union, the Race Equality Directive and the Gender Equal Access to Goods and Services provide a framework for the implementation of the principle of equality to services provided to the public and exclude transactions occurring in the core of the family life.[217] Moreover, both Directives provide for the respect for the private life.[218] However, when an individual advertises a service, such as the rent of a room in their property, it is understood that the service is available to the public, and therefore, the owner does not have the right to exclude clients/tenants based on their protected grounds.[219] The only exception resides in the gender criteria. For reasons of privacy, landlords who will share some spaces of the property, such as the kitchen and other facilities, may exclude a prospective guest/tenant based on their gender.[220] Therefore, all the listed properties falling under this condition in platforms offering accommodation are outside of the scope of European and national antidiscrimination laws.

Finally, rules of secondary liability (i.e., vicarious liability) have little use to hold platforms focused on accommodation – when they are not defined as Internet Service Providers – liable for illegal discrimination of their users both in Europe and in the United States.[221] While traditional places offering services to the public, such as hotels or real estate agencies, might be liable for the illegal conduct of their agents, including discrimination against prospective clients, these rules are unlikely to apply to online platforms in relation to the illegal conduct of their users. Vicarious liability theories are mostly founded in the principles of subordination and authority existent between a particular corporation and its agents. These principles do not guide the relationship that most online platforms have with their users.

In the present title, I develop the challenges that platforms focused on housing and accommodation pose to the principle of equality. In Chapter 1, I present the evolution of these online spaces and the challenges to apply housing

---

[217]   Recital 4, Race Equality Directive; Recital 13 and Article 3,1, Gender Equal Access to Goods and Services Directive.

[218]   *Ibid.*

[219]   Brussels, 17.1.2014 COM(2014) 2 final Report From the Commission to the European Parliament and the Council: Joint Report on the Application of Council Directive 2000/43/EC of 29 June 2000 Implementing the Principle of Equal Treatment Between Persons Irrespective of Racial or Ethnic Origin (Racial Equality Directive) and of Council Directive 2000/78/EC of 27 November 2000 establishing a general framework for equal treatment in employment and occupation (Employment Equality Directive), p 11.

[220]   *See* chapter 1.

[221]   In Europe, the vicarious liability of corporate real estate agencies or any other company involved in the intermediation of housing transaction is regulated by the laws of member states. However, there is a certain convergence of the criteria of agency and subordination to establish secondary liability. *See* Helmut Werner, Eugenia Caracciolo di Torella, Bridgette McLellan, *Gender Equal Access to Goods and Services Directive 2004/113/EC: European Implementation Assessment* (January 2017), online: EPRS European Parliamentary Research Service Ex-Post Impact Assessment Unit <https://www.europarl.europa.eu/RegData/etudes/STUD/2017/593787/EPRS_STU(2017)593787_EN.pdf>, p 69.

and public accommodation antidiscrimination laws to these online markets, including the tensions involving publisher liability, Internet Service Providers' liability, vicarious liability, freedom of association, and the right for respect of private life. In Chapter 2, I deepen my argument that the platform economy challenges the implementation of the principle of equality in Europe and in the United States through a case-based analysis involving four different platforms: Craigslist, Roommates, Daft, and Airbnb.[222]

---

[222] *Chicago Lawyers' v Craigslist Inc*, No. 07–1101 (7th Cir. 2008); *Fair Housing Council of San Fernando Valley v Roommates, LLC*, 521, F.3d 1157 (9th Cir. 2008); *Irish Human Rights and Equality Commission v Daft Media Limited t/a Daft/ie*, ADJ-00005960, WRC, 2019; *Selden v Airbnb*, INC., No. 16-cv-00933 (CRC) (D.C. Nov. 1, 2016). (Hereinafter, *Selden v Airbnb*).

CHAPTER 1

FIGHTING AGAINST DISCRIMINATION IN THE HOUSING AND ACCOMMODATION MARKETS

SECTION I. EQUAL ACCESS TO HOUSING AND ACCOMMODATION: TRANSITION TO A DIGITAL WORLD

1. TYPES OF ONLINE HOUSING AND ACCOMMODATION MARKETPLACES

Online spaces focused on the intermediation of housing and accommodation transactions have evolved in the past 20 years.[223] First, the internet has experienced the expansion of classified advertisement billboards with sections devoted to housing. In these online spaces, internet users can directly publish offers to rent or sell their properties. These publications initially had no professional editorial control and were similar to bulletin boards. The primary popular example was Craigslist, which allowed users to advertise their offers free of charges.[224] Craigslist was followed by successful models of online classified advertising spaces, including eBay and the classified ads of Yahoo!.[225] In these cases, users did not have their profiles published with their photographs and personal information. The main purpose of these ads was to inform about the offer. Several years later, social networking platforms and search engine platforms have expanded their business towards advertising housing and accommodation offers with more sophisticated tools. Roommates, Spareroom, Immoweb, and Daft developed matching mechanisms to connect house owners and house seekers.[226]

---

223 David S Evans, "The Online Advertising Industry: Economics, Evolution and Privacy" (2009) 23:3 Journal of Economic Perspectives 37.

224 Susan M Freese, *Craigslist: The Company and Its Founder* (ABDO, 2011); Rigel C Oliveri, "Discriminatory Housing Advertisements Online: Lessons from Craigslist" (2010) 43 Indiana Law Review 1125.

225 David S Evans, "The Online Advertising Industry: Economics, Evolution and Privacy" (2009) 23:3 Journal of Economic Perspectives 37, p 38 and 45.

226 Immoweb, *hostpage* (December 2019), online: Immoweb <https://www.immoweb.be/fr>; Roommates, *Find Your Perfect Match* (June 2019), online: Roommates <https://www.

After a short period of time, the hospitality industry followed the real estate industry. Online intermediaries focused on the offer of hotel rooms emerged in Europe and in the United States. The startup company now known as Booking. com was founded in Amsterdam in 1996 with the mission to "make it easier for everyone to experience the world."[227] Booking.com first invested in technology that connects travelers to hotels, and later they expanded to offer transportation options. Booking.com has successful competitors including the American platforms Expedia and Hotel.com. These platforms have become the world's largest travel marketplaces by enabling hotels around the world to reach a global audience. Booking.com is currently available in 43 languages and offers more than 28 million accommodation listings.[228]

In the 2000s, the internet facilitated the global emergence of a new market within the hospitality industry: the offer of private accommodation for short-term periods to travelers from places all over the world. First, in 2004 the platform Couchsurfing was created to connect individuals with a network of people interested in providing their couch or a room in their home for free.[229] Through Couchsurfing, the offers did not consist of a mere listing. Instead, users were encouraged to create profiles with photographs, names, and reflections about their lifestyle, mission, and preferences. Having a complete profile facilitated the connection between strangers and fostered users' willingness to host travelers on their couch for the sake of having an experience. A few years later in 2008, Airbnb was inaugurated to efficiently allocate empty home spaces.[230] Similar to Couchsurfing, users were able to create detailed profiles to offer or to seek an accommodation. Different from Couchsurfing, users on Airbnb rent their places, or part of it, for a pre-established price, and the platform receives a percentage of the charged price. Over the years, new platforms have been developed to explore the "holidays" market. For example, through Homeway and Abritel homeowners can offer their entire property, generally for a short period of time.[231] Contrarily to the first models of billboard platforms,

---

roommates.com>; Spareroom, *Find Home Together* (December 2019), online: spareroom, <https://www.spareroom.co.uk>.

[227] Booking, *About Booking.com,* (December 2019), online: booking.com <https://www.booking. com/content/about.html?aid=356980&label=gog235jc-1DCBQoggJCBWFib3V0SA1YA2gV iAEBmAENuAEHyAEN2AED6AEB-AECiAIBqAIDuALqu4XyBcACAQ&sid=817cd163dc7a5 ba9ff86c78592d43de6&tmpl=docs%2Fabout&lang=en-us&soz=1&lang_click=other;cdl=fr; lang_changed=1>.

[228] *Ibid.*

[229] Couchsurfing, *About Us* (December 2019), online: <https://www.couchsurfing.com/about/ about-us/>.

[230] Leigh Gallagher, *Airbnb Story: How Three Ordinary Guys Disrupted an Industry, Made Billions, and Created Plenty of Controversy* (New York: Houghton Mifflin Harcourt, 2017), p 34.

[231] HomeAway, *List Your Property* (December 2019), online: HomeAway <https://homeaway. com>; Abritel, *Publiz Votre Annonce sur Arbitrel.fr et Dites Bonjour à de Nouveaux Revenues* (December 2019), online: Arbitrel <https://abitrel.fr>.

these new intermediaries intervene more actively on the transaction. They might suggest a rental price for the homeowner, rank the offers, provide insurance for third-party damages, and develop matching tools to connect homeowners with home seekers.

2. DISCRIMINATION IN THE HOUSING AND ACCOMMODATION SECTORS: NEW SPACES BUT SAME BIASES

In 2014, researchers from the Harvard Business School published the state of inequality between White and Black American users who listed their properties on Airbnb in New York City. After analyzing hosts' profile images, rental fees, location, and information about the quality of the property, researchers found that Black American hosts earned approximately 12% less than White hosts for equivalent rental properties.[232] Another study found that Asian Americans and Hispanic hosts receive 8%–10% less in San Francisco.[233] The impact of how users' photographs distorted rental prices was also indicated with users based in Stockholm.[234]

Another field experiment conducted with 6,400 listings detected that requests from individuals with markedly Black American names were 16% less likely to be accepted than guests with characteristically white names across five American cities.[235] This acceptance rate difference remained whether hosts shared the property with guests or whether the property was expensive or inexpensive. In Seattle, Chicago, and Boston, guests with typically Black American names were welcomed 29% of the time, compared to 48% for white guests.[236] In Austin, guests with typically Black American names received positive answers for 42% of their requests compared to 53% for white guests.[237]

In May 2016, Gregory Selden, a self-identified Black American residing in Philadelphia, filed a putative class action suit against Airbnb for race discrimination on behalf of himself and fellow Black American travelers who had reported being

---

[232] Benjamin G Edelman, Michael Luca, *Digital Discrimination: The Case of Airbnb.com* (January 2014), online: Harvard Business School <https://www.hbs.edu/faculty/Publication%20Files/Airbnb_92dd6086–6e46–4eaf-9cea-60fe5ba3c596.pdf>.

[233] Venoo Kakar, Joel Voelz, Julia Wu, Julisa Franco, "The Visible Host: Does Race Guide Airbnb Rental Rates in San Francisco? (2018) 40 Journal of Housing Economics 25.

[234] Eyal Ert, Aliza Fleischer, Nathan Magen, "Trust and Reputation in the Sharing Economy: The Role of Personal Photos in Airbnb" (2016) 55 Tourism Management 62.

[235] Benjamin Edelman, Michael Luca, Dan Svirsky, "Racial Discrimination in the Sharing Economy: Evidence from a Field Experiment" (2017) 9 American Economic Journal: Applied Economics 1, p 4.

[236] Ruomeng Cui, Jun Li, Dennis Zhang, "Reducing Discrimination with Reviews in the Sharing Economy: Evidence from Field Experiments on Airbnb" (2019) Management Science 1.

[237] *Ibid.*

discriminated against on Airbnb.[238] In this same year, housing advocates and hotel companies funded a television campaign in the United States reporting widespread discrimination against Black Americans by private hosts advertising their accommodation on the platform. Through this campaign, a Black American guest confirmed he "gets declined all the time. Hosts have one excuse after another."[239] The media has also reported the refusal of an Asian American in California[240] and of a transgender person in Minneapolis[241] due to their protected characteristics.

In Europe, the French comedian Jhon Rachid – officially called Mohamed Ketfi – has complained of being discriminated against because of his nam3e.[242] In Toulouse, Djamila Cariou was refused, under suspicious excuses, the rental of a house for her summer vacation. Feeling she was discriminated against, she asked her friend Isabelle to request the house for the same period. Isabelle had a positive response three hours after having contacted the host.[243]

In addition, researchers have documented discrimination on the grounds of sexual orientation and disability. Across 48 states in the United States, hosts have accepted in advance (i.e., preapproved) 75% of guests without disabilities; however, only 50% of blind guests and 25% of guests who required a wheelchair were preapproved.[244] Moreover, male guests in a same-sex relationship were approximately 25% less likely to be accepted to rent a property than guests in a heterosexual relationship in Dublin, Ireland.[245]

Moreover, discrimination against protected classes has been reported in billboard platforms.[246] Users in the United States seeking housing opportunities have come across rental ads stating requests such as "African-American and Arabians tend to clash with me so that won't work out," "No minorities," "No children," and "No women of color need to apply."[247] An empirical study

---

238 *Selden v Airbnb*, INC., No. 16-cv-00933 (CRC) (D.C. Nov. 1, 2016). *See* chapter 2, section 4.

239 *Ibid.*

240 Olivia Solon, *Airbnb Host Who Canceled Reservation Using Racist Comment Must $5,000* (July 2017), online: The Guardian <https://www.theguardian.com/technology/2017/jul/13/airbnb-california-racist-comment-penalty-asian-american>.

241 Nellie Bowles, *Airbnb Faces Outcry After Transgender Guest Was Denied Stay by a Host* (June 2016), online: The Guardian <https://www.theguardian.com/technology/2016/jun/06/airbnb-criticism-transgender-guest-denied-super-host>.

242 Henri Seckel, *Pour Réserver sur Airbnb, Mieux Vaut S'Appeler Isabelle que Djamila* (August 2018), online: LeMonde <https://www.lemonde.fr/societe/article/2018/08/24/airbnb-abritel-discriminations-en-ligne_5345587_3224.html>.

243 *Ibid.*

244 Manson Ameri, Sean Rogers, Lisa Schur, Douglas Kruse, "No Room at the Inn? Disability Access in the New Sharing Economy" (2019) Academy of Management 1.

245 Rishi Ahuja, Ronan C Lyons, "The Silent Treatment: LGBT Discrimination in the Sharing Economy" (2017) Trinity Economics Papers, Trinity College Dublin, Department of Economics 1.

246 Nathaniel Decker, "Housing Discrimination and Craigslist" (2010) 14.1 The Public Policy Journal of the Cornell Institute for Public Affairs 43.

247 Rigel C Oliveri, "Discriminatory Housing Advertisements Online: Lessons from Craigslist" (2010) 43 Indiana Law Review 1125.

demonstrated that more than 10,000 discriminatory ads existed on Craigslist in 10 American cities.[248] Another report, published by the National Fair Housing Alliance, identified more than 7,500 discriminatory advertisements.[249] The matching systems of some platforms have also been designed to incorporate protected aspects, such as sexual orientation, family status[250], and rental social compliment[251], and these systems allow users to select or exclude flat mates based on these aspects.

SECTION II. LEGAL FRAMEWORK AGAINST DISCRIMINATION IN HOUSING AND PUBLIC ACCOMMODATION TRANSACTIONS

1. UNITED STATES

In the course of the twentieth century, the American Congress legislated federal statutory laws to address widespread discrimination in spaces of public accommodation and housing transactions.[252] Particularly, legislation to prohibit racial discrimination was urgent, considering that throughout the South Black Americans were excluded from both public and private facilities under Jim Crow laws.[253] In this regard, two main federal statutes were enacted to prohibit racial discrimination in spaces of public accommodation and housing transactions: Title II of the Civil Rights of 1964 (Public Accommodation Act) and Title VIII of the Civil Rights Act of 1968 (Fair Housing Act).[254]

1.1. EQUAL ACCESS TO PLACES OF PUBLIC ACCOMMODATION: FRAMEWORK AGAINST DISCRIMINATION

Title II of the Civil Rights Act of 1964 prohibits discrimination based on race, color, religion, and national origin in the access to goods, services, facilities,

---

248 *Ibid.*
249 National Fair Housing Alliance, *2010 Fair Housing Trends Report* (May 2010), online: National Fair Housing <https://nationalfairhousing.org/wp-content/uploads/2017/04/fair_housing_trends_report_2010.pdf>.
250 *See* chapter 2, Roommates section.
251 *See* chapter 2, Daft section.
252 Nick Kotz, *Judgement Days: Lyndon Baines Johnson, Martin Luther King Jr, and the Laws that Changed America* (Mariner Books 2006); Jonathan Zasloff, "The Secret History of the Fair Housing Act" (2016) 53 Harvard Journal of Legislation 247.
253 James W Fox Jr, "Intimations of Citizenship: Repressions and Expressions of Equal Citizenship in the Era of Jim Crow" (2006) 50 Howard Law Journal 113, p 138.
254 42 U.S.C. §2000a (Title II) and 42 U.S.C. §3605 (FHA).

and places of public accommodation.[255] Places of public accommodation are described and listed by the statute regarding three different categories: 1) establishments focused on providing lodging to guests, such as hotels, inns, and motels[256]; 2) establishments engaged in selling food for consumption on their premises, such as restaurants, cafeterias, and places located in gasoline stations[257]; and 3) places of exhibition or entertainment, such as movie theatres and sporting arenas.[258]

Regarding the first category of places that offer lodging, the text provides an exception for establishments located in a building with less than five units for rent and for establishments where the owners of the property reside.[259] This exception was conceived to protect the First Amendment right to freedom of association of businesses owners.[260]

Title II is clear that the provisions against discrimination have a material scope for places of public accommodation and do not apply to private clubs or other establishments not open to the public.[261] Some state laws have a broader scope regarding the definition of places of public accommodation compared to the one provided by Title II. For example, the Civil Code of California provides that all citizens are entitled to the full enjoyment of public accommodations in all business establishments of every kind.[262] Therefore, it does not limit its scope to hotels, restaurants, and places of public entertainment; instead, it also includes retail shops, for instance. Moreover, several states define a broader personal scope against discrimination in the access to public accommodation compared to the Federal Title II.[263] In this respect, all states prohibit discrimination based on sex, 21 states prohibit discrimination based on gender identity, 25 states prohibit discrimination based on sexual orientation, and 19 states prohibit age-based discrimination regarding public accommodation.[264]

In 1990, the American Congress passed the Americans with Disabilities Act (ADA) which also has provisions prohibiting discrimination against persons

---

[255] 42 U.S.C. §2000a (a), (b) and (c), title II of the Civil Rights Act (Public Accommodations). The Title II does not cover the grounds of disability, sex, sexual orientation, and age.
[256] 42 U.S.C. §2000a (b), 1.
[257] 42 U.S.C. §2000a (b), 2.
[258] 42 U.S.C. §2000a (a), (b) and (c), title II of the Civil Rights Act (Public Accommodations).
[259] *Ibid.*
[260] Nancy Leong, "The First Amendment and Fair Housing in the Platform Economy" (2017) 78 Ohio State Law Journal 1001.
[261] 42 U.S.C. §2000a, (e).
[262] California Civil Code §51(b). Utah also has a very similar provision, *see* Utah Code Ann. §13–7-2(1)(a).
[263] *See* National Conference of State Legislatures, *State Public Accommodation Laws* (December 2019), online: NCSL <https://www.ncsl.org/research/civil-and-criminal-justice/state-public-accommodation-laws.aspx#ftn8>.
[264] *Ibid.*

with disabilities in the access to places of public accommodation.[265] The material scope of the ADA is much broader than Title II. Aside from prohibiting discrimination against individuals with disabilities in the access to places offering lodging, food, and entertainment, the ADA also includes retail stores, such as bakeries, grocery stores, clothing stores, barber shops, beauty shops, museums, day cares, and health spas.[266]

1.2. ANTIDISCRIMINATION VERSUS FREEDOM OF ASSOCIATION

The principle of antidiscrimination applicable to the access to places of public accommodation has been challenged in light of the right to freedom of association.[267] The United States Supreme Court held a restrictive interpretation regarding the balance of equal access to public accommodation places and the First Amendment right of freedom of association in the landmark case *Boy Scouts of America v Dale*.[268] The case involved Boys Scouts, a nonprofit organization, and its former member James Dale. Dale entered the Boy Scouts in 1978, at the age of eight, and was a member until he turned 18 years old, when he was recognized as an Eagle Scout, one of the highest honors of the organization. At this time, he required an adult membership and was approved for the position of assistant scoutmaster. In the following years, he publicly announced he was gay and was appointed as the co-president of the Gay Alliance at his university. Not long after, Dale received a letter revoking his Boy Scouts adult membership.

Dale filed a complaint against Boy Scouts of America, alleging that the organization had violated New Jersey's public accommodation statute by revoking his membership based only on his sexual orientation. New Jersey's

---

[265] 42 U.S.C. §12181. (ADA). *See* Matthew a Stowe, "Interpreting Place of Public Accommodation Under Title III of the ADA: A Technical Determination with Potentially Broad Civil Rights Implications" (2000) 50:1 Duke Law Journal 297.

[266] 42 U.S.C. §12181, (7) (A) until (L). (ADA).

[267] The freedom of association includes the freedom of intimate association and the freedom of speech, both provided by the First Amendment to the United States Constitution. *See* John D Inazu, "The Unsettling 'Well-Settled' Law of Freedom of Association" (2010) 43: 1 Connecticut Law Review 149. Regarding the provision of goods, in *Masterpiece Cakeshop v Colorado Civil Rights Commission*, 584 U.S. S.Ct., the United States Supreme Court limited the application of the Colorado Antidiscrimination law on the ground of sexual orientation because of the service provider religious belief.

[268] *Boy Scouts of Am. V Dale*, 530 U.S. 640, 644 (2000). The case was vastly commented. *See* Samuel R Bagenstos, "The Unrelenting Libertarian Challenge to Public Accommodations Law" (2014) 66 Stanford Law Review 1205, p 1229; For arguments disagreeing with such a vison, *see* Richard A Epstein, "Public Accommodations Under the Civil Rights Act of 1964: Why Freedom of Association Counts as a Human Right" (2014) 66 Stanford Law Review 1241; For arguments criticizing the decision: Andrew Koppelman, "Signs of the Times: Dale v Boy Scouts of America and the Changing Meaning of Nondiscrimination" (2002) 23 Cardozo Law Review 1819.

public accommodation statute prohibits discrimination based on sexual orientation, in addition to other grounds. When the case reached the New Jersey Supreme Court, the Court held that the Boy Scouts was a place of public accommodation. Therefore, Dale could not be banished from the organization based only on his sexual orientation under New Jersey's antidiscrimination law.

However, the United States Supreme Court ruled that the application of the New Jersey public accommodation law to prohibit Boy Scouts from banishing an openly gay member violated the organization's First Amendment right of expressive association. Boy Scouts claimed that one of its common values was that it considered homosexuality to be immoral. Therefore, allowing an openly gay member would impair this message. The Supreme Court consented that Dale's presence in the organization would force the Boy Scouts to send a message "both to the youth members and the world, that the Boy Scouts accepts homosexual conduct as a legitimate form of behavior."[269] The Supreme Court then concluded that the State interests embodied in New Jersey's public accommodations law do not justify such "a severe intrusion on the Boy Scout's rights to freedom of expressive association."[270]

1.3. EQUAL ACCESS TO HOUSING OPPORTUNITIES: FRAMEWORK AGAINST DISCRIMINATION

Regarding housing transactions, the Fair Housing Act (FHA), passed in 1968, specifically prohibits discrimination grounded on race, color, religion, and national origin from the process of residential real estate-related transactions.[271] At that time, 60% of the American States already had legislation prohibiting discrimination in real estate transactions based on racial criteria, but the issue was yet not addressed at the federal level, which allowed some states, especially in the South, to avoid enacting antidiscrimination housing legislation.[272] Later, sex became a protected aspect under the FHA after the act was amended in 1974.[273] In 1988 and 1990, protection against discrimination in housing transactions was expanded to persons with disabilities and families with children.[274]

Overall, the FHA prohibits discrimination in the terms and conditions, refusal to deal, discriminatory advertising, falsely representing availability, denying use of or participation in real estate services, and making representations regarding the entry or prospective entry of persons of a

---

[269]   *Boy Scouts of Am. V Dale*, 530 U.S. 640, 644 (2000), §653.
[270]   *Ibid*, §659.
[271]   FHA, 42 U.S.C. §3605 (a)(b).
[272]   Jean Eberhart Dubofsky, "Fair Housing: A Legislative History and a Perspective" (1969) 8 Washburn Law Journal 149, p 155.
[273]   FHA, 42 U.S.C. 3604 (a).
[274]   For the contents of the amended Fair Housing Act *see*: National Fair Housing Advocate Online, *Fair Housing Act* (January 2018), online: Fair Housing <http://fairhousing.com/legal-research/fha/history/fair-housing-act>.

protected class in a neighborhood.[275] The FHA also provides home seekers who are victims of discrimination with remedies such as actual damages, punitive damages, attorney's fees, injunctive relief, and civil penalties in cases enforced by the Secretary of Housing of Attorney General.[276]

1.4. ANTIDISCRIMINATION VERSUS FREEDOM OF ASSOCIATION

The FHA, similarly to Title II, includes an exception that allows individuals to discriminate against persons belonging to one of the protected grounds in housing transactions. This exception concerns single-family privately owned homes and multifamily properties of four units or less where the owner lives in one of the units.[277] In these cases, the owners are exempt from the requirements of the FHA. This so-called "Mrs. Murphy" exemption allows property owners and landlords to discriminate on the grounds of religion, national origin, sex, disability, and family status in housing transactions when they live in a property with people with the above specified aspects. The same rule applies when landlords rent one room of their property and remain living in the home. This exception, similar to one in the Title II, was justified under the constitutional right to freedom of association, which protects individuals against government interference with their intimate relationships and includes both the "affirmative right to associate with desired persons and a negative right to be free to not associate with undesired persons."[278] Voices to amend this exception, particular regarding the racial criteria, have been raised.[279] Even if the administrative authority were to take the position that racial discrimination is not allowed in shared places[280], Courts of Appeals for the Circuits have held that the right to freedom of association applies to shared living spaces.[281]

---

[275] FHA, 42 U.S.C. §3604 (a) (b).

[276] FHA, 42 U.S.C. §3613 (c)-(d).

[277] FHA, 42 U.S.C. §3603 (b) (1).

[278] Tim Iglesias, "Does Fair Housing Law Apply to 'Shared Living Situations'? Or, the Trouble with Roommates" (2014) 22:2 Journal of Affordable Housing & Community Development Law 111, p 115.

[279] See Brenna R McLaughlin, "#Airbnbwhileblack Repealing the Fair Housing Act's Mrs. Murphy Exemption to Combat Racism on Airbnb" (2018) Wisconsin Law Review 149; Nancy Leong, "The First Amendment and Fair Housing in the Platform Economy" (2017) 78 Ohio State Law Journal 1001; James D Walsh, "Reaching Mrs. Murphy: A Call for Repeal of the Mrs. Murphy Exemption to the Fair Housing Act" (1999) 34 Harvard Civil Rights-Civil Liberties Law Review 605; and David M Forman, "A Room for 'Adam and Steve' at Mrs Murphy's Bed and Breakfast: Avoiding the Sin of Inhospitality in Places of Public Accommodation" (2012) 23 Columbia Journal of Gender and Law 326.

[280] Rigel C Oliveri, "Discriminatory Housing Advertisements Online: Lessons from Craigslist", op. cit., p 1135.

[281] See Fair Housing Council of San Fernando Valley v Roommates.com, LCC, 521 F3d 1157 (9th Circuit 2012); US v Space Hunters, Inc, 429 F.3d 416 (2d Circ. 2005), concerning racial and

When this exception was included in the FHA, it was argued that it would have no relevance.[282] At the time, it was estimated that the exception would affect 3% of the places for sale and rent across the country.[283] Currently, scholars argue that the Mrs. Murphy exemption did not consider the development of the home sharing economy[284], in which a significant number of places rented either are occupied by the owner, when they rent a single room, or are the main residence of the owner who makes the property available for rent temporarily when they are away on vacation.[285]

It is worth noting that the exemption does not apply if the property is sold or rented through a broker or agent.[286] Moreover, discriminatory advertisements are not allowed even in the occasion of the sale and rental of single-family owned properties in which the owner lives.[287] For example, a landlord willing to rent a room of the home where they live cannot publish an advertisement stating, "no colored people" accepted, even if refusing a person on this basis in cases of shared residences is a legal criterion under the FHA.[288]

1.5. THE FIGHT AGAINST HOUSING DISCRIMINATORY ADVERTISEMENTS: LIABILITY OF PUBLISHERS

In the United States, the freedom of expression, protected by the First Amendment, is a core constitutional value. Therefore, the right to freedom of expression is only limited in exceptional circumstances. One of these circumstances regards the publication of discriminatory advertisements concerning housing offers. The prohibition to discriminate against protected classes in housing transactions applies to advertising. When home owners and landlords publish discriminatory requirements regarding any housing transaction, they are overtly providing proof of discrimination, which is outlawed by the FHA.[289] Even in cases in which home owners can legally

---

disability discrimination.

[282] James D Walsh, "Reaching Mrs. Murphy: A Call for Repeal of the Mrs. Murphy Exemption to the Fair Housing Act" (1999) 34 Harvard Civil Rights-Civil Liberties Law Review 605, p 606.

[283] *Ibid.*

[284] Brenna R McLaughlin, "#Airbnbwhileblack Repealing the Fair Housing Act's Mrs. Murphy Exemption to Combat Racism on Airbnb" (2018) Wisconsin Law Review 149, p 150.

[285] Leigh Gallagher, *Airbnb Story: How Three Ordinary Guys Disrupted an Industry, Made Billions, and Created Plenty of Controversy* (New York: Houghton Mifflin Harcourt, 2017).

[286] FHA, 42 U.S.C. §3603 (b)(1). Also, even though the statute does not state that there should be an exception for the ground of sex in ads regarding shared housing, the HUD recognized that social norms and personal concerns such as safety and morality support such exception. Rigel C Oliveri, "Discriminatory Housing Advertisements Online: Lessons from Craigslist", *op. cit.*, p 1135.

[287] FHA, 42 U.S.C. 3603, (b)(1)(B).

[288] FHA, 42 U.S.C. §3603 (b) (1).

[289] FHA, 42 U.S.C. §3605 (a)(b).

discriminate due to the Mrs. Murphy exception, they cannot advertise such a discriminatory preference (apart from the ground of sex).[290] In addition to these limitations, the FHA also holds liable the publisher of a third-party discriminatory housing advertisement, such as newspapers.[291] In this case, both the home owner, who created the advertisement, and the publisher are liable in a circumstance of a tort charge of illegal discrimination. The inclusion of publishers within the FHA's personal scope was originally relevant to address housing discrimination, because newspapers commonly published third-party racial discriminatory advertisements at the time the statute was enacted in 1968.[292] Newspapers often included a "colored" section in their classifieds that listed properties that were available for sale and rent to Black Americans.[293] The Statute later became extensive and made it illegal to "make, print, or publish, or cause to be made, printed, or published any notice, statement, or advertisement, with respect to the sale or rental of a dwelling that indicates any preference or any intention to make such preference, limitation, or discrimination" based on the protected grounds of race, color, religion, sex, disability, familial status, or national origin.[294]

Although the practice of publishing "colored" columns did not last long after the FHA was enacted, newspapers kept publishing ads with more implicit forms of discrimination on the grounds of race and nationality, including advertisements explicitly stating that a place available for rent was a "white home" or that potential tenants were required to speak the same language as the neighborhood, in this case English.[295] In several occasions, Courts held newspapers liable for illegal discrimination regarding housing advertisements, even in cases of non-explicit discrimination.[296]

In *Ragin v New York Times Company*, for instance, the publisher of the *New York Times* was considered liable for continuously publishing advertisements with only white models in offers dedicated to real estate properties in a certain area of the city.[297] The Court of Appeals for the Second Circuit held that only including white models in ads indicated a preference grounded on race, and,

---

[290]   FHA, 42 U.S.C. 3603, (b)(1)(B). Rigel C Oliveri, "Discriminatory Housing Advertisements Online: Lessons from Craigslist", *op. cit.*, p 1135.

[291]   FHA, 42 U.S.C., §3604, (c).

[292]   Hugh J Cunningham, "Fair Housing Act: Newspaper Liability for Discriminatory Advertisements (1992) 37 Loyola Law Review 981, 982.

[293]   Margot S Rubin, "Advertising and Title VIII: The Discriminatory Use of Models in Real Estate Advertisements" (1988) 98 Yale Law Journal 165, 178.

[294]   FHA, 42 U.S.C., §3604, (c).

[295]   *United States v Hunter* 459 F.2 205 (4th Circuit), 409 U.S. 934 (1972) and *Holmgren v Little Village Community Reporter* 342 F. Supp. 512 (N.D. III 1971).

[296]   Margot S Rubin, "Advertising and Title VIII: The Discriminatory Use of Models in Real Estate Advertisements" (1998) *op. cit.*, p 165 referring to *Saunders v General Services Corp.* 659 F. Supp. 1042 (E.D. Va. 1987) *and Spann v Carley Capital Group* 734 F. Supp. 1 (D.D.C. 1988).

[297]   *Ragin v New York Times Company*, 923 F.2d 995 (2d Cir. 1991), §997.

therefore, the publisher had breached the provision that prohibits the publication of a real estate ad "that indicates any preference based on race."[298]

1.6. IMMUNITY FOR ONLINE PLATFORMS FOR DISCRIMINATORY ADVERTISEMENTS WITH HOUSING OFFERS

The FHA was enacted well before the internet was ubiquitously used as a tool for housing opportunity searches. However, the FHA provision that holds liable publishers of illegal third-party housing advertisements does not apply to online platforms. Even if some online platforms, such as Craigslist, have a similar function as newspaper classifieds, they may not have any liability for an advertisement published by a third-party user containing the preference "no colored tenants need to apply." This immunity from liability is because online platforms are legally identified as Internet Service Providers (ISPs).

1.6.1. Back to the Past: Early Cases

In the early 1990s, the matter of whether ISPs were liable for illegal third-party content was not addressed by any federal statute. The liability of ISPs was unregulated not only for what concerns illegal advertisements but also for third-party content in general. The lack of legal statutorily provision regarding the liability of ISPs for illegal third-party content resulted in court decisions that were considered inadequate by the emerging online industry.[299]

In the landmark case *Stratton Oakmont v Prodigy*, the Supreme Court of New York held the ISP Prodigy liable for illegal third-party publications.[300] Prodigy had over two million subscribers who published on its online bulletin boards. In the early 1990s, several defamatory statements were published on one of its boards named "Money Talk," which was dedicated to financial topics, such as stocks and investments. Prodigy used a software program that automatically identified offensive language published on its bulletin boards. Moreover, it had a policy that insulting language would be removed from its boards.

In the State of New York, the law provides that one who repeats or republishes a defamation statement is liable just as the one who originally published the

---

298   *Ibid.*
299   Jeff Kosseff, "Defending Section 230: The Value of Intermediary Immunity" (2010) 15:2 Journal of Technology Law & Policy 123 and Douglas B Luftman, "Defamation Liability for Online Services: The Sky is Not Falling" (1996) George Washington Law Review 1071.
300   *Stratton Oakmont, Inc. v Prodigy Services Company*, (S. Ct. N.Y. 1995), §§323.
       Susan Freiwald, "Comparative Institutional Analysis in Cyberspace: The Case of Intermediary Liability for Defamation" (2000) 14 Harvard Journal Law & Technology 569.

statement.[301] However, a carrier or distributor of defamatory content is not liable if it delivers it as passive conduit and in the absence of fault.[302] Newspapers are not considered as carrier of their articles, comments, and ads, for instance, because they have an editorial board that ultimately decides what should be published.[303]

In *Stratton Oakmont v Prodigy Services Companies,* the Supreme Court had to decide whether Prodigy had enough "editorial control" over the content published on its bulletin boards. If Prodigy was considered to have such editorial control, the Supreme Court should rule Prodigy as a "publisher with the same responsibilities as a newspaper."[304] Prodigy alleged that too much information was posted by users on its boards to allow it to efficiently check all the content. However, the Court held that Prodigy was a publisher rather than a distributor, because, first, it had a special software to screen illegal content and, second, it had announced that it did not tolerate illegal content on its bulletin boards as a public policy. Therefore, Prodigy should be held as a publisher and face the same consequences as a publisher regarding the liability for third-party illegal content present on its bulletin boards. The fact that Prodigy could not efficiently process complaints of illegal defamation on its bulletin boards did not minimize that it had "uniquely arrogated to itself the role of determining what is proper for its member to post on its bulletin boards."[305]

Through its ruling, the Supreme Court of the State of New York distinguished Prodigy from another well-commented case, *Cubby v CompuServe.*[306] In *Cubby,* the ISP CompuServe was released from liability because it did not arrogate to itself the role of monitoring and reviewing the content of third-party publications before they were published online. In this sense, CompuServe was not comparable to traditional printed media because, contrarily to Prodigy, it had not claimed diligence over third-party content.

The *Stratton Oakmont, Inc. v Prodigy Services* ruling was criticized because it held that an ISP taking diligent measures to remove unlawful content was liable for illegal third-party publications, while the ISP that was not diligent and did not monitor third-party content was not liable for third-party illegal content.[307] The online industry was manifestly against the ruling of *Stratton Oakmont, Inc. v Prodigy Services,* alleging that it would undermine any initiative of private self-regulation to tackle online unlawful content.[308]

---

[301] Restatement, Second Torts §578 (1977).
[302] *Ibid.*
[303] *Stratton Oakmont, Inc. v Prodigy Services Company,* §§326.
[304] *Ibid.*
[305] *Ibid.*
[306] *Cubby, Inc. v CompuServe Inc.,* 776 F. Supp. 135 (S.D.N.Y. 1991).
[307] Douglas B Luftman, "Defamation Liability for Online Services: The Sky is Not Falling" (1996) George Washington Law Review 1071.
[308] R Hayes Johnson Jr, "Defamation in Cyberspace: A Court Takes a Wrong Turn on the Information Superhighway in *Stratton Oakmont, Inc. v Prodigy Services Co*" (1996) Arkansas

1.6.2. Communications Decency Act, 1996

This context of legal instability around ISPs' liability for third-party content, in addition to increasing defamatory and pornographic publications and a strong lobby of companies operating online, pushed the American Congress to pass the federal statute Communications Decency Act of 1996 (CDA) as part of the Telecommunications Act.[309] In the Act's section dedicated to the "protection for private blocking and screening of offensive material," the "Good Samaritan" provision aims to protect ISPs from liability for third-party content. The provision determines that ISPs may not be treated as publishers or speakers of "any information provided by another information content provider,"[310] and that ISPs shall not face tort liability in cases it takes "any action in good faith to restrict access to or availability of material that the provider or user considers to be objectionable."[311] This legal framework does not hold ISPs liable for illegal third-party content, even when they acknowledge it and do not remove it.[312] The "Good Samaritan" provision explicitly does not apply to cases related to obscenity, sexual exploitation of children, intellectual property instances, and privacy cases.[313]

Concerning intellectual property, for instance, the Digital Millennium Copyright Act (DMCA) establishes the regime of "notice-and-taken-down."[314] In cases related to copyright, but also trademark, ISPs have the duty to take any third-party infringing content down once they are aware of it.[315] This regime is similar to the one implemented in Europe by the Directive on Electronic Commerce to all sorts of content, and not only, copyrighted ones.[316]

Scholars argue that Congress had two key policy goals when it legislated the CDA. First, it wanted to allow companies to keep investing in innovation without the fear of holding liability for the action of third-party users. Second, it wanted to engage ISPs in voluntary self-regulation to remove illegal content without having the burden to be liable for it in cases of failure.[317]

Law Review 589 p 594.

[309]   47 U.S.C. Communications Decency Act of 1996 (CDA) (Title V, Telecommunications Act of 1996).

[310]   §230, c, CDA.

[311]   §230, 2, A, CDA.

[312]   For an overview of how this regime applies, *see* David S Ardia, "Free Speech Savior or Shield for Scoundrels: An Empirical Study of Intermediary Immunity Under Section 230 of the Communication Decency Act" (2009) 43 Loyola of Los Angeles Law Review 373.

[313]   Communications Decency Act of 1996 (CDA), section 230 (e) (1) – (4).

[314]   17 U.S.C., (c)(1)(A), DMCA.

[315]   Also, *Tiffany (NJ) Inc. v eBay Inc*, 600 F. 3d 93 (2d Circuit 2010) shows that even in case of counterfeit pieces, the ISP eBay only had the duty and liability to remove the products that it was expressly notified of.

[316]   Article 14, 1 (b), Directive on Electronic Commerce.

[317]   Mark A Lemley, "Rationalizing Internet Safe Harbors" (2007) 6 Journal on Telecommunication & High Technology Law 101, p 102; Jeff Kossef, "Defending Section 230:

Many cases that litigated ISPs' liability for third-party illegal content have involved instances of defamation.[318] The *Barnes v Yahoo!* case illustrates how the matter stands in light of the "Good Samaritan" provision in the United States.[319] In this case, the Court of Appeals for the Ninth Circuit was asked if the CDA protected an ISP that failed to remove serious defamatory content. The case involved the plaintiff Cecilia Barnes who had broken up with her boyfriend. As a reaction to the breakup, he created several public profiles of Cecilia on a website run by Yahoo!. These profiles could be seen by anyone and included nude photographs of Cecilia, which were taken without her knowledge, as well as messages suggesting that she was open to engaging in "sexual intercourses."[320] The ex-boyfriend then used these non-authorized profiles to chat with users in Yahoo!'s chat room. He provided users with Cecilia's employment address and phone numbers. As a result, several men came to Cecilia's workplace and called her in the expectation of having intimate "intercourses" with her. When Cecilia became aware of why these men were looking for her, she emailed Yahoo! requesting the immediate removal of such profiles. After one month, Yahoo! had not taken any measure to remove the fake profiles, and Cecilia continued to be approached by unknown men. She inquired a few more times to have the fake profiles removed, but she still did not have any response. A local television station decided to report the issue. One day before the station planned to broadcast the incidence, Yahoo!'s manager called Cecilia and promised to remove the profiles. Two months passed after the call and Yahoo! had not taken any measure to take the profiles down. Cecilia then sued Yahoo! for negligence to remove the defamatory content. The Court of Appeal upheld the District Court on the "ground that the CDA holds Yahoo! immune against any liability for the content that Barnes' former boyfriend had posted."[321]

Even if many of the cases litigating the liability of ISPs involve such instances of defamation, other cases have been raised and taken into litigation, including cases of discriminatory messages such as housing advertising overtly stating, "no Blacks," "no women of color," and "no Muslim,"[322] among others.[323]

The Value of Intermediary Immunity" (2010) 15:2 Journal of Technology Law & Policy 123.

318   David S Ardia, "Free Speech or Shield for Scoundrels: An Empirical Study of Intermediary Immunity Under Section 230 of the Communications Decency Act" (2009) 43 (2) Loyola of Los Angeles Law Review 373, p 452.

319   *Barnes v Yahoo Inc.*, no 05–36189 (9th Circuit, 2009). For comments on the case, *see* Nancy S Kim, "Web Site Proprietorship and Online Harassment" (2009) 3 Utah Law Review 993; Joshua A Fairfield, "The God Paradox" (2009) 89:3 Boston University Law Review 1017.

320   *Barnes v Yahoo Inc.*, no 05–36189 (9th Circuit, 2009), §§II.

321   *Barnes v Yahoo Inc.*, no 05–36189 (9th Circuit, 2009), §§IV.

322   *Chicago Lawyers' v Craigslist Inc.*, No. 07–1101 (7th Cir. 2008) and *Fair Housing Council of San Fernando Valley v. Roommates, LLC*, 2012 WL 310849 (9th Cir. February 2, 2012); *Doe v MySpace Inc.*, 528, F.3d 413 (5th Circuit, 2008); *Flowers v Carville*, 210 F.3d 1118 (9th Circuit, 2002).

323   Douglas B Luftman, "Defamation Liability for Online Services: The Sky is Not Falling" (1997) 65 George Washington Review 1071; Kate Klonick, "The New Governs: The People,

1.7. THEORY OF VICARIOUS LIABILITY APPLIED TO COMPANIES: LIABILITY FOR THIRD-PARTY DISCRIMINATION

Aside from newspapers' tort liability for discriminatory third-party advertisements against protected classes, courts have also held real estate companies and companies that offer places of public accommodation, such as hotels, liable for discrimination conducted by their agents against protected classes of housing seekers or clients.[324] This sort of third-party liability is referred to as vicarious liability, and as *responsibility du fait d'autrui*, in civil law traditions.[325] It alludes to a situation in which a person or a company is held liable for the actions or omissions of another person.[326] This context includes two main views about the vicarious liability of businesses for third-party misconduct. First, companies shall be liable when their employees conduct illegal actions under the doctrine of *respodeat superior*.[327] In these cases, the company's agents or employees were acting within the course of their employment responsibilities. No fault on the part of the company is required, and they will be liable for their agents' wrongdoings exclusively because of their responsibility and duty to supervise and control the action of its agents or employees in a circumstance of tort lawsuit. Second, companies shall be vicariously liable only in cases of negligence, such as being notified about the employee wrongdoing and not acting accordingly.[328]

In tort legal actions, punitive damages have the role to compensate harmed victims of wrongdoings, to penalize an individual or business for their illegal behavior, and, particularly, to discourage them and others in a similar position from engaging in similar conduct in the future.[329] Aside from compensatory

---

Rules, and Processes Governing Online Speech" (2017) 131 Harvard Law Review 1598; Corey Omer, "Intermediary Liability for Harmful Speech: Lessons From Abroad" (2014) 28 Harvard Journal Law & Technology 289; Julie Adler, "The Public's Burden in a Digital Age: Pressures on Intermediaries and the Privatization of Internet Censorship" (2011) Journal Law & Policy 231; David S Ardia, "Free Speech or Shield for Scoundrels: An Empirical Study of Intermediary Immunity Under Section 230 of the Communications Decency Act" (2009) 43 (2) Loyola of Los Angeles Law Review 373.

324   Michael Todisco, "Share and Share Alike: Considering Racial Discrimination in the Nascent Romm-Sharing Economy" (2014) 67 Stanford Law Review 121, p 127 and *Meyer v Holley*, 123 S.Ct. 824,829 (2003).

325   Vassilis Hatzopoulos, *The Collaborative Economy and the EU Law* (Oregon: Hart Publishing, 2018), p 22.

326   John C P Goldberg, *Torts* (New York: OUP, 2010), p 60.

327   Joy S Kimbrough, "The Federal Housing Act: No More Absolute Owner Liability When Employees Discriminate" (2003) 31 Southern University Law Review 109 p 116 and 121.

328   *Ibid.*

329   John C P Goldberg, *Torts* (New York: OUP, 2010); Linda L Schlueter, *Punitive Damages* (LexisNexis, 2015). For independent contractors, *see* Deanna N Conn, "When Contract Should Preempt Tort Remedies: Limits on Vicarious Liability for Acts of Independent Contractors" (2010) 15 Fordham Journal of Corporate and Financial Law 179; Gregory C

damages, punitive damages are considered relevant to discourage illegal behavior. When companies hold vicarious liability for their agents' actions, they must compensate the victims for both punitive and compensatory damages. As a result, corporate vicarious liability may serve as an incentive for companies to properly train and manage their employees. In some cases, corporate vicarious liability is also essential to redress victims of wrongdoings because companies often have more assets or financial means to compensate the victims than the individual agents of misconducts.

Over the past decades, the question whether real estate agencies should be liable for punitive damages in cases of discrimination perpetrated by their real estate agents against home seekers has been discussed in light of vicarious liability.[330]

In this context, the FHA explicitly prohibits any "person" or other entity whose business includes engaging in residential real estate-related transactions or business transactions in public accommodations to discriminate against home seekers because of their race or any other protected aspect.[331] The act includes that "person" comprises not only individuals but also corporations.[332] The FHA itself does not mention vicarious liability theories. However, it has been established that it provides for vicarious liability in cases of discrimination, because lawsuits filed for compensation by a victim of a housing or public accommodation discrimination are by definition tort actions.[333] Precedents have ruled that vicarious liability rules apply to tort actions.[334] Moreover, it is precedential that traditional vicarious liability rules ordinarily make companies liable for the acts of their agents in the scope of their authority.[335] A company might be liable for both negligent and intentional torts committed by its agent. Furthermore, in the absence of special circumstances, it is the company and not its owner or officer who is subject to vicarious liability for torts committed by its agents.[336]

Keating, "The Theory of Enterprise Liability and Common Law Strict Liability" (2001) 54 Vanderbilt Law Review 1285, p 1286–1287, Gregory C Keating, "The Idea of Fairness in the Law of Enterprise Liability" (1997) 95 Michigan Law Review 1266, p 1267.

[330]   Andrene N Plummer, "A Few New Solutions to a Very Old Problem: How the Fair Housing Act Can Be Improved to Deter Discriminatory Conduct by Real Estate Brokers" (2003) Howard Law Journal 163; Jessica Reingold Katz, "Finding Fault: Implications of Importing the Title VII Standard for Vicarious Punitive Liability to the Fair Housing Act" (2008) 29 Cardozo Law Review 2749.

[331]   FHA, 42 U.S.C. §3605(a) and Civil Rights Act of 1964, 42 U.S.C. §2000a.

[332]   FHA, §3602(a) and Civil Rights Act of 1964, 42 U.S.C. §2000a.

[333]   Joy S Kimbrough, "The Federal Housing Act: No More Absolute Owner Liability When Employees Discriminate" (2003), *op. cit.*, p 113, referring to: *Curtis v Loether*, 415 US 189 (1974).

[334]   *Ibid*, p 121, citing *Montrey v Del Monte Dunes at Montrey*, Ltd, 526 U.S. 687 (1999).

[335]   *Ibid.*

[336]   *Ibid.*

In *Meyer v Holley*, for instance, the United States Supreme Court ruled that the FHA imposes liability without fault upon a real estate agency under traditional vicarious liability principles.[337] In this case, the Holleys wanted to buy a property in California, and one of the partners was a Black American. The real estate agency Triad had announced a house for sale. Grove Crank, in his capacity as a Triad salesman, was convicted to have refused to sell the property to the couple for racially discriminatory reasons. Nevertheless, the court also found the real estate agency Triad liable for the discrimination perpetrated by its agent, and therefore, it was equally responsible for putative damages.[338]

Rules of vicarious liability traditionally apply to corporations that establish a relationship of subordination with their agents, typically through employment or similar arrangements. However, in recent years, victims of discrimination have questioned the liability of online platforms for discriminatory actions perpetrated by its users. One could speculate if a theory of vicarious liability would apply in such a case if these platforms are not considered Internet Services Providers in the terms of the CDA.[339] Precedents have shown that a theory of vicarious liability is not applicable in cases where companies lack authority over their agents, which is usually the case between companies that own online platforms and their users.

2. EUROPEAN UNION

At the level of the European Union, specific protection against discrimination concerning housing transactions and services available to the public is provided on the grounds of race, ethnic origin, and sex. In this regard, two instruments are relevant: the Race Equality Directive and the Gender Equal Access to Goods and Services Directive.[340] They both establish a minimum legal framework against discrimination beyond employment matters in the member states. Moreover, they both address discrimination against these grounds in such contexts for the first time at the core of the EU secondary legislation.[341]

So far, the European Equality Directives do not cover discrimination in housing transactions and services available to the public on the basis of religion,

---

[337] *Meyer v. Holley*, 537 U.S. 280 (2003).

[338] *Ibid.*

[339] *Selden v Airbnb*, INC., No. 16-cv-00933 (CRC) (D.C. Nov. 1, 2016). This view is supported by Agnieszka A McPeak, "Sharing Tort Liability in the New Sharing Economy" (2016) 49:1 Connecticut Law Review 171.

[340] Article 3, (h), Race Equality Directive; Article 3, 1, Gender Equal Access to Goods and Services Directive.

[341] Mark Bell, "Beyond European Labour Law? Reflections on the EU Racial Equality Directive" (2002) 8:3 European Law Journal 384, 385, and Sandra Fredman, "Equality: A New Generation?" (2001) 2:1 Industrial Law Journal 145, p 151.

belief, disability, age, and sexual orientation.[342] A proposal to implement the principle of antidiscrimination outside the scope of employment in relation to these classes was introduced in 2008, but it is still on hold at the time this book was submitted.[343]

2.1. EQUAL ACCESS TO HOUSING OPPORTUNITIES AND ACCOMMODATION SERVICES

Both the Race Equality Directive and the Gender Equal Access to Goods and Services Directive have provisions against direct and indirect discrimination on the grounds of race, ethnic origin, and sex in the access and supply of goods and services, but only the former specifically mentions housing.[344] The latter does not indicate any definition for housing, but it is inferred that the meaning goes beyond the equality of treatment for individuals belonging to a certain ethnic origin or "race" in housing transactions.[345] In other words, the term housing must cover homeowners or real estate agencies when they are deciding who to sell or rent their properties to as well as the equal treatment in the allocation to social and housing assistance.[346]

---

[342] These grounds are also provided by article 19 of the Treaty on the Functioning of the European Union (TFEU). At the present time, these 4 grounds are covered in employment-related discrimination by the Employment Equality Directive (Council Directive 2000/78/EC of 27 November 2000 Establishing a General Framework for Equal Treatment in Employment and Occupation, OJ L 303, 2.12.2000).

[343] COM (2008) 426, 2.2.2008. European Commission, *Proposal for a Council Directive on Implementing the Principle of Equal Treatment Outside the Labour Market, Irrespective of Age, Disability, Sexual Orientation or Religious Belief* (July 2008) online: European Commission <https://eur-lex.europa.eu/legal-content/EN/TXT/PDF/?uri=CELEX:52008PC0426&from =EN>; European Parliament, *Legislative Train Schedule: Anti-Discrimination Directive* (May 2022), online: European Parliament <https://www.europarl.europa.eu/legislative-train/ theme-area-of-justice-and-fundamental-rights/file-anti-discrimination-directive>.

[344] Article 3, (h), Race Equality Directive; Article 3, 1, Gender Equal Access to Goods and Services Directive.

[345] Fundamental Rights Agency (FRA), *Handbook on European Non-Discrimination Law* (Luxembourg: Publications Office of the European Union, 2018), p B134. The text suggests that the scope of term housing, in the Race Equality Directive, might be interpreted in light of international law, including the Article 7 of the Charter of Fundamental Rights of the European Union (respect for private and family life); the Article 8 of the European Convention on Human Rights (respect for private and family life), Article 11 of the International Covenant on Economic Social and Cultural Rights (adequate housing conditions). Also, Article 3 of the International Convention on the Elimination of All Forms of Racial Discrimination imposes the prevention, prohibition and eradication of racial segregation. And, the General Recommendation XIX Regarding Article 3 of the Convention, §3 (Committee on the Elimination of Racial Discrimination) prohibits segregation caused by both government policies and by private parties.

[346] *Ibid*, p B135. Also, the Article 34(3) of the Charter of Fundamental Rights of the European Union recognizes the right to social and housing assistance to ensure a decent living for those who lack sufficient resources. Scholars support that even if the term housing is not mentioned

For the purpose of this title, the equal treatment of persons irrespective of their racial, ethnic origin, and gender in the public transaction and offer of housing as well as in the access to private services available to the public is included in the scope of both Directives and, more specifically, in the provision that makes discrimination in the "access and supply of goods and services" illegal.[347] The prohibition of discrimination in transactions involving real estate and access to services and goods available to the public is nearly absolute and only comprises few exceptions.[348]

Even though scholars call attention to the usual intersectionality between nationality and racial/ethnic origin discrimination, the Race Equality directive does not apply to the grounds of nationality.[349] However, several EU member states include nationality as a protected class in their national antidiscrimination laws.[350] Moreover, other European legal texts protect nationality against discrimination in housing transactions under certain circumstances. For instance, nationals of member states who live in the territory of another member state have the same rights accorded to nationals regarding housing.[351] Moreover, long-term residents from third-countries have the right to equal treatment

---

in the Gender Equal Access to Goods and Services Directive it might be construed from the terms "goods and services, which are available to the public". *See* Julie Ringelheim, Nicolas Bernard, *Discrimination in Housing: Thematic Report of the European Network of Legal Experts in the Non-Discrimination Field* (February 2013), online: European Commission Directorate General for Justice and Consumers <https://op.europa.eu/en/publication-detail/-/publication/c8cf0ff7–8676–4751–8d36–59eeffe379ee/language-en>, p 12.

[347] Article 3, 1(h), Race Equality Directive; Article 3, 1, Gender Equal Access to Goods and Services Directive.

[348] For private life, *see* section 2.2. Both directives admit discrimination based on sex, race and ethnic origin to compensate for disadvantages (positive actions): Article 5, Race Equality Directive and Article 6, Gender Equal Access to Goods and Services Directive; Also, regarding the difference of treatment between women and men, the establishment of single sex shelters is justified to the protection of victims of sex-related violence. Recital 16, Gender Equal Access to Goods and Services Directive. For positive action, *see* Lisa Waddington, Mark Bell, "Exploring the Boundaries of Positive Action under EU Law: a Search for Conceptual Clarity" (2011) 48 Common Market Law Review 5; Olivier De Schutter, Natalie Boccadoro, *Le Droit au Logement Dans l'Union Européenne* (February 2005) online: CRIHO Working Paper Series <https://cridho.uclouvain.be/documents/Working.Papers/CridhoWPs022005.PDF>, p 25.

[349] Lilla Farkas, *The Meaning of Racial or Ethnic Origin in EU Law: Between Stereotypes and Identities* (January 2017), online: European Commission Directorate General for Justice and Consumers <https://op.europa.eu/en/publication-detail/-/publication/c1cf6b78–094c-11e7–8a35–01aa75ed71a1> p 113; Olivier De Schutter, *Links Between Migration and Discrimination: A Legal Analysis of the Situation in EU Member States, European Network of Legal Experts in Gender Equality and Non-Discrimination* (July 2016) online: European Commission Directorate General for Justice and Consumers <https://www.equalitylaw.eu/downloads/3917-links-between-migration-and-discrimination>, p 31.

[350] *See* chapter 3.

[351] Article 9(1), Regulation (EU) No 492/2011 of the European Parliament and of the Council of 5 April 2011 on Freedom of Movement for Workers Within the Union, OJ L 141/1 27 May 2011.

in relation to the supply of goods and services made available to the public, including housing.[352]

The term "service" is not defined in the Race Equality Directive. The text only provides that the scope of protection against racial and ethnic discrimination is limited to "services which are available to the public."[353] Alternatively, the directive on Gender Equal Access to Goods and Services determines that the services it refers to are within the meaning of Article 57 TFEU.[354] Despite the lack of a definition for the term "services" in the Race Equality Directive, the notion shall be construed in the light of this same article.[355] In this regard, the principle of equal treatment applies to the services that are provided for remuneration and involve activities of the commercial and industrial sectors.[356] This definition encompasses a broad spectrum of activities available to the public, including access to retail stores, restaurants, hotels, and travel services. Litigation, at the national level, involving the clause of equal treatment in the provision of services has included discrimination in access to discotheques, bars, and cafes and in the sale of insurance policies and pets, for example.[357]

Overall, the EU member states have more grounds of protection against discrimination regarding real estate transactions or access to goods and services than the ones enshrined in the Equality Directives.[358] Aside from sex, racial and ethnic origin, the protection against discrimination on the grounds of nationality is specifically provided in the access of goods and services,

---

[352]   Article 11(1), Council Directive 2003/109/EC of 25 November 2003 Concerning the Status of Third-Country Nationals Who are Long-Term Residents, OJ L 16 of 31 January 2004.

[353]   Article 3, 1 (h) Race Equality Directive.

[354]   Recital 11, Gender Equal Access to Goods and Services Directive mentions Article 50 of the Treaty establishing the European Community (EC), which is the actual Article 57 of the Treaty on the Functioning of the European Union (TFEU).

[355]   *See* Julie Ringelheim, "The Prohibition of Racial and Ethnic Discrimination in Access to Services under EU Law" (2010) 10 European Anti-Discrimination Law Review 11, p 11.

[356]   Art 57, TFEU. In the same sense, the article 4(1) of Directive 2006/123/EC of the European Parliament and of the Council of 12 December 2006 on Services in the Internal Market, OJ L 376, 12.12.2006, p 36 defines services as "any self-employed economic activity, normally provided for remuneration".

[357]   Fundamental Rights Agency (FRA), *Handbook on European Non-Discrimination Law, op. cit.*, p 135. It provides the cases taking place in Hungary (Equal Treatment Authority, Case 72, 2008); Sweden (*Escapade Bar and Restaurant v Ombudsman Against Ethnic Discrimination* T-2224–07, 2008; and *Ombudsman Against Discrimination on Grounds of Sexual Orientation v A.S.*); in Austria (Bezirksgericht Döbling, GZ17C 1597/05f-17, 2006); France (*Lenormand v Balenci*, N 08/00907, Nîmes).

[358]   Alexandra Timmer, Linda Senden, *How Are EU Rules Transposed into National Law in 2018? Thematic Report of the European Network of Legal Experts in the Non-Discrimination Field* (January 2019), online: European Commission Directorate-General for Justice and Consumers <https://www.equalitylaw.eu/downloads/4830-gender-equality-law-in-europe-2018-pdf-554-kb> p 70. Also, Nathalie Wuiame, *How are EU Rules Transposed into National Law? Country Report Gender Equality, Belgium* (February 2019) online: European Commission Directorate-General for Justice and Consumers <https://www.equalitylaw.eu/downloads/4992-belgium-country-report-gender-equality-2019-pdf-1-0-mb>.

under certain circumstances, by the laws in Belgium, Denmark, Finland,
France, Greece, Italy, Liechtenstein, Lithuania, Poland, Romania, Slovakia, and
Spain.[359] Furthermore, the grounds of religion, belief, and sexual orientation are

---

[359] Emmanuelle Bribosia, Isabelle Rorive, with the collaboration of Areg Navasartian, Assal
Sharifrazi, *Country Report Non-Discrimination: Transposition and Implementation at
National Level of Council Directives 2000/43 and 2000/78 Belgium* (January 2019), online:
European Commission Directorate-General for Justice and Consumers <https://www.
equalitylaw.eu/downloads/5034-belgium-country-report-non-discrimination-2019-pdf-
2–09-mb>, 61–62; Pia Justesen, *Country Report Non-Discrimination: Transposition and
Implementation at National Level of Council Directives 2000/43 and 2000/78 Denmark*
(January 2019), online: European Commission Directorate-General for Justice and
Consumers <https://www.equalitylaw.eu/downloads/4985-denmark-country-report-non-
discrimination-2019-pdf-1-51-mb> p 43; Rainer Hiltunen, *Country Report Non-
Discrimination: Transposition and Implementation at National Level of Council Directives
2000/43 and 2000/78 Finland* (January 2019), online: European Commission Directorate-
General for Justice and Consumers <https://www.equalitylaw.eu/downloads/4964-finland-
country-report-non-discrimination-2019-pdf-1-27-mb>, p 31–32; Sophie Latraverse,
*Transposition and Implementation at National Level of Council Directives 2000/43 and
2000/78, Country Report Non-Discrimination, France* (January 2019), online: Equality Law
<https://www.equalitylaw.eu/downloads/5000-france-country-report-non-discrimination-
2019-pdf-1-94-mb>, p 58–59; Athanasios Theodoris, *Country Report Non-Discrimination:
Transposition and Implementation at National Level of Council Directives 2000/43 and
2000/78 Greece* (January 2019), online: European Commission Directorate-General for
Justice and Consumers <https://www.equalitylaw.eu/downloads/4962-greece-country-
report-non-discrimination-2019-pdf-1-28-mb>, p 42–45; Chiara Favilli, *Country Report Non-
Discrimination: Transposition and Implementation at National Level of Council Directives
2000/43 and 2000/78 Italy* (January 2019), online: European Commission Directorate-
General for Justice and Consumers <https://www.equalitylaw.eu/downloads/5014-italy-
country-report-non-discrimination-2019-pdf-1-36-mb>, p 32–35; Patricia Hornich,
*Country Report Non-Discrimination: Transposition and Implementation at National Level
of Council Directives 2000/43 and 2000/78 Liechtenstein* (January 2019), online: European
Commission Directorate-General for Justice and Consumers <https://www.equalitylaw.eu/
downloads/4966-liechtenstein-country-report-non-discrimination-2019-pdf-1-09-mb>,
p 34–37; Biruté Sabatauskaité, *Country Report Non-Discrimination: Transposition and
Implementation at National Level of Council Directives 2000/43 and 2000/78 Lithuania*
(January 2019), online: European Commission Directorate-General for Justice and
Consumers <https://www.equalitylaw.eu/downloads/5015-lithuania-country-report-
non-discrimination-2019-pdf-1-77-mb>, p 55–57; Lukasz Bojarski, *Country Report Non-
Discrimination: Transposition and Implementation at National Level of Council Directives
2000/43 and 2000/78 Poland* (January 2019), online: European Commission Directorate-
General for Justice and Consumers <https://www.equalitylaw.eu/downloads/4801-poland-
country-report-non-discrimination-2018-pdf-2-79-mb>, p 84–86; Romanita Iordache,
*Country Report Non-Discrimination: Transposition and Implementation at National Level
of Council Directives 2000/43 and 2000/78 Romania* (January 2019), online: European
Commission Directorate-General for Justice and Consumers <https://www.equalitylaw.eu/
downloads/4971-romania-country-report-non-discrimination-2019-pdf-1-27-mb>, p 48–49;
Vanda Durbakova, *Country Report Non-Discrimination: Transposition and Implementation
at National Level of Council Directives 2000/43 and 2000/78 Slovakia* (January 2019), online:
European Commission Directorate-General for Justice and Consumers <https://www.
equalitylaw.eu/downloads/4975-slovakia-country-report-non-discrimination-2019-pdf-1-
40-mb>, p 54–55; Lorenzo Cachón, *Country Report Non-Discrimination: Transposition and
Implementation at National Level of Council Directives 2000/43 and 2000/78 Spain* (January
2019), online: European Commission Directorate-General for Justice and Consumers

specifically enshrined in the antidiscrimination laws regarding access to goods and services in Croatia, Cyprus, Czech Republic, Finland, Greece, Liechtenstein, Lithuania, Luxembourg, the Netherlands, Romania, Slovakia, Slovenia, and Sweden.[360] In these cases, landlords, real estate agencies, and hotels cannot legally decide to refuse to rent or sell an accommodation based on these grounds.

Even though studies have shown that a significant level of discrimination exists in the private rental market across the member states[361], especially based on the grounds of nationality and racial and ethnic origin, court cases concerning discrimination in these markets are less extensive.[362] The reasons

<https://www.equalitylaw.eu/downloads/4963-spain-country-report-non-discrimination-2019-pdf-1-32-mb>, p 41–42.

[360] Ines Bojic, *Country Report Non-Discrimination: Transposition and Implementation at National Level of Council Directives 2000/43 and 2000/78 Croatia* (January 2019), online: European Commission Directorate-General for Justice and Consumers <https://www.equalitylaw.eu/downloads/4965-croatia-country-report-non-discrimination-2019-pdf-1-18-mb>, p 47–48; Corina Demetriou, *Country Report Non-Discrimination: Transposition and Implementation at National Level of Council Directives 2000/43 and 2000/78 Cyprus* (January 2019), online: European Commission Directorate-General for Justice and Consumers <https://www.equalitylaw.eu/downloads/5067-cyprus-country-report-non-discrimination-2019-pdf-2-07-mb>, p 63–64; Jakub Tomsej, *Country Report Non-Discrimination: Transposition and Implementation at National Level of Council Directives 2000/43 and 2000/78 Czech Republic* (January 2019), online: European Commission Directorate-General for Justice and Consumers <https://www.equalitylaw.eu/downloads/4959-czech-republic-country-report-non-discrimination-2019-pdf-1-21-mb>, p 44–45; Tania Hoffmann, *Country Report Non-Discrimination: Transposition and Implementation at National Level of Council Directives 2000/43 and 2000/78 Luxembourg* (January 2019), online: European Commission Directorate-General for Justice and Consumers <https://www.equalitylaw.eu/downloads/4967-luxembourg-country-report-non-discrimination-2019-pdf-781-kb>, p 23–34; Karin de Vries, *Country Report Non-Discrimination: Transposition and Implementation at National Level of Council Directives 2000/43 and 2000/78 Netherlands* (January 2019), online: European Commission Directorate-General for Justice and Consumers <https://www.equalitylaw.eu/downloads/4970-the-netherlands-country-report-non-discrimination-2019-pdf-1-92-mb>, p 44–45; Neza Kogovsek Salamon, *Country Report Non-Discrimination: Transposition and Implementation at National Level of Council Directives 2000/43 and 2000/78 Slovenia* (January 2019), online: European Commission Directorate-General for Justice and Consumers <https://www.equalitylaw.eu/downloads/4974-slovenia-country-report-non-discrimination-2019-pdf-1-31-mb>, p 42–43; Paul Lappalainen, "*Country Report Non-Discrimination: Transposition and Implementation at National Level of Council Directives 2000/43 and 2000/78 Sweden* (January 2019), online: European Commission Directorate-General for Justice and Consumers <https://www.equalitylaw.eu/downloads/4973-sweden-country-report-non-discrimination-2019-pdf-1-44-mb>, p 45–47; Lucy Vickers, *Country Report Non-Discrimination: Transposition and Implementation at National Level of Council Directives 2000/43 and 2000/78 United Kingdom* (January 2019), online: European Commission Directorate-General for Justice and Consumers <https://www.equalitylaw.eu/downloads/4976-united-kingdom-country-report-non-discrimination-2019-pdf-1-39-mb>, p 34–35; for Finland, Greece, Liechtenstein, Lithuania, Romania and Slovakia *see* note above 372.

[361] *See* section I above.

[362] Julie Ringelheim, Nicolas Bernard, *Discrimination in Housing: Thematic Report of the European Network of Legal Experts in the Non-Discrimination Field* (February 2013), online: European Commission Directorate General for Justice and Consumers <https://op.europa.eu/

are mainly related to an asymmetry of information that potential discriminated tenants or clients have about the causes of their refusal.[363] Apart from cases of overt discrimination, or close contact with the person who ultimately rented or bought the property, refused tenants or home buyers have little possibilities to know whether they were discriminated against. Therefore, situation testing is relevant to address discrimination in the sector.[364]

2.2. ANTIDISCRIMINATION VERSUS THE RIGHT TO PRIVATE AND FAMILY LIFE

The principle of equal treatment between persons irrespective of their sex, race, ethnic origins, and the other grounds the member states might provide is limited in scope to services available to the public.[365] Nevertheless, the Race and Gender Equality Directives stress the importance of respecting private and family life and, thus, limit their material scope to transactions that are performed out of this context.[366] They emphasize the relevance to respect the right for private life and family.[367] Country reports of transposition and implementation at the national level of the Equality directives also emphasize the need to balance the right of privacy with the one of antidiscrimination.[368] Therefore, the principle of equal treatment must be balanced with the respect for private and family life in the context of access of services and goods, including housing.[369]

In EU law, the balance between the right to private and family life and the principle of equality has been long debated in cases of domestic employment.[370] Employment laws have the most extensive grounds against discrimination in the EU Equality Directives and in the EU countries. However, in the past,

---

en/publication-detail/-/publication/c8cf0ff7-8676-4751-8d36-59eeffe379ee/language-en>, p 47.

[363] *Ibid.*

[364] *See* chapters 2 and 4.

[365] Article 3, 1 (h), Race Equality Directive; Recital 13, Article 3, 1, Gender Equal Access to Goods and Services Directive.

[366] Recital 4, Race Equality Directive; Recital 3, Gender Equal Access to Goods and Services Directive.

[367] Recital 4, Race Equality Directive; Recital 16, Gender Equal Access to Goods and Services Directive. The latter provides the example of cases of "memberships of single-sex private clubs".

[368] *See* chapter 1, section II, 2.2.

[369] The right to respect for private and family life is also enshrined in the Article 8 of the European Convention on Human Rights and Article 7 of the Charter of Fundamental Rights of the European Union.

[370] For an overview of the balance between the principle of equality and private life *see* Emmanuelle Bribosia, Isabelle Rorive, *In Search of a Balance Between the Right to Equality and Other Fundamental Rights* (February 2010), online: European Commission Directorate General for Employment, Social Affairs and Equal Opportunities <https://tandis.odihr.pl/bitstream/20.500.12389/21232/1/07052.pdf>, 29–32.

member states have argued for the possibility for employers to discriminate against employees on the basis of respect for private life. Particularly, the UK had statutes that excluded jobs in households and in companies with less than five employees from the scope of its Act that prohibited discrimination grounded on sex.[371] In practice, employers were able to refuse to hire someone based solely on their sex due to a genuine occupational requirement. The case was assessed by the Court of Justice that ruled that the principle of equal treatment between men and women might be indeed balanced with the right for private life in the context of employment in households, but the exception to discriminate on the ground of sex should be more specific than the text provided by the UK Act.[372]

Regarding the access to services and goods, the European Commission, through reports about the application of the Race Equality Directive and Gender Equal Access to Goods and Services Directive, has indicated that the line between public and private is sometimes blurred in some member states, without giving more detailed information about which member states and in which situations.[373] However, when a good, service, or employment is somehow advertised, either in a newspaper, in a website, or as a notice in a window, it shall be considered under the meaning as available to the public, and, therefore, under the scope of the Race Equality Directive.[374] Moreover, some countries do not permit exceptions to discriminate because of race even in contexts of private life involving accommodation, such the rental of a room in someone's house.[375]

---

[371]   Case C-165/82 *Commission v UK* ECR 3431 ECLI:EU:C:1983:311.

[372]   *Ibid.*

[373]   Brussels, 15.12.2006 COM (2006)643 final/2 Report from the Commission to the Council and the European Parliament: The Application of Directive 2000/43/EC of 29 June 2000 implementing the principle of equal treatment between persons irrespective of racial or ethnic origin, p 3.

[374]   Brussels, 15.12.2006 COM (2006)643 final/2 Report from the Commission to the Council and the European Parliament: The Application of Directive 2000/43/EC of 29 June 2000 implementing the principle of equal treatment between persons irrespective of racial or ethnic origin, p 3. The commission reinforced this view several years later, in Brussels, 17.1.2014 COM(2014) 2 final Report From the Commission to the European Parliament and the Council: Joint Report on the Application of Council Directive 2000/43/EC of 29 June 2000 Implementing the Principle of Equal Treatment Between Persons Irrespective of Racial or Ethnic Origin (Racial Equality Directive) and of Council Directive 2000/78/EC of 27 November 2000 establishing a general framework for equal treatment in employment and occupation (Employment Equality Directive), p 11. Some national laws specifically provide that antidiscrimination laws apply to advertisement, such as the case of Hungary. *See* Andras Kadar, *Report on Measures to Combat Discrimination Directives 2000/43/EC and 2000/78/ EC Country Report Hungary* (January 2013), online: European Commission European Network of Legal Experts in the Non-Discrimination Field <https://www.equalitylaw.eu/ downloads/4177-hungary-country-report-non-discrimination-2013-1-23-mb>, p 80.

[375]   It is the case of the UK, *see* Equality and Human Rights Commission, *What Equality Means for Advertisers and Publishers* (February 2016), online: Equality and Human Rights Commission <https://www.equalityhumanrights.com/sites/default/files/ehrc_advertising_-_ equality_law_12.pdf>, p 9.

With respect to the equal treatment between men and women, the concept of services and goods offered in the context of private life encompasses personal physical proximity.[376] Privacy and decency are considered legitimate aims that justify difference in treatment on the grounds of sex in cases of a provision of accommodation as part of the person's home.[377] In this context, the Commission considers that when services and goods are somehow advertised they are "available to the public."[378] However, private individuals are allowed to discriminate on the grounds of sex when "the proximity to the personal sphere of the person offering goods or services influences the choice of the contractual partner more than economic considerations."[379] The Commission gave the example of someone subletting a room in a house or apartment where they live. In this case, personal proximity is a legitimate aim that justifies sex discrimination, even when the concerned room is advertised in a newspaper or on the internet.[380]

2.3. THE FIGHT AGAINST DISCRIMINATORY ADVERTISEMENTS: LIABILITY OF PUBLISHERS

The freedom of expression is a protected value in most foundational legal instruments in Europe[381], including the Charter of Fundamental Rights of the European Union[382] and the European Convention on Human Rights (ECHR).[383] In addition to comprehensive provisions in national constitutions, this freedom is also enshrined amongst the fundamental rights in the Universal Declaration of Human Rights (UDHR)[384] and the International Covenant on Civil and Political

---

[376] Recital 16, Gender Equal Access to Goods and Services.

[377] *Ibid.*

[378] Brussels, 5.5.2015 COM (2015) 190 final, Report From the Commission to the European Parliament, the Council and the European Economic and Social Committee, Report on the Application of Council Directive 2004/113/EC Implementing the Principle of Equal Treatment Between Men and Women in the Access to and Supply of Goods and Services, p 4.

[379] *Ibid.*

[380] *Ibid.*

[381] The unilateral removal of online content by platforms/private companies has also been pointed as a threat to the freedom of expression. *Delfi AS v Estonia* (2015) ECtHR 64669/09. See Lisl Brunner, *"The Liability of an Online Intermediary for Third-Party Content: The Watchdog Becomes the Monitor: Internet Liability after Delfi v Estonia" (2016) Human Rights Law Review 163.*

[382] The Charter of Fundamental Rights of the European Union, Article 11. Article 11.1. "Freedom of Expression and Information": "Everyone has the right to freedom of expression. This right shall include freedom to hold opinions and to receive and impart information and ideas without interference by public authority and regardless of frontiers".

[383] The European Convention on Human Rights, article 10,1 "Everyone has the right to freedom of expression".

[384] The 1948 Universal Declaration of Human Rights, Article 19: "Everyone has the right to freedom of opinion and expression".

Rights 1966 (ICCPR).[385] However, the exercise of the freedom of expression "carries with it special duties and responsibilities"[386] and might be restricted in certain circumstances that are specifically provided by law. These circumstances may regard the protection of the rights of others and reputation.[387]

In this context, media publishers are liable for illegal content they may communicate under certain circumstances.[388] They have the duty to remove the content from the sight of consumers, when it is possible, and grant putative damages to the persons whose rights were violated. When newspapers, magazines, and publishing companies issue or print third-party material that breaches legal requirements they might be held jointly liable with the author of the content in certain circumstances. In the EU, this sort of liability is regulated at the national level. Member states often have sectorial legislation that impose liability on publishers.

Regarding the liability of housing and accommodation advertisements containing illegal discrimination, the set of liabilities is twofold. First, the content provider of the illegal discriminatory advertisement (i.e., the advertiser) is liable under antidiscrimination laws. Second, the publisher of the advertisement is liable in some circumstances under tort laws for distributing, printing, and disseminating the illegal content. In this respect, the framework provisions against discrimination in the Race Equality Directive do not admit any exception to advertisements and fully apply to the content of advertisement. All member states except from Austria have transposed the Race Equality Directive properly. In Austria, the law still admits that a differentiation regarding ethnicity in housing ads focused on shared places is justified by the nature of the intimate relationship that it engages.[389] The Gender Equal Access to Goods and Services Directive admits that advertisements are outside of its scope, and the principal of equal treatment between women and men is *a priori* not enforceable in this context.[390] However, when several member states transposed the Directive into their national laws, they did not exclude advertising or media content from the antidiscrimination principle. These countries are Belgium,

---

[385] International Covenant on Civil and Political Rights 1966 (ICCPR), art 19.2 "Everyone shall have the right to freedom of expression"

[386] ICCPR, Article 19.2.

[387] The European Convention on Human Rights, Article 10.2.

[388] Vassilis Hatzopoulos, *The Collaborative Economy and the EU Law* (Oregon: Hart Publishing, 2018), p 27.

[389] The principle for respect of private life should not be interpreted in a way to admit the advertisement of ethnic preferences regarding the rental of shared places. The rapporteur of Austria considers that the country is breaching the Race Equality Directive, because it admits a possibility to discriminate that is not provided in the Directive. Dieter Schindlauer, *Country Report Non-Discrimination: Transposition and Implementation at National Level of Council Directives 2000/43 and 2000/78* (January 2019), online: European Commission Directorate General for Justice and Consumers <https://www.equalitylaw.eu/downloads/4984-austria-country-report-non-discrimination-2019-pdf-1-49-mb>, p 23.

[390] Recital 13 and Article 3, 3 Gender Equal Access to Goods and Services Directive.

Bulgaria, Croatia, Czech Republic, Denmark, Estonia, France, Hungary, Ireland, Latvia, Luxembourg, the Netherlands, Portugal, Slovakia, and Spain.[391]

Some countries have specific legal provisions for the liability of publishers in cases of discriminatory advertisements. In Ireland, for instance, the Equal

---

[391] Nathalie Wuiame, *Country Report Gender Equality Belgium* (January 2019), online: European Commission Directorate General for Justice and Consumers <https://www.equalitylaw.eu/downloads/4992-belgium-country-report-gender-equality-2019-pdf-1-0-mb>, p 54; Genoveva Tisheva, *Country Report Gender Equality Bulgaria* (January 2019), online: European Commission Directorate General for Justice and Consumers <https://www.equalitylaw.eu/downloads/5068-bulgaria-country-report-gender-equality-2019-pdf-1-21-kb>, p 63; Adrijana Martinovic, *Country Report Gender Equality Croatia* (January 2019), online: European Commission Directorate General for Justice and Consumers <https://www.equalitylaw.eu/downloads/4995-croatia-country-report-gender-equality-2019-pdf-1-20-mb>, p 68; Kristina Koldinska, *Country Report Gender Equality Czech Republic* (January 2019), online: European Commission Directorate General for Justice and Consumers <https://www.equalitylaw.eu/downloads/5030-czech-republic-country-report-gender-equality-2019-pdf-825-kb>, p 40; Stine Jorgensen, *Country Report Gender Equality Denmark* (January 2019), online: European Commission Directorate General for Justice and Consumers <https://www.equalitylaw.eu/downloads/5031-denmark-country-report-gender-equality-2019-pdf-828-kb>, p 32; Anu laas, *Country Report Gender Estonia* (January 2019), online: European Commission Directorate General for Justice and Consumers <https://www.equalitylaw.eu/downloads/5060-estonia-country-report-gender-equality-2019-pdf-1-18-mb>, p 57; Marie Mercat-Bruns, *Country Report Gender Equality France* (January 2019), online: European Commission Directorate General for Justice and Consumers <https://www.equalitylaw.eu/downloads/5043-france-country-report-gender-equality-2019-pdf-1-6-mb>, p 73; Lidia Hermina Balogh, *Country Report Gender Equality Hungary* (January 2019), online: European Commission Directorate General for Justice and Consumers <https://www.equalitylaw.eu/downloads/5044-hungary-country-report-gender-equality-2019-pdf-1-26-mb>, p 61; Frances Meenan, *Country Report Gender Equality Ireland* (January 2019), online: European Commission Directorate General for Justice and Consumers <https://www.equalitylaw.eu/downloads/5047-ireland-country-report-gender-equality-2019-pdf-1-14-mb>, p 63; Kristine Dupate, *Country Report Gender Equality Latvia* (January 2019), online: European Commission Directorate General for Justice and Consumers <https://www.equalitylaw.eu/downloads/5049-latvia-country-report-gender-equality-2019-pdf-1-1-mb>, p 18; Nicole Kerschen, *Country Report Gender Equality Luxembourg* (January 2019), online: European Commission Directorate General for Justice and Consumers <https://www.equalitylaw.eu/downloads/5074-luxembourg-country-report-gender-equality-2019-pdf-860-kb>, p 47; Marlies Vegter, *Country Report Gender Equality The Netherlands* (January 2019), online: European Commission Directorate General for Justice and Consumers <https://www.equalitylaw.eu/downloads/5050-the-netherlands-country-report-gender-equality-2019-pdf-1-25-mb>, p 66; Maria do Rosário Palma Ramalho, *Country Report Gender Equality Portugal* (January 2019), online: European Commission Directorate General for Justice and Consumers <https://www.equalitylaw.eu/downloads/4998-portugal-country-report-gender-equality-2019-pdf-976-kb>, p 57; Zuzana Magurová, *Country Report Gender Equality Slovakia* (January 2019), online: European Commission Directorate General for Justice and Consumers <https://www.equalitylaw.eu/downloads/5076-slovakia-country-report-gender-equality-2019-pdf-1-1-mb>, p 71; Amparo Ballester, *Country Report Gender Equality Spain* (January 2019), online: European Commission Directorate General for Justice and Consumers <https://www.equalitylaw.eu/downloads/4994-spain-country-report-gender-equality-2019-pdf-1-19-mb>, p 64; Grace James, *Country Report Gender Equality The United Kingdom* (January 2019), online: European Commission Directorate General for Justice and Consumers <https://www.equalitylaw.eu/downloads/5064-united-kingdom-country-report-gender-equality-2019-pdf-1-39-mb>, p 54.

Status Act has a specific section dedicated to advertisements that holds liable the publisher of ads that discriminate against protected classes.[392] Other countries have this sort of liability provided in general rules. In the UK, for instance, publishers are liable for disseminating illegal housing advertisements when they negligently engage with advertisers.[393]

2.4. ONLINE PLATFORMS' IMMUNITY FOR DISCRIMINATORY ADVERTISEMENTS

2.4.1. Back to the Past: Early Cases

Around the turn of the twentieth century, three major cases addressing the liability of Internet Service Providers for illegal third-party content were assessed by national courts of the EU member states. These cases were notably related to pornography, defamation, and racism.

The first case concerned the Internet Service Provider CompuServe Inc., headquartered in the United States, and its subsidiary CompuServe GmbH in Germany.[394] CompuServe provided access to the internet and other related services, such as online billboards and groups where users could post and discuss a variety of topics. In the late 1990s, CompuServe Inc. hosted a significant amount of illegal content related to child pornography and violence. At the time, CompuServe GmbH allowed German users to access this illegal material by supplying them with local dial-up internet. Following investigation, German law enforcement warned CompuServe GmbH and its German director Felix Somm to take down the illegal content. Mr. Somm argued that CompuServe GmbH did not have the technical capability to take down the required content and, thus, he directly asked CompuServe Inc., in the United States, to do it. CompuServe removed most of the indicated content. However, CompuServe Inc. announced online that they were not obliged to intervene more in such cases because they created the software Cyber Patrol, free of charge and available to all users in

---

[392] Section 12, Equal Status Act 2000–2016. (Ireland). <https://www.lawreform.ie/_fileupload/ RevisedActs/WithAnnotations/HTML/EN_ACT_2000_0008.HTM#PARTII-SEC12>.

[393] Equality and Human Rights Commission, *Advertising What Equality Law Means for Advertisers and Publishers* (February 2016), online: Equality and Human Rights <https:// www.equalityhumanrights.com/sites/default/files/ehrc_advertising_-_equality_law_12.pdf>.

[394] AG München, NJW, 51 (1998), 2836 (lower court) and LG München Az Ns 465 Js 173158/95 (December 28, 1999) (appeal court). More details of the case in English, *see* Lothar Determann, "Case Update: German CompuServe Director Acquitted on Appeal" (1999) 23:1 Hastings International and Comparative Law Review 109; Gunnar Bender, "Bavaria v Felix Somm: The Pornography Conviction of the Former CompuServe Manager" (1998) International Journal of Communication Law and Policy 1. The case is also commented by Benoit Frydman, Isabelle Rorive, "Regulating Internet Content through Intermediaries in Europe and the USA" (2002) 23:1 Zeitschrift Für Rechtssoziologie 41.

German and English, which allowed users to block access to any groups available on CompuServe.

Law enforcement did not consider the implementation of the tool as a justifiable reason to exempt CompuServe GmbH and Mr. Somm from liability for the illegal content in Germany, because the tool did not completely remove the content from public access. Mr. Somm and CompuServe were then charged and convicted for facilitating access to violent and child pornography content.[395] Later, the court of appeals overruled the conviction, because CompuServe GmbH did not have the technical capability to remove the illegal content and thus was not at fault.[396]

The second case involving the liability of an ISP for illegal third-party content occurred in the UK.[397] The content at stake concerned defamatory statements. The ISP Demon hosted several newsgroups (i.e., public forums where users post messages) that focused on varied subjects. Once messages were posted on newsgroups, they could be read by anyone who had access to the internet. In January 1997, the defamatory message stating that "all Thai women were intellectually deficient and as a result were only suited to employment as prostitutes"[398] was posted in one of the groups by the name of Lawrence Godfrey, a physics and computer-science professor in London. Once the professor became aware of the offending material, he immediately sent a fax to Demon's managing director informing him that he had not posted such content and demanding that Demon immediately remove it from its services. Nevertheless, Demon did not succeed to take down the publication before it was automatically removed a few weeks later.

Mr. Godfrey filed a tort action against Demon for defamation, because Demon controlled the server on which the newsgroup was hosted, and, therefore, it was effectively the publisher of the defamatory content under the terms of the UK defamation statutory law.[399] According to the UK law, a defamation charge cannot be filed against individuals who are not "the author, editor, or publisher of the statement complained of" and "take reasonable care in relation to its publication" and "neither knew nor had reason to suspect that what he did caused or contributed to the publication of a defamatory statement."[400]

---

[395] AG München, NJW, 51 (1998), 2836 (Lower Court).
[396] LG München Az Ns 465 Js 173158/95 (December 28, 1999) (Court of Appeal). *See* Lothar Determann, "Case Update: German CompuServe Director Acquitted on Appeal" (1999) 23:1 Hastings International and Comparative Law Review 109, p 110–115.
[397] *Godfrey v Demon Internet Ltd*, 1999 AII E.R.4 342 (1999). For comments on the case, *see* Kit Burden, "Case Report: Liability of ISPs for Third Party Postings to Newsgroups Godfrey v Demon" (1999) 15:4 Computer Law & Security 260; also, Gavin Sutter, "Don't Shoot the Messenger? The UK and Online Intermediary Liability" (2003) 17:1 International Review of Law 73;
[398] *Godfrey v Demon Internet Ltd*, 1999 AII E.R.4 342 (1999).
[399] Defamation Act 1996 (UK).
[400] Section 1 (1), Defamation Act 1996 (UK).

Ultimately, the court held Demon as the "publisher" of the defamatory content because it did not take reasonable care to remove it when received the fax notice from Mr. Godfrey.

The third relevant early case involving ISP liability for hosting illegal content regards Yahoo! Inc. in France.[401] Yahoo! Inc. was charged for illegally publicly displaying the sale of Nazi memorabilia in its auction website and for hosting several pro-Nazi webpages. In France, the public exhibition and sale of pro-Nazi objects might follow some statutory law requirements.[402] Following the charge, a court in Paris issued an injunction order against Yahoo! Inc. to block individuals physically located in France from having access to such a content.[403] Moreover, the judge held that Yahoo! had violated the French law and was required to pay all the expenses related the lawsuit.[404]

In the years following these cases, several rulings involving intermediary liability hold ISPs as simple carriers or intermediaries of third-party content across European countries.[405] For instance, a German court ruled that Yahoo! Inc. was not liable for the Nazi memorabilia transacted through its auction website because Yahoo! Inc. had merely hosted the illegal transaction without being an active part of it.[406] Moreover, in a legal dispute involving the French antiracist association J'Accuse, several ISPs, and the Association of Internet Service Providers (AFA), a court in Paris considered that French law, at the time, did not impose liability over illegal third-party content.[407] The case concerned the American website front14.org, which hosted neo-Nazi and xenophobic material. At the time, the judge went further and ruled that ISPs have no filtering obligation and shall be free to determine the measures they deem necessary to remove from the public access to illegal content.[408] The outcome of these cases anticipates the regime later imposed by the European Directive on Electronic Commerce that member states were obliged to transpose by January 2002.[409]

---

[401] UEJF et LICRA c/ Yahoo! Inc. et Yahoo France, TGI Paris (22 mai 2000); For details of the case in English, *see* Benoit Frydman, Isabelle Rorive, "Regulating Internet Content through Intermediaries in Europe and the USA" (2002) 23:1 Zeitschrift Für Rechtssoziologie 41.

[402] R645–1 Penal Code. (France).

[403] *Yahoo! Inc. v La Ligue Contre le Racisme*, 433 F.3d 1199 (9th Circuit 2006).

[404] Benoit Frydman, Isabelle Rorive, "Regulating Internet Content through Intermediaries in Europe and the USA" (2002) 23:1 Zeitschrift Für Rechtssoziologie 41, 48.

[405] Caroline Vallet, *La Réglementation des Contenus Illicites Circulant sur Internet: Étude en Droit Comparé"* (Éditions Universitaires Européenes 2012).

[406] Yulia A Timofeeva, "Hate Speech Online: Restricted or Protected. Comparison of Regulations in the United States and Germany (2003) 12 Transatlantic Law & Policy 253.

[407] *J'accuse c. AFA et autres*, TGI Paris, ord. réf., 30 octobre 2001, Comm. comm. électr. Janvier 2002. n°1, 30, n°8.

[408] *Ibid.*

[409] Directive 2000/31 of 8 June 2000 on certain legal aspects of information society services, in particular electronic commerce, in the Internal Market (Directive on electronic commerce), OJ L 178, 17.07.2000 (Hereinafter, Directive on Electronic Commerce).

Debates prior to the approval of the Directive on the Electronic Commerce focused on removing legal obstacles to electronic commerce in different member states.[410] The idea was to enable the free movement of information society services between EU countries. Moreover, uncertainties over the legal obligations expected from ISPs would negatively interfere on the EU's ambitions regarding electronic commerce. At the time, the member states achieved a rough consensus that Internet Service Providers should not be unconditionally liable for the third-party content they hosted.[411] Following this line, the Directive on Electronic Commerce sought to bring a common framework to ISP liabilities across different member states.

2.4.2. Directive on Electronic Commerce (2000)

Since 2002, the European Union framework for the liability of Internet Service Providers for illegal third-party content has been set by the Directive on Electronic Commerce and its transposed legal provisions.[412] Contrarily to the American federal statutory regime, the Directive presents a horizontal approach to liability because it applies to several sorts of illegal content, including defamation, hatred speech, and discriminatory advertisement, and provides immunity for tort, direct, and vicarious liability.[413]

Internet Service Providers are exempted under Article 14 of the Directive on Electronic Commerce from civil liability for illegal third-party content if they have no knowledge that such illegal content is available through their services.[414] Therefore, hosting services are only immune from liability for such illegal content while they are not aware of its existence. Once they are aware of it, they must assess whether the content is illegal and then expeditiously act to remove the access to it.[415] This system of liability exemption is commonly named as the notice-and-take down mechanism.[416] It has placed Internet Service Providers as

---

[410] Graham Pearce, Nicholas Platten, "Promoting the Information Society: The EU Directive on Electronic Commerce" (2000) 6:4 European Law Journal 363, 367.

[411] *Ibid*, p 372.

[412] The Directive does not mention the term Internet Service Provider, but instead Internet Service Society.

[413] Article 14 to 15, Directive on Electronic Commerce. The Regulation (EU) 2021/784 of the European Parliament and of the Council of 29 April 2021 on addressing the dissemination of terrorist content online, OJ L 172, 17.4.2021 provides new accountability rules for online platforms on the topic of terrorist content. The Digital Services Act will provide new rules on the topic of targeted advertising.

[414] Article 14, 1 (a), Directive on Electronic Commerce.

[415] Article 14, 1 (b), Directive on Electronic Commerce.

[416] Vassilis Hatzopoulos, *The Collaborative Economy and the EU Law* (Oregon: Hart Publishing, 2018), p 47. For a general view of notice and take down mechanisms, *see* OECD, *The Role of Internet Intermediaries in Advancing Public Policy Objectives*, DSTI/ICCP (2010)11/FINAL (June 2011), online: OECD Directorate for Science, Technology and Industry <www.oecd.org/internet/ieconomy/48685066.pdf>, p 14ss.

private gatekeepers of which content might remain published online and which content should be removed.[417] This issue has raised concerns about the freedom of expression of internet users.[418] Scholars have argued that European law should protect the right to freedom of expression when it regulates the responsibility of online platforms to moderate content.[419] However, several voices support that the notice-and-take down system has the benefit to provide relief in a brief frame of time, avoiding serious harm to happen, especially in cases of defamation and reputation.[420] For many years, some scholars have argued that to keep a balance between freedom of expression and other rights, the EU should have a fragmented approach towards the mechanism of notice-and-take down in cases of copyright, defamation, and hate speech.[421] In this case, the moderation of content with copyright, defamation, and hate speech[422] should be regulated differently. More recently, the Copyright Directive has implemented new rules for the use of protected content by online platforms that provide content-sharing services.[423]

---

[417] Aleksandra Kuczerawy, "The Power of Positive Thinking: Intermediary Liability and the Effective Enjoyment of the Right to Freedom of Expression" (2017) 8:3 Journal of Intellectual Property, Information, Technology and Electronic Commerce Law 226, p 227; more on the concept of gatekeeper, *see* Aleksandra Kuczerawy, *Intermediary Liability and Freedom of Expression in the EU: From Concepts to Safeguards* (Intersentia, 2018), p 15–23.

[418] Aleksandra Kuczerawy, "The Power of Positive Thinking", *op. cit.*, p 227. The concern about the right to freedom of expression has been debated since the Directive on Electronic Commerce has passed, *see* Rosa Julia-Barcelo, Kamiel J Koelman, "Intermediary Liability: Intermediary Liability in the E-Commerce Directive, So Far, So Good, But It's Not Enough" (2000) 16:4 Computer Law & Security Review 231; More recent perspective, *see* Sophie Stalla-Bourdillon, "Sometimes One Is Not Enough! Securing Freedom of Expression, Encouraging Private Regulation, or Subsidizing Internet Intermediaries or All Three at the Same Time: The Dilemma of Internet Intermediaries' Liability (2012) 7:2 Journal of International Commercial Law and Technology 154.

[419] Sophie Stalla-Bourdillon, "Internet Intermediaries as Responsible Actors? Why It Is Time to Rethink the e-Commerce Directive as Well", in: Luciano Floridi, Mariarosaria Taddeo, *The Responsibilities of Online Service Providers* (Springer, 2017), p 275.

[420] Etienne Montero, Quentin Van Enis, "Enabling Freedom of Expression in Light of Filtering Measures Imposed on Internet Intermediaries: Squaring the Circle? (2011) 27:1 Computer Law & Security Review 21.

[421] Christina Angelopoulos, Stijn Smet, "Notice-and-Fair Balance: How to Reach a Compromise Between Fundamental Rights in European Intermediary Liability" (2016) 8:2 Journal of Media Law 266; Against fragmentation, *see* Giancarlo F Frosio, "Reforming Intermediary Liability in the Platform Economy: A European Digital Single Market Strategy" (2018) 112 Northwestern University Law Review 18, p 45. He argues that a sectorial approach to the liability of ISPs is an attempt to get around "the lack of consensus behind an amendment to the intermediary liability regime" set by the Directive on Electronic Commerce. He considers that a sectorial approach might create conflicts between norms.

[422] *See* the EU initiative: European Commission, Communication from the Commission to the European Parliament and the Council, *A More Inclusive and Protective Europe: Extending the List of EU Crimes to Hate Speech and Hate Crimes*, Brussels, 9.12.2021 COM (2021) 777 final.

[423] Directive (EU) 2019/790 of the European Parliament and of the Council of 17 April 2019 on copyright and related rights in the Digital Single Market and amending Directives 96/9/EC and 2001/29/EC, OJ L 130, 17.5.2019, p. 92–125.

The CJEU has ruled that to establish whether the liability of an Internet Service Provider might be excluded under the terms of the Directive on Electronic Commerce, it is necessary to examine whether the role played by that service provider is neutral.[424] The Court construed that neutrality means that the service provider merely conducts the content in a technical, automatic, and passive fashion and lacks knowledge or control over the content stored.[425] Internet Service Providers are not merely hosting content when they assist to promote it by optimizing the presentation of third-party offers, for instance.[426]

Internet Service Providers may obtain knowledge about illegal hosted content through different ways, including self-monitoring activities or third-party notification. Nevertheless, it is worth noting that the Directive prohibits member states from imposing general monitoring obligations on ISPs.[427] Rather, ISPs may freely decide whether to implement self-monitoring mechanisms.[428] In addition, the Directive on Electronic Commerce provides two possibilities from which to receive third-party notifications: first, from public authorities, such as courts or administrative bodies[429]; and second, from private entities.[430] In the case of private notification, the provider of a hosting service must assess whether such content is illegal and decide whether to take it down or not. Moreover, the Directive provides no guidelines regarding the implementation of notice-and-take down mechanisms. The Directive left the decision regarding the implementation of such mechanisms up to the member states, and, therefore, no harmonized notice-and-takedown procedure exists across member states.[431] In most European Union member states, no guidelines or legal framework on how

---

[424] Case involving Facebook and concerning defamation: C-18/18 Glawischnig-Piesczek v Facebook, ECLI:EU:C:2019:821. Case concerning counterfeited products: Case C-236/08 *Google France v Louis Vuitton* EU:C:2010:159, §114. For a balanced approach, *see* Patrick Van Eecke, "Online service providers and liability: A plea for a balanced approach" (2011) 48:5 Common Market Law Review 1455.

[425] Cases C-236/08 *Google France v Louis Vuitton* EU:C:2010:159, §114.

[426] Case C-324/09 *L'Oreal v eBay* EU:C:2011:474, §123.

[427] Art 15, 1, Directive on Electronic Commerce.

[428] Report on some of these initiatives: Article 19, *Self-Regulation and "Hate Speech" on Social Media Platforms* (March 2018), online: article 19 <https://www.article19.org/wp-content/uploads/2018/03/Self-regulation-and-'hate-speech'-on-social-media-platforms_March2018.pdf>; Compact, *Report on Current Policies and Regulatory Frameworks* (February 2019), online: European Commission <http://compact-media.eu/wp-content/uploads/2019/11/D2.1-Report-on-current-policies-and-regulatory-frameworks.pdf>.

[429] Article 14, 3, Directive on Electronic Commerce.

[430] Article 14, 1 (b) Directive on Electronic Commerce.

[431] Recital 46, Directive on Electronic Commerce. For a comprehensive view of how the 47 Member States of the Council of Europe have implemented the notice and take down system, *see* Council of Europe, *Comparative Study on Blocking, Filtering and Take-Down of Illegal Internet Content* (January 2017), online: CoE <https://edoc.coe.int/fr/internet/7289-pdf-comparative-study-on-blocking-filtering-and-take-down-of-illegal-internet-content-.html>. Also, the proposal for the Digital Services Act has called for an harmonization at the EU level on the rules concerning "notice and action" mechanisms. Recital 41.

such mechanisms should work were created nor implemented.[432] As a result, online service providers have developed private self-regulation on notice-and-take down mechanisms across the European Union.[433] This reality may change with the Digital Services Act.

Over the past years, the European Commission has increasingly indicated that ISPs and, more specifically, online platforms should take responsibility for their content governance.[434] In this regard, in 2018 the Commission published detailed non-binding recommendations for online platforms on measures to effectively tackle illegal content online.[435] The recommendations expressed the need for companies to implement transparent notice-and-take down policies. Online platforms might include fast-track paths for "trusted flaggers" to avoid the unfair removal of content that is actually legal. Moreover, users who have their content removed shall be notified and given the possibility to argue against the measure. The Commission also recommended that companies develop cutting-edge technologies to automatically recognize and remove illegal content, especially for content related to terrorism, child pornography, and counterfeited goods.[436] Second, in April 2019 the European Parliament adopted the Directive on Copyright[437] and the Regulation on Fairness in Platform-to-Business Relations. Both texts address illegal content provided by online platforms.[438] In 2021, the European Union adopted the Regulation 2021/784 that addresses the dissemination of terrorist content online.[439] In April 2022, members of the European Parliament reached a political agreement on the Digital Services Act, which will significantly change the accountability and transparency duties of online platforms, in particular considerably large online platform, once it is entirely in force.[440]

---

[432] Aleksandra Kuczerawy, "Intermediary Liability & Freedom of Expression: Recent Developments in the EU Notice & Action Initiative" (2015) 31 Computer Law & Security Review 46, p 49.

[433] *Ibid*, p 49.

[434] European Commission, Brussels, 1.3.2018 C(2018) 1177 final Commission Recommendation on Measures to Effectively Tackle Illegal Content Online.

[435] The recommendations are non-binding. *Ibid*.

[436] *Ibid*, §25.

[437] Directive (EU) 2019/790 of the European Parliament and of the Council of 17 April 2019 on Copyright and Related Rights in the Digital Single Markets and Amending Directives 96/9/EC and 2001/29/EC, OJ L 130, 17.5.2019, p 92–125.

[438] Regulation (EU) 2019/1150 of the European Parliament and of the Council of 20 June 2019 on Promoting Fairness and Transparency for Business Users of Online Intermediation Services, OJ L 186, 11.7.2019, p 57–79.

[439] Regulation (EU) 2021/784 of the European Parliament and of the Council of 29 April 2021 on Addressing the Dissemination of Terrorist Content Online, OJ L 172, 17.5.2021, p 79.

[440] European Parliament, *Digital Services Act: Agreement for a Transparent and Safe Online Environment* (23 April 2022), online: European Parliament Press Release <https://www.europarl.europa.eu/news/en/press-room/20220412IPR27111/digital-services-act-agreement-for-a-transparent-and-safe-online-environment>.

2.4.3. Digital Services Act: Liability and the Future of Online Platforms' Accountability

Over the past two decades, the Directive on Electronic Commerce has been applied with differences across the European Union.[441] Member states have increasingly imposed diligence duties on Internet Service Providers, and courts have interpreted the liability regime provided by the Directive on Electronic Commerce and transposed it to national laws differently. This occurrence has resulted in a fragmented approach of online platform liability within the European Union. Scholars have argued that the CJEU precedents on the matter do not provide clear guidance on the topic of online intermediary liabilities for third-party illegal content.[442] Moreover, since the Directive on Electronic Commerce has entered into force, the diversification of methodologies, purposes, and design innovations implemented by Internet Service Providers have, in several instances, impeded the determination of whether they are under the scope of the definition of information society services, which ultimately can be exempted from liability immunities.

These challenges have pushed European policymakers to work on regulatory alternatives for information society services. In this regard, in March and April 2022, a political agreement was achieved on the Digital Markets Act and on the Digital Services Act (DSA), respectively.[443] Online intermediaries and platforms analyzed in this book are primarily concerned by the DSA, once it enters into force. Among its purposes, the Act harmonizes rules for the better protection of the fundamental rights of online platform users and the implementation of a comprehensive framework for transparency and accountability practices of online platforms. On the one hand, the Act suggests ambitious reforms on the legal regime applicable to online platforms, and on the other hand, it maintains some core principles of the Directive on the Electronic Commerce, including aspects of liability immunity and the general prohibition for member states to impose monitoring duties for information society services.[444]

The DSA has various scopes and may apply differently according to the nature of the information service provider and the risks they pose to certain core EU

---

[441]   Joris Van Hoboken, João Pedro Quintais, Joost Poort, Nico van Eijk, *Hosting Intermediary Services and Illegal Content Online: An Analysis of the Scope of Article 14 ECD in Light of Developments in the Online Service Landscape* (2018), online: European Commission <https://op.europa.eu/en/publication-detail/-/publication/7779caca-2537-11e9-8d04-01aa75ed71a1/language-en>.

[442]   *Ibid*, pp 28 to 42.

[443]   European Commission, *The Digital Services Act Package* (April 2022), online: European Commission <https://digital-strategy.ec.europa.eu/en/policies/digital-services-act-package>. For the latest amendments available at the time of the submission, *see* European Parliament, *Amendments Adopted by the European Parliament on 20 January 2022 on the Proposal for a Regulation of the European Parliament and of the Council on a Single Market for Digital Services (Digital Services Act) and Amending Directive 2000/31/EC* (2022), online: European Parliament <https://www.europarl.europa.eu/doceo/document/TA-9-2022-0014_EN.html>.

[444]   Article 7, Proposal for a Regulation of the European Parliament and of the Council on a Single Market for Digital Services (Digital Services Act) and amending Directive 2000/31/EC. COM/2020/825 final.

values, such as democracy and nondiscrimination.[445] Special rules will regulate very large platforms, and some rules concerning transparency duties shall not apply to online providers that are micro- or small enterprises.[446] The former is defined as those with a significant reach in the European Union market with more than 45 million service users.[447] This number is susceptible to be changed regularly to constantly correspond to 10% of the European Union population.

The DSA reproduces in its provisions the Directive on Electronic Commerce liability regime and the CJEU rulings on the liability rules for online intermediary services. Most importantly, the Act complements but does not entirely replace the Directive of Electronic Commerce.[448] In particular, it has substituted Articles 12–15 of the Directive on Electronic Commerce but has maintained the liability immunity of information service providers in accordance with the vast CJEU case law. Internet Service Providers will continue to be exempt from liability for third-party illegal content until they have awareness of it. From this point, online intermediaries should act expeditiously to take down or disable access to the illegal content.[449] It is interesting to note that the DSA defines illegal content as any "information relating to illegal content, products, services and activities."[450] This definition also explicitly refers to unlawful discriminatory content and activities and covers discrimination against protected classes in housing and accommodation platforms.

Whereas the Act has not introduced significant changes for the liability of online platforms, when compared to the Directive on Electronic Commerce it has established an extensive regulatory framework for the accountability and transparency duties of these players operating in the European Union.[451]

---

[445]   Recital 3, Proposal for a Regulation of the European Parliament and of the Council on a Single Market for Digital Services (Digital Services Act) and amending Directive 2000/31/EC. COM/2020/825 final.

[446]   Recital 39, Proposal for a Regulation of the European Parliament and of the Council on a Single Market for Digital Services (Digital Services Act) and amending Directive 2000/31/EC. COM/2020/825 final.

[447]   Article 25 (1), Proposal for a Regulation of the European Parliament and of the Council on a Single Market for Digital Services (Digital Services Act) and amending Directive 2000/31/EC. COM/2020/825 final.

[448]   Recital 9, Proposal for a Regulation of the European Parliament and of the Council on a Single Market for Digital Services (Digital Services Act) and amending Directive 2000/31/EC. COM/2020/825 final.

[449]   Articles 3, 4 and 5, Proposal for a Regulation of the European Parliament and of the Council on a Single Market for Digital Services (Digital Services Act) and amending Directive 2000/31/EC. COM/2020/825 final.

[450]   Recital 12, Proposal for a Regulation of the European Parliament and of the Council on a Single Market for Digital Services (Digital Services Act) and amending Directive 2000/31/EC. COM/2020/825 final.

[451]   During the DSA negotiations, this framework was criticized by multiple stakeholders. For an overview, *see* Ilaria Buri, Joris van Hoboken, *The Digital Services Act (DSA) Proposal: A Critical Overview* (October 2021), online: DSA Observatory, Institute for Information Law <https://dsa-observatory.eu/wp-content/uploads/2021/11/Buri-Van-Hoboken-DSA-discussion-paper-Version-28_10_21.pdf>.

These duties include the obligation for online platforms to designate a single point of contact who is easily accessible under request and the appointment of a legal representative in the EU[452]; the definition of terms and conditions with unambiguous wording on expected content moderation policies[453]; and the implementation of transparency requirements that will translate into the provision of a comprehensive report on the content moderation put in place in the referred period of time.[454] Additionally, hosting services and online platforms will be required to create a notice-and-action mechanism available to any users willing to indicate content they consider illegal. Once implemented, this mechanism will give rise to awareness of the potential illegal content and may trigger the liability of the service provider in case of inaction to address the referred content.[455] Content removal should also be explained by hosting services with a clear and specific statement of the reasons for the decision.[456]

The DSA has created more specific duties for internet providers defined as online platforms. These additional provisions encompass the implementation of an internal complaint-handling system[457], an out-of-court dispute settlement[458], trusted flaggers[459], and the requirement to suspend their services to users who often provide manifestly illegal content after prior warning and for a reasonable period of time.[460] Moreover, transparency reporting obligations are stricter for

---

[452]   Article 10 and 11, Proposal for a Regulation of the European Parliament and of the Council on a Single Market for Digital Services (Digital Services Act) and amending Directive 2000/31/EC. COM/2020/825 final.

[453]   Article 12, Proposal for a Regulation of the European Parliament and of the Council on a Single Market for Digital Services (Digital Services Act) and amending Directive 2000/31/EC. COM/2020/825 final.

[454]   Article 13, Proposal for a Regulation of the European Parliament and of the Council on a Single Market for Digital Services (Digital Services Act) and amending Directive 2000/31/EC. COM/2020/825 final.

[455]   Article 14, Proposal for a Regulation of the European Parliament and of the Council on a Single Market for Digital Services (Digital Services Act) and amending Directive 2000/31/EC. COM/2020/825 final.

[456]   Article 15, Proposal for a Regulation of the European Parliament and of the Council on a Single Market for Digital Services (Digital Services Act) and amending Directive 2000/31/EC. COM/2020/825 final.

[457]   Article 17, Proposal for a Regulation of the European Parliament and of the Council on a Single Market for Digital Services (Digital Services Act) and amending Directive 2000/31/EC. COM/2020/825 final.

[458]   Article 18, Proposal for a Regulation of the European Parliament and of the Council on a Single Market for Digital Services (Digital Services Act) and amending Directive 2000/31/EC. COM/2020/825 final.

[459]   Article 19, Proposal for a Regulation of the European Parliament and of the Council on a Single Market for Digital Services (Digital Services Act) and amending Directive 2000/31/EC. COM/2020/825 final.

[460]   Article 20, Proposal for a Regulation of the European Parliament and of the Council on a Single Market for Digital Services (Digital Services Act) and amending Directive 2000/31/EC. COM/2020/825 final.

online platforms.[461] Finally, very large platforms will be submitted to additional obligations to address systemic risks, including discrimination.[462] At the time of the submission of this manuscript, the DSA was not yet published in the official journal and was not in force in the EU.

Concerning the topic of the present title, several online housing markets will be bound by the DSA notice-and-action system because they work as hosting service providers. Platforms focused on housing transactions will continue to be required to take down any illegal content, including housing discriminatory advertisements, once they are aware of the illegal content. Failing to take expeditious action to remove third-party illegal content makes hosting service providers liable for the damages caused by the third-party illegal content. In this regard, the DSA does not differ from the Directive on Electronic Commerce. This liability regime differs from the American one, because hosting service providers in the United States are not liable for third-party illegal content even when they acknowledge it and do not take any expeditious measure to remove it, except in cases related to copyrighted content, trademark infringement, and criminal and electronic communications privacy law breaches.[463] This issue is further developed in the following chapter.[464]

2.5. THEORIES OF VICARIOUS LIABILITY APPLIED TO COMPANIES: LIABILITY FOR THIRD-PARTY DISCRIMINATION

In cases in which online service providers are not legally defined under the concepts of Internet Service Providers or online platforms, they could be susceptible to the vicarious liability regimes available across the member states. This possibility could theoretically make them responsible for third-party discrimination occurring in their online spaces. This strategy has been frequently used in litigation. Interested parties often attempt to question the identity of online platforms as Internet Service Providers.[465]

Concerning the housing and accommodation markets, cases have been reported of discrimination implicating real estate agents against potential

---

[461]   Articles 17 to 23, Proposal for a Regulation of the European Parliament and of the Council on a Single Market for Digital Services (Digital Services Act) and amending Directive 2000/31/EC. COM/2020/825 final.

[462]   Article 25 to 33, Proposal for a Regulation of the European Parliament and of the Council on a Single Market for Digital Services (Digital Services Act) and amending Directive 2000/31/EC. COM/2020/825 final.

[463]   CDA, section 230 (e) (1)-(4).

[464]   See chapter 2, section Airbnb.

[465]   See, for instance, C-390/18 Airbnb Ireland, ECLI:EU:C:2019:1112 and C-434/15 Asociación Profesional Elite Taxi v Uber Systems Spain, ECLI, EU:C:2017:981.

home seekers, whether they were required to do so or not by the house owner. In this respect, the manager of a house broker in Toulouse, France had overtly stated in a telephone call that she followed her client's requests and only selected potential tenants based on whether their names sounded French.[466] She alleged that she could not rent the property "to colored people."[467] She was condemned to pay € 1,500 to the victim. In two other cases in Belgium, real estate agents were condemned, first, for using flyers advertising that only tenants who were "naturally Belgian" would be considered[468] and, second, for refusing a male house seeker under the justification that the landlord wanted to restrict the entire accommodation to female tenants.[469]

When property owners require real estate agents not to rent or sell their properties to certain individuals because of a protected aspect, they are practicing direct discrimination. Both directives and transposed laws provide that an instruction to discriminate against persons on grounds of racial, ethnic origin, and sex might be deemed as discrimination.[470] In this case, real estate agents who discriminate against house seekers following property owners' instructions are also committing direct discrimination under the purposes of both directives.[471] Therefore, real estate agents should refuse to meet any discriminatory request from the property owner and should ideally report it to the competent authorities.[472]

The issue whether companies would face vicarious liability if their agents perpetrate direct discrimination against prospective tenants and clients is regulated by the laws of the member states.[473] Overall, companies/employers are

---

[466] See Sophie Latraverse, *Country Report on Measures to Combat Discrimination Directives 2000/43/EC and 2000/78/EC France* (January 2012), online: European Network of Legal Experts in the Non-Discrimination Field <https://www.refworld.org/pdfid/525534b70.pdf>, p 57. Court of Cassation (Criminal Chamber) 7 June 2005 No 04–87354. The phone call was recorded in a testing conducted by the NGO SOS Racism.

[467] *Ibid.*

[468] Corr. Anvers, 21 June 1996, *T. Vreemd*, 1996, p 165. Referred by Julie Ringelheim, Nicolas Bernard, *Discrimination in Housing: Thematic Report of the European Network of Legal Experts in the Non-Discrimination Field* (February 2013), online: European Commission Directorate General for Justice and Consumers <https://op.europa.eu/en/publication-detail/-/publication/c8cf0ff7–8676–4751–8d36–59eeffe379ee/language-en>, p 48.

[469] European Network of Legal Experts in Gender Equality and Non-Discrimination, *"Girls Only" Housing Illegal"* (April 2015), online: Equality Law <https://www.equalitylaw.eu/downloads/2743-13-be-ge-girls-only-housing-illegal>.

[470] Art 2(4), Race Equality Directive; Art 4(4), Gender Equal Access to Goods and Services Directive.

[471] Art 2(1), Race Equality Directive; Art 4(1), Gender Equal Access to Goods and Services Directive.

[472] In France, a real estate agent reported a landowner for having refused to sell his property to a man with Algerian origin. The landowner was eventually condemned. Natalie Boccadoro, "Housing Rights and Racial Discrimination" (2009) 9 European Anti-Discrimination Law Review 21, p 27.

[473] Helmut Werner, Eugenia Caracciolo di Torella, Bridgette McLellan, *Gender Equal Access to Goods and Services Directive 2004/113/EC: European Implementation Assessment* (January

vicariously responsible for the illegal behavior of their employees. This situation is particularly clear in the legal statutes in Austria, Belgium, Denmark, Ireland, and the UK.[474] Some convergence is also found regarding the conditions by which the company/employer might be responsible for its employees' actions, including if the illegal conduct was committed during the time and duties of work and if the company was negligent to prevent the employee from acting unlawfully.[475] Cases of non-employment vicarious liability are limited among the member states[476] and mostly concern the responsibility of schools over their students.[477]

The matter of whether companies should be vicariously liable for the illegal actions conducted by their users in their contractual relations with other users has been argued in contexts other than discrimination in online platforms in the member states.[478] For example, in France Airbnb was held liable for allowing users to rent their apartment through the platform without the proper consent of the apartment owner, which is illegal in France.[479]

2017), online: EPRS European Parliamentary Research Service Ex-Post Impact Assessment Unit <https://www.europarl.europa.eu/RegData/etudes/STUD/2017/593787/EPRS_STU(2017) 593787_EN.pdf>, p 69 (I-29).

[474] *Ibid*, p 69 (I-29). In the UK, the Equality Act 2010 (UK) s109, Employment Equality Acts 1998–2011 (IE)s 15(1) and (3). Also, the Supreme Court ruled that a grocery store was vicariously liable for its employees assault on a customer, *see Mohamud v Wm Morrison Supermarkets plc* (2016) UKSC 1.

[475] *Ibid.*

[476] In the UK, employment-related arrangements have been considered sufficient to apply vicarious liability. *Cox v Ministry Justice* [2016] UKSC 10. See Phillip Morgan, "Certainty in Vicarious Liability: A Quest for a Chimaera?" (2016) 75:2 The Cambridge Law Journal 202.

[477] Aileen Mc Colgan, *National Protection Beyond the Two EU Anti-Discrimination Directives: The Grounds of Religion and Belief, Disability, Age and Sexual Orientation Beyond Employment* (September 2013), online: European Commission Directorate for Consumers and Justice <https://tandis.odihr.pl/handle/20.500.12389/21745>, p 45.

[478] Vassilis Hatzopoulos, *The Collaborative Economy and the EU Law* (Oregon: Hart Publishing, 2018), p 22.

[479] Tribunal d'Instance, Paris, Jugement du 6 février 2018, RG 11–17–000190. There was a reported case in the Netherlands. Rosalie Koolhoven, *Impulse Paper on Specific Liability Issues Raised by the Collaborative Economy in the Accommodation Sector, Paris-Amsterdam-Barcelona* (May 2016), online: <https://sharingcitiesalliance.knowledgeowl.com/help/ impulse-paper-on-specific-liability-issues-raised-by-the-collaborative-economy-in-the-accommodation-sector>, p 12. Referring to *Duinzigt* Hoge Raad 16 October 2015, NL:HR:2015:3099, Prejudiciele beslissing op vraag van NL:RBDHA:2015:1437.

CHAPTER 2

HOUSING AND PUBLIC ACCOMMODATION ONLINE PLATFORMS

Following a case-based approach, this chapter explores how the liability for third-party discrimination against protected classes has been addressed in the context of online platforms in housing and accommodation transactions. I selected litigated cases related to three online platforms focused entirely or in part on accommodation and housing: Craigslist, Daft, and Airbnb. While Craigslist and Airbnb have operations in the United States and Europe, Daft restricts its services to the European market. I address the differences of the approach to the liability of online intermediaries in the United States and in member states of the European Union. I argue that the Directive of Electronic Commerce might provide more tools in the fight against discrimination in these online spaces in the European Union.

1. CRAIGSLIST

1.1. BUSINESS MODEL

Founded in 1995, Craigslist has dedicated its activities to classified advertisements in different sectors, including the rental and sale of accommodation.[480] The platform provides listing billboards for individuals who want to buy, sell, and rent properties as well as other goods and services. Contrarily to similar marketplaces, Craigslist does not equip its users with the possibility to create a personal profile, and therefore, the platform primarily serves as an advertisement listing. Advertisements are categorized into regions and sectors to prevent misunderstandings.

Over the years, Craigslist has replaced newspapers to some extent in the function of advertising housing in several places.[481] By 2017, over 50 million

---

[480] Susan M Freese, *Craigslist: The Company and Its Founder* (ABDO, 2011), p 15.
[481] Craig Smith, *Craigslist Statistics and Facts* (May 2019), online: Business Statistics <https://expandedramblings.com/index.php/craigslist-statistics/>.

internet users had access to Craigslist's advertisements across the world, which made the platform a leader in the classifieds sector.[482] Craigslist was originally designed to be free of charges, but it has charged fees for the listing of certain advertisements so far.[483]

In the late 2000s, Craigslist had thousands of third-party discriminatory advertisements against protected classes in its housing section.[484] Once these ads were discovered, a group of civil rights lawyers, based in Chicago, working to secure racial equality for all sued Craigslist for publishing illegal discriminatory housing advertisements online.[485]

1.2. LITIGATION: LIABILITY IMMUNITY FOR INTERNET SERVICE PROVIDERS

In the *Chicago Lawyers Committee for Civil Rights under Law v Craigslist*[486], the Committee for Civil Rights presented the discriminatory ads as a *prima facie* condition for the tort action against Craigslist. The Committee grounded its claim on the Fair Housing Act; aside from forbidding discrimination against housing renters and buyers based on their race, color, religion, national origin, disability, sex, and family status, the Act holds liable publishers of third-party discriminatory advertisement against these classes.[487]

In the case, the Committee tried to extend to Craigslist the same tort liability publishers and traditional newspapers have under the FHA. Craigslist argued that it could not be held as a publisher in the sense provided by the FHA[488], because it was an Internet Service Provider. Internet Service Providers are immune from liability of third-party illegal content, including housing discriminatory advertisements, under the terms of the CDA.[489]

By the time of the legal action, Craigslist was supported by the Internet Commerce Coalition, which included members such as Amazon, Google, Yahoo!, and eBay. The Coalition filed an *amicus curiae* to endorse Craigslist's immunity for the third-party discriminatory advertisements.[490] The main point

---

[482]   *Ibid.*

[483]   Susan M Freese, *Craigslist: The Company and Its* Founder, *op. cit.*, p 39.

[484]   Rigel C Oliveri, "Discriminatory Housing Advertisements Online: Lessons from Craigslist" (2010) 43 Indiana Law Review 1125, p 1143; National Fair Housing Alliance, *2010 Fair Housing Trends Report* (May 2010), online: National Fair Housing <https://nationalfairhousing.org/wp-content/uploads/2017/04/fair_housing_trends_report_2010.pdf>.

[485]   *Chicago Lawyers' v Craigslist Inc*, No. 07–1101 (7th Cir. 2008).

[486]   *Chicago Lawyers' v Craigslist Inc*, No. 07–1101 (7th Cir. 2008).

[487]   FHA, 42 U.S.C. 3604, (a) (b).

[488]   FHA, 42 U.S.C. 3604 (c).

[489]   CDA, 47 U.S.C., §230, (1).

[490]   Motion by Amicus Parties, *Brief of Amici Amazon.com, Inc, AOL llc, eBay Inc, Google Inc, Yahoo! Inc, Electronic Frontier Foundation, Internet Commerce Coalition, NetChoice, NetCoalition, and United States Internet Service Provider Association in support of Craigslist's*

raised by the Coalition was that Craigslist, like most Internet Service Providers, had no centralized prior control over third-party publications. Contrarily to newspapers or magazines, the high number of publications make prior review of third-party content online impossible. Precedents involving companies of the Coalition supported the view that online platforms are neither liable for illegal third-party content nor third-party wrongdoings. In *Schneider v Amazon*[491], the latter was exempted from tort liability for a high number of defamatory users' reviews about an author of a book. After being notified, Amazon did not take down the defamatory reviews for several days.[492] In *Gentry v eBay Inc.*[493], eBay was held immune for their users selling fake autographed sport memorabilia. Several consumers bought sport items with forged signatures of professional athletes on eBay's marketplace, which had several sports product categories focused on sports memorabilia and autographs. The platform had never asked from its sellers for a certificate of authenticity, which is a legal requirement imposed to retail stores.[494] These cases were both dismissed on the grounds of the section 230 (c) of the CDA, which provides that Internet Service Providers must not be held as a publisher of illegal information.[495]

Not unexpectedly, the Court of Appeals for the Seventh Circuit exempted Craigslist from tort liability for the thousands of discriminatory housing advertisements published by third-party users on its billboard.[496] Even if the primary aim of the Communications Decency Act was not to render the effects of the Fair Housing Act void in certain online contexts, the text was clear that Internet Service Providers shall not be treated as the publisher or speaker of any information provided by someone else. In the case, only in the capacity of publisher could Craigslist be liable under the terms of the FHA[497], because the platform was not the author of the advertisements. The Court also added that the burden to monitor content in this context would be too high, considering that at the time Craigslist had over 30 million notices posted and a staff of only 30 people in California.[498]

The case was vastly discussed because since the FHA was enacted overt discrimination against protected classes in housing advertisements had

Motion for Judgement on the Pleadings (June 2017), online: Justia <https://docs.justia.com/cases/federal/district-courts/illinois/ilndce/1:2006cv00657/195440/24/1.html>.

491 *Schneider v Amazon.com, Inc.*, 31 P3d 37, 108 (Wash. Ct. App., 2001).
492 See Karen Alexander Horowitz, "When Is §230 Immunity Lost? The Transformation from Website Owner to Information Content Provider" (2007) 3:4 Washington Journal of Law, Technology & Arts 14; Mark A Lemley, "Rationalizing Internet Safe Harbors" (2007) 6 Journal on Telecommunication & High Technology Law 101.
493 *Gentry v. eBay, Inc.*, 121 Cal. Rptr. 2d 703, 99 Cal. App. 4th 816 (California Ct. App. 2002).
494 Bob Rietjens, "Trust and Reputation on eBay: Towards a Legal Framework for Feedback Intermediaries" (2006) 15:01 Information & Communications Technology Law 55.
495 CDA §230 (c).
496 *Chicago Lawyers' v Craigslist Inc.*, No. 07–1101 (7th Cir. 2008).
497 §3604, (c), FHA.
498 *Chicago Lawyers' v Craigslist Inc.*, No. 07–1101 (7th Cir. 2008), §669.

sensibly disappeared from the view of house seekers in the United States.[499] The pervasiveness of the internet in the sector of advertising housing, notably without a central edition board, took discriminatory advertisements with housing offers back to the public view. Moreover, commentators argued that the fair housing bodies would have difficulty finding the real authors of the advertisements at stake. The Court of Appeal suggested that the Committee for Civil Rights should investigate the cases one by one and collect proper damages from house owners or landlords who engaged in discrimination.[500] However, Craigslist did not have further details about them.[501]

1.3. SELF-REGULATORY MEASURES: A NEW FAIR HOUSING FORUM

Craigslist implemented an antidiscrimination policy to raise awareness against discrimination in housing advertisements. To serve this purpose, Craigslist created a specific section available to all users, with extensive and accessible explanation of federal statutory law against discrimination in the housing sector.[502] In this context, Craigslist warned users that both intentional and unintentional discrimination based on stated preferences related to race or color, national origin, religion, sex, familial status, and handicap and disability were, in general, outlawed.

The platform clarified that direct discrimination might encompass the usage of language discouraging a protected category from trying to rent or buy the advertised offer. Craigslist offered some examples, such as noting an apartment is "perfect for a single or couple" or "ideal for working professionals" can be discouraging for families with children, advertising that the property is in a "Christian neighborhood" can be discouraging towards non-Christian tenants, and mentioning that a property is located in a "predominately Latino neighborhood" can also discourage other groups from being interested in the advertisement.[503]

---

[499] James D Shanahan, "Rethinking the Communications Decency Act: Eliminating Statutory Protection of Discriminatory Housing Advertisements on the Internet" (2007) 60 Federal Communications Law Journal 135; Stephen Collins, "Saving Fair Housing on the Internet: The Case for Amending the Communication Decency Act" (2008) 102:3 Northwestern University Law Review 1471; Shahrzad T Radbod, "Craigslist: A Case for Criminal Liability for Online Service Providers?" (2010) 25 Berkeley Technology Law Journal 597.

[500] *Chicago Lawyers' v Craigslist Inc.*, No. 07–1101 (7th Cir. 2008), §672.

[501] Rigel C Oliveri, "Discriminatory Housing Advertisements Online: Lessons from Craigslist" (2010) 43 Indiana Law Review 1125, p 1172.

[502] Craigslist, *Fair Housing is Everyone's Right! Stating a Discriminatory Preference in a Housing Post is Illegal* (March 2018), online: Craigslist <https://www.craigslist.org/about/FHA>.

[503] *Ibid.*

In addition, Craigslist created an open forum available to all users to debate overt discrimination on housing advertising[504] in which it encouraged users to flag posts as "prohibited" if they believed it violated the Fair Housing Laws.

These self-regulatory measures, such as the publication of administrative regulations and flagging systems, have been largely implemented by online platforms to both increase users' awareness of potential wrongdoings and to report breaches of the law. To my knowledge, the results of such policies implemented by Craigslist in the fight against discrimination have not been analyzed or published.

2. ROOMMATES

One year after Craigslist addressed tort action against illegal housing discriminatory content published in its billboards, Roommates faced litigation for its drop-down menu designed to match individuals looking for a shared place to live based on protected grounds under antidiscrimination statutes.[505]

2.1. BUSINESS MODEL

Roommates is specialized in matching people renting spare rooms in their houses or apartments with people looking for a room to live.[506] Over the years, Roommates has become a popular service, receiving over 50,000 visits per day.[507] The platform operates more than a simple advertising list and has distinctive aspects when compared to Craigslist. First, Roommates is only available in the United States. Second, it is sectorial and solely focused on housing advertisements. Third, it requires users to create personal profiles with several pieces of mandatory information about themselves.

In the late 2000s, individuals who used Roommates' services mandatorily had to answer a questionnaire about their gender, sexual orientation, familial status, and whether they had children.[508] In other words, the platform required subscribers to specify, using an automatically provided drop-down menu, whether they were "male" or "female," whether there were currently "straight

---

504 Craigslist, *Forum* (May 2018), online: Craigslist <https://forums.craigslist. org/?forumID=3604>.

505 *Fair Housing Council of San Fernando Valley v Roommates, LLC*, 521, F.3d 1157 (9ᵗʰ Cir. 2008).

506 Roommates, *Find Your Perfect Match* (June 2019), online: Roommates <https://www. roommates.com>

507 Numbers available in the legal action: *Fair Housing Council of San Fernando Valley v Roommates, LLC*, CV 03–9386 PA (RZx) (C.D. Cal. Nov. 7, 2008), p 3450.

508 *Fair Housing Council of San Fernando Valley v Roommates, LLC*, CV 03–9386 PA (RZx) (C.D. Cal. Nov. 7, 2008), p 3462.

male(s)," "gay male(s)," "straight female(s)," or "lesbian(s)," whether they wanted to live with straight or gay males/females, only with gay males/females or with no males/females. Moreover, the platform encouraged users to provide further information about themselves and their desired roommate in an "additional comments" box, by prompting users to "take a moment to personalize your profile by writing a paragraph or two describing yourself and what you are looking for in a roommate."[509]

Based on the above-mentioned profiles and preferences, Roommates matched users and provided them a list of available room-seekers meeting their criteria. In addition, the platform enabled users to search available rooms based on the individuals' characteristics, including gender, sexual orientation, and familial status. This information was allegedly included to help subscribers decide which users they wanted to contact.[510]

2.2. LITIGATION: DESIGN AT STAKE IN CASES OF IMMUNITY FOR ISPS

In 2007, the Fair Housing Council of the San Fernando Valley[511] filed a lawsuit against Roommates on the grounds that the platform had breached the federal Fair Housing Act and the California Fair Employment and Housing Act (FEHA) as the matching tool allowed users to include or exclude individuals seeking a spare room based on their gender, sexual orientation, and family status. Both statutes outlaw discrimination against house seekers based on these criteria.[512] Moreover, the Council sought liability from the platform about the discriminatory preferences stated on several comment boxes, including statements such as "prefer white male roommates," "the person applying for the room must be a Black gay male," "to live without kids," and "not looking for Black Muslims."[513]

In the lawsuit, the Council argued that Roommates had a far greater active role compared to other ISPs. When the platform actively created a drop-down menu with questions and choices for answers that were illegal under the terms of statutory antidiscrimination laws, the platform was not solely the carrier of

---

509 *Fair Housing Council of San Fernando Valley v Roommates, LLC*, CV 03-9386 PA (RZx) (C.D. Cal. Nov. 7, 2008), p 3462.

510 *Ibid*, p 3451.

511 The Fair Housing Council of the San Fernando Valley is a private, non-profit, civil rights advocacy organization founded in 1958 to eliminate housing discrimination. It is the second Fair Housing Council in the United States and provides services in all Los Angeles County.

512 The FHA 42 U.S.C. §3601 et seq. and Section 804 [42 U.S.C. 3604], FEHA, §12955 (a). The FEHA provides more grounds of protection against discrimination in housing transaction than the FHA and, includes sexual orientation

513 *Fair Housing Council of San Fernando Valley v Roommates, LLC*, CV 03-9386 PA (RZx) (C.D. Cal. Nov. 7, 2008) p 3472.

the illegal questions but also the author. In this context, Roommates was the "information content provider" in addition to acting as the Internet Service Provider.[514] The Council alleged that a real estate agent, when intermediating a housing transaction, cannot inquire about the sexual orientation and the family status of a prospective tenant.[515]

The District Court in California dismissed the tort action, by holding that Roommates was wholly immune to the choices of its users under section 230 of the CDA.[516] The Council appealed, and the Court of Appeals for the Ninth Circuit initially reversed the ruling on the basis that Roommates was shielded by the CDA only for the third-party discriminatory comments published in the "additional comments" box. However, the Court of Appeals held that the platform was not protected from tort liability regarding the other claims. First, the CDA would not protect Roommates when it implemented questionnaires that required potential tenants to disclose their sex, sexual orientation, and familial status. Second, limiting the scope of searches according to the users' preferences based on the potential tenants' sex, sexual orientation, and familial status was not protected by the CDA. Third, implementing a matching system for landlords and tenants based on those preferences was also not protected by the immunity regime of the CDA. The Court of Appeals for Ninth Circuit endorsed that the CDA only gives immunity for publishing third-party illegal content, as long as the illegal content is wholly created by third-parties and not by the provider itself.[517]

The Court of Appeals for the Ninth Circuit sent the case back on remand to the District Court, which ultimately ruled that the questionnaires and the matching tools *by design* violated the FHA and FEHA and, thus, required Roommates to cease these practices.[518]

Through this ruling, the District Court held that both Roommates' users and Roommates itself were information content providers. They both created illegal content that breached federal and State statutory housing antidiscrimination laws. On the one hand, Roommates' users were information content providers who created their own profiles by selecting among the options in the drop-down menu automatically given by Roommates, and on the other hand, Roommates was also an information content provider when it created the menus with a limited amount of prefilled answers that included protected grounds, particularly sex, sexual orientation, and family status, and used this information to match landlords with tenants. Therefore, Roommates was not only the carrier

---

514   *Fair Housing Council of San Fernando Valley v Roommates, LLC*, CV 03–9386 PA (RZx) (C.D. Cal. Nov. 7, 2008), p. 3455.
515   FEHA, §12955 (a).
516   CDA, 47 U.S.C. §230.
517   CDA, 47 U.S.C. §230, (c)(2).
518   *Fair Housing Council of San Fernando Valley v Roommates, LLC*, CV 03–9386 PA (RZx) (C.D. Cal. Nov. 7, 2008).

of messages in this case.[519] The Appeal Court then ruled that inducing landlords to express illegal preferences is not shielded by the CDA.[520]

Roommates appealed the decision. Four years later in February 2012, the Court of Appeals for the Ninth Circuit reversed the District Court ruling by holding that even though Roommates' design was indeed not sheltered by the CDA it violated neither the FHA nor the FEHA.[521]

The issue at stake was whether the antidiscrimination provisions in the FHA and FEHA extended to the selection of roommates. While the FHA specifically provides that it does not apply to single-family privately owned houses and multifamily properties of four units or less where the owner lives in one of the units, the FEHA defines that the protected aspects cannot be considered in the sale or rental of a dwelling.[522] The Court of Appeals for the Ninth Circuit thus reasoned that a spare room cannot be considered a dwelling, and, therefore, the rental transaction of a single room – which is the purpose of Roommates – is not bound by the protections provided by the FHA and FEHA, as their ultimate scope is not shared spaces.[523] These statutes together do not aim at interfering with private relationships. In this regard, the First Amendment right to freedom of association applies to shared living spaces and may serve as a grounds for landlords to discriminate against protected classes including sex, sexual orientation, and family status but also race, color, religion, national origin, and disability.[524]

The case is interesting because it highlights the relationship between the design of a platform and the immunity for liability provided by the CDA to ISPs.[525] The Ninth Circuit ruled that Roommates' design was not protected by the CDA immunity of liability regime. Therefore, when companies in their capacity as ISPs design matching tools, such as the drop-down menu, that make users discriminate against other users the ISPs' liability is direct and not exempted by the CDA.

In the case of Roommates, the platform did not have to change its matching tools (i.e., the drop-down menu), because the FHA and the FEHA do not apply for shared places, which is the focus of Roommates.[526] Ultimately, the criteria

---

[519] *Fair Housing Council of San Fernando Valley v Roommates, LLC*, CV 03–9386 PA (RZx) (C.D. Cal. Nov. 7, 2008).

[520] *Fair Housing Council of San Fernando Valley v Roommates, LLC*, CV 03–9386 PA (RZx) (C.D. Cal. Nov. 7, 2008), p 3456.

[521] *Fair Housing Council of San Fernando Valley v. Roommates, LLC*, 2012 WL 310849 (9th Cir. 2012).

[522] FHA, 42 U.S.C. §§3604 and FEHA, Cal. Gov't Code §12955.

[523] *Fair Housing Council of San Fernando Valley v. Roommates, LLC*, 2012 WL 310849 (9th Cir. February 2, 2012).

[524] *Ibid.*

[525] *See* Varty Defterderian, "Fair Housing Council v Roommates.com: A New Path for Section 230 Immunity" (2009) 24 Berkeley Technology Law Journal 563; Bradley M Smyer, "Interactive Computer Service Liability for User-Generated Content After Roommtes.com" (2009) 43 University of Michigan of Law Reform 811.

[526] *Fair Housing Council of San Fernando Valley v Roommates, LLC*, 2012 WL 310849 (9th Cir. February 2, 2012).

used in the matching tool – sex, sexual orientation, and familial status – were not illegal. Considering the reasoning of the Court of Appeals' decision, if the criteria used in the matching tools were illegal under the federal and state antidiscrimination laws, the platform would likely have held tort liability for discrimination against its users.

3. DAFT.IE

3.1. BUSINESS MODEL

Daft is a platform focused on advertising and matching property seekers with homeowners, landlords, and real estate professionals in Ireland.[527] It accepts properties for sale, rent, sharing, commercial use, short-term rent, and holidays as well as foreign properties. The platform was founded as a housing marketplace in 1997. Since then, it has become a leader in the sector. It has listed 90% of the properties available for sale in the country, 70,000 properties for sale in total, and it has 1,000 property searches every minute and over two million unique users' visits monthly.[528]

Property owners, real estate professionals, or individuals willing to share their properties can gain access to the platform by paying a € 1 standard fee or a € 25 premium one.[529] Depending on the deal, they can advertise their properties for 90 days, post unlimited photographs, select the size of the advertisement, and opt for a high priority listing. When announcing the property, users have the possibility to describe it in an "overview" box. In this same space, they may state some preferences regarding future tenants or owners. House seekers are not required to pay any fee to use Daft's services. They are also given the possibility to contact the landlord directly through the platform.

3.2. LITIGATION: ONLINE PLATFORMS AS REAL ESTATE COMPANIES

In 2016, the Irish Human Rights and Equality Commission filed a complaint seeking adjudication against Daft for publishing discriminatory housing advertisements on its platform.[530] Several third-party advertisements for rental

---

[527] Daft.ie, *About Us* (December 2019), online <https://www.daft.ie/about/>.

[528] *Ibid.*

[529] Daft.ie., *Instant Access to Ireland's Largest Property Audience List Your Place Today* (December 2019), online: Daft.ie <https://www.daft.ie/ad-entry/sharing>.

[530] *Irish Human Rights and Equality Commission v Daft Media Limited t/a Daft/ie*, ADJ-00005960, WRC, August 2019. Available online <https://www.workplacerelations.ie/en/cases/2019/august/adj-00005960.html>.

properties were displayed on the platform with statements such as would "suit family only"[531] (excluding persons who are not under the meaning of family provided by the Equal Act), "would suit young professionals" (excluding older tenants)[532], and "rent allowance not accepted" and "work letter of reference needed"[533] (excluding persons who receive public rent supplement).

The Commission found that the advertisements discriminated against prospective tenants on the grounds of age, family status, and social economic status. Moreover, the Equal Status Act expressly provides that "a person shall not publish or display or cause to be published or displayed" advertisements that indicate intention to discriminate or "might reasonably be understood as indicating such an intention."[534]

The Irish Human Rights and Equality Commission sent a letter to Daft in 2016 about the concerned advertisements alleging that Daft breached the Equal Status Act by publishing illegal discriminatory housing advertisements. Daft disagreed that it had breached the Equal Status Act, because it was not the publisher of the advertisements, but alternatively it was an ISP. The Irish Human Rights and Equality Commission proposed to withdraw the complaint if Daft compromised by providing a written statement that declared it would "refrain from publishing" discriminatory ads.[535] The Commission provided a long list of terms and sentences that should not be published.

Daft refused to make such a commitment for several reasons. First, it argued that it is not the advertiser nor the publisher of the illegal content, but it is an ISP as defined by the Directive on Electronic Commerce and the transposed Irish law.[536] Both of these legal instruments do not impose any duty on Internet Service Providers to monitor the content published by third-parties (advertisers) and renders it immune for liability on such illegal content.[537] Second, it had undertaken several measures to help advertisers comply with the Equal Status Act, including the implementation of a pending section that receives advertisements containing terms previously reported as discriminatory. These advertisements are reviewed by Daft's staff prior to publication. Daft also implemented a "notice-and-take-down" policy. All users can report a discriminatory advertisement with a flag system. In addition, they have the possibility of directly sending an email to Daft. Finally, Daft educates advertisers

---

[531] Section 2, (c), Equal Status Act 2000–2015. (Family status). The act defines "family status" as individuals "being pregnant or having responsibility "(a) as a parent or as a person *in loco parentis* in relation to a person who has not attained the age of 18" (b) "the resident primary carer in relation to a person with disability", see Part I, 2, F4, Equal Status Act.

[532] Section 3, (f), Equal Status Act 2000–2015. (Age status).

[533] Section 3, (3B), Equal Status Act 2000–2015. (housing assistance status).

[534] Section 12, I, Equal Status Act 2000–2015.

[535] *Irish Human Rights and Equality Commission v Daft Media Limited t/a Daft/ie*, ADJ-00005960, WRC, 2019.

[536] Article 14, Directive on Electronic Commerce and Regulation 2003, (S.I. 68 of 2003) (Ireland).

[537] *Ibid.*

about the use of illegal discriminatory language in a dedicated part of the platform.

The case was referred to the Workplace Relation Commission (WRC), which has the authority to adjudicate employment and non-employment related cases of discrimination. The WRC opted to construe the Equal Status Act in the most liberal way possible. First, it ruled that Daft provides services related to accommodation. Second, the WRC found that Daft had vicarious liability for advertisements listed on the platform when they breached the Equal Status Act, which forbids discrimination in the provision of accommodation.[538] The WRC refused to recognize that the Directive on Electronic Commerce protected Daft from liability imposed by the Equal Status Act. Third, the WRC determined that Daft had breached the Article 12 of the Equal Status Act for publishing the illegal advertisements. Finally, the WRC ordered Daft to "refrain from publishing or, displaying, or permitting to be published or displayed on its website advertisements" that discriminate against protected classes.[539] In practice, the WRC imposed on Daft the duty to monitor third-party housing advertisements prior to their publication. Until December 2019, the WRC decision was not appealed to a Circuit Court.

In my view, the decision is problematic because the WRC imposed on Daft the duty to monitor several thousand posts of third-party content published daily on its server. This inverts the logic settled by the Directive on Electronic Commerce that services such as Daft should not be imposed to monitor illegal content, but instead should be compelled to take it down once it is aware of it.

4. AIRBNB

4.1. BUSINESS MODEL

Airbnb was founded in San Francisco in 2008 as a private company that operates an online marketplace dedicated to the rental market of houses, apartments, rooms, or any related place for the accommodation of individuals normally for short-term stays.[540] In 14 years, Airbnb has reached international success, having listed over four million accommodations across 65,000 cities in 191 countries.[541]

---

[538] Article 6 (1)(c), Equal Status Act 2000–2015.

[539] *Irish Human Rights and Equality Commission v Daft Media Limited t/a Daft/ie*, ADJ-00005960, WRC, 2019.

[540] Leigh Gallagher, *Airbnb Story: How Three Ordinary Guys Disrupted an Industry, Made Billions, and Created Plenty of Controversy* (New York: Houghton Mifflin Harcourt, 2017), p 34.

[541] Craig Smith, *Airbnb Statistics and Facts* (September 2019), online: Business Statistics <https://expandedramblings.com/index.php/airbnb-statistics/>.

After the United States, Airbnb has its most important market in France.[542] Between January 2016 and January 2017, eight million travelers booked accommodation through the platform in France. Airbnb's economic impact on the French economy was over € 6.5 billion in 2016.[543] Part of its success is credited to its capacity to tackle inefficiencies in the accommodation market by allowing individuals to rent empty properties or a fraction of a property for a short term.[544] This system benefits property owners as well as individuals looking for a more authentic or, in some cases, more affordable option than a hotel.

Airbnb affirms to connect hosts and guests under a large number of circumstances, where the former can rent their entire property, a room, a bed, or even the living room couch.[545] Hosts may or may not be present when having the guest for the contracted period. A survey revealed that over 57% of the announced places are entire homes, 41% are private rooms, and 2% are shared rooms.[546] Moreover, property owners are free to choose the price to be charged for the rental, even if Airbnb suggests a fare reflecting the average price charged for places located in the same area. Airbnb retains around 6%–12% of the final price for each transaction as a fee for usage of their services.[547]

To register on Airbnb, users are asked to provide their first and last name, sex, birth date, email address, phone number, preferred language, real address, profile photograph, and, more generally, a personal description. As a personal description, Airbnb suggests that users indicate what they appreciate doing, things they cannot live without, and their favorite travel destination, books, movies, and food.[548] In the section dedicated to the provision of a personal description, Airbnb reminds users that its platform is "built on relationships. Help other people get to know you."[549]

Regarding the profile photograph, Airbnb notes that clear face photographs are important for hosts and guests to get to know each other, as they note "It's not much fun to host a landscape!"[550] With this respect, Airbnb encourages users to use a photograph that clearly presents their face and does not include

---

[542] Emmanuel Marill, *La Communauté Airbnb en France en 2016* (January 2017), online: Airbnb <http://hr-infos.fr/wp-content/uploads/2017/04/EIS-France.pdf> p 4–5.

[543] Emmanuel Marill, *La Communauté Airbnb en France en 2016* (January 2017), online: Airbnb <http://hr-infos.fr/wp-content/uploads/2017/04/EIS-France.pdf> p 4–5.

[544] Benjamin G Edelman, Michael Luca, *Digital Discrimination: The Case of Airbnb.com* (January 2014), online: Harvard Business School <https://www.hbs.edu/faculty/Publication%20Files/Airbnb_92dd6086-6e46-4eaf-9cea-60fe5ba3c596.pdf>.

[545] Airbnb, *Homepage* (November 2019), online: Airbnb <https://www.airbnb.com>.

[546] Daniel Guttentag, "Airbnb: Disruptive Innovation and the Rise of an Informal Tourism Accommodation Sector" (2015) 18 Current Issues in Tourism 1192, 1193.

[547] *Ibid,* p 1193.

[548] *See* annex 1.

[549] *Ibid.*

[550] *See* annex 2.

any personal or sensitive information they would not want other guest and hosts to be aware of.

Moreover, the users' public profile lists the date they joined Airbnb. Next to this information is a flag with the text "Report this user." Users can anonymously report other users if "1. This profile shouldn't be on Airbnb; 2. Attempt to share contact information; 3. Inappropriate content or spam."[551] In the section "trust and verification," users are informed about the need to provide a copy of an official identity card to book any accommodation. Moreover, Airbnb verifies the user's email address and telephone number.[552]

Host and guests can receive and give reviews about their experience.[553] Airbnb has also created the category of "super hosts" to award hosts who have received over 10 guests, have maintained a rental request response rate over 90%, have had zero cancellations with the exception of extenuating circumstances, and have over a 4.8-star overall rating.

4.2. DESIGN IS A CHOICE!

In several occasions, homeowners rent parts or all of their own home through Airbnb. Contrarily to traditional housing transactions, renting one's own space with one's personal belongings or with one's personal presence involves not only monetary risks, but also personal security risks. Airbnb has maintained that such transactions are only possible if a minimum relationship of trust between guests and hosts is developed beforehand.[554]

Airbnb supports that a trustworthy relationship between users is built upon transparence on (1) how hosts and guests appear in the offline world (photographs and names), (2) narratives on past experiences (reviews), and (3) a system of verification of identity cards, telephone numbers, and address that is managed exclusively by the company's staff.[555]

Several reported cases of discrimination, mainly related to the refusal of hosts belonging to statutorily protected classes[556], have pushed scholars to challenge Airbnb's platform design choices, particularly the ones that immediately disclose ethnic origin markers, such as guests' photographs and first and last names. Ethnic origin markers coupled with the possibility for the host's discretion for approved guests has raised concerns that long-term issues

---

[551] *See* Annex 4.
[552] *See* Annex 3.
[553] *See* Annex 5.
[554] The platform alleges that Airbnb is built on relationships. Annex 1 and Annex 2.
[555] Leigh Gallagher, *Airbnb Story: How Three Ordinary Guys Disrupted an Industry, Made Billions, and Created Plenty of Controversy* (New York: Houghton Mifflin Harcourt, 2017), p 60.
[556] *See* chapter 1.

of racial discrimination in traditional housing markets would widely persist in rental transactions on Airbnb.

The disclosure and prominence of ethnic origin markers, notably through photographs and names, are part of the choices made by Airbnb's designers.[557] Other online housing markets have voluntarily opted for different formats. For example, HomeAway, a platform dedicated to vacation rental properties, opts to display only the photographs of the properties. Once the transaction is concluded, hosts and guest photographs are then disclosed.[558] This example illustrates that the design of housing marketplaces is not static and can be rethought to avoid bias.

4.3. LITIGATION: ONLINE PLATFORMS AS PLACES OF PUBLIC ACCOMMODATIONS?

In 2015, Gregory Selden, a Black American Airbnb guest, was refused accommodation by a host in Philadelphia under the justification that the property was not available on Selden's required dates. Suspecting that he was discriminated against, Selden then created two fake profiles, Jessie and Todd, both with profile photographs of typical white Americans. He tried to book the same property again, on the same dates he had inquired about before. This time, the host accepted the bookings of Jessie and, subsequently Todd, which confirmed Selden's suspicion that he had been discriminated against. He contacted the host explaining what had happened and received the response that "people like you were simply victimizing yourself."[559] He then filed a complaint within the Airbnb's customer service area, but he did not receive a response.[560] Selden then tweeted his story, launching the hashtag #airbnbwhileblack. The tweet went viral and was retweeted by thousands of individuals who vocalized their experiences of similar discriminatory treatment from Airbnb hosts.[561]

In May 2016, Selden filed a putative class action suit against Airbnb for race discrimination on behalf of himself and fellow Black American guests who had reported similar treatment on the platform. Selden claimed that Airbnb

---

[557]   Ray Fisman, Michael Luca, "Fixing Discrimination in Online Marketplaces" (2016) Harvard Business Review 1.

[558]   Airbnb, for instance, experimented to hold host photos from the main search results page to measure the effects on booking outcomes, however it did not make those results available to the public. Benjamin Edelman, Michael Luca, Dan Svirsky, "Racial Discrimination in the Sharing Economy: Evidence from a Field Experiment" (2017) 9 American Economic Journal: Applied Economics 1.

[559]   *Selden v Airbnb*, INC., No. 16-cv-00933 (CRC) (D.C. Nov. 1, 2016). (Hereinafter, *Selden v Airbnb*), p 7.

[560]   *Ibid.*

[561]   Twitter, *#airbnbwhileblack* (November 2019), online: twitter <https://twitter.com/hashtag/airbnbwhileblack?lang=fr>.

violated several provisions of the Civil Rights Acts, notably the one that forbids discrimination in the access to public accommodation[562], the one that forbids race discrimination in the formation of contracts[563], and the one that prohibits race discrimination in the rental of housing.[564]

Rather than suing the host, Selden opted to litigate with Airbnb. The reason why Selden did not sue the host is not clear in the text of the class action. One could speculate that the host might have fit under the Fair Housing Act's Mrs. Murphy exception that allows differentiations in cases in which the homeowner lives in the unit they rent.[565]

Airbnb promoted itself, since the beginning of its operations, as a platform with the utmost role to connect individuals. Under this intermediation label, how could one hold Airbnb liable for breaching housing federal and state antidiscrimination laws and make them liable for hosts' discriminatory behavior against guests?

The class action related Airbnb to a (1) hotel and (2) real estate agency and related its hosts to (3) hotel employees and (4) rental agents. The strategy to compare Airbnb with traditional housing and lodging agents, who are overall responsible and might pay victims punitive damages for the illegal actions implemented by their "agents, representatives, or employees,"[566] aimed to seek liability from Airbnb. Plaintiffs claimed that independent of how Airbnb shall be labeled by the court, the platform had violated several different antidiscrimination statutory laws, including Title II of the Civil Rights Act of 1964 (Public Accommodations), Title VIII of the Civil Rights Act of 1968 (Fair Housing Act), and the Federal Civil Rights Statute 42 U.S.C §1981. These statutes together prohibit housing and lodging agents to refuse the transaction of an accommodation on the basis of the race of the tenant/guest.[567] Moreover, agency theories impose vicarious liability on companies that manage these agents.

The question of whether a housing market such as Airbnb could be considered a place of public accommodation had been answered before in relation to other online businesses. First, in a previous case involving the liability of an online chat room and third-party harassing comments that blasphemed and defamed Islamic religion[568], the United States District Court for the Eastern District of Virginia ruled that the examination of Title II makes it clear that "places of public accommodation are limited to actual, physical places and structures and, thus, cannot include chat rooms, which are not actual physical facilities, but instead

---

[562]   Title II of the Civil Rights Act of 1964, 42 U.S.C. §2000a.
[563]   Civil Rights Act of 1866, 42 U.S.C §1981.
[564]   FHA, 42 U.S.C. §3604.
[565]   The derogation concern single-family privately owned houses and multifamily properties of four units or less where the owner lives in one of the units; see FHA, 42 U.S.C. §3603 (b) (1).
[566]   *Selden v Airbnb*, §13.
[567]   Title VIII of the Civil Rights Act of 1968.
[568]   *Noah v AOL Time Warner, Inc.*, 261 F. Supp. 2d 532 (E.D. Va. 2003).

virtual forums for communication provided by an Internet Service Provider."[569] Second, in *Access Now, Inc. v Southwest Airlines*[570], plaintiffs claimed that the airline company Southwest Airlines had violated Title III of the Americans With Disability Act[571], because its website was not compatible with "screen reader" programs, and, therefore, it was inaccessible to blind persons. The issue whether the airline's website constituted a place of public accommodation under the ADA was relevant, because in case of a positive answer, the website should provide reasonable accommodation for blind users. However, the United States District Court for the Southern District of Florida decided that the ADA restricts places of public accommodation to physical structures, and therefore, the website was not one of such places.[572]

However, more recent precedents concerning the material scope of the ADA have construed broader meaning to the term "place of public accommodations." In *National Federation of the Blind v Scribd*, the District Court for the District of Vermont ruled that websites under certain circumstances are public accommodation and, therefore, must comply with ADA's requirements.[573] Scribd has a membership program that allows subscribers to read eBooks from its library for a small fee. Scribd's website and application were not accessible through special screen reader software. This fact prevented blind persons to access Scribd services. The District Court found that Scribd is a place of public accommodation under the category of library or service establishment. The court reasoning was based on the fact that currently internet spaces play a fundamental role in the personal and professional lives of Americans and, therefore, "excluding disabled persons from access to covered entities that use it as their principle means of reaching the public would defeat the purpose of this important civil rights legislation (ADA)."[574]

Some scholars defend Airbnb as a space of public accommodation by referring to the precedent *National Federation of the Blind v Scribd*.[575] However, in my view, the difference between Airbnb and the above examples, Southwest Airlines and Scribd, is that Airbnb does not directly provide the hosting service.

---

[569]   In the *Welsh v Boy Scouts* case, the Court of Appeals for the Seventh Circuit decided that *Boy Scout* was not a place of public accommodation because it is not "closely connected to a facility". The case involved the right of *Boy Scout* to discriminate on the ground of religion when deciding the individuals entitled to be memberships. *Welsh v Boy Scouts of America*, 993 F.2d 1267 (7ᵗʰ Circuit, 1993).

[570]   *Access Now, Inc. v Southwest Airlines, Co.*, 227 F. sup. 2d 1312, 1316 (S.D. Fla. 2002).

[571]   42 U.S.C. §12182, Title III.

[572]   *Access Now, Inc. v Southwest Airlines, Co.*, 227 F. sup. 2d 1312, 1316 (S.D. Fla. 2002).

[573]   *National Federation of the Blind v Scribd, Inc.*, case 2:14-cv-162 (United States District Court for the District of Vermont 2015).

[574]   *Ibid*, p 23–24.

[575]   Nancy Leong, Aaron Belzer, "The New Public Accommodations: Race Discrimination in the Platform Economy" (2017) 105 The Georgetown Law Journal 1271. In this article, the authors defend both possibility of framing Airbnb either under the concept of public accommodation or real estate broker.

In this regard, Airbnb does not own the properties, it does not select which lodgings will be available on the platform and how hosts will proceed in the selection of their guest.

Moreover, trying to fit Airbnb under the label of a real estate agency has also encountered limitations similar to its comparison with a space of public accommodation, because the link of subordination between Airbnb and its hosts can be hardly proved. Airbnb hosts, contrarily to traditional real estate agents, have the freedom to make their own accommodation available and to select the price to be charged and the rental time frame. Moreover, even if Airbnb is compared to a real estate agency, not all accommodations are included under the limitations of the FHA, but only the ones that are entirely rented (and not only a fraction) and owned by someone who has more than four properties.[576]

Partially based on the above arguments, Airbnb denied that it is either a place of public accommodation or a real estate agency, and, therefore, it is not liable under any agency theory for the harm caused to Gregory Selden and individuals in a similar position.[577] Airbnb stressed that it simply operates a platform and is not under the position to make decisions regarding the motivation a host has in each case.[578] Traditional businesses that provide public accommodation spaces or real estate agencies are liable for the harm caused by its agents because there is a relationship of subordination, and companies have the duty to train and monitor their agents. However, the difficulty to apply any agency theory and vicarious liability concerning Airbnb lies on the lack of subordination between Airbnb and the hosts.

Airbnb also alleged that in a condition of an Internet Service Provider it is immune to liability for any discriminatory content posted by hosts under the exemptions provided by Section 230 of the CDA.

Ultimately, Airbnb's liability for damages was not subject to the District Court's assessment. The case was entirely dismissed, because Airbnb's terms of service – which Selden had accepted by signing up to use Airbnb - contained a clause requiring all disputes to be resolved by an arbitrator. In this sense, civil lawsuits were prohibited as well as class actions. Selden tried to argue that the sign-up process did not adequately notify him when he agreed to Airbnb's terms of service, including mandatory arbitration.[579] However, the Court ruled that no matter how controversial the practice of requiring consumers to renounce

---

[576] Nancy Leong, "The First Amendment and Fair Housing in the Economy Platform" (2017) 78 Ohio State Law Journal 1001, p 1002–1009.

[577] *Selden v Airbnb.*

[578] *Ibid.*

[579] For comments on the case, *see* Caitlin Toto, "Sharing Economy Inequality: How the Adoption of Class Action Waivers in the Sharing Economy Presents a Threat to Racial Discrimination Claims" (2017) 58 BCL Review 1355; David Restrepo Amariles, Gregory Lewkowicz, "Global Contract Governance: Selden V Airbnb", in: Horatia Muir Watt, Lucia Bizíková, Agatha Brandao de Oliveira, Diego P Fernandez Arroyo, *Global Private International Law* (Edward Elgar Publishing, 2019). Also, *see* chapter 5, Arbitration.

on their fundamental right to a jury trial and to pursue class actions, the law is clear that mutual arbitration provisions in electronic contracts are enforceable in commercial disputes and discrimination cases as well.[580]

4.4. AIRBNB GLOBAL ANTIDISCRIMINATION POLICY: AN OUTCOME OF LITIGATION AND RESEARCH

Even though Airbnb's liability in the *Selden v Airbnb* case could not be assessed by the District Court of Columbia, the platform did not take long to act. Following the repercussion of the litigation and of the academic studies suggesting widespread discrimination on the platform by the media, Airbnb hired a team of experts, led by Laura Murphy, to address the issue. Prior to her work for Airbnb, Laura Murphy had been an activist in the cause of racial and gender equality during her career as a lawyer and as the Director of the American Civil Liberties Union (ACLU) where she specifically fought for LGBT, minorities, and women's reproductive rights.[581]

Laura Murphy was hired to create new strategies to tackle discrimination against guests who transact on the platform. In this regard, in September 2016, Airbnb released the report "Airbnb's Work to Fight Discrimination and Build Inclusion"[582] authored by Laura Murphy with the help of a team composed of diverse members including hosts, victims of discrimination, employees, civil rights organizations, federal and state regulatory agencies, elected and appointed officials, and travel and tourism executives.[583] Accommodating all these perspectives was a challenge stressed by Laura Murphy in the report. Particularly demanding was the need to balance the hosts' freedom to determine who stays in their houses and the company's mission of not tolerating discrimination based on statutorily protected features.[584] The report details nine steps to be followed by Airbnb in its mission to tackle hosts' discrimination against potential guests.

The first step concerns the implementation of a contractual general clause against discrimination that hosts and guests must accept to join the platform across the world, and not only in the United States. Airbnb explicitly requires new and old users to agree to treat all other members of Airbnb with respect and without judgement or bias no matter their race, religion, national origin, ethnicity, skin color, disability, sex, gender identity, sexual orientation, or

---

580   *Selden v Airbnb Inc.*, §70; also, the Federal Arbitration Act (FAA), 9 U.S.C. §2 and chapter 5.
581   Laura W Murphy, *Airbnb's to Fight Discrimination and Build Inclusion: A Report Submitted to Airbnb* (September 2016), online: Airbnb <https://blog.atairbnb.com/wp-content/uploads/2016/09/REPORT_Airbnbs-Work-to-Fight-Discrimination-and-Build-Inclusion_09292016.pdf>.
582   *Ibid.*
583   Laura W Murphy, *Airbnb's to Fight Discrimination and Build Inclusion: A Report Submitted to Airbnb*, p 5–8.
584   *Ibid*, p 5.

age.[585] This commitment is broader than the FHA in scope given the inclusion of sexual orientation and gender identity. So far, over one million Airbnb users have refused to accept Airbnb's general clause against discrimination, and consequently they have been denied to use the platform.[586]

Second, the report stressed Airbnb's new engagement to hire a team of engineers, data scientists, researchers, and designers whose work consists of excluding bias and advancing inclusion in the platform. Moreover, a new product team was appointed to explore reducing the role of guest and host photographs in the booking process, while highlighting other parts of the profiles' description. In this context, Airbnb sponsored experiments conducted by technologists to assess reducing the prominence of users' photographs in the booking process.[587] The report agreed that emphasizing guests' photographs can foster discrimination based on the statutory protected aspect. However, the report suggested that guests and hosts profile photographs should not be entirely excluded, and users should not be hidden under a curtain of anonymity to prevent discrimination. Ultimately, in October 2018 Airbnb globally changed how the guest profile photographs are showed in the booking request process. Currently, hosts see the guest's photograph only after they have accepted to conclude the transaction instead of having access to a potential guest's profile photograph during the booking request.[588] Moreover, Airbnb removed users' photographs from its main page, leaving only the photographs of the properties in the main page. However, the photographs are still available when users search for more details about the property.

Third, Airbnb committed to encouraging hosts to provide instant book listings. In these cases, the accommodation is available immediately after the guest's request with no need for the host's prior approval. Airbnb promised a million of instant bookable listings by January 2017. By July 2019, around 70% of all six million global listings can be booked with the instant book feature.[589] Moreover, by default, when hosts create a new listing, the reservation mode is pre-checked to be immediate. When hosts do not want to have their

---

585 *Ibid*, p 10. *"I agree to treat everyone in the Airbnb community – regardless of their race, religion, national origin, ethnicity, skin color, disability, sex, gender identity, sexual orientation or age – with respect and without judgment or bias."* This message was displayed in 24 October 2018, when I created a profile. Check the annex 6.

586 Laura Murphy, *Three Year Review – Airbnb's Work to Fight Discrimination and Build Inclusion* (September 2019), online: Airbnb <https://news.airbnb.com/wp-content/uploads/sites/4/2019/09/Airbnb_Work-to-Fight-Discrimination_0909_3.pdf>, p 6.

587 Airbnb, *An Update on Airbnb's Work to Fight Discrimination* (September 2019), online: Airbnb <https://news.airbnb.com/an-update-on-airbnbs-work-to-fight-discrimination/>, and Laura Murphy, *Three Year Review – Airbnb's Work to Fight Discrimination and Build Inclusion* (September 2019), online: Airbnb <https://news.airbnb.com/wp-content/uploads/sites/4/2019/09/Airbnb_Work-to-Fight-Discrimination_0909_3.pdf>.

588 Laura Murphy, *Three Year Review – Airbnb's Work to Fight Discrimination and Build Inclusion*, *op. cit.*, p 6.

589 *Ibid.*

accommodation available on the instant book mode, they must manually turn on the option to "review every request."[590] Moreover, at present, guests can filter their search to only view listings that are available through instant booking.[591]

Fourth, Airbnb implemented an "open door policy" to ensure accommodation for guests who could not find one because they were discriminated against by Airbnb's hosts.[592] Between October 2016 and March 2019, Airbnb made a total of 6,045 open door offers, and 512 of these were accepted.[593]

Fifth, Airbnb committed to offer special training for users willing to address unconscious bias. In this context, it developed self-teaching tools with videos, testimonies, tests, and special tips to help hosts avoid unconscious bias behavior when approving a guest's request for accommodation.[594]

Sixth, Airbnb compromised to have a more diverse workforce among its permanent staff. The new "Diversity Rule" requires women and unrepresented individuals to be mandatorily included within candidate pools for senior-levels positions.[595]

Seventh, Airbnb committed to hold hosts accountable in cases in which they refuse a guest based on the justification that the accommodation is already booked for the dates required. Currently, when hosts refuse a guest under this justification, Airbnb automatically blocks the calendar for the period required.[596]

Eighth, Airbnb compromised to expedite its response to complaints involving discrimination and to enforce its antidiscrimination policies by implementing antidiscrimination protocols. The aim was to implement a technology that allows guests to rapidly flag an instance of discriminatory behavior and to immediately forward the reported case to a group of specialists hired specifically for this purpose. The promised deadline to implement such a measure was January 2017, but, at the moment, no further information is available apart from a general link made available to report users for wrongdoings.

Ninth, Airbnb committed to develop a new antidiscrimination policy to which all members shall accept to register or remain in the platform. The new policy has been in place since September 2016 and contains principles of inclusion and respect. It explicitly provides that "bias, prejudice, racism,

---

[590] *See* annex 7.

[591] Airbnb, *What is Instant Book?* (March 2018), online: Airbnb <https://www.airbnb.com/help/article/523/what-is-instant-book>.

[592] Laura W Murphy, *Airbnb's to Fight Discrimination and Build Inclusion: A Report Submitted to Airbnb, op. cit.*, p 10–12.

[593] Laura Murphy, *Three Year Review – Airbnb's Work to Fight Discrimination and Build Inclusion, op. cit.*, p 9.

[594] Airbnb hired Robert W. Livingston Professor and Psychologist from Harvard University to develop its toolkit. Also, Airbnb, *Toolkit* (May 2018), online: Airbnb <https://www.airbnb-toolkits.com/outline/8y7bu00k/cover>.

[595] Laura W Murphy, *Airbnb's to Fight Discrimination and Build Inclusion: A Report Submitted to Airbnb, op. cit.*, p 10–12.

[596] Laura W Murphy, *Airbnb's to Fight Discrimination and Build Inclusion: A Report Submitted to Airbnb, op. cit.*, p 20.

and hatred" shall have no place.[597] Moreover, it particularly engages Airbnb to do more "than comply with the minimum requirements established by the law."[598] Furthermore, the policy provides guidance for hosts regarding illegal discrimination against guests based on preferences related to their race, color, national origin, religion, sexual orientation, gender identity, age, disability, or marital status in the United States and EU member states. However, the policy recognizes that some countries may allow or require individuals to make distinctions based on marital status, national origin, gender, or sexual orientation in housing-related transactions. In these cases, it recommends hosts to not breach the law, but when communicating such restrictions, hosts shall use "clear, factual, non-derogatory terms."

Airbnb's antidiscrimination policy was first implemented in the United States and was later required for users everywhere it operates. The guidance on race, color, national origin, religion, sexual orientation, gender identity, age, disability, or marital status was notably inspired by American fair housing statutes, including the federal FHA and the Californian FEHA, which contains a broader scope of protection than the FHA.[599]

The FHA with the FEHA prohibit the refusal of potential renters because of their race, color, ethnicity, national origin, religion, sexual orientation, gender, identity, or marital status.[600] However, it is precedential that both statutes do not apply in cases of a single-family property being rented by the owner – and not through a broker – or in cases that only a fraction of the accommodation (e.g., a room) is being rented out.[601] In these cases, the policy does not provide for further limitation but completely rejects stated preferences based on the "race" of the host.[602] Furthermore, the policy provides that hosts are not allowed to ask their potential guests about any eventual disability they might experience. In the case, it was also mentioned that hosts shall spontaneously provide reasonable accommodation, including the acceptance of an assistant animal or the use of an available parking space near the accommodation. However, the policy specifies

---

[597] All the following quotes from this paragraph were taken on Airbnb's antidiscrimination policy, accessed when I created my profile. *See* annex 8.

[598] *Ibid.*

[599] It is worth noting that the FHA provides minimum grounds, but States can have aws with more grounds of protection.

[600] In line with the FHA that allows, in certain conditions, difference of treatment concerning prospective tenants, especially if the owner shares same spaces in the house, or if the owner owns maximum 4 units of a property and lives in one of them. However, there is nothing in the FHA that allows homeowners to advertise discriminatory preferences regarding the ethnic origin of the person.

[601] *See* chapter 1, section II, 1.4. Right of intimate association.

[602] Airbnb, *Politique de Non-Discrimination d'Airbnb: Notre Engagement en Matière d'Inclusivité et de Respect* (March 2018), online: Airbnb <https://www.airbnb.fr/help/article/1405/airbnb-s-nondiscrimination-policy--our-commitment-to-inclusion-and-respect>.

that hosts may refuse to rent their accommodation based on aspects that are not prohibited by law, including declining guests who smoke or have pets.[603]

Airbnb's global antidiscrimination policy is the outcome of the significant repercussion of (unsuccessful) litigation and the rise of extensive academic studies demonstrating numerous instances of discrimination on the platform. The practical results of the implementation of such a policy on the refusal of guests based on their protected aspects are still largely undocumented. However, the policy has shed light on the necessity to be proactive and inform users conducting housing transactions of the illegality of certain forms of differentiation against guests. The prevailing question is whether users *de facto* read and are aware of such a policy.

4.5. CONSIDERING FURTHER SOLUTIONS: SITUATION TESTS?

Commentators have suggested that one of the missing aspects among the new Airbnb's antidiscrimination policy is the lack of a provision for external auditing or situation tests to assess ongoing discrimination. In recent years, researchers have faced obstacles to conduct experiments to assess discrimination on the platform.[604] When researchers created fake profiles to inquire hosts about accommodation opportunities, they consistently had their accounts taken down, as having a fake or non-verifiable profile is against Airbnb's terms of services.

In general, collecting evidence related to discrimination in house transactions has proven difficult, because (1) often only two private parties are involved in the transaction – the house owner (or real estate agent) and tenants/buyer – and therefore no witness is present; and (2) evidence may be subtle, with house owners announcing that the place is not available anymore and choosing, among different propositions, a tenant who corresponds to their expectations.

Given this context, since the 1960s situation testing has been implemented to prove cases of direct discrimination against protected classes.[605] In the United States, this method was used as evidence in trials related to housing discrimination as well as a method to evaluate how segregation in certain neighborhoods was due to private discrimination.[606] In the second case, the

---

[603]   *See* annex 9.

[604]   Benjamin Edelman, Michael Luca, Dan Svirsky, "Racial Discrimination in the Sharing Economy: Evidence from a Field Experiment", *op. cit.*

[605]   Situation testing is also called by the specialized literature and by public officers as situational tests, testing, auditing, pair-comparison testing, and discrimination testing. I will keep the expression situation testing in this thesis.

[606]   Veronica M Reed, "Civil Rights Legislation and the Housing Status of Black Americans: Evidence from Fair Housing Audits and Segregation Indices", *op. cit.*; Marc Bendick Jr, *Discrimination Against Racial and Ethnic Minorities in Access to Employment in the United*

purpose was mainly to provide evidence to public authorities and foster the creation of policies against discrimination.

The implementation of situation tests could be facilitated and have been considered in Airbnb's antidiscrimination policy. Contrarily to traditional real estate agencies, Airbnb has proper technology to prevent the implementation of such tests. This is detrimental to an external and independent assessment of ongoing discrimination in the platform. Furthermore, running experiments on online platforms is simpler and demands less human resources than conducting such experiments through a real estate agency.

In 2016, Airbnb reached an agreement with the Department of Fair Employment and Housing of the State of California (DFEH) with respect to the implementation of situation tests.[607] Following its legal competence, the DFEH had started an investigation concerning administrative complaints of racial discrimination in housing and public accommodations managed through the platform. In the occasion, the DFEH's director Kevin Kish alleged potential harm to a group of statutorily protected individuals in the state of California.

The terms of the agreement were to last two years and were applicable to all Airbnb listings physically located in the State of California.[608] Airbnb committed to report on collected data regarding the average acceptance rate for Caucasian, Black American, Hispanic, and Asian American guests; the frequency that Californian hosts reject based on claimed unavailability; the number of discrimination complaints raised by guests who were rejected by Californian hosts; and the number of Californian hosts who are de-listed from the platform based on the host's discriminatory conduct.[609] In addition, the agreement settled that Airbnb shall allow the DFEH to conduct fair housing testing in some instances. Under the terms of the documents signed by Airbnb and the DFEH, the enforcement body or a contractor were apt to conduct fair housing testing against Californian hosts who had been subject to one or more discrimination complaints and had three or more listings.

States: Empirical Findings from Situation Testing (Employment Department International Labor Office 1996).

[607] The Department of Fair Employment and Housing is the state agency charged with enforcing the Fair Employment and Housing Act. It exercises its law enforcement power under the California Fair Employment and Housing Act of 1959. It has also the authority to enforce the Unruh Civil Rights Act (Unruh Act) (Civ. Code, §51) which is expressly incorporated into FEHA (Gov. Code, §12948). *Voluntary Agreement,* Complainant v Airbnb, INC., a Delaware Corporation Respondent. Case Nos. 574743–231889 and 574743–231624. DFEH, *Voluntary Agreement* (April 2017), online: DFEH <https://www.dfeh.ca.gov/wp-content/uploads/sites/32/2017/06/04–19–17-Airbnb-DFEH-Agreement-Signed-DFEH-1–1.pdf>.

[608] *Voluntary Agreement,* Complainant v Airbnb, INC., a Delaware Corporation Respondent. Case Nos. 574743–231889 and 574743–231624.

[609] *Voluntary Agreement,* Complainant v Airbnb, INC., a Delaware Corporation Respondent. Case Nos. 574743–231889 and 574743–231624. The compliance of this measure could not be found online.

The scope was quite limited, considering that there were approximately 76,000 hosts in California but only 6,000 had three or more listings. It was settled that Airbnb could not interfere with the creation of accounts and profiles created to be used for the tests and could not intentionally remove any of them. The agreement, reached before the implementation of Airbnb's global antidiscrimination policy, was a relevant step regarding the possibility to implement situation tests, but it was too limited geographically (California) and temporally (two years).

4.6. AIRBNB IN THE EUROPEAN UNION: AN INTERNET SERVICE PROVIDER

Despite Airbnb's extensive presence across EU countries, members of the European Network of Legal Experts in Non-Discrimination have reported no specific lawsuit regarding the discriminatory refusal of guests because of their protected aspect in the level of national courts[610], even though cases of ethnic origin discrimination against Airbnb guests have been reported by the press.[611]

Overall, the lack of attention public authorities have given to the issue in the past is striking. For instance, in 2016 the European Commission published the comprehensive document "European Agenda for the Collaborative Economy" to address concerns over uncertainty about rights and obligations of different actors engaging in the collaborative economy.[612] In the document, the European Commission attentively expressed several concerns related to the consumer protection of users, employment rights, taxation, market access requirements, and liability regimes, but it overlooked any possible impact of platforms similar to Airbnb on equality rights.[613] Airbnb's practices and design have been closely followed by the European Commission, but nothing has been mentioned regarding the potential vulnerability to discrimination – grounded on protected

---

[610] Eugenia Caracciolo di Torella, Bridgette McLellan, *Gender Equality and the Collaborative Economy* (March 2018), online: European Commission <https://www.equalitylaw.eu/downloads/4573-gender-equality-and-the-collaborative-economy-pdf-721-kb>. Also, Isabelle Chopin, Carmine Conte, Edith Chambrier, *A Comparative Analysis of Non-Discrimination Law in Europe 2018, European Network of Legal Experts in Gender Equality and Non-Discrimination* (November 2018), online: European Commission Directorate-General for Justice and Consumers <https://www.equalitylaw.eu/downloads/4804-a-comparative-analysis-of-non-discrimination-law-in-europe-2018-pdf-1–02-mb>.

[611] Henri Seckel, *Pour Réserver sur Airbnb, Mieux Vaut S'Appeler Isabelle que Djamila* (August 2018), online: LeMonde <https://www.lemonde.fr/societe/article/2018/08/24/airbnb-abritel-discriminations-en-ligne_5345587_3224.html>.

[612] Brussels, 2.6.2016 COM(2016) 356 final. Communication from the Commission to the European Parliament, the Council, the European Economic and Social Committee and the Committee of the Regions: A European Agenda for the Collaborative Economy.

[613] *Ibid.*

aspects – to which Airbnb users might or might not be exposed.[614] Alternatively, Airbnb has been required to modify the way it presents information on pricing, ensuring that when a property is offered the consumer has easy access to the entire price, including all charges and fees, such as cleaning and service charges.[615] In addition, the platform has also been required to unequivocally state when the offer is made by a private or professional host, because consumer protection rules are different for each of type of host.[616] Furthermore, the Commission has also requested Airbnb to bring its terms of services into conformity with the Unfair Contract Terms Directive (93/13/EEC), especially regarding imbalances to the detriment of the consumer.[617]

On the litigation side, national courts have assessed whether Airbnb was liable for its host's illegal activities. For instance, Airbnb was ruled liable for non-harm and harm damages in a case related to illegal subletting in Paris in 2018.[618] In this occasion, the host Romuald L. had listed and rented the apartment where he lived through Airbnb without the agreement of his landlord Léon D. The lease contract signed between Romuald L. and Léon D. explicitly prohibited subletting. In 2017, Romuald asked Léon to sublet his property on Airbnb and Léon refused. Romuald ignored his contractual obligations and rented the apartment through the platform anyway. In total, he sublet the apartment 119 times through Airbnb for more than four months in a unique year and received € 49,301.71 from Airbnb stays. Law enforcement went to the apartment four times during the period it was illegally sublet. Moreover, Romuald did not give notice to public authorities that he was renting his apartment in a housing platform. French law obliges hosts renting their place in housing platforms such as Airbnb to have a written authorization from the public office.[619] It also prohibits individuals from renting the property where they live for more than four months per year.[620]

---

[614] European Commission, *EU consumer rules: the European Commission and EU consumer authorities push Airbnb to Comply* (July 2018), online: European Commission <http://europa.eu/rapid/press-release_IP-18-4453_en.htm>.

[615] *Ibid.* Airbnb's pricing presentation and the distinction between private and professional hosts did not comply with the Unfair Commercial Practices Directive (2005/29/EC). Article 6 (d) and article 7 (c), Directive 2005/29/EC.

[616] *Ibid.*

[617] Article 3, Directive 93/13/EEC. European Commission, *EU consumer rules: Airbnb commits to complying with European Commission and EU consumer authorities' demands* (September 2018), online: European Commission <http://europa.eu/rapid/press-release_IP-18-5809_en.htm>. Such as the platform "should not mislead users by going to a court in a different country from the one in their Member State of residence"; "Airbnb cannot decide unilaterally and without justification which terms may remain in case of termination of a contracts"; "Airbnb cannot unilaterally change the terms and conditions without clearly informing consumers in advance and without giving them the possibility to cancel the contract"; "terms of services cannot confer unlimited and discretionary power to Airbnb on the removal of content".

[618] *Tribunal d'Instance, Paris,* Jugement du 6 février 2018, RG 11-17-000190.

[619] Article L 324-2-1, Code du Tourisme, modifié para la loi du 7 Octobre 2016.

[620] Article L 324-2-1, Code du Tourisme, modifié para la loi du 7 Octobre 2016.

The court found that Airbnb should have verified if the host Romuald L. was authorized by his landlord to sublet the apartment, or at least, had obtained a declaration from Romuald affirming that he could legally rent the property through the platform. Moreover, the court ruled that Airbnb should have informed Romuald about his obligation to request a written authorization from the public office to rent his place for more than four months. Finally, Airbnb should have checked that Romuald rented his place for more than four months and should have acted accordingly.

Airbnb received notice from public authorities about the four-month rule and the requirement of public authorization to rent properties on Airbnb in such cases. Even after being notified about its obligations, Airbnb did not suspend Romuald L.'s account. In addition, Airbnb made profits from the illegal rental transactions by charging fees for each transaction. The court also highlighted that more than 20,000 properties may be illegally sublet in Paris through Airbnb. Due to Airbnb's negligence and abstention, Romuald L. consistently breached the French law.

Airbnb alleged that it is only a platform that connects hosts and guests and that it has no control over the 450,000 apartments listed on its services in Paris. However, the court ruled that by negligence and imprudence Airbnb allowed the host to illegally rent his apartment and made profit over it. Airbnb was condemned to pay the owner of the apartment € 3,000 for non-material harm damages (prejudice moral), € 1,664 for material harm damages, € 1,869 for the fees obtained by the illegal rental transactions, and, finally, € 1,500 for the judicial fees.

The question whether Airbnb provides information society services or real estate brokerage ultimately reached the CJEU in 2018.[621] In January 2017, the association AHTOP (Association for Professional Tourism and Hosting) and two hotels filed a legal complaint against Airbnb in Paris, claiming that the company does not merely connect two parties through its platform, but it also provides services comparable to intermediary real estate activities. Considering this factual reality, Airbnb would not have complied with the French law that requires real estate agencies/brokers to have a professional license issued by the local chamber of industry and commerce.[622] The French Law regulating the conditions for the exercise of activities relating to the transaction of real property is applicable to all natural or legal persons who give assistance on

---

[621]   Case C-390/18, Eion Michael Hession and Airbnb Ireland UC v Hôtelière Turenne SAS and Association pour un Hébergement et un Tourisme Professionnel (AHTOP) and Valhotel, ECLI:EU:C:2019:1112. For previous comments on the case, *see* Christoph Busch, "The Sharing Economy at the CJEU: Does Airbnb pass the Uber test? Some observations on the pending case c-390/18 Airbnb Ireland" (2018) 7:4 *Journal of European Consumer and Market Law* 172.

[622]   Loi Hoguet, loi n 70–9 du 2 janvier 1970 réglement les conditions d'exercice des activités relatives à certaines opérations portant sur les immeubles et les fonds du commerce. Article 3(1) and 5. (Hoguet Law).

a regular basis, even in an auxiliary capacity, to any transaction affecting real estate. These activities include "the purchase, sale, search for, exchange, leasing or sub-leasing, seasonal or otherwise, furnished or unfurnished, of existing buildings or those under construction."[623] Moreover, the legislation specifically provides that the assistance to such real estate transaction can only be exercised by a legal or natural person holding a professional license that has been issued by the appropriate public authority.[624] The license is only awarded to applicants who demonstrate their professional qualification and a professional liability insurance. Providing such real estate-related activity without having the proper license is punishable by six months of imprisonment and a fine of € 7,500 if there is no remuneration[625] or € 30,000 and two years of imprisonment if there is remuneration.[626] AHTOP argued that, in this occasion, those provisions limiting the activities of real estate brokers applied to Airbnb because the platform provides services that come under the Directive on services in the internal market.[627]

Airbnb argued before the French court that it does not act as a real estate agency and, therefore, it is not bound by laws that regulate real estate brokerage. Airbnb stressed that its activities concern the services provided under the Directive on Electronic Commerce. Moreover, requiring Airbnb, which is allegedly an Internet Service Provider, to obtain a special license breaches the European Directive on Electronic Commerce and its transposed French law.[628] Article 3 (2) of the Directive on Electronic Commerce states that, aside from a few exceptions, member states may not restrict the freedom to provide information society services from another member state.[629] The primary objective of the Directive is to enable the freedom of information society services between member states.[630] For this reason, member states might immediately notify the Commission about any draft or technical regulation imposed on information society services[631], considering that such technical regulation may hamper the freedom companies have to provide information society services across member states.

In June 2018, the *Tribunal de Grande Instance de Paris* sent a request for a preliminary ruling to the CJEU on whether the services provided by Airbnb

---

[623] Article 1, Hoguet Law.

[624] Article 3, Hoguet Law.

[625] Article 14, Hoguet Law.

[626] Article 16, Hoguet Law.

[627] Directive 2006/123/EC of the European Parliament and of the Council of 12 December 2006 on Services in the Internal Market, OJ L 376, 27.12.2006, p 36–68.

[628] Article 3(2), Directive on Electronic Commerce.

[629] The exceptions include criminal investigation and prevention; the protection of public health; public security; the protection of consumers. Art 3(4)(a)(i), Directive on Electronic Commerce.

[630] Recital 8, Directive on Electronic Commerce.

[631] Article 5(1), Directive 2015/1535.

fell under the freedom of services provided by the Directive on Electronic Commerce[632] or, in other words, if Airbnb should be classified as an information service provider. Moreover, the French court requested whether the restrictive provisions concerning the profession of the real estate brokers shall be invoked against Airbnb even in its condition as an information service provider.[633]

The CJEU construed that the activity of intermediation provided by Airbnb comes under the concept of service within the meaning of Article 56 TFEU and Directive 2006/123.[634] However, the Directive 2006/123 does not apply in cases of conflict with other EU legislation regulating the access or the exercise of specific services and professions.[635]

To determine whether Airbnb activities shall be regulated under the terms of the Directive 2006/123 of the Directive on Electronic Commerce, the CJEU had to assess whether such a service shall be qualified as an "information society service" within the meaning of Article 2(a) of the Directive on Electronic Commerce.

Under EU law, "information society services" have been defined as involving any service provided for remuneration, at a distance, by electronic means and at individual request.[636] The Court stressed that Airbnb provides services for remuneration that are intended to connect potential guests looking for accommodation with professional or non-professional hosts offering shot-term accommodation by means of an electronic platform. Moreover, the service provided by Airbnb is electronic and at a distance because hosts, guests, and Airbnb itself do not come into contact in means other than through the Airbnb electronic platform.[637] Finally, Airbnb's service is provided under request since hosts and guests might voluntarily place their offers and interests in renting accommodation.[638] The CJEU concluded, therefore, that Airbnb meets the conditions to be qualified as an "information society service" within the meaning of EU law.[639]

In a prior ruling related to the activities supplied by Uber, the CJEU have found that in some contexts companies providing information society services can do it as part of an "overall service" whose main component is a service

---

[632] Article 3(2), Directive on Electronic Commerce.

[633] Act n. 70–9 of 2 January 1970 (Hoguet Law).

[634] Directive 2006/123/EC of the European Parliament and of the Council of 12 December 2006 on services in the internal market OJ L 376, 27.12.2006, 36–69. (Hereinafter, Directive 2006/123/EC).

[635] Article 3(1), Directive 2006/123/EC.

[636] Article 2(a), Directive on Electronic Commerce; and Art 1(1)(b), Directive (EU) 2015/1535 of the European Parliament and of the Council of 9 September 2015 laying down a procedure for the provision of information in the field of technical regulations and of rules on information society services, OJ L 241, 17.9.2015, 1–15. (Hereinafter, Directive 2015/1535).

[637] C-390/18 *Airbnb Ireland*, ECLI:EU:C:2019:1112, §47.

[638] C-390/18 *Airbnb Ireland*, ECLI:EU:C:2019:1112, §48.

[639] C-390/18 *Airbnb Ireland*, ECLI:EU:C:2019:1112, §49.

regulated by another EU legislation.[640] The court decided that Uber, for instance, provides information society services ancillary to its main transportation service. In these cases, the Directive on Electronic Commerce does not entirely apply. Aligned to this precedent, AHTOP argued that the information society service provided by Airbnb is only an ancillary activity part of the overall service whose main component is the provision of an accommodation service, similar to intermediary activities in real estate transactions.

The CJEU found that even if the only purpose of the intermediation provided by Airbnb is to allow users to rent accommodation, the nature of this purpose does not serve as a justification to depart from the application of the Directive on Electronic Commerce. Among the reasons given by the court, Airbnb does not exercise a significant role on the conditions related to the provision of the accommodation services because, first, hosts have autonomy to determine the rental price, and second, guests are free to select which hosts and accommodation listed on the platform they want to request (i.e., the matching service is not automatic). These two pieces of evidence distinguish Airbnb from Uber.

Overall, Airbnb does not decide the price of the rentals for users listing their properties in the platform, even if it has available in its services a tool for estimating rental price. Although the tool considers the average price of similar properties offered in the same region through the platform, Airbnb leaves the responsibility for setting the rent to the host. Moreover, Airbnb provides hosts with a template for presenting the content of their offer, a facultative photography service for the rental of the property, and a system for rating hosts and guests, and this information is then made available to future users. However, these elements do not present evidence for the same level of control found by the court in the case concerning Uber.

The CJEU also ruled that restrictive provisions concerning the profession of real estate brokers included in the Hoguet Law shall not be invoked against Airbnb in its condition as an information society service provider. First, such limitation is not compatible with Article 3(2) of the Directive on Electronic Commerce, which provides that member states may not restrict the freedom to provide information society services from another member state. In this regard, it should be stressed that Airbnb Ireland UC, established in Dublin under Irish law, is the company that offers an electronic platform to connect hosts and guests offering and looking for accommodation in the EU market. Airbnb France SARL is only a supplier to Airbnb Ireland. In this capacity, Airbnb France SARL is simply in charge of promoting the platform in the French market and organizing, for instance, local advertisement content. The Hoguet Law applied in such a context restricts the freedom to provide information society services.[641]

---

[640]   *See* C-434/15 *Asociación Profesional Elite Taxi*, EU:C:2017:981 Also, chapter 6.
[641]   C-390/18 *Airbnb Ireland*, ECLI:EU:C:2019:1112, §81.

Second, the possibility to limit the provision of information society services is authorized by the Directive on Electronic Commerce in a few circumstances, such as when a public policy is implemented to prevent, investigate, and detect criminal offenses as well as in cases regarding the protection of public health, public security, and consumers.[642] However, the CJEU concluded that the Hoguet Law does not fall under any of these circumstances.[643] Moreover, the Directive on Electronic Commerce provides that when member states derogate the freedom to provide information society services because of the above-cited circumstances, they should inform both the European Commission and the member state in which the concerned service provider is established before taking any restrictive measure.[644] The French Government has never notified the Commission or Ireland about the restrictive limitations provided by the Hoguet Law. Failing to meet the duty to inform both the Commission and the member state about the technical rules restricting freedom of service provision makes the concerned legislation void against individuals.[645] Therefore, even if the Hoguet Law was under the scope of the authorized exception of the freedom to provide information society services, the fact that the French Government had not notified the Commission about its existence would make this law unenforceable against individuals in a situation such as that with Airbnb Ireland.[646]

---

[642]   Art 3(4)(a)(i), Directive on Electronic Commerce.
[643]   C-390/18 *Airbnb Ireland*, ECLI:EU:C:2019:1112, §82.
[644]   Art 3(4)(b), Directive on Electronic Commerce.
[645]   C-390/18 *Airbnb Ireland*, ECLI:EU:C:2019:1112, §96.
[646]   C-390/18 *Airbnb Ireland*, ECLI:EU:C:2019:1112, §99.

CONCLUSION OF TITLE I

Platforms focused on the housing and accommodation sectors bring great opportunities to connect property owners and individuals seeking properties for rental and sale. Moreover, they have enhanced the possibility for individuals to efficiently allocate empty places by renting them through short-term arrangements. These positive aspects combine with the fact that housing and accommodation platforms intermediate relationships in a market that has long been marked by instances of discrimination.

My aim in this title was to demonstrate how these platforms challenge the principle of equality by scaling the number of offers visibly available to the public, by scaling the number of individuals renting a fraction of their properties, and by their design, that either enhances protected markers, such as gender and ethnic origin, or implements matching tools to exclude protected classes from housing offers.

Concerning the publication of discriminatory advertising, I argue that, on the one hand, the full immunity provided by the Communications Decency Act of 1996 to Internet Service Providers limits the possibilities victims of discrimination have to be redressed in the United States.[647] On the other hand, in Europe, the more balanced approach concerning the liability of online intermediaries over third-party illegal content provides more safeguards to take the illegal content down.[648] However, both sets of liabilities cannot avoid the aspect of the scale that illegal content has online.

Moreover, antidiscrimination laws provide limited possibilities to address cases in which hosts, renting a fraction of their properties, refuse to accept guests through online platforms either in countries of the European Union or in the United States. While in the EU, the right for respect for private life is more limited and only sex discrimination is exempt in cases of shared spaces, in the United States the constitutional right of freedom of association allows further differentiations in cases in which the host owns a single-family property or a multifamily property of four units or less.

Finally, rules of vicarious liability do not apply to most online platforms because the principles of subordination and agency do not guide the relationship that most online platforms have with their users. In Europe, more particularly

---

[647] §230, c, 47 U.S.C. Communications Decency Act of 1996 (CDA) (Title V, Telecommunications Act of 1996).

[648] Article 14, Directive on Electronic Commerce.

in France, Airbnb was condemned to redress an infringed third-party due to an illegal action of its user, because the judge considered Airbnb to be negligent.[649] In this case, Airbnb was informed several times that the user was subletting his apartment through the platform without proper license to do so. Even after being informed, Airbnb did not take reasonable measures to prohibit the user from continuing to sublet his apartment illegally through the platform. Following the logic of the liability regime of the Directive on Electronic Commerce[650], courts should rule in the same way in cases in which Airbnb was warned several times that a certain host illegally refused hosts because of their protected grounds and did not take any measure to stop the situation. This possibility is theoretical, since, to my knowledge, no case of legal dispute regarding discrimination has been reported in courts in Europe.

Finally, the self-regulatory responses provided by Airbnb and Craigslist against discrimination show that social pressure is also a tool for change. After the media, strategic litigation, and academics have vocally drawn attention to the issue, both platforms agreed to implement antidiscrimination policies, while the former energetically engaged a team headed by the civil rights activist Laura Murphy, who worked with engineers, data scientists, and others to reflect on practical improvements regarding the platform's design and booking practices. I consider that engaging the civil society and academia is absolutely necessary to produce real change in the fight against discrimination. Strategies to push companies to revise their practices and recognize their flaws must be constantly undertaken to change the *status quo*. The history of antidiscrimination rights is profoundly related to these sorts of social actions. However, in my view, self-regulatory responses pushed by social pressure should not be the only remedy to address discrimination, because the attention Airbnb and Craigslist received from the different sectors is mainly due to their size and importance within their market segment. A balanced liability regime is necessary to redress victims of discrimination placed in platforms that are less important, less known and, therefore, less likely to mobilize social action.

---

[649] *Tribunal d'Instance, Paris,* Jugement du 6 février 2018, RG 11–17–000190.
[650] The Digital Services Act has not changed the liability regime provided by the Directive on Electronic Commerce.

TITLE II

ONLINE ADVERTISING MARKETS: WIDESPREAD DATA COLLECTION AND UNEQUAL ACCESS TO EMPLOYMENT, GOODS, AND SERVICES

INTRODUCTION

Businesses have sponsored traditional media through advertising campaigns for a long time.[651] Commonly, television shows and radio broadcasts are interrupted by commercials, and magazines have pages dedicated to advertising third-party goods and services. In this context, advertising campaigns have labeled and targeted audiences to reach consumers in their market segment.[652] Content-related targeting used to be the most popular form to reach potential consumers.[653] To illustrate this idea in content-related targeting, advertisements for toys are likely broadcasted on the Disney Channel and men's athletic shoes are likely advertised on ESPN. When advertisers opt for content-related targeting, they base their choices both on customers' preferences and stereotypes. For this reason, a study revealed that a "typical" female publication has up to 60% of all ads related to clothes and cosmetics, while 5% of the ads are related to high-tech devices.[654]

So far, the marketing industry has gone beyond content-related targeting to reach segmented audiences. In the past decades, this same industry has developed advanced profiling techniques to grasp its consumers' needs more accurately. One of these well-known techniques is referred to as behavioral targeting. With this technique, consumers are categorized by their personal traits as well as by their actions and practices.[655] Years ago, in the United States the department store Target asked its analytics department if it was possible to discover consumers' pregnancies through their purchasing habits.[656] Knowing whether a consumer is pregnant is relevant for the retail industry, because it is a time when consumers' needs change, and they seek new products. Target's analytics sector reviewed the shopping files of all female customers who had

---

651   Larry D Kelly, Donald W Jugenheimer, Kim Bartel Sheehan, *Advertising Media Planning: A Brand Management Approach* (Routledge 2011), chapter 5; Helen Katz, *The Media Handbook: A Complete Guide to Advertising Media Selection, Planning, Research, and Buying* 3rd ed (Lawrence Erlbaum Associates 2009), p 2–3.

652   Viktor Mayer-Schönberger, Kenneth Cukier, *Big Data: A Revolution That Will Transform How We Live, Work and Think* (Houghton Mifflin Harcourt 2013), p 50.

653   *Ibid.*

654   Emmanuella Plakoyiannaki, Yorgos Zotos, "Female Role Stereotypes in Print Advertising: Identifying Associations with Magazine and Product Categories" (2009) 43 European Journal of Marketing 1411.

655   Marcel Gommans, Krish S Krishman, Katrin B Scheffold, "From Brand Loyalty to e-Loyalty: A Conceptual Framework (2001) 3:1 Journal of Economic & Social Research 43, p 47.

656   Viktor Mayer-Schönberger, Kenneth Cukier, *Big Data: A Revolution That Will Transform How We Live, supra* note 2, p 57.

registered for baby gift listings. The team discovered over 24 products that, used as proxies, allowed them to calculate a pregnancy prediction score for every client who had a loyalty card. The pregnancy score was then used to target direct personalized advertisement to clients. One day, a man complained to Target's service sector and alleged that his teenage daughter had received coupons in the mail for baby products, and he accused the store of trying to convince his daughter to get pregnant. Later, the man apologized confirming that his daughter was indeed pregnant.[657]

Over the past 20 years, the marketing industry has actively invested in the internet. Currently, advertisements are omnipresent in every user's online experience. One of the reasons for this is the economic model adopted by most services online: they are frequently completely free of charge to the users. This model is especially essential for the most popular ones, such as Google, Facebook, and YouTube. These platforms are able to provide their activities free of charge to the final consumer by selling online space to third-party advertisements.

Similarly to its offline counterpart, online advertising also targets consumers. However, the possibilities to track consumers' behavior, traits, and preferences are much wider online, considering that activities online are easily traceable and registered. Consumers are targeted to receive specific ads in expected and unexpected places, including in banners on the top placement of their social networking media or when they search for a term in search engines.[658] The ads are displayed in multiple forms, such as hyperlinks with a short text, banners, or videos. Moreover, advertisements can be targeted based on content context, on consumers' demographics, and on consumers' behavior online.[659]

Most advertisers (82.5%) and advertising companies (90.7%) have reported that they use digital audience targeting in the United States.[660] In 2018, online advertising revenues increased 23% compared to 2017 and totaled $49.5 billion dollars.[661] Across the pond, the European online advertising sector has doubled in the past 5 years.[662] The growth of online advertising is due to the ubiquity of the internet, mobile phones, and pervasive trust in e-Commerce. Studies

---

[657]   Viktor Mayer-Schönberger, Kenneth Cukier, *Big Data: A Revolution That Will Transform How We Live, Work and Think*, *supra* note 2, p 58.

[658]   Avi Goldfarb, "What Is Different About Online Advertising?" (2014) 44 Review of Industrial Organization 115, p 116–119.

[659]   *See* chapter 3.

[660]   Soontae An, Hannah Kang, Hyun Seug Jin, "Self-Regulation for Online Behavioral Advertising (OBA): Analysis of OBA Notices" (2018) 24 Journal of Promotion Management 270, p 272.

[661]   The Interactive Advertising Bureau, *IAB Internet Advertising Revenue Report* (November 2018), online: IAB <https://www.iab.com/wp-content/uploads/2018/11/IAB-WEBINAR-HY18-Internet-Ad-Revenue-Report1.pdf>.

[662]   IAB Europe, *IAB Europe recording: European Digital Advertising Spend 2017* (December 2017), online: IAB <https://iabeurope.eu/iab-europe-webinar-recording-european-digital-advertising-spend-2017/>.

have demonstrated that consumers have been increasingly purchasing in online markets.[663] As a result of the consumption transition to online markets, the online advertising industry has blossomed.

It is worth noting that online targeted advertising is not limited to the offer of goods. It currently includes a broad spectrum of services, including credit offers, education opportunities, political campaigns, and employment offers. In particular, over the past two decades the use of online recruitment has grown rapidly and companies have increasingly spent more in advertising employment offers online.[664] In the United States and Europe, this practice has replaced newspapers' classified ads, to a certain extent.[665] Furthermore, employment ads are not only displayed in specialized platforms, such as LinkedIn, but they are also displayed in social networks such as Facebook or through search engine platforms such as Google.[666] Several companies and employment agencies also have pages on Facebook, where they post information about job opportunities.[667] Moreover, these entities use Facebook's targeting tools to deliver employment advertisements to selected users.[668] Companies have increasingly advertised employment offers online, because the costs are lower, they may reach a wide range of workers, and ultimately, they can target potential employees by their location and, in some instances, by their demographics.[669]

Targeted advertisement has become a widespread practice in online platforms for several reasons. First, digital advertising has proved to not necessarily engage internet users.[670] Clicks on digital advertisements were

663 Steven C Bennett, "Regulating Online Behavioral Advertising" (2011) 44:4 The John Marshall Law Review 889.
664 Yioula Melanthiou, Fotis Pavlou and Eleni Constantinou, "The Use of Social Network Sites as an E-Recruitment Tool" (2015) 20 Journal of Transnational Management 31; Emma Parry, Shaun Tyson, "An Analysis of the Use and Success of Online Recruitment Methods in the UK" (2008) 18 Cranfield School of Management Human Resource Management Journal 257, p 258.
665 Yioula Melanthiou, Fotis Pavlou and Eleni Constantinou, "The Use of Social Network Sites as an E-Recruitment Tool" (2015) 20 Journal of Transnational Management 31.
666 Chapter 4.
667 In 2015, a survey revealed that 92% of employment recruiters, in the US, use social media to recruit applicants for employment. A study led by the Society for Human Resource Management, in 2016, indicated that 66% of employers who recruit via social network use Facebook. AdWeek, *Survey: 92% of Recruiters Use Social Media to Find High-Quality Candidates* (September 2015), online: AdWeek <www.adweek.com/socialtimes/survey-96-of-recruiters-use-social-media-to-findhigh-qualitycandidates/627040>; SHRM, *Survey Findings: Using Social Media for Talent Acquisition. Recruitment and Screening* (January 2016), online: SHRM <https://www.shrm.org/hr-today/trends-and-forecasting/research-andsurveys/Documents/SHRM-Social-Media-Recruiting-Screening-2015.pdf>, p 9.
668 *See* chapter 4.
669 Yioula Melanthiou, Fotis Pavlou, Eleni Constantinou, "The Use of Social Network Sites as an E-Recruitment Tool", *op. cit.*, p 38.
670 Juan Miguel Carrascosa, Jakub Mikians, Ruben Cuevas, Vijay Erramily, and Nikolaos Laoutaris, "I Always Feel Like Somebody's Watching Me: Measuring Online Behavioural Advertising" (2015) Proceedings of the 11th ACM Conference on Emerging Networking

often low. To address this problem, advertisers with the help of data scientists and engineers have been incentivized to develop sophisticated targeting tools to reach the right audience and to personally cater to every user it could reach with personalized advertisements. Second, targeting users for marketing purposes is ubiquitous because the audiences in social network platforms and search engines are diverse. Social media and search engines are not sectorial.[671] Instead, they are available to a broad range of users. As a result, platforms such as Facebook and Google have introduced algorithms that tailor advertisements based on the users' traits and behavior.[672] Contextual advertising is less viable in these platforms when compared to websites with niche content, such as newspapers.

Over the past decades, online platforms have increasingly become emergent gatekeepers for marketing in general.[673] These online actors handle information overload by accessing and categorizing valuable information that has been collected, processed, filtered, and personalized for each individual user. Google, for instance, makes use of personal and non-personal data, including location and previous search words, to deliver advertisements to its users.[674] Facebook collects users' personal and non-personal data and registers how users generally interact with the available social gestures of the platform including likes, shares, and comments.[675] Third-party advertising represents their main source of revenue. To illustrate the dimension of the marketing industry, in 2018 Facebook generated $55 billion in ad revenues, while Google generated $116.3 billion.[676]

In this title, I analyze how targeted advertising, which is enabled and incentivized by online platforms, poses risks to the principle of equality in the access to certain goods, services, and employment in the European Union and the United States. The evolution of technology has given the possibility for advertisers to differentiate which individuals will have access to their content by completely or partially excluding certain groups who have access to it. In the

---

Experiments and Technologies 13; Alexander Bleier, Maik Eisenbeiss, "Personalized Online Advertising Effectiveness: The Interplay of What, When, and Where" (2015) 34 Marketing Science 669.

[671] Jianqing Chen, Jan Stallaert, "An Economic Analysis of Online Advertising Using Behavioral Targeting" (2014) 38 MIS Quartely 429; V Kumar and Gupta Shaphali, "Conceptualizing the Evolution and Future of Advertising" (2016) 45:3 Journal of Advertising 302.

[672] Anja Lambrecht, Catherine Tucker, "When Does Retargeting Work? Information Specificity in Online Advertising" (2013) 50 Journal of Marketing Research 561.

[673] Engin Bozdag, "Bias in Algorithmic Filtering and Personalization" (2013) 15 Ethics Information Technology 209, p 209.

[674] *Ibid*, p 211.

[675] *Ibid.*

[676] *See* United States Securities and Exchange Commission, *Annual Report Pursuant to Section 13 15 (d) of the Securities Exchange Act* (December 2018), online: Facebook Commission File <https://www.sec.gov/Archives/edgar/data/1326801/000132680119000009/fb-12312018x10k. htm#s7598225E01E95F77950D4736C39C55F1> and United States Securities and Exchange Commission, *Annual Report Pursuant to Section 13 15 (d) of the Securities Exchange Act* (December 2018), online: Alphabet Inc. Commission File <https://www.sec.gov/Archives/edgar/data/1652044/000165204419000004/goog10-kq42018.htm>.

past, printed magazines did not have the option to advertise job vacancies only in copies that went to male readers, but sectorial advertisements were still possible, such as by publishing an employment ad in a magazine typically read by males. However, women who bought this magazine could still read the advertisement. Advertising only for targeted groups belongs to the possibilities that platforms like Facebook and Google currently provide. They can direct their third-party advertising only for women, men, users under 40 years old, people residing in a specific geographic location, and an infinite range of possibilities given by data provided spontaneously or collected by the platforms.

Discrimination in the employment market is well documented in Europe and in the United States, and the figures that demonstrate the frequency of occurrence are compelling. Discrimination primarily occurs in relation to ethnicity, age, and gender. For instance, in Belgium, job applicants with foreign sounding names have 30% less chances of being invited to a job interview compared to applicants with a similar profile but Flemish sounding names.[677] In the UK, older workers are 4.2 times less likely to be selected for an interview than their 28-year-old counterparts.[678] Across Europe, on average, the employment rate for women is 12% less than men, and women are more representative in lower-paid sectors, such as retail salespeople, cleaners, personal care workers, pre-primary and primary school teachers, and secretaries.[679] In the United States, white employment applicants receive, on average, 36% more callbacks than Black applicants, and 24% more callbacks than Latino applicants with similar CVs.[680] In the past two decades, the number of employment discrimination charges against older workers filed with the EEOC has risen by 47%.[681] Finally, the callback rate for high-skilled male workers is four times greater than for high-skilled women workers.[682]

---

[677] European Network Against Racism (ENAR), *Racism & Discrimination in Employment in Europe 2013–2017* (March 2017), online: European Commission <https://ec.europa.eu/migrant-integration/?action=media.download&uuid=F613A27D-A960–4FB3-FD3AD6A629C8FBE7> p 4.

[678] House of Commons, *Older People and Employment Fourth Report of Session 2017–19* (May2019), online: Age UK <https://www.ageuk.org.uk/globalassets/age-uk/documents/reports-and-publications/later_life_uk_factsheet.pdf> p 14–15.

[679] European Commission, *2018 Report on Equality Between Women and Men in the EU* (March 2018), online: European Commission <https://www.google.com/url?sa=t&rct=j&q=&esrc=s&source=web&cd=1&ved=2ahUKEwjput3EqbDkAhXFPFAKHdXwAL8QFjAAegQIAhAC&url=https%3A%2F%2Fec.europa.eu%2Fnewsroom%2Fjust%2Fdocument.cfm%3Fdoc_id%3D50074&usg=AOvVaw3utWtG8Lntp1lfCf4PMbOa>, p 9.

[680] Lincoln Quillian and others, "Meta-Analysis of Field Experiments Shows No Change in Racial Discrimination in Hiring Over Time" (2017) 114 Proceedings of the National Academy of Sciences 10870, p 10871.

[681] Equal Employment Opportunity Commission, *Age Discrimination in Employment Act Charges Filed with EEOC* (December 2018), online: EEOC <https://www.eeoc.gov/eeoc/statistics/enforcement/adea.cfm>.

[682] David S Pedulla, *Pathways the Poverty and Inequality Report – Gender* (November 2018), online: Stanford <https://inequality.stanford.edu/sites/default/files/Pathways_SOTU_2018.

In some sectors, discrimination in the provision of certain goods, such as credit, is also widely documented.[683] For instance, a study released by the Federal Reserve of Boston about the mortgage loan denial rate revealed that racial and ethnic disparities exist in the provision of credit. In this context, "Black and Hispanic applicants were denied loans two to three times more often than whites."[684] In France, a situation testing conducted at 12 commercial banks revealed that individuals with Northern-African origin receive worse treatment than typical French individuals[685]: all the testers had the same salary and guarantees, and they were seeking either a mortgage loan or credit to start a business. In 19 out of 28 agencies, individuals with Northern-African origins were accepted for a significantly shorter amount of time, had much less information about their credit possibilities, and, on several occasions, met with the financial professional in the public lobby, instead of being invited to a reserved room, as was common for individuals with "typical" French origins. Moreover, the individuals with Northern-African origin did not receive in many occasions a loan simulation, while the clients with French origins received a loan simulation in almost all occasions, according to the study.

Discrimination against protected classes regarding employment offers or the provision of goods and services can be deepened by online targeted advertising because the practice enables the exclusion of protected classes from having access to it.

In this title, I present the challenges online targeted advertising pose to the principle of equality by introducing empirical studies and lawsuits regarding the topic in the United States and in Europe. I review the legal instruments provided by the Civil Rights Acts in the United States and the Equality Law Directives in the EU. I use their statutory protected grounds and their judicial construed meanings to determine whether targeted advertising illegally limits access to employment, goods, and services in a discriminatory fashion.

Most of the legal literature about targeted advertising is related to privacy or data protection rights. This academic literature is broad and has been developed since the early 2000s. In the last decade, scholars in the European Union have

---

pdf> p 36.

[683] In the US, it is considered structural discrimination. *See* Douglas S Massey, Jacob S Rugh, Justin P Steil, Len Albright, "Riding the Stagecoach to Hell: A Qualitative Analysis of Racial Discrimination in Mortgage Lending" (2016) 15:2 City and Community 118; and Christine Barwick, "Patterns of Discrimination Against Blacks and Hispanics in the US Mortgage Market" (2010) 25 Journal of Housing and the Built Environment 117.

[684] Peter Swire, *Lessons from Fair Lending Law for Fair Marketing and Big Data* (September 2014), online: Federal Trade Commission <https://www.ftc.gov/system/files/documents/public_comments/2014/09/00042-92638.pdf>, p 2.

[685] Villeurbanne, *Testing (tests de discrimination) sur l'accès au prêt immobilier et au prêt à la création d'entreprise réalisé par la ville de Villeurbane* (July 2017), online: Défenseur des Droits <https://www.defenseurdesdroits.fr/sites/default/files/atoms/files/170921_synthese_testing_credit_villeurbanne.pdf>.

vastly raised the problem of discrimination in automated systems. However, the issue is often referred to in general terms, such as "automated systems present risk for discrimination" or "the troubles big data analytics bring about is that of discrimination."[686] The generalization of the term and its lack of scope sounds unfamiliar to antidiscrimination scholars, who are used to assessing equality and discrimination through statutory specific "grounds," "classes," "protected aspects."[687]

Through my exploratory literature and lawsuits research, I understood that targeted advertisements are, first, vastly addressed by "data-legal" experts[688], and second, are found in the docks of data authorities as well as data case-law[689] in Europe and in the United States. However, I also discovered that the issue is generally more approached by civil rights lawyers in the United States than in Europe.[690] Actually, the European literature includes few papers on the

[686] Tal Z Zarsky, "Understanding Discrimination in the Scored Society" (2014) 89 Washington Law Review 1375; Elena Gil González and Paul de Hert, "Understanding the Legal Provisions That Allow Processing and Profiling of Personal Data – an Analysis of GDPR Provisions and Principles" (2019) 19 ERA Forum 597; Sophie C Boerman, Sanne Kruikemeier and Frederik Zuiderveen Borgesius, "Online Behavioral Advertising: A Literature Review and Research Agenda" (2017) 46 Journal of Advertising 363; Sandra Wachter, "Normative Challenge of Identification in the Internet of Things: Privacy, Profiling, Discrimination, and the GDPR" (2018) 34 Computer Law & Security Review 436.

[687] These terms are vastly found in the antidiscrimination academic literature and also in legal documents.

[688] *See* in the EU: Desiree de Lima, Adam Legge, "The European Union's Approach to Online Behavioural Advertising: Protecting Individuals or Restricting Business? (2014) 30:1 Computer Law & Security Review 67; Edith G Smit, Guda Van Noort, Hilde AM Voorveld, "Understanding Online Behavioural Advertising: Use Knowledge, Privacy, Concerns and Online Coping Behavior in Europe"(2014) 32 Computer in Human Behavior 15; Frederik Zuiderveen Borgesius, "Singling Out People Without Knowing Their Names: Behavioural Targeting, Pseudonymous Data, and the New Data Protection Regulation", (2016) 32 Computer Law & Security Review 256; Frederik Zuiderveen Borgesius and others, "Tracking Walls, Take-It-or-Leave-It Choices, the GDPR, and the ePrivacy Regulation" (2017) 3 European Data Protection Law Review 353; Frederik Zuiderveen Borgesius, *Improving Privacy Protection in the Area of Bahavioural Targeting* (Alphen aan den Rijn: Kluwer Law International 2015). In the United States: Chris J Hoofnagle, Ashkan Soltani, Nathaniel Good, Dietrich J Wambach, Mika Ayenson, "Behavioral Advertising: the Offer You Cannot Refuse", (2012) 6:1 Harvard Law & Policy Review 673; Omer Tene, Jules Polenetsky, "To Track or Do Not Track: Advancing Transparency and Individual Control in Online Behavioral Advertising" (2012) 13 Minnesota Journal of Law 281; Avi Goldfarb, Catherine E Tucker, "Privacy Regulation and Online Advertising" (2011) 57:1 Management Science 57.

[689] *See* in the EU: chapter 4, section I.

[690] *See* in the EU: Sandra Wachter, "Affinity Profiling and Discrimination by Association in Online Behavioral Advertising" (2020) 35:2 Berkeley Technology Law Journal 367; David Jacobus Dalenberg, "Preventing Discrimination in the Automated Targeting of Job Advertisements" (2018) 34 Computer Law & Security Review 615; Frederik Zuiderveen Borgesius, *Discrimination, Artificial Intelligence, and Algorithmic Decision-Making. Council of Europe Study* (December 2018), online: Council of Europe <https://rm.coe.int/discrimination-artificial-intelligence-and-algorithmic-decision-making/1680925d73>;   In the US: Ifeoma Ajunwa, "Age Discrimination by Platforms" (2019) 40 Berkeley Journal of

specific topic of discrimination and targeted advertising.[691] In the United States, some class actions were filed challenging discriminatory practices of targeted advertising under the Civil Rights Acts.[692] In Europe, antidiscrimination lawyers have given less attention to the issue in the light of traditional antidiscrimination law.

In this title, I argue that online platforms in general as well as Google and Facebook in particular have the potential to engender discrimination in the access to employment, goods, and services by massively tracking their users' behavior online, collecting and processing their personal data, and allowing advertisers to target ads according to the internet users' personal features, including their ethnicity, gender, age, and geographic location among other innumerous possibilities. The disruptive aspect of online targeted advertising is the amount of data available to the sector about their consumers and applicants. This data is mainly owned, managed, processed, and used by online platforms. Facebook and Google were chosen for the analysis given their representativeness in the sector. In 2018, Facebook had 78.96% and 50.85% of the market share of social media platforms in Europe and in the United States, respectively.[693] Google had 92.8% and 88.07% of the market share of search engines in Europe and in the United States, respectively.[694]

My hypothesis is that the set of traditional regulations in the United States and the EU are only partially equipped to tackle illegal discrimination occurring in the online targeted advertising industry. On the one hand, privacy laws in the United States do not provide enough protection to internet users from being tracked and having their personally identifiable information collected and processed for online targeting purposes. Moreover, the set of immunities enshrined in Section 230 of the Communications Decency Act and in the precedents exempt online platforms from liability for providing tools that allow companies to discriminate against protected classes. In Europe, data protection laws offer a structured composite of rules to protect personal data from being collected and processed and used in a discriminatory fashion; however, these overarching rules do not provide any strong definition of discrimination – and this context implies practical obstacles to address concrete cases of discrimination. On the other hand, the Equality Directives in the EU

Employment & Labor Law 1; Pauline T Kim and Sharion Scott, "Discrimination in Online Employment Recruiting" (2019) 63 St. Louis University Law Journal 1.

[691]   *Ibid.*

[692]   *Onuoha v. Facebook, Inc.*, No. 5: 16-cv-06440-EJD (N.D. Cal. Apr. 7, 2017). *Bradley v. T-Mobile US, INC.*, No. 17-cv-07232-BLF (N.D. Cal. June 4, 2019); *National Fair Housing Alliance v. Facebook, Inc.*, No. 1:18-cv-02689-JGK (S.D. N.Y. Aug. 08, 2018); *Riddick v. Facebook, Inc.*, No. 3:18-cv-04429 (N.D. Cal. Mar. 19, 2019).

[693]   Social Media Stats Worldwide, *Statcounter* (July 2019), online: GlobalStats <http://gs.statcounter.com/social-media-stats/all/united-states-of-america/2018>.

[694]   Search Engines Stats Worldwide, *Statcounter* (July 2019), online: GlobalStats <http://gs.statcounter.com/search-engine-market-share/all/united-states-of-america>.

and their transposed domestic laws are potentially equipped with appropriate tools to tackle discrimination in online targeted advertisements, especially in the employment sector, but these instruments have neither been mobilized by lawyers nor deeply investigated by scholars. Alternatively, in the United States antidiscrimination laws have been proposed in the fight against discrimination within the advertising industry. Ultimately, the United States and the EU might have valuable assets to exchange regarding their antidiscrimination and privacy legal practices.

To present the problem and develop my hypothesis, Chapter 3 provides definitions and the context of online targeted advertising, including its technical elements such as digital profiling, data mining, and tracking cookies. I also explore different targeting modalities, the essential role of online platforms to the targeted advertising industry, and examples of bias and illegal discrimination. Furthermore, I present the possible legal practices and frameworks to address discrimination in the sector. Chapter 4 addresses how real models of online platforms – Google and Facebook – have extensively used online targeted advertisement as a business model and as their main source of revenue and profits and, in turn, have been exposing their users to privacy intrusions as well as to illegal discrimination in the access to offers of employment, services, and goods.

CHAPTER 3

DISCRIMINATION IN TARGETED ADVERTISING: A PATH THROUGH DATA COLLECTION AND PROFILING

SECTION I. DEFINITIONS AND CONTEXT

In 1994, the webpage Hotwired inaugurated the business of online advertising by selling an online banner space to the telecommunication company AT&T.[695] The banner was charged based on the number of impressions it had. This model is referred to as "cost-per-mille," and the costs are determined for each thousand views the advertisement has. The cost-per-mille model remained predominant until 1996, when Yahoo! launched the "cost-per-click" and was paid accordingly to the number of clicks the advertisement had.[696]

In 1994, at the beginning of search engines' activities, they also monetized their business with third-party advertisements. First, they followed the model of selling banner advertisements on a cost-per-mille basis.[697] Second, they switched their banner ad model to the keywords search model. In this new fashion, as soon internet users typed keywords to find information in the search engine, some of the first responses displayed were sponsored by the websites themselves. Yahoo! adopted this system and Google still operates in this way.

In the past 25 years, the online advertising sector has evolved at the same pace as the internet. The pervasiveness of information about users has enabled the marketing sector to be even more data-driven than before. Profiling and targeting techniques have reshaped the online advertising business, because advertisers can granularly include or exclude their audience and consumers.

---

[695]   Ryan Singel, *Oct. 27, 1994: Web Gives Birth to Banner Ads* (October 2010), online: Wired <https://www.wired.com/2010/10/1027hotwired-banner-ads/>; Barbara K Kaye, Norman Medoff, *Just a Click Away: Advertising on the Internet* (Massachusetts: Allyn and Bacon, 2001).

[696]   David S Evans, "The Online Advertising Industry: Economics, Evolution, and Privacy" (2009) 23:3 Journal of Economic Perspectives 37, p 39.

[697]   *Ibid.*

1. MONITORING, PROFILING, AND DELIVERING

Online targeted advertising is defined as a practice of delivering an ad to a specific audience or individual.[698] The practice encompasses four different steps: 1) the monitoring of internet users' activities, 2) the collection users' data, 3) the creation of their digital profiles, and 4) the delivery of the advertisement to the "right" consumer/individual.[699]

1.1. MONITORING AND COLLECTION OF DATA

Targeted advertising reaches consumers based both on information spontaneously provided by them, such as in the cases of social networking, and on information tracked by cookies. Cookies are files designed to collect data about internet users' activity online.[700] They were originally developed to support e-commerce platforms identify items added in online shopping carts and personal login information.[701] In the 2000s, companies started using tracking cookies for advertising purposes.[702] Cookies collect information about users' browsing activities, such as the websites they visited, and share this data with the advertisement networking. In this respect, researchers found that Google placed over 6,000 cookies on the devices of users who visited the top popular online websites only to collect information about consumers' online behavior for advertising purposes.[703] Some cookies can be blocked, but studies have demonstrated that a few users try to do it through specific software programs.[704] Moreover, studies have shown that blocking tools were not entirely effective in some internet browsers.[705]

---

[698]   Avi Goldfarb, "What Is Different About Online Advertising?", *op. cit.*, p 116; David S Evans, "The Online Advertising Industry: Economics, Evolution, and Privacy", *op. cit.*, p 40.

[699]   Jenny Van Doorn, Janny C Hoekstra, "Customization of Online Advertising: The Role of Intrusiveness" (2013) 24 Marketing Letters 339.

[700]   Joseph Turow, *The Daily You: How the New Advertising Industry Is Defining Your Identity and Your Worth* (Yale University Press 2011), p 23.

[701]   *Ibid.* They are also called authentication cookies.

[702]   *Ibid.*

[703]   Ibrahim Altaweel, Nathaniel Good, Chris Jay Hoofnagle, *Web Privacy Census* (December 2015), online: Technology Science <https://techscience.org/a/2015121502/>.

[704]   Tae H Baek and Mariko Morimoto, "Stay Away from Me: Examining the Determinants of Consumers Avoidance of Personalized Advertising" (2012) 41 Journal of Advertising 59.

[705]   Specifically, with Firefox. Tae H Baek and Mariko Morimoto, "Stay Away from Me: Examining the Determinants of Consumers Avoidance of Personalized Advertising" (2012) 41 Journal of Advertising 59.

1.2. THE CREATION OF PROFILES AND PROFILING TECHNIQUES

The creation of users' digital profiles comprises the aggregation, storage, and processing of their tracked and spontaneously provided data.[706] The creation of profiles aims to make predictions about consumers' preferences based on the data spontaneously provided by them and inferred from their online behavior.[707] These predicted preferences will serve as a basis to determine which advertisement will be delivered to the sight of the internet user. Currently, the creation of internet user's digital profiles depends both on big data and data mining automated processes.[708] They are both used to identify patterns between variables in a dataset or to make predictions.[709]

To illustrate the dimensions of digital profiles, in 2016 Facebook had stored individual profiles of 1.65 billion people and a notorious ad networking company, named Add This, had profiles of 1.9 billion people in the same year.[710]

---

[706] Mireille Hildebrandt, "Defining Profiling: A New Type of Knowledge?" in Mireille Hildebrandt and Serge Gutwirth (eds), *Profiling the European Citizen* (Springer 2008), p 17.

[707] The creation of profiles to make predictions about individual behavior is used in different sectors. For advertising, see Sophie C Boerman, Sanne Kruikemeier, Frederik Zuiderveen Borgesius, "Online Behavioral Advertising: A Literature Review and Research Agenda", *op. cit.*, p 364; Edith G Smit, Guda Van Noort, Hilde A Voorveld, "Understanding Online Behavioural Advertising: User Knowledge, Privacy Concerns, and Online Coping Behaviour in Europe" (2014) 32 Computers in Human Behavior 15, p 15; for criminal justice assessment, see Rosamunde Van Brakel, Paul De Hert, "Policing, Surveillance and Law in a Pre-Crime Society: Understanding the Consequences of Technology Based Strategies" (2011) 165 Technology-Led Policing 20 p 167–170; Alexandra Chouldechova, "Fair Prediction with Disparate Impact: A Study of Bias in Recidivism Prediction Instruments" (2017) 5 Big Data 153 p 154; Mireille Hildebrandt, "Criminal Law and Technology in a Data-Driven Society" in M Dubber and T Hörnle (eds), *The Oxford Handbook of Criminal Law* (Oxford: OUP 2014), p 174–176; for immigration policies see Olivier De Schutter, Julie Ringelheim, "Ethnic Profiling: A Rising Challenge for European Human Rights Law" (2008) 71 Modern Law Review 358; for setting prices see Frederik Zuiderveen Borgesius and Joost Poort, "Online Price Discrimination and EU Data Privacy Law" (2017) 40 Journal of Consumer Policy 347; For insurance assessment see Tal Z Zarsky, "Understanding Discrimination in the Scored Society", *op. cit.*, p 1376. Danielle Keats Citron, Frank Pasquale, "The Scored Society: Due Process for Automated Predictions" (2014) 89 Washington Law Review 1, p 12–13.

[708] Usama Fayyad, "The Digital Physics of Data Mining" (2001) 44 Communication of the ACM; Michael JA Berry, Gordon S Linoff, *Data Mining Techniques: For Marketing, Sales, and Customer Relationship Management* (Indianapolis: John Wiley & Sons 2004); Jonathan R Mayer and John C Mitchell, "Third-Party Web Tracking: Policy and Technology" [2012] IEEE Symposium on Security and Privacy 413; Jan Ahrens, James R Coyle, "A Content Analysis of Registration Processes on Websites: How Advertisers Gather Information to Customize Marketing Communications" (2011) 11 Journal of Interactive Advertising 12.

[709] Machine learning and data mining are included in the broad research field of Artificial Intelligence. Ethem Alpaydin, *Machine Learning: The New AI* (New Haven: MIT Press 2016); David Lehr and Paul Ohm, "Playing with the Data: What Legal Scholars Should Learn About Machine Learning" (2017) 51 U C Davis Law Review 653.

[710] AddThis, *about us* (June 2019), online: AddThis <www.addthis.com/about>.

Digital profiles are described as digital identities[711], and digital identities singularize and identify internet users. They are available to ad networking companies. They are especially useful for advertisers to target their audiences online.[712] Internet users are often unaware of the details and full extent of their digital identity, considering most of the information composing it is not entirely and spontaneously provided by them, but instead, it is externally constructed through their behavior and by inferential analytics.[713]

1.3. ADVERTISEMENT DELIVERY

Advertising delivery practices include content and contextual targeting, time targeting, sociodemographic targeting, geographic and location based targeting, and behavioral targeting. Contextual and time targeting do not particularly involve internet users' data. While in the former advertisers choose to place their ads in location online in which content is related to the advertisement[714], the latter focuses on the time the ad is displayed.[715] For instance, a certain advertiser can schedule its ad to be displayed from 7 a.m. to 8 a.m., when a user commutes to school and uses their mobile device. The delivery based on users' sociodemographic data focuses on the personal traits of internet users and potential consumers, including traits such as their language, gender, age, and nationality. The purpose is to target users based on one or several cross-referenced personal features.

The delivery based on online behavior focuses on predictions relying on the users' browsing activities. This practice is also known as online behavioral advertising (OBA), and it depends on tracking cookies to monitor the internet users' browsing data.[716] Data collected for OBA includes the internet users' visited webpages, read articles, watched videos, online purchases, click-through responses to ads, email content, and words searched in search engines, such as

---

[711] Sandra Wachter, "Normative Challenge of Identification of the Internet of Things", *op. cit.*, p 440.

[712] *Ibid.*

[713] Paul Hitlin, Lee Raine, *Facebook Algorithms and Personal Data Complete Report* (January 2019), online: Pew Research Center <https://www.pewinternet.org/2019/01/16/facebook-algorithms-and-personal-data/>.

[714] Avi Golfarb, Catherine Tucker, "Implications of Online Display Advertising and Obtrusiveness" (2011) 30:3 Marketing Science 389, p 345.

[715] Jun Wand, Weinan Zhang, Shuai Yuan, "Display Advertising with Real-Time Bidding (RTB) and Behavioural Targeting" (2017) 11:5 Foundations and Trends in Information Retrieval 297, p 300.

[716] Edith G Smit, Guda Van Noort, Hilde A Vooveld, "Understanding Online Behavioural Advertising: User Knowledge, Privacy Concerns, and Online Coping Behaviour in Europe", *op. cit.*, p 20.

Google.[717] In OBA, the level of personalization varies widely, because it depends on the data collected and processed.[718] The delivery based on geographic location involves targeting internet users with reference to their real physical location.[719]

2. THE ROLE OF ONLINE PLATFORMS IN THE ADVERTISEMENT SECTOR

Online platforms either directly deal with advertisers or rely on advertising network companies/brokers. Some platforms, notably Google and Facebook, have their own ad network brokers. Advertising network brokers serve as an intermediary between a group of publishers (websites) and a group of advertisers. They assist advertisers to buy available ad space – also known as inventories – across multiple websites (publishers).[720] The role of platforms in online targeted advertising is twofold. First, it relates with the collection of user's data (spontaneously provided or tracked by cookies). Second, it concerns the ad delivery (display) to the targeted users.

An ad network broker normally provides an amount of inventory (ad spaces) to advertisers on an auction basis. The advertiser decides the campaign parameters, including targeted audiences, budget, and the frequency the ad shall be displayed. In general, publishers (websites) do not have direct contact with the advertisers but only with the ad network company. In addition, websites (publishers) and ad network companies share the revenue received from the advertiser.

The number of ad network companies have increased at the rate of available publishers (websites) willing to sell inventories (ad spaces).[721] Some examples of popular advertisement network brokers include AddThis, Facebook Audience Networking (FAN), and AdSense (Google).

On the one hand, for publishers the benefit of this broker system is to sell inventories that had not been sold via direct negotiations with advertisers; on the other hand, advertisers also benefit from the system because it scales their

---

717   Chang-Dae Ham, Michelle R Nelson, "The Role of Persuasion Knowledge, Assessment of Benefit and Harm, and Third-Person Perception in Coping with Online Behavioral Advertising" (2016) 62 Computer in Human Behavior 689.

718   Frederik Zuiderveen Borgesius, *Improving Privacy Protection in the Area of Bahavioural Targeting, op. cit.*, p 60; Elizabeth Aguirre et al, "Unraveling the Personalization Paradox: The Effect of Information Collection and Trust-Building Strategies on Online Advertisement Effectiveness" (2015) 91 Journal of Retailing 34, p 40.

719   Howard Beales, "The Value of Behavioral Targeting" (2010) 1 Network Advertising Initiative 1, p 5. Internet Protocol (IP) addresses indicate the location of internet users.

720   Catherine E Tucker, "Social Networks, Personalized Advertising, and Privacy Controls", *op. cit.*, p 555.

721   Anja Lambrecht and Catherine Tucker, "When Does Retargeting Work? Information Specificity in Online Advertising", *op. cit.*, p 566.

campaign, saves time, and offers an aggregated view of the campaign results. In terms of scale, advertisers can buy several inventories from multiple publishers (websites) through a unique ad network broker. It saves time because advertisers can distribute the campaign to one broker instead of dealing separately with different publishers (websites). Finally, the ad network broker provides a global perspective of the clicks and impressions of the campaign across multiple publishers (websites).

There is a continuing dispute for market share between websites (publishers) and ad network brokers. Both compete for advertising revenue. Publishers make more profit when they negotiate directly with advertisers. However, publishers may not have demand to supply all their inventories. As a result, publishers (websites) and advertisers often cooperate and provide functionalities to one another.

The ad network and the publisher, in most part of the cases, own the information about the users. Cookies are placed on the internet user's device by either the website (publisher) or by the ad network company that is allowed primarily by the website publisher to place the cookie, to collect data to build a profile of the particular internet user based on their browsing history for targeting purposes.

Some commercial platforms entirely and exclusively manage their own advertisements. Google and Facebook, for instance, have their own ad network brokers.[722] Moreover, they have an entire platform dedicated only to advertisers in which they provide the tools to create the ads as well as the possibilities to target the users who are going to see them.[723] Both companies have invested enormously over the years in research, capacity development, artificial intelligence, big data structures, data mining, and machine learning studies to improve their know-how on collecting, storing, and processing data. They have implemented sophisticated ways of targeting with all the data collected from their users.

3. DOCUMENTED DISCRIMINATION AGAINST PROTECTED CLASSES

In recent years, numerous studies have focused on understanding how online targeted advertisements work and the consequences in terms of bias and stereotypes.[724] To illustrate problems related to bias and potential illegal discrimination against internet users, I selected four of these studies.

---

[722]   *See* chapter 4.
[723]   *Ibid.*
[724]   Amit Datta, Michael Carl Tschantz and Anupam Datta, "Automated Experiments on Ad Privacy Settings: A Tale of Opacity, Choice and Discrimination" (2015) 1 Proceedings

In 2015, researchers from Carnegie Mellon University created identical fake internet users who self-declared to be male or female in their Google settings.[725] These same fake users visited hundreds of webpages related to employment to make Google ad networking understand that they were looking for a job. Google showed the male group ads from a certain company that promised higher salaries 1,852 times, while this same advertisement was displayed only 318 times to the female group. "A finding suggestive of discrimination."[726]

In 2013, a study developed by a Harvard University researcher demonstrated that when internet users typed typically considered Black-American names on Google's search engine, Google displayed advertisements about law enforcement and crime prevention up to 95% of the time.[727] Alternatively, when she entered typically considered white-American names, Google displayed the same advertisements only 23% of the time. The data collection was probably biased in the process of machine learning.

In 2018, Spanish researchers found that 73% of Facebook users in the European Union, which corresponds to 40% of the overall EU population, were labeled with interests linked to sensitive personal data.[728] This labeling with sensitive personal data, such as political opinion, religious belief, and sexual orientation, was aimed exclusively for targeted online advertising. After extensive research, the authors of the study found that Facebook had approximately 5.5 million ad preferences assigned to more than 4,500 Facebook users. Facebook provides these labels to third-party advertisers interested in advertising on the platform. These preferences were tracked by cookies based on the users' activity online, what they see, which videos they watch, their geographic location, and their personal information provided spontaneously by the users.

Specifically, the researchers demonstrated that Facebook commercially exploits sensitive personal data to target advertising, by running three Facebook advertising campaigns using sensitive aspects, including "religious beliefs" (targeting users with interest in Islam, Judaism, Christianity, Buddhism), "political opinions" (targeting users with interest in communism, anarchism,

---

on Privacy Enhancing Technologies 92; Latanya Sweeney, "Discrimination in Online Ad Delivery" (2013) 56 ACM 44; José González Cabañas, Ángel Cuevas and Rubén Cuevas, "Facebook Use of Sensitive Data for Advertising in Europe" 2018 arXiv preprint arXiv:1802.05030; Paul Barford et al, "Adscape: Harvesting and Analyzing Online Display Ads" [2014] Proceedings of the 23rd International Conference on World Wide Web 597; Bin Liu et al, "AdReveal: Improving Transparency into Online Targeted Advertising" [2013] Proceedings of the 12th ACM Conference on Emerging Networking Experiments and Technologies 12; Till Speicher et al, "Potential for Discrimination in Online Targeted Advertising" (2018) 81 Proceedings of Machine Learning Research 1.

[725] Amit Datta, Michael Carl Tschantz and Anupam Datta, "Automated Experiments on Ad Privacy Settings: A Tale of Opacity, Choice and Discrimination", *op. cit.*, p 92.

[726] *Ibid*, p 93.

[727] Latanya Sweeney, "Discrimination in Online Ad Delivery", *op. cit.*.

[728] José González Cabañas, Ángel Cuevas and Rubén Cuevas, "Facebook Use of Sensitive Data for Advertising in Europe", *op. cit.*, p 10.

radical feminism, socialism) and "sexual orientation" (targeting users with interest in transsexualism or homosexuality). These labels associated to Facebook users were used by the researchers to direct specific advertisements. Ultimately, their ad campaigns reached over 25,000 users with some of the sensitive aspects, and they only spent € 35 for the advertisements. The advertisements were displayed for users in Germany, Spain, France, and Italy.[729]

In 2018, an experiment developed by professors from the London Business School and MIT demonstrated empirically that employment ads for the science, technology, engineering, and mathematics (STEM) sector was shown over 20% more to men than women in 191 countries.[730] The campaign was run on Facebook and targeted at women and men over 18 years old. After crossing different data sets, the researchers had three hypotheses for the discriminatory outcome. First, the algorithm learned to discriminate against women from consumer behavior. Considering women were less prone to click on the advertisement, an algorithm aiming at increasing engagement probability with the ad (click probability) would more likely display the advertisement to men. Second, the algorithm learned to discriminate against women from alternative data sources used to train it. These alternative data sources might have simply expressed a pattern of discrimination against women in different locations. Third, the difference might have been a result of the economics around advertisement delivery. In targeted online advertisement, numerous advertisers compete at the same time to display their campaigns to individuals with particular characteristics (called "same set of eyeballs"). The researchers revealed evidence from different data sources that "on average across the world, female eyeballs are more expensive than male eyeballs." They discovered that the price advertisers pay to display advertisement campaigns to women is more pronounced than ads targeted at men. In short, women are more valuable to the market of targeted advertisements. Ultimately, the researcher concluded that the discriminatory delivery outcome was not intentional. It was a result of the economics of ad delivery.

These four studies present how internet users' data, including their personal features, in addition to their behavior online, determine the advertisements users will be shown. They also show how online targeting can result in discriminatory ad delivery. Profiling and targeting are *per se* discriminatory, if the definition of discrimination as "selecting or distinguishing based on identifiable characteristics" is considered.[731] Profiling and targeting in the advertising context consist of differentiating internet users to direct to them the most suitable ad. Profiling and targeting give advertisers the power to

---

729   *Ibid.*
730   Anja Lambrecht and Catherine Tucker, "Algorithmic Bias? An Empirical Study of Apparent Gender-Based Discrimination in the Display of STEM Career Ads" [2019] Management Sicence 1.
731   Oxford English Dictionary, *Lexico* (June 2019), online: Oxford <https://en.oxforddictionaries.com/definition/discrimination>.

discriminate internet users based on a number of identifiable characteristics, such as personal interests, age, race, gender, location, and behavior, among others. These differentiation practices are not necessarily illegal.

SECTION II. WHEN TARGETING DOES NOT ACCOUNT FOR EQUALITY: LEGAL BOUNDARIES

In the United States and in the EU, Civil Rights Acts, equality laws, and privacy and data protection legislation protect individuals with some demographic aspects against discrimination in advertising.[732] For instance, it is illegal to discriminate based on racial origin when advertising a job offer under the both United States' and the EU's antidiscrimination legal framework.[733] In this context, an advertiser cannot legally target only alleged white internet users to receive a job offer. Moreover, in the EU, data protection laws can be partially mobilized in the fight against online discrimination, because in many cases even collecting data, such as a user's race, for advertising purposes is not legal.[734]

EU law does not regulate advertising **content** directly. Conversely, it imposes obligations on member states through a set of directives concerning misleading advertising, in addition to some provisions regarding advertisements targeted at children[735], some practices related to advertising medicine[736], and tobacco advertisements.[737] This reality is different from online advertisements that make use of internet users' personal data via automated systems. In this case, the EU counts on the General Data Protection Regulation (GDPR), which is directly applied in all EU member states and enforced by national courts, to resolve private and public conflicts. Furthermore, the European Commission has been working to establish boundaries and guidance for a variety of technologies that

---

[732] In Europe, the term data protection is used while data privacy is more common in the United States. To distinguish from the traditional privacy rights, that mainly regards the respect of family life, home and correspondence, I will use in this text the term data protection and data privacy depending on the jurisdiction.

[733] Title VII, 42 U.S.C., subchapter VI, §2000e-3 (b). In the EU, specifically mentioned in the Council Directive 2000/43/EC of 29 June 2000 implementing the principle of equal treatment between persons irrespective of racial or ethnic origin, art 3.

[734] The GDPR establishes limit for profiling (article 21).

[735] Directive 2005/29/EC of the European Parliament and of the Council of 11 May 2005 concerning unfair business to consumer commercial practices in the internal market, and amending Council Directive 84/450/ECC, Directives 97/7/EC, 98/27/EC and 2002/65/EC of the European Parliament and of the Council and Regulation (EC) No 2006/2004 of the European Parliament and of the Council, OJ L 149/22, 11.6.2005.

[736] Directive 2004/27/EC of the European Parliament and of the Council of 31 March 2004 Amending Directive 2001/83/EC on the Community Code Relating to Medicinal Products for Human Use, OJ L 136/34, 30.04.2004.

[737] Directive 2003/33/EC of the European Parliament and of the Council of 26 May 2003 on the Approximation of Laws, Regulations and Administrative Provisions of the Member States Relating to the Advertising and Sponsorship of Tobacco Products, OJ L 152, 20.6.2003.

encompass automated decisions.[738] Ultimately, the Digital Services Act proposal has explicitly ruled on targeted advertising.[739] Beyond protecting privacy, the European data protection legal framework aims to prevent discrimination against individuals by automated systems.

Furthermore, the European Equality Directives, and member states' transposed antidiscrimination laws, provide a legal framework to protect some groups from being excluded from employment offers and from the provision of goods and services because of their protected characteristics, including their gender, ethnic origin, religion or belief, disability, age, or sexual orientation.[740] Since online targeted advertising considers personal characteristics – that can be a protected ground or not – to include or exclude individuals from receiving such offers, this European legal framework could provide guidance on whether certain targeting practices are legal or illegal. The European Equality Directives are particularly relevant to this regulatory direction because they were transposed into domestic law of the member states.[741]

In the United States, federal statutes regulate unfair and deceptive marketing[742] and advertisements aimed at children[743] as well as advertisements for alcohol[744], tobacco[745], and medicine.[746] In addition, the collection of data for targeted advertising purposes is by analogy regulated by the Federal Trade Commission Act (FTC Act) and several Federal Trade Commission's

---

[738] European Commission, Guidelines on Automated Individual Decision Making and Profiling for the Purposes of Regulation 2016/679, (wp251rev.01), revised in August 2018; Brussels, 8.4.2019 COM (2019)168 final. Communication from the Commission to the European Parliament, the Council, the European Economic and Social Committee and the Committee of the Regions: Building Trust in Human Centric Artificial Intelligence; Brussels, 25.4.2018 COM (2018)237 final. Communication from the Commission to the European Parliament, the European Council, the European Economic and Social Committee and the Committee of the Regions: Artificial Intelligence for Europe.

[739] Article 24, 26, 27, 30, Proposal for a Regulation of the European Parliament and of the Council on a Single Market for Digital Services (Digital Services Act) and amending Directive 2000/31/EC. Brussels, 15.12.2020 COM (2020)825 final. Proposal for a Regulation of the European Parliament and of the Council on a Single Market for Digital Services (Digital Services Act) and amending Directive 2000/31/EC.

[740] Race Equality Directive; Employment Equality Directive; Gender Equality Directive; Gender Equal Access to Goods and Services Directive.

[741] Article 288, TFEU. *See* European Network of Legal Experts in Gender Equality and Non-Discrimination, *A comparative analysis of non-discrimination law in Europe 2018* (November 2018), online: European Commission <https://www.equalitylaw.eu/downloads/4804-a-comparative-analysis-of-non-discrimination-law-in-europe-2018-pdf-1-02-mb>; European Network of Legal Experts in Gender Equality and Non-Discrimination, *A comparative analysis of gender equality law in Europe 2018* (January 2019): online: European Commission <https://www.equalitylaw.eu/downloads/4829-a-comparative-analysis-of-gender-equality-law-in-europe-2018-pdf-807-kb>.

[742] Federal Trade Commission Act, 15 U.S.C.

[743] Children's Online Privacy Protection Act (COPPA, 15 U.S.C. §§6501–6506).

[744] Federal Alcohol Administration Act, 27 U.S.C.

[745] Family Smoking Prevention Tobacco Control Act, 21 U.S.C.

[746] Federal Food, Drug, and Cosmetic Act, 21 U.S.C. §301 *et seq.*

guidelines.[747] Contrarily to the EU, laws regulating the protection of personal data – or personally identifiable information[748] – are not overarching but instead are fragmented into several pieces of legislation.[749] Overall, the compromise to protect personally identifiable information is looser in the United States.

At the federal level, the United States counts on a set of statutory laws prohibiting discrimination in the employment, credits and housing sectors. They regulate marketing practices and might fully apply to online advertising.

The following sections contemplate the regulatory possibilities for addressing online targeted advertisements in the United States and in the EU in light of data protection and equality laws.

1. PRIVACY LEGAL FRAMEWORK IN THE UNITED STATES

1.1. REGULATING THE USE OF PERSONALLY IDENTIFIABLE INFORMATION: A FRAGMENTED AND SELF-REGULATORY APPROACH TOWARDS PRIVACY

The United States has sectorial laws to protect personally identifiable information (PII).[750] No federal legislation exists that comprehends privacy and the protection of personally identifiable information from unconsented data collection, misuse, or abuse like the European GDPR.

1.1.1. Fragmented Approach

In the United States, the protection of personal information is enshrined in several federal and state laws, administrative regulations, and specific self-

---

[747] See chapter 3, section II, 1.2.

[748] In the United States, personal data is referred as personally identifiable information in the legal texts and literature.

[749] Esteve Asunción, "The Business of Personal Data: Google, Facebook, and Privacy Issues in the EU and the USA" (2017) 7 International Data Privacy Law 36.

[750] Some legislation related to data protection in the federal level: The Federal Trade Commission Act (FCT Act, 15 U.S.C.§§41–58); Children's Online Privacy Protection Act (COPPA, 15 U.S.C. §§6501–6506); Financial Services Modernization Act (GLB Act, 15 U.S.C. §§6801–6827); Health Insurance Portability and Accountability Act (HIPAA, 42 U.S.C. §§1301 et seq.); Controlling the Assault of Non-Solicited Pornography and Marketing Act (CAN-SPAN Act 15 U.S.C. §§7701–7713 and 18 U.S.C., §1037); the Fair Credit Reporting Act (15 U.S.C., §1681); Electronic Communications Privacy Act (18 U.S.C., §2510); the Computer Fraud and Abuse Act (18 U.S.C., §1030). These statutory laws were enacted prior to significant personal use of the internet. See Shawn Marie Boyne, "Data Protection in the United States" (2018) 66 The American Journal of Comparative Law 299.

regulation guidelines. This legal framework applies to different sectors such as private communications, education, healthcare, and financial organizations.[751]

This fragmented approach leaves some areas that deal with the collection and processing of personally identifiable information unregulated by specific statutes at the federal level.[752] For instance, no statute specifically addresses the practices of data collected by online companies such as ad networks, Facebook or Google.[753] Courts and the Federal Trade Commission have construed the Federal Trade Commission Act (FTC) to address some practices regarding the collection of personal identifiable information for online targeted advertisement.[754] The FTC Act was initially legislated to outlaw unfair practices regarding trade and commerce, and it has no particular provision related to privacy.

Some states, including California, Arizona, Delaware, and Missouri, have passed legislation that addresses some practices related to the use of personally identifiable information by companies, and, consequently, by targeted advertising.[755] The California's Online Privacy Protection Act, for instance, provides that any company, organization, or person that collects personally identifiable information online from Californian residents for commercial purposes should publish the categories of information that it collects. In addition, they must post a privacy policy on their websites or online services.[756] However, the Act does not require users' consent to have their personal data collected.

1.1.2. Defining Personally Identifiable Information

The concept of personally identifiable information (personal data) is as fragmented as the legal framework for data privacy is in the United States.[757] In 2010, the Federal Trade Commission recognized that the blurred distinction

---

751 Shawn Marie Boyne, "Data Protection in the United States" (2018) 66 The American Journal of Comparative Law 299, p 302.

752 Neil Richards, Andrew Serwin and Tyler Blake, "Understanding American Privacy" in Gloria González Fuster, Rosamunde Van Brakel and Paul De Hert (eds), Research Handbook on Privacy and Data Protection Law: Values, Norms and Global Politics (Edward Elgar Publishing 2018) p 22.

753 Some call for a comprehensive federal privacy legislation. See Hayes Hagan, "How to Protect Consumer Data? Leave It to the Consumer Protection Agency: FTC Rulemaking as a Path to Federal Cybersecurity Regulation" (2019) 2019 Columbia Business Law Review 735; Jaqueline May Tom, "A Simple Compromise: The Need for a Federal Data Breach Notification Law" (2010) 84 St. John's Law Review 1569.

754 See chapter 3, section II, 1.2. (FTC) and 1.3.

755 Daniel Castro, "Benefits and Limitations of Industry Self-Regulation for Online Behavioral Advertising" [2011] The Information Technology & Innovation Foundation 1.

756 The Online Privacy Protection Act of 2003, California Business & Professions Code §§22575–22579.

757 See Paul M Schwartz and Daniel Solove, "The PII Problem: Privacy and a New Concept of Personally Identifiable Information" (2011) 86 New York University Law Review 1814.

between personally identifiable information and anonymous or de-identified information can harm consumer's privacy rights.[758]

In that sense, the Video Privacy Protection Act (VPPA) defines personally identifiable information as data that "identifies a person."[759] The Gramm-Leach-Bliley Act (GLBA), which regulates financial services, defines it as "nonpublic personal information."[760] The statute does not define nonpublic, but the term is largely understood to reach information not found within the public domain.[761] The problem of this approach is that it excludes data that can identify a person. A name or address identify a person, but can be found on the public domain in telephone books, for example. The Children's Online Privacy Protection Act (COPPA), which regulates the collection and use of children's information by online services, defines personally identifiable information as first and last name, physical address, social security number, telephone number, e-mail address, and any other identifier that the Federal Trade Commission determines that permits the physical or online contacting of a specific individual.[762] The Federal Trade Commission has extended the concept of personally identifiable information under the COPPA to a "persistent identifier, such as a customer number held in a cookie or a processor serial number, where such identifier is associated with individually identifiable information."[763]

1.2. LEGAL FRAMEWORK FOR ONLINE TARGETED ADVERTISEMENT: OPTIONAL PRIVACY

1.2.1. The Role of the Federal Trade Commission

The collection of personally identifiable information to online targeted advertising purposes is currently addressed in light of the FTC Act.[764] Although the Act does not specifically mention privacy, it prohibits unfair and deceptive practices towards consumers.[765] The concept of unfairness and deceptiveness

---

[758] Federal Trade Commission, *Protecting Consumer Privacy in an Era of Rapid Change* (December 2010), online: FTC <https://www.ftc.gov/sites/default/files/documents/reports/federal-trade-commission-bureau-consumer-protection-preliminary-ftc-staff-report-protecting-consumer/101201privacyreport.pdf>; or alternatively Paul M Schwartz and Daniel Solove, "The PII Problem: Privacy and a New Concept of Personally Identifiable Information" (2011) 86 New York University Law Review 1814, p 1828.

[759] Video Privacy Protection Act of 1988, 18 U.S.C. §2710.

[760] Gramm-Leach-Bliley Act of 1999, 15 U.S.C. §6809 (4)(A)(2006).

[761] Paul M Schwartz and Daniel Solove, "The PII Problem: Privacy and a New Concept of Personally Identifiable Information", *op. cit.*, p. 1830.

[762] Children's Online Privacy Protection Act of 1998, 15 U.S.C, §6501(8)(A)-(E) and (8)(F).

[763] 16 C.F.R. §312.2(2011).

[764] FTC Act, 15 U.S.C., §§41–58.

[765] FTC Act, 15 U.S.C., §§45.

are broadly defined.[766] Practices that are likely to mislead a reasonable consumer have been interpreted as deceptive and unfair.[767] Breaching the privacy of personally identifiable information when companies have privacy terms of services has been outlawed under the concept of unfair and deceptive actions.[768] Failing to give sufficient motive for privacy invasive practices has been also considered a deceptive practice.[769]

The Federal Trade Commission is currently the federal agency responsible for conducting investigation and enforcing the FTC Act in the context of privacy issues and online advertising.[770] The commission was not conceived to enforce privacy policies just as the FTC Act was not enacted to deal with personally identifiable information privacy.[771] The commission was created to investigate companies engaged in unfair and deceptive practices.[772] However, since the 1990s, the Federal Trade Commission has enforced companies' privacy policies through its authority to enforce the FTC Act against unfair and deceptive trade practices.[773] Scholars highlight that the commission started enforcing privacy on the internet when the European Data Protection Directive was about to come into effect in 1995.[774] This European law required the United States to have adequate privacy protection over personal data transferred from Europe to the United States. By this time, no authority was competent to ensure privacy online in the United States, and therefore, to ensure compliance with the Safe Harbor agreement; therefore, the Federal Trade Commission took responsibility for it.[775]

The commission only brings action against companies that violate their own privacy policies, because the FTC Act does not require that companies must have

---

[766]   To assess unfairness courts and the FTC must demonstrate three criteria: [the practice] "(1) causes or is likely to cause substantial injury to consumers (2) which is not reasonable avoidable by consumers themselves and not (3) outweighed by countervailing benefits to consumers". See FTC Act, 15 U.S.C. §45. See Gautam Hans, "Privacy Policies, Terms of Service, and FTC Enforcement: Broadening Unfairness Regulation for a New Era" (2012) 19 Michigan Telecommunications and Technology Law Review 163, p 172.

[767]   Compilation of cases in Daniel J Solove and Woodrow Hartzog, "The FTC and the New Common Law of Privacy", op. cit., p 628–629.

[768]   Ibid.

[769]   Ibid.

[770]   Woodrow Hartzog and Daniel J Solove, "The Scope and Potential of FTC Data Protection" (2015) 83 The George Washington Law Review 2230 p 2247.

[771]   Federal Trade Commission, Protecting Consumer Privacy in an Era of Rapid Change, op. cit., p 69–79.

[772]   "The Commission's authority cover virtually every sector of the economy, except for certain excluded industries, such as common carrier activities and the business of insurance, Airlines and banks". Federal Trade Commission, How to Make Effective Disclosures in Digital Advertising (March 2013), online: FTC <https://www.ftc.gov/system/files/documents/plain-language/bus41-dot-com-disclosures-information-about-online-advertising.pdf>.

[773]   Daniel J Solove and Woodrow Hartzog, "The FTC and the New Common Law of Privacy", op. cit., p 585.

[774]   Chris Jay Hoofnagle, Federal Trade Commission Privacy Law and Policy (Cambridge University Press 2016), p 156.

[775]   Ibid.

or disclose privacy policies to inform users how their personable identifiable information will be used.[776] However, the understanding exists that if a company voluntarily has privacy policies in its terms and services, they must comply with it under the risk of deceiving its customers.[777] Even if no statutory law requires it, nearly every large online company voluntarily has privacy policies.[778] With this respect, the FTC has already decided that companies violated the FTC Act when they changed their privacy policy without providing data subjects a chance to opt out of the new policy.[779] Most cases regarding internet user's privacy have resulted in settlement agreements and consent orders, which serve as a guide to other online companies' privacy practices.[780] The non-respect of the commission order may result in a monetary civil penalty.[781] Many scholars argue that that self-regulation is not the most effective way to protect internet users against data misuse.[782]

1.2.2. Optional Privacy and Online Targeted Advertising

Online targeted advertising is an allowed practice according to the Federal Trade Commission's understanding of the FTC Act.[783] The Commission has overtly stated that several types of targeted advertising present minimal privacy intrusion and are consistent with consumer expectations.[784] Moreover, they are likely to benefit the consumers in their online experience. In this sense, when an internet user frequently accesses retailing websites, targeted ads related to the same retail website are expected and would not represent intrusion, for example.

In 1999 the Federal Trade Commission organized its first public workshop on online profiling – which was directly related to targeted advertising.[785] In 2000, in a report submitted to the American Congress, the FTC admitted that online

---

776 FTC Act, §§15 U.S.C.
777 Daniel J Solove and Woodrow Hartzog, "The FTC and the New Common Law of Privacy", *op. cit.*, p 588.
778 For example: Google, *Google Privacy Policy* (June 2019), online: Google <https://policies.google.com>; Facebook, *Data Policy* (June 2019), online: Facebook <https://www.facebook.com/full_data_use_policy>.
779 *FTC v Facebook.Inc*, docket no. C-4365 (2011); *Google Inc.*, docket no. C-4336 (2012).
780 Daniel J Solove and Woodrow Hartzog, "The FTC and the New Common Law of Privacy", *op. cit.*, p 585.
781 FTC Act, 15 U.S.C., §45 (l).
782 Gordon Hull, "Successful Failure: What Foucault Can Teach Us About Privacy Self-Management in a World of Facebook and Bid Data" (2015) 17 Ethics and Information Technology 89.
783 Federal Trade Commission, *FTC Staff Report: Self-Regulatory Principles for Online Behavioral Advertising* (February 2009), online: FTC <https://www.ftc.gov/sites/default/files/documents/reports/federal-trade-commission-staff-report-self-regulatory-principles-online-behavioral-advertising/p085400behavadreport.pdf > p 4–5.
784 *Ibid.*
785 Siona Listokin, "Does Industry Self-Regulation of Consumer Data Privacy Work?" (2017) 15 IEEE Security & Privacy 92.

profiling and more specifically targeted advertising had several advantages, including avoiding waste in advertising money by selecting individuals who were potential consumers, improving consumer's online experience by preventing users from being exposed to the same ads, and helping websites maintain their activities free of charge for the users.[786]

However, by the time the report was sent to the American Congress, the FTC slightly shifted its position about online profiling by expressing particular concerns about the misuse of internet users' personally identifiable information in the determination of prices for goods and services.[787] The Commission feared that online companies could "web line"[788] users notably in the real estate and financial markets.[789]

In 2009, the FTC launched the first guidelines for online targeted advertising: the FTC Self-Regulatory Principles for Online Behavioral Advertising.[790] The principles recommended, for the first time, that websites should notify their users about their data collection practices related to online behavioral advertising. Moreover, it suggested that internet users should be able to opt out of these practices. The self-regulatory principles also recommended that websites should obtain expressed consent only before using sensitive personally identifiable information[791], which is defined in the same document as financial data, data about children, health information, precise geographic location information, and social security numbers.[792] Therefore, consent was not specifically required for collecting and processing data such as gender, race, nationality, age, political beliefs, and innumerous others that were not considered sensitive.

In general, individuals do not have to provide their consent before companies collect and process their personally identifiable information for commercial purposes. The FTC Act does not have any requirement in that regard. However, for targeted advertisement purposes, the Federal Trade Commission has developed the above principles advising companies to require consent when collecting sensitive personal information. In summary, personally identifiable information collected for targeted advertising other than the five sensitive types specified above does not need the user's consent to be collected and processed.

---

786   *Ibid.*
787   Steven C Bennett, "Regulating Online Behavioral Advertising", *op. cit.*, p 906.
788   Weblining refers to the practice of redlining. The practice of redlining consists in denying products and services to inhabitants of particular neighborhoods. These neighborhoods were normally marked with a red line on a map.
789   Steven C Bennett, "Regulating Online Behavioral Advertising", *op. cit.*, p 906.
790   Federal Trade Commission, *FTC Staff Report: Self-Regulatory Principles for Online Behavioral Advertising* (February 2009), online: FTC <https://www.ftc.gov/sites/default/files/documents/reports/federal-trade-commission-staff-report-self-regulatory-principles-online-behavioral-advertising/p085400behavadreport.pdf >.
791   "Companies should collect sensitive data for behavioral advertising only after they obtain affirmative express consent from the consumer to receive such advertising". *Ibid* p 39.
792   *Ibid,* p 44.

Furthermore, internet users do not have the right to access their personally identifiable data collected by companies nor the right to request the deletion of their data.[793] To conclude, the FTC's self-regulatory principles are voluntary in nature. In other words, they are optional and not legally binding.

1.3. REGULATING TRACKING COOKIES

1.3.1. Optional Privacy

Tracking cookies do not identify internet users by their names, but alternatively they use an alphanumerical code that is installed in the users' devices. Is such identification considered personally identifiable information? The answer cannot be found in any statute. Cookies are neither regulated nor defined as personally identifiable information by any federal statute. The advertising industry has tried to claim that tracking cookies do not violate internet user's privacy.[794] Moreover, given that cookies are not defined as sensitive personally identifiable information by the FTC's self-regulatory principles on behavioral advertisement, companies are not required to request consent from their users to implement cookies on their devices. Companies are only advised to request consent for tracking cookies that collect sensitive personally identifiable information, being financial data, data about children, health information, precise geographic location information, and social security numbers.[795]

The FTC's self-regulatory principles on behavioral advertising recommend that websites disclose their data collection practices related to online behavioral advertising when they rely on the use of cookies. Moreover, the principles advise companies to obtain affirmative expressed consent from consumers before they change their privacy policies regarding cookies. Companies are also advised to disclose that consumers can opt out of tracking cookies and to provide a mechanism for opting out. Again, these principles are not binding. They are only optional. The Federal Trade Commission has engaged in regulatory enforcement and private class action lawsuits against companies that failed to disclose or misrepresented their use of tracking cookies, when **they promised** to do so in their private policies, under the charge of deceptive practices and, therefore, violation of the FTC Act.[796]

In some enforcement actions, the Commission has gone further to its "broken promises approach" concerning tracking cookies to adopt a concept of privacy more related to transparency. In a 2009 case, the Commission concluded

---

[793]   FTC Act §§15 U.S.C.
[794]   *See* Paul M Schwartz and Daniel Solove, "The PII Problem: Privacy and a New Concept of Personally Identifiable Information", *op. cit.*, p 1859.
[795]   *See* above.
[796]   *See* section chapter 4, section II (*Google*).

that a particular online company had undertaken unfair trade practices by failing to disclose to which extent it had tracked its consumers.[797] The privacy license agreement contained too obscured language.

Moreover, the Federal Computer Fraud and Abuse Act (CFAA)[798], the Electronic Communications Privacy Act (ECPA)[799], and the Video Privacy Protection Act[800] have been mobilized to bring legal claims against the use of cookies for behavioral advertising, where the cookies enabled deep inspection of the computer on which they were placed without proper consent.[801] However, courts have been resistant to interpret existing statutes enacted before the invention of cookies or enacted for other technologies in a manner that applies to cookies.[802]

1.3.2. Self-Regulatory Initiatives

In addition to the FTC Act and the Federal Trade Commission principles and enforcement practices, industry groups have also released several self-regulatory guidelines that are not legally binding but are considered best practices to be followed in the online advertising industry.[803] These guidelines largely mirror the Federal Trade Commission's principles.

The Network Advertising Initiative (NAI), founded in 1999, is exclusively composed of third-party digital advertising companies. The organization has a self-regulatory code of conduct[804] that requires transparency, an opt-in choice before sensitive information is collected and processed for behavioral advertising, and reasonable security provisions. The NAI may impose sanctions and/or revocation of the membership for those who do not respect the code of conduct, and, ultimately, may give notice to the Federal Trade Commission for non-compliance. In that same sense, the Digital Advertising Alliance (DAA)[805]

---

[797] Complaint 13–14, Sears Holdings Mgmt. Corp., FTC, Docket No C-4264 (31 August 2009). Same way at: FTC v EchoMetrix, Inc. No CV10–5516 (E.D.N.Y Nov 30, 2010).

[798] Computer Fraud and Abuse Act (CFAA), 18 U.S.C. §1030, 1986.

[799] Electronic Communications Privacy Act (ECPA), 18 U.S.C. §2510, 1986.

[800] Video Privacy Protection Act (VPPA), 18 U.S.C. §2710, 1988.

[801] See Eric C Bosset and others, "Private Actions Challenging Online Data Collection Practices Are Increasing: Assessing the Legal Landscape" (2011) 23 Intellectual Property & Technology Law Journal 3; Michael R Siebecker, "Cookies and the Common Law: Are Internet Advertisers Trespassing on Our Computers?" (2003) 76 Southern California Law Review 893.

[802] "Mortensen v. Bresnan Commc'ns LLC, No. 1:10-cv-0013-RFC (D. Mon.) (filed Feb. 16, 2010); Deering v. CenturyTel, Inc., No. 10-cv-00063-RFC (D. Mon.) and Kirch v. Embarq Mgmt. Co., No. 2:10-cv-02047-JAR-GLR (D. Kan.) referred by Eric C Bosset and others, "Private Actions Challenging Online Data Collection Practices Are Increasing: Assessing the Legal Landscape" (2011), op. cit..

[803] Andrew Serwin, "The Federal Trade Commission and Privacy: Defining Enforcement and Encouraging the Adoption of Best Practices" (2011) 48 San Diego Law Review 809.

[804] Network Advertising Initiative, NAI Code of Conduct: Enforcement (May 2018), online: NAI <https://www.networkadvertising.org/sites/default/files/nai_code2018.pdf>.

[805] Digital Advertising Alliance, About (June 2019), online: DAA <https://digitaladvertisingalliance.org>.

has also developed principles of transparency and control for data used across devices and self-regulatory principles for online behavioral advertising. The DAA's members include major online players, such as Google, Amazon, LinkedIn, Netflix, and Yahoo!.

These self-regulation measures and the Federal Trade Commission enforcement actions offer the privacy framework for collecting and processing personally identifiable information in the online advertising industry in the United States.[806]

Scholars have stressed that the fragmented privacy laws in the United States do not provide enough protection against the misuse of personally identifiable information.[807] The processing of personally identifiable information, the creation of internet users' profiles, and, consequently, targeted advertisements are eased by the lack of explicit legal requirement for consent for many types of personal data.[808]

2. DATA PROTECTION LEGAL FRAMEWORK IN THE EUROPEAN UNION

2.1. THE USE OF PERSONAL DATA: OVERARCHING AND MANDATORY LEGAL APPROACH TO ENFORCE DATA PROTECTION AND PREVENT DISCRIMINATION

In contrast to the United States, the EU has comprehensive legislation with a set of general principles related to personal data protection.[809] The overarching data protection framework aims not only to ensure privacy but also to prevent discrimination by automated systems. In this sense, first, the European Union and the member states of the Council of Europe have long settled a tradition of regulatory responses to protect personal data. Second, the legal protection of personal data to specifically avoid discrimination against citizens by automated systems has been the subject of increasing concern from the EU and Council of Europe. The term "discrimination" was recently inserted and stressed in foundational legal texts addressing the protection of personal data.[810]

---

[806] Woodrow Hartzog and Daniel J Solove, "The Scope and Potential of FTC Data Protection", *op. cit.*, p 2269.

[807] Paul M Schwartz and Daniel Solove, "The PII Problem: Privacy and a New Concept of Personally Identifiable Information", *op. cit.*, p 1288.

[808] Gregory Voss and Kimberly A Houser, "GDPR: The End of Google and Facebook or a New Paradigm in Data Privacy?" (2018) 25 Richmond Journal of Law & Technology 1; Andrew Serwin, "The Federal Trade Commission and Privacy: Defining Enforcement and Encouraging the Adoption of Best Practices" (2011) 48 San Diego Law Review 809.

[809] *See* European Union Agency for Fundamental Rights, *Handbook on European Data Protection Law, op. cit.*.

[810] The texts of the Data Protection Directive or the original text of the Council of Europe Convention for the Protection of Individuals with regard to Automatic Processing of Personal Data did not explicitly mentioned discrimination. Directive 95/46/EC of the European

2.1.1. Personal Data as a Fundamental Right

The European Union recognizes personal data protection as a fundamental right.[811] The Charter of Fundamental Rights of the European Union provides that everyone has the right to the protection of their personal data, and personal data processing is only allowed if the data controller has a legal basis for processing it.[812] The Council of Europe Convention for the Protection of Individuals with regard to Automatic Processing of Personal Data, named Convention 108, was adopted in 1980[813] and served as a basis for the European Data Protection Directive[814] that came into effect in 1995. Neither the original Convention 108 nor the European Data Protection Directive specifically mentioned the risks of discrimination against citizens when automated systems process personal data. More recently, however, the updated Convention 108+ has raised concerns that processing sensitive data may present risks for individuals, "notably a risk of discrimination."[815] With this respect, the Council of Europe Guidelines on Artificial Intelligence and Data Protection also stress the risk of discrimination against individuals posed by automated systems. The guidelines urge AI developers to implement in their systems a human right by design approach and avoid "any potential biases, including unintentional or hidden, and the risk of discrimination" against data subjects.[816] In addition, the document guides policymakers to encourage cooperation between data protection supervisory authorities and antidiscrimination bodies.[817] Ultimately, the General Data Protection Regulation, which was enacted in 2016 and entered into force on May 25, 2018, provides that discrimination is a risk to the rights and freedoms of natural persons that may result from personal data processing, including

---

Parliament and of the Council of 24 October 1995 on the protection of individuals with regard to the processing of personal data and the free movement of such data, OJ L 281, 23.11.1995, (Data Protection Directive).

[811]   GDPR, recital (1); The Charter of Fundamental Rights of the European Union, Article 8 (1); the Treaty on the Functioning of the European Union (TFEU), Article 16 (1). On the right to privacy, *see* also Charter of Fundamental Rights of the European Union, Article 7; European Convention on Human Rights, Article 8.

[812]   Charter of Fundamental Rights of the European Union, art. 8 (1) and (2).

[813]   The Convention has been modernized with the adoption of an amending protocol: Protocol CETS No 233. The aim was to reinforce the protection of privacy in the digital environment. The protocol preserves the general and flexible aspect of the Convention and enhances its potential as a universal instrument of data protection law.

[814]   Directive 95/46/EC of the European Parliament and of the Council of 24 October 1995 on the protection of individuals with regard to the processing of personal data and the free movement of such data, OJ L 281, 23.11.1995, at 31–50 (Data Protection Directive).

[815]   Convention 108+ for the Protection of Individuals with Regard to the Processing of Personal Data, art. 6 (2).

[816]   T-PD(2019)01, Consultative Committee of the Convention for the Protection of Individuals with Regard to Automatic Processing of Personal Data, Convention 108, *Guideline on Artificial Intelligence and Data Protection, Guidance for Developers, Manufacturers and Service Providers* (January 2019), online: COE <https://rm.coe.int/guidelines-on-artificial-intelligence-and-data-protection/168091f9d8>.

[817]   *Ibid*, p 3.

profiling.[818] In this regard, the Article 29 Working Party (WP29) issued guidelines on profiling, stressing that the practice can perpetuate existing stereotypes, social segregation, and unjustified discrimination.[819]

2.1.2. Defining Personal Data

The GDPR comprehensively defines personal data as "any information relating to an identified or identifiable natural person."[820] The information can encompass a name, an identification number, location data, an online identifier, or aspects related to the physical, physiological, genetic, mental, economic, cultural, or social identity of that natural person.[821] For instance, pseudonymous identifiers[822], IP addresses, and tracking cookies are defined as personal data. Among the general concepts of personal data, the GDPR specifies that processing *special categories* of personal data is *a priori* prohibited, and this data should only be processed after explicit consent from the data subject.[823] Special categories of personal data comprise data disclosing racial or ethnic origin, political opinions, religious beliefs, philosophical beliefs, trade union membership, genetic data, biometric data for the purpose of uniquely identifying a natural person, data concerning health, and data concerning a natural person's sex life or sexual orientation.[824] The compromise of the EU on protecting sensitive data is so strong that the GDPR explicitly allows member states to fully prohibit the processing this kind of data, even in the case of explicit consent.[825]

Data defined as personal by the GDPR is often collected for targeted advertising purposes. The Article 29 Working Party has provided that behavioral targeting commonly encompasses personal data processing. When a company uses data to single out a person to target an advertisement, these data should be considered personal data.[826]

2.2. DIGITAL PROFILING

The GDPR definition of profiling is inspired by the Council of Europe's explanation that profiling may involve three different phases including (i)

---

[818]   Recital 75, GDPR.
[819]   WP25, *Guidelines on Automated Individual Decision Making and Profiling for the Purposes of Regulation 2016/679* (February 2018), online: European Commission <https://ec.europa.eu/newsroom/article29/item-detail.cfm?item_id=612053> p 5–6.
[820]   Art 4 (1), GDPR.
[821]   Article 4 (1), GDPR.
[822]   Recital 26, GDPR.
[823]   Art 9 (2), GDPR.
[824]   Art 9 (1), GDPR.
[825]   Art 9 (2)(a), GDPR.
[826]   This view is supported by Frederik Zuiderveen Borgesius, "Singling Out People Without Knowing Their Names: Behavioural Targeting, Pseudonymous Data, and the New Data Protection Regulation", (2016) 32 Computer Law Security Review 256 p 257.

personal data collection, (ii) automated analysis to identify correlations, and (iii) application of the correlation to an individual to identify characteristics of present or future behavior.[827] The GDPR defines profiling as any kind of automated processing of personal data used to evaluate particular personal aspects to specifically *analyze* or *predict* a "natural person's performance at work, economic situation, health, personal preferences, interests, reliability, behavior, location or movements."[828] The GDPR applies to profiling and therefore to targeted advertising practices because they presuppose the collection, storage, and processing of personal data.[829]

2.3. LEGAL FRAMEWORK FOR ONLINE TARGETED ADVERTISEMENT: PRIVACY AND NON-DISCRIMINATION

The approach in the EU towards targeted advertising greatly diverges from the United States.[830] Profiling and targeted advertising are legal as long as companies meet all the GDPR principles and have legal grounds for processing personal data. The GDPR is based on six sets of principles that must guide profiling and should therefore be applicable to any targeted advertising practice: (1) lawfulness, fairness, and transparency[831]; (2) legitimacy of purposes[832]; (3) data minimization[833]; (4) accuracy[834]; (5) time storage limitation[835]; and (6) integrity and confidentiality.[836] These principles are rooted in the Fair Information Practices (FIPs), which were the core of the previous regulatory framework of the Data Protection Directive.[837]

---

[827] Council of Europe Recommendation CM/Rec (2010)13, and WP25, *Guidelines on Automated Individual Decision Making and Profiling for the Purposes of Regulation 2016/679, op. cit.*.

[828] Art 4 (4), GDPR.

[829] When companies use cookies to monitor users' data, the Directive 2002/58/EC also applies (the Directive of the European Parliament and of the Council of 12 July 2002 concerning the processing of personal data and the protection of privacy in the electronic communication sector, OJ L 201, 31.7.2002, p 37–47. Frederik Zuiderveen Borgesius, *Improving Privacy Protection in the Area of Behavioural Targeting, op. cit.*.

[830] Philip Yannella, "The Differing US and EU Regulatory Responses to Rise in Algorithmic Profiling" (2018) 33 Forum Committee on Communications Law American Bar Association 19.

[831] Art. 5 (1)(a), GDPR. Personal data must be processed in compliance with the GDPR and other applicable data protection laws.

[832] Art. 5(1)(b), GDPR.

[833] Art. 5(1)(c), GDPR.

[834] Art. 5(1)(d), GDPR.

[835] Art. 5 (1)(e), GDPR.

[836] Art. 5 (1)(f), GDPR.

[837] These FIPs are similar to the ones contained in the US Privacy Act of 1974 (5 U.S.C. §552a). They are also similar to the previous and updated OECD "Guidelines on the Protection of Privacy and Transborder Flows of Personal Data" in 1980.

The requirement that companies should follow lawfulness, fairness, and transparency when creating profiles for targeted advertising is fundamental for addressing discrimination. The methods of profiling are not commonly visible to internet users. Moreover, the creation of profiles often implies data inferred about internet users. Even when users spontaneously provide their data, they are not necessarily aware that the data will be used for profiling purposes. First, the concept of lawfulness requires that companies comply with antidiscrimination laws when processing any personal data. Second, transparency compels companies to make internet users aware of what kind of data are collected about them and for which purpose. Moreover, the principle of transparency requires companies to make data subjects informed about the logic involved in the processing. In this sense, companies should provide individuals with concise, transparent, intelligible, and easily accessible information about the processing of their personal data.[838] If companies fully comply with their data protection obligations, internet users will be given the possibility to understand, for instance, what kind of personal data were used and determinant to expose them to certain targeted advertising content. Third, beyond being lawful and transparent, profiling and, therefore, targeted advertising, must be fair. The concept of fairness is correlated with avoidance of discrimination by the WP29. The advisory body recommends that fair profiling cannot have a discriminatory outcome by excessively targeting individuals and denying them access to employment opportunities, for instance.[839]

Additionally, legitimate purpose means that data should only be collected for specific objectives and cannot be processed in a way that is inconsistent with these objectives. Vague purposes are not acceptable, such as the promotion of consumer satisfaction or improvement of the quality of the service.[840] Thus, when companies use personal data for targeting advertisements, they must be clear about this when they inform internet users. In this sense, the principle of data minimization requires that companies should only collect and process data that are useful for legitimate purposes. Companies cannot, according to the principle of data minimization, collect data only because they could be useful in the future.[841]

Furthermore, accuracy should be considered at all levels of profiling, including collecting data, analyzing data, building a profile for an individual, and

---

[838] GDPR, art. 12 (1). In addition, Article 29 Data Protection Working Party, Guideline on Transparency Under Regulation 2016/679 WP260, (November 2017), online: European commission <http://ec.europa.eu/newsroom/just/document.cfm?doc_id=48850>.

[839] *Ibid*, p 10. Also, *see* Michael Veale and Lilian Edwards, "Clarity, Surprises, and Further Questions in the Article 29 Working Party Draft Guidance on Automated Decision-Making and Profiling" (2018) 34 Computer Law & Security Review 398.

[840] Michael Veale and Lilian Edwards, "Clarity, Surprises, and Further Questions in the Article 29 Working Party Draft Guidance on Automated Decision-Making and Profiling" (2018) 34 Computer Law & Security Review 398.

[841] *Ibid*, p 78.

applying a profile to make a decision that impacts the individual.[842] When data are not accurate, the profile will be flawed and may lead to incorrect predictions about the data subject. Companies must proactively ensure that data subjects have the possibility to correct their data in case it is not accurate. Moreover, the requirement to limit the storage time means that personal data identifying internet users shall only be kept for the amount of time that is strictly necessary to achieve the aims for which the data was collected and processed. Ultimately, companies should guarantee the security of personal data against unauthorized and unlawful processing, accidental loss, and destruction and damage to meet the requirements of confidentiality and integrity.

In addition to the six principles that must be met by companies, the GDPR provides six legal grounds on which profiling is legal.[843] In the case of targeted advertising, the legal ground for legal profiling is valid consent.[844] Valid consent requires a clear indication of intention. Furthermore, companies cannot obtain valid consent by implementing an opt-out system in which failing to oppose it leads to consent. Additionally, the terms "specific" and "informed" do not allow unclear consent requests, such as "to use your data for commercial purposes." Rather, the data processor/platform must state that it uses one's personal data for targeted advertising purposes. Furthermore, Article 7(2) of the GDPR requires that consent must be "clearly distinguishable from the other matters, in an intelligible and easily accessible form, using clear and plain language." Consequently, consent requests cannot be required in small clauses of a data policy document. For tracking purposes, websites normally make a box pop out, requiring user consent for data collection and processing. Finally, consent for processing data does not exempt the processor from the GDPR fair practice principles such as transparency, fairness, legitimate purposes, data minimization, accuracy, time storage limitation, integrity, and confidentiality.[845]

Currently, online companies have different strategies to require user consent for online tracking. Some websites use tracking walls, which are barriers that internet users can overcome only if they consent to the tracking policies of the website. Tracking walls are ultimately controversial under the GDPR's

---

[842] GDPR, art. 5(1) d.

[843] For consent, GDPR art 4(11), 6(1), 7, and recs 32, 33 and 40 to 47: (1) unambiguous consent of data subject; (2) necessity due to a contract with data subject; (3) compliance with a legal requirement; (5) protection of the life of a data subject; (5) necessity of accomplishing public tasks; (6) legitimate interests.

[844] Hunton & Williams LLO, *Centre for Information Policy Leadership GDPR Implementation Project, Recommendations for Implementing Transparency, Consent and Legitimate Interest under the GDPR* (May 2017), online: IOP <https://www.informationpolicycentre.com/uploads/5/7/1/0/57104281/cipl_recommendations_on_transparency_consent_and_legitimate_interest_under_the_gdpr_-19_may_2017-c.pdf>; Also, regarding the previous Directive, *see* Article 29 Working Party, Opinion 03/2013 on purpose limitation, WP 203 (April 2013), online: EC <https://ec.europa.eu/justice/article-29/documentation/opinion-recommendation/files/2013/wp203_en.pdf> p 46.

[845] GDPR, art 4(11), 6(1), 7, and recitals 32, 33, 42 and 43 for consent.

requirement of freely given consent.[846] In addition, some websites only enable users to have access if they accept their cookie policies.[847]

Finally, aside from the GDPR, self-regulatory initiatives aim to preserve consumer privacy. These initiatives provide information to consumers about the practices involving the collection and processing of their personal data. For instance, the European Interactive Digital Advertising Alliance (EDAA) was founded by a European coalition representing several actors in the industry, including advertisers, the advertising agency sector, the direct marketing sector, and the media sector.[848] The Alliance's main purpose is to assess and label companies engaged in online behavioral advertising with the OBA icon in all Europe. The OBA icon is an interactive symbol usually displayed on top of an ad that links consumers to the website youronlinechoices.eu. In this website, consumers can find accessible information about the practice of online behavioral advertising as well as their rights to exercise informed choice about it. The Alliance also provides its guiding principles that are established in the Interactive Advertising Bureau Europe OBA Framework (IAB Europe)[849] and the Best Practice Recommendation for Online Behavioral Advertising of the European Advertising Standards Alliance.[850]

2.4. DIGITAL SERVICES ACT: FURTHER REQUIREMENTS FOR TARGETED ADVERTISING

The Digital Services Act will establish new accountability rules for online platforms and their targeted advertising practices in the European Union in the

---

[846] See generally on Do Not Track and European law: Frederik Zuiderveen Borgesius, J Van Hoboken, K Irion, M Rozendaal, "An Assessment of the Commission's Proposal on Privacy and Electronic Communications" (June 2017), online: Directorate-General for Internal Policies, Policy Department Citizen's Rights and Constitutional Affairs <https://ssrn.com/abstract=2982290>.

[847] Frederik Zuiderveen Borgesius et al., Tracking Walls, Take-It-or-Leave-It Choices, the GDPR, and the ePrivacy Regulation, *op. cit.*, p 353.

[848] EDAA, *European Interactive Digital Advertising Alliance* (June 2019), online: edaa <https://www.edaa.eu/about/>.

[849] The framework consists on seven principles: "notice, user choice over online behavioral advertising, data security, sensitive segmentation, education, compliance and enforcement programs, review". *See* IAB, *IAB Europe EU Framework for Online Behavioural Advertising* (April 2011), online: IAB <https://www.edaa.eu/wp-content/uploads/2012/10/2013–11–11-IAB-Europe-OBA-Framework_.pdf>.

[850] The document relies on five principles: notice, user choice, sensitive segmentation (which forbids creating segments that are specifically designed to target children, and advises that advertisers seeking to use sensitive personal data for targeted advertising have to obtain prior explicit consent from the internet user), compliance and enforcement, and review. EASA, *Best Practice Recommendation on Online Bahavioural Advertising* (October 2016), online: EASA <www.easa-alliance.org/sites/default/files/EASA%20Best%20Practice%20Recommendation%20on%20Online%20Behavioural%20Advertising_0.pdf>.

near future.[851] In addition to personal data processing and antidiscrimination law requirements, companies operating online targeted advertising will have to comply with transparency and risk management obligations.

The proposal for the Digital Services Act requires that online platforms that display advertisements on their services must ensure that users are fully aware that what they see is an advertisement, that users are fully aware about the natural or legal person who finances the advertisement, and, most importantly for the purpose of this manuscript, that users must have "clear, meaningful, and uniform information about the parameters used to determine the recipient to whom the advertisement is displayed."[852] This last measure may present positive impact on the fight against discrimination in online targeted advertising, considering users and interested stakeholders will have access to the criteria used to include or exclude users from receiving a certain offer based on their demographic aspect, including protected ones related to ethnic origin, sex, and age data. Amendments to the original proposal suggest that very large platforms must inform users whether a certain advertisement "was intended to be displayed to one or more particular groups of recipients of the service and if so, the main parameters used for that purpose including any parameters used to exclude particular groups."[853] Users may also be given the possibility to modify these parameters. In this case, very large online platforms should make available at least one parameter that is not based on profiling.[854]

---

[851] Proposal for a Regulation of the European Parliament and of the Council on a Single Market for Digital Services (Digital Services Act) and amending Directive 2000/31/EC. COM/2020/825 final; and European Parliament, *Amendments Adopted by the European Parliament on 20 January 2022 on the Proposal for a Regulation of the European Parliament and of the Council on a Single Market for Digital Services (Digital Services Act) and Amending Directive 2000/31/EC* (2022), online: European Parliament <https://www.europarl.europa.eu/doceo/document/TA-9-2022-0014_EN.html>.

[852] Art 24, proposal for a Regulation of the European Parliament and of the Council on a Single Market for Digital Services (Digital Services Act) and amending Directive 2000/31/EC. COM/2020/825 final; and amendment 287, Article 24, paragraph 1, point c European Parliament, *Amendments Adopted by the European Parliament on 20 January 2022 on the Proposal for a Regulation of the European Parliament and of the Council on a Single Market for Digital Services (Digital Services Act) and Amending Directive 2000/31/EC* (2022), online: European Parliament <https://www.europarl.europa.eu/doceo/document/TA-9-2022-0014_EN.html>.

[853] Amendment 335 to art 30, paragraph 2, point d, European Parliament, *Amendments Adopted by the European Parliament on 20 January 2022 on the Proposal for a Regulation of the European Parliament and of the Council on a Single Market for Digital Services (Digital Services Act) and Amending Directive 2000/31/EC* (2022), online: European Parliament <https://www.europarl.europa.eu/doceo/document/TA-9-2022-0014_EN.html>.

[854] Art 29 (1), Proposal for a Regulation of the European Parliament and of the Council on a Single Market for Digital Services (Digital Services Act) and amending Directive 2000/31/EC. COM/2020/825 final; and amendment 330, art 29, paragraph 1, European Parliament, *Amendments Adopted by the European Parliament on 20 January 2022 on the Proposal for a Regulation of the European Parliament and of the Council on a Single Market for Digital Services (Digital Services Act) and Amending Directive 2000/31/EC* (2022), online: European Parliament <https://www.europarl.europa.eu/doceo/document/TA-9-2022-0014_EN.html>.

In addition to the transparency of the requirements used to target users, the DSA contemplates other special rules for very large online platforms and their advertising practices. First, they must conduct a regular basis risk assessments to identify whether their advertising practices have a negative effect on the prohibition to discriminate provided by the Charter of Fundamental Rights of the European Union.[855] Second, amendments to the proposal suggest that when very large platforms conduct their risk assessments, they must consult with representatives of the groups potentially impacted as well as with independent experts and civil society organizations.[856] Third, the documents produced during the risk assessment should be reported to the European Commission.[857]

Further accountability measures should eventually include the implementation of the mitigation of risks once they are identified and the publication of comprehensive reports with the most prominent and recurrent systemic risks reported in the period of assessments.[858] In addition, the DSA provides that very large online platforms shall be subject to independent audit to assess their compliance with the requirements provided in Chapter III of the proposal, which includes requirements related to online advertising transparency and reporting obligations.[859] Auditors must have access to all relevant data necessary to properly perform the audit.[860] When receiving negative external audit reports, very large online platforms will likely have to take the necessary measures to address their recommendations.[861]

---

[855] Referring to art 21, Charter of Fundamental Rights of the European Union. Art 26 (1), b and (2), proposal for a Regulation of the European Parliament and of the Council on a Single Market for Digital Services (Digital Services Act) and amending Directive 2000/31/EC. COM/2020/825 final.

[856] Amendment 300, art 26, paragraph 2 (a), European Parliament, *Amendments Adopted by the European Parliament on 20 January 2022 on the Proposal for a Regulation of the European Parliament and of the Council on a Single Market for Digital Services (Digital Services Act) and Amending Directive 2000/31/EC* (2022), online: European Parliament <https://www.europarl.europa.eu/doceo/document/TA-9-2022-0014_EN.html>.

[857] Amendment 301, article 26, paragraph 2(b), European Parliament, *Amendments Adopted by the European Parliament on 20 January 2022 on the Proposal for a Regulation of the European Parliament and of the Council on a Single Market for Digital Services (Digital Services Act) and Amending Directive 2000/31/EC* (2022), online: European Parliament <https://www.europarl.europa.eu/doceo/document/TA-9-2022-0014_EN.html>.

[858] Art 27, proposal for a Regulation of the European Parliament and of the Council on a Single Market for Digital Services (Digital Services Act) and amending Directive 2000/31/EC. COM/2020/825 final.

[859] Art 28, proposal for a Regulation of the European Parliament and of the Council on a Single Market for Digital Services (Digital Services Act) and amending Directive 2000/31/EC. COM/2020/825 final.

[860] Amendment 318, art 28, paragraph 1 (a), European Parliament, *Amendments Adopted by the European Parliament on 20 January 2022 on the Proposal for a Regulation of the European Parliament and of the Council on a Single Market for Digital Services (Digital Services Act) and Amending Directive 2000/31/EC* (2022), online: European Parliament <https://www.europarl.europa.eu/doceo/document/TA-9-2022-0014_EN.html>.

[861] Article 28, (4), proposal for a Regulation of the European Parliament and of the Council on a Single Market for Digital Services (Digital Services Act) and amending Directive 2000/31/EC. COM/2020/825 final.

Finally, additional online advertising transparency requirements will apply to very large online platforms. One of the most interesting requirements in the fight against discrimination includes the obligation for these companies to indicate whether the advertisements were intended to be primarily displayed to one or more groups. The companies must also indicate the total number of users reached by the targeted advertisements for specific groups.[862]

The proposal for the Digital Services Act received criticism from activists and researchers concerned with the protection against discrimination in targeted advertising. First, activists have advocated for regulatory obligations that are beyond transparency requirements.[863] Second, interested stakeholders have argued that the transparency requirements are not enough to sufficiently inform users on the criteria used to their inclusion or exclusion from a certain targeted advertisement offer, considering the technology implemented to granularly profile certain demographics.[864] Finally, it is argued that these transparency obligations should be extended to other online intermediary services and not only to very large online platforms.[865]

At the time of the submission of this manuscript, the Digital Services Act was not yet in force. The proposal represents significant changes to the expected regulatory governance and accountability of online platforms, especially considerably large ones, regarding their targeted adverting practices. The implementation of the new requirements will provide a better perspective on the opportunities and gaps this new regulatory framework presents to the fight against discrimination on targeted advertising. In any case, similarly to the GDPR, the Digital Services Act does not provide any strong legal definition of discrimination. The act references the Charter of Fundamental Rights of the European Union, which provides that any discrimination based on the grounds of sex, race, color, ethnic or social oaring, genetic features, language, religion or belief, political or any other opinion, national origin, property, birth,

---

862 Art 30 of the proposal, proposal for a Regulation of the European Parliament and of the Council on a Single Market for Digital Services (Digital Services Act) and amending Directive 2000/31/EC. COM/2020/825 final.

863 Amnesty International, *Position on the Proposals for a Digital Services Act and a Digital Markets Act* (March 2021), online: Amnesty International <https://www.amnesty.eu/wp-content/uploads/2021/04/Amnesty-International-Position-Paper-Digital-Services-Act-Package_March2021_Updated.pdf>.

864 BEUC, *The Digital Services Act Proposal BEUC Position Paper* (April 2021), online: BEUC <https://www.beuc.eu/publications/beuc-x-2021–032_the_digital_services_act_proposal.pdf>.

865 European Parliament Committee on Civil Liberties, Justice and Home Affairs, *Opinion on the Proposal for a Regulation of the European Parliament and of the Council on a Single Market for Digital Services (Digital Services Act) and Amending Directive 2000/31/EC* (June 2021), online: European Parliament <https://www.europarl.europa.eu/doceo/document/LIBE-AD-692898_EN.pdf>.

disability, age, or sex orientation must be prohibited.[866] Despite this reference, differentiation in treatment based on these aspects are not constantly deemed to be illegal discrimination according to European Union antidiscrimination law and precedents.[867] Given this circumstance, when addressing discrimination in online targeted advertising, interested parties will have to make use of the Digital Services Act with the support of antidiscrimination laws.

3. ANTIDISCRIMINATION LAW APPROACH TO ADVERTISING IN THE UNITED STATES

In the past 50 years, federal courts and enforcement agencies have ruled that Title VII of the Civil Rights of 1964, the FHA, and the Equal Credit Opportunity (ECOA) Act have provided a cause for litigation against entities engaged in discriminatory advertising, marketing, or recruitment, not only when the content expresses bias for or against a particular group but also when certain individuals or communities are targeted to receive relevant materials or are excluded from receiving relevant materials, regardless of the content of the materials.[868]

3.1. TARGETING EMPLOYMENT ADVERTISEMENTS

No specific statutory law addresses targeted employment offers in the United States. However, at the federal level, statutory laws specifically impose restrictions to employment recruitment procedures. In practice, employment targeted advertising means excluding individuals from the employment offer. Some of these exclusions might be legal but others might not. In this respect, Title VII of the Civil Rights Act of 1964[869], the Age Discrimination in Employment Act of 1967 (ADEA)[870], and the Americans with Disabilities Act of 1990 (ADA)[871] prohibit – with some exceptions – employers from refusing to hire any qualified individual because of such individual's "race, color, religion, sex, national origin," "age," and "disability" or from implementing any apparent

---

[866] For instance, art 26 (b) of the proposal for the Digital Services Act refers to article 21 of the Charter of Fundamental Rights of the European Union.
[867] For more details, *see* section 4 of this chapter, chapter 1, and chapter 5.
[868] Willy E Rice, "Race, Gender, 'Redlining' and the Discriminatory Access to Loans, Credit, and Insurance: A Historical and Empirical Analysis of Consumers Who Sued Lenders and Insurers in Federal and State Courts, 1950–1995" (1996) 33 San Diego Law Review 583.
[869] Title VII, 42 U.S.C. §2000e-2(a)(1).
[870] ADEA, 29 U.S.C. §621 et seq.
[871] ADA, 42 U.S.C. §12112 (a).

neutral measure that has a disparate impact on individuals having one of these protected classes.[872]

3.1.1. Protection of Prospective Employees in Employment Recruitment

Title VII of the Civil Rights Act of 1964 was enacted by the American Congress in response to a reality of widespread and harmful discrimination, especially against Black Americans, in the employment context.[873] The statute protects employment applicants against direct and indirect discrimination based on race, color, national origin, sex, and religion.[874] In the United States, direct and indirect discrimination are referred to as disparate treatment and disparate impact, respectively. Direct discrimination regarding employment applicants involves intentionally excluding prospective employees because of their protected aspects. Case law regarding Title VII is extensive. In particular, in *Griggs v Duke Power Co*, a landmark case involving discrimination related to employment application, the Supreme Court of the United States first articulated the disparate impact theory.[875] This theory holds employers liable for discrimination even when they do not intend to discriminate against individuals; as employers implement apparent neutral policies regarding the conditions and access to work, they disproportionately affect protected classes in a negative way.

In *Griggs v Duke Power Co*, an electric power holding company (Duke Company) required from job applicants and employees willing to change their department to pass a standardized general intelligence test as a condition of being hired or changing department in their power generating plant. The test was applied to all candidates, but because Black American candidates had long had worse education in segregated schools, their success rate in the test was much lower than white candidates. To avoid accusation of discrimination, the company allowed Black American candidates to present a high school diploma instead of passing the test. Nevertheless, most of the Black American applicants did not have a high school diploma. The Supreme Court held that the requirement was not related to a successful job performance and that the requirement disqualified Black Americans at a much higher proportion than white applicants.[876] In addition, white employees had long filled the concerned employment position. The company had 95 employees at the Dan River Stations, 14 of whom were Black Americans, and 13 of these individuals were petitioners in the lawsuit. The energy station was located in Rockingham County, North

---

[872] Title VII, 42 U.S.C. §2000e-2(k).
[873] David J Garrow, "Toward a Definitive History of Griggs v Duke Power" (2014) 67 Vanderbilt Law Review 197, p 201.
[874] Title VII, 42 U.S.C. §2000e-2 (a)(1), (b), (c)(2), (d).
[875] *Griggs v Duke Power Co.*, 401 U.S. 424, 91 S. Ct. 849, 28 L. Ed. 2d 158 (1971).
[876] *Griggs v Duke Power Co.*, §362.

Carolina, in the South of the United States, where a significant part of the population was Black.

A classic example of a neutral policy with discriminatory outcomes involves accepting applicants only from particular areas of a certain city or applying apparent neutral tests to applicants that ultimately systematically eliminate a statutorily protected class. Under the indirect discrimination theories, apparent neutral employment practices that have negative effect on protected classes may only be legal if the employer can prove that the policy is important for job performance or is part of a business necessity.[877]

After the ruling of *Griggs v Duke Power Co*, the Supreme Court refused the indirect discrimination theories in a series of case law.[878] The most emblematic case was *Wards v Atonio* in which the business necessity test favored the employer.[879] Considering the inconstancy of precedents regarding the matter, the disparate impact theory was ratified and endorsed by the American Congress in 1991 when it amended Title VII of the Civil Rights Act of 1964.[880]

When plaintiffs present a case under the disparate impact theory, they must provide evidence that a particular employment practice has caused negative impact to a protected class.[881] To determine whether a neutral policy has disproportional adverse impact on a statutorily protected group, the Equal Employment Commission (EEOC) has set a guideline establishing that the

---

[877] Title VII, 42 U.S.C §2000e-2(k)(I)(A)(i). Some practices such as evaluations involving personal criteria such as weight and height, and physical tests have been challenged with success as not having a business justification/necessity. *Fickling v New York State Department of Civil Service*, 909 F. Supp. 185, 193 (1995). U.S. District Court for the Southern District of New York; *Merritt v WellPoint, Inc*, 615 F.Supp. 2d 440, 440 (2009). U.S. District Court E.D. Virginia. Cassandra Jones Havard, "'On the Take': The Black Box of Credit Scoring and Mortgage Discrimination" (2011) 20 Boston University Public Interest Law Journal 241, p 243.

[878] The Supreme Court ruled a series of cases that destabilized the disparate impact doctrine by requiring strict statistical evidence, by increasing the role of the plaintiff's burden to provide statistical data; and by dismissing the sufficiency of the plaintiff's statistical evidence in the cases *New York City Transit Authority v Beazer*, 440 U.S. 568 (1979); *Watson v Fort Worth Bank & Trust*, 487 U.S. 977 (1988); and *Wards Cove Packing Co v Atonio*, 490 U.S. (1989). See comments on these cases: Nicole J DeSario, "Re-conceptualizing Meritocracy: The Decline of Disparate Impact Discrimination Law" (2003) 38 Harvard Civil Rights Civil Liberties Law Review 479, p 493–501; Linda Lye, "Title VII's Tangled Tale: The Erosion and Confusion of Disparate Impact and the Business Necessity Defense" (1998) 19 Berkeley Journal of Employment & Labor Law 315. On the evolution of disparate impact, also David Oppenheimmer, "Sources of United States Equality Law: The View from 10000 Meters" (2010) European Antidiscrimination Law Review" 19, p 26.

[879] *Wards Cove Packing Co. v Atonio*, 490 U.S. 642, 109, S. Ct. (1989).

[880] The Congress enacted the amendment by introducing provisions on the burden of proof in disparate impact cases. Title VII, 42 U.S.C. §2000e-2(k). Susan D Carle, "A Social Movement History of Title VII Disparate Impact Analysis" (2011) 63 Florida Law Review 251, p 252–255.

[881] Title VII, 42 U.S.C., §2000e-2(k)(1)(A)(i) (2006).

protected group should have lower than 80% success chance in relation to a comparison group.[882]

Three years after Title VII of the Civil Rights Act was enacted, the Congress passed the Age Discrimination in Employment Act (ADEA)[883] to address the systemic age discrimination that older workers faced in the employment market.[884] The ADEA makes it illegal to treat employment applicants less favorably because of their age.[885] Age was suggested to be a protected class in Title VII, but it was not immediately included.[886] Congress considered that older employees were frequently discarded when competing with younger ones and recognized that arbitrary age limits had become a common practice in employment recruitment, and these practices could have consequences for a higher incidence of unemployment among older workers.[887] Employment agencies and employers in several industries frequently exclude older workers from recruiting processes.[888] This reality is particularly prominent in the technology sector.[889]

The statute covers workers who are 40 years old or older[890] and does not protect workers under the age of 40.[891] In other words, it is legal for an employer to favor an older worker – when they are 40 years old or over – over a younger one.[892] Age-related proxies in advertising language cannot be used to discriminate against potential applicants. For instance, the term "recent graduate" or the requirement of maximum years of experience should not be

---

882   Equal Employment Opportunity Commission, "Adoption of Question and Answers to Clarify and Provide a Common Interpretation of the Uniform Guidelines on Employee Selection Procedures", available at: https://www.eeoc.gov/policy/docs/qanda_clarify_procedures.html. Michael Selmi, "Was the Disparate Impact Theory a Mistake?" (2006) 53 UCLA Law Review 701.

883   ADEA, 29 U.S.C. §621 to §634. It was passed in December 1967.

884   ADEA, 29 U.S.C., §621 (b): "it is therefore the purpose of this chapter to promote employment of older persons based on their ability rather than age; to prohibit arbitrary age discrimination in employment; to help employers and workers find ways of meeting problems arising from the impact of age on employment".

885   ADEA, 29 U.S.C., §623, (a) (1) and (b).

886   Laurie McCann, "The Age Discrimination in Employment Act at 50: When Will It Become a "Real" Civil Rights Statute" (2018) 33 ABA Journal of Labor & Employment Law 89, p 89–91.

887   Ibid, p 91. This goal was not achieved.

888   Laurie A McCann, "The Age Discrimination in Employment Act at 50: When Will It Become a 'Real' Civil Rights Statute?", op. cit., p 91; AARP Public Policy Institute, "Boomers and the Great Recession: Struggling to Recover" (2012), p 21–23; Sara E Rix, The Employment Situation, May 2011: Average Duration of Unemployment for Older Jobseekers Continues to Rise (May 2011), online: AARP Public Policy Institute <https://assets.aarp.org/rgcenter/ppi/econ-sec/fs226-employment.pdf>.

889   Ifeoma Ajunwa, "Age Discrimination by Platforms", op. cit., 3. Referring to discrimination against older workers in the Silicon Valley, notably by IBM, Facebook and Google.

890   ADEA, 29 U.S.C., §631, (a).

891   Some State laws protect younger workers from age discrimination.

892   The Supreme Court of the United States decided that way in the case General Dynamics Land Systems, Inc. v Cline, 540 U.S. 581, 124 S.Ct. 1236, 157 L Ed. 2d 1094.

used except under limited situations.[893] The word "junior" should only be used if it is part of the job title. Otherwise, both terms could be considered to discourage older people to apply. When companies claim in an employment advertisement they have a culture comprised of "digital natives," they could also be deterring older people from applying.[894] Terms such as "college student," "recent college graduate," and "young blood" were previously noticed as being likely to violate the ADEA by the Equal Employment Opportunity Commission.[895]

Moreover, prospective employees with disabilities are also protected from discrimination in employment recruitment under the Americans with Disabilities Act (ADA).[896] The statute defines disability as a "physical or mental impairment that substantially limits one or more of the major life activities of such individual."[897] In addition, the Act provides that a qualified applicant with a disability is an individual who can perform the essential functions of the position in question with or without reasonable accommodation.[898] The employer may reasonably accommodate the employee's needs when it does not impose "undue hardship" on the employer's operations.[899] Over the years, litigation regarding the personal scope of the ADA was intense and was limited by the Supreme Court decisions.[900] In 2008, the Act was amended to address the issue.[901]

3.1.2. Exceptions to Discrimination Liability in Employment Recruitment

Title VII of the Civil Rights Acts of 1964 and the Americans With Disabilities Act only applies to employers who have more than 15 employees[902], whereas the Age Discrimination in Employment Act applies to employers with more than 20 employees.[903] Employers who do not fall under this limitation can lawfully exclude the protected classes from the delivery of their advertisements.

---

893   Ifeoma Ajunwa, "Age Discrimination by Platforms", *op. cit.*, p 8. Referring to case *Hodgson v Approved Personnel Services* no 75–1158 (1975), (4th Circuit). In this case, the circuit ruled that the term *recent graduate* in an employment advertisement deterred older workers from applying to the position and thus violated the ADEA.

894   Jessica k Sink, Richard Bales, "Born in the Bandwidth: Digital Native as Pretext for Age Discrimination in Hiring" (2016) 31 ABA Journal of Labor & Employment Law 521, p 522.

895   *Ibid*, p 524.

896   ADA, 42 U.S.C. §12102.

897   ADA, 42 U.S.C. §12102(2).

898   ADA, 42 U.S.C. §12111(8).

899   ADA, 42 U.S.C. §12111(9) and (10).

900   The Supreme Court has defined individuals with disability by excluding individuals whose impairment is mitigated with the use of devices or medication. *See Albertson's, Inc. v Kirkingburg*, 527 U.S. 555, 199 S. Ct. (1999); For the courts limits to disability, *see* Stephen F Befort, "An Empirical Examination of Case Outcomes Under the ADA Amendments Act" (2013) 70: Washington & Lee Law Review 2027, p 2035.

901   In 2008, the American Congress passed the ADA Amendments Act (ADAAA).

902   ADA, 42 U.S.C. §12112(a).

903   ADEA, 29 U.S.C., §630(b).

Moreover, Title VII and the ADEA admit that employers can intentionally exclude protected classes from their recruitment processes when there is a *bona fide* occupational qualification reasonably necessary for the normal operation of the business.[904] For instance, female applicants can be excluded from the recruitment process regarding a male football team under the *bona fide* occupational qualification provision.[905] However, the ADA does not provide for *bona fide* occupation qualification defense. Applicants with disabilities can only be excluded from employment recruitment based on their disability if the employer proves the measure is consistent with business necessity, such as in the case of safety risk that cannot be eliminated through reasonable accommodation.

Finally, employers can justify disparate impact over a protected ground when there is a business necessity.[906] The Title VII provision of disparate impact applies to other statutory antidiscrimination laws, even when they do not mention it in their text. Most rulings have followed this understanding even though controversies have arisen over the topic.[907] In the past decades, the theory of disparate impact has had moderate to low success rates in litigation.[908] Courts have required precise statistical evidence to constitute a cause of action, which bars many cases.[909] Moreover, the "employer business necessity" and "job-relatedness" aspects have been interpreted without a necessary link to the required employment practices of the future job performance.[910] In other words, strict requirements on statistical evidence to justify *prima facie* discrimination in addition to broad interpretations of business necessity have weakened the success rate of indirect discrimination in courts.[911]

Scholars have argued that online platforms and automated systems have been largely excluded from the public authorities and academic debates about

---

[904] Title VII, 42 U.S.C. §2000e-2(e)(1) and ADEA, 29 U.S.C., §623, (f)(1).

[905] Michael Selmi, "Was the Disparate Impact Theory a Mistake?" (2006) 53 UCLA Law Review 701.

[906] Title VII, 42 U.S.C., §2000e-e(k)(1)(A)(i).

[907] The Supreme Court of the United States has extended disparate impact to cases related to ADEA. *See Smith v City of Jackson*, 544 U.S. 228, 125 S. Ct. (2005), Supreme Court of the United States. Also, Judith J Johnson, "Reasonable Factors Other than Age: The Emerging Specter of Ageist Stereotypes" (2009) 33 Seattle University Law Review 49, p 50.

[908] Michael Selmi, "Was the Disparate Impact Theory a Mistake?" (2006) 53 UCLA Law Review 701. Selmi demonstrates that disparate impact cases won only 19.2% in federal appellate courts and only 25.1% in federal district courts. Other analysis: Stacy E Seischnaydre, "Is Disparate Impact Having Any Impact: An Appellate Analysis of Forty Years of Disparate Impact Claims under the Fair Housing Act" (2013) 63 American University Law Review 357; Lawrence Rosenthal, "Saving Disparate Impact" (2012) 34 Cardozo Law Review 2157.

[909] *Shah v New York State Department of Civil Service*, no 94 Civ. 9193 (S.D.N.Y. Dec 9, 1997); *Chavez v Coors Brewing Co*, n 98–1109, 1999 U.S. App (10th Circ. Mar. 25, 1999); *EEOC v Joe's Stone Crab*, Inc. 220 F.3d 1263, 1268 (11th Cir. 2000).

[910] *Shah v New York State Department of Civil* Service no 94 Civ. 9193 (S.D.N.Y. Dec 9, 1997).

[911] Nicole J DeSario, "Reconceptualizing Meritocracy: The Decline of Disparate Impact Discrimination Law", *op. cit.*, p 507.

employment discrimination in the United States.[912] The use of targeted advertising to deliver employment offers holds potential forms of discrimination, particularly when it is used to exclude statutorily protected classes such as race, color, religion, sex, national origin, age, and disability.[913] The possibility to select or exclude such protected grounds for employment targeted advertisement consisted as a basis for a class action against Facebook.[914]

3.2. TARGETING CREDIT AND HOUSING ADVERTISEMENTS

Despite the risks of stereotypes when advertisers target their audiences for the offer of goods and services, two sectors are explicitly covered by statutory law against discrimination in the federal level: credit and housing. The issue of housing advertisements was the topic of Title I. The distinctive aspect of Title II is the possibility of excluding protected classes from receiving housing advertisements. Regarding housing, precedents have ruled that targeting practices in the advertisement content are not legal under the FHA.[915] For example, when a newspaper constantly published real estate advertisement only with white models, a certain precedent considered that the ads were targeting white prospective tenants and excluding Black prospective tenants. In this case, the newspaper as a publisher of the illegal content was held liable under the terms of the FHA.[916] Contrarily to other antidiscrimination statutes, the FHA holds liable the publisher of discriminatory advertisements.[917] The exclusion of certain areas for advertised credit opportunities has been assessed as disparate impact.[918]

3.3. PROTECTION OF CREDIT APPLICANTS AGAINST DISCRIMINATION

The Equal Credit Opportunity Act (ECOA)[919] was enacted to give protected groups the equal opportunity to apply for loans from banks and other credit

---

912 Ifeoma Ajunwa, "Age Discrimination by Platforms", *op. cit.*, p 7.
913 For issues concerning big data and disparate impact, *see* Andrew Selbst, Solon Barocas, "Big Data's Disparate Impact" (2016) 104 California Law Review 671.
914 *See* chapter 4.
915 Ross D Petty, Anne-Marie G Harris, Toni Broaddus, "Regulating Target Marketing and Other Race-Based Advertising Practices" (2003) 8:2 Michigan Journal of Race & Law 335, p 375.
916 *Ragin v New York Times Company,* 923 F.2d 995 (2d Cir. 1991), §997.
917 FHA, 42 U.S.C. §3604(c).
918 *See* following section 3.3.
919 15 U.S.C. §1691 et seq, ECOA. (The Act was enacted 1974).

organizations.[920] Initially, the Act only outlawed creditors from discriminating against sex and marital status grounds. At the time, women were often denied credit because credit organizations did not consider them to be economically liable.[921] In this regard, banks resisted providing credit to single-working women due to general assumptions that women would eventually get married and would not be economically active.[922] Two years after the Act was enacted, Congress passed an amendment to include race, color, religion, national origin, and age as grounds of protection against discrimination. At the time, credit institutions redlined minority neighborhoods and refused loans based on the property location.[923]

The current ECOA prohibits credit institutions and intermediaries, such as credit brokers, to discriminate against credit applicants on the grounds of their race, color, religion, national origin, sex, marital status, and age.[924] Moreover, credit organizations are also not allowed to include in their credit scores the fact that applicants' income is currently, or was ever, derived from public assistance.[925] A set of exceptions exist regarding marital status, age, and public assistance.[926] Furthermore, the definition of a credit institution is broad and includes "any person who regularly extends, renews, or continues credit."[927]

Proving direct discrimination under the ECOA is not easy, considering that discrimination in loan transactions is likely to be subtle, especially given the implementation of automated scoring systems to evaluate applicants.[928] In this respect, disparate impact theories have been accepted even though it is not unequivocally provided by the statute.[929]

Targeting credit offers have been restrictively accepted by fair credit authorities because of its potential to disparately impact certain groups.[930]

---

[920] See Winnie F Taylor, "The ECOA and Disparate Impact Theory: A Historical Perspective" (2018) 26:2 Journal of Law and Policy 576; Benjamin Howell, "Exploiting Race and Space: Concentrated Subprime Lending as Housing Discrimination" (2006) 94: 1 California Law Review 101; Jackelyn Hwang, Michael Hankinson, Kreg Seven Bown, "Racial and Spatial Targeting: Segregation and Subprime Lending within and Across Metropolitan Areas" (2015) 93:3 Social Forces 1081.

[921] Winnie F Taylor, "The ECOA and Disparate Impact Theory: A Historical Perspective" (2018) 26:2 Journal of Law and Policy 576, p 602.

[922] Ibid.

[923] Willy E Rice, "Race, Gender, 'Redlining' and the Discriminatory Access to Loans, Credit, and Insurance: A Historical and Empirical Analysis of Consumers Who Sued Lenders and Insurers in Federal and State Courts, 1950–1995" (1996) 33 San Diego Law Review 583.

[924] 15 U.S.C., §1691a (e), ECOA and 15. U.S.C., §1961(a)(1), ECOA.

[925] 15 U.S.C., §1961(a)(2)(3), ECOA.

[926] 15 U.S.C. §1691, (b) and (c), ECOA.

[927] ECOA, 15 U.S.C. §1691a.

[928] See Cassandra Jones Havard, "'On the Take': The Black Box of Credit Scoring and Mortgage Discrimination" (2011) 20 Boston University Public Interest Law Journal 241 and Winnie Taylor, "Proving Racial Discrimination and Monitoring Fair Lending Compliance: The Missing Data Problem in Nonmortgage Credit" (2011) 31:1 Review of Banking and Financial Law 199, p 208.

[929] See Garcia v Johanns, 444 F 3d 625, 633 (D.C. Circ. 2006).

[930] Linda E Fisher, "Target Marketing of Subprime Loans: Racialized Consumer Fraud & Reverse Redlining" (2010) 18 Journal of Law and Policy 121.

For instance, the United States Department of Justice sued the Chevy Chase Federal Saving Bank for having refused to advertise its credit offers and services in neighborhoods with a predominantly Black American population.[931] When the bank settled the case, it consented to proactively advertise its services regarding credit offers and target calls offering housing credit opportunities in neighborhoods where Black Americans were overrepresented. Moreover, enforcement bodies also consider if credit institutions make "a lower level of marketing effort towards prohibited basis groups or geographies."[932] More recently, the credit institution GE Capital was condemned to penalties for excluding credit to customers who have indicated they communicate in Spanish.[933]

A credit institution may target credit advertisements to protected classes online, but it is prohibited to exclude these same classes from credit advertisements.[934] Even if the ECOA does not mention discrimination related to advertising, authorities' practices and enforcement actions provide guidance on online targeted credit advertisement.[935]

Advertisers and credit institutions have direct liability under the terms of the ECOA when they exclude protected classes from their online credit offers (advertisements).[936] The relevant question is if other players involved in advertising credit offers, such as online platforms and ad network companies, would be also liable for illegal targeting in these cases. The precedent involving Roommates.com might offer some clue to this question. Roommates' matching tool that allowed the exclusion of protected classes was considered to breach the terms of the Fair Housing Act. Moreover, the Court of Appeals understood that because the platform developed the tool and the content of the tool, it was not covered by the exception for liability imposed by the Communications Decency Act.[937]

---

[931] *United States v Chevy Chase Federal Saving Bank,* civil action n. CV94–1824JG (D.D.C. 1994).

[932] Federal Reserve Bank of Chicago, *Banker's Guide to Risk-Based Fair Lending Examinations* (January 1999), online: Federal Reserve Bank of Chicago <https://www.chicagofed.org/digital_assets/others/utilities/about_us/cca/bankers_guide_to_risk_based_fair_lending_examinations.pdf>.

[933] Press Release, *CFPB Orders GE Capital to Pay $225 Million in Consumer Relief for Deceptive and Discriminatory Credit Card Practices* (June 2014), online: Consumer Finance <www.consumerfinance.gov/newsroom/cfpb-orders-ge-capital-to-pay-225-million-in-consumer-relief-for-deceptive-and-discriminatory-credit-card-practices/>.

[934] Peter Swire, "Lessons from Fair Lending Law for Fair Marketing and Big Data", *op. cit.,* p 8. Also, Carol Evans, Westra Miller, "From Catalogs to Clicks: The Fair Lending Implications of Targeted, Internet Marketing" (2019) 3 Consumer Compliance Outlook 9.

[935] Peter Swire, "Lessons from Fair Lending Law for Fair Marketing and Big Data", *op. cit.,* p 8.

[936] 15. U.S.C., §1961(a)(1), ECOA.

[937] *Fair Housing Council of San Fernando Valley v. Roommates, LLC,* 2012 WL 310849 (9th Cir. 2012).

4. ANTIDISCRIMINATION LAW APPROACH TO ADVERTISING IN THE EUROPEAN UNION

In the European Union, no secondary **equality** laws particularly regulate the practice of targeted advertising. Alternatively, the frame of protection against discrimination regarding this practice is provided by regulations involving data protection, when advertisers use personal data to target their audiences, the Digital Services Act in the near future, and antidiscrimination laws that impose restrictions on the exclusion of protected classes from recruitment processes or from the **access** to the provision of services and goods. Whereas the Equality Directives and case law may provide guidance for targeting employment offers, the issue is less certain regarding the offer of services and goods.

The Race Equality Directive and Gender Equal Access to Goods and Services Directive protect the grounds of race, ethnic origin, and gender against discrimination in the provision of goods and services. It is worth noting that most member states have more grounds protected against discrimination in the access to the provision of goods and services than the framework provided by the Equality Directives.[938] Uncertainties related to scope of the Gender Equal Access to Goods and Services Directive on targeted advertisement is related to the fact that the Directive explicitly excludes advertisement from its scope.[939] However, one could question whether the clause of the Directive that excludes advertisements from its scope is only related to content and not related to profiling and targeting practices. So far, it is accepted that advertisements may neither include discriminatory terms against protected classes nor have excluding terms, such as "this insurance offer is limited to men." However, it is less clear whether companies may exclude protected classes when they deliver their marketing either online or offline. In this respect, the European Commission has affirmed that institutions offering insurance may target their market either to men or women even if they may not discriminate against these classes when estimating insurance primes.[940] Nevertheless, further clarification about this issue might be necessary in the context of online targeting. When advertisers market their offers online, they have technical possibilities to target their offers in a way that is not feasible in the physical reality. The practice

---

[938] *See* chapter 1.

[939] Article 3(3), Gender Equal Access to Goods and Services. Also, it is worth noting that several member states did not include this limitation when they transposed the Directive into their national laws. For an updated overview, *see* Eugenia Caracciolo di Torella, *Directive 2004/113/EC on Gender Equality in Goods and Services – In Search of the Potential of a Forgotten Directive* (2021) online: European Commission Directorate General for Justice and Consumers <https://www.equalitylaw.eu/downloads/5614-directive-2004–113-ec-on-gender-equality-in-goods-and-services-in-search-of-the-potential-of-a-forgotten-directive-1–38-mb>.

[940] Guidelines on the application of Council Directive 2004/113/EC to insurance, in the light of the judgement of the court of Justice of the European Union in case C-236/09.

involves more than targeting a neighborhood by means of IP addresses. Rather, it entails the possibility of granularly targeting audiences based on their personal traits. For instance, would it be acceptable to exclude internet users from receiving a hotel offer based on their gender? This issue needs further clarification in the content of online marketing.

4.1. TARGETED EMPLOYMENT ADVERTISEMENTS

4.1.1. Protection of Prospective Employees in Employment Recruitment

The Gender Equality Directive, the Racial Equality Directive, and the Employment Equality Directive provide a comprehensive framework to implement the principle of nondiscrimination in the context of employment and occupation. The prohibition of direct or indirect discrimination on the grounds of race, ethnic origin, sex, religion, belief, age, sexual orientation, and disability might orient work conditions as well as access to employment, including recruitment practices.[941] In particular, individuals applying for employment are under the personal scope of the Directives and their transposed laws. In this respect, the European Commission instructed that employment advertising must not contain any explicit or non-explicit discriminatory requirement concerning the protected grounds of prospective employees.[942] These instances include naming an employment position in the feminine or masculine form in some languages; requiring experience in the army, as more men are often in the military service; demanding native language skills; or specifying a preference for recent graduates when no genuine requirement exists for such specification.

The CJEU has broadly interpreted "access to employment" by including into the concept of "access" both recruitment circumstances and selection requirements.[943] In addition, the Court has ruled that the exclusion of protected

---

[941] Gender Equality Directive, Article 14 (1)(a); Racial Equality Directive, Article 3(1)(a); Employment Equality Directive, Article 3 (1)(a).

[942] Brussels, 17.1.2014 COM(2014) 2 final. Report From the Commission to the European Parliament and the Council: 'Joint Report on the application of Council Directive 2000/43/EC of 29 June 2000 implementing the principle of equal treatment between persons irrespective of racial or ethnic origin ('Racial Equality Directive) and of Council Directive of 27 November 2000 establishing a general framework for equal treatment in employment and occupation (Employment Equality Directive)', p 7.

[943] *See*, for instance, C-116/94 *Meyers v Chief Adjudication Officer*, ECLI:EU:C:1995:247; C-180/95 *Draehmpaehl v Urania Immobilienservice OHG*, ECLI, EU:C:1997:208; C-415/10 *Galina Meister v Speech Design Carrier Systems GmbH*, ECLI:EU:C:2012:217; C-317/14 *European Commission v Kingdom of Belgium*, ECLI:EU:C:2015:63; C-416/13 *Mario Vital Pérez v Ayuntamiento de Oviedo*, ECLI:EU:C:2014:2371; C-507/18 *N.H. c. Associazione Avvocatura per i diritti LGBTI – Rete Lenford*, ECLI:EU:C:2020:289. *See* Emmanuelle Bribosia, Isabelle Rorive, "Les Paroles Ont des Ailes et Peuvent Discriminer: Regard sur l'Arrêt N.H. c. Associazione

classes from employment recruitment is illegal.[944] The Feryn case illustrates the position of the Court about this matter.[945] Feryn is a business focused on repairing and installing sophisticated doors in private properties. They were looking for employees to work as door fitters in Belgium, and they placed employment advertisements on billboards along Belgian motorways. In a public interview, one of the company's directors, Mr. Pascal Feryn, stated that his company would not hire individuals with a certain origin (implicitly Moroccan origin) because his customers were allegedly against it. Following the statement, the Belgian national equality body charged Feryn for having implemented a discriminatory recruitment policy that excluded a protected class (ethnic origin). In this scenario, no prospective employees had presented themselves as a victim.

The Belgian judge referred the issue to the Court of Justice by asking whether the exclusion of protected classes from an employment offer when no victim was identified was sufficient to establish direct discrimination. The CJEU ruled that the existence of direct discrimination is not conditioned to the identification of a victim. The exclusion of a protected class from the employment offer was already a sufficient ground to establish direct discrimination.[946]

The CJEU's reasoning in the *Feryn* case may be extended to targeted employment offers online. An employer may directly discriminate against prospective employees with one or more protected grounds by completely excluding them from receiving the online advertisement with the employment offer. In this case, direct discrimination might occur even if no victim is identified. It should be sufficient to identify that the advertiser has excluded a protected ground from its targeting options to configure direct discrimination. Therefore, if an employment campaign is created to only reach male internet users, direct discrimination has occurred regardless of whether the victims of discrimination file a complaint or not.[947] Concerning the means of proving direct discrimination, the CJEU has taken the line that proof may be founded on the relation of causation and not necessarily on intention.[948] No internal motive or explicit intention on the part of the discriminator are required to be

---

Avvocatura per I diritti LGBTI – Rete Lenford, rendu en Grand Chambre par la CJUE le 23 avril 2020 (C-507/18) Journal Européen des Droits de l'Homme 2020.

[944] C-54/07 *Centrum voor gelijkheid van kansen en voor racismebestrijding v Firma Feryn NV*, ECLI:EU:C:2008:397; C-81/12 *Asociaţia Accept v Consiliul Naţional pentru Combaterea Discriminării*, ECLI:EU:C:2013:275.

[945] C-54/07 *Centrum voor gelijkheid van kansen en voor racismebestrijding v Firma Feryn NV*, ECLI:EU:C:2008:397.

[946] *Ibid.*

[947] *Ibid.*

[948] "But for" tests. C-303/06 *Coleman v Attridge Law*, ECLI:EU:C:2008:415 and C-506/06 *Mayr v Flöckner OHG*, ECLI:EU:C:2008:119. Evelyn Ellis, Philippa Watson, "EU Anti-Discrimination Law", *op. cit.*, p 167.

demonstrated to hold individuals liable for discrimination against protected classes.[949]

Indirect discrimination may also occur in the context of employment targeted adverting. Under EU law, indirect discrimination is established when "an apparently neutral provision, criterion or practice would put persons [with protected characteristic] at a particular disadvantage compared with other persons" in a similar position.[950] To illustrate this idea, targeting a specific IP address to advertise employment may disproportionately impact certain groups in cities that have neighborhoods with spatial ethnic concentrations. In this case, the disproportionate impact would only be justified if business legitimate and proportionate needs exist. Moreover, statistical data is not required to prove indirect discrimination in Europe. Even if statistics might assist charges of indirect discrimination, the only requirement is that the neutral policy put the person in a particular disadvantaged position.[951]

4.1.2. Exceptions to Discrimination in Employment Recruitment

A derogation to discriminate against applicants in employment advertising, as part of the employment recruitment, may be authorized in limited circumstances when a genuine occupational requirement exists.[952] The list of permissible exceptions is limited. Following the text of the three directives[953], the CJEU's case law[954], and legal scholars' findings[955], the genuine occupational requirement must be demonstrated by the employers first, when there is a legitimate objective;

---

[949] National courts have also taken the causation approach as a matter of proof for direct discrimination, *see* UK *R (on the application of E) v Governing Body of JFS and the admissions Appeal Panel of JFS* (2009) UKSC. Evelyn Ellis, Philippa Watson, "EU Anti-Discrimination Law", *op. cit.*, p 168.

[950] Gender Equality Directive, art 2(1)(b); Race Equality Directive, art 2(2)(b); Employment Equality Directive, art 2(2)(b).

[951] In *O'Flynn*, the Court of Justice of the European Union understood that indirect discrimination did not require statistical evidence. "It is not necessary in this respect to find that the provision in question does in practice affect a substantially higher proportion of migrant workers. It is sufficient that it is liable to have such an effect", paragraph 21, C-237/94 *O'Flynn v Adjudication Officer*, ECLI:EU:C:1996:206.; Also, *see* Sandra Fredman, *Discrimination Law*, *op. cit.*, p 187.

[952] Race Equality Directive, recital 18; Employment Equality Directive, recital 23. *See also* Gender Equality Directive, recital 19. *See* CJEU cases in European Union Agency for Fundamental Rights & Council of Europe, *Handbook on European Non-Discrimination Law* (Luxembourg: Publications Office of the European Union, 2018), p 97–102.

[953] Gender Equality Directive, art. 14(2); Employment Equality Directive, art. 4(1); Racial Equality Directive, art. 4.

[954] *See* C-54/07 *Centrum voor gelijkheid van kansen en voor racismebestrijding v Firma Feryn NV*, ECLI:EU:C:2008:397; C-81/12 *Asociația Accept v Consiliul Național pentru Combaterea Discriminării*, ECLI:EU:C:2013:275; and C-188/15 *Asma Bougnaoui and ADDH v Micropole SA*, ECLI:EU:C:2017:204.

[955] Evelyn Ellis, Philippa Watson, *EU Anti-Discrimination Law*, *op. cit.*, p 381–394. Richard Painter, Ann Holmes, *Cases and Materials on Employment Law* 10th ed (Oxford: OUP 2015),

---

second, when the protected ground excluded must constitute a *genuine and determining* motive for performing the concerned employment position; and third, when the particular aspect required shall be appropriate, necessary, and proportionate for effectively carrying out the particular function.

The European Commission has cited examples regarding racial requirement, such as "authenticity in a dramatic performance, or where the holder of a particular job provides persons of a particular ethnic group with personal services promoting their welfare and those services can most effectively be provided by a person of that ethnic group."[956] Another possibility to justify direct discrimination based on protected grounds in a job advertisement occurs when the company has a positive action program to hire applicants with aspects that are underrepresented.[957]

EU law also allows for additional exceptions regarding religion and age. For instance, legislation may authorize a difference of treatment, in certain conditions, based on religion if the employment activities are to be carried out within churches and ethos-based organizations.[958] In this case, the individual's religious belief may constitute a genuine, legitimate, and justified occupational requirement for recruitment. Concerning age, exceptions may include a minimum age requirement to meet professional experience necessary to perform the job.[959]

4.2. TARGETING INSURANCE OFFERS

The Race Equality Directive and the Gender Equal Access to Goods and Services Directive provide protection against racial, ethnic origin, and sex discrimination in the provision and supply of goods and services, but with exceptions. Moreover, the Gender Directive expressly provides that neither media content nor advertising are under its material scope.[960] Through these Directive, the

---

p 281. Hazel Oliver, "Sexual Orientation: Perceptions, Definitions and Genuine Occupational Requirements" (2004) 33 Industrial Law Journal 1.

[956] Catherine Barnard, *EU Employment Law* 4th Edition (Oxford: Oxford University Press, 2012), p 367.

[957] Gender Equality Directive, art. 3; Racial Equality Directive, art. 5; Employment Equality Directive, art. 7(1);

[958] Employment Equality Directive, art 4(2). *See* C-414/16 *Egenberger v Evangelisches Werk Für Diakonies un Entwicklung eV,* ECLI:EU:C:2018:257 and for different developments at Emmanuelle Bribosia, Isabelle Rorive, "Equality and Non-Discrimination: Column" (2014) 2 European Journal of Human Rights 205; Emmanuelle Bribosia, Isabelle Rorive, "Equality and Non-Discrimination: Column" (2016) 2 European Journal of Human Rights 254; Emmanuelle Bribosia, Isabelle Rorive, "Equality and Non-Discrimination: Column" (2017) 2 European Journal of Human Rights 191; Emmanuelle Bribosia, Isabelle Rorive, "Equality and Non-Discrimination: Column" (2018) 2 European Journal of Human Rights 126.

[959] Employment Equality Directive, art 6 (1) (a)(b)(c).

[960] Article 3 (3), Gender Equal Access to Goods and Services Directive.

European Union has left member states free to regulate and set the boundaries on how goods and services can be advertised.[961]

The *Association Belge des Consomateurs Test-Achats v Conseil des Ministres* case demonstrates how the EU understands targeted marketing involving the offer of insurance services.[962] In this case, the CJEU held that insurance companies are prohibited from considering the gender of the insurance holder to determine their benefits or premiums.[963] National insurers across Europe had to adhere to this provision over the years. Despite the obligation of insurance companies to follow the new construed standard, the European Commission guidelines on the application of the directive in light of the case *Association Belge des Consomateurs Test-Achats v Conseil des Ministres* made it clear that the directive does not apply to advertising. The guidelines provide that "it [still] remains possible for insurers to use marketing and advertising to influence their portfolio mix, e.g., by targeting advertising at either men or women."[964] The guidelines expressly indicate that insurance companies may target their offers based on sex, even if they cannot differentiate the amount of premiums based on that same ground.[965]

---

[961]   Evelyn Ellis, Philippa Watson, "EU Anti-Discrimination Law", *op. cit.*, p 368.

[962]   C-236/09 *Association Belge des Consomateurs Test-Achats v Conseil des Ministres*, ECLI:EU:C:2011:100.

[963]   *Ibid.* Differential premium rates are only justified where there are objective physical reasons why a risk is more likely to materialize in one gender than another. For example, a family breast cancer is relevant to assess the risk of it happening in a woman where it is not the case for a man. *See* Annick Masselot, "The State of Gender Equality Law in the European Union" (2007) 13 European Law Journal 152.

[964]   Guidelines on the application of Council Directive 2004/113/EC to insurance, in light of the judgement of the court of Justice of the European Union in case C-236/09.

[965]   Christa Tobler, "Case C-236/09, Association Belge Des Consommateurs Test-Achats ABSL, Yann Van Vurgt, Charles Basselier v Conseil Des Ministres" (2011) 48 Common Market Law Review 2041; Philippa Watson, "Equality, Fundamental Rights and the Limits of Legislative Discretion: Comment on Test Achats" (2011) 36 European Law Review 896; Eugenia Caracciolo di Torella, "Gender Equality after Test Achats" (2012) 12 ERA Forum 59.

CHAPTER 4

ONLINE PLATFORMS: GATEKEEPERS OF ADVERTISEMENTS

This chapter uses a case-based approach to address how companies have increasingly developed targeted advertisements to monetize their businesses. I particularly explore the business model adopted by Facebook and Google in Section I. In Section II, I present how privacy and equality laws have been mobilized (or not) to address the misuse of personal data and discrimination within their targeting practices.

Regarding Facebook, I develop the issues existent in the cases *Onuoha v Facebook, Bradley v T-Mobile US, National Fair Housing Alliance v Facebook, Riddick v Facebook,* and *Spees et al. v Facebook* litigated in the United States. These cases bring to light how targeting tools, developed by the platform, allow businesses (advertisers) to exclude protected classes from receiving their offers and, therefore, how this practice poses great risks to the principle of equality in the access to good, service, and employment offers.

Moreover, through litigation against Google and Facebook involving personal data rights, I present how the debate about online targeted advertisements is to a great extent circumscribed by data protection law in the EU. The cases *Authorities Persoonsgegevens v Facebook* in the Netherlands, *Commission Nationale de l'Informatique et des Libertés v Facebook* in France, and *Agencia Española de Datos v Facebook* in Spain illustrate that data protection law should be articulated with antidiscrimination rights in the fight against discrimination occurring with the use of targeting tools in the EU. This articulation has scantly occurred so far.

SECTION I. SOCIAL NETWORK AND SEARCH ENGINE PLATFORMS

1. FROM FACE MASH TO FACEBOOK

A face book, with individual photographs and names – originally printed and more recently available online – is used by several American universities at the beginning of the academic year to help students to get to know each other.

Inspired by this book, Mark Zuckerberg developed a website called FaceMash in his second year of college in 2003.[966] FaceMash had 450 visitors and 22,000 photograph views in its first four hours online.[967] Despite its success among students, Harvard administration disapproved of it, because it had breached the university web security and violated students' individual privacy.[968]

After FaceMash's success, Zuckerberg with Dustin Moskovitz, Andrew McCollum, Chris Hughes, and Eduardo Saverin, launched the social networking service Facebook.[969] The service was initially limited to the Harvard alumni, and within its first 24 hours over 1,500 individuals registered.[970] The social networking was gradually expanded to other universities. In 2005, Facebook was available to 21 universities in the United Kingdom, and, in this same year, it became accessible to high school students. In September 2006, any person with a valid email address and older than 13 years old could register.

In December 2005, Facebook had over six million users.[971] In July 2019, it had 2.2 billion monthly active users.[972] Currently, Facebook is a publicly traded corporation, headquartered in Menlo Park, California, and incorporated under the laws of the State of Delaware.[973]

1.1. BUSINESS MODEL

Facebook, a platform to connect people and an advertising apparatus

In 2004, Facebook had a simple design. The welcome webpage presented its purpose of being "an online directory that connects people through social networks at colleges"[974] and, specifically, informed its users that Facebook had been made available for popular consumption at Harvard University to allow its users to: "1. Search for people at your school; 2. Find out who are in your classes;

---

[966] Sarah Phillips, "A Brief History of Facebook" *the Guardian* (2007).

[967] Ellen McGirt, *Facebook's Mark Zuckerberg: Hacker. Dropout. CEO* (May 2007), online: Fast Company <https://www.fastcompany.com/59441/facebooks-mark-zuckerberg-hacker-dropout-ceo>.

[968] Sarah Phillips, "A Brief History of Facebook" *the Guardian* (2007).

[969] The network was created under the name *thefacebook.com*. *Ibid.*

[970] Nicholas Carlson, "At Last – The Full Story of How Facebook Was Founded" *Business Insider* (2010).

[971] Niels Brügger, "A Brief History of Facebook as a Media Text: The Development of an Empty Structure" (2015) 20 First Monday. <https://s21.q4cdn.com/399680738/files/doc_financials/2018/Q2/Q218-earnings-call-transcript.pdf>.

[972] United States Securities and Exchange Commission Washington, "Annual Report Pursuant to Section 13 or 15(d) of The Securities Exchange Act of 1934 for the Fiscal Year Ended December 31, 2019" (2019). <https://www.sec.gov/Archives/edgar/data/1326801/000132680118000009/fb-12312017x10k.htm>.

[973] *Ibid.*

[974] Annex 9.

3. Look up your friends' friends; 4. See a visualization of your social network."[975] Users' profiles consisted of an image, information about where they were connected, and personal information such as their name, date of membership, last update, email, status (e.g., alumnus), sex, year at college, concentration (e.g., computing sciences, mathematics), telephone, and high school. The profiles also included some extended information, such as what the person was looking for, which could include friendship, dating, a relationship, a random play, or "whatever I can get"; who the user was interested in (e.g., women, men); relationship status; political views (liberal); and general interests.[976]

Facebook has been a free of charge service since its creation. Selling advertising spaces is how it has monetized its business and has become one of the wealthiest online companies in the world. By 2004, advertisements were placed as simple flyers and banners on Facebook's main webpage. Advertising placements were generally purchased by students promoting events and local business.[977] From 2005, Facebook has increasingly developed its ad business and sealed profitable deals with Apple, Microsoft, and JP Morgan Chase, only to cite a few examples.[978] In 2006 the tool Facebook Ads was created, allowing any company to directly buy advertising placements on the platform. By the late 2000s, companies willing to advertise on Facebook were increasingly offered cookie-based targeting options for their ads.[979] In addition, ads were not restricted to banners and flyers on the top and side of the webpage but were introduced among users' feeds. In 2013 Facebook released the lookalike audiences tool, which enables advertisers to reach users sharing similar characteristics to their existing customers.[980]

From 2004 to 2019, Facebook has been transformed from a student social networking site to one of the wealthiest companies in the world due to advertising. Facebook's annual fiscal report to the United States Securities and Exchange Commission reveals that it makes 95% of its revenues by selling

---

[975]   *Ibid.*

[976]   Annex 10.

[977]   Stefan Des, "The History of Facebook Ads: How Facebook Advertising Evolved in the Last 13 Years" (*Leadsbridge*, 2017) <https://leadsbridge.com/infographic-history-facebook-ads/>.

[978]   Brad Stone, "Microsoft to Pay $240 Million for Stake in Facebook" (*the New York Times*, 2007). Available at: https://news.microsoft.com/2007/10/24/facebook-and-microsoft-expand-strategic-alliance/; Press Announcement, "Facebook and Microsoft Expand Strategic Alliance" *Microsoft* (2007).

[979]   Joseph Turow, *The Daily You: How the New Advertising Industry Is Defining Your Identity and Your Worth*, *op. cit.*, p 145.

[980]   *See* Huajung Li, "Generating Clusters of Similar Users for Advertisement Targeting" [2013] U.S Patent Application No 13/297 117, p 118. Facebook created the lookalike tool to enable advertisers to cluster users with similar tastes and behavior. The tool clusters users that have expressed interests in a brand and previously engaged with its advertisements with users who have similar demographics that will be eventually targeted to receive a particular advertisement.

advertisement placements.[981] Marketers pay for advertisement placements either
directly or through advertising agencies. The price to be paid is mostly based on
the number of impressions and the number of actions, such as clicks.[982] With
over two billion monthly active users, Facebook is a profitable environment for
companies that want to advertise their services and products.

1.2.   TARGETING PRACTICES

"Target the Right People for Your Business."[983]

Targeting tools have assisted marketers to reach their audience in ways that are
often not feasible in traditional media. Facebook confirmed that advertisers
may reach users "based on a variety of factors including age, gender, location,
interests, and behaviors."[984] The platform has also stated that "with our
powerful audience selection tools, you can target the people who are right for
your business. Using what you know about your customers, like demographics,
interests, and behaviors, you can connect with people similar to them."[985]

Advertisers may create ads on Facebook by using the tools Ad Creation Tool
and Ads Manager. Audiences can be targeted by using both Facebook's original
data, provided spontaneously by users, and non-original Facebook data, which is
tracked by cookies.[986]

The platform provides three ways to target users: first, by targeting core
audiences, in which the advertiser selects its audience manually based on
demographics. Second, by targeting customer audiences, in which the advertiser
uploads its contact list to connect with its customers on Facebook. Third, by
targeting lookalike audiences, in which advertisers use information about its
customer to find users with similar traits.[987]

---

981   In 31 December 2017, Facebook made over 39 billion dollars in profits selling spaces on its
      platforms for third party advertisement. United States Securities and Exchange Commission
      Washington, *Annual Report Pursuant to Section 13 or 15(d) of The Securities Exchange
      Act of 1934 for the Fiscal Year Ended December 31* (February 2018), online: Facebook
      Commission File <https://www.sec.gov/Archives/edgar/data/1326801/000132680118000009/
      fb-12312017x10k.htm> p 41.
982   *Ibid* p 41.
983   See "Facebook business" section: "Help Your Ads Find the People Who Will Love Your
      Business" <https://www.facebook.com/business/products/ads/ad-targeting>.
984   *Ibid.*
985   *Ibid.*
986   Joseph Turow, "The Daily You", *op. cit.*, p 50.
987   Asma AI Vranaki, "Regulating Social Networking Sites: Facebook, Online Behavioral
      Advertising, Data Protection Laws and Power", *op. cit.* and *Onuoha v Facebook, INC.*, No. 5:
      16-cv-06440-EJD (United States District Court Northern District California. Apr. 7, 2017),
      First Amended Complaint, p 8–18. A graphic representation can be found in annex 5.

Facebook specifies the steps advertisers may engage to manually target a particular group of people. They can include certain types of profiles or groups and exclude others. The inclusion and exclusion of the audiences that will receive advertisements is based on their "demographics," "interests," and "behaviors." These three categories are also composed of subcategories, allowing advertisers to precisely target and reach their final audience.[988]

The following offers an example of a specific final audience who may be selected: "(1) people in the United States; (2) who are between the ages of 15–35; (3) and are also men; (4) who must also use either an iPhone 6 or an iPhone 6 plus; (5) who must also be interested in action games to be in my audience; (6) However, if they meet all the above, but have a 2G network connection, then they'll be excluded from my audience."[989]

Moreover, through demographics categories, Facebook has allowed advertisers to target or exclude users who may have access to the advertisement according to their ethnic origin or perceived ethnic origin. Facebook has labeled these categories of multicultural affinity. Multicultural affinities available to advertisers have been described as: "African American (US), Asian American (US), Hispanic (US-all), Hispanic (US-bilingual), Hispanic (US-English dominant); Hispanic (US-Spanish dominant)."[990]

To test the possibilities of targeting audiences to receive advertisements on the platform, in 2016 Propublica, an independent nonprofit organization[991], purchased advertisement placements to advertise housing offers.[992] They were able to target an audience of house seekers and exclude through the tool provided by the platform all users identified as being part of the Black American, Asian American, and Hispanic ethnic affinity groups.[993] The housing advertisements excluding Black Americans, Asian Americans, and Hispanic were approved 15 minutes after Propublica placed the order. Propublica affirmed that they could empirically check that "Facebook's business model is based on allowing advertisers to target specific groups using huge realms of personal data the company has collected."[994] The publication identified over 50,000 unique categories in which Facebook could place its users.[995]

---

[988]   See Facebook, *Ad Targeting* (December 2019), online: Facebook <https://www.facebook.com/business/a/online-sales/ad-targeting-details/>.

[989]   *Onuoha v Facebook, INC.*, No. 5: 16-cv-06440-EJD (United States District Court Northern District California. Apr. 7, 2017), First Amended Complaint, p 11.

[990]   *Ibid.*

[991]   <https://www.propublica.org/about/>.

[992]   <https://www.propublica.org/article/facebook-lets-advertisers-exclude-users-by-race>.

[993]   *Ibid.*

[994]   *Ibid.*

[995]   *Ibid.*

2. FROM GOOGLE TO ALPHABET

Google was created in 1998 by Larry Page and Sergey Brin when they were Ph.D. researchers in computer science at Stanford University.[996] Both were reportedly frustrated with the search engines that existed in the United States at the time, because they did not efficiently rank the results of their queries. For instance, AltaVista was the best search engine in 1998, and the first full-text search database that allowed users to search content on the web.[997] It enabled users to search for things using "natural language," meaning that when a user typed "what is a computer" the engine would return results about computers rather than results about the words "what," "is," and "a." Over time, to monetize its activities AltaVista diversified its features, turning into a more complex web portal with a significant amount of information clustered on its homepage.[998]

Google outpaced AltaVista by offering a clean homepage design with the valuable ability to produce prompt and relevant responses to almost any of the user's queries.[999] Google's ability to fast-find users' queries in the vast ocean of information of the web has transformed it into the most popular search engine platform of the internet. The search engine considerably changed the way people find information and have access to knowledge online. For many, Google has become an indispensable tool for the use of the internet.

Google's search engine is so ubiquitous across the world that "to Google" is a verb that means "to search" not only in English but also in Portuguese, French, and German. Annually, more than one billion users make over one trillion searches on the engine.[1000] The search engine registers over three billion searches daily.[1001] It has turned into the most popular application since the invention of e-mail.[1002]

Even though the search engine is still one of the company's core products, Google has diversified from its first mission to organize and list all the digital world's information and make it available globally. Currently, Google is a technology company specialized in internet services, including online

---

[996]   Eric Schmidt, Jonathan Rosenberg, *How Google Works* (London: John Murray, 2015) p 4.

[997]   Bernard J Jansen, Amanda Spink, "How Are We Searching the World Wide Web? A Comparison of Nine Search Engine Transaction Logs" (2006) 42:1 Information Processing & Management 248.

[998]   *Ibid.*

[999]   David A Vise, Mark Malseed, *The Google Story: Inside the Hottest Business, Media and Technology Success of Our Time,* (New York: Bantam Books, 2018), p 28.

[1000] *Ibid,* p 34.

[1001] Google Ads, *Basics of Online Marketing* (June 2019), online: Google Ads <https://ads.google.com/intl/en_uk/home/resources/internet-marketing/>.

[1002] Scott Galloway, *The Four: The Hidden DNA of Amazon, Apple, Facebook, and Google* (New York: Portfolio, 2017).

advertising technologies, search engines, and cloud computing as well as a company that invests in disruptive future-oriented businesses.[1003]

Over the past years, Google has digitized millions of academic books from the public libraries with the purpose of making them available outside of these physical places.[1004] With this same future-oriented vein, Google has invested in promising fields ranging from artificial intelligence to molecular biology to genetics.[1005] Recording thousands of millions of genes seems to be a promising undertaking for Google's search engine.[1006] The willingness to disruptively innovate is the company's moto. To cite a few more developments, Google has heavily invested in its branches Brain (responsible for artificial intelligence)[1007], Wing (to build drones that deliver emergency medicines and goods)[1008], Waymo (to develop driverless cars)[1009], and Loon (to create stratospheric balloons that provide internet access in remote places that have been devastated by natural disasters).[1010]

To structure all these contrasting parts of the company, Google has created the holding company named Alphabet.[1011] Alphabet holds all the subsidiaries including Google's search engine, Gmail, YouTube, the Google Chrome browser, Blogger, the Android operating system, Google Docs, Google Maps, Waze, and all the other disruptive innovative initiatives.

2.1. BUSINESS MODEL

"Don't Be Evil"[1012]

Google's search engine, Gmail, YouTube, Waze, and Google Maps are all free of charge for internet users. These services and the heavy investments in the expansion of cutting-edge technologies are sponsored by Google's advertising

---

[1003] David A Vise, Mark Malseed, *The Google Story: Inside the Hottest Business, Media and Technology Success of Our Time, op. cit.*, p 40.

[1004] Paul Conway, "Preservation in the Age of Google, Digitization, Digital Preservation, and Dilemmas" (2010) 80:1 The Library Quarterly 61.

[1005] David A Vise, Mark Malseed, *The Google Story: Inside the Hottest Business, Media and Technology Success of Our Time, op. cit.*, p 50.

[1006] *Ibid*, p 52.

[1007] Google AI, *Google Brain Team* (June 2019), online: Google <https://ai.google/research/teams/brain/> AI is currently used in all sectors of the company from photos identification to advertising.

[1008] Google Wing, *Transforming the Way Goods Are Transported* (June 2019), online: Google <https://x.company/projects/wing/>

[1009] Google Waymo, *Introducing Waymo One* (June 2019), online: Google <https://waymo.com>.

[1010] It delivered internet in Puerto Rico when it was devastated by the hurricane Maria.

[1011] Google Loon, *Ballons Designed to Extend Connectivity* (June 2019), online: Google <https://loon.com>

[1012] "Don't Be Evil" is the motto of Google's corporate code of conduct and reflects the CEO's purposes of creating unbiased and objective technologies.

business to a great extent. Google alone has half of all digital advertising in the United States[1013], and 97% of the company total revenue is due to advertising.[1014] From the beginning, investors saw Google above all as an advertising industry.[1015]

The fast-growing migration of advertising from mass communication means, including television and printed media, to the online world made Google's ad business a great success. Google's search engine became highly profitable mainly because of the development of sophisticated targeted advertisements that appear to users when they are searching for information. Later, the company expanded its advertising business by creating its own ad network service: Google Display Network (GDN).

2.2. TARGETING PRACTICES

Google has two main approaches to allow third-party business advertising: AdWords – currently named Google Ads – Google Display Network.

One of Google's first main successful advertising initiatives was AdWords.[1016] With AdWords, advertisers choose the keywords they want to match with words searched by internet users in the search engine. For instance, if a company wants to advertise credit loan offers, it might choose words such as "looking for credit," "bank credit lines," "mortgage," and so forth. When the internet user searches for these terms, ads related to these terms will be listed on the top of Google's index in a form of a response link or, in some cases, an image. This system is one of the most profitable ad businesses for Google and was launched in 2000. Google profits every time an internet user clicks on one of the ads it displays. The price of keywords depends on the demand. Popular search terms are more expensive.[1017]

The second advertising possibility within Google is to contract Google Display Network (GDN), which is an advertising network service that intermediates the relationship between advertisers and hundreds of thousands of websites/publishers that belong to Google or not. These websites are also

---

[1013] David A Vise, Mark Malseed, *The Google Story: Inside the Hottest Business, Media and Technology Success of Our Time, op. cit.*, p xi.

[1014] United States Securities and Exchange Commission, *Annual Report Pursuant to Section 13 15 (d) of the Securities Exchange Act* (December 2018), online: Alphabet Inc. Commission File <https://www.sec.gov/Archives/edgar/data/1652044/000165204419000004/goog10-kq42018.htm>.

[1015] David A Vise, Mark Malseed, *The Google Story: Inside the Hottest Business, Media and Technology Success of Our Time, op. cit.*, p 139.

[1016] Harold Davis, *Google Advertising Tools: Cashing in With AdSense, AdWords, and the Google APIS* (Sebastopol: O'Reilly Media, 2006).

[1017] David A Vise, Mark Malseed, *The Google Story: Inside the Hottest Business, Media and Technology Success of Our Time, op. cit.*, p 129.

called Google's affiliated websites, and GDN operates within millions of them, including major commercial players such as AOL, *The New Yorker*, *Le Monde*, and *The Guardian*. Estimates indicate that GDN reaches over 90% of all internet users.[1018] Moreover, Google owns several platforms, including Blogger and YouTube, where independent content producers place their content. Google monetizes these contents through ads, which are delivered by the GDN, and their revenue is shared between the content producer and Google.

Both advertising systems use a complex set of auctions that involves the price offered by the advertisers per click and the relevance of the ad content to the internet user. These two factors determine which ads will be displayed and how they will be ranked. Advertisers using AdWords and the GDN can target their ads by choosing several internet users' individual aspects. Google overtly encourages advertisers to target their ads by affirming that "targeting ads is an essential part of a successful advertising campaign. You may have designed the perfect ad, but you'll need to show it to the right people at the right time to better reach your goal."[1019]

For both systems, audience targeting may include geographic location, age, and gender; "in-market" tools which display ads that are similar to what users searched to buy online; "custom intent" that is related to internet user's preferences; "similar audiences" that target users with similar traits of the advertiser clients; and "remarketing" tools that target users who have interacted online with the brand or the store.[1020] Google also offers the possibility to target content or topics.[1021] Advertisers can also target where they want to have their ads displayed according to the content published in the webserver.

Regarding audience targeting, only Google has the information concerning the internet users that will be targeted. The advertisers are given the option to select aspects of the audiences who will see the ads, but they will not directly have information about individual users. This set of detailed information about internet users is acquired through tracking cookies and other technologies. Ultimately, Google's services are not free for internet users, as the cost is their personal and non-personal data.[1022]

[1018] *Ibid*, p 141.

[1019] Google, *Google Ads Help* (June 2019), online: Google <https://support.google.com/google-ads/answer/1704368?hl=en>.

[1020] *Ibid*.

[1021] *Ibid*.

[1022] *See* section II below.

SECTION II. FIGHTING FOR PRIVACY AND EQUALITY: LITIGATION

1. LITIGATION AGAINST DATA MISUSE AND DISCRIMINATION IN ADVERTISING PRACTICES

1.1. UNITED STATES: TRACKING COOKIES

1.1.2. Google

In 2012, the Federal Trade Commission imposed charges of over $22 million on Google for misleading users about their privacy.[1023] After investigation, the Commission concluded that Google misrepresented to users in the United States that it would not place tracking cookies to serve targeted advertisements when in fact it did. Google placed tracking cookies on the devices of users who visited sites that were part of Google Ad Network.[1024] In its privacy policy, Google informed users using the browser Safari that they would be opted out of tracking cookies, but in fact by default they were opted in.

In the United States, online platforms are not obliged to inform their users that they are tracked by cookies, but when they have a privacy policy disclaiming that they do not place tracking cookies in their users' devices, they must comply with it under the risk of being charged for misleading trade practice.[1025] Contrarily to the EU law requirements, online platforms in the United States are not obliged to require users' consent for collecting their personal data, which is normally obtained through tracking cookies. However, major online platforms, as a general practice, have a privacy policy informing their users about it. Moreover, some platforms, including Google, are part of self-regulatory initiatives that request members to comply with their self-regulatory code of conducts.[1026]

In this particular settlement, Google paid charges to the FTC because it had violated its users' trust as well as a previous FTC order.[1027] The Commission had investigated Google a few years before for this same reason and had officially issued an order requiring the company to stop breaching its own

---

[1023] *Google Inc.*, docket no. C-4336. FTC, *Decision and Order* (August 2012), online: FTC <https://www.ftc.gov/sites/default/files/documents/cases/2012/08/120809googlestatement.pdf>.

[1024] Named by the time DoubleClick Advertising Network.

[1025] *See* chapter 3.

[1026] Google, for instance, is member of the Network Advertising Initiative. NAI, *Nai Members* (June 2019), online: NAI <https://www.networkadvertising.org/participating-networks/?page=1>.

[1027] *Google Inc.*, docket no. C-4336. FTC, *Decision and Order* (October 2011), online: FTC <https://www.ftc.gov/sites/default/files/documents/cases/2011/10/111024googlebuzzdo.pdf>.

privacy policies.[1028] The settlement and the previous order were part of the Commission's effort to ensure that companies follow the promises they make to their consumers. In 2016, Google accepted to pay over $5 million to settle a private class action involving the same conduct.[1029] In 2019, Google paid almost $200 million to settle allegations by the Federal Trade Commission that YouTube, which is a Google subsidiary, illegally collected personal information from children without having the consent of their parents.[1030] The practice is against the Children's Online Privacy Protection Act (COPPA), one of the few statutory laws that protect personal data.

1.1.3. Facebook

The Federal Trade Commission has also conducted several investigations against Facebook for misleading, deceptive, and unfair trade practices towards its consumers for breaching its privacy policy.

The FTC has charged Facebook for unfairly misleading its users about who could have access to their personally and non-personally identifiable information.[1031] According to the Federal Commission, Facebook stored users' profile information, including their name, gender, birthday, hometown, who they are interested in (men/women), relationship status, political and religious views, and other data on a computer network that the platform controlled.[1032] Facebook designated each user with an identification number – a unique number – that advertisers could access to obtain user's profile information. However, Facebook's central privacy page overtly guaranteed to users that they could control who was able to see their profile information. The options included "only friends" or "friends of friends." Nothing in the privacy page indicated that advertisers would have access to their personally identifiable information. Despite Facebook's privacy policy, users had their personal information shared with third-party advertisers.

In that particular case, Facebook allowed advertisers to target their ads based on the user's disclosed personal traits, including, but not limited to, the information the user listed under the fields of geographic location, age, sex, birthday, interested in (women/men), relationship status, likes, education, and name of employer. In its privacy policy, Facebook disclosed that it would use

---

[1028]   *Ibid.*

[1029]   *Google Inc. Cookie Placement Consumer Privacy Litigation*, 806 F.3d 125, 130–32 (3d Cir. 2015).

[1030]   Federal Trade Commission, *Google and YouTube Will Pay Record $ 170 Million Alleged Violations of Children's Privacy Law* (September 2019), online: Federal Trade Commission <https://www.ftc.gov/news-events/press-releases/2019/09/google-youtube-will-pay-record-170-million-alleged-violations>.

[1031]   *Facebook Inc.*, docket no. C-923184. FTC, *Complaint* (November 2011), online: FTC <https://www.ftc.gov/sites/default/files/documents/cases/2011/11/111129facebookcmpt.pdf>.

[1032]   *Ibid.*

information about users' profiles without identifying them for the purposes of personalized advertisement.[1033] However, Facebook shared information about users with advertisers by identifying who had clicked on the ads. Moreover, the FTC found that advertisers could access users' identification number to get detailed information about them. This information consisted of their profile photographs, sex, name, location, list of friends, and pages liked.

The FTC considered the practices unfair and deceptive because they violated the platform's privacy policy. In the consent order, Facebook agreed, among other things, to make sure that protected information would not be accessed by advertisers without users' knowledge.[1034] As part of the agreement, Facebook accepted that a third-party examiner may conduct privacy audits for 20 years.[1035]

After the consent agreement with the FTC, Facebook privacy practices continued under the spotlight of lawyers and journalists in the United States. The main criticism relates to the amount of personally identifiable information that is collected and the practice of continually sharing this data with advertisers.[1036] The apex of the tensions came with the Facebook and Cambridge Analytical political scandal in 2018.[1037] Cambridge Analytica, a private company, had harvested personal information of more than 87 million Facebook users for political targeted advertising purposes.[1038] This data was allegedly used to target political advertisements in the American presidential elections and in the Brexit referendum in 2016.[1039] Cambridge Analytica built psychographic profiles correlating users' personality to their political beliefs. This data helped politicians to target voters. The scandal took Zuckerberg to testify before the United States Congress and the British Parliament.[1040] After Zuckerberg's hearings, a few Congress representatives proposed legislation to regulate personal data policies.

The Consent Act proposal, for instance, requires explicit opt-in consent before online companies are allowed to use, share, or sell any of their users' personal data as well as explicit notification whenever data is collected,

---

[1033] *Ibid*, p 12.
[1034] *Facebook Inc.* docket no. C-4365. FTC, *Agreement Containing Consent Order* (July 2011), online: FTC <https://www.ftc.gov/sites/default/files/documents/cases/2011/11/111129faceboo kagree.pdf>.
[1035] *Ibid.*
[1036] Natasha Simmons, "Facebook and the Privacy Frontier" (2012) 33:3 Business Law Review 58.
[1037] Jim Isaak and Mina J Hanna, "User Data Privacy: Facebook, Cambridge Analytica, and Privacy Protection" (2018) 51 Computer 56; Roberto J Gonzalez, "Hacking the Citizenry? Personality Profiling, Big Data and the Election of Donald Trump" (2017) 33 Anthropology Today 9; Nathaniel Persily, "The 2016 US Election: Can Democracy Survive the Internet?" (2017) 28 Journal of Democracy 63.
[1038] *Ibid*, p 57.
[1039] Roberto J Gonzalez, "Hacking the Citizenry? Personality Profiling, Big Data and the Election of Donald Trump" (2017) 33 Anthropology Today 9; Nathaniel Persily, "The 2016 US Election: Can Democracy Survive the Internet?" (2017) 28 Journal of Democracy 63.
[1040] Ewan McGaughey, "Could Brexit Be Void?" (2018) 29 King's Law Journal 331.

shared, or sold to a third party.[1041] The proposal for the Social Media Privacy Protection and Consumer Rights Act of 2018 provides similar obligations, but it adds restrictions on modifications to privacy terms, provisions concerning withdrawal of consent, and procedures when a violation of privacy occurs.[1042]

In 2019, Facebook settled a consent agreement with the Federal Trade Commission to pay the largest civil penalty for breaching privacy promises and conducting deceptive and unfair practices.[1043] The penalty amounted to $5 billion. After the investigations, the Commission discovered that Facebook breached its 2011 agreement. The platform continued to share its users' personally identifiable data with third-party partners, violating several provisions of the agreement. The settlement mandated fundamental privacy changes and removed Mark Zuckerberg from the charge of consumer privacy decision-maker. It created an independent committee to oversee Facebook's privacy decisions and an independent third-party committee to assess the performance of the platform's privacy policy. The first members of the committee were appointed in May 2020.[1044]

1.2. EUROPE: TRACKING COOKIES BREACH PRIVACY AND FOSTER DISCRIMINATION IN EUROPE

1.2.1. Google

In 2019, the French data protection authority the Commission Nationale de l'Informatique et des Libertés (CNIL) imposed a financial penalty of € 50 million on Google for breaching the GDPR.[1045] The French authority concluded that Google's privacy policies regarding advertising personalization lacked transparency, did not inform users adequately, and lacked valid consent. Only eight days after the GDPR entered into force, the CNIL received collective complaints with more than 1,000 signatures from two organizations: None of Your Business (NOYB) and La Quadrature du Net (LQDN). The complaint

1041 Senator Edward Markey, *S.2639 Consent Act* (October 2018), online: US Congress <https://www.congress.gov/bill/115th-congress/senate-bill/2639>.

1042 Senator Amy Klobuchar, *S.2728 Social Media Privacy and Consumer Protection Act of 2018* (April 2018), online: US Congress <https://www.congress.gov/bill/115th-congress/senate-bill/2728>.

1043 *Facebook Inc.* docket no.19-cv-2184. FTC, *Stipulated Order for Civil Penalty, Monetary Judgement, and Injunctive Relief* (July 2019), online: FTC <https://www.ftc.gov/system/files/documents/cases/182_3109_facebook_order_filed_7-24-19.pdf>.

1044 Rob Price, *Facebook Has Appointed the Privacy Committee on Its Board Designed to Prevent Another Cambridge Analytica Scandal* (May 2020), online: Business Insider <https://www.businessinsider.com/facebook-announces-privacy-committee-board-of-directors-2020-5?r=US&IR=T>.

1045 Deliberation of the Restricted Committee SAN-2019–001 of 21 January 2019 Pronouncing Financial Sanction Against Google LLC.

alleged that Google did not have a valid legal basis to process the personal data of its users, especially for targeted advertisements.

The CNIL concluded that Google's operation was illegally intrusive. Moreover, the purposes of data processing were described in a too vague manner and the period of storage was not provided for a set of personal data collected. The Committee concluded that the consent obtained to operate all these personal data were not valid, specific, or unambiguous.[1046] The fine imposed on Google was the first to be applied with the new limits provided by the GDPR.[1047] The determination of the amount considered the importance Google had in the French market.

1.2.2. Facebook

Over the past few years, data protection authorities have investigated Facebook for breaching users' privacy for targeted advertising. The CNIL condemned Facebook to pay € 150,000 for collecting personal data and displaying targeted advertisements without a legal basis.[1048] The CNIL stressed that Facebook unfairly tracked its users via *datr* cookies outside the platform without making its users understand that their data were systematically collected as soon as they navigated to a third-party website. The sanction was implemented in 2017 before the GDPR entered into force and was grounded on a breach of French data protection law[1049] – which was framed by the General Data Protection Directive. Contrarily to the United States, EU member states have data protection laws requiring online companies to request consent to collect and process personal data since the Data Protection Directive, enacted in 1995, was transposed into domestic laws.

Moreover, data protection authorities (DPAs) in Belgium, the Netherlands, Spain, and Germany have investigated and sanctioned Facebook for having created a massive compilation of personal data about its users to display targeted advertisements without their knowledge and consent.[1050] In 2018 in

---

[1046] *Ibid.*

[1047] Article, 83(5), GDPR. It ranges from up to 4% annual of the global turnover of the preceding fiscal year or twenty million euros.

[1048] Facebook Sanctioned for Several Breaches of the French Data Protection Act in 2017. Délibération nSAN-2017 du 6 mai 2017 pronançant une sanction pécuniaire à l'encontre de la société Facebook.

[1049] Décret n° 2005–1309 du 20 octobre 2005 pris pour l'application de la loi n° 78–17 du 6 janvier 1978 relative à l'informatique, aux fichiers et aux libertés. Updated after the GDPR, in 2018, to: Ordonnance n° 2018–1125 du 12 décembre 2018 prise en application de l'article 32 de la loi n° 2018–493 du 20 juin 2018 relative à la protection des données personnelles et portant modification de la loi n° 78–17 du 6 janvier 1978 relative à l'informatique, aux fichiers et aux libertés et diverses dispositions concernant la protection des données à caractère personnel.

[1050] Autoriteit Persoonsgegevens, *Common Statement by the Contact Group of the Data Protection Authorities of the Netherlands, France, Spain, Hamburg and Belgium* (May 2017), online: DPA <https://autoriteitpersoonsgegevens.nl/sites/default/

Belgium, the Tribunal de Première Instance de Bruxelles ruled Facebook to stop breaking privacy laws by tracking its users while they are navigating on third-party websites or to face a fine of € 250,000 to € 125 million.[1051] In 2018, a German Regional Court in Berlin condemned Facebook for having violated data protection laws by using tracking cookies without the users' proper consent.[1052] In 2017, the Spanish DPA sanctioned Facebook for the same reason.[1053]

In the Netherlands, the Dutch DPA, the Autoriteit Persoonsgegevens, revealed that Facebook had used the personal data of 9.6 million Dutch people for targeted advertising without having their explicit consent. After investigations, the DPA found that the platform enabled advertisers to select "men who are interested in other men" for targeted advertising purposes. The DPA condemned Facebook for not having required its users to process this sensitive data and concluded that data relating to sexual preferences to show targeted advertisements could lead to discrimination.[1054]

2. LITIGATION AGAINST TARGETED ADVERTISEMENTS: EMPLOYMENT, CREDIT, AND HOUSING OFFERS

The advertisement targeting tools implemented by Facebook did not go unnoticed by civil rights lawyers in the United States. Between 2016 and 2018, charges of discrimination and class actions were filed against Facebook, seeking declaratory and injunctive relief, penalties, and monetary damages to redress racial, sex, and age discrimination, among other protected grounds, based on what the lawyers then called the "exclude people" button used by Facebook

---

files/atoms/files/common_statement_16_may_2017.pdf>. *See* also the campaign #stopspyingonus started in the June 2019 in several countries of the European Union: Ligue des Droits Humains, *communiqué de presse* (June 2019), online: LDH <http://2ur2r.r.ca.d.sendibm2.com/mk/mr/UrbaMII0WjtmxReLSprj_R7V06S93d_CzxiYS6on0Hc0KrHFTpgYjto0M6OpQwMaxuSsWJfJASPqf2MraSfdwjBjnYydKivSTy6hgUaq5_rVmvht>.

[1051] Civ. Tribunal de Première Instance (néerl.), Bruxelles, 24e Chambre, 16 février 2018. <https://www.autoriteprotectiondonnees.be/sites/privacycommission/files/documents/jugement_facebook_16022018.pdf>.

[1052] *Urteil des Landgerichts Berlin vom 16.01.2018, Az. 16 O 341/15* <https://www.vzbv.de/sites/default/files/downloads/2018/02/12/facebook_lg_berlin.pdf>.

[1053] Agencia Española de Datos, *Procedimiento no. PS/00219/2017 – Resolución: R/00259/2018* <https://www.aepd.es/media/resoluciones/PS-00219-2017_Resolucion-de-fecha-02–03–2018_Art-ii-culo-11–6-LOPD.pdf>.

[1054] Autoriteit Persoonsgegevens, Informal English Translation of the Conclusions of the Dutch Data Protection Authority in its Final Report of Findings About Its Investigation Into the Processing of Personal Data by Facebook Group (February 2017), online: DPA <https://autoriteitpersoonsgegevens.nl/sites/default/files/atoms/files/conclusions_facebook_february_23_2017.pdf>.

ads.[1055] The lawyers alleged that the platform and its third-party advertisers had breached innumerous civil rights acts by excluding protected classes from receiving advertisements with housing, credit, and employment offers.

2.1. ETHNIC AFFINITY AND GEOGRAPHIC LOCATION TARGETS

In *Onuoha v Facebook,* a class action was filed by three plaintiffs on behalf of all Black American, Latino, and Asian American Facebook users located within the United States who were interested in receiving employment, housing, and credit opportunities and were denied by Facebook targeting policies.[1056] The first plaintiff, Suzanne-Juliette Mobley, self-identified as a Black American and worked as a community engagement manager. She declared to reside in New Orleans where more than 70% of the population is composed of Black Americans. The second plaintiff, Daniel Adrian Manriquez, self-identified as Latino, lived in Phoenix, Arizona in an area where 53% of the inhabitants were Latinos and 13% were Black Americans. The third plaintiff, Victor Onuoha, self-identified as a Black American and was based in Gretna, Louisiana, in a predominantly non-white neighborhood. In his zip code, 38% of residents were Black Americans and 15% were Latinos. All the plaintiffs alleged to be frequent Facebook users and to have sought housing, employment, and credit opportunities on Facebook through the advertisements the platform chose to show them.[1057]

They charged Facebook of racial discrimination when advertising housing, employment, and credit opportunities. According to the lawyers, some statutory protected groups were excluded from receiving marketing advertisements for housing, employment, and credit opportunities, because Facebook had created and provided filters that enabled companies and advertisers to exclude them from receiving the ads.[1058] Through this action, Facebook was engaging in practices that had an unjustified disparate impact on Black Americans, Latinos, and Asian Americans.

The group of people potentially affected by the discriminatory targeting was considered so numerous that it was not feasible to join all members in the class action. In the United States, the platform assumed to have 26 million users

---

[1055] Onuoha v Facebook, Inc., No. 5: 16-cv-06440-EJD (N.D. Cal. Apr. 7, 2017). Bradley v T-Mobile US, INC., No. 17-cv-07232-BLF (N.D. Cal. June 4, 2019); National Fair Housing Alliance v Facebook, Inc., No. 1:18-cv-02689-JGK (S.D. N.Y. Aug. 08, 2018); Riddick v Facebook, Inc., No. 3:18-cv-04429 (N.D. Cal. Mar. 19, 2019); Spees et al v Facebook, Inc. (EEOC, September 2018).

[1056] *Onuoha v Facebook*, p 19.

[1057] *Onuoha v Facebook*, p 7–8.

[1058] *Onuoha v Facebook*, p 19.

who identified as "African Americans," 8 million users who identified as "Asian American," and 32 million users who identified as "Hispanic."[1059]

The lawyers claimed that in the past decade Facebook had become the most popular platform for businesses to advertise their products and offers. However, they were convinced that Facebook, on the one hand, had become a relevant means for companies to specifically advertise employment positions, housing opportunities, and credit offers online, and, on the other, a popular means for individuals to seek and pursue these three opportunities. Essentially, the plaintiffs claimed that Facebook itself provided the tools and filters that enabled advertisers to exclude groups of individuals, more precisely, African Americans, Latinos, and Asian Americans – based on information the platform had collected, analyzed, and categorized. The lawyers did not find filters to specifically target white users.[1060]

By designing filters that redlined certain groups protected by federal and state laws, Facebook had "engaged in a practice of providing racially discriminatory marketing, recruitment, sourcing, advertising, branding, information, and hiring services for and on behalf of employers, housing providers, and creditors in violation of federal and state civil rights law."[1061] When companies interested in advertising on Facebook used the suggested filters to select which users would receive their advertisements, Facebook kept encouraging them to show their marketing to the right people in the right places. The platform provided a specific page to assist advertisers to target its users, and included information such as "easier, more effective ways to reach the right people on Facebook" and "targeting tips to reach the right people."[1062]

The plaintiffs pleaded that Facebook assisted companies and advertisers in the housing, employment, and credit sectors to identify users who would be seeking these three opportunities. The way Facebook assisted businesses was by categorizing certain individuals as employment seekers, housing seekers, and credit seekers based on what Facebook users had interacted with, liked, shared, or stated in their profiles regarding their interests. For example, once a user was categorized as an employment seeker, advertisements related to the job market would specifically reach this user.[1063]

In addition to the categorization of users as employment, housing, and credit seekers, the problem was that Facebook had allowed advertisers to target individuals in these three categories and to target their ethnic affinity. Furthermore, beyond ethnic affinity categories, Facebook also had other

---

[1059]   *Ibid*, p 19.
[1060]   *Ibid*, p 1.
[1061]   *Ibid*, p 1–2. The practice of redlining traditionally consisted in the exclusion of whole communities from economic opportunities, such as mortgage, lending or housing purchases.
[1062]   See Facebook, *Help Your Ads Find the People Who Will Love Your Business* (July 2019), online: Facebook <https://www.facebook.com/business/products/ads/ad-targeting>.
[1063]   *Onuoha v Facebook*, p 12–13.

targeting possibilities that could work as proxies for ethnicity, such as geographic location. The lawyers demonstrated that when an advertiser follows Facebook's encouragement to exclude or include people who live in certain zip codes, a "mapping tool draws a bright red line around the zip code that is being excluded (and whose residents will not receive the ad) and a blue line around the zip code that is being included (and whose residents will receive the ad)."[1064] In this way, companies advertising employment, housing, and credit opportunities on Facebook can redline an entire zip code or a group of zip codes.

Through the filters created and made available by Facebook, advertisers can place advertisements that could disproportionally reach people of a particular ethnic background and exclude users from different ethnic origins.[1065] Allowing employment, housing, or credit opportunities to be advertised based on the zip code where potential interested users reside is a way to exclude certain ethnic affinities, particularly Black Americans, Latinos, and other non-white communities.[1066]

The plaintiffs alleged that Facebook specifically instructs advertisers to understand their target audiences, especially based on demographics: "because when you narrow your targeting you can focus on reaching the people who matter the most to your business, including by targeting a Custom Audience, and reach interested and engaged audiences, by finding more people on Facebook who share traits – like location, age, gender, and interests – with your customers."[1067]

According to the lawyers, for an undetermined period of time, members of the proposed class have not received – or have not regularly received – Facebook ads for employment, housing, and credit opportunities from Facebook and companies that use Facebook's advertising tools to seek job applicants, house seekers, and credit seekers. As a result, "plaintiffs and members of the proposed class have been denied employment, housing, and credit opportunities by Facebook and such businesses."[1068]

The class action alleged that Facebook was not a passive player in its advertising business. Instead, the tools provided by the platform were a central aspect for companies to selectively advertise in a discriminatory manner. While Facebook decided that it was desirable to limit which Facebook users would see an advertisement based on their race, national origin, and location, federal and state laws prohibit racial and national origin discrimination in advertising employment, housing, and credit opportunities.[1069]

1064   *Onuoha v Facebook*, p 13.
1065   *Ibid*, p 14.
1066   *Ibid.*
1067   *Ibid* p 15.
1068   *Ibid* p 24.
1069   *Onuoha v Facebook*, p 5.

2.2. AGE TARGETS

Less than two years after the *Onuoha v Facebook* case was filed, another class action was initiated alleging illegal age targeting for employment advertisement offers.[1070] The case was headed by the Communications Workers of America (CWA), which is an international labor union headquartered in Washington D.C. Across the United States, Canada, and Puerto Rico, the CWA represents over 700,000 workers within several industries, including information technologies, news media, and telecommunications. The union's mission is to help workers protect their rights, mainly through collective bargain and public advocacy.[1071]

The class action advocated for the right of older workers against the practice of age discrimination in employment advertising through Facebook in the United States. According to the complaint, Facebook and third-party advertisers frequently excluded older workers from receiving their employment advertisements with recruitment offers and, therefore, denied older workers to be informed about employment positions. They excluded older workers from receiving the advertisements with the offers by targeting their ads to younger workers. They could do so via Facebook's ad tools. The practice potentially breached the ADEA and state law that forbid age discrimination in employment recruitment.

In the complaint, the lawyers could not precisely determine the number of companies that had illegally targeted age in their employment offers on the platform, but the defendant class comprised hundreds of major American employers and employment agencies.[1072] Among the hundreds of identified companies that allegedly discriminated grounded on applicants' age were Facebook, T-Mobile US, Amazon.com, and Cox Communications.

T-Mobile, based in Delaware, provides wireless communication services such as voice, messaging, and data to over 71 million clients across the United States.[1073] T-Mobile advertised employment opportunities in 42 American states and in the District of Columbia through Facebook.[1074] In 2016 Amazon.com had employed over 300,000 full-time and part-time employees in the United States.[1075] Amazon had advertised employment opportunities on Facebook

---

[1070] *Bradley et al v T-Mobile US, Inc. et al,* (cv 07232, United States California Northern District Court, 2017), amended complaint, p. 8. (hereinafter *Bradley v T-Mobile US*).

[1071] *More* Communications Workers of America, *about* (June 2019), online: CWA <https://cwa-union.org>.

[1072] *Bradley v T-Mobile US,* first amended complaint, p 11.

[1073] United States Securities and Exchange Commission Washington, *Annual Report Pursuant to Section 13 or 15(d) of The Securities Exchange Act of 1934 for the Fiscal Year Ended December 31* (December 2016), online: secgov <https://www.sec.gov/Archives/edgar/data/1283699/000128369917000010/tmus12312016form10-k.htm>.

[1074] *Bradley v T-Mobile US,* p 10.

[1075] United States Securities and Exchange Commission, *Annual Report Pursuant to Section 13 15 (d) of the Securities Exchange Act* (February 2017), online: Amazon Commission File <https://

for job opportunities in the United States. Cox Communications, the third largest cable company in the United States[1076], also used Facebook to advertise employment opportunities. In the condition of employer, Facebook itself also advertised employment offers on its own platform. All these companies targeted preselected users to receive their employment offers.

T-Mobile published employment ads to recruit for customer care job positions available in stores located in the United States and limited the Facebook users who would receive the ad to individuals 18–38 years old. Amazon.com restricted employment ads for part-time jobs to users ranging 18–54, 18–50, 28–55, and 22–40 years old. Cox Communications restricted various employment ads to users who were 20–45, 20–50, 19–55, and 20–55 years old. Facebook itself advertised employment positions to users ranging 21–55 and 25–60 years old.[1077] The ads themselves did not state any age limit, but it was possible to know such information through the option "Why am I seeing this ad?" When users clicked on it, they were informed that "one reason you're seeing this ad is that T-Mobile Careers wants to reach people interested in customer services, based on your activity such as liking pages or clicking on ads. There may be other reasons you're seeing this ad, including that T-Mobile Careers wants to reach people ages to 18 to 38 who live or were recently in the United States. This is information is based on your Facebook profile and where you've connected to the Internet."[1078] The same message appeared for the other advertisements.[1079]

These companies have excluded older internet users from receiving advertisements with employment recruitment offers via Facebook's paid advertising platform. As a consequence, they have denied thousands of older users the opportunity to learn about and obtain employment opportunities.

One of the excluded older users was Linda Bradley, a 45-year-old resident in Ohio. By the time the class action was filed, she had been fired from her job at a call center. She was a regular Facebook user and had accessed the platform to seek jobs opportunities. Once, she had seen an employment advertisement on the platform's news feed and contacted the company to be informed about the open position. In the class action, the lawyers alleged that she had the required skills for the available positions advertised by T-Mobile, Amazon, Cox, Facebook, and several other class members.[1080] She was also available for employment opportunities outside her current geographic area of Ohio. The lawyers claimed that she had never received an employment ad from T-Mobile, Amazon, Cox,

www.sec.gov/Archives/edgar/data/1018724/000101872417000011/amzn-20161231x10k.htm>.

[1076] Cox, *about* (June 2019), online: COX <https://www.coxenterprises.com/about-us#.WjkkTGyosl1>.

[1077] In the class action is not specified the title of all jobs advertised by these companies. *Bradley v T-Mobile US*, first amended complaint, p 28.

[1078] *Bradley v T-Mobile US*, first amended complaint, p 26.

[1079] *Ibid.*

[1080] *Bradley v T-Mobile US*, first amended complaint, p 8.

and Facebook among other offers they were not aware of. She confirmed that if she had received one of those ads, she would have clicked on it to have more information about it, and, eventually, she would have applied for it.[1081]

Maurice Anscombe, 57 years old, lived in Maryland and was also affected by the age targeting. He had worked as a cable technician and also in law enforcement. By the time the class action was filed, he was unemployed and had used the platform to look for job opportunities.[1082] Similarly to Mrs. Bradley, Mr. Anscombe had a range of skills to work for T-Mobile, Amazon, Cox, and Facebook, but he had never received their ads on his news feed. He would have applied to one of the offered positions if he had received it.

The last class representative was Lura Callahan, a 67-year-old resident in Ohio. Similarly to Mrs. Bradley, she worked for a long time in a call center and was laid off by the time the class action was filed. She used Facebook to seek job opportunities but never received an employment ad from T-Mobile, Amazon, Cox, Facebook, or other class defendants.[1083]

According to the lawyers, employment advertising, recruiting, and hiring practices have transformed over the past decade. For several sectors, social media platforms, particularly Facebook, have become an important force in the labor market. As companies advertise increasingly more job opportunities on Facebook, workers increasingly seek job opportunities on the platform.

The class allegations argued that Facebook's advertising platform was an important place for employers and employment agencies to recruit workers.[1084] Facebook overtly collected information about its users, including age, and allowed employers and employment agencies to target them when advertising employment positions. Facebook informed employers which workers were available for job positions or were looking for a job. Facebook provided employers the possibility to choose the age of the users who would receive employment advertisements with recruitment offers. When advertisers targeted users' age, they excluded older workers.[1085] In addition, Facebook assisted employers to select users who were demographically similar to their current employees with the tool lookalike audiences.[1086] Ultimately, hundreds of major employers, including Facebook, and employment agencies have reportedly excluded millions of older workers from receiving employment ads on the platform.[1087]

[1081]   *Ibid*, p 9.
[1082]   *Ibid*, p 10.
[1083]   *Ibid*, p 13.
[1084]   *Bradley v T-Mobile US*, first amended complaint, p 12.
[1085]   *Ibid*, p 17.
[1086]   *Ibid*, p 19.
[1087]   *Ibid*, p 24.

2.3. GENDER TARGETS

In *Spees et al. v Facebook*, the international labor union Communications
Workers of America (CWA) and female class representatives accused Facebook
of discriminating by targeting and sending employment advertisements
and related recruitment and hiring opportunities to male Facebook users
"while excluding female prospective job applicants from receiving the job
advertisements and opportunities."[1088] They alleged that Facebook asked its
users to identify their gender when subscribing to the platform. Next, Facebook
enabled employers' advertising employment opportunities to target users who
would receive the advertisement according to their gender with the options:
"all," "male," and "female."

2.4. DEFENSE STRATEGIES: LIABILITIES

In the above-mentioned cases, lawyers compared Facebook to a traditional
publisher, employer, employment agency, credit institution, and housing agency
to seek liability for the application of filters to be used by advertisers. The liability
of publishers, employers, employment agencies, creditors, and housing agencies
for discrimination in the offer of credit, housing, and employment is backed
by Title VII of the Civil Rights Act, the Fair Housing Act, the Equal Credit
Opportunity Act (ECOA), and the Civil Rights Act of 1866 (Section 1981 and
Section 1982).[1089]

Facebook alleged that as an Internet Service Provider it could not be liable
for the acts of its users.[1090] First, Facebook claimed that third-party advertisers,
and not the platform, controlled the content of the ads and the criteria used to
target their audience.[1091] Second, Facebook argued that its policies do not allow
any unlawful discrimination in advertising and require companies to certify
that their ads comply with antidiscrimination laws.[1092] At the time, the policy
specifically stated that "advertisers may not use our audience selection tools to
wrongfully target specific groups of people for advertising or wrongfully exclude
specific groups of people from seeing their ads; or include discriminatory
content in their ads."[1093]

[1088] Spees et al v Facebook, Inc. (EEOC, September 2018).

[1089] The defense also referred to State statues including the Fair Employment and Housing Act
(FEHA), the Unruh Civil Rights Act (Unruh Act), and the Unfair Competition Law (UCL). In
the thesis, I focus my analyses on the federal level.

[1090] Particularly in the cases Onuoha v Facebook and Bradley v T-Mobile US.

[1091] *Bradley v T-Mobile US*, motion to dismiss first amended complaint, p 12.

[1092] "Targeting: You must not use targeting options to discriminate against, harass, provoke, or
disparage users or to engage in predatory advertising practice". Facebook, *Advertising Policy*,
(7)(1) (June 2019), online: Facebook <https://www.facebook.com/policies/ads/>.

[1093] *Bradley v T-Mobile US*, motion to dismiss first amended complaint, p 3.

Facebook argued that the CDA exempts it from tort responsibility for the third-party content and third-party targeted advertisements.[1094] According to Facebook, advertisers are the only ones responsible for the targets they chose. Ultimately, the platform only provided neutral tools to them. The fact that the CDA does not allow imposition of liability based on third-party content should be enough to dismiss the complaint entirely.

However, the plaintiffs raised that the CDA did not encompass targeted advertisement, because Facebook had the data about the users who would see the ads, created filters that allowed advertisers to target users, incentivized its advertisers to use its targeting tools as an efficient method to reach their target audience, and made all its business profits on targeted third-party advertisements. Given this context, Facebook would also be considered a content provider.

2.5. FACEBOOK'S AD POLICY CHANGES: CLASS ACTIONS SETTLEMENT

Increasing pressure from journalists[1095], Congress members[1096], civil rights commissions and activists[1097], academia[1098], and litigation against discriminatory targeting advertisement encouraged Facebook to react.

[1094] CDA 47 U.S.C. §230 (c)(1). "No provider or user of an interactive computer service shall be treated as the publisher or speaker of any information provided by another information content provider".

[1095] Julia Angwin and Terry Parris, "Facebook Lets Advertisers Exclude Users by Race" *ProPublica* (2016), available at: https://www.propublica.org/article/facebook-lets-advertisers-exclude-users-by-race; Stephen Engelberg, "HUD Has 'Serious Concerns' About Facebook's Ethnic Targeting" *ProPublica* (2016), available at: https://www.propublica.org/article/hud-has-serious-concerns-about-facebooks-ethnic-targeting.; Julia Angwin, Ariana Tobin and Madeleine Varner, "Facebook (Still) Letting Housing Advertisers Exclude Users by Race" *ProPublica* (2017), available at: https://www.propublica.org/article/facebook-advertising-discrimination-housing-race-sex-national-origin; Julia Angwin, Noam Scheiber and Ariana Tobin, "Dozens of Companies Are Using Facebook to Exclude Older Workers From Job Ads" *ProPublica* (2017), available at: https://www.propublica.org/article/facebook-ads-age-discrimination-targeting.; Ariana Tobin and Jeremy B Merril, "Facebook Is Letting Job Advertisers Target Only Men" *ProPublica* (2018), available at: https://www.propublica.org/article/facebook-is-letting-job-advertisers-target-only-men.

[1096] Congress of the United States, Letter to Zuckerberg about "Ethnic Affinities" filters, 1 November 2016, available at: https://cbc.house.gov/uploadedfiles/facebook_housing_letter.pdf.

[1097] ACLU, *Facebook Settles Civil Rights Cases by Making Sweeping Changes to its Online Ad Platform* (March 2019), online: ACLU <https://www.aclu.org/blog/womens-rights/womens-rights-workplace/facebook-settles-civil-rights-cases-making-sweeping>. Also the EEOC and the FHA.

[1098] Ifeoma Ajunwa, "Age Discrimination by Platforms" (2019) *op. cit.*; Pauline T Kim, Sharion Scott, "Discrimination in Online Employment Recruiting" (2019) *op. cit.*.

Over the years, Facebook has promised to address discrimination in advertising a few times.[1099] At the end of 2017, Facebook representative Sheryl Sandberg publicly responded to several questions related to discrimination, content, and advertising posed by the chairman of the Congressional Black Caucus (CBC).[1100] First, she stressed that multicultural marketing was a common practice in the advertising industry. She revealed that since 2013 advertisers have had the option to specifically deliver their ads to people belonging to different "multicultural affinity groups." These groups consisted of Facebook users whose activities on the platform suggested that they may be interested in advertisements related to African American, Hispanic American, and/or Asian American communities. However, she also recognized that the platform is aware that "African Americans have been the victims of divisive and abusive content online."[1101] On Facebook's behalf, she committed to address discrimination perpetuated by the advertising tools to ensure that Facebook would not be a "vehicle for discrimination or division."[1102]

In March 2019, Facebook settled the lawsuits and charges of discrimination filed between November 2016 and September 2018 by the National Fair Housing Alliance (NFHA), Communications Workers of America (CWA), and several other organizations.[1103] In the settlement, Facebook engaged with practical measures to prevent discrimination in housing, employment, and credit advertising not only on Facebook but also in the other platforms owned by it, including Instagram.

The first measure included the implementation of a separate advertising portal for the creation of housing, employment, and credit ads that would contemplate limited targeting options to avoid discrimination. In this separate portal, gender, age, multicultural affinity, race, religion, family status, disability, and

---

[1099] In December 2016, the platform announced updates to ethnic affinity marketing. Facebook, *Improving Enforcement and Promoting Diversity: Updates to Ethnic Affinity Market* (November 2016), online: Facebook <https://newsroom.fb.com/news/2016/11/updates-to-ethnic-affinity-marketing/>. In February 2017, the platform published its efforts on improving enforcement and promoting diversity updates to ads policies and tools. Facebook, *Improving Enforcement and Promoting Diversity: Updates to Ads Policies and Tools* (February 2017), online: Facebook <https://newsroom.fb.com/news/2017/02/improving-enforcement-and-promoting-diversity-updates-to-ads-policies-and-tools/>.

[1100] Sheryl Sandberg, *Letter to Chairman Richmond* (November, 2017), online <https://www.documentcloud.org/documents/4312370-Facebook-Sheryl-Sandberg-Letter-2017–11–29.html>.

[1101] *Ibid.*

[1102] *Ibid.*

[1103] The following cases were settled: *Onuoha v Facebook*, Inc., No. 5: 16-cv-06440-EJD (N.D. Cal. Apr. 7, 2017); *Bradley v T-Mobile US*, INC., No. 17-cv-07232-BLF (N.D. Cal. June 4, 2019); *National Fair Housing Alliance v Facebook, Inc.*, No. 1:18-cv-02689-JGK (S.D. N.Y. Aug. 08, 2018); *Riddick v Facebook*, Inc., No. 3:18-cv-04429 (N.D. Cal. Mar. 19, 2019) and *Spees et al v Facebook, Inc.* (EEOC, September 2018). Summary of Settlements Between Civil Rights Advocates and Facebook, <https://www.aclu.org/sites/default/files/field_document/3.18.2019_joint_statement_final_0.pdf>.

sexual orientation are not available anymore among the targeting possibilities. Moreover, advertisements related to housing, credit, and employment would have a minimum geographic distance of 15 miles from a specific address or from the city center. Furthermore, specific zip code targeting would also not be allowed in cases of credit, employment, and housing advertising. In addition, the "lookalike audience" tool would no longer include gender, age, religious views, zip codes, or specific Facebook group membership to advertise employment, credit, and housing opportunities.[1104] Second, Facebook made available a specific webpage where users can consult all housing offers available regardless of whether they were targeted or not to receive it. Third, Facebook now requires advertisers to certify that they are complying with the antidiscrimination polices and antidiscrimination laws. Fourth, Facebook provides educational materials and features to inform advertisers about its antidiscrimination polices. Fifth, Facebook's representatives meet on a regular basis with the plaintiffs to report the implementation of the terms of the settlements. Sixth, Facebook is required to engage antidiscrimination bodies in situational testing to ensure the terms of the settlements were implemented effectively. Seventh, Facebook started to train its employees on antidiscrimination laws. Finally, Facebook started to cooperate with academics, researchers, experts, and civil rights and liberties advocates to study the potential for unintended biases in the algorithmic modeling used by the platform.

[1104] Summary of Settlements Between Civil Rights Advocates and Facebook, <https://www.aclu.org/sites/default/files/field_document/3.18.2019_joint_statement_final_0.pdf>.

CONCLUSION OF TITLE II

In this second title, I indicated how online platforms have disrupted the advertising industry in the past two decades by granularly profiling and targeting consumers based on their personal demographic information and online behavioral patterns. I particularly selected Google and Facebook because their business models are based on advertising revenue. Although they are different platforms, they have both developed similar, sophisticated ways of monetizing their activities that are ultimately free of monetary charge for internet users. The abundance of personal data coupled with cutting-edge technologies has allowed both platforms to become leaders in the advertising business. While targeted advertisement can improve consumers' experience by giving them access to content related to their interests, it can also replicate stereotypes and, in some cases, pose a major risk of discrimination against certain groups of individuals.

Having this in mind, I addressed the question of whether the legal frameworks in the EU and the United States are equipped to address discrimination in online targeted advertising. I conclude that data protection legal instruments and authorities in Europe are no longer silent on the risks of discrimination as a result of targeting practices. By setting a strong regulatory regime that outlines how companies can process data, the European legal framework offers safeguards to prevent unlawful discrimination. Data authorities have also acted by enforcing the principles of data protection laws in the past few years. However, even if European data protection law makes special room for addressing risks of discrimination, it does not set what discrimination precisely means. *Per se*, the regulation does not determine what kind of discrimination is unlawful with the same level of detail as EU antidiscrimination law does. In general, the regulation mentions in its Recital 71 that data processing practices should prevent discriminatory outcomes on the basis of individuals' racial or ethnic origin, political opinion, religion or beliefs, and sexual orientation aspects. However, it does not define in which contexts such differentiations are illegally discriminatory. In the light of EU antidiscrimination law, not all sorts of differentiations based on these grounds are illegal, as described in Chapters 1 and 3. In this regard, the regulation shall be completed and construed in the light of European and national antidiscrimination laws. With this in mind, it is striking to note that even though data protection authorities have already investigated and fined Facebook and Google for illegal targeted advertising with possible discriminatory outcomes, none of these cases have been mobilized in the field of antidiscrimination law. The European and member states' laws offer several answers and legal tools to address discrimination in this sector, and an investment should be made in the near future to investigate this context.

The situation is different in the United States, where civil rights lawyers have been on the front line to combat discrimination perpetuated by online advertisements. The recent legal battles against Facebook have made the platform change its design to accommodate special conditions for employment, credit, and housing advertisements. Nevertheless, the problem resides in the lack of protection guaranteed for personal data through the federal and state legal frameworks. These frameworks do not offer safeguards to all sophisticated targeting systems that might fall out of the sight of civil rights lawyers.

Finally, American companies processing the personal data of EU citizens or residents that is transferred from the EU to the United States should comply with the GDPR.[1105] In this regard, personal data used for commercial purposes, such as targeted advertisements, might be collected and processed under the principles and rules of the regulation. In February 2016 the United States and the European Union reached a political agreement on a framework, the EU-US Privacy Shield IP/16/216, for the transatlantic exchange of personal data for commercial purposes. Such agreement protected the fundamental rights of individuals in the EU whose personal data was transferred to the United States. It shed light on the principles businesses should meet when working with transatlantic data transfers. Nevertheless, in July 2020 the CJEU ruled that this agreement was no longer valid to guide the transfer of personal data from the European Union to the United States, because the United States' legal framework does not provide adequate protection, under the terms of the GDPR, for personal data.[1106] Following the decision, the European Commission announced to have initiated discussions with the United States Department of Commerce to reach an updated shield agreement to comply with the CJEU judgement.[1107] In March 2022, the United States and the European Commission announced they have reached an agreement for a new transatlantic data privacy framework.[1108]

[1105] Art 45, GDPR.

[1106] C-311/18, *Data Protection Commissioner v Facebook Ireland and Maximillian Schrems*, ECLI:EU:C:2020:559.

[1107] European Commission, *Joint Press Statement from European Commissioner for Justice Didier Reynders and US Secretary of Commerce Wilbur Ross* (August 2020), online: Press Release <https://ec.europa.eu/info/news/joint-press-statement-european-commissioner-justice-didier-reynders-and-us-secretary-commerce-wilbur-ross-7-august-2020-2020-aug-07_en>.

[1108] European Commission, *European Commission and United States Joint Statement on Trans-Atlantic Data Privacy Framework* (March 2022), online: Press Release <https://ec.europa.eu/commission/presscorner/detail/en/ip_22_2087>.

TITLE III

ONLINE LABOR MARKETS: PERFORMANCE EVALUATION AND DISCRIMINATORY TERMINATION OF PLATFORM WORKERS

INTRODUCTION

The rise of online labor platforms has resulted in a significant transformation in the employment market in the past decade.[1109] Their success is attributed to the fact that they easily connect workers and hiring individuals or entities with minimal bureaucratic barriers. Simply put, online labor platforms are regarded in two distinct ways: first, as traditional companies that provide services[1110], and second, as innovative technology companies that only intermediate the relationship of the two sides of the labor market.[1111] These two conceptual frames share the view that online labor platforms highly decentralize workforces through a system of self-employment or subcontracting.[1112]

Studies have demonstrated that the internet was related to the decentralization of the workforce in modern economies even before the emergence of online labor platforms.[1113] At the beginning of the twenty-first century, the World Summit of the Information Society recognized that information and communication technology (ICT) was changing working practices.[1114] The emergence of online labor platforms has further increased the speed to which ICT has been changing

---

[1109] Janine Berg, Marianne Furrer, Ellie Harmon, Uma Rani, Six Silberman, *Digital Labour Platforms and the Future of Work Towards Decent Work in the Online World* (September 2018), online: International Labour Organisation <https://www.ilo.org/wcmsp5/groups/public/---dgreports/---dcomm/---publ/documents/publication/wcms_645337.pdf > p xv.

[1110] Janine Berg, Marianne Furrer, Ellie Harmon, Uma Rani, Six Silberman, *Digital Labour Platforms and the Future of Work Towards Decent Work in the Online World, op. cit.*, p xv.

[1111] Mark N Wexler, "Reconfiguring the Sociology of the Crowd: Exploring Crowdsourcing" (2010) 31:1 International Journal of Sociology and Social Policy 6; Alek Felstiner, "Working the Crowd: Employment and Labor Law in the Crowdsourcing Industry" (2011) 32 Berkeley Journal of Employment & Labor Law 143; Aniket Kittur, Jeffrey V Nickerson, Michael Bernstein, Elizabeth Gerber, Aaron Shaw, John Zimmerman, Matt Lease, John Horton, "The Future of Crowd Work" (2013) Proceedings of the 2013 Conference on Computer Supported Cooperative Work (ACM) 1301.

[1112] The difference between self-employed and contractors exists in EU countries, where several employment laws apply also to dependent and non-dependent self-employed workers.

[1113] Ajay Agrawal, John Horton, Nicola Lacetera, Elizabeth Lyons and others, "Digitization and the Contract Labor Market: A Research Agenda" in Avi Goldfarb, Shane M Greenstein and Catherine E Tucker (eds), *Economic Analysis of the Digital Economy* (Chicago: University of Chicago Press, 2015) p 219; Laura Abramovsky, Rachel Griffith, "Outsourcing and Offshoring of Business Services: How Important Is ICT?" (2006) 4 Journal of the European Economic Association 594.

[1114] World Summit on the Information Society (WSIS), Declaration of Principles: Building the Information Society: A Global Challenge in the New Millennium. Document WSIS-03/Geneva/Doc/4-E/2003 (December 2003) online: ITU <www.itu.int/net/wsis/docs/geneva/official/dop. html > §47.

labor. The European Commission has reported that 32% of Europeans provide services through online platforms.[1115] The number of independent workers have been growing in Europe and the United States since the popularization of sharing economy platforms.[1116] The ubiquity of online platforms in the modern economy led the European Commission, several EU member states, American states' governments, the Organisation for Economic Cooperation and Development (OECD), and the International Labour Organisation (ILO) to undertake numerous multi-stakeholder initiatives to address the challenges involving workforce conditions in this ICT age.[1117]

Even though online labor platforms might expand competition, give easier access to the labor market to unemployed individuals, and generate economic growth, concerns have emphasized the threat this model represents to labor rights and employment standards.[1118] Notably, several online platforms controversially classify their workers as self-employees or independent

---

[1115] European Commission, *The Use of Collaborative Platforms: Flash Eurobarometer 438* (July 2016) online: EU Open Data Portal <ec.europa.eu/ COMMFrontOffice/PublicOpinion/index.cfm/ResultDoc/download/DocumentKy/72885 >.

[1116] Valerio de Stephano, "The Rise of the Just-in-Time Workforce: On-Demand Work, Crowdwork, and Labor Protection in the Gig-Economy" (2016) 37 Comparative Labor Law & Policy Journal 471; Antonio Aloisi, "Commoditized Workers: Case Study Research on Labor Law Issues Arising from a Set of on-Demand/Gig Economy Platforms" (2016) 37 Comparative Labor Law & Policy Journal 653.

[1117] The European Commission has published several studies and trends on the impact of new technologies including online platforms on the working practices and workers. To cite only a few: Annarosa Pesole, Maria Cesira Urzi Brancati, Enrique Fernandez Macias, Federico Biagi, Ignacio Gonzalez Vasquez, *Platform Workers in Europe Evidence from the COLLEEM Survey* (December 2018), online: EUR Scientific and Technical Research Reports <https://publications.jrc.ec.europa.eu/repository/handle/JRC112157>; European Group on Ethics in Science and New Technologies, *Future of Work, Future of Society* (December 2018), online: European Commission Directorate-General for Research and Innovation <https://ec.europa.eu/info/sites/info/files/research_and_innovation/ege/ege_future-of-work_opinion_122018.pdf>; Chris Warhusrt, Wil Hunt, "The Digitalisation of Future Work and Employment: Possible Impact and Policy Responses (2019) European Commission JRC117404 1; United Kingdom Government, *Good Work: A Response to the Taylor Review of Modern Working Practices* (February, 2018) online: Government UK <assets.publishing.service.gov.uk/government/uploads/system/uploads/attachment_data/file/679767/ 180206_BEIS_Good_Work_Report Accessible_A4_pdf >; OECD, *Policy Responses to New Forms of Work* (Paris: OECD Publishing, 2019); In August 2019, California created the Future of Work Commission to address, among other things, the impact of technology on work, workers, employers, jobs and society: Future of Work Commission, *Future of Work* (August 2019), online: Labor & Workforce Development Agency <https://labor.ca.gov/fowc/>; In 2017, the ILO launched a commission on the future of work focused on a human-centered agenda. The outcome of their work can be consulted in the report: Global Commission on the Future of Work, *Work for a Brighter Future* (January 2019), online: ILO <https://www.ilo.org/global/publications/books/WCMS_662410/lang--en/index.htm>;

[1118] Valerio de Stefano, Antonio Aloisi, *European Legal Framework for Digital Labour Platforms* (October 2018) online: European Commission <jrc112243_legal_framework_digital_labour_platforms_final.pdf> p 4.

contractors, which has the effect of depriving them of the protections of labor law in the United States and, to a lesser extent, in EU member states.[1119]

In the field of employment, American Federal Statutes and EU law provide the most robust and comprehensive set of rules against discrimination. In the EU, employees and dependent self-employed workers enjoy protection against discrimination in numerous contexts, including unfair termination based on the employee's gender[1120], race or ethnic origin[1121], religion or belief, disability, age, and sexual orientation.[1122] Under EU law, the grounds of race, ethnic origin, and gender are protected against discrimination in other areas such as the access to and supply of goods and services, and the grounds of religion, belief, age, and sexual orientation are only covered against discrimination in employment circumstances.[1123] In the United States, federal statutory law also offers several grounds of protection against discrimination in the employment context, notably for race, color, religion, sex, national origin, age, and disability.[1124]

The personal scope of some of those rules is essentially related to the worker's employment status. In the United States, employers shall comply with the protections of Title VII and the Americans with Disabilities Act (ADA) when they have more than 15 employees or with the Age Discrimination in Employment Act (ADEA) when they have more than 20 employees.[1125] Self-employed workers are out of scope. Alternatively, the European Union Equality framework and its transposed laws across the member states present a more protective approach, including in their personal scope – against discriminatory dismissal based on gender, ethnic origin, religion or belief, disability, age, and sexual orientation – for **dependent** self-employed workers but not for genuine or entrepreneurial self-employed workers.[1126] All in all, genuine self-employed workers are outside these protections in the United States and in the EU countries. For this reason, when online labor platforms blur the boundaries of employment qualification, they touch the foundation of some labor-related antidiscrimination laws.[1127]

Currently, the conditions for working for labor platforms are essentially set unilaterally in the terms of services, which govern crucial topics related to workers' rights such as how and when they will be paid, how their work will be

---

[1119] *See* chapter 6.
[1120] Article 14, 1 (c) Gender Equality Directive.
[1121] Article 3, 1 (c) Race Equality Directive.
[1122] Article 3, 1 (c), Employment Equality Directive.
[1123] Article 1, Gender Equal Access to Goods and Services Directive; Article 3, Race Equality Directive.
[1124] Title VII 42 U.S.C., §2000e-2(a)(1); ADA, 42 U.S.C., §12112 (a), ADEA, 29 U.S.C., §623 (a)(1).
[1125] Title VII, 42 U.S.C., §2000e(b); ADEA, 29 U.S.C., §630 (b) and ADA, 42 U.S.C., §12112 5(A).
[1126] *See* Catherine Barnard, *EU Employment Law* 4th Edition (Oxford: Oxford University Press, 2012), p 347; Nicola Countouris, *The Changing Law of the Employment Relationship* (Aldershot: Ashgate, 2007), chapter 5. Also, *see* below chapter 5, section II, 4, 4.1.
[1127] *See* chapter 5, section II.

evaluated, and what remedies workers have when there are problems.[1128] In this regard, the methods used by most labor platforms to evaluate their workers have raised concerns amongst academic circles.[1129] By design, labor platforms manage their workforce through a system of feedbacks and ratings. In short, after a service is concluded, workers receive a score that reflects the satisfaction of the client. Rating systems are quite simply designed and often include the possibility of assigning to workers one to five stars or equivalent measures. This system is implemented by major online labor platforms including Uber, Lyft, TaskRabbit, Amazon Mechanical Turk, and Clickworker only to cite a few. The main documented consequence of low ratings for workers is the unilateral termination of their contract with the platform.

The concerns with scored rating systems largely lie in their design.[1130] First, rating systems express an aggregated set of clients' evaluations about their experience. Therefore, the scores expressed in a rating system are highly subjective even if the metrics expressed in stars or similar features give the impression that it is an objective measure free of bias. Second, rating systems have been proved to be permeated by biased decisions instead of objective assessment in some occasions.[1131] Protected groups, including women and ethnic minorities, have reportedly received lower ratings when providing services on online labor platforms.[1132] Legal scholars and social scientists agree that the use of customer ratings – an instrument that appears to be neutral – in decisions related to workers' risks engenders discriminatory outcomes by enhancing existing biases embedded in society.[1133]

[1128] Some argue that the internet has created a new kind of sweatshops regarding the precariousness of working conditions and rights. *See* Cristiano Codagnone, Federico Biagi, Fabienne Abadie, *The Passions and the Interests: Unpacking the Sharing* Economy (Luxembourg: European Commission, 2016), JRC Science for Policy Report, p 32.

[1129] Rating systems are a pervasive practice in multiple sectorial platforms. Their ubiquity gave rise to the term *scored* society. Also, Danielle Keats Citron, Frank Pasquale, "The Scored Society" (2014) 89:1 Washington Law Review 1; Michael Luca, "Designing Online Marketplaces: Trust and Reputation Mechanisms" (2017) 17 Innovation Policy and the Economy 77; and Alex Rosenblat, Karen E C Levy, Solon Barocas, Tim Hwang, "Discriminating Tastes: Uber's Customer Ratings as Vehicles for Workplace Discrimination" (2017) 9:3 Policy & Internet 256.

[1130] Rating and reputation mechanism are pervasively implemented and studied across several sectors in online marketplaces. *See* Michael Luca, "Designing Online Marketplaces: Trust and Reputation Mechanisms" (2017) 17 Innovation Policy and the Economy 77 and Rossana Ducato, Miriam Kullmann, Marco Rocca, "European Legal Perspectives on Customer Ratings and Discrimination", in Tindara Addabbo, Ylenia Curzi, Olga Rymkevich, *Performance Appraisal in Modern Employment Relations: An Interdisciplinary Approach* (Palgrave Macmillan, 2019), p 256.

[1131] *See* chapter 5.

[1132] *See* chapter 5.

[1133] Solon Barocas, Andrew D Selbst, "Big Data's Disparate Impact" (2016) 104:3 California Law Review 671, p 732; Devin G Pope, Justin R Syndor, "Implementing Anti-Discrimination Policies in Statistical Profiling Models" (2011) 3:3 American Economic Journal 206.

With this context in mind, this title demonstrates how scored rating systems implemented to evaluate platform workers 1) serve as an instrument of control and management of their decentralized workforce and 2) can lead to the discriminatory termination of statutorily protected groups.[1134] I argue that when platforms outsource work by forging a complex system of intermediation where all workers providing work through the platform are entrepreneurial or genuine self-employed, such platforms put their workers outside the personal scope of several legal instruments that forbid the dismissal of employees because of their gender[1135], race or ethnic origin[1136], religion or belief[1137], disability[1138], age[1139], and sexual orientation.[1140] In this sense, scored systems that have as an outcome the termination of genuinely self-employed workers are not under the scope of the protections enshrined by these rules in the United States and EU countries (to a lesser extent), which outlaw direct and indirect discrimination based on all (or most of) these grounds.[1141]

To examine whether the antidiscrimination rules enshrined in the above mentioned legal instruments can be potentially enforced in the termination of platform workers, this title is structured in two parts: Chapters 5 and 6.

Chapter 5 presents and defines the types of online labor platforms and their organizational practices. This definitional step is necessary because platforms connecting workers to hiring parts are not a uniform block. They present substantial differences. Since this Title examines cases of discrimination in the termination of workers' contracts due to biased rating systems, I prioritized the illustration of on-demand platforms in which workers provide their service locally, have direct contact with clients, and are often evaluated by them. In this regard, I indicate several studies that conclude how scored systems that evaluate workers often do not reflect their proper work, but instead they reflect the personal preferences and biases of the evaluator. In the following section, I illustrate how legal systems in the United States and in the European Union address discrimination regarding rating systems that evaluate workers. I argue that rating systems can be compared to previous cases where employers have discriminated against their employees based on the clients' discriminatory preferences. For that matter, I demonstrate how Title VII of the Civil Rights Act, the Age Discrimination in Employment Act (ADEA), and the Americans with Disabilities Act (ADA) in the United States as well as the Gender Equality

---

[1134] *See* chapter 5.

[1135] Title VII 42 U.S.C., §2000e-2(a)(1); art 14, 1 (c) Gender Equality Directive.

[1136] Title VII, 42 U.S.C., §2000e-2(a)(1); art 3, 1 (c) Race Equality Directive.

[1137] Title VII, 42 U.S.C., §2000e-2(a)(1); art 3, 1 (c) Employment Equality Directive.

[1138] ADA, 42 U.S.C., §12112 (a); art 3, 1 (c) Employment Equality Directive.

[1139] ADEA, 29 U.S.C., §623 (a)(1); art 3, 1 (c) Employment Equality Directive.

[1140] The American Federal framework does not encompass sexual orientation; art 3, 1 (c) Employment Equality Directive.

[1141] *See* chapter 5, section II.

Directive, the Race Equality Directive, and the Employment Directive in the EU and their transposed laws are partially equipped to hold employers liable for terminating their employees based on customers' discriminatory preferences.

I follow this argument by highlighting the obstacles platform workers face to challenge discriminatory rating systems both in the United States and in the EU. In the United States, protections grounded on Title VII, the ADEA, and the ADA against discriminatory rating systems do not apply to platform workers if they are classified as contractors. Moreover, discriminatory outcomes of apparent neutral policies, which are comparable to rating systems, have been ruled justifiable under the business necessity exemption. Moreover, cases regarding the misclassification and discrimination of platform workers have been prevented from being assessed by American District Courts because of arbitration clauses. Alternatively, EU equality laws regarding discrimination in the termination of workers cover employees as well as dependent self-employed workers on the grounds of race, ethnic origin, sex, religion or belief, age, disabilities, and sexual orientation. Sex, race, and ethnic origin are also covered against discrimination in the access to and supply of goods and services. In this regard, the relation of dependence between workers and the platform determines whether workers have access to a set of antidiscrimination rights. In addition, arbitration clauses are void in most cases regarding employment disputes. However, even if workers generally enjoy a wider range of protection in EU countries, precedents have so far enhanced that eventual discriminatory outcomes against employees due to organizational policies/practices are acceptable in certain circumstances, such as maintaining an image of neutrality *vis-à-vis* clients. These precedents ultimately put at stake whether scored rating systems that potentially discriminate against protected groups would be justifiable by the legitimate aim of providing services with quality.[1142]

In Chapter 6, I analyze in depth one real case to illustrate my above arguments.[1143] I selected the on-demand platform Uber among several others operating in the online markets because of its ubiquity across the United States and many European countries. By reviewing the platform, organizational practices, and judicial cases, I note that in the United States, the UK, and France the misclassification of employment contracts of Uber drivers has made its path to the courts.[1144] Most cases involving the reclassification of work contracts are aimed at redressing issues related to the minimum wage, right of unionization,

---

[1142] For neutrality policies, *see Achbita v G4S Solutions NV* case-157/15 ECLI:EU:C:2017:203; Also, chapter 5, section II, 3.

[1143] Benoît Frydman, "Les Défis du Droit Global", in Caroline Bricteux, Benoit Frydman, *Grands Défis du Droit Global, op. cit.*, pp 11–17.

[1144] *O'Connor v Uber Technology Inc.*, 82 F Supp 3d 1133, 1135–38 (ND Cal 2015); *Yucesoy et al v Uber Technology Inc. et al*, Civil Action No 1:14-cv-13938-IT (US District Court for the District of Massachusetts); *Uber BV v Aslam* [2018] EWCA civ 2748; Cour d'Appel de Paris, pôle 6, chamber 2, arrêt du 10 janvier 2019, sn rg 18/08357, n portalis 35L7-V-B7C-B6AZK.

and other traditional employment rights.[1145] All these cases have raised a similar aspect that evaluating workers with scored rating systems represents a mechanism of control typical of employment relationships.[1146] However, to my knowledge, only two cases have challenged discriminatory employment termination due to biased ratings, as of the date of this research. One concerned an Asian American driver whose contract was terminated unilaterally by Uber based on his low ratings[1147]; and the other case concerned a female driver in the UK who claimed before the London Employment Tribunal that the Uber rating system put women in a disadvantaged position.[1148]

It is striking to note that in the United States, the employment status of Uber drivers, which could define whether they are under the personal scope of Title VII, the ADEA, and the ADA, could not be assessed by the District Courts, because drivers have waived their trial and class action rights by accepting arbitration clauses as a mean of resolution to all employment disputes. The only option for these workers is to initiate arbitration resolution procedures, one by one, against Uber. In Europe, alternatively, with the restrictive legal possibilities of arbitration, employment courts in the UK have ruled Uber drivers as workers – a middle term category between employment and genuine self-employment – which falls under the scope of the Equality Act 2010. This case opened the path to further legal challenges to Uber's employment organizational practices, including its rating system. However, the case brought to court in the UK is still too minor, considering the pervasiveness of online labor platforms across EU countries. For the sake of equal treatment in online labor platforms, courts should be given more opportunities to assess this common platform organizational practice that manages thousands of workers across the EU member states and the United States. The number of platform workers is no longer negligible.

In the United States, over 40 million workers have provided work through an online labor platform.[1149] Amid this sample, workers have primarily offered services related to home repair and moving (11%), ride-sharing transportation

---

[1145]   *Ibid.*

[1146]   *Ibid.*

[1147]   *Thomas Liu v Uber, Inc.*, EEOC. Equal Employment Opportunity Commission. Charges of employment discrimination investigated and settled by the EEOC are not available to the public. This case was particularly publicized on the attorney's law office webpage. *See* Dan Adams, *Boston-Based Attorney Argues Uber's Star Ratings Are Racially Biased* (October 2016) online: Lichten & Liss-Riordan, P.C. <https://www.llrlaw.com/wp-content/uploads/2015/04/Boston-based-Attorney-Argues-Uber's-Star-Ratings-are-Racially-Biased.pdf>.

[1148]   The claim was brought by the GMB union, on behalf of the women who wanted to remain anonymous. Some details of the case were published on the plaintiff's law firm website. Leigh Day, *British Female Driver Launches Sex Discrimination Claim Against Uber Over Practices* (September 2017), online: Leigh Day Office <https://www.leighday.co.uk/News/News-2017/September-2017/British-female-driver-launches-sex-discrimination>.

[1149]   Burson-Marsteller, *The On-Demand Economy Survey* (2015), online: The Aspen Institute <https://www.aspeninstitute.org/publications/demand-economy-survey/>.

(10%), and food delivery (7%).[1150] Racial, ethnic minorities, and young people (Millennials) are overrepresented in the platform economy. Around 67% of the sample belongs to a racial minority group, and 57% were born after the 1980s.[1151]

In Europe, 11.5% of the active labor force has worked for online platforms at least once in Portugal, 12.5% in Spain, 7.9% in Croatia, 7.6% in France, 7.6% in Sweden, 6.9% in Slovakia, 6.9% in Hungary, and 6.5% in Finland.[1152] In the UK, 3.6% of the entire active workforce provides work exclusively through platforms, followed by 2.8% in the Netherlands, 2.7% in Spain, 2.6% in Germany, and 2.4% in both Lithuania and Italy.[1153]

[1150]   *Ibid.*
[1151]   *Ibid.*
[1152]   *Ibid*, p 9.
[1153]   Cesira Urzi Brancati, Annarosa Pesole, Enrique Fernandez-Macías, *Digital Labour Platforms in Europe: Numbers, Profiles, and Employment Status of Platform Workers* (January 2019), online: Publications Office of the European Union <https://publications.jrc.ec.europa.eu/repository/bitstream/JRC117330/jrc117330_jrc117330_dlp_counting_profiling.pdf> p 9.

CHAPTER 5

LABOR RELATIONS IN THE PLATFORM ECONOMY

SECTION I. DEFINING LABOR PLATFORMS AND WORKER EVALUATION SYSTEMS

1. TYPES OF ONLINE LABOR PLATFORMS

Online labor platforms are primarily focused on the service sector. The specialized literature generally labels them under two distinct categories: professional crowdsourcing platforms and on-demand work platforms.[1154] On the one hand, both models use the internet to create a marketplace where workers and hiring entities can meet; on the other hand, they provide different types of services and working methods.

Journalist Jeff Howe first used the word "crowdsourcing" in 2006 to describe "the act of taking a job traditionally performed by a designated agent, usually an employee, and outsourcing it to an undefined generally large group of people in the form of an open call."[1155] In other words, crowdsourcing platforms allow third-party companies to fragment a particular chore and assign it to a community of crowd workers.[1156] The content of crowd tasks range from creative

---

[1154] Janine Berg, Valerio de Stefano, *Regulating Work in the Gig Economy* (July, 2015) online: ILO <https://iloblog.org/2015/07/10/regulating-work-in-the-gig-economy/>; Also, a detailed typology of online labor platforms is elaborated by Cristiano Codagnone, Federico Biagi, Fabienne Abadie, *The Passions and the Interests: Unpacking the 'Sharing Economy'* (October, 2016) online: European Commission <https://publications.jrc.ec.europa.eu/repository/bitstream/JRC101279/jrc101279.pdf>; Wilma B Liebman, Andrew Lyubarsky, "Crowdwork, the Law, and the Future of Work" (2016) 1 Perspectives on Work 22; OECD, *New Forms of Work in the Digital Economy* (June 2016) online: OECD Digital Economy Papers <https://www.oecd-ilibrary.org/science-and-technology/new-forms-of-work-in-the-digital-economy_5jlwnklt820x-en>; Jon Messenger, Oscar Vargas Llave, Lutz Gschwind, Simon Boehmer, Greet Vermeylen, Mathijn Wilkens, *Working Anytime, Anywhere: the Effects on the World of Work* (February, 2017) online: Eurofond <https://www.eurofound.europa.eu/publications/report/2017/working-anytime-anywhere-the-effects-on-the-world-of-work>.

[1155] Enrique Estellés-Arolas, Fernando González, "Towards an Integrated Crowdsourcing Definition" (2012) 38:2 Journal of Information Science 189.

[1156] Individuals working for crowdsourcing platforms are typically named crowdworkers. *See* Valerio de Stefano, Antonio Aloisi, *European Legal Framework for Digital Labour Platforms*, *op. cit.*, p 12.

to repetitive work, including the creation of marketing campaigns, coding, proofreading academic pieces, designing, and human intelligence tasks (HITs), such as data entry.[1157] Considering the nature of the crowd tasks, crowdsourcing platforms may have a geographic global dimension in which workers may provide their work remotely. Moreover, the payment system may be performed according to the output or based on hours worked.[1158]

Amazon Mechanical Turk and Clickworker are two prominent examples of crowdsourcing platforms. Both platforms facilitate outsourcing work to a distributed workforce that can perform tasks virtually.[1159] They typically offer micro-task jobs related to cleaning online directories, testing new software, categorizing items, transcribing audio documents, editing texts, managing surveys, detecting images with obscene content, or detecting images in general, such as "identifying the red apple in this image of a fruit basket."[1160] The numbers are not negligible. The platform Clickworker is based in the United States and Germany, but its workforce – more than 1.8 million individuals – is located in 136 countries.[1161] Clickworker highlights its importance in offering micro-tasks to hundreds of thousands of workers to help optimize AI-based searches, for instance.[1162] Furthermore, it stresses how the future of AI depends on a significant workforce of human teachers.[1163] Amazon Mechanical Turk also offers access to a global 24/7 workforce, and 2,000–5,000 workers are estimated to be active on the platform at any given time.[1164]

The average age of crowd platform workers is 33.2 years old worldwide.[1165] They are slightly educated, and fewer than 18% have a high school diploma or less, 25% have a technical certificate or some university studies, 37% have a bachelor's degree, and 20% have a postgraduate degree.[1166] Reasons for working on a crowd platform vary from supplementing one's pay from other jobs to avoiding unemployment.[1167] An ILO worldwide survey identified that in 2017

[1157] Debra Howcroft, Birgitta Bergvall-Kareborn, "A Typology of Crowdwork Platforms" (2019) 33:1 Work, Employment and Society 21.

[1158] Birgitta Bergvall-Kareborn, Debra Howcroft, "Amazon Mechanical Turk and the Commodification of Labour" (2014) 29:3 New Technology, Work and Employment 213.

[1159] Amazon Mechanical Turk, *Overview* (November 2019), online: mturk <https://www.mturk.com>, and Clickworker, *Our Solutions at a Glance* (November 2019), online: clickworker <https://www.clickworker.com>.

[1160] Amazon Mechanical Turk, *Overview* (November 2019), online: mturk <https://www.mturk.com>.

[1161] Clickworker, *Our Solutions at a Glance* (November 2019), online: clickworker <https://www.clickworker.com>.

[1162] *Ibid.*

[1163] *Ibid.*

[1164] Amazon Mechanical Turk, *Overview* (November 2019), online: mturk <https://www.mturk.com>.

[1165] Janine Berg, Marianne Furrer, Ellie Harmon, Uma Rani, Six Silberman, *Digital Labour Platforms and the Future of Work Towards Decent Work in the Online* World, *op. cit.*, p XVI.

[1166] *Ibid*, p XVI.

[1167] *Ibid.*

a crowd worker earned $4.43 per hour.[1168] Almost two-thirds of American workers providing services to the Amazon Mechanical Turk platform made less than the minimum federal wage of $7.25 per hour; while 7% of German workers surveyed on the ClickWorker platform indicated earnings above the German minimum wage of € 8.84 per hour.[1169] Moreover, workers spend over 20 minutes on unpaid activities for every hour of paid work, particularly searching for more work.[1170]

On the other side of the spectrum of online labor marketplaces, on-demand work platforms refer to services that are executed mainly locally. They have a geographic local dimension, considering that the execution of the task depends on the worker's physical presence. This type notably includes tasks involving manual content, such as household and transport services.[1171] Payment is often based on the number of hours worked, and the platform makes its revenue from a percentage of the amount paid to the worker. On-demand work platforms generally focus on services such as delivery, maintenance of households, cleaning services, babysitting, and transportation, which are the most common services. The example of companies that have invested in on-demand work platforms are numerous: Foodora, Etece.es, TaskRunner, Helpling, Handy, TaskRabbit, Deliveroo, and, the well-known transportation networking companies, Uber and Lyft. In short, on-demand work platforms are classified in three different service sectors: (1) small task provision, (2) food delivery, and (3) transportation.

One of the most notorious exponents of small task provision is TaskRabbit, a two-sided marketplace that connects TaskPosters (hiring parties or clients), described as individuals who need help, with Taskers (workers), described as individuals who are pre-approved and background-checked.[1172] The platform provides services related to mounting and installation, moving and packing, furniture assembly, cleaning, general handyman, and heavy lifting. Taskers are assigned to tasks instead of choosing them; they are asked to wear a uniform (the platform's shirt); they must use the Tasker mobile app for scheduling, chatting, and booking tasks; and they must use that Tasker calendar for availability and scheduling.[1173] When TaskRabbit started, TaskPosters posted jobs and quoted a price for it generally lower than the minimum wage.[1174] In an attempt to win the

---

[1168] *Ibid.*

[1169] *Ibid.*

[1170] *Ibid.*

[1171] Valerio de Stefano, Antonio Aloisi, *European Legal Framework for Digital Labour Platforms*, *op. cit.*, p 14.

[1172] TaskRabbit, *The Convenient & Affordable Way to Get Things Done Around the Home* (November 2019), online: TaskRabbit <https://www.taskrabbit.com>.

[1173] TaskRabbit, *How Task Rabbit Works Insights Into Business Revenue Model* (November 2019) online: TaskRabbit <https://jungleworks.com/how-task-rabbit-works-insights-into-business-revenue-model/>.

[1174] Miriam A Cherry, "Beyond Misclassification: The Digital Transformation of Work" (2016) 37 Comparative Labor Law & Policy Journal 577, p 604.

bid for the job posted, Taskers accepted all kinds of jobs regardless the price paid or the difficulty. Recently, the platform changed this model allowing Taskers to specify their hourly rate. Moreover, they do not have to bid for a task anymore. Alternatively, they are automatically assigned to execute the task. TaskPosters often were misleading about the number of hours the job they announced required. Taskers often previously worked more hours than they were paid on a regular basis. To fix this issue, TaskRabbit established that TaskPosters have to pay a charge based on the hourly rate.

On-demand work platforms focused on food delivery have popped up in the past few years.[1175] They allow customers to order from a wide variety of restaurants with a single tap on their phone. They enable consumers to compare menus, scan and post reviews, and place orders directly. In these cases, workers are selected by the platform to take the order from the restaurant to the final consumer. Workers accomplish their mission by bicycle or car. The notorious examples on this sector in Europe and in the United States are Uber Eats, Deliveroo, Just-Eat, and Takeaway.

Finally, transportation has the most established examples of on-demand work platforms, which are often called transportation network companies (TNC). Uber is a well-known example, but it has direct and specialized competitors around the world, such as Lyft, Didi Chuxing, and Ola Cabs among many others.

2. EVALUATION SYSTEMS: RATINGS, SCORES, AND FEEDBACK

"Customers are the bosses."

Catchy sayings such as "customers are the bosses," "customers are the kings," or "management by customers" are the mainstream within the service sector, where organizational structures often have a triangular dimension comprising companies, workers, and customers.[1176] The concrete manner to implement customers' preferences into the practices of companies operating in the service sector is by giving customers a voice. With this concern, several companies have implemented performance review systems, which are also called performance appraisals or appraisal reviews.[1177] In essence, these reviews are managerial tools

---

[1175] Alex Veen, David Oliver, Caleb Goods, Tom Barrat, "The 'Gigification' of Work" in Russell D Lansbury, Anya Johnson, Diane Van de Broek, *Contemporary Issues in Work and Organisations: Actors and Institutions* (Routledge 2019), p 28.

[1176] Einat Albin, "A Worker Employer Customer Triangle: The Case of Tips" (2011) 40 Industrial Law Journal 181, p 182.

[1177] Liza Estino Daoanis, "Performance Appraisal System: its Implication to Employee Performance" (2012) 2:3 International Journal of Economics and Management Sciences 55.

used to evaluate workers and assist in the making of organizational decisions, including in areas such as worker termination (layoffs), promotions, transfers, and salary determination.[1178] In other words, performance review shapes several concrete aspects of working conditions. Currently, performance review is a pervasive managerial practice and was not invented by online on-demand work platforms, even if they are extensively used by the latter.

Several on-demand work platforms rely on customer ratings as a strategy to both manage their workforce and to build their users' trust and confidence. Integrating ratings and review systems into online marketplaces is largely regarded as a fundamental element to enhance trustworthiness. Reputational systems remarkably use star ratings to give users a reputation in online peer-to-peer platforms, regardless if they are devoted to labor or to the access to goods and services.[1179] However, on-demand work platforms also use rating systems as a tool to manage and regulate their workforces. For instance, Uber's passenger ratings on the services provided by drivers serve as the basis for their inclusion or exclusion from the platform.[1180] When drivers have low ratings and risk being banned, Uber sends an email with suggestions of which kind of behavior would likely improve their evaluations.[1181] TaskRabbit also alerts its Taskers that if they have a negative review, including a "thumbs down" or two stars or below out of five stars, they will no longer be paired for tasks.[1182] Lyft has a two-way rating system: at the end of the ride, passengers and drivers are able to rate each other on a scale of 1–5 stars. After passengers rate their drivers, they have the option to tell the platform more about the experience. If a ride is rated with less than 5 stars, passengers will be able to flag specific areas to improve. The platform considers any rate higher than 4.8 to be "awesome." Anything below that might be subject to improvement. Consistently low ratings put the driver at risk of deactivation.[1183] All in all, the main consequences of low ratings are, first, the adjustment of the worker's behavior, and then the termination of the contract with the platform.

[1178] Hubert S Field, William H Holley, "The Relationship of Performance Appraisal System Characteristics to Verdicts in Selected Employment Discrimination Cases" (1982) 25:2 Academy of Management Journal 392 p 392.

[1179] Will Qiu, Palo Parigi, Bruno Abrahao, "More Stars or More Reviews? Differential Effects of Reputation on Trust in the Sharing Economy" (2018) Proceedings of the CHI 20.

[1180] *See* more at chapter 6.

[1181] Such as offering passengers bottled water, mints, phone chargers; or advising them to keep their vehicle clean and well maintained, to dress appropriately, to open the door, to take the best route or to be nice. *See O'Connor v Uber and Yucesoy et al v Uber Technology Inc.* et al, Civil Action No 1:14-cv-13938-IT, US District Court for the District of Massachusetts.

[1182] TaskRabbit, *Ratings and Reviews on the Task Rabbit Platform* (November 2019), online: TaskRabbit <https://support.taskrabbit.com/hc/en-us/articles/213301766-Ratings-and-Reviews-on-the-TaskRabbit-Platform>.

[1183] Lyft, *Driver and Passenger Ratings* (November 2019), online: Lyft <https://help.lyft.com/hc/en-us/articles/115013079948-Driver-and-passenger-ratings>.

The strategy of using customer feedback about employees as a managerial tool has long been practiced by corporations worldwide.[1184] However, in online platforms the novelty resides in the methodological and technological instruments firms implement to gather customer feedback. In the past 30 years, businesses began moving away from informal feedback measurements to implement sophisticated ratings, comment sheets, focus groups, hidden shoppers, interviews, testing, and telephone call surveys.[1185] The focus on these strategies indicates that boosting customer satisfaction is pivotal to mass consumption society.[1186]

The emergence of the internet has fundamentally increased the possibilities to measure clients' satisfaction. Ratings systems embedded in apps, email surveys, dedicated evaluation spots in all sorts of e-services, community discussion groups, and sites devoted to reviews allow companies to reach customers faster and inexpensively. In reality, companies currently receive customer feedback without even requesting it, with the proliferation of independent online pages in which customers may share their evaluations about different services and experiences, such as through Yelp, Amazon, and Google.[1187]

Traditionally, in the United States and in countries across the EU, employers have taken customers' feedback into consideration in several instances of business decision-making, including employment-related resolutions, such as who should be disciplined, promoted, and terminated.[1188] Not rarely, employees' pay rates and bonuses are based on aggregated customer preferences.[1189] A survey has demonstrated that nearly half of large American businesses used customers' feedback to award their employees with incentive compensation.[1190] Another qualitative study found that detailed customer feedback about certain

---

[1184] Atul Parvatiyar, Jagdish N Sheth, "Customer Relationship Management: Emerging Practice, Process, and Discipline" (2001) 3:2 Journal of Economic & Social Research 1.

[1185] Dallan F Flake, "When Should Employers Be Liable for Factoring Customer Feedback into Employment Decisions" (2018) 102:5 Minnesota Law Review 2169, p 2175.

[1186] Nigel Hill, Greg Roche, Rachel Allen, *Customer Satisfaction: The Customer Experience Through the Customer's Eyes* (Cogent Publishing, 2007).

[1187] Dallan F Flake, "When Should Employers Be Liable for Factoring Customer Feedback into Employment Decisions" (2018), *op. cit.*, p 2176.

[1188] Mike Bourne, Pippa Bourne, *Handbook of Corporate Performance Management* (Cornwall: John Wiley & Sons 2011) p 149; Ramesh Neupane, "Relationship Between Customer Satisfaction and Business Performance: A Case Study of Lloyds Bank UK" (2014) 1:2 International Journal of Social Sciences and Management 74; Marisa Salanova, Sonia Agut, José Maria Peiró, "Linking Organizational Resources and Work Engagement to Employee Performance and Customer Loyalty: The Mediation of Service Climate" (2005) 90:6 Journal of Applied Psychology 1217.

[1189] Gary W Loveman, "Employee Satisfaction, Customer Loyalty, and Financial Performance: An Empirical Examination of the Service Profit Chain in Retail Banking" (1998) Journal of Service Research 18.

[1190] Jeff Marr, *Tying Employee Compensation to Customer Feedback* (August 2019), online: customer think <http://customerthink.com/tying-employeescompensation to-customer feedback>.

employees was added into the personal directory of employees to be used by evaluation systems.[1191] The same study discovered that an insurance agency and a grocery store chain included customer feedback as an element of quantitative performance reviews that were used as a base to determine wage rises and promotion and to initiate the first stages of disciplinary actions and, eventually, terminations.[1192]

In the United States and in the EU, the fact that employers utilize customer feedback to decide about their employees' work conditions, advantages, sanctions, or termination is relevant because such decisions are understood as employment actions under antidiscrimination law, which protects classes of employees against illegal discrimination.[1193] In other words, an employer can be held liable for discriminatory treatment if a protected ground motivates the decision and the employee is negatively impacted as a result.[1194] This typically happens in cases where client feedback is biased. Biased client evaluations or preferences used as a basis for employment decisions have been litigated and ruled as illegal by courts in the United States and in certain contexts in the EU.[1195] The judicial assessment of whether customers' preferences motivate or serve as basis for discriminatory employment actions is relevant, considering that discrimination against protected classes exists in the labor markets of the United States and the EU.

3. BIASED EVALUATION OF WORKERS' PERFORMANCE

Discrimination regarding the management of workforces, particularly implicit biases on the managerial evaluation of workers, has been long documented by social science research.[1196] Studies have demonstrated that racial and gender

---

[1191]   Linda Fuller, Vicki Smith, "Consumers' Reports: Management by Customers in a Changing Economy" (1991) Work, Employment and Society 1, p 5.

[1192]   *Ibid.*

[1193]   *See* Dallan F Flake, "When Should Employers Be Liable for Factoring Customer Feedback into Employment Decisions" (2018), *op. cit.,* in the United States. In the EU Equality framework, notably in the Race, Employment and Gender Directives, the scope of employment actions covered are provided in art 3 and 14 respectively.

[1194]   Title VII, 42 U.S.C. §2000e-2(m) (2012); Dallan F Flake, "When Should Employers Be Liable for Factoring Customer Feedback into Employment Decisions" (2018), *op. cit.,* referring to *Tibbs v Calvary United Methodist Church*, 505 F Appx 508, 515 (United States Court of Appeals, 6th Circuit 2012) and *Richardson v Monitronics International*, Inc., 434 F3d 327, 333 (United States Court of Appeals, 5th Circuit 2005).

[1195]   *See* section chapter 6, section II, 2, 2.3.

[1196]   George C Thornton III, Deborah E Rupp, Alyssa M Gibbons, Adam J Vanhove, "Same-Gender and Same-Race Bias in Assessment Center Ratings: A Rating Error Approach to Understanding Subgroup Differences" (2019) 27:1 International Journal of Selection and Assessment 54; Emilio J Castilla, "Bringing Managers Back In: Managerial Influences on

biases negatively impact managers' evaluation of workers through subjective appraisals.[1197] Companies using managers' subjective appraisals as the only criteria to reward employees has resulted in racial and gender wage inequality among workers with the same level of responsibility and experience.[1198] These cases include supervisors delivering a higher level of in-depth review when evaluating employees with statutorily protected grounds.[1199] Social scientists have also revealed that shared demographic characteristics between managers and employees might positively influence managers' subjective evaluation of the employee performance.[1200] Researchers suggest that when objective appraisal methods including strict productivity criteria are implemented to evaluate employees, they tend to reduce racial bias.[1201]

Biased evaluations have been attested in the relationships between employees and managers as well as in the relationships between employees and customers. Particularly, academic studies focused on the food sector have concluded that customers evaluated the agility and diligence of waiters with similar demographic aspects more positively.[1202] Moreover, empirical studies have indicated how rater biases impacts customer satisfaction scores in medical clinics.[1203] In this context, researchers analyzed over 12,000 patient satisfaction evaluations about their doctors and found that female and Black American

---

Workplace Inequality" (2011) 76:5 American Sociological Review 667; Patrick F McKay, Michael A McDaniel, "A Reexamination of Black-White Mean Differences in Work Performance: More Data, More Moderators" (2006) 91:3 Journal of Applied Psychology 538; Marta Elvira, Robert Town, "The Effects of Race and Worker Productivity on Performance Evaluations" (2001) 40:4 Industrial Relations a Journal of Economy and Society 571.

[1197] Stan Malos, "Overt Stereotype Biases and Discrimination in the Workplace: Why haven't We fixed this by now?" (2015) 27:4 Employee Responsibilities and Rights Journal 271, p 272.

[1198] For gender, see Tindara Addabbon, "Wage Discrimination by Gender and Performance Evaluation", in Tidara Addabbo, Edoardo Ales, Ylenia Curzi, Tommaso Fabbri, Olga Rymkecivh, Iacopo Senatori (eds) (Palgrave Macmillan: Performance Appraisal in Modern Employment Relations, 2019), p 35; Emilio J Castilla, "Merit and Discrimination within Organizations: Gender and Racial Differences in the Evaluation and Compensation of Employees" (2010) 129 Revista Espanola de Investigaciones Sociologicas 61, p 62.

[1199] For gender, see Victor S Maas, Raquel Torres-González, "Subjective Performance Evaluation and Gender Discrimination" (2011) 101 Journal of Business and Ethics 687; for race, see Joseph Stauffer, Ronald Buckley, "The Existence and Nature of Racial Bias in Supervisory Ratings" (2005) 90:3 Journal of Applied Psychology 586.

[1200] Victor S Maas, Raquel Torres-González, "Subjective Performance Evaluation and Gender Discrimination" (2011), op. cit., p 688.

[1201] John S Heywood, Patrick L O'Halloran, "Racial Earnings Differentials and Performance Pay" (2005) 40:2 The Journal of Human Resources 435, p 436.

[1202] Michael Lynn, Michael C Sturman, "Is the Customer Always Right? The Potential for Racial Bias in Customer Evaluations of Employee Performance" (2011) 41:9 Journal of Applied Social Psychology 2312.

[1203] Robin L Snipes, Neal F Thomson, Sharon L Oswald, "Gender Bias in Customer Evaluations of Service Quality: An Empirical Investigation" (2006) 20:4 Journal of Services Marketing 274, p 262.

doctors received lower satisfaction marks compared to their white and male colleagues.[1204]

The scenario is not much different within traditional transportation sectors. Researchers collected data on more than 1,000 tips given to taxi drivers in Connecticut.[1205] They found the tipping had one potential racial effect: Black American cab drivers were tipped on average one third less than white cab drivers. Taxicab tipping has a similar dimension of consumer evaluation because both are discretionary behaviors and are potentially observable.[1206]

Shifting to on-demand work platforms, a recent publication has revealed racial and gender discrimination against TaskRabbit and Fiverr workers on their reviews.[1207] Researchers collected 13,500 worker profiles and gathered information about the workers' sex, race, customer reviews, ratings, and position in search rankings. They found that the workers' perceived sex and race were significantly correlated with the workers' evaluations. On both platforms, perceived Black workers received 32% lower ratings compared to qualified workers who were perceived to be white.[1208] Moreover, on TaskRabbit, researchers observed that sex and gender are significantly correlated with search ranks.[1209]

If the above results are replicable and generalizable, they may indicate that evaluation and rating systems as an employment organizational practice may lead to discrimination against statutorily protected groups. Specifically regarding online platforms, if companies are concerned about the equal treatment of their workers, they might not count only on customer ratings to manage their workforce.[1210]

In light of this scenario, since most on-demand work platforms use customer ratings to maintain or terminate employees' work activities, making use of biased customer evaluations to determine termination could expose the platforms to lawsuits when customer appraisals contain illegal biases, including racial and gender biases. Detecting biased customer's feedback has become increasingly difficult, especially in rating systems that use stars or scores.

1204 *Ibid.*
1205 Ian Ayres, Frederick E Vars, Nasser Zakariya, "To Insure Prejudice: Racial Disparities in Taxicab Tipping" (2005) 114: The Yale Law Journal 1613, p 1616.
1206 *Ibid*, p 1617.
1207 Ánikó Hannák, Claudia Wagner, David Garcia, Alan Mislove, Markus Strohmaier, Christo Wilson, "Bias in Online Freelance Marketplaces: Evidence from TaskRabbit and Fiverr" (2017) Proceedings of the 2017 ACM Conference on Computer Supported Cooperative Work and Social Computing 1914.
1208 *Ibid*, p 1923.
1209 *Ibid*, p 1925.
1210 Dallan F Flake, "When Should Employers Be Liable for Factoring Customer Feedback into Employment Decisions" (2018) 102:5 Minnesota Law Review 2169, p 2180.

SECTION II. LEGAL FRAMEWORK FOR THE EVALUATION SYSTEM OF PLATFORM WORKERS

Rating systems may present a facially neutral path for discrimination related to online labor platforms' decisions when customers tend to give biased ratings to workers based on protected characteristics. This section explores the challenges to hold platforms liable for this sort of discrimination in the United States and in the EU.

1. UNITED STATES

1.1. EMPLOYMENT CLASSIFICATION AND PERSONAL SCOPE OF NON-DISCRIMINATION RIGHTS

As long as Title VII of the Civil Rights Act, the ADA, and the ADEA only cover discrimination against employees[1211], the employment status of the platform workers matters as it entitles them to claim any discrimination linked to their termination grounded on these three statutory bills. The situation is entirely different with regards to the EU and transposed work-related antidiscrimination law.

Defining the factual employment status of a worker is not an easy task in the United States. The problem of the misclassification of employees remains a reality in different sectors. The core element underlying the employment and independent contractor dichotomy is the nature and level of control that employers can exercise over their workers.[1212] However, courts and government agencies at the state and federal levels use different criteria and standards to classify employees; the tests to distinguish independent contractors from employees are not homogeneous; and statutory law, in general, does not provide any clear definition of employment relationships or employee status.[1213]

[1211] The Title VII, 42 U.S.C., §2000e(b); ADEA, 29 U.S.C., §630 (b) and ADA, 42 U.S.C., §12112 5(A) define that they apply to employees who are individuals employed by an employer, and that the term employer "means a person engaged in an industry affecting commerce who has 15 or more employees for each working day in each of 20 or more calendar weeks". The Supreme Court confirmed that part-time employees should be included. *Equal Employment Opportunity Commission and Walters v Metropolitan Educational Enterprises*, Inc., 117 S.Ct. 660, 666 (1997).

[1212] Guy Davidov, "The Three Axes of Employment Relationships: A Characterization of Workers in Need of Protection" (2002) 52 The University of Toronto Law Journal 357.

[1213] Mitchell H Rubenstein, "Our Nation's Forgotten Workers: The Unprotected Volunteers" (2006) 9 Journal of Labor and Employment Law 147. *See* the tensions about the classification of workforce in the "on-demand" economy: Benjamin Means, Joseph A Seiner, "Navigating the Uber Economy" (2016) 49 University of California Davis Law Review 1511; Keith Cunningham-Parmeter, "From Amazon to Uber: Defining Employment in the Modern

Two important national labor regulations vaguely define "employee." The National Labor Relations Act (NLRA), which regulates collective bargaining, has a definition section (§153(3)), which includes the terms "person," "employer," and "employee." The definitions are not self-explicatory: "the term 'employer' includes any person acting as an agent of an employer," and "the term 'employee' shall include any employee, and should not be limited to the employees of a particular employer."[1214] The Fair Labor Standards Act (FLSA), which regulates minimum wages and overtime, among other rights, defines employees as "any individual employed by an employer."[1215]

The National Labor Relations Board (NLRB)[1216] and courts have case-based definitions of employment. The Supreme Court recognizes that no uniform and easily applicable test exists to define who employees are in a work relationship.[1217] Courts and the NLRB created and applied several tests to distinguish employees. The most common are the "right to control" and the "economic realities" tests. On the one hand, the common-law right to control test focuses on the employer's control over the tasks that are performed by the worker.[1218] Courts generally apply this test to determine if a worker is an employee under the scope of federal antidiscrimination statutes.[1219] On the other hand, the economic realities test seeks to determine whether the worker uniquely relies on the hiring part to earn a living.[1220] Positive response is *indicia* of an employment relationship. This test is used to determine whether the federal minimum wage and overtime rules apply.

In 1992 the Supreme Court ruled that the "right to control test" shall be used to define whether an employment relationship exists when statutes specify

---

Economy" (2016) 96 Boston University Law Review 1673; Miriam A Cherry, "Beyond Misclassification: The Digital Transformation of Work" (2016) 37 Comparative Labor Law & Policy Journal 577; Brishen Rogers, "Employment Rights in the Platform Economy: Getting Back to Basics" (2016) 10 Harvard Law & Policy Review 479.

[1214] NLRA, s 2 §152: "The term 'employee' shall include any employee, and shall not be limited to the employees of a particular employer, unless this subchapter explicitly states otherwise".

[1215] FLSA, s 203 §203. Other Federal regulations define employees in the same way: the Employment Retirement Income Security Act (ERISA) of 1974; the Family and Medical Leave Act (FMLA) of 1993; the Civil Rights Act of 1964, title VII, the Age Discrimination in Employment Act (ADEA) of 1967; American with Disabilities Act, 1990.

[1216] The NLRB is a US governmental agency responsible for investigating and prosecuting unfair labor practices mainly in the cases that have interstate commerce. For more information see <www.nlrb.gov >.

[1217] *Nationwide Mutual Insurance Co v Darden* 503 US 318 (1992).

[1218] Mitchell H Rubenstein, "Our Nation's Forgotten Workers: The Unprotected Volunteers" (2006), *op. cit.*, p 161.

[1219] The common law "right to control test" is clearly articulated in US Supreme Court decision *Nationwide Mutual Insurance Co v Darden* 503 US 318 (1992).

[1220] Noah Zatz, "Working Beyond the Reach or Grasp of Employment Law" in Anette Bernhardt, Heather Boushey, Laura Dresser, Chris Tilly, *The Gloves-Off Economy: Workplace Standards at the Bottom of America's Labor Market* (Champaign: Labor and Employment Relations Association, 2008), p 35.

---

differently.[1221] In that sense, the implementation of the NLRA is conditioned to the common-law test when the status of the worker is in doubt. Conversely, the FLSA specifically relates the definition of employee to economic realities and focuses on (1) the opportunity for profit or loss, (2) investment in equipment or materials, and (3) the extent to which the service rendered is an integral part of the employer's business.[1222]

The following factors are generally considered among the criteria for the tests: (1) the control that the business has over the worker's performance, and (2) the entrepreneurial potential the worker has, which means the possibility to handle different activities and clients and not perform functions that are an essential part of the company's normal operations.[1223]

The differentiation between an employee and an independent contractor is the most relevant limitation on employment law coverage. Independent contractors working outside an employment relationship are considered too powerful within an organization to be given special protection. Therefore, independent contractors are not entitled to receive employment law protections, except in some forms of social insurance.[1224] In this regard, independent contractors are outside the reach of minimum wage, unemployment compensation, occupational safety and health laws, collective bargaining laws, and employment antidiscrimination laws. For instance, the statute that prohibits companies from discharging any individual based on their race, color, religion, sex, or national origin only applies to employees.[1225] The same applies to the prohibition of discrimination of older workers and workers with disabilities.[1226] These antidiscrimination statutes define the term "employee" as "any individual employed by an employer".[1227] Considering the vagueness of the definition, the assessment of the employment relationship is conditioned to the verification of factual elements according to the common-law test, since the Supreme Court set the precedent.

In this light, the debate around the misclassification of workers' status has become prominent with the emergence of online work platforms.[1228] In

---

1221 *Nationwide Mutual Insurance Co v Darden* 503 US 318 (1992).

1222 Guy Davidov, "The Three Axes of Employment Relationships: A Characterization of Workers in Need of Protection" (2002) 52 The University of Toronto Law Journal 357, p 368–369.

1223 Micah Jost, "Independent Contractors, Employees, and Entrepreneurialism Under National Labor Relations Act: A Worker-by-Worker Approach" (2011) 68 Washington & Lee Law Review 311, 334–335.

1224 Noah Zatz, "Working Beyond the Reach or Grasp of Employment Law" in Anette Bernhardt, Heather Boushey, Laura Dresser, Chris Tilly, *The Gloves-Off Economy: Workplace Standards at the Bottom of America's Labor Market* (Champaign: Labor and Employment Relations Association, 2008) p 34.

1225 Title VII, 42 U.S.C., §2000e-2(a)(1).

1226 ADEA, 29 U.S.C., §623 (a)(1) and ADA, 42 U.S.C., §12112 (a).

1227 Title VII, 42 U.S.C., §2000e(f); ADEA, 29 U.S.C. §630(f); and 42 U.S.C. §12111(4).

1228 Robert L Redfearn III, "Sharing Economy Misclassification: Employees and Independent Contractors in Transportation Network Companies" (2016) 31 Berkeley Technology Law

September 2019 the State of California, birthplace of the largest technology companies in the peer-to-peer market, enacted a new bill clarifying the standards for assessment of the existence of real employment relationships. The California Assembly Bill 2019, also named AB 5, replaces previous uncertainties around the employment tests, notably the standards set in the case *Borello* decided by the Californian Supreme Court in 1989[1229] and the federal common law standards. The AB 5 prescribes that a person providing services for remuneration shall be considered an employee rather than an independent contractor when the three following conditions are met: (1) the person is not independent from the control and direction of the hiring entity who dictates details about the performance of work; (2) the person does not perform work for other hiring parts; (3) the person is not frequently engaged in an independent occupation of the same nature as the one involved to the hiring part to other hiring parts.[1230] The bill expressly excludes physicians, lawyers, architects, engineers, private investigators, and accountants from the new test, by determining that the status of employee or independent contractor for individuals in these sectors shall still be governed by the Borello test.[1231] Despite the attention in the media, commentators are still divided whether this new regulation will change the status of platform workers.[1232]

1.2. DISCRIMINATORY RATING SYSTEMS: LAWS AND PRECEDENTS

Employees' performance reviews (including rating systems) are used to guide employers through a variety of organizational decisions, such as termination, promotions, and wage rises. However, performance review may pose challenges to the principle of equal treatment of workers, particularly regarding intentional and non-intentional biases.[1233] Employers should carefully execute any type of systems focused on evaluating employees, otherwise they may face charges of direct or indirect discrimination if their performance review system

---

Journal 1023; Veena B Dubal, "Winning the Battle, Losing the War: Assessing the Impact of Misclassification Litigation on Workers in the Gig Economy (2017) Wiscosin Law Review 739; Andrei Hagiu, Julian Wright, "The Status of Workers and Platforms in the Sharing Economy" (2019) 28:1 Journal of Economics & Management Strategy 97; Orly Lobel, "The Gig Economy & the Future of Employment and Labor Law" (2017) 51 University of San Francisco Law Review 51.

[1229] *SG Borello & Sons, Inc. v Department of Industries Relations*, Case No S003956 (SC Cal 1989).

[1230] Assembly Bill No 5, Chapter 296, §2, 2750.3 (a)(1) (A).

[1231] Assembly Bill No 5, Chapter 296, §2, 2750.3 (b) (2) and (3).

[1232] Particularly, Uber announced that the enactment of AB5 does not compel it to reclassify its drivers. See JDSupra, *California Assembly Bill Five Excepts Certain Categories of Workers From Independent Contractor Classification Overhaul* (September 2019), online: JDSupra <https://www.jdsupra.com/legalnews/california-assembly-bill-five-excepts-58372/>.

[1233] *See* chapter 5, section I, 2, 2.1.

discriminates employees of protected classes, notably because of their "race," religious affiliation, sex, national origin, disability, or age.[1234]

In general, on-demand labor platforms base their workers' performance reviews on the clients' ratings. Would these platforms be liable for direct or indirect discrimination in cases in which they terminate the contract of their worker with protected classes based on biased clients' ratings? Thus far, no court cases involving discrimination against platform workers based on biased rating systems have been published, even though the *O'Connor v Uber* case approached the issue accessorily and a complaint regarding adverse impact of Uber's rating system was filed before the Equal Employment Opportunity Commission (EEOC).[1235] Nevertheless, if rates attributed by clients are understood as an expression of their preference regarding workers, instead of a neutral assessment of their performance, then case law addressing the liability of employers for direct and indirect discrimination of employees based on clients' preferences might shed some light on how courts would decide such cases.[1236]

1.2.1. Direct Discrimination Based on Clients' Preferences (Disparate Treatment)

District courts have already held employers liable for direct discrimination against their employees in cases involving customer's harassment and customer's discriminatory preferences.[1237]

Customer's harassment of employees is one example of employer liability for third-party direct discrimination addressed by district courts. Several lawsuits involving allegations of clients harassing employees because of their sex, "race," religion, and national origin have been filed since the enactment of Title VII.[1238]

[1234] Title VII, 42 U.S.C., §2000e-2(a)(1); ADEA, 29 U.S.C., §623 (a)(1) and ADA, 42 U.S.C., §12112 (a).

[1235] *O'Connor v Uber Technologies, Inc.*, 82 F. Supp. 3d 1133 (N.D. Cal. 2015), also *see* chapter 6, section II, 2, 2.1; and *Thomas Liu v Uber Technologies,* Equal Employment Opportunity Commission, 2014, *see* chapter 6, section II, 2, 2.3.

[1236] *See* particularly *Diaz v Pan American World Airways, Inc.*, 442 F2d 385 (United States Court of Appeals, 5th Circuit 1971); *Marenette v Michigan Host Inc.* 506 F. Supp 909 (United States Court for the Eastern District of Michigan, 1980); *Chaney v Plainfield Healthcare Center* 612 F.3d 908, 912–15 (United States Court of Appeals, 7th Circuit 2010); *Williams v G4S Secure Solutions* 1:17CV51 (United States District Court for the Middle District of North Carolina 2018); *EEOC v Sephora USA, LLC* 419 F.Supp.2ed 408 (United States District Court New York 2005) and the other referred on the footnotes of this section and the following section 3.2.2 and 3.2.3. These cases are listed by Dallan F Flake, "Employer Liability for Non-Employee Discrimination" (2017) 58 Boston College Law Review 1169, as several other cases in this subtopic.

[1237] *See* Lu-in Wang, "When the Customer is King: Employment Discrimination as Customer Service (2016) 23 Virginia Journal of Social Policy & the Law 249; Noah D Zatz, "Managing the Macaw: Third-Party Harassers, Accommodation, and the Disaggregation of Discriminatory Intent" (2009) 109 Columbia Law Review 1357.

[1238] Cases listed by Dallan F Flake, "Employer Liability for Non-Employee Discrimination", *op. cit: Beckford v Florida Department of Corrections*, 605 F.3d 951, 957–58, 921 (United States

One of the leading cases happened in Michigan almost four decades ago.[1239] In this instance, the employer required the waitresses to wear provocative uniforms, which subjected them to verbal and physical sexual harassment from the clients of the restaurant. The employer was aware that his clients were sexually harassing his employees, but he did not take any corrective action. In addition, male employees were not required to wear similar revealing and provocative clothes. The District Court sustained, in its ruling, that employers shall be liable for third-party illegal actions (e.g., customers' harassment) when they are negligent.[1240] When employers might have known or should have known about the harassment and fail to take any action to fix the situation, they might face direct liability, instead of any vicarious – indirect – liability.[1241] In this case, the lack of an agency link between the employer and the customer did not matter, and the employer was held directly liable for the harassment charges.[1242]

Aside from customer harassment, courts have held employers liable for direct discrimination against employees when they justified discrimination stemming from a customer's preferences in early cases involving Title VII of the Civil Rights Act.[1243] In this respect, the airline company Pan American World Airways (Pan Am) had the policy of exclusively hiring women as flight cabin attendants.[1244] The company argued, based on surveys, that passengers preferred to be served by female flight attendants. The airline company sustained that clients' preferences should constitute a reason to discriminate against men under Title VII. The statute allows direct discrimination when there is a *bona fide* occupational qualification.[1245] Based on this policy, Pan Am refused the application of Celio Diaz to the employment position of flight attendant. However, Diaz considered the exclusion of men unfair and discriminatory. He filed a lawsuit against Pan

---

Courts of Appeal, 11th Circuit 2010); *Santos v Puerto Rico Children's Hospital*, No. 11–1539 (United States District Court for the District of Puerto Rico, 2012); *Freeman v Dal-Tile Corporation*, 750 F.3d 413, 426 (United States Court of Appeal, 4th Circuit 2014); *Muldrow v Schmidt Baking Co*, No. WDQ-11–0519 (United States District Court for the District of Maryland, 2012); *Aguilar v Elite Care Management*, No. 12 C 6245, (United States District Court Northern District of Illinois, 2012); *Dunn v Washington County Hospital* 429 F.3d 689,690,693(United States Court of Appeals, 7th Circuit 2005).

[1239] *Marentette v Michigan Host Inc.* 506 F. Supp 909 (United States Court for the Eastern District of Michigan, 1980).
[1240] *Ibid.*
[1241] *Ibid.*
[1242] See Dallan F Flake, "Employer Liability for Non-Employee Discrimination" (2017) 58 Boston College Law Review 1169, 1196.
[1243] *See Rucker v Higher Educational Aids Board*, 669 F2d 1179 (United States Court of Appeals, 7th Circuit 1982); *Fernandez v Wynn Oil Company*, 653 F2d 1273 (United States Court of Appeals, 9th Circuit 1981); *Diaz v Pan American World Airways, Inc.*, 442 F2d 385 (United States Court of Appeals, 5th Circuit 1971).
[1244] *Diaz v Pan American World Airways, Inc.*, 442 F.2d 385 (United States Court of Appeals, 5th Circuit 1971).
[1245] Title VII, 42 U.S.C. §2000e-2(e)(1).

Am grounded on the prohibition that Title VII imposes on employers against sex discrimination in hiring processes.

Ultimately, the United States Court of Appeals for the Fifth Circuit ruled that clients' preferences should not serve as a reason to discriminate against men in the access to the employment position at stake. The ruling sustained that the substance of the business would not be undermined if the airline hired male flight attendants. The main function of an airline is to transport passengers safely from one point to another. In this particular case, both genders could perform this job. Therefore, the discriminatory policy of excluding men from being employed as flight attendants consisted of employer direct discrimination against employees. The ruling highlighted that it would be aberrant if they allowed the preferences and prejudices of customers to determine whether sex discrimination was valid: "It was, to a large extent, these very prejudices the [Civil Right] Act [of 1964] was meant to overcome."[1246]

The *Diaz v Pan American World Airlines Inc.* case provides the rationale adopted by courts for holding employers liable when they act based on discriminatory customer preferences, despite the employer allegedly lacking the intention to discriminate against protected classes. Pan Am alleged that it had no intention to discriminate against men, but instead wanted to accommodate its client requirements. Even in this context, the United States Court of Appeals for the Fifth Circuit found that allowing customers' preferences to guide the company's employment decisions was sufficient to determine liability for direct discrimination.

Since the *Diaz v Pan American* case, courts have ruled several instances of direct discrimination against employers who discriminated against their employees under the justification of accommodating customers' preferences.[1247] In this light, a United States District Court in North Carolina condemned the company G4S Secure Solutions, which is focused on providing staff for other businesses, for direct discrimination grounded on sex, because G4S refused to place a female employee, Ms. Williams, as a security guard after the client requested to have only-male security guards.[1248] In addition, in *Chaney v Plainfield Healthcare Center*, the employer was held liable for direct discrimination grounded on race for reassigning a Black American nurse to different job duties because certain patients refused to be treated by Black American nurses.[1249] The United States Court of Appeals for the Seventh

---

[1246] *Diaz v Pan American World Airways, Inc.*, 442 F2d 385 (United States Court of Appeals, 5th Circuit 1971), §389.

[1247] *Tamosaitis v URS Energy & Construction* 781 F3d 468, 476,489 (9th circuit 2015); *Olsen v Marriot International Inc.* 75 F Supp 2d 1052, (United States District Court D. Arizona 1999).

[1248] *Williams v G4S Secure Solutions* 1:17CV51 (United States District Court for the Middle District of North Carolina 2018).

[1249] *Chaney v Plainfield Healthcare Center* 612 F.3d 908, 912–15 (United States Court of Appeals, 7th Circuit 2010).

Circuit highlighted that accommodating customers' racial preferences is not allowed under Title VII.[1250] Another comparable case of direct discrimination was settled by a neonatal intensive care in Michigan. The agreement followed the claims that a Black American nurse was not allowed to take care of a white baby because the baby's father did not want his child to be treated by a Black American woman.[1251] Moreover, in *Bradley v Pizzaco of Nebraska*, the United States Court of Appeals for the Eight Circuit rejected customers' preferences for clean-shaven deliverymen because it had a disparate impact on Black American men, a large percentage of whom cannot shave because of a skin condition.[1252]

These aforementioned cases collectively involve the fact that employer action against the employee was based on one of the latter's protected aspects. This link is a condition for direct discrimination charges. It is also typically referred as a *but-for* test, which is applied in both tort and criminal law to determine causation. In the Pan Am case, Diaz was excluded from the job position because he was a man. Similarly, in *G4S Secure Solutions* and *Chaney,* the guard and the nurse were excluded because they were a woman and a Black American, respectively.

There are few cases in which employers were admitted to direct discriminate against employees based on the client's preference. These cases comprised contexts where privacy, safety, and genuineness were at stake and, then, considered as a *bona fide* occupational qualification.[1253] In *Wade v Napolitano*, the United States District Court in Tennessee dismissed a claim of sex discrimination against a transportation security company that required that one-third of its screeners should be female. In this case, the requirement of a particular sex constituted a *bona fide* occupational qualification necessary to ensure the privacy interests of passengers.[1254] In *Dothard v Rawlinson*, the United States Supreme Court maintained the State of Alabama's creation of male-only and female-only employment positions as guards for its prison system based on security reasons.[1255] The court considered that the requirement met the *bona fide* occupational qualification provided in Title VII.

[1250]   *Ibid.*

[1251]   EEOC, *Hurley Medical Center Agrees to Settle EEOC Race Discrimination Case* (November 2019), online: EEOC <https://www.eeoc.gov/eeoc/newsroom/release/9-26-13e.cfm>. The assignment of employees based on customers' racial preference violates Title VII of the Civil Rights Act of 1964.

[1252]   *Bradley v Pizzaco of Nebraska, Inc.* 7F.3d 795, 799 (8th Circuit 1993).

[1253]   Cases in which courts acknowledged that customer preference can form the basis of a *Bona Fide* Occupational Qualification under certain conditions: *Swint v Pullman-Standard*, 624 F.2d 525, 535 (United States Court of Appeals, 5th Circuit 1980); *EEOC v Sedita*, 816 F Supp 1291, 1295 (United States Court for the Northern District of Illinois 1993); Slivka v Camden-Clark Memorial Hospital, 594 S.E.2d 616, 620–21 (Supreme Court of Appeals of West Virginia 2004).

[1254]   *Wade v Napolitano* No. 3–07–0892 (United States District Court for the Middle District of Tennessee 2009).

[1255]   In *Dothard v Rawlinson*, 433 U.S. 321, 333 (1977).

1.2.2. Indirect Discrimination Based on Clients' Preferences (Disparate Impact)

When victims of discrimination cannot establish that an employment practice was motivated by their own personal statutorily protected aspects, such as race, gender, national origin, religion, age, or disability, the victims still have the possibility to challenge the action under a disparate impact claim. They can make a *prima facie* case by showing that the employment practice disproportionally affected a statutorily protected class. This *prima facie* involves 1) identifying the policy or practice, 2) demonstrating that a disparity exists, and 3) establishing a causal link between the policy and the disproportional impact.[1256] In response, employers can avoid liability for indirect discrimination if they prove that their facially neutral practice is coherent with their business necessity.[1257] In this scenario, the only possibility the victim has to succeed is by demonstrating that the employer refuses to adopt an available alternative practice that has less disproportional effects and serves the employer's legitimate needs.[1258]

A case brought by the EEOC against Sephora elucidates how courts address customer preferences involving indirect discrimination claims.[1259] Sephora, a cosmetics store chain, implemented an internal policy compelling its employees to speak "English-only" in the store when any client was around. The policy was based on the client's convenience and preferences. Sephora estimated that clients shopping in the store would feel more welcomed if they heard the entire staff speaking in English. The EEOC initiated the action alleging that the policy discriminated against five former employees, Leydis Rodriguez, Angela Sarnboy, Solange Bernal, Julissa Bautista, and Mariela Del Rosario, and a potential class of Hispanic employees in violation of Title VII of the Civil Rights Act, that forbids discrimination on the ground of national origin.[1260] They were all to some level bilingual in Spanish and English.

Prior to the action, Sephora's human resources had conducted a conference call with the directors to address the expectation that all employees spoke only English in the stores. Sephora expected employees who were on stage during business hours to speak only English whenever clients were around. In response, the employees alleged that they had some difficulty expressing some particular issues with their colleagues in English and this was why they spoke Spanish on a few occasions. They alleged to have an unconscious tendency to begin to speak

---

[1256] 42 U.S.C. §2000e-2(k)(1)(A)(I).
[1257] 42 U.S.C. §2000e-2(k)(1)(A)(i).
[1258] 42 U.S.C. §2000e-2(K)(1)(A)(ii).
[1259] *EEOC v Sephora USA, LLC* 419 F.Supp.2ed 408 (United States District Court New York 2005). *See* Lauren M Weinstein, "The Role of Labor Law in Challenging English-Only Policies" (2012) 47 Harvard Civil Rights-Civil Liberties Law Review 219; Andrew J Robinson, "Language, National Origin, and Employment Discrimination: The Importance of the EEOC Guidelines" (2009) 157 University of Pennsylvania Law Review 1513;
[1260] Title VII, 42 U.S.C., §2000e-2(a)(1).

in Spanish when addressed in that language, and because of that, they could not completely comply with Sephora's expectations on some occasions. Since they switched the language as a matter of involuntary habit, they were triggered to speak Spanish not as a matter of personal preference and convenience, but as a matter of necessity. They also complained about being disciplined for speaking Spanish in circumstances such as in the break room and during their lunch hour without the presence of clients. The victims were not against the fact that it was a job requirement to speak English, but rather they defended that requiring employees to speak only English with their colleagues when having a client in the store was discrimination grounded on their national origin.

The United States District Court in New York denied that the English-only policy violated Title VII. Even if the policy disproportionally impacted Hispanic staff, and "customer preference is not a valid defense to discrimination against employees,"[1261] Sephora had demonstrated a business necessity to implement such a policy. Sephora maintained that speaking English in the presence of customers was consistent with its "business needs of politeness and approachability as components of customer service."[1262] They characterized their policy as a "common sense rule against offending customers."[1263] Moreover, customers "feel welcome"[1264] when they hear employees speak English. The District Court ruled that the relationship between customer preference and the employment requirement to speak English only was sufficiently justified under business necessity in this case.

1.2.3. Rating Systems: Direct and Indirect Discrimination Under Federal Law

Rating scores and any quantitative method that potentially evaluates employees in a biased-discriminatory manner is most likely to fit under a disparate impact charge if the evaluation policy is indistinctly applicable to all workers.[1265] In the case of an indirect discrimination charge, the court's focus resides in the disproportional effect of the employment practice. Regarding scored systems, victims may establish a *prima facie* violation by demonstrating that facially neutral policies exist that disproportionately affect employees with protected classes.

Thus far, no published decisions concern allegations that customer feedback embedded in platforms' rating systems has resulted in indirect discrimination against protected classes of workers. However, plaintiffs have relied on disparate impact theories, first, to challenge facially neutral policies designed

---

[1261]   *EEOC v Sephora USA, LLC* 419 F.Supp.2ed 408 (United States District Court New York 2005), §417.

[1262]   *Ibid*, §416.

[1263]   *Ibid*, §416.

[1264]   *Ibid*, §417.

[1265]   42 U.S.C. §2000e-2(k)(1)(A)(i).

to accommodate customers' preferences, and, second, to challenge different subjective evaluations, generally performance reviews conducted by supervisors. In this context, Microsoft faced a class action discrimination lawsuit on the grounds that the company's method for evaluating performance systematically rates female engineer employees lower than their male colleagues.[1266]

Even if disparate impact claims are a suitable way to challenge rating systems that evaluate workers, disparate impact case-law has revealed one main drawback.[1267] The rate of success of disparate impact claims is low in courts. An analysis of years of disparate impact lawsuits demonstrates that the rate of success of disputes ruled by courts of appeals is 19.2%.[1268] One of the reasons attributed to this low success rate is the extensive meaning courts attribute to "business necessity."[1269]

1.3.   ARBITRATION

The assessment of on-demand platforms' organizational practices, such as rating systems, risks being permanently excluded from the jurisdiction of district courts because of the pervasiveness of arbitration clauses waiving trial rights imposed on most platform workers in the United States.[1270] As developed in Chapter 6, numerous litigations have occurred regarding the misclassification of Uber drivers' employment contracts, and cases of discrimination regarding these same drivers were dismissed by district courts and courts of appeals based on the fact that they consented to arbitration clauses when they agreed to work for the platform.[1271] In short, judges have ruled that the non-dismissal of such actions breaches the core of the Federal Arbitration Act (FAA).[1272]

[1266]   *Moussouris v Microsoft Corporation* 2:15-cv-01483 (Washington Western District Court 2015).

[1267]   *See* Michael Selmi, "Was the Disparate Impact Theory a Mistake" (2005) 53 UCLA Law Review 701, p 738; Stacy E Seischnaydre, "Is Disparate Impact Having Any Impact: An Appellate Analysis of Forty Years of Disparate Impact Claims under the Fair Housing Act" (2013) 63 American University Law Review 357; Richard a Primus, "Equal Protection and Disparate Impact: Round Three" (2003) 117 Harvard Law Review 493; Elaine W Shoben, "Disparate Impact Theory in Employment Discrimination: What's *Griggs* Still Good For? What Not?" (2004) 42 Brandeis Law Journal 597; Sandra F Sperino, "Disparate Impact or Negative Impact? The Future of Non-Intentional Discrimination Claims Brought by the Elderly" (2005) 13 Elder Law Journal 339, p 363.

[1268]   Michael Selmi, "Was the Disparate Impact Theory a Mistake" (2005) 53 UCLA Law Review 701, p 738.

[1269]   *Ibid*, p 749.

[1270]   Jill Gross, "The Uberization of Arbitration Clauses" (2017) 9 Arbitration Law Review 43, p 45.

[1271]   For instance, in *O'Connor v Uber Technologies*, Inc, 82 F. Supp. 3d 1133 (N.D. Cal. 2015); *Kendall Reese v Uber Technologies, Inc.* (2:18-cv-03300, United District Court for The Eastern District of Pennsylvania, Aug 2018); and *Mohamed v Uber Technologies, Inc.*, 848 F.3d 1201 (9th Circuit 2016).

[1272]   *See* chapter 6.

The FAA was enacted in an attempt to reverse courts' widespread refusal to enforce arbitration agreements.[1273] In this regard, the FAA specifies that a "written provision (...) to settle by arbitration a controversy thereafter arising out of such contract or transaction (...) shall be valid, irrevocable, and enforceable, save upon such grounds as exists at law or equity for the revocation of any contract."[1274] The American Congress essentially aimed for the FAA, and therefore arbitration, to apply to contracts between equal parties and not parties with unbalanced bargaining power.[1275] Initially, the FAA was not intended to apply to consumer cases or employment contracts of any sort but rather only to commercial cases.[1276]

Nevertheless, courts' understanding of the FAA has weakened the American constitutional right to judicial trials.[1277] Over the years, there has been an increasing adoption of arbitration clauses taking the resolution of all kinds of commercial, consumer, and employment disputes to the scope of professional arbitration instead of to court trial.[1278] The United States Supreme Court and Court of Appeals' expansive interpretation of the FAA have noticeably contributed to the privatization of consumer and employment-related litigation.[1279] Currently, arbitration clauses can frequently be found on individual employment contracts, even when the terms of the contracts are not genuinely negotiated between employers and employees, such as in the case of contracts of adhesion, also known as "take it or leave it" contracts.[1280] Arbitration clauses have been interpreted as enforceable in cases of employment age discrimination[1281], race discrimination[1282], and consumer protection.[1283]

[1273] Eric V Moyé, "Outsourcing American Civil Justice: Mandatory Arbitration Clauses in Consumer and Employment Contracts" (2012) 44 Texas Tech Law Review 281 p 287.

[1274] FAA, 9 U.S.C. §2 (2000).

[1275] Craig Smith, Eric V Moyé, "Outsourcing American Civil Justice: Mandatory Arbitration Clauses in Consumer and Employment Contracts" (2012) 44 Texas Tech Law Review 281.

[1276] *Ibid,* p 287.

[1277] Specifically, the Seventh Amendment right to a jury trial, Craig Smith, Eric V Moyé, "Outsourcing American Civil Justice: Mandatory Arbitration Clauses in Consumer and Employment Contracts" (2012) 44 Texas Tech Law Review 281 p 295.

[1278] Marc Galanter, "The Vanishing Trial: An Examination of Trials and Related Matters in Federal and State Courts (2004) 1 Journal of Empirical Legal Studies 459. From 1962 to 2002, the annual number of civil trials declined by more than 20%.

[1279] FAA, 9 U.S.C. (2000). *See, Gilmer v Interstate Johnson Lane Corporation,* 500 U.S. 20, 42 (1991); *Rent-a-Center W Inc. v Jackson,* 130 S. Ct. 2772, 2775 (2010); *AT&T Mobility LCC v Conception,* 131 S. Ct. 1740, 1744 (2010); *Southland Corporation v Keating,* 465 U.S. (1984); *See* David Horton, "Arbitration About Arbitration" (2018) 70 Stanford Law Review 363, p 363.

[1280] Alexander J S Colvin, "Mandatory Arbitration and Inequality of Justice in Employment" (2014) 25 Berkeley Journal of Employment & Labor Law 71; and Andrea Doneff, "Arbitration Clauses in Contracts of Adhesion Trap 'Sophisticated Parties' Too" (2010) Journal of Dispute Resolution 235.

[1281] *Gilmer v Interstate Johnson Lane Corporation,* 500 U.S. 20, 42 (1991).

[1282] *Rent-a-Center W Inc. v Jackson,* 130 S. Ct. 2772, 2775 (2010).

[1283] *AT&T Mobility LCC v Conception,* 131 S. Ct. 1740, 1744 (2010).

Commentators argue that, on the one hand, arbitration provides a faster, more flexible, more affordable, and often simpler procedural and evidentiary regime than judicial litigation[1284]; on the other hand, in the context of consumer and employment contracts, particularly in cases involving discrimination, private arbitration is perceived as detrimental because (1) it regularly strips the weaker party with less bargaining power to pursue claims as class or collective action, (2) it lacks publicity, (3) it does not create publicly binding precedents in the common-law sense and prevents the development of the law, and (4) it tends to favor repeat player corporations with superior bargaining power.[1285]

In this regard, courts have dismissed claims to make arbitration clauses void based on the fact that there was an imbalance in the bargaining power between the parties several times in the context of employment.[1286] Moreover, the fact that arbitration is a private and confidential system of dispute resolution has raised concerns because it deprives individuals in the same context from having access to the rationale of the decision. Cases litigated in courts are mostly accessible to the public, which ensures that individuals outside of the case can acknowledge it.[1287]

2. EUROPEAN UNION

2.1. EMPLOYMENT CLASSIFICATION AND PERSONAL SCOPE OF ANTIDISCRIMINATION RIGHTS

As long as the Employment Equality Directive only applies to employees and self-employed workers, and does not apply to entrepreneurs, the employment status of platform workers entitles them to claim any discrimination regarding their termination grounded on religion, belief, disability, age, and sexual

---

[1284] Thomas J Stipanowich, J Ryan Lamare, "Living with ADR: Evolving Perceptions and Use of Mediation, Arbitration and Conflict Management in Fortune 1000 Corporations" (2014) 19 Harvard Negotiation Law Review 1.

[1285] Lisa B Bingham, "Employment Arbitration: The Repeat Player Effect (1997) 1 Employment Rights & Employment Policy Journal 189, p 190; Craig Smith, Eric V Moyé, "Outsourcing American Civil Justice: Mandatory Arbitration Clauses in Consumer and Employment Contracts" (2012) 44 Texas Tech Law Review 281 p 296; Also, Jean R Sternlight, *Disarming Employees: How American Employers are Using Mandatory Arbitration to Deprive Workers of Legal Protection* (2015) 80 Brook. Law Review 1309, p 1310; Katherine Van Wezel Stone, "Mandatory Arbitration of Individual Employment Rights: The Yellow Dog Contract of the 1990's" (1996) 73 Denver University Law Review 1017; David Horton, "Arbitration as Delegation" (2011) 86 New York Law Review 437; Lisa Bingham, "On Repeat Players, Adhesive Contracts, and the Use of Statistics in Judicial Review of Employment Arbitration Awards" (1998) 29 McGeorge Law Review 223.

[1286] *Gilmer v Interstate Johnson Lane Corporation*, 500 U.S. 20, 42 (1991).

[1287] Craig Smith, Eric V Moyé, "Outsourcing American Civil Justice: Mandatory Arbitration Clauses in Consumer and Employment Contracts" (2012) 44 Texas Tech Law Review 281, p 297.

orientation. The situation is different regarding the grounds of race, ethnic origin, and sex. First, the Race Equality Directive protects the grounds of race and ethnic origin in employment relationships as well as in the access to goods and services. Second, sex is also protected against discrimination in the access to goods and services by the Gender Equal Access to Goods and Services Directive. Therefore, when platforms in the EU have a contract to provide services, such as matching two sides of the market, with platform workers they must comply with antidiscrimination rules regarding the grounds of race, ethnic origin, and sex. Under the general EU Equality Directives, rating systems that adversely discriminate against race, ethnic origin, and sex are illegal, no matter if the workers are employees, self-employed, or clients of the platform. However, the reality is different regarding the other grounds provided by the Employment Equality Directive. In this case, the contractual classification of platform workers matters given the scope of the directive.[1288]

European Law limits the liberty of member states to decide the scope of their labor law legislations.[1289] The idea behind this limitation is to, primarily, harmonize and guarantee social protection to employees and, ultimately, to avoid economic distortions between different EU member states.[1290] Currently, EU member states have no unique clear-cut criteria to differentiate employees from genuine self-employed workers.[1291] The EU Parliament has raised concerns about the lack of unique legal tests to distinguish self-employment from employment across EU member states.[1292] Such a lack of definition has led to increased numbers of false self-employment.[1293] Member states were invited in several occasions to undertake initiatives to make clear distinctions between employees and genuine self-employed workers.[1294]

In the UK, for instance, self-employed workers are considered dependent when they have only one client, have no authority to hire and dismiss employees, and have no extended decision-making-autonomy.[1295] Moreover, the hiring

---

[1288] It is worth noting that certain Member States went further than the provisions of the Employment Equality Directive.

[1289] Catherine Barnard, *EU Employment Law* 4th Edition (Oxford: Oxford University Press, 2012), p 253.

[1290] Taco Van Peijpe, "EU Limits for the Personal Scope of Employment Law" (2012) 3:1 European Labour Law Journal 35, p 37.

[1291] Frans Pennings, "The European Union and the Issue of the Employment Relationship" in Frans Pennings, Claire Bosse, *The Protection of Working Relationships* (Wolter Kluwer, 2011) p 30; Opinion of the European and Social Committee on 'abuse of the status of self-employed' (own-initiative opinion), OJ C 161, 6.6.2013, p 14–19.

[1292] European Parliament Resolution of 14 January on Social Protection for All, Including Self-Employed Workers (2013/2111(INI)).

[1293] *Ibid.*

[1294] European Parliament Resolution of 6 May 2009 on the Renewed Social Agenda (2008/2330 (INI)).

[1295] Catherine Barnard, *EU Employment Law* 4th Edition (Oxford: Oxford University Press, 2012) p 147.

party has control over the party who will perform the service.[1296] The absence of control and subordination are likely to indicate that the individual is self-employed.[1297] However, courts rarely use one single criterion to determine the worker's status, but instead they take a multiple or pragmatic approach balancing several factors, including the level of integration of the individual into the business, an allocation of risks, and a mutuality of obligation.[1298]

Contrarily to the EU law that only has the categories of employed and self-employed, a number of EU countries recognize a tripartite classification of the personal scope of the relations in the employment field, including the categories of employees, self-employed/workers, and self-employed/entrepreneurs.[1299] The first category concerns those who are under usual employment contracts. The second category self-employed/workers, also called dependent self-employed, includes those who are largely dependent on one particular hiring party. The category of dependent self-employment is covered by employment law.[1300] The third category encompasses self-employed persons who work for a number of hiring parties (also called customers or clients) and who do not have any relationship of dependence with any of them. This last category is covered by civil or commercial statues and is outside the scope of employment laws.

In this context, an extensive amount of literature is focused on the distinctions and concepts of workers, employees, dependent self-employed persons, and genuinely self-employed persons.[1301] Even though most of EU labor law has not exhaustively defined these categories[1302], the CJEU has ruled

---

[1296]   See *Byrne Brothers (Formwork) Ltd v Baird* [2002] IRLR 96; *Bates van Winkelhof v Clyde & Co LLP* [2014] UKSC 32; *Cotswold Developments Construction Ltd v Williams* [2006] IRLR 181.

[1297]   Simon Deakin, "Interpreting Employment Contracts: Judges, Employers and Workers" (2004) 20:2 International Journal of Comparative Labour Law and Industrial Relations 201.

[1298]   The mutuality of obligation requirement lay down whether there is an obligation on the employer to provide work and an obligation on the employee to accept work offered. *Carmichael v National Power* [2000] IRLR 43. Simon Deakin, "Interpreting Employment Contracts: Judges, Employers and Workers" (2004) 20:2 International Journal of Comparative Labour Law and Industrial Relations 201.

[1299]   Catherine Barnard, Alysia Blackham, *Self-Employed: The Implementation of Directive 2010/41 on the Application of the Principle of Equal Treatment Between Men and Women Engaged in an Activity in a Self-Employed Capacity* (March 2015), online: European Commission Directorate-General for Justice and Consumers <https://www.equalitylaw.eu/component/edocman/self-employed-en>, p 4.

[1300]   *Ibid.*

[1301]   Nicola Countouris, "The Concept of 'Worker' in European Labour Law: Fragmentation, Autonomy, and Scope" (2018) 47:2 Industrial Law Journal 192; Charlotte O'Brien, Eleanor Spaventa, Joyce De Coninck, *Comparative Report 2015: The Concept of Worker Under Article 45 TFEU and Certain Non-Standard Forms of Employment* (April 2016), online: European Commission <http://dro.dur.ac.uk/18690/1/18690.pdf?DDC72+DDC71+DDD19+dla0es+d700tmt>; Bernd Waas, "The Legal Definition of the Employment Relationship" (2010) 1:1 European Labour Law Journal 45; Nicola Countouris, *The Changing Law of the Employment Relationship* (Aldershot: Ashgate, 2007).

[1302]   For instance, the Treaty of Rome has several provisions regarding "workers", including the equal pay for equal work and the freedom of movement for workers, but it did not offer

in several instances on the personal scope of EU labor legislation.[1303] EU law has left a margin of appreciation to member states and to their courts, as long as national definitions of employment do not circumvent the purposes of EU legislation regarding the freedom of movement and social and equal protection of workers.[1304]

Concerning the freedom of movement, the CJEU has ruled that the main criteria of an employment relationship consist of subordination, remuneration[1305], and the fact that the worker is engaged in "effective and genuine activities, to the exclusion of activities on such a small scale as to be regarded as purely marginal or ancillary."[1306] National courts must decide whether a relationship of subordination exists because it is a matter of fact.[1307] In the context of freedom of movement, the Court of Justice has already ruled that, unlike employees, self-employed workers are outside of a relationship of subordination when they handle the risk of success and failure of their business and when they are paid directly and in full.[1308]

Regarding the protection against discrimination in working conditions and the termination of work contracts, the personal scope of the Employment Equality Directive is less limited than Title VII of the Civil Rights Act, the ADA, and the ADEA, but it still sets outer limits. The text provides that it shall be applicable to all persons in the public and private sectors concerning

---

any proper definition to the terms. Also, concerning equal treatment, the directive on the application of the principle of equal treatment between men and women engaged in an activity in a self-employed capacity broadly defines that self-employed workers pursue a gainful activity for their own account under the conditions defined by national law. Directive 2010/41/EU of the European Parliament and of the Council of 7 July 2010 on the application of the principle of equal treatment between men and women engaged in an activity in a self-employed capacity and repealing Council Directive 86/613/EEC, OJ L 180, 15.7.2010, p 1–6, art 2(a).

[1303] The Court of Justice has held its competence to define the term worker in the context of the free movement of workers. *See* C-75/63 *Hoekstra v Bestuur der Bedrijfsvereniging voor Detailhandel en Ambachten* ECLI:EU:C:1964:19; C-66/85 *Lawrie-Blum v Land Baden-Württemberg* ECLI:EU:C:1986:284; C-3/87 *Agegate* ECLI:EU:C:1989:650; C-196/87 *Steymann Staatssecretaris van Justitie,* ECLI:EU:C:1988:475; C-344/87 *Bettray v Staatssecretaris Van Justitie,* ECLI:EU:C:1989:226;C-456/02 *Trojani v Centre public d'aide sociale de Bruxelles,* ECLI:EU:C:2004:488.

[1304] Nicola Countouris, "The Concept of 'Worker' in European Labour Law: Fragmentation, Autonomy, and Scope" (2018) 47:2 Industrial Law Journal 192, p 194. Also, *see* European Commission, "Communication from the Commission to the European Parliament, the Council, the European Economic and Social Committee and the Committee of the Regions – A European Agenda for the Collaborative Economy" COM (2016) 356 final, p 12.

[1305] "The worker performs services under the direction of another person for a certain period of time in return for which he/she receives remuneration", *see* C-66/85 *Lawrie-Blum v Land Baden-Württemberg* ECLI:EU:C:1986:284, paragraphs 16–17. Also, the requirement to be engaged in an economic activity has been ruled in: C-10/05 *Mattern v Ministre du Travail et de l'Emploi,* ECLI:EU:C:2006:220, paragraph 21.

[1306] C-337/97, *Meeusen v Hoofddirectie van de Informatie Beheer Groep,* ECLI:EU:C:1999:284.

[1307] *Ibid,* paragraph 15.

[1308] C-268/99, *Jane and others v Staatssecretaries van Justitie,* ECLI:EU:C:2001:616.

the conditions for access to employment and to self-employment.[1309] Notwithstanding, it also applies to employment and working conditions, including dismissals and pays.[1310] The first subheading makes it clear that it aims to reach employees as well as self-employed individuals. This inclusive understanding of the personal scope was supported by the *Allonby* case and later the *Danosa* case, which involve sex discrimination.[1311]

However, according to scholars, the fact that the scope of the Equality Directives expressly relates to employment and occupation[1312] implies that some sort of subordination, economic or personal, must be present in the relationship between the hiring party and the individual.[1313] In that sense, the Directives' personal scope would be confined to employees, workers, and dependent self-employed persons and should not reach the genuine self-employed worker.[1314] EU case law regarding equal pay between women and men supports the view that EU equality law applies to employed and dependent self-employed workers, but not to genuinely self-employed workers.[1315] In this light, the CJEU ruled

---

[1309]   Art(s) 3(1)(a) of the Race Equality Directive and Employment Equality Directive; Art 14(a) of the Gender Equality Directive. *See* Sandra Fredman, "Pasts and Futures: EU Equality Law", in (eds), *Research Handbook on EU Labour Law* (Edward Elgar Publishing, 2016), p 391.

[1310]   Art(s) 3(1)(c) of the Race Equality Directive and Employment Equality Directive; Art 14(c) of the Gender Equality Directive. Also, the Directive 2010/41/EU of the European Parliament and of the Council of 7 July 2010 on the application of the principle of equal treatment between men and women engaged in an activity in a self-employed capacity and repealing Council Directive 86/631/EEC, OJ L 180/1, 15.7.2010 applies to self-employed workers but does not comprise discrimination in the termination of the contract, which is the scope of the present title. *See* more Catherine Barnard, Alysia Blackham, *Self-Employed: The Implementation of Directive 2010/41 on the Application of the Principle of Equal Treatment Between Men and Women Engaged in an Activity in a Self-Employed Capacity* (March 2015), online: European Commission Directorate-General for Justice and Consumers <https://www.equalitylaw.eu/component/edocman/self-employed-en>.

[1311]   In the Case C-256/01, C-256/01 *Allonby v Accrington & Rossendale College*, ECLI:EU:C:2004:18 the Court of Justice ruled that the right to equal pay for equal work is applicable to all workers; C-232/09 *Danosa v LKB Līzings SIA* ECLI:EU:C:2010:674, paragraph 74 provided that a pregnant woman without the "worker" status would still fall within the scope of the Gender Equality Directive 2006/54 in case of dismissal based on her pregnancy. *See* Catherine Barnard, *EU Employment Law* 4th Edition (Oxford: Oxford University Press, 2012), p 347; Nicola Countoris, *The Changing Law of the Employment Relationship* (Aldershot: Ashgate, 2007), chapter 5; Nicola Countouris, Mark Freedland, *The Personal Scope of the EU Sex Equality Directives* (April 2012), online: European Commission European Network of Legal Experts in the Field of Gender Equality <https://op.europa.eu/en/publication-detail/-/publication/d6139fa9-b67b-4bfb-99c6-526d016f7a7d>.

[1312]   Art 1 of the Race Equality Directive, Employment Equality Directive and Gender Equality Directive.

[1313]   Catherine Barnard, *EU Employment Law* 4th Edition (Oxford: Oxford University Press, 2012), p 347; Nicola Countouris, *The Changing Law of the Employment Relationship* (Aldershot: Ashgate, 2007), chapter 5.

[1314]   *Ibid.*

[1315]   Case C-256/01, *Debra Allonby v Accrington & Rossendale College* (2004) ECLI:EU:C:2004:18. Also, *See* Nicola Countouris, Mark Freedland, *The Personal Scope of EU Sex Equality Directives* (April 2013), online: European Commission Directorate-General for Justice and

that the personal scope of the Gender Equality Directive includes dependent self-employed workers when it decided that the dismissal of a pregnant women would fall into the prohibitions of discrimination because she was a dependent self-employed person.[1316] However, the CJEU has not yet been asked if the Employment Equality Directive approaches the issue of personal scope differently from how it has been considered in the gender equality or free-movement cases, or in other words, if it reaches genuine self-employed workers.[1317]

With this backdrop in mind, the definition of the employment status of platform workers is relevant to determine whether they are covered by the scope of the Employment Equality Directive. The above-mentioned precedents and legal literature indicate that the Directive certainly applies to employed and dependent self-employed workers, but it does not apply to genuine self-employed workers/entrepreneurs.

2.2. DISCRIMINATORY RATING SYSTEMS: LAWS AND PRECEDENTS

On-demand labor platforms use clients' ratings to evaluate the performance of platform workers. These clients' ratings influence organizational decisions, such as the termination of worker's contract with the platform. In other words, rating systems determine which workers can provide services through the platform and the ones who cannot. Would online platforms – either as an employer or service provider–be liable for direct or indirect discrimination in cases they terminate the contract of protected classes of workers based on discriminatory clients' ratings? Up to the present, EU case law has only sparsely addressed employers' discrimination that addresses customer preferences.

2.2.1. Client's Preferences as a Basis for Direct Discrimination

The Court of Justice has assessed the legality of treating workers in a discriminatory fashion based on customer preferences in a few cases related

---

Consumers <https://op.europa.eu/en/publication-detail/-/publication/d6139fa9-b67b-4bfb-99c6–526d016f7a7d>.

[1316] C-232/09 *Danosa v LKB Līzings SIA* ECLI:EU:C:2010:674, paragraph 74.

[1317] Nicola Countouris argues that because the two directives (Race and Employment) place greater emphasis on their fundamental rights dimension, if the CJEU once faces the question of their personal scope it might decide that the principles provided by them apply to "many working persons as possible, regardless of their state of economic or formal dependency". *See* Nicola Countouris, *The Changing Law of the Employment Relationship: Comparative Analyses in the European Context* (Ashgate: Aldershot, 2007) p 184; Also, *see* Alysia Blackham, Catherine Barnard, "The Self-Employed and the Welfare State in the EU: Insights from Gender and Race Equality Law", in Mies Westerveld, Marius Olivier (eds), *Social Security Outside the Realm of Employment Contract* (Edward Elgar Publishing, 2019), p 83.

to the protected aspects of ethnic origin and religion. First, the *Feryn* case, discussed in Title II, concerns an employer who publicly declared that he would not hire individuals with a certain origin (implicitly Moroccan) because his customers would not like to give them access to their houses.[1318] He claimed his decision was based on customer's preferences and not on his own: "I must comply with my customers' requirements. If you say, 'I want that particular product or I want it like this and like that' and I say, 'I'm not doing it, I'll send those people', then you say, 'I don't need that door'. Then I'm putting myself out of business. We must meet the customers' requirement. This isn't my problem. I didn't create this problem in Belgium. I want the firm to do well and I want us to achieve our turnover at the end of the year, and how do I do that? I must do it the way the customer wants it done."[1319] The CJEU found that regardless of whether the discriminatory preferences did or did not come from the employer, the employer's action of discouraging individuals with a certain ethnic origin from applying to the position hinders their access to the job market and, therefore, constitutes direct discrimination in respect to recruitment within the meaning of the Race Equality Directive.[1320] The intention to discriminate is irrelevant to demonstrate direct discrimination.[1321]

The second case – *Bougnaoui* – concerns more specifically the termination of an employment relationship because of the customer's discriminatory preference. In this particular instance, the customer of a commercial company called Micropole SA (i.e. employer) requested that there "should be no veil next time."[1322] In this situation, the employee, a Muslim design engineer, worked wearing an Islamic headscarf, and after the complaint of a customer, the French company required Ms. Bougnaoui not to wear the headscarf anymore. She refused to do so and was then dismissed in the interests of the business. The company also did not have a written internal policy of neutrality *vis-à-vis* its customers. The employee considered the dismissal to be discriminatory

---

[1318] Case C-54/07, Feryn, ECLI:EU:C:2008:397, *see* title II, chapter 2.

[1319] §18(1), Case C-54/07, Feryn, ECLI:EU:C:2008:397.

[1320] Case C-54/07, Feryn, ECLI:EU:C:2008:397.

[1321] Besides the case *Feryn, see* C-507/18, *N.H. c. Associazione Avvocatura per i diritti LGBTI – Rete Lenford,* ECLI:EU:C:2020:289 and Emmanuelle Bribosia, Isabelle Rorive, "Les Paroles Ont des Ailes et Peuvent Discriminer: Regard sur l'Arrêt N.H. c. Associazione Avvocatura per I diritti LGBTI – Rete Lenford, rendu en Grand Chambre par la CJUE le 23 avril 2020, C-507/18", (2020) Journal Européen des Droits de l'Homme. *Also,* the motivation or intention to discriminate is not a necessary element of direct discrimination. It is enough that the discriminatory treatment is grounded on, or caused by, a prohibited classification. "This causation-based approach is reflected in the so-called 'but-for' test. According to this test, 'but for' the person's sex/race (and other protected grounds) they would have enjoyed the more favorable treatment experience by the comparator". Direct discrimination is unlawful unless it can be justified by a legal exception/derogation. These exceptions can be found on the equality directives. *See* Catherine Barnard, *EU Employment Law* 4th Edition (Oxford: Oxford University Press, 2012), p 278. Also, title II.

[1322] C-188/15, *Asma Bougnaoui and ADDH v Micropole SA*, ECLI:EU:C:2017:204.

and brought the case to litigation. The Court of Appeals in Paris ruled that Ms. Bougnaoui's termination related to the religious beliefs of the employee, considering she was allowed to wear the veil within internal service, but the restriction was justified by a legitimate reason arising from the preferences of the clients.

Ms. Bougnaoui appealed to the Court of Cassation arguing that the embarrassment or sensitivity of the customers of a commercial company when facing an employee wearing the Islamic headscarf is neither a relevant nor a legitimate criterion that is free from any discrimination "that might justify the company's economic or commercial interests being allowed to prevail over the fundamental freedom of religion of an employee."[1323] The Court of Cassation stressed that the CJEU in the *Feryn* case did not specifically determine whether the Race Equality Directive[1324] might allow an employer's *customer discriminatory preference* to be interpreted as a genuine and determining occupational requirement. Therefore, the Court of Cassation referred the question of whether the Employment Equality Directive must be interpreted as meaning that the wish of a customer of a commercial company asking its employee not to wear an Islamic headscarf should be held as a genuine and determining occupational requirement by reason of the nature of the particular occupational activities concerned.

The CJEU held that customers' preferences cannot be considered a genuine and determining occupational requirement justifying a direct discrimination based on religion.[1325] The Court found that Micropole SA directly discriminated against its employee on the ground of religion, since the decision to terminate her contract was not based on a general neutrality policy.[1326]

[1323] *Ibid.*

[1324] Art 4(1), Race Equality Directive.

[1325] Case C-188/15, *Asma Bougnaoui and ADDH v Micropole SA*, ECLI:EU:C:2017:204, paragraph 41.

[1326] This case along with *Achbita v G4S Solutions NV* were vastly commented. *See* Emmanuelle Bribosia, Isabelle Rorive, "Affaires Achbita et Bougnaoui: Entre Neutralité et Préjugés" (2017) 112:3 Revue Trimestrielle des Droits de L'Homme 1018; Erica Howard, "Islamic Headscarves and the CJEU: Achbita and Bougnaoui" (2017) 24:3 Maastricht Journal of European and Comparative Law 348; Schona Jolly, "Islamic Headscarves and the Workplace Reach the CJEU: the Battle for Substantive Equality" (2016) 6 European Human Rights Law Review 622; Erica Howard, *Religious Clothing and Symbols in Employment: A Legal Analysis of the Situation in the EU Member States* (November 2017), online: European Commission European Network of Legal Experts in Gender Equality and Non-Discrimination <https://www.equalitylaw.eu/downloads/4493-religious-clothing-and-symbols-in-employment-pdf-928-kb>, p 62–80; Eva Brems, *European Court of Justice Allows Bans on Religious Dress in the Workplace* (March 2017), online: IACL-AIDC <https://blog-iacl-aidc.org/test-3/2018/5/26/analysis-european-court-of-justice-allows-bans-on-religious-dress-in-the-workplace>; Eleanor Spaventa, *What is the Point of Minimum Harmonization of Fundamental Rights? Some Further Reflection on the Achbita Case* (March 2017), online: EU Law Analysis <http://eulawanalysis.blogspot.com/2017/03/what-is-point-of-minimum-harmonization.html>. *For more* on customer preference, Sophie Robin-Olivier, "French Labour Law: Testing the

2.2.2. The Crossroads Between Clients' Preferences and Neutrality Policies: A Real Basis for Indirect Discrimination?

In the *Achbita* case, Ms. Achbita, a Muslim woman, worked for G4S, a Belgian company specialized in the provision of reception services for customers in both public and private sectors, and after three years of working for the company she manifested her intention to wear an Islamic headscarf during her working hours.[1327] In response, G4S approved an amendment to the written workplace regulation expressly providing that employees were prohibited from wearing any visible signs of their political, philosophical, or religious beliefs due to their neutrality policies *vis-à-vis* clients. A month after the regulation entered into force, Ms. Achbita was dismissed because of her continued insistence to wear the headscarf. The company alleged that Ms. Achbita's behavior breached the neutrality policy in force. She sued G4S by claiming that her dismissal constituted religion or belief discrimination contrary to the Employment Equality Directive and the transposed law. Both the Labor Court and the Higher Labor Court in Antwerp, Belgium, rejected the claim.[1328]

Contrarily to the *Bougnaoui* case, the CJEU found no direct discrimination against the employee, because the neutrality rule treated all workers of the company in the same way.[1329] Therefore, such an internal rule did not introduce a difference of treatment that is directly based on religion or belief under the scope of the Employment Equality Directive.[1330] In that sense, the Court recognized that such internal policy apparently imposing neutral obligation on its employees could result in placing persons adhering to a particular religion or belief at a disadvantageous position. However, this disadvantageous position would not amount to indirect discrimination if it was objectively justified by a legitimate aim and if the means of achieving that aim were appropriate and necessary. In this respect, it was ultimately for the national court, which is the jurisdiction to assess the facts, to determine whether the requirements that justify indirect discrimination in this case were present. However, the CJEU stressed that employers manifesting interest to project an image of neutrality towards

---

Possibility of a Legal Transplant", in Reasonable Accommodation for Religion, and Other Motives, Bulletin of Comparative Labour Relations, Vol 93, 2016, p 145.

[1327] C-157/15, *Achbita v G4S Solutions NV* ECLI:EU:C:2017:203, paragraph 12.

[1328] *Ibid*, §10–20.

[1329] Several commentators disagreed with the Court's position affirming that in fact the case concerned direct discrimination. *See* Emmanuelle Bribosia, Isabelle Rorive, "Affaires Achbita et Bougnaoui: Entre Neutralité et Préjugés" (2017), *op. cit.*; Amnesty International, ENAR, *Wearing the Headscarf in the Workplace: Observation on Discrimination Based on Religion in the Achbita and Bougnaoui Cases* (October 2016), online: Amnesty <https://www.amnesty.org/en/documents/eur01/5077/2016/en/>; Open Society Justice Initiative, *Employer's Bar on Religious Clothing and European Union Discrimination Law* (2016), online: Justice Initiative <https://www.justiceinitiative.org/uploads/3ee205fb-ad07–4ef2–9d45–2af0ec8101dc/briefing-cjeu-headscarves-20160712.pdf>.

[1330] Art 2(2)(a) Employment Equality Directive.

customers is essentially connected to their freedom to conduct a business, under the terms of Article 16 of the Charter, and, in principle, it is legitimate according to their freedom to conduct their business to involve employees in the pursuit of projecting the image of neutrality, especially when they directly deal with the employer's customers and when the policy is genuinely pursued in a consistent and systematic manner.[1331] Once the legitimacy of the policy was attested, the question of necessity of the prohibition should be assessed. Ultimately, the CJEU found that requiring employees not to wear a headscarf was a necessary and proportionated mean to project the company's image of neutrality.

The decision was strongly criticized for allowing private companies to exclude women wearing Islamic headscarves from the contact with customers as a necessary and appropriate mean aligned to their legitimate aim of pursuing an image of neutrality as part of their general freedom to conduct business.[1332] Moreover, some commentators disagreed that the case concerned indirect discrimination.[1333] The CJEU found that the case regarded indirect discrimination on the ground that the neutrality rule applicable by the enterprise prohibited the wearing of *any* visible signs of political, philosophical, or religious convictions and, thus, indifferently targeted *any* manifestation of such convictions. Therefore, the court considered that this rule did not result in direct discrimination based on the religion ground because it treated all workers the same way, by imposing clothing neutrality on them in a general and undifferentiated manner. However, commentators argued that the verification of direct discrimination – which in cases of religious discrimination imposes a stricter possibility of justification[1334] – does not depend on the verification of a general rule that applies indistinctively to all workers but on the fact that a rule does not have the effect of subjecting a person to a less favorable treatment based on religious convictions, compared to another who is in a comparable situation.[1335]

In both cases, the values under dispute are freedom to conduct a business and freedom of religion. Ultimately, the question to be considered is whether

---

[1331] C-157/15, *Achbita v G4S Solutions NV* ECLI:EU:C:2017:203 paragraph 38. Even if limits to the pursuit of these aims could be borne out from the case law of the European Court of Human Rights, regarding the Article 9 of the ECHR. *Eweida and others v United Kingdom* CE:ECHR:2013:0115JUD004842010, §94.

[1332] Lucy Vickers, "Achbita and Bougnaoui: One Step Forward and Two Steps Back for Religious Diversity in the Workplace" (2017) 8:3 European Labour Law Journal 232; Elke Cloots, "Safe Harbour or Open Sea for Corporate Headscarf Ban? Achbita and Bougnaoui" (2018) 55:2 Common Market Law Review 589; Emmanuelle Bribosia, Isabelle Rorive, "Affaires Achbita et Bougnaoui: Entre Neutralité et Prejugés" (2017) 112:3 Revue Trimestrielle des Droits de L'Homme 1018.

[1333] Emmanuelle Bribosia, Isabelle Rorive, "Affaires Achbita et Bougnaoui: Entre Neutralité et Prejugés" (2017), *op. cit.*.

[1334] Article 5 §1, and Article 4 §2 Employment Equality Directive.

[1335] Emmanuelle Bribosia, Isabelle Rorive, "Affaires Achbita et Bougnaoui: Entre Neutralité et Prejugés" (2017) 112:3 Revue Trimestrielle des Droits de L'Homme 1018, p 1026.

companies can limit their employees' freedom of religion to project an image of political, ideological, and religious neutrality or to accommodate their clients' preferences. In a pending case, the CJEU was requested to answer whether employers' instructions that prohibit the wearing of any visible sign of political, ideological, or religious belief constitutes direct or indirect discrimination against female employees who wear a headscarf due to their faith.[1336] One of the interests of the request is also to determine whether such a condition not to wear a headscarf would constitute gender discrimination, and, therefore, multidimensional discrimination based on gender and religion. Moreover, the Court was requested to determine whether the fundamental right to conduct a business justifies discrimination on the grounds of religion.

2.2.3. Rating Systems: Direct and Indirect Discrimination Under EU Law

Some scholars suggest that the CJEU's reasoning in the cases *Achbita* and *Bougnaoui* may be useful to predict how the Court would assess the use of biased-customer ratings to base employment-related decisions.[1337] They justify that ratings are the expression of customers' preferences. Regarding the above-mentioned cases, first, the Court construed that customer preferences could not serve as a genuine occupational requirement to justify the company's discrimination against its employee on the ground of religion in the *Bougnaoui* case.[1338] Second, in *Achbita* the Court controversially construed that the implementation of an organizational policy (e.g., requiring workers to not wear their headscarf in the presence of their clients) to project the company's image of neutrality *vis-à-vis* the clients was a legitimate aim aligned with the freedom to conduct a business.[1339]

Based on these cases, scholars have argued that the CJEU would likely assess the eventual negative impact on protected classes (e.g., the termination of their contract) by the implementation of a rating system as justifiable under the freedom to conduct a business.[1340] Since the Court construed in *Achbita* that an organizational policy implemented to project the image of neutrality was legitimate under the freedom to conduct a business, the Court would likely accept rating systems that put certain classes of employees in a disadvantageous

---

[1336] C-804/18, *IX v WabeeV and MH Müller Handels GmbH v MJ* ECLI:EU:C:2021:594.

[1337] Rossana Ducato, Miriam Kullmann, Marco Rocca, "European Legal Perspectives on Customer Ratings and Discrimination", in Tindara Addabbo, Ylenia Curzi, Olga Rymkevich, *Performance Appraisal in Modern Employment Relations: An Interdisciplinary Approach* (Palgrave Macmillan, 2019), p 255.

[1338] C-188/15, *Asma Bougnaoui and ADDH v Micropole SA*, ECLI:EU:C:2017:204.

[1339] C-157/15 *Achbita v G4S Solutions NV* ECLI:EU:C:2017:203, paragraph 38. Freedom to conduct a business protected by Article 16 of the Charter of Fundamental Rights of the European Union.

[1340] Rossana Ducato, Miriam Kullmann, Marco Rocca, "European Legal Perspectives on Customer Ratings and Discrimination", *op. cit.*, p 261.

position as a legitimate aim to project an image of quality under the company's freedom to conduct a business.

I do not fully agree with this argument because expanding the reasoning of the Court in the *Achbita* case to a rating system policy means neglecting many contextual aspects that the Court used to justify its decision. First, the Court did not ground the decision to limit the employee's freedom of religion because of the preference of the clients, but instead because the image of "neutrality" that the company wanted to project to the clients.[1341] In the case, it was not demonstrated that the clients would prefer to be in contact with an employee who did not wear a headscarf, but instead that the company wanted to express that it holds to neutral values, and, therefore, it does not allow its employees to display any religious symbols.[1342] Second, the ruling in *Achbita* was in great part confirmed in *Wabe*.[1343] Third, the issue of wearing a headscarf in places of public accommodation has been contentious across several European countries and is not easily compared to other grounds of discrimination.[1344] It seems an extrapolation to compare the "acceptance" of neutral policies implemented to limit women from wearing a headscarf, considering the context of the debate in Europe, with the acceptance of rating systems that put other classes, such as sexual orientation or disability, under a disadvantageous position because of the company's legitimate aim to project a neutral image or the legitimate aim to guarantee the quality of the services provided.

2.3. ARBITRATION

In contrast to the United States, arbitration for most individual employment disputes, including cases of employment-related discrimination and misclassification of employment contract, is simply not allowed in several EU countries.[1345] The main reason behind prohibiting arbitration in employment-

---

[1341] This argument was very controversial, because "neutral values" have been used as justification to discriminate against women wearing a headscarf on the ground of religion. *See* Erica Howard, "Islamic Headscarves and the CJEU: Achbita and Bougnaoui" (2017) 24:3 Maastricht Journal of European and Comparative Law 348.

[1342] C-157/15 *Achbita v G4S Solutions NV* ECLI:EU:C:2017:203.

[1343] C-804/18, IX v WabeeV and MH Müller Handels GmbH v MJ ECLI:EU:C:2021:594.

[1344] Erica Howard, *Religious Clothing and Symbols in Employment: A Legal Analysis of the Situation in the EU Member States* (November 2017), online: European Commission European Network of Legal Experts in Gender Equality and Non-Discrimination <https://www.equalitylaw.eu/downloads/4493-religious-clothing-and-symbols-in-employment-pdf-928-kb>, p 62–80.

[1345] For instance, the Court of Cassation in France has ruled that employment rights lack of arbitrability, while in the UK and the Netherlands, very specific cases of arbitration agreed on voluntary basis may be allowed depending on the amount of the litigation and restricted contractual clauses. *See* Cour de Cassation 30 November 2011, Arrêt no 2512 (pourvoi 11–12.905 and 906); Rob Jagtenberg, Annie de Roo, "Employment Disputes and Arbitration:

related disputes is attributed to the perceived imbalance of power between employee and employer.

The vast majority of EU countries have specialized labor courts to adjudicate employment matters. Conciliation is commonly offered as an option to employees and employers prior to court adjudication, but conciliatory systems are usually integrated into the labor courts.[1346] Several EU countries allow collective disputes aside from individual ones.[1347] In collective disputes, voluntary arbitration is often accepted, even though in such cases negotiation-based solutions are more frequently applied.[1348] Individual employment litigation, often preceded by conciliation through labor courts, is the traditional mode of labor-related dispute resolution. Conciliation and negotiation approaches are preferred because, unlike arbitration, they acknowledge the autonomy of the partners, especially the employees. When an agreed solution is not achieved, the case can be brought to a state court. Considering this backdrop, contrarily to the United States, some courts of member states have ruled the status of platform workers without dealing with the voidance of arbitration clauses.[1349]

An Account of Irreconcilability, with Reference to the EU and the USA" (2018) 68 Zbornik PFZ 171, p 173.

[1346] In Germany, the *Arbeitsgerichte*, in France, the Conseils de Prud'Hommes, in the UK, the ACAS Advisory Conciliation and Arbitration Service.

[1347] Tony Cole, Ilias Bantekas, Frederico Ferretti, Christine Riefa, Barbara Warwas, Pietro Ortolani, *Legal Instruments and Practice of Arbitration in the* EU (November 2014), online: European Parliament <https://www.europarl.europa.eu/RegData/etudes/STUD/2015/509988/IPOL_STU%282015%29509988_EN.pdf>; Mike Eisner, Christian Welz, *Collective Dispute in an Enlarged European Union* (November 2008) online: Eurofound <https://www.eurofound.europa.eu/publications/report/2006/industrial-relations-law-and-regulation/eiro-thematic-feature-collective-dispute-resolution-in-an-enlarged-european-union>; John Purcell, *Individual Disputes at the Workplace: Alternative Dispute Resolution* (April 2010), online: Eurofound <https://www.eurofound.europa.eu/publications/report/2010/individual-disputes-at-the-workplace-alternative-disputes-resolution>.

[1348] Yasmine Taraseviwicz, Niki Borofsky, "International Labor and Employment Arbitration: A French and European Perspective" (2013) 28 ABA Journal of Labor and Employment Law 349, p 351.

[1349] *Uber BV v Aslam* [2018] EWCA civ 2748 and Cour d'Appel de Paris, pôle 6, chamber 2, arrêt du 10 janvier 2019, sn rg 18/08357, n portalis 35L7-V-B7C-B6AZK.

CHAPTER 6

TRANSPORTATION NETWORK COMPANIES: A CASE-BASED ANALYSIS

Currently, transportation network companies are one of the most established examples of on-demand work platforms in the e-market. Uber, along with its direct and specialized competitors Lyft[1350], Didi Chuxing[1351], and Ola Cabs[1352], have recruited hundreds of thousands of drivers, have supplied them with service requests, and have managed the transportation of a large number of passengers across the world.

Similar to other online platforms, transportation network platforms self-identify their business under the label of intermediary information society services, which essentially consists of connecting two sides of the market: drivers and riders. This model has faced regulatory challenges both in the United States and in European countries.[1353] At the present moment, one of the main disputes regarding transportation network companies relates to their workforces and the way different countries address the legal perception and conditions of an employment relationship.

In that regard, litigation faced by transportation network companies may shape how they develop their activities and manage their workforce across countries. Notwithstanding the fact that labor law is traditionally a national matter, global transportation network companies have created similar labor challenges in several countries almost simultaneously – notably the alleged misclassification of their driver contracts.

This chapter explores the legal consequences workers face when transportation network companies outsource their main service – transportation – to contractors/self-employed workers. Even though other transportation network companies have faced lawsuits regarding the misclassification of their workforce[1354], this chapter focuses on Uber, considering its global reach and its

---

[1350]   Uber's competitor in the US. Lyft, *About us* (November 2019) online: Lyft <www.lyft.com>.
[1351]   Uber counterpart in China. Didi, *About Us* (November 2019) online: Didi <https://www.didiglobal.com>.
[1352]   OlaCabs, *About Us* (November 2019) online: OlaCabs <www.olacabs.com>.
[1353]   Mainly issues related to unfair competition with taxis, lack of professional licenses to the transportation of passengers and the misclassification of the drivers. *See Section I* below.
[1354]   Notably Lyft, *see Cotter v Lyft Inc.*, 60 F Supp 3d 1067, 1070 (ND Cal 2015).

representativeness in the sector in European countries and in the United States. The Uber model opened up long debates about sharing economies as one of the economic forces of the twenty-first century and the hurdles of regulating it.[1355] The way the platform is structured gave rise to the word "uberization" to either indicate a certain business model or the degradation of a certain workforce's rights.[1356] The platform practices also made courts in several countries deal with the question of whether Uber provides a transportation or information society service. The company has faced massive litigation so far due to its ambiguous identity in several sectors[1357] and particularly regarding the status of its main

---

[1355] Brishen Rogers, "The social costs of Uber" (2016) 82 University of Chicago Law Review Dialogue 85; Stephen R Miller, "First Principles for Regulating the Sharing Economy" (2016) 53 Harvard Journal on Legislation 147; Ryan Calo, Alex Rosenblat, "The Taking Economy: Uber, Information and Power (2017) 117 Columbia Law Review 1623; Rachel Botsman, Roo Rogers, *What's Mine is Yours: The Rise of Collaborative Consumption* (New York: HarperCollins, 2010); Russel Belk, "You Are What You Can Access: Sharing and Collaborative Consumption Online" (2014) 67:8 Journal of Business Research 1595; Vanessa Katz, "Regulating the Sharing Economy" (2015) 30:4 Berkeley Technology Law Journal 1067; Molly Cohen, Arun Sundararajan, "Self-Regulation and Innovation in the Peer-to-Peer Sharing Economy" (2015) 82 University of Chicago Law Review 116; Philipe Aigran, *Sharing: Culture and the Economy in the Internet Age* (Amsterdam: Amsterdam University Press, 2012), Sofia Ranchordás, "Does Sharing Mean Caring? Regulating Innovation in the Sharing Economy" (2015) 16:1 Minnesota Journal of Law, Science & Technology 413; Vassilis Hatzopoulos, "Vers un Cadre de la Régulation des Plateformes?" (2019) 3 Revue Internationale de Droit Économique 399; Adrian J Hawley, "Should Europe Regulate Labor Platforms in the Sharing Economy?" in Russell W Belk, Giana M Eckhardt, Fleura Bardhi, *Handbook of the Sharing Economy* (Edward Elgar Publishing, 2019), p 424.

[1356] Geoffrey Dudley, David Banister, Tim Schwanen, "The Rise of Uber and Regulating the Disruptive Innovator" (2017) 88:3 The Political Quartely 493.

[1357] For cases in which the company's technology identity were disputed for achieving different regulatory purposes, *see* Ana Maria Corrêa, "Regulatory Risks Faced by the Transportation Sharing Economy: Workforces at Stake" (2018) 9:4 European Journal of Risk Regulation 641: "unfair competition and lack of licences: Spain (*Asociacion Madrileña del Taxi v Uber Technologies INC*, Juzgado de lo Mercantil No 2, Madrid, Recurso 707/2014, 9/12/2014 and Case C-434/15, Asociación Profesional Elite Taxi v Uber System Spain Case); Belgium (AS Radio Taxi Bruxellois v SPRL Uber Belgium, Tribunal de Commerce de Bruxelles, Chambre des Actions en Cessation, 31/03/14); France (Uber France SAS, Conseil Constitutionnel, Décision n° 2015–484 QPC, 22/09/2015 & Uber France, Cour de Cassation, Arrêt n 699, 23/06/2015); Italy (Soc Coop. Taxiblu e altri v Uber international holding BV a altri, Tribunale di Milano, ordinanza, 9/07/2015); Germany (Taxi Deutschland Servicegesellschaft v Uber BV, Landgericht Frankfurt am Main, Zivilkammer, Aktenzeichen 2–03 O 329/14, 25/08/ 2014); Canada (City of Toronto v Uber Canada Inc, Uber BV and Rasier Operations BV, Ontario Superior Court of Justice, 2014); Brazil (Simtetaxi, sp Sindicato dos Motoristas e Trabalhadores nas Empresas de Taxi no Estado de São Paulo v Uber do Brasil Tecnologia Ltda, Tribunal de Justiça do Estado de São Paulo, 12a Vara Cível, Processo digital 1040391–49.2015.8.26.0100); Taxation: Australia (Uber BV v Commissioner of Taxation, Federal Court of Australia, NSD 904 of 2015, 17/02/2017); discriminatory treatment: USA (National Federation of the Blind of California v Uber Technologies, Inc, United States District Court, California, 2015; Thomas Liu v Uber, Equal Employment Opportunity Commission, 2014); misclassification of workers: Brazil (Rodrigo Leonardo Silva Ferreira v Uber do Brasil Tecnologia LTDA, 33a Vara do Trabalho de Belo Horizonte, 13 de Fevereiro de 2017. Processo n. 0011369–34.2016.5.03.0112); UK (Aslam v Uber London), USA (O'Connor v Uber and

workforce as independent contractors.[1358] The apex of the conflict between Uber and its workforce came a few days before the company went to initial public offering (IPO), when drivers from diverse places such as Lagos, Santiago, London, São Paulo, and Sydney initiated a worldwide strike demanding better work conditions and pay.[1359]

With this backdrop in mind, I review judicial cases in the United States and the United Kingdom to explore how the company recruits its drivers, develops its contracts and terms of service, and manages its workforces through a scored rating system. I illustrate how potential discrimination embedded in the scored rating system has been challenged in the past years.

SECTION I. UBER'S OPERATIONAL CONFIGURATION: FROM RIDESHARING TO TEMPORARY WORK

1. BUSINESS MODEL

Uber was founded in 2009 as an online platform that offered peer-to-peer ridesharing services in San Francisco, United States. Ten years later, Uber operated in over 69 countries and diversified its products to include UberXL (vehicles that hold up to six passengers), UberBlack (luxurious vehicles), UberPool (a less expensive option with multiple riders), food delivery, and bike rental.[1360] In October 2019 the company launched Uber Works to match job seekers with employers looking for temporary staff, and at first it operated only in Chicago.[1361] This rapid expansion made Uber the world's most valuable privately held technology company, and in 2019 it became an IPO, allowing public and private investors to buy its shares.[1362]

Yucesoy *et al* v Uber Technology Inc. *et al*, Civil Action No 1:14-cv-13938-IT, US District Court for the District of Massachusetts)".

[1358] Alex Rosenblat, *Uberland: How Algorithms Are Rewriting the Rules of Work* (University of California Press, 2018); Min Kyung Lee, Daniel Kusbit, Evan Metsky, Laura Dabbish, "Working with Machines: The Impact of Algorithmic and Data-Driven Management on Human Workers" (2015) Proceedings of the 33rd Annual ACM Conference on Human Factors in Computing Systems 1603, p 1607.

[1359] Alexia Fernández Campbell, *The Worldwide Uber Strike is a Key Test for the Gig Economy* (May 2019) online: Vox <https://www.vox.com/2019/5/8/18535367/uber-drivers-strike-2019-cities>.

[1360] Uber, *Country List* (October 2019) online: Uber <https://www.uber.com/en-BE/country-list/>.

[1361] Uber, *Uber Works* (October 2019) online: Uber <https://www.works.co>.

[1362] Financial Times, *Uber IPO* (October 2019) online: FT <https://www.ft.com/content/b3e70e9e-5c4d-11e9-9dde-7aedca0a081a>.

In 2009, Uber emerged with the purpose of efficiently allocating empty car spaces in urban areas. With this goal, the platform offered the necessary technology to connect riders and drivers in urban areas. The idea that Uber was a technology company whose only purpose was to connect passengers and drivers has been long disputed.[1363] Despite being advertised as such, Uber decides the fare rates[1364], receives payment for all rides and retains a percentage of them[1365], sets the cancellation policy, and selects the driver when a ride is requested.[1366] In relation to its main suppliers, it requires drivers to have an appropriate driver's license (in some jurisdictions this implies a professional driving license), an eligible vehicle with four doors, and insurance certificates.[1367] In addition, Uber also conducts a criminal record check and a personal interview with the driver.[1368] Even if the company was created to efficiently allocate empty car spaces, the reality is that most drivers work for Uber as their only means of living, and they buy cars to exclusively transport people through Uber. In this sense, the idea that Uber is either a sharing economy platform or an exclusive technological intermediary is controversial, considering the way goods (car spaces) and work are traded and the degree of management Uber that has over the activities developed through the platform.[1369]

Regarding the business model, Uber's main source of revenue comes from a share of every trip conducted by a driver and charged through its platform. In most countries, drivers do not process the payment in the car with cash. Alternatively, Uber collects payment directly through the app at the time of the ride completion, and pays the driver on a weekly basis. Moreover, drivers pay for their gas, the maintenance of the car, and the insurance. On top of that, each driver has an independent contract, making Uber a platform connected to thousands of independent drivers who provide the main and final service available to the passenger via the platform.

[1363] Brishen Rogers,"The social costs of Uber" (2016) 82 University of Chicago Law Review Dialogue 85; Veena Dubal, "The Drive to Precarity: A Political History of Work, Regulation, & Labor Advocacy in San Francisco's Taxi & Uber Economies" (2017) 38:1 Berkeley Journal of Employment & Labor Law 73; Jillian Kaltner, "Employment Status of Uber and Lyft Drivers: Unsettlingly Settled" (2018) 29 Hastings Women's Law Journal 29.

[1364] Uber, *Terms and Conditions & Payment* (September 2019) online: Uber <www.uber.com/legal/terms/gb/ >.

[1365] *Ibid.*

[1366] Uber, *Terms of Use & Acceptance of Booking as Agent of the Transportation Provider* (September 2019) online: Uber <https://www.uber.com/legal/terms/gb/>.

[1367] Uber, *Get Started* (September 2019) online: Uber <www.uber.com/en-GB/drive/resources/get-started/ >. These requirements can vary in different jurisdictions.

[1368] Those requirements were found in the judicial decisions: *O'Connor v Uber Technology Inc*, p 3 and *Aslam v Uber London, op. cit.*, pp 3–16.

[1369] Donald N Anderson, "Not Just a Taxi? For Profit Ridesharing, Driver Strategies, and VMT" (2014) 41:5 Transportation 1099; Mareike Glöss, Moira McGregor, Barry Brown, "Designing for Labour: Uber and the On-Demand Mobile Workforce" (2016) Proceedings of the 2016 CHI conference on Human Factors in Computing Systems 1632.

2. UBER'S APP DESIGN

Uber has two different apps dedicated to its ridesharing activities: one for drivers and one for riders. The app for riders provides a map and requires the rider to indicate their pickup location and destination. Once these two positions are chosen, riders can select which kind of car they want. Uber issues an estimate of the price and function of different cars available. As soon as the car is chosen, Uber's algorithm chooses a driver.[1370] The rider does not have access to the driver's profile photograph, name, or rating until the trip is confirmed.

The app the drivers use displays which other drivers are available close by and their precise location on the map. Once Uber's algorithms choose the driver, they will receive a request that has details about the passenger, such as their name, location, photograph, and rating. If the driver accepts the passenger's request, the passenger gets a notification, and the driver goes to the passenger's location to provide the riding service. Drivers can see riders before accepting the trip. Notably, female drivers often do "not accept male passengers without pictures at night because of safety concerns."[1371]

3. CONSEQUENCES OF RATINGS FOR RIDERS AND DRIVERS

Drivers and riders are given the option to rate each other on a 1–5-star score at the end of each trip. As part of its internal policy, Uber suspends low-scored drivers. In addition, drivers can refuse to take a low-rated passenger. However, when drivers refuse many rides in a row, they are automatically logged out from the platform and are not able to accept any rides for a period of time.[1372]

The rating system is presented as a suitable alternative to keep quality control over a remote workforce.[1373] Rider's feedback provides immediate evaluations that allow Uber to record workers' performance. The ratings serve as the basis for termination of drivers' contracts or suggestions for amelioration for under-performing workers. Individual ratings are not displayed to the drivers, but only the total number of rated trips and their average rating score are available.

[1370] Min Kyung Lee, Daniel Kusbit, Evan Metsky, Laura Dabbish, "Working with Machines: the Impact of Algorithmic and Data-Driven Management on Human Workers" (2015) Proceedings of the 33rd Annual ACM Conference on Human Factors in Computing Systems 1603, p 1607.

[1371] *Ibid,* p 1609.

[1372] Min Kyung Lee, Daniel Kusbit, Evan Metsky, Laura Dabbish, "Working with Machines: The Impact of Algorithmic and Data-Driven Management on Human Workers", *op. cit.,* p 1609.

[1373] Alex Rosenblat, Karen Levy, Solon Barocas, Tim Hwang, "Discriminating Tastes: Uber's Customer Ratings as Vehicles for Workplace Discrimination" (2017) 9:3 Policy & Internet 256, p 261.

To keep their contract with Uber, drivers must have an average score above 4.6 out of 5 stars.[1374] The company's policy provides that drivers who are under the local performance goals risk permanent termination or short-term suspension from the application. The rating system has incentivized Uber drivers, especially in the beginning of the operations, to maintain a friendly attitude and to offer candy and snacks, and this context has generally led to the perception that Uber drivers provided better service than taxis because they were motivated by their ratings.[1375]

SECTION II. UBER LABOR LITIGATION

1. UNITED STATES

1.1. MISCLASSIFICATION OF EMPLOYMENT STATUS

A significant legal battle started in the United States between 2013 and 2015. In California and Massachusetts, two class actions representing an average of 300,000 drivers challenged Uber's business configuration.[1376] In the cases of *O'Connor v Uber Technology* and *Yucesoy v Uber Technology*[1377], the core question was crucial for guarantees and benefits for Uber's main workforce: "Are the drivers employees or independent contractors?"[1378] The consequences of requalifying the drivers could have massively changed the company's structure and, most importantly, the drivers' rights. In these two class actions, drivers claimed that they were misclassified as independent contractors; they were denied reimbursement of their necessary business expenses, which would include gas, smartphones, phone data, and insurance; and their termination

---

[1374] It changes according to the city.

[1375] Alex Rosenblat, Karen Levy, Solon Barocas, Tim Hwang, "Discriminating Tastes: Uber's Customer Ratings as Vehicles for Workplace Discrimination" (2017) 9:3 Policy & Internet 256, p 261.

[1376] *O'Connor v Uber Technologies*, Inc, 82 F. Supp. 3d 1133 (N.D. Cal. 2015). This case was followed by several others. Cases reported by Jill Gross, "The Uberization of Arbitration Clauses" (2017) 9 Arbitration Law Review 43, p 47: "*Singh v Uber Techs. Inc.*, No. CV 16–3044 (FLW), 2017 WL 396545 (D.N.J. Jan. 30, 2017); *Richmond v Uber Techs., Inc.*, No. 16-CV-23267, 2017 WL 416123 (S.D. Fla. Jan. 27, 2017); *Gunn v Uber Techs., Inc.*, No. 116CV01668SEBMJD, 2017 WL 386816 (S.D. Ind. Jan. 27, 2017); *Scroggins v Uber Techs., Inc.*, No. 116CV01419SEBMJD, 2017 WL 373299 (S.D. Ind. Jan. 26, 2017); *Zawada v Uber Techs., Inc.*, No. 16-CV-11334, 2016 WL 7439198 (E.D. Mich. Dec. 27, 2016) (appeal filed); *Razak v Uber Techs., Inc.*, No. CV 16–573, 2016 WL 7241795 (E.D. Pa. Dec. 14, 2016); *Marc v Uber Techs.*, No. 216CV579FTM99MRM, 2016 WL 7210886, (M.D. Fla. Dec. 13, 2016); *Rimel v Uber Techs., Inc.*, No. 615CV2191ORL41KRS, 2016 WL 6246812 (M.D. Fla. Aug. 4, 2016)".

[1377] The District Court in Massachusetts joined the *Yucesoy* case the *O'Connor* case in California, because drivers have signed the contract with a clause of exclusive jurisdiction in California.

[1378] *Yucesoy v Uber*, Memorandum of Law in Support of Defendants' Motion to Dismiss or in the Alternative to Transfer Venue, p 4.

practices based on a rating system exclusively attributed by customers was unfair.[1379]

One of the legal arguments for reclassifying the drivers' status was rooted in the technological identity of the company, even if control over the drivers should be the main criterion to classify them as employees according to the common law legal tests of federal and state legislation.[1380] Accordingly, in its terms of service, the platform has consistently been presented as a software technology company headquartered in San Francisco, California. Uber has emphatically denied that it is a transportation business, "and consequently, it did not have any vehicles or employ drivers. The company claimed to provide technologic services that allowed users to locate a participating driver 'on demand' through a mobile application."[1381]

Uber established two types of contracts in the United States: a software license and online services agreement and/or a transportation provider service agreement, specific to collective partners or transportation companies, such as taxi-cab drivers.[1382] Drivers should declare that they were not in an employment relationship under these contracts. Moreover, the terms of service required riders to clearly state that Uber had no obligation to provide them with rides at all and that the "services constitute a technology platform that enables the user to pre-book and schedule transportation, logistic, delivery, and/or vendors' services with independent party providers."[1383] In short, the company defined its role in the terms of services as that of an intermediary.

Drivers did not perceive Uber in the same way that the company did. They claimed that despite the fact that Uber legally denied that it was a transportation business, it was deeply involved in marketing its transportation services, and it has referred to itself before as an "On-Demand Car Service," it had the slogan "Everyone's Private Drive," and it had stated "Uber provides the best transportation system."[1384] The drivers also claimed that Uber did not sell its software as typical technology companies do and that the company's revenue was mainly due to its transportation services. The software itself did not cost anything to the users. For those reasons, it would be completely illogical to deny its transportation nature.[1385]

The United States District Court in California denied Uber the status of simply being a digital platform because recognizing it as such would mean

---

[1379] *Ibid.*

[1380] *O'Connor v Uber*, Order Denying Defendants Motion for Summary Judgment, pp 11–15.

[1381] *Yucesoy v Uber*, Memorandum of Law in Support of Defendants' Motion to Dismiss or in the Alternative to Transfer Venue, p 1.

[1382] Uber, *Legal Terms* (September 2019) online: Uber <www.uber.com/fr/legal/terms/us/;https://www.uber.com/fr/legal/terms/gb/>.

[1383] Uber, *Legal Terms* (September 2019) online: Uber <www.uber.com/fr/legal/terms/gb/ >.

[1384] *O'Connor v Uber, op. cit.*, Order Denying Defendants Motion for Summary Judgment, pp 4–5.

[1385] *Ibid.*

reaffirming Uber as an intermediary for transportation purposes. The matter of whether Uber was a technology or transportation company, in the United States, is not *res judicata*. The District Court of Northern California stated in the early stages of the litigation that Uber "is ultimately a transportation company, albeit a technologically sophisticated one."[1386] The argument was based on three elements: (1) Uber's existence is due to transportation services, (2) it does not sell any software, and (3) it sells and provides transportation. Defining Uber as a technology company would focus only on the way the platform operates – the use of the internet and applications – instead of relying in what the company truly does, which is to enable customers to book and receive rides. The intermediary frame was too narrow to define the larger context of the business.

1.2. DRIVER'S RECRUITMENT AND MONITORING

The manner in which Uber recruits and monitors its drivers was used by the plaintiffs to strengthen the employment argument. Allegedly, drivers became partners with Uber after completing an application process. The applicants had to upload a copy of their drivers' license, their vehicle registration, and their insurance; they had to pass a background check; and they were required to pass a city knowledge test and attend an interview with an Uber employee for which they were advised "to bring their car, dress professionally and be prepared to stay for an hour."[1387] The background check, city knowledge exam, vehicle inspection, and personal interview were considered essential measures by the company because "Uber provided the best transportation service and to keep it this way, they would be taking some major steps to improve both driver and vehicle quality in the Uber system."[1388]

When applicants were finally successful in their application requirements and interview, they signed a contract stating that the relationship between the transportation provider and Uber was solely that of independent contracting parties.[1389] Both parties specifically agreed that there was no employment agreement or employment relationship.

Uber drivers claim that the company controls them in two different manners: (1) prescribing how they should act with clients, and (2) monitoring their activities through the rating system. In all countries where Uber operates, the drivers' performance is a condition to keep them connected and using the platform. The company regards the quality of the service provided as indispensable to keep its clients loyal to the application. Drivers considered

---

[1386]   *Ibid*, p 11.
[1387]   *O'Connor v Uber*, Order Denying Defendants Motion for Summary Judgment, p 3.
[1388]   *Ibid*, p 12.
[1389]   Service Agreement at 7, Other Provisions, see <www.uber.com/legal/terms/us/ >.

that the performance monitoring Uber imposes is typical of an employment relationship.

Some documents attached by David O'Connor's lawyers showed how Uber tried to constrain its drivers with commands or orders related to the way they should dress, the way they should treat the passengers, and what they expected the atmosphere in the car to be. Uber instructs: "(1) make sure you are dressed professionally; (2) send to the client a text message when 1–2 minutes away from the pickup location (this is very important); (3) make sure the radio is off or on soft jazz or on National Public Radio; (4) make sure to open the door for your client."[1390]

In the United States, like in other countries where Uber operates, the company can terminate its contract with the drivers based on their low performance, which is solely evaluated by passengers, who are encouraged to write comments about how the drivers behaved, the cleanliness of the car, any unpleasant smells, the music, and the trip in general.[1391] The fact that passengers constantly evaluate drivers allowed Uber to have an enormous amount of surveillance and control over the manner of its workers' performance, according to the lawsuits. Several documents reported by the judge in the *O'Connor* case revealed that the company regularly terminated the accounts of drivers who did not comply with Uber's performance standards. An email from an Uber San Francisco manager to an employee stressed this point: "We will be deactivating Uber accounts regularly of drivers who are in the bottom 5% of all Uber drivers and not performing up to the highest standards. We believe that the removal of underperforming drivers will lead to more opportunities for our best drivers."[1392]

When Judge Chen from the District Court of Northern District of California denied Uber's motion for summary judgement, he affirmed that ratings are not only a customer feedback tool, but alternatively, they represent a new level of monitoring that is far more unescapable than that of any vigilant boss. Judge Chen considered that the rating system gives Uber an "arguably tremendous amount of control over the manner and means of its drivers."[1393] Monitoring performance is treated as evidence of a relationship between employers and employees in the cases analyzed. In the United States, for instance, in a case involving FedEx, a precedent was established as a matter of law stating that monitoring job performance was essential to determine that FedEx's drivers

---

[1390]   *O'Connor v Uber*, Order Denying Defendants Motion for Summary Judgment, p 21.

[1391]   *Ibid.*

[1392]   Email from UBER SF Community Manager instructing a fellow Uber employer to "get rid of this guy. We need to make serious cuts of guys below": *O'Connor v Uber*, Order Denying Defendants Motion for Summary Judgment, p 11.

[1393]   *O'Connor v Uber*, Order Denying Defendants Motion for Summary Judgment, p 24.

were employees. In Uber's case, the drivers could be monitored many times a day.[1394]

Regarding working hours, Uber claimed that it gives complete freedom to its drivers to choose when and how much they want to work, with the condition that they do at least one trip in every 180 days to keep the contract valid. In addition, Uber alleges that the company exerted no pressure on or control over its drivers' working hours. There is no question of permitting or authorizing breaks because drivers are free agents, according to Uber. Thus, they can take breaks whenever they feel it is necessary.[1395] Despite this Uber claim, the break-time aspect was a subject of litigation because Uber established a limitation to it by contract. If the drivers were logged into the application and they refused more than three trips, they would be compulsorily logged out of the platform for a certain amount of time, regardless of whether the drivers refused the trips for a fair reason such as a problem with the car or even a timed break. For this reason, drivers believed that Uber had control over their break time.

To define the status of Uber's drivers, Judge Edward Chen analyzed the case in light of the factors ruled by the Supreme Court of California in the *SG Borello & Sons, Inc. v Dep't of Industries Relations* case.[1396] These factors are used by courts in California to determine whether the element of control exists, and they include the following: "whether the worker completes the work individually or under supervision; the skill required in the particular occupation; whether the hiring part or the worker supplies the tools and the place of work for the person doing work; the length of time they have to complete the work; the method of payment whether by time or by job; whether or not the work is a part of the regular business of the principal; whether or not the parties believe they are creating the relationship of employer-employee."[1397] In *O'Connor v Uber Technology*, it was first decided that the status of the drivers was ambiguous according to the *Borello* factors. There was evidence that demonstrated that the drivers were independent contractors, such as the complete freedom to choose their worktime as long as they were not connected to the platform, their breaks, the fact that they owned their own vehicles, and the possibility of employing other drivers to drive on their behalf.[1398] However, there was also evidence that showed they were employees, given that the frequent monitoring of performance

---

[1394] FedEx controlled the appearance of its drivers and their vehicles, their worktime, and how and when they should deliver the packages: *Alexander v FedEx Ground Package Sys Inc.*, Case No 05-cv-00038-EMC (ND Cal 2016), pp 16– 20.

[1395] *O'Connor v Uber, op. cit.*, Order Denying Defendants Motion for Summary Judgment, pp 18–19.

[1396] *SG Borello & Sons, Inc. v Department of Industries Relations*, Case No S003956 (SC Cal 1989).

[1397] *SG Borello & Sons, Inc. v Department of Industries Relations*, Case No S003956 (SC Cal 1989). See Robert Sprague, "Worker (Mis)Classification in the Sharing Economy: Trying to Fit Square Pegs into Round Holes" (2015) 31:1 ABA Journal of Labor & Employment Law 53.

[1398] *O'Connor v Uber, op. cit.*, Order Denying Plaintiffs Mot for Preliminary, p 17.

was a regular and integral part of Uber's business. Therefore, factors under the Borello analysis supported both status qualifications of the drivers.

1.3. LEGAL APPROACHES TO TACKLE MISCLASSIFICATION CHALLENGES

Considering the financial risks of going on trial and after three years of considerably active and highly contested litigation, a settlement between the drivers and Uber was submitted to the District Court of California in March 2016.[1399] The agreement established a monetary payment and non-monetary relief.

Uber proposed a non-revisionary payment that would be distributed to all class members in function of the number of miles that drivers had transported Uber passengers. Moreover, the non-monetary agreement consisted of including more transparency in the company policies with the creation of a "Comprehensive Deactivation Policy," a procedure to seek redress from deactivation led by a Driver Appeal Panel, and drivers' better bargaining power with Uber in case of future disputes through the means of a Driver Association.[1400]

According to the proposed "Comprehensive Deactivation Policy," Uber would no longer be able to deactivate drivers at will, but only for sufficient cause, including drivers' low ratings. Drivers would have the right to receive two prior written warnings with an explanation justifying the deactivation and a chance to fix any problematic issues before the termination of their contract and their deactivation from the platform.[1401] The purpose of this clause was to limit the power Uber has to dispose of its main workforce. This change aimed at placing Uber as an intermediary between passengers and drivers instead of the drivers' manager.

The creation of the Driver Appeal Panel, composed of highly-rated drivers, was designed to resolve issues related to the termination of drivers. Drivers could appeal to the panel in cases in which they think their contract has been terminated unjustly. In cases of non-agreement with the panel's decision, the driver would have a neutral arbitrator to decide whether there was sufficient cause for termination of the contract and deactivation of the account. This neutral arbitrator was supposed to be paid by Uber. Uber would also fund and facilitate the formation of a Driver Association, which is not a union, but which

---

[1399] The entire terms of the agreement can be found at *O'Connor v Uber*, Notice of Motion and Motion for Preliminary Approval and Memorandum of Points and Authorities in Support Thereof.

[1400] *O'Connor v Uber*, Notice of Motion and Motion for Preliminary Approval and Memorandum of Points and Authorities in Support Thereof, p 6.

[1401] Except in cases of fraud, safety, discrimination or illegal conduct: *Ibid*, p 8.

would have elected driver leaders. The Driver Association would discuss issues regarding drivers' concerns with Uber management. The management, in turn, has committed to meet, discuss, and address the issues facing Uber drivers.[1402]

The settlement was rejected in June 2016 because it was considered "not fair, adequate, and reasonable,"[1403] mainly because the amount of money was considered to be insufficient[1404], and deactivation continued to be a bone of contention, even if the company proposed clearer standards in a comprehensive written deactivation policy.[1405]

Uber agreed to lose its discretionary power when deactivating accounts of drivers. According to their new policy, a driver could only be deactivated for sufficient cause. The fact that a driver accepts few ride requests was not included among these sufficient causes. It would be considered excessive control under an independent contractor activity. Drivers could accept as many rides as they want. However, Uber imposed a condition considered by the judge to be inadequate to the liberty of the drivers. In cases where a driver declined a ride request, Uber could temporarily log the driver out of the application for a limited period of time. Uber suggested that this helped to maintain the quality of the service and that the drivers spontaneously had the option to turn off the application, instead of declining rides.[1406]

Uber's strategy seemed to create a similar situation to an employment relation, but without the same benefits. The company wanted to facilitate the creation of an association of drivers to bargain for driver entitlements, but it did not recognize this as a union. The drivers would not have the right to minimum wage and hour claims. Moreover, the drivers would not be entitled to any protection provided by Title VII, ADEA, and ADA.

Ultimately, Uber was successful in the class action litigation to keep drivers as independent contractors. In September 2018 the United States Court of Appeals for the Ninth Circuit issued a decision reversing the district court decision on the ground that Uber's arbitration clause prohibits class and individual court actions.[1407] When drivers signed their contract with Uber, they agreed to waive their right to trial in favor of arbitration, a private path that in general favors corporations over individuals.[1408] The *O'Connor* plaintiffs had argued that their arbitration agreements with Uber were unenforceable in part because they

---

[1402] *Ibid*, p 9.
[1403] *Ibid*, p 2.
[1404] It was estimated that the cause would reach the amount of $800 million dollars *O'Connor v Uber*, Order Denying Plaintiffs' Motion for Preliminary Approval, p 8.
[1405] *Ibid*, p 10.
[1406] *O'Connor v Uber*, pp 24–25.
[1407] *O'Connor v Uber, Inc.* n 14–16078 (United States Court of Appeal, 9th Circuit 2018).
[1408] Lauren Guth Barnes, "How Mandatory Arbitration Agreements and Class Action Waivers Undermine Consumer Rights and Why We Need Congress to Act (2015) 9:2 Harvard Law & policy Review 329; Craig Smith, Eric V Moyé, "Outsourcing American Civil Justice: Mandatory Arbitration Clauses in Consumer and Employment Contracts" (2012) 44 Texas

contained class-action waivers that violated the National Labor Relations Act (NRLA).[1409] The panel rejected the drivers' arguments, noting that their NLRA argument was overruled by the United States Supreme Court's 2018 divided decision (5–4) in *Epic Systems v Lewis*.[1410] After the appeal ruling, the last option for drivers pursuing misclassification claims – who opted for the agreement clause – was to engage in individual arbitration. The United States Court of Appeals for the Ninth Circuit's ruling in the *O'Connor v Uber* is an important incidence of a federal court invoking the Supreme Court's recent decision in *Epic Systems*. The case could prove discouraging for future complaints in similar situations. The main expected consequence of the decision made by the United States Court of Appeals for the Ninth Circuit is that Uber will likely only face a handful of complaints from drivers who are willing to arbitrate a single matter to a conclusion that will not be likely to bring meaningful financial benefit for either the litigants or attorneys.

For the drivers who did not opt for the arbitration clause in *O'Connor v Uber*, the District Court of Northern California accepted the settlement that in exchange for class members' release of their claims they would enjoy monetary and non-monetary benefits, including $15 million to be split among all class member and a policy guaranteeing that low acceptance rates will not be ground for deactivation.[1411] However, all policy modification due to this settlement shall expire two years after final approval or "change to any applicable statute, regulation, or other law that Uber reasonably believes would require a modification to any of the provisions."[1412]

1.4. ARBITRATION CLAUSES: UNDERMINING ANTIDISCRIMINATION LAW AND JUDICIAL TRIALS

Over the past five years, drivers across the United States have challenged several of Uber's employment-related discrimination practices and corporate policies in courts. These legal actions were entirely dismissed on the ground that Uber's arbitration clause forbids civil litigation by requiring any dispute between drivers and the company to be settled by private arbitration.[1413]

A notable case concerned employment-related racial discrimination. In August 2018 Kendall Reese, after having exhausted his administrative remedies

---

Tech Law Review 281; Hiro N Aragaki, "Equal Opportunity for Arbitration" (2011) 58 UCLA Law Review 1189.

[1409] Section 7, National Labor Relations Act, 29 U.S.C. §§151–169.

[1410] *Epic Systems Corporation v Lewis*, 138 S. Ct. 1612, 584 US, 200L.

[1411] *O'Connor v Uber, Inc.* case n13-cv-03826-EMC (United States District Court Northern District of California, March 2019).

[1412] *Ibid.*

[1413] Jill Gross, "The Uberization of Arbitration Clauses" (2017) 9 Arbitration Law Review 43.

at the EEOC, sued Uber for discrimination following the termination of his alleged employment as a driver.[1414] He sought declaratory and injunctive relief, damages, and punitive damages. His complaint was grounded on Title VII of the Civil Rights Act among other statutes and the Constitution of the United States.[1415]

Kendall Reese is a Black American residing in Philadelphia, Pennsylvania. He claimed that he was an Uber employee for one year from May 2017 to May 2018. He applied to work at the company after having seen an advertisement in which Uber "promoted itself as a so-called second chance employer."[1416] Prior to start working for Uber, he bought a car with a car trader referred by Uber with the only purpose of working as a driver. Uber often leases or serves as a guarantor in the purchase of vehicles by its drivers in the United States. During the entire year he drove for Uber, Kendall transported more than 2,000 passengers. On May 15, 2018, Uber terminated Kendall's account and did not allow him to use the app anymore as a driver, because he did not pass a new criminal background check.

Kendall had committed minor criminal offenses 33 and 30 years before he sued Uber, in 1985 and 1988, respectively, when he was 18 and 19 years old. In the cases, he was convicted to terms of 11 and 23 months.

He alleged that Uber did not consider the nature of the offense nor the amount of time that had passed since the completion of the sentence. The company did not provide him with any form of due process to resolve the issue and unilaterally terminated his contract. Furthermore, Kendall did not have any knowledge of this new background check and, consequently, had not voluntarily agreed to having it performed.

Employers, in general, cannot discriminate against persons with criminal records and criminal convictions after a certain amount of time.[1417] At the federal level, the Fair Credit Reporting Act (FCRA) sets no limit for how many years employers may conduct a background check if there was a conviction.[1418] However, the FCRA protects potential employees from credit and criminal background reports because misreported information might, and does often, have serious consequences for the job seeker. Therefore, the Act provides that before taking any disadvantageous employment related action based on a

---

[1414] *Kendall Reese v Uber Technologies, Inc.* (2:18-cv-03300, United District Court for The Eastern District of Pennsylvania, Aug 2018). (Hereinafter *Reese v Uber*).

[1415] Title VII, 42 U.S.C. §§1981, 1985, 1986 and 1988 and the first, fifth and fourteenth amendments to the United States Constitution.

[1416] *Reese v Uber*, amended civil action complaint, p 3.

[1417] The issue is currently disputable. Several lawsuits claiming disparate impact on Black and Hispanic men when employers settled automatic ban to those with arrest and conviction records won in courts between the 1970s and 1980s. The situation has changed since then. *See* Alexandra Harwin, "Title VII Challenges to Employment Discrimination against Minority Men with Criminal Records" (2012) 14:1 Berkeley Journal of African-American Law & Policy 1.

[1418] FCRA, 15 U.S.C. §1681c (2).

consumer and criminal background report, the employer must provide to the applicant (1) a copy of the consumer report, (2) a description in writing of the rights of the consumer under the FCRA, and (3) a reasonable opportunity to dispute the information before rendering the disadvantageous employment decision.[1419] Moreover, employers shall comply with the disclosure requirement even when the information provided by consumer and criminal background report would automatically disqualify the individual from employment.[1420] These FCRA provisions came as a recognition of the potential discriminatory impact arising from sharing personally identifiable information contained in credit and background reports used to inform private actors about which decision to take. When employers use credit and backgrounds check to hire or terminate someone, they should comply with the FCRA.[1421]

Many states allow minor cases not to be publicly available after a certain amount of time has passed. In Pennsylvania the period is 10 years for misdemeanors and 5 years for summary offenses.[1422] In the lawsuit Kendall sustained that the policy and practice of terminating Black American men with criminal convictions that occurred decades ago had a disparate impact on Black American men who are overrepresented in the prison system.[1423] Moreover, the termination of his contract based on criminal convictions dated more than 30 years before constituted *prima facie* evidence of intentional and willful discrimination against Kendall based on his race.[1424]

Uber filed a motion to dismiss the cases based on the fact that Kendall entered into a valid and enforceable arbitration agreement to arbitrate any disputes arising out of his relationship with Uber and expressly waived his right to pursue actions in courts.[1425] Uber requested the lawsuit to be completely dismissed pursuant to the Federal Arbitration Act[1426] due to the fact Kendall Reese had entered into a valid and enforceable arbitration agreement in July 2017, when he started driving for Uber.[1427]

[1419] FCRA, 15 U.S.C. §1681 (b)(3)(A). California state law contains similar provisions in addition it requires company to provide a copy of any consumer report to other similarly situated applicants or employee California Civil Code §1785.20(a). Massachusetts has similar provisions, see Massachusetts Civil Rights Act, M.G.L.c.93 §62.

[1420] Federal Trade Commission, 40 Years of Experience with the Fair Credit Reporting Act: An FTC Staff Report with Summary of Interpretations (July 2011) online: FTC <https://www.ftc.gov/sites/default/files/documents/reports/40-years-experience-fair-credit-reporting-act-ftc-staff-report-summary-interpretations/110720fcrareport.pdf> p 53.

[1421] *See* Title II, chapter 3.

[1422] House Bill 1419, Clean Slate, §9122.1(1) and (2).

[1423] Amanda Agan, Sonja Starr, "Ban the Box, Criminal Records, and Racial Discrimination: A Field Experiment" (2018) 133:1 The Quarterly Journal of Economics 191.

[1424] *Reese v Uber,* amended civil action complaint, p 8.

[1425] *Reese v Uber,* memorandum of law in support of defendant Uber's motion to dismiss the case.

[1426] Federal Arbitration Act, 9 U.S.C. §§3,4.

[1427] *Reese v Uber,* Memorandum of Law in Support of Defendant Uber's Motion to Dismiss the case, p 1.

The arbitration agreement broadly requires the drivers – who are called transportation providers – to individually arbitrate all disputes with Uber, including allegations of discrimination regarding Title VII, 42 U.S.C. §1981. The agreement eliminates the possibility of the drivers bringing their claims to court either individually or collectively. In that sense, the agreement reads "this arbitration provision is intended to apply to the resolution of disputes in a court of law or before any forum other than arbitration (…). This arbitration provision requires all such disputes to be resolved only by an arbitrator through final and binding arbitration on an individual basis only and not by way of court or jury trial, or by way of class, collective, or representative action."[1428]

In a reply to the motion to dismiss the case, Reese claimed that the arbitration agreement was defective and, therefore, invalid.[1429] The lawyer grounded his argument on the fact that the Federal Arbitration Act does not bind to interstate transportation workers. Uber would also be an interstate transportation and commerce company engaged in the transportation of people and delivery of goods in the flow of interstate commerce, because one of the lines of Uber business is the Uber Eats Delivery service. Moreover, customers routinely take advantage of Uber's provision of a car and driver for "off menu services," including package delivery and "lost and found" retrieval services.[1430] The FAA states the arbitration provisions do not bind "seamen, railroad employees, or any other class of workers engaged in foreign or interstate commerce."[1431]

Another case alleging racial adverse impact resulted in arbitration discussions. Abdul Kadir Mohamed, residing in Boston, Massachusetts, after having previously worked for Uber as an "Uber Black" driver since 2012, applied to work as an Uber X driver using his own car in 2014. Mohamed was told he would need a new car for this position and he, therefore, purchased a new car in late September 2014. In October 2014 he started working as an Uber X driver using his new car. By the end of this same month, he received an email stating that he would be unable to fill the position as the result of information obtained through the Consumer and Background Reporting Agency Hirease.[1432] At the same time, Mohamed's access to the Uber app, which previously enabled him to work as an Uber driver, was turned off.

In November 2014, Mohamed brought a class action against Uber and its contractors Rasier and Hirease for having accessed consumer and background

---

[1428] *Reese v Uber*, Memorandum of Law in Support of Defendant Uber's Motion to Dismiss the case, p 3.
[1429] *Reese v Uber*, Reply in Opposition to the Defendant Motion to Dismiss, p 3.
[1430] *Ibid*, p 4.
[1431] FAA, 9 U.S.C. §1. In the case *Circuit City Stores Inc. v Adam*, the Supreme Court held that arbitration agreements enforceable under employment contexts exempt the class of the §1 FAA.
[1432] *Mohamed v Uber Technologies, Inc.*, 848 F.3d 1201 (9th Circuit 2016) p 4. (Hereinafter *Mohamed v Uber*).

reports about himself and all the class of drivers to make decisions about hiring and terminating them without sending them a copy or informing them about the content of such report.[1433] Mohamed believed that Uber terminated his account because Hirease's consumer report concerning him indicated he had a minor criminal record "that stems from his seven children receiving Medicaid benefits."[1434] The lawyers grounded the complaint on the Federal Credit Reporting Act (FCRA)[1435] and California and Massachusetts state laws[1436] that impose that an employer first discloses its intent to use a background report in its hiring decision and must obtain the potential employee's written authorization to do so.

Uber's defense in this case was based on the arbitration clause. The ridesharing company alleged that Uber drivers have the option to opt out of the arbitration requirement, which waives their right to pursue labor and employment claims as a group and makes the arbitration agreements legal under the National Labor Relations Act. In the specific case, Mohamed and similar class members had accepted the clause requiring all disputes with Uber to be settled by an arbitrator and on an individual basis only. The clause excluded any possibility to take disputes to jury trial and collective actions.[1437] Furthermore, all questions related to the arbitrability of the case should also be resolved by an arbiter according to the contract. Mohamed had accepted this agreement and had not opted out with Uber and Rasier in 2014.

The District Court in the Northern District of California denied Uber's motion to compel arbitration of the claims due to conflicts in the terms of the provisions to arbitration.[1438] In addition, Uber did not provide real possibility for the drivers to reject the contract and did not notify drivers that they would be asked to pay important charges to arbitrate individually. However, Uber appealed and the United States Court of Appeals for the Ninth Circuit ruled that these conflicts were artificial and the arbitration agreement was valid.[1439] Moreover, the Ninth Circuit ruled that the District Court did not have authority to decide whether the arbitration agreement was enforceable, because even the "arbitrability" of the matter should be decided by an arbiter according to the original arbitration agreement.[1440]

These cases, along with *O'Connor*, demonstrate the difficulties to resolve employment issues, including claims of discrimination, by courts in the

---

[1433] *Mohamed v Uber*, class action complaint, p 2.

[1434] *Ibid*, p 6.

[1435] FCRA, 15 U.S.C. §1681b(b)(2)(A).

[1436] California Civil Code §1785.20.5(a).

[1437] *Mohamed v Uber*, opinion by Judge Clifton Sept 2016, p 8.

[1438] *Mohamed v Uber Technologies, Inc.*, 848 F.3d 1201 (9th Circuit 2016).

[1439] *Mohamed v Uber Technology, Inc.*, 836 F.3d 1102 (United States Court of Appeals, 9th Circuit, September 2016).

[1440] *Ibid*.

United States, because of arbitration clauses. When these cases are resolved by an arbitrator, they lack publicity, and therefore, prevent individuals placed in similar contexts of the litigation to have access to the rationale of the decision. Furthermore, arbitrated cases do no create binding precedents.

1.5. DISCRIMINATION BY DESIGN: OBJECTION TO THE RATING SYSTEM AS GROUNDS FOR TERMINATION

Apart from general concerns of the fairness of the rating system exclusively scored by clients that is used by Uber to terminate its contract with drivers, one specific case challenging the rating system regarding possible discriminatory outcomes was initiated in 2016. Shannon Liss-Riordan, the same attorney who represented the class of drivers in *O'Connor v Uber*, filed a Title VII-based complaint with the Equal Employment Opportunity Commission on behalf of Thomas Liu in California.[1441] Liu, an Asian-American Uber driver, alleged that his contract was terminated based on low passenger ratings that he received because of his racial origins. The complaint within the EEOC claimed that the app's system for rating drivers from one to five stars is racially discriminatory and, therefore, Uber was accused of violating Title VII, which provides that employers cannot have policies in place that have a disparate impact on minorities.[1442]

One of the attorney's arguments to challenge the policy of using the rating system to base termination decisions *vis-à-vis* Uber's workforce is the fact that the company had publicly refused to implement tips because "unconscious racial biases would result in white drivers earning more tips than Black drivers."[1443] In this case, the same unconscious biases are likely to impact the passenger ratings that Uber uses as a basis of driver's termination. The platform should not admit that customers decide whether drivers remain active on the service while also saying that customers are likely to discriminate. The attorney admitted that she did not have access to data from Uber's system showing drivers with a statutorily protected aspect received lower ratings, and she hoped the EEOC complaint would allow her to obtain such data. The developments of the case remained largely undocumented. Complaints and procedures within the EEOC are not publicized and, to my knowledge, the case did not make it to any district court.

[1441] *Thomas Liu v Uber, Inc.*, EEOC. The case was publicized in the attorney's law office webpage. *See* Dan Adams, *Boston-Based Attorney Argues Uber's Star Ratings Are Racially Biased* (October 2016) online: Lichten & Liss-Riordan, P.C. <https://www.llrlaw.com/wp-content/uploads/2015/04/Boston-based-Attorney-Argues-Uber's-Star-Ratings-are-Racially-Biased.pdf>.

[1442] Title VII, 42 U.S.C., §2000e-2(a)(1); ADEA, 29 U.S.C., §623 (a)(1) and ADA, 42 U.S.C., §12112 (a).

[1443] Tipping is currently possible, but it was not by 2016. *See* Uber, *In-App Tips on Uber* (October 2019) online: Uber <https://www.uber.com/be/en/ride/how-it-works/tips/>.

Precedents have settled that employers shall serve as an intermediary force to ensure workers are not suffering discrimination based on customers' preferences.[1444] However, workers are only suitable to Title VII protections if they are employees, not independent contractors. Several antidiscrimination rights are related to the employment classification.

Back to the first settlement proposals in the *O'Connor v Uber* case, the platform promised to provide additional information to drivers about their star ratings and their rankings relative to other drivers and to provide more clarity about what customer ratings thresholds a driver must maintain.[1445] Nevertheless, this promise to increase clarity and transparency for drivers did not substantially address problems of biases related to Uber's customer evaluations.

2. EUROPE

Europe was Uber's primary international expansion when it started operating in Paris in December 2011. Since then, the UberPop app, the first Uber service that allowed drivers who are not licensed to commercially transport passengers, has been banned by courts in several cities across Spain, France, Belgium, Italy, Germany, Spain, Norway, Finland, Hungary, and Bulgaria.[1446] Most European cities currently have the service only provided by professional drivers – UberX. However, intensive litigation did not stop there. Taxi associations in European countries have challenged the company's practices for misleading acts and unfair competition.[1447]

In that regard, a professional taxi driver association in Barcelona sued Uber Systems Spain before the Commercial Court, seeking to hold the activities of the company illegal for misleading practices and acts of unfair competition.[1448] The lawsuit was grounded on the fact that neither Uber Systems Spain nor the drivers of the vehicles had the proper licenses and authorizations required by the regulation of taxi services in Barcelona. The Spanish judge referred the question to the CJEU. Before the case in Spain, the question had been referred

---

[1444] *See* chapter 5, section II, 3, 3.2.

[1445] *O'Connor v Uber*, Notice of Motion and Motion for Preliminary Approval and Memorandum of Points and Authorities in Support Thereof, p 10.

[1446] *See* France: Conseil Constitutionnel, Décision n 2015–484 QPC, 22.09.2015; Belgium: Tribunal de l'Entreprise Francophone de Bruxelles, 00031, A/18/02920, 16.01.2019; Italy: Tribunale di Torino, Prima Sezione Civile, Sezione Speciallizzata in Materia di Impresa, sentenza n 1553/2017, 22.03.2017; The Netherlands: College Van Beroep Voor Het Bedrijfsleven ECLI:NL:CBB:2017:312, 21.09.2017; Eurofound, *Bulgaria: Supreme Court Shuts Down Smartphone Car Service Uber* (January 2016) online: Eurofound <https://www.eurofound.europa.eu/publications/article/2016/bulgaria-supreme-court-shuts-down-smartphone-car-service-uber>.

[1447] *See* chapter 6.

[1448] *Jizgado de lo Mercantil* No 3 de Barcelona.

to the European Court by a Belgian judge in the context of a dispute between Uber and the company Taxi Radio Bruxellois.[1449] However, in the absence of sufficient information, the CJEU ruled that the request for a preliminary ruling was inadmissible. The case brought before the Spanish judge offered the CJEU a new opportunity to determine whether European member states may submit Uber operation to a prior authorization.

To establish if Uber was conducting unfair practices that breached the Spanish rules on competition, the court considered it indispensable to define whether or not Uber required prior administrative authorization. For that purpose, the court deemed that it should be determined if the services provided by Uber should be labeled as transportation services, information society services, or a combination of both. Prior administrative authorization must rely on the definition of the activities Uber provided, because if the platform only provided information society services, it should be included in the scope of the freedom to provide services, in general, as well as the directive on services in the internal market and the directive on electronic commerce.[1450] In this case, Uber's practices – without proper member state previous authorization – could not be regarded as unfair practices.

Ultimately, the CJEU ruled that the intermediation service provided by Uber "must be regarded as being inherently linked to a transport service and, accordingly, must be classified as a service in the field of transport within the meaning of EU law."[1451] Therefore, member states have the competence to regulate the conditions under which transportation services are to be provided

---

[1449] CJEU, 27 October 2016, *Uber Belgium BVBA v Taxi Radio Bruxellois* NV C-526/16. *See* Jean-Victor Maublanc, *Uberpop Est un Service de Transport Avant d'Etre un Service de Mise en Relation par Voie Électronique* (March 2018), online: Journal d'Actualité des Droits Européens <https://revue-jade.eu/article/view/2184>.

[1450] When qualified as an "information society service", the activity of a service provider can hardly be subject to authorization, because it falls within the competence of the European Union, and the freedom to provide services protected by Article 56 TFEU. Directive 2006/123/EC of the European Parliament and of the Council of 12 December 2006 on services in the internal Market (OJ L 367, p 36); and Directive 2000/31/EC of the European Parliament and of the Council of 8 June 2000 on certain legal aspects of information society services, in particular electronic commerce, in the Internal Market (Directive on electronic commerce) (OJ 2006 L 178, p 1).

[1451] C-434/15 *Asociación Profesional Elite Taxi* ECLI:EU:C:2017:981. Also, *see* Philipp Hacker, "Uber Pop, UberBlack, and the Regulation of Digital Platforms after the Asociación Profesional Elite Taxi Judgement of the CJEU" (2018) 14:1 European Review of Contract Law 80; Michèle Finck, "Distinguishing Internet Platforms from Transport Services: Elite Taxi v Uber Spain" (2018) 55:5 Common Market Law Review 1619; Martien Y Shaub, "Why Uber Is an Information Society Service?" (2018) 7:3 Journal of European Consumer and Market Law 109; Alberto de Franceschi, "Uber Spain and the Identity Crisis of Online Platforms" (2018) 7:1 Journal of European Consumer and Market Law 1; Massimiliano Delfino, "Work in the Age of Collaborative Platforms Between Innovation and Tradition" (2018) 9:4 European Labour Law Journal 346.

in conformity with the general rules of the Treaty on the Functioning of the European Union.[1452]

The CJEU found that Uber provides more than information society services, because it organizes the transportation activity by determining the conditions under which the drivers provide their services. In that sense, Uber's online intermediation must be considered as forming an integral part of the service whose main aspect is a transport service, and, therefore, must be classified as "a service in the field of transport" and not as "an information society service."

Any attempt to extrapolate the Uber decision to other platforms does not seem appropriate, because the case ruled by the CJEU clearly relates only to the way Uber operates in the transportation sector. However, the rationale of the CJEU decision has served as inspiration for employment misclassification rulings, especially the fact that the platform is not limited to intermediation or the provision of information society services and provides, in fact, transportation services by the way it manages and controls the selection of the drivers, the clients available to the drivers, and the regulation of the price of the service provided by them.[1453] Even if subordination and control are some key concepts to the definition of employment in many jurisdictions[1454], some judges rooted their legal arguments for reclassifying the drivers' status in the transportation identity of the company.[1455]

In Europe, drivers have sued Uber to have their contractual relationship classified as employment in France and in the UK.[1456] In the next section, I analyze how driver-employment litigation has been developed in the UK because of the importance given to the rating system in the case law.

2.1. MISCLASSIFICATION OF EMPLOYMENT STATUS

Similar to the understanding in the United States, the employment status of Uber drivers in the European member states is relevant to the determination of the applicability of a large set of rights, including paid leave and the protection these workers have against some potential discriminatory practices implemented by the company.[1457] In contrast to the United States, the personal scope of employment-related equality directives, and the subsequently transposed equality legislation, reach not only employees, but also dependent self-employed workers. However, the question of whether these rules protect genuine self-

---

[1452] Art 56 TFEU.
[1453] *See Uber BV v Aslam* [2018] EWCA civ 2748.
[1454] Among others such as mutuality of obligation.
[1455] *Aslam v Uber BV* [2016] EW Misc B68 (ET), 28 October 2016, p 27.
[1456] Cour d'Appel de Paris, pôle 6, chamber 2, arrêt du 10 janvier 2019, sn rg 18/08357, n portalis 35L7-V-B7C-B6AZK.
[1457] *See* chapter 5, section.

employed workers (contractors of services) is by far not a consensus and has not been answered by the CJEU regarding the Race Equality Directive and the Employment Equality Directive.[1458]

2.2. EMPLOYMENT (MIS)CLASSIFICATION IN THE UK

Two years after the *O'Connor v Uber* class action was filed in the United States, drivers in the UK filed a lawsuit claiming their employment status before the Employment Tribunal in London.[1459] The drivers argued that the platform misclassified their contracts and failed to pay minimum wage time and paid leave.[1460] In the case *Aslam, Farrar v Uber BV, Uber London Ltd, and Uber Britannia Ltd*, the Employment Tribunal assessed the conditions of work of the drivers in London. The Tribunal ruled, for the first time in Europe, that Uber drivers were employed as "workers" and not as contractors, as the company had originally decided. This change of the drivers' classification was based on the legal design that linked the drivers to the platform and the control Uber had over them.[1461] In the UK, worker status is regarded as a half-way between employed and self-employed statutes.[1462] Workers are entitled to some legal rights similarly to employees, including protection from discrimination[1463], protection against unlawful deduction from wages[1464], and entitlement to the national minimum wage.[1465]

[1458] *Ibid.*

[1459] *Aslam v Uber BV* [2016] EW Misc B68 (ET), 28 October 2016, p 3–7. In its early stages, this case was described in Ana Maria Correa, "Regulatory Risks Faced by the Transportation Sharing Economy: Workforces at Stake" (2018) 9:4 European Journal of Risk Regulation 641. Also, for comments on the case and related issues, *see* Sandra Fredman, Darcy Du Toit, "One Small Step Towards Decent Work: *Uber v Aslam* in the Court of Appeal" (2019) 48:2 Industrial Law Journal 260; Ewan McGaughey, "Uber, the Taylor Review, Mutuality and the Duty Not to Misrepresent Employment Status" (2019) 48:2 Industrial Law Journal 180; Jeff Kenner, "Uber Drivers Are Workers: The Expanding Scope of the Worker Concept in the UKs Gig Economy", in Jeff Kenner, Izabela Florczak, Marta Otto, *The Challenge of Labour Law in Europe* (Edward Elgar Publishing, 2019), p 288; Mark Freedland, Jeremias Adams-Prassl, "Employees, Workers, and the 'Sharing Economy" (2017) Oxford Legal Studies Research Paper No.19 1; Debra Howcroft, Tony Dundon, Cristina Inversi, "Fragmented Demands and Gig-Working in the UK", in: M Sullivan (ed), *Zero Hours and On-Call Work in Anglo-Saxon Countries: Work, Organization, and Employment* (Springer, 2019), 215.

[1460] The claims were based on the following statutory law: Employment Rights Act 1996 (ERA); National Minimum Wage Act 1998 (NMWA) and Working Time Regulations 1998 (WTR).

[1461] *See* comments Jeff Kenner, "Uber Drivers Are Workers: The Expanding Scope of the "Worker Concept in the UK's Gig Economy", chapter 11, *in* Jeff Kenner, Isabela Florczak, Marta Otto (eds), *Precarious Work: The Challenge for Labour Law in Europe* (London: Edward Elgar, 2019).

[1462] René Böheim, Ilrike Muehlberger, "Dependent Forms of Self-Employment in the UK: Identifying Workers on the Border between Employment and Self-Employment" (2009) 42:2 Journal of Labour Market Research 182.

[1463] Equality Act 2010, part 5, chapter 1, 41.

[1464] ERA 1996, Section 13–14.

[1465] NMWA 1998, Section 1 (2)(a).

The plaintiffs Aslam and Farrar claimed that Uber exerted excessive control over the activity of its "allegedly" independent drivers. They claimed that Uber instructed, managed, and controlled them. Conversely, Uber provided that the company merely gives instructions to guarantee the common interest of ensuring a good ride experience for passengers. When drivers start working for Uber UK, they receive a welcome pack containing instructions of what is expected from them. As part of these instructions, Uber states that it expects high-quality service, demonstrated by the rating given by the clients, and low cancellation rates or high acceptance rates, in which the driver should accept at least 80% of trip requests to retain their account status. Drivers are forcibly logged out of the Uber app for 10 minutes when they reject three trips in a row. Uber also lists its safety and quality preferences: "polite and professional drivers; zero tolerance to any form of discrimination; avoid inappropriate topics of conversation; do not contact the rider after the trip has ended."[1466] All of these recommendations are followed by "please remember that there are some recommendations that if not followed, may constitute a breach of your partner terms or license conditions."[1467]

The UK courts apply common law tests to determine employment status, which includes aspects such as control, economic dependency, subordination, or mutuality of obligation.[1468] The mutuality of obligation criteria has been a relevant guide used to identify employment status since the late 1970s.[1469] It considers the existence of the mutual obligation to provide work and to accept any work that is offered; the duration of the employment; the regularity of employment; the right to refuse work; and custom in the trade. In that sense, the Employment Tribunal verified that once drivers have their app switched on, they have the obligation to accept the rides just as Uber must provide them with available rides. Moreover, to have skilled drivers, Uber recruits, interviews, instructs drivers, and decides the fees drivers will receive for the service they provide to the client, making them dependent.[1470] Furthermore, the Employment Tribunal considered that Uber managed and controlled the drivers by the rating system, which has direct consequences, varying from a warning email to removal from the platform. Uber additionally administered passengers' complaints about the drivers in this monitoring role.

The Employment Tribunal decided that the contractual terms that linked Uber and its drivers did not correspond with the reality: "The notion that Uber in London is a mosaic of 30,000 small businesses linked by a common platform is

---

1466 *Aslam v Uber BV* [2016] EW Misc B68 (ET), 28 October 2016, p 14.
1467 *Aslam v Uber BV* [2016] EW Misc B68 (ET), 28 October 2016, p 15.
1468 Sandra Fredman, Darcy Du Toit, "One Small Step Towards Decent Work: *Uber v Aslam* in the Court of Appeal" (2019), *op. cit.*, p 264.
1469 *See* cases *O'Kelly v Trusthouse Forte* [1983] IRLR 369 (CA); see also *Nethermere (St Neots) v Gardiner* [1984] ICR 612 (Court of Appeal).
1470 *Aslam v Uber BV* [2016] EW Misc B68 (ET), 28 October 2016, p 29.

to our minds faintly ridiculous."[1471] For Uber, each car with a driver constituted
an independent business, and in this business, the driver and passenger would
have a binding contract without knowing details retrospectively, including their
full names or telephone numbers. Uber also retains all the information about
the passengers to be picked up, including their credit cards. The driver has none
of this information, only the first name and a photograph when it is provided by
the client. In addition, this same contract provides that the driver will start a ride
without knowing the destination until the ride begins with a route prescribed
by a stranger to the contract and for a fee also set by a stranger to the contract.
Grounded on these facts, the Tribunal considered that the contract between
driver and passenger was a fiction with no relation to the real legal reality. For
all these reasons, it ruled that the drivers provided work for Uber and were
"workers" of ULL, the Uber branch in London.

In 2016 Uber appealed to the Employment Appeal Tribunal against the above
decision, which was upheld in 2017.[1472] Uber appealed again, and, in December
2018 the Court of Appeal – Civil Division – upheld the first and second instance's
decisions by ruling that Uber drivers are workers of the platform.[1473] Based on
the fact – among 12 other reasons – that Uber submits drivers to a rating system,
which amounts to a performance management/disciplinary procedure.[1474] The
Court of Appeal confirmed that ratings are monitored, and drivers with average
scores below 4.4 become subject to a graduated series of quality interventions
aimed at assisting them to improve. Experienced drivers, that is to say those who
have undertaken 200 trips or more, whose figures do not improve to 4.4 or better
are removed from the platform and their accounts are deactivated.[1475]

Moreover, the Court of Appeals relied in a precedent of the Supreme
Court to support that the terms of a contract are not sufficient to determine
the employment status of workers, because "the relative bargaining power of
the parties must be taken into account in deciding whether the terms of any
written agreement in truth represent what was agreed and the true agreement
will often have to be gleaned from all circumstances of the case, of which the
written agreement is only a part."[1476] Uber appealed to the Supreme Court of
the UK, which unanimously dismissed the platform's appeal.[1477] The Court
considered that Uber drivers have no say over their pay and working conditions,
and therefore, they should be protected by labor legislation because they are in a
subordinate and dependent position in relation to Uber. The platform ultimately

---

[1471]   *Aslam v Uber BV* [2016] EW Misc B68 (ET), 28 October 2016, p 28.
[1472]   *Uber BV v Aslam* [2017] UKEAT 0056171011, 10 November 2017.
[1473]   *Uber BV v Aslam* [2018] EWCA civ 2748.
[1474]   *Uber BV v Aslam* [2018] EWCA civ 2748, p 68.
[1475]   *Uber BV v Aslam* [2018] EWCA civ 2748, p 69.
[1476]   *Autoclenz Ltd v Belcher* [2011] UKSC 41, §45. *See* Alan L Bogg, "Sham Self-Employment in the
        Supreme Court" (2012) 41:3 Industrial Law Journal 328;
[1477]   *Uber BV v Aslam* [2021] UKSC.

controls how drivers' work is conducted. The Court concluded that one of the methods of control is the use of a ratings system, considering that any driver who fails to maintain a required average rating will suffer a series of consequences, including potentially having their relationship with Uber terminated.

In the meantime, Uber drivers in the UK, including James Farrar, have requested the data that Uber had collected about them in compliance with the GDPR.[1478] As a response to the request, the company has provided a limited data sample, with GPS data, pick-up and drop-off points, and fare details, but Uber has not provided the full data the drivers sought to obtain, including accurate log-on and log-off times, all location data, individual ratings and reviews, and any detail about how Uber's drivers' personal information and profile impacts the work they are assigned. This data will support the drivers' claims that Uber manages its drivers through its algorithms.

2.3. DISCRIMINATION BY DESIGN: OBJECTION TO THE RATING SYSTEM AS A GROUND FOR TERMINATION

The London Employment Appeal Tribunal's ruling that Uber drivers are workers opens the path for the drivers to the potential protection against discrimination enshrined in the Equality Act 2010 (EA 2010). The Act has a wider scope than other employment laws.[1479] It protects not only employees under a contract of service but also any person "under a contract personally to do work."[1480] This personal scope is aligned to the Race, Employment, and Gender Equality Directives, which are not restricted in scope for traditional employment relationships nor for self-employed workers who have a relationship of dependence with one employer.[1481] In that sense, the Supreme Court of the UK has ruled that an element of subordination is necessary for the purposes of domestic employment discrimination law.[1482]

In 2017 a female Uber driver filed a sex discrimination lawsuit against Uber before the Central London Employment Tribunal, claiming that Uber's working practices unfairly disadvantage women.[1483] The unfair working practices

---

[1478] Melissa Heikkilä, *Uber Drivers Wage Battle to Obtain their Data* (October 2019), online: Politico <https://www.politico.eu/article/uber-drivers-wage-battle-to-obtain-their-data/>.

[1479] Catherine Barnard, "Discrimination, Self-Employment and the Liberal Professions" (2011) 12 European Anti-Discrimination Law Review 21.

[1480] Section 83, EA 2010.

[1481] *See* chapter 5.

[1482] *Jivraj v Hashwani* [2011] UKSC 40. *See* Christopher McCrudden, "Two Views of Subordination: The Scope of Employment Discrimination Law in *Jivraj v Hashwani*" (2012) 41 Industrial Law Journal 30.

[1483] The claim was brought by the GMB union, on behalf of the women who wanted to remain anonymous. Some details of the case were published on the plaintiff's law firm website. Leigh Day, *British Female Driver Launches Sex Discrimination Claim Against Uber Over Practices*

comprise the design of the app, which allows drivers to know their passenger's destination only after they accept the ride, and the rating system. In the case, the plaintiff argued that requiring drivers to accept rides before knowing the destination has led her to unsafe areas. Canceling accepted rides is possible, but drivers are penalized by being logged off the platform, and ultimately, their contract with Uber may be permanently terminated. In addition, when customers have become aggressive in the car and were required to leave it, drivers were low rated with the ultimate outcome of having their contract terminated. The claim argues that the company should allow drivers to challenge complaints and low ratings, so that drivers do not risk having their contract terminated if they ask passengers to leave their cars for their own safety. In short, the design of the platform has put women at greater risk and, therefore, has particularly discriminated female drivers. The outcome of the case is not acknowledged, but it would give a court the chance to examine whether Uber's design discriminates against women drivers under the terms of the EA 2010, which prohibits discrimination in the termination of employment/work contract for several protected groups including women.[1484] The case also stresses how the classification of the contractual relationship between drivers and Uber is relevant to protect its workers against organizational practices of discrimination.

(September 2017), online: Leigh Day Office <https://www.leighday.co.uk/News/News-2017/September-2017/British-female-driver-launches-sex-discrimination>.

[1484] Part 5, chapter 1, 39 (2)(c), EA 2010.

CONCLUSION OF TITLE III

Across the United States and EU member states, the methods used by online labor platforms to manage their workforce – through scored rating systems – have raised the attention of scholars considering their possible discriminatory outcomes against statutorily protected classes of workers.[1485] With this in mind, I aimed to bring to light the possible adverse impact of implementing rating systems to manage platform workers, specifically as a criterion for dismissal, and the legal challenges platform workers face when disputing it. So far, scholars have sparsely analyzed managerial workforce practices, such as rating systems, in the light of antidiscrimination laws, particularly in Europe.

I conclude that the first obstacle lies in how platforms place themselves as intermediaries between workers and clients (or hiring parties), by subcontracting their service providers. This arrangement prevents *a priori* workers – or in the words of online platforms, "entrepreneurs" – from having the protection of employment-related rights. The legal consequences of being classified as self-employed workers or employees have brought platform workers to the courts both in the United States and in EU member states. In the United States, protections against discriminatory dismissals of employees based on their statutorily protected aspects (provided by Title VII, the ADA, and the ADEA) are considerably restricted in their personal scope and only reach employees employed by companies with 15 or more employees. In EU member states, the personal scope of the Race, Employment, and Gender Equality Directives and their member states' counterparts are less rigid and also apply to dependent self-employed persons, but they are less likely to apply to genuine self-employed workers – also named entrepreneurs. The second obstacle lies on how courts in the United States and the CJEU have so far accessed "neutral policies" implemented by companies to accommodate their clients' preferences. Precedents have up to this point have guaranteed the maintenance of apparent neutral policies to accommodate clients' preferences that might have a disparate

---

[1485] Michael Luca, "Designing Online Marketplaces: Trust and Reputation Mechanisms" (2017) 17 Innovation Policy and the Economy 77; and Alex Rosenblat, Karen E C Levy, Solon Barocas, Tim Hwang, "Discriminating Tastes: Uber's Customer Ratings as Vehicles for Workplace Discrimination" (2017) 9:3 Policy & Internet 256; not specifically for ratings, but big data in general: Solon Barocas, Andrew D Selbst, "Big Data's Disparate Impact" (2016) 104:3 California Law Review 671. About algorithmic decision and gender discrimination, *see* Miriam Kullmann, "Platform Work: Algorithmic Decision-Making, and EU Gender Equality Law (2018) 34:1 International Journal of Comparative Labour Law and Industrial Relations 1.

impact on protected groups in the name of the business' necessity or freedom to conduct business.[1486]

Finally, arbitration clauses have also been placed as a barrier for courts to assess the employment status of Uber drivers as well as any other claim regarding these workers in the United States. Contrarily, in Europe the legal possibilities of arbitrating employment-related disputes are limited, when not forbidden. This limitation has given courts the possibility to rule drivers as workers and has allowed judicial disputes to assess Uber's rating system in the UK. However, considering the pervasiveness of rating systems across online labor platforms, the case brought to court in the UK is still too minor and has not yet established whether Uber's rating system indeed adversely impacts protected groups nor whether the policy would fall under business necessity if the answer were affirmative.

[1486] *EEOC v Sephora USA, LLC* 419 F.Supp.2ed 408 (United States District Court New York 2005); and *Asma Bougnaoui and ADDH v Micropole SA*, Case C-188/15, ECLI:EU:C:2017:204.

GENERAL CONCLUSION

1. PROBLEM FRAMING

Discrimination against statutorily protected classes has been increasingly documented in online environments.[1487] Concerns include how the design of online platforms, the pervasive collection of data, automated decisions, and scant control over users' activities might enhance forms of structural discrimination, such as the denial of ethnic minorities from the access of goods and services[1488], the exclusion of women from receiving employment offers[1489], and the removal of protected classes from platform servers due to evaluation systems.[1490] With this backdrop in mind, this book explores the challenges the online platform economy poses to the principle of equality enshrined in both European and American antidiscrimination laws with regards to the access to goods, services, and labor markets.

The research was oriented by two main inquiries. First, it investigated the structural challenges online platforms present to the nondiscriminatory treatment of their users. Second, it examined whether antidiscrimination legal frameworks in the United States and in the European Union are equipped to address discrimination in these online spaces. After conducting case-based research, my thesis demonstrates that the structural challenges to the principle of equality rely on the aesthetic design, matching tools, evaluation systems, and the network effect of online platforms, and these aspects ultimately reinforce old biases against protected classes. Subsequently, my thesis argues that antidiscrimination laws in the United States and in member states of the

---

[1487] *See* chapter 2, 3, and 6. Also, Benjamin Edelman, Michael Luca, Dan Svirsky, "Racial Discrimination in the Sharing Economy: Evidence from a Field Experiment" (2017), *op. cit.*; Andrew Selbst, Solon Barocas, "Big Data's Disparate Impact" (2016), *op. cit.*; Alex Rosenblat, Karen E C Levy, Solon Barocas, Tim Hwang, "Discriminating Tastes: Uber's Customer Ratings as Vehicles for Workplace Discrimination" (2017), *op. cit.*; Miriam Kullmann, "Platform Work: Algorithmic Decision-Making, and EU Gender Equality Law" (2018), *op. cit.*.

[1488] *Selden v Airbnb*, INC., No. 16-cv-00933 (CRC) (D.C. Nov. 1, 2016).

[1489] Anja Lambrecht and Catherine Tucker, "Algorithmic Bias? An Empirical Study of Apparent Gender-Based Discrimination in the Display of STEM Career Ads" (2019), *op. cit.*.

[1490] *Thomas Liu v Uber, Inc.*, EEOC. Equal Employment Opportunity Commission; Leigh Day, *British Female Driver Launches Sex Discrimination Claim Against Uber Over Practices* (September 2017).

European Union are only partially equipped to hold these businesses liable for discrimination occurring in their online spaces.

Regarding the structural challenges, I indicate that online platforms might enhance discrimination against protected classes. This outcome first occurs by their aesthetic design choices that over-emphasize users' protected markers before prospective transactions are concluded.[1491] Second, this outcome occurs by the design of cutting-edge matching tools that allow users to exclude protected classes from receiving goods, services, and work offers.[1492] Third, the development of facially objective evaluation systems may result in the permanent exclusion of protected classes or their poor ranking in search algorithms.[1493] Fourth, discrimination might be enhanced by the platform's network effect and its consequent impossibility and undesirability to implement prior central control over the users' conduct.

Concerning the aforementioned legal challenges, I argue that the legal systems in the United States and in the European Union member states are only partially equipped to address these structural challenges posed by online platforms to the equality principle for three reasons. First, they do not address certain flaws of the platforms' aesthetic choices, such as the salience of their users' protected markers. Second, most criteria used by matching tools are not apparent and evident to the users.[1494] Third, rating systems provide an aggregate of opinions and, therefore, no clear evidence that the evaluated user was discriminated against due to one of their protected aspects. With respect to these three challenges, based on my research, my thesis demonstrates that the co-regulatory system that involves private and public actors provided by the Directive on Electronic Commerce (2000) in the EU is more equipped to hold online platforms liable for third-party discrimination in the particular circumstance they become aware of the illegal conduct. Alternatively, the general set of immunities online platforms have over the illegal activities of their users provided by the Communications Decency Act of 1996 prevents online platforms in the United States from being liable for discrimination occurring through their online intermediation, in most cases. I argue that, aside from pressure from civil

---

[1491] *See* chapter 1 and 2. Particularly, *Airbnb*.

[1492] *See* chapter 3 and 4. Also, *Fair Housing Council of San Fernando Valley v Roommates, LLC*, 2012 WL 310849 (9th Cir. February 2, 2012); *Irish Human Rights and Equality Commission v Daft Media Limited t/a Daft/ie*, ADJ-00005960, WRC, August 2019; *Onuoha v Facebook, Inc*, No. 5: 16-cv-06440-EJD (N.D. Cal. Apr. 7, 2017); *Bradley v T-Mobile US, Inc.*, No. 17-cv-07232-BLF (N.D. Cal. June 4, 2019); *National Fair Housing Alliance v Facebook, Inc.*, No. 1:18-cv-02689-JGK (S.D. N.Y. Aug. 08, 2018); *Spees et al v Facebook, Inc.* (EEOC, September 2018).

[1493] *See* chapter 5 and 6. Also, *Thomas Liu v Uber, Inc.*, EEOC. Equal Employment Opportunity Commission; Leigh Day, *British Female Driver Launches Sex Discrimination Claim Against Uber Over Practices* (September 2017).

[1494] In cases of targeted advertisement.

society[1495], legal accountability is also relevant to incite companies to implement policies against discrimination.

However, even though the co-regulatory system of the Directive on Electronic Commerce provides more remedies in the fight against discrimination, it does not address flawed aesthetic choices and the opacity of matching and rating systems.[1496] Ultimately, in the light of these challenges, my thesis asserts that the fight against discrimination in online platforms might produce the best results when also oriented by a model of regulation that encourages online platforms to implement the principle of transparency and fairness in their interactions with users[1497], coupled with the cooperation of antidiscrimination bodies and private businesses.

The structural and legal challenges are developed in Sections 2 and 3, respectively. An alternative path consisting of private cooperation as well as transparent and fair policies to address these factual challenges is presented in Section 4.

2. STRUCTURAL CHALLENGES: DESIGN, NETWORK EFFECT, AND DISCRIMINATION

Throughout the past two decades, online platforms described as intermediaries that connect individuals as well as different sides of the market has become a driving force in several economic sectors.[1498] Concerning markets, online platforms' success is mainly attributed to the fact that they enable supply and demand to easily connect at local and global scales by challenging physical and regulatory barriers.

Goods, services, and labor markets are generally permeated by information asymmetries.[1499] Consumers do not have perfect information about the state of the product or the quality of the service provision in advance in the same way that hiring parties do not have flawless information about workers prior to hiring them. Traditionally, strong and consolidated brands, experts' opinions, recommendation letters, and CVs mitigate the impact of information asymmetries by increasing confidence about the service, the product, or the worker's quality. These resources guide consumers and hiring parties in their

---

[1495] Such was the cases of *Craigslist*, *Airbnb* and *Facebook* in the United States.
[1496] The opacity of matching system may be eventually addressed by the Digital Services Act, once in force in the European Union.
[1497] Inspired by Regulation (EU) 2019/1150 of the European Parliament and of the Council of 20 June 2019 on Promoting Fairness and Transparency for Business Users of Online Intermediation Services, OJ L 186, 11.7.2019, p 57–79. *See* section 4 below. Some of these remedies were eventually included in the proposal for the Digital Services Act.
[1498] Orly Lobel, "The Law of The Platform" (2016), *op. cit.*
[1499] *See* chapters 1, 3, and 6.

decision-making.[1500] In online platforms, to mitigate the presence of frequent non-professional providers or consolidated brands, design is carefully considered to handle information asymmetries and, therefore, increase trustworthiness and the efficiency of transactions.

Initially, online platforms, such as eBay and Amazon, mainly dealt with retailers that were unknown to consumers by the fact that they could not assess the quality of the purchase before concluding it, because of the physical distance.[1501] Additionally, the barriers to entry in online platforms are, at present, scant. The selection criteria of service providers are often non-existent or considerably loose. To illustrate the matter, Airbnb only requires hosts to provide their ID card, names, email address, telephone number, geographic address, and profile photographs; Amazon Mechanical Turk only requests workers to provide their address of residence, name, and phone number; and TaskRabbit includes simple background checks and social networking control through Facebook or LinkedIn verification.[1502] Aside from these loose selection criteria, there is also a general lack of training or supervision from the side of the platforms towards their providers, given that online platforms supposedly only intermediate supply and demand. In this respect, when Uber first started operating Uber Pop, it simply required drivers to submit their regular driver's license without assessing their driving experience or providing any sort of training.[1503]

Given that online platforms' ultimate goal is to foster networking between the two sides of the market and increase transactions, over the years they have invested in mechanisms to attenuate the consequences of information asymmetries to improve users' confidence in the quality of the products or services offered through their intermediation, and, as a result, efficiently enable networking. These mechanisms include aesthetic design, matching tools, and evaluation systems. They are mainly conceived and implemented to guide users in their decision-making by improving their confidence in the platform market, which is typically comprised of individuals with no branding.[1504]

[1500] Sofia Ranchordás, "Public Values, Private Regulators: Between Regulation and Reputation in the Sharing Economy" (2019) 13:2 The Law & Ethics of Human Rights 203; Lynn Frewer, Hans Van Trijp, *Understanding Consumers of Food Products, op. cit.*, p 168.

[1501] Ray Fisman, Michael Luca, "Fixing Discrimination in Online Marketplaces" (2016), *op. cit.*.

[1502] Zoe Cullen, Chiara Farronato, "Outsourcing Tasks Online: Matching Supply and Demand on Peer-to-Peer Internet Platforms", *op. cit.*, P 7.

[1503] As a response, authorities in several places in the United State and in the European Union countries ruled the transportation of private passengers mandatorily required drivers with professional licenses, forcing Uber to launch UberX and to discontinue Uber Pop in these locations. *See* chapter 6.

[1504] Ray Fisman, Michael Luca, "Fixing Discrimination in Online Marketplaces" (2016), *op. cit.*.

2.1. AESTHETIC DESIGN CHOICES

The number of demographic aspects available about users and how they are displayed to other users are platform-specific. Platforms greatly diverge in this aspect. For instance, Uber only displays the identity of its drivers once the ride is accepted. HomeAway only discloses the identity of potential tenants for short-term vacation rentals once the deal is concluded. Airbnb provides users' personal demographic aspects when guests are looking for hosts. On Facebook, personal information concerning users' demographics is vastly shared.

If on the one hand, the disclosure of personal demographic information has proven to increase or decrease trustworthiness amid users in online platforms[1505], on the other hand, it has exposed statutorily protected classes to discrimination they have faced in offline markets. Even though, in this case, online platforms are not the source of the discrimination, their aesthetic design choices, such as how they reveal their users' personal markers, might enhance or mitigate the adverse treatment against individuals with protected aspects.

Airbnb provides several examples of how a platform's aesthetic choices might negatively impact statutorily protected classes and particularly facilitate racial discrimination. Airbnb has encouraged users to provide accurate and detailed personal information with the ultimate aim to foster trust and improve networks in the rental and accommodation market, which are typically pervaded by safety and privacy concerns. However, after several cases involving the alleged refusal of guests with protected classes in European member states and in the United States, the viral hashtag #airbnbwhileblack, in which thousands of Black guests reported discrimination by hosts on Airbnb, trended on Twitter. In addition, the publication of several studies that presented the scale of discrimination against protected classes on the platform have captured the attention of scholars and antidiscrimination activists for the adverse impact aesthetic choices have on protected classes.[1506] The disclosure and prominence of ethnic origin markers, notably photographs and names, are the result of choices made by Airbnb's designers to guide users to make their decisions. Other online housing markets have voluntarily opted for different formats. For example, HomeAway has opted to display only the photographs of the properties. Once the transaction is concluded, hosts and guest photographs are then disclosed. This example illustrates that the aesthetic design choices of online platforms' marketplaces are not static and can be rethought to avoid bias.

[1505] *See* chapter 1 and 2. Also, Jefferson Duarte, Stephan Siegel, Lance Young, "Trust and Credit: The Role of Appearance in Peer-to-Peer Lending" (2012), *op. cit.*.

[1506] *See* chapter 1 and 2.

2.2. EVALUATION TOOLS

Through evaluation tools, users' performance is assessed by a score or comment that might reflect their counterparts' satisfaction. Online platforms develop and implement evaluation tools to build up their private providers' reputations, to somehow reassure users about the quality of the services and products offered, and to certify that users are aligned with the platform's values.[1507] Evaluation tools might, on some occasions, encourage users to improve their behavior. Ultimately, however, evaluation tools aim to increase trust between users and, consequently, increase the number of transactions intermediated by the platform.

While online platforms implement evaluation tools to build the reputation of their users, increase trust, assure quality, and certify that users are aligned with their main values, they also implement evaluation tools to guide users in their decision-making and directly manage the inclusion or exclusion of users in their online market. For instance, Airbnb hosts and guests are both able to publicly evaluate their experiences. Given that these evaluations will be available to the entire community, they serve as a basis to guide users to make decisions concerning the acceptance or refusal of guests and hosts. The platform might terminate hosts' and guests' contracts when they repeatedly receive poor ratings or reviews.[1508] Uber also uses its peer-to-peer evaluation scored tools to terminate their driver and rider contracts unilaterally.

Evaluation tools have raised the attention of antidiscrimination scholars due to their potential adverse impact on statutorily protected classes, considering that one of their outcomes might be the user's exclusion from the platform.[1509] Evaluation tools have raised concerns because of their design. In theory, evaluation tools, especially the scored ones, depict an aggregated expression of users' assessments of their experience. Even though they might be perceived as being objective measures of satisfaction, they have been proven to be permeated by biased assessments instead of objective ones. Statutorily protected classes have reportedly received lower scores when providing services through online platforms.[1510] Making decisions based on evaluation systems that are biased might illegally prevent statutorily protected classes from accessing goods and services or may result in the termination of workers from the platforms of which they depend on for their livelihoods.

The reality of biased customer evaluation has been long observed in corporate environments that use this practice to assess their workers' performance.

[1507] Sofia Ranchordás, "Public Values, Private Regulators: Between Regulation and Reputation in the Sharing Economy" (2019) 13:2 The Law & Ethics of Human Rights 203.

[1508] Airbnb, *Terms of Services* (January 2020), online: Airbnb <https://pt.airbnb.com/terms#sec201910_10>, Article 15.5.

[1509] *See* chapter 5.

[1510] *Ibid.*

As developed in Chapter 5, in the section dedicated to "Biased Evaluation of Workers' Performance," female Black American doctors consistently received lower satisfaction rates compared to their white and male counterparts in an American medical clinic. In this case, 12,000 evaluations were analyzed. These findings reveal that patients persistently evaluated doctors with two protected grounds (sex and ethnicity) less favorably – and these grounds are enshrined and protected against discrimination in Title VII of the Civil Rights of 1964. Thus, the clinic's decisions on salary rates, promotion, and termination of doctors based on the biased patient evaluations likely adversely impacted female and Black doctors, which is illegal under Title VII.

This pattern has also been observed in on-demand work platforms. Gender and ethnic origin were related to less favorable client evaluations in TaskRabbit and Fiverr.[1511] In these cases, data related to protected aspects of workers and customer reviews was collected on over 10,000 workers of both platforms. Female and workers with minority ethnic backgrounds were consistently lower rated.[1512] In these platforms, customer evaluations were used to rank workers in the platform search results, resulting in the workers with lower ratings appearing towards the bottom. These results consist of thousands of workers offering their services in the platform. When a poorly evaluated worker is ranked on the bottom of a list of thousands, their chance to be contacted by a potential customer is significantly reduced. If workers with protected grounds such as gender and ethnicity are consistently evaluated less favorably by clients, any platform decision concerning these workers and based on such evaluations will adversely impact workers with protected grounds both under European law and the American Federal Civil Rights Act.

Therefore, the use of evaluation systems as the only organizational practice to manage users by online platform businesses might lead to discrimination against statutorily protected groups when these evaluations are biased against a protected ground.[1513]

Additionally, detecting biased customer feedback is considerably difficult in systems that use stars or scores, because they represent an aggregate of multiple client opinions. These scores are not comparable to client evaluation with openly stated discriminatory and derogatory terms. Any disparate impact, in which protected classes are disproportionally and negatively impacted, might only be uncovered by statistical studies conducted by specialists. Finally, many platforms do not disclose to the public the evaluation of all their workers or users. The knowledge and disclosure of data regarding the evaluation of all workers

---

[1511] Ánikó Hannák, Claudia Wagner, David Garcia, Alan Mislove, Markus Strohmaier, Christo Wilson, "Bias in Online Freelance Marketplaces: Evidence from TaskRabbit and Fiverr" (2017), *op. cit.*.

[1512] *See* chapter 5, section I, subsection 2.1 (Biased Evaluation of Workers' Performance).

[1513] Dallan F Flake, "When Should Employers Be Liable for Factoring Customer Feedback into Employment Decisions" (2018) 102:5, *op. cit.*, p 2180.

together in addition to data related to their protected grounds is a necessary step to determine if any protected class is being adversely impacted by the platform evaluation system. Most platforms do not disclose such data, and, in Europe, for instance, the collection of data concerning certain protected grounds, such as ethnic origin, is mostly forbidden.

2.3. MATCHING TOOLS

Matching efficiency is the core value of the intermediation role of online platforms, given the high number of users available to provide services in networked markets. Matching tools reduce or eliminate searching costs and potentially increase the number of transactions between the two sides of the market. In other words, when platforms provide tools that enable suppliers with the right characteristics to meet the demand, they boost the chance that a transaction will be concluded. Consequently, online platforms' matching capability is the pivotal element to their economic growth, considering that the more transactions that occur through their intermediation, the more profitable they become, either by charging a percentage of each individual transaction or by being an attractive marketplace for advertisers. While pipeline business models sell goods and services, platform models sell matchmaking capability. Thus, mismatching and rejections impact an online platform's economic growth. The consequence of rejections might be attenuated if the search costs are low and users can easily find a replacement for their demand. Therefore, scale, or the number of users available in online platforms, is essential for their success.

Matching capability is also platform-specific. Some online platforms design tools in which the demand can select the category, location, and time for a given service. Based on these criteria, the platform algorithm ranks possible suppliers and offers them to the discretion of the demand. Examples of platforms using such a matching method include Airbnb, Roommates, Daft, and TaskRabbit. For instance, Airbnb's algorithms place hosts on the webpage of guests based on the specific requirements guests might have, including geographic location, type of real estate, and price.[1514] Potential guests begin their research on Airbnb by submitting their travel preferences, such as a city, time frame, and price range, to the platform's search engine. The platform's algorithm replies with an inventory of listings available in the selected location according to a ranking algorithm.[1515] Inventory listings are placed for each request based on their algorithmically determined scores. Listings with the highest scores appear first. If any listed option is attractive, the potential guest has the chance to inquire

---

[1514]   *See* chapter 2.
[1515]   Andrey Fradkin, "Search Frictions and the Design of Online Marketplaces" (2015), *op. cit.*, p 10.

about the availability and further details about the property. To improve its match capability and fulfill the demand for accommodation at any time, Airbnb depends on scale or a wide inventory of available listings.[1516]

Some other platforms such as Uber automatically match supply – drivers – with demand – riders – based on their geographic location. Uber's algorithms place a driver on the app of a rider based on their geographic proximity with the purpose of "providing an experience with low waiting time for both riders and drivers."[1517] In this case, the demand (riders) is largely time-sensitive, because if the supplier takes too much time to arrive to the pick-up location, the rider might take another alternative such as a taxi or public transportation. To address this issue, Uber relies on having as many cars as possible to meet the demand at a specific time and place. The platform tends to be accurate as possible by sending drivers to a specific location, based on the number of users (riders) in the geographic location and by analyzing statistics on the demand in the location/time frame. This model is only possible because Uber has such data about its users. This data is updated in real time.

Matching tools are also implemented to deliver advertisements with offers of goods, services, and work opportunities. The practice is referred to as targeted advertising and consists of differentiating internet users to direct them to the most suitable offers. Targeting gives companies the power to differentiate internet users based on a number of identifiable characteristics, such as their personal interests, age, race, sex, location, or behavior, among others. The possibility to target marketing with offers online is enhanced by the amount of data online platforms have about their internet users. This data is mainly collected, owned, managed, and processed by online platforms.

Google and Facebook, for instance, deliver advertisements with offers based on their user demographics and behaviors.[1518] They use personal and non-personal data such as sex, ethnic origin, age, sex, interests, geographic location, spoken language, previously used search words, and online interaction to deliver advertisement offers to their users.[1519] Facebook indicates the steps advertisers must follow to target a group of people with suitable personal aspects for their advertisement. The platform gives advertisers the possibility to include profiles with certain demographic aspects and to exclude others. Targeted users may be as precise as users in the United States, who are between the ages of 15–35, are also men, and use an iPhone 10.[1520] Additionally, companies are given the possibility to exclude users with certain aspects such as having a 2G network

---

[1516] Zoe Cullen, Chiara Farronato, "Outsourcing Tasks Online: Matching Supply and Demand on Peer-to-Peer Internet Platforms", *op. cit.*, p 35.

[1517] Dawn Woodard, "Dynamic Pricing and Matching in Ride-Hailing Platforms" (2019), *op. cit.*.

[1518] *See* chapter 4, section I.

[1519] *Ibid.*

[1520] *Onuoha v Facebook, INC.*, No. 5: 16-cv-06440-EJD (United States District Court Northern District California. Apr. 7, 2017), First Amended Complaint, p 11.

connection. Google allows advertisers to target internet users they want to reach when they do research on Google's search engine. With AdWords, advertisers can choose keywords they want to match with words searched by internet users in the search engine. When a company wants to advertise credit loan offers, it might choose words or phrases such as "looking for credit," "bank credit lines," "mortgage," and so forth. When the internet user with the target demographic markers search for these terms, ads related to it will be listed on the top of Google's index in the form of response links or, in some cases, images.

Matching or targeting tools are discriminatory when they exclude protected classes from the offer of certain services, such as housing, accommodation, credit offers, and employment positions. In the Roommates case, for instance, the platform required potential tenants to mandatorily answer a questionnaire using a drop-down menu that was provided automatically, about whether they were "male" or "female"; whether there were currently "straight male(s)," "gay male(s)," "straight female(s)," or "lesbian(s)"; whether they wanted to live with "straight or gay males/females," "only with gay males/females" or with "no males/females"; and whether they have children.[1521] Based on these mentioned profiles and preferences, Roommates matched users and provided them with a list of available room-seekers meeting their criteria. In short, the platform enabled users to search available rooms based on characteristics such as sex, sexual orientation, and familial status. Likewise, users were allowed to exclude potential tenants based on their sex, sexual orientation, and familial status, which, in principle, is not allowed by the Fair Housing Act in the United States.

In targeted advertisements, online platforms might increase discrimination against statutorily protected classes in the access to employment, goods, and services by allowing advertisers to granularly exclude internet users from receiving offers based on their personal features, including their ethnicity, sex, sexual orientation, age, and geographic location. The distinctive aspect of targeted advertising is the discriminatory delivery of offers and not their content. Discriminatory delivery based on sex, sexual orientation, ethnic origin, and age has been documented in the employment, credit, accommodation, and housing sectors.[1522] By design, internet users are only shown offers proposed by advertisements specifically addressed to them.

In *Onuoha v Facebook*, for instance, Facebook was charged for racial discrimination for allowing advertisers to exclude Black Americans, Hispanics, and Asian Americans from receiving their advertisements with housing, accommodation, employment, and credit offers.[1523] The class action was filed in the name of persons belonging to these protected classes who were based in the

---

[1521] *Fair Housing Council of San Fernando Valley v Roommates, LLC*, CV 03–9386 PA (RZx) (C.D. Cal. Nov. 7, 2008), p 3462.
[1522] *See* chapter 3.
[1523] *Onuoha v Facebook, Inc*, No. 5: 16-cv-06440-EJD (N.D. Cal. Apr. 7, 2017).

United States and were interested in receiving employment, housing, and credit opportunities, but they were ultimately excluded by Facebook's targeting tools. In the case, Facebook was charged for providing a design that had an unjustified disparate impact on Black Americans, Hispanics, and Asian Americans. This case was followed by other lawsuits against Facebook alleging that the platform's targeting tools allowed the exclusion of older workers and women from receiving employment opportunities.[1524]

In the cases against Facebook and Roommates, even though the platforms provided the means to include or exclude protected classes from receiving housing, accommodation, employment, and credit offers, advertisers had to deliberately choose to exclude protected classes. The process of choosing particular users or groups of users to receive the offers was not automatic, but instead based on a deliberate choice. In other words, discrimination was triggered by a human choice.

However, discrimination based on algorithmic choices has also been documented in the practice of targeted advertising. While it might be appealing to assume that algorithmic decisions are neutral from bias, algorithmic-generated discrimination has occurred on online platforms several times. On one occasion, an advertisement with employment offers for the STEM sector was proven to be shown over 20% more to men than to women in 191 countries[1525], even though the campaign targeted both men and women Facebook users to receive the employment offer. The hypothesis for such a disparity is that the algorithm used to target the offer had learned that female users were less interested in STEM from their behavior online; or, still, the algorithm had learned such bias when it was trained by an external data set; or, ultimately, the disparity may have reflected the economics of targeted advertising delivery. In any case, the 20% disparity was not a result of a deliberate choice of the advertiser of the employment offer to reach more male users than female users – it was an algorithmic decision. Other cases of algorithmic-generated bias in targeted delivery have been documented, including gender disparity and racial discrimination for employment offers on Google.[1526]

Discrimination against statutorily protected classes in targeted advertising is difficult to be detected. In some cases, online platforms allow users to know why they see a particular offer. This is the case with Facebook. When users

---

[1524] *Bradley v T-Mobile US, Inc.*, No. 17-cv-07232-BLF (N.D. Cal. June 4, 2019); *National Fair Housing Alliance v Facebook*, Inc., No. 1:18-cv-02689-JGK (S.D. N.Y. Aug. 08, 2018); *Spees et al v Facebook, Inc.* (EEOC, September 2018).

[1525] Anja Lambrecht and Catherine Tucker, "Algorithmic Bias? An Empirical Study of Apparent Gender-Based Discrimination in the Display of STEM Career Ads" (2019), *op. cit.*.

[1526] *See* chapter 3. Amit Datta, Michael Carl Tschantz and Anupam Datta, "Automated Experiments on Ad Privacy Settings: A Tale of Opacity, Choice and Discrimination", *op. cit.*; Latanya Sweeney, "Discrimination in Online Ad Delivery", *op. cit.*.

are interested, they may click on the button "Why am I seeing this ad?"[1527] In the class action charging Facebook for having a targeting policy that might disparately impact older workers, users were informed that they received a certain employment offer because the employer wanted to reach people interested in customer services, they were targeted based on their activities such as liking pages or clicking on ads, and the employer wanted to reach people ages 18–38 who live in a certain area of the United States.[1528] The difficulty resides on the fact that users who receive the targeted offer are able to know the reasons why they receive them, but the users who are excluded are not able to see the offers they were excluded from nor the reasons they were excluded. In the cases against Facebook, the class actions were triggered by equality organizations focused on promoting antidiscrimination policies because regular users were not aware of the reasons they were excluded from receiving advertisements with offers related to employment, credit, housing, or accommodation opportunities. In other cases, involving algorithmic discrimination and targeting based on online behavior, the only possibility to acknowledge a disparity is through statistic and experimental studies. The cases reported on Google were discovered in such studies.[1529]

2.4. SCALE, NETWORK EFFECT, AND LACK OF BUSINESS CONTROL

Online platforms create value by connecting the highest number of users interested in transacting or interacting with each other. Contrarily to the pipeline structure, where value is generated by the supplier of a product or a service, online platforms create value by fostering networks between individuals willing to provide services or goods and individuals willing to consume them.[1530] In this regard, online platforms are valuable for their network effects or, in other words, their capacity to build networks where any additional user will enhance the experience of all existing users. Given that users produce material value for the platform, scale is ultimately important for their business model. The more users a platform has, the more transactions are likely to happen.

Network platform structures raise concerns regarding discrimination because, contrary to pipelines businesses, network platforms have less control

---

[1527] *See* chapter 4.

[1528] *Bradley v T-Mobile US*, first amended complaint, p 26. Also, chapter 4.

[1529] Amit Datta, Michael Carl Tschantz and Anupam Datta, "Automated Experiments on Ad Privacy Settings: A Tale of Opacity, Choice and Discrimination", *op. cit.*; Latanya Sweeney, "Discrimination in Online Ad Delivery", *op. cit.*.

[1530] Geoffrey G Parker, Marshall W Van Alstyne, Sangeet Paul Choudary, *Platform Revolution: How Networked Markets Are Transforming the Economy and How to Make Them Work for You, op. cit.*, p 7.

and monitoring capacity in addition to no agency over the actions of their agents. The purpose of online platforms in their capacity as intermediaries is not to provide goods and services but instead to connect people willing to do so. In this context, discrimination against protected classes may scale when platforms do not have any incentive to monitor or train their users against it.

The housing market provides a comprehensive understanding of the above ideas of how networking effect and lack of central control have allowed pervasive discriminatory statements to remain online without further consequences. For instance, more than 10,000 of Craigslist's housing offers contained discriminatory statements and preferences against women and people of color in the United States.[1531] In this example, the number of property owners offering opportunities were neither limited by physical space, as with printed media; costs, because it was free of charge; nor any sort of central control, as the publications were not moderated. Over the years, the number of housing offers containing discriminatory preferences and statements against protected classes have come to the attention of the public.[1532] In other markets, such as Facebook, employers could exclude protected classes amongst their two billion users from receiving employment offers.[1533]

3. LEGAL CHALLENGES: LIABILITY OF ONLINE PLATFORM BUSINESSES, PURPOSES OF ANTIDISCRIMINATION LAWS, AND BUSINESS NECESSITY

3.1. AESTHETIC DESIGN CHOICES: SALIENCE OF PROTECTED MARKERS

Over the years, the design of online platforms have evolved from simple classifying listings into elaborated markets. The use of detailed demographic information, including names, gender, age, photographs, and personal preferences about suppliers, consumers, workers, or users – in the case of social networking – is widespread. Anonymity is not a threshold in these online places. As mentioned in the above section, the salience of personal markers aims to foster networking and trust.[1534] Nevertheless, the salience of protected markers, such as ethnic origin, sex, and age, when displayed before deals are concluded coupled with the total discretion users have over the conclusion of certain transactions intermediated by online platforms have proved to have a negative

---

[1531] National Fair Housing Alliance, *2010 Fair Housing Trends Report* (May 2010), *op. cit.*.
[1532] *See* chapter 1.
[1533] *See* chapter 3 and 4.
[1534] *See* chapter 1.

impact on users with protected aspects, particularly in housing, accommodation, and work offers.[1535] In other words, these users are more often refused by service providers.

The European Union, its member states, and the United States have comprehensive legislation to address discrimination against protected classes in housing transactions, in the access to places of public accommodations, and in the access to and termination from work positions and contracts.

In the EU, the Race Equality Directive, the Employment Equality Directive, the Gender Equality Directive, and the Gender Equal Access to Goods and Services Directive provide a legal framework that prohibits direct and indirect discrimination on the grounds of race, ethnic origin, and sex in the provision of services available to the public and employment/dependent self-employment work offers.[1536] Moreover, the Employment Equality Directive provides a framework for protection against discrimination on the grounds of religion, belief, disability, age, and sexual orientation in the context of employment and dependent self-employment.[1537]

In the United States, federal statutes prohibit discrimination on the grounds of race, color, religion, national origin, and disability in the provision of services and access to places of public accommodation.[1538] Moreover, federal fair housing statutes protect the grounds of sex and family status in addition to race, color, religion, national origin, and disability in the specific context of housing transactions.[1539] Ultimately, Title VII, concerning employment, protects the classes of race, color, religion, national origin, disability, age, and sex against discrimination in the access and conditions of employment.[1540]

Even though these comprehensive legal frameworks in the EU and in the United States prohibit direct and indirect discrimination against protected classes, they do not have any specific reference to platforms' design nor do they prohibit the disclosure of protected markers before transactions related to housing, accommodation, employment, and goods and services offers are concluded. In offline transactions, protected markers are ubiquitously disclosed when job seekers apply for a job, potential tenants visit a real estate property, customers buy a certain product, or individuals seek credit. In the lawsuits against Airbnb and Uber, the aesthetic design chosen by those platforms were not sufficiently challenged by plaintiffs or assessed by the judges.[1541]

[1535] See Airbnb, chapter 2.

[1536] Article 3, Race Equality Directive; Article 1, Gender Equal Access to Goods and Services Directive.

[1537] Article 3, Employment Equality Directive; Article 1, Gender Equality Directive. several European Member States have laws with broader personal scope.

[1538] 42 U.S.C. §2000a (a), (b) and (c), title II of the Civil Rights Act (Public Accommodations) and 42 U.S.C. §12181 (ADA).

[1539] FHA, 42 U.S.C. §3605 (a)(b).

[1540] 42 U.S.C. §2000e(b) (2006) and §2000e(b) (Title VII).

[1541] See chapter 2 and 6.

Antidiscrimination laws, in the United States and in the EU, do not aim to hide individuals to protect them against discrimination.

When faced with charges of discrimination because users have refused to provide a service due to the alleged reason of other users' protected aspects, online platforms have consistently used as a basis of defense the liability exemption attributed to online intermediaries for the wrongdoings of their users.[1542] Even if scholars and researchers have raised the possibility of the platform's aesthetic design to facilitate certain forms of discrimination, so far, this approach has been less used in litigation, because hiding protected markers to avoid discrimination was never a strategy embedded in legislation or desired by certain antidiscrimination groups.[1543]

In the Airbnb case, for instance, Gregory Selden, in the name of racial minorities in the United States who might have faced discriminatory refusals when requiring about an accommodation, charged Airbnb in its condition as a hotel or real estate agency of illegally discriminating against prospective hotel guests or tenants on the basis of race. The reason to relate Airbnb to a hotel or real estate agency is founded on the fact that, generally, Internet Service Providers, such as Airbnb, have no liability over their users' illegal actions.

In the United States, since the last century, the federal statute Communications Decency Act of 1996 protects Internet Service Providers from liability for third-party wrongdoings and content. In this regard, the statute determines that Internet Service Providers may not be treated as publisher or speaker of "any information provided by another information content provider"[1544] and that Internet Service Providers shall not support tort liability in cases it takes "any action in good faith to restrict access to or availability of material that the provider or user considers to be objectionable."[1545] This regime does not hold Internet Service Providers liable for illegal third-party content/wrongdoings, even when they acknowledge it and do not remove it or take it down.[1546] Online platforms in their capacity as Internet Service Providers have been exempted from liability for their users' wrongdoings by district courts and courts of appeals based on this provision.[1547]

Given this exemption of liability for Internet Service Providers, antidiscrimination lawyers have attempted to frame online platforms, not as Internet Service Providers, but instead as the businesses that provide the main

---

[1542] *See* chapter 2,4 and 6.
[1543] Laura W Murphy, *Airbnb's to Fight Discrimination and Build Inclusion: A Report Submitted to Airbnb*, p 5–8.
[1544] §230, c, CDA.
[1545] §230, 2, A, CDA.
[1546] *See* chapter 1.
[1547] Examples: Noah v AOL Time Warner, Inc., 261 F. Supp. 2d 532 (E.D. Va. 2003); Barnes v Yahoo Inc, no 05–36189 (9th Cir., 2009); Chicago Lawyers' for Civil Rights v Craigslist, 519 F.3d 666 (7th Cir. 2008).

service, such as hotels, real estate agencies, publishers, or even transportation companies.[1548] These businesses, contrarily to Internet Service Providers, may face vicarious liability for the wrongdoings of their representatives, including discrimination against clients.[1549]

The strategy to compare online platforms with other businesses is not free of problems. So far, in the United States, district courts and courts of appeals have held, for instance, real estate companies and companies that offer places of public accommodation, such as hotels, liable for discrimination conducted by their agents against protected classes of home seekers or clients.[1550] However, vicarious liability in the United States is conditioned by agency theories.[1551] In this sense, companies are liable for their representatives' illegal actions when there is a relationship of subordination between the company and their representatives. This context often happens in employment relationships.[1552] In such cases, the company's representatives were acting within the course of their employment responsibilities. No fault on the part of the company is required, and they will be liable for their employees' wrongdoings because of their duty to supervise and control the action of their agents or employees. Some lawyers sustain that on top of a subordination relationship, companies must be vicariously liable only in cases of negligence.[1553]

In any case, vicariously liability results in monetary compensation for the victim of the wrongdoing. When companies are held vicariously liable for their agents' actions, they must redress the victims for both punitive and compensatory damages. As a result, corporate vicarious liability incentivizes companies to properly train and manage their employees. In some cases, corporate vicarious liability is also essential to redress victims of wrongdoings because companies often have more financial means than the agents of misconduct.[1554]

The problem of relating Internet Service Providers such as Airbnb and Uber to traditional real estate, transportation business, or publishers to charge them with vicarious liability in cases of discrimination perpetrated by their users is that rules of vicarious liability apply to corporations that establish a

---

[1548] Particularly in the cases: Selden v Airbnb, Inc, No. 16-cv-00933 (CRC) (D.C. Col., 2016); Onuoha v Facebook, Inc, No. 5: 16-cv-06440-EJD (N.D. Cal., 2017); Yucesoy v Uber Technologies, Inc., 109 F. Supp. 3d 1259 (N.D. Cal. 2015); O'Connor v Uber Technologies, Inc, 82 F. Supp. 3d 1133 (N.D. Cal. 2015); Airbnb, Uber, Facebook.

[1549] *See* chapter 1.

[1550] Michael Todisco, "Share and Share Alike: Considering Racial Discrimination in the Nascent Room-Sharing Economy" (2014) *op. cit.*, p 127 and *Meyer v Holley*, 123 S.Ct. 824,829 (2003).

[1551] *See* chapter 1.

[1552] Joy S Kimbrough, "The Federal Housing Act: No More Absolute Owner Liability When Employees Discriminate" *op. cit.*, p 116 and 121.

[1553] *See* chapter 1.

[1554] Jessica Reingold Katz, "Finding Fault: Implications of Importing the Title VII Standard for Vicarious Punitive Liability to the Fair Housing Act" (2008), *op. cit.*.

relationship of subordination with their agents, in typical employment or similar arrangements. Precedents have shown that a theory of vicarious liability is not applicable in cases where companies lack authority over their agents, which is the most common relationship between companies that own online platforms and their users.[1555]

As a consequence, in the United States, when users discriminate against others in the provision of services – facilitated by aesthetic design choices – online platforms will likely avoid vicarious liability either because they are held as Internet Service Providers, and they fall into the scope of Section 230 of the CDA 1996, or because they are held as the service's company (main provider), but there is no relationship of subordination between them and their users, and, the rules of vicarious liability are conditioned to a subordination relationship.

In the European Union, Internet Service Providers have also been exempted from the wrongdoings of their users with some exceptions. The legal framework for the liability of Internet Service Providers for illegal third-party content/ wrongdoings has been set by the Directive on Electronic Commerce and its transposed legal provisions. Internet Service Providers are exempted under Article 14 of the Directive on Electronic Commerce from civil liability for illegal third-party wrongdoings/content when they have no knowledge about it.[1556] Therefore, hosting services, such as online platforms, are only immune to liability for users' illegal conduct while they are not aware of their illegal existence. Once they are aware of it, they must assess its legality and act expeditiously to remove access to it.[1557] This system referred to as the notice-and-takedown mechanism[1558] places Internet Service Providers in Europe as private gatekeepers of what shall remain online.[1559] The liability of online platforms for third-party wrongdoings will remain similar to what the Directive on Electronic Commerce has established, once the Digital Services Act (DSA) enters into force.[1560] The DSA creates substantial changes regarding the accountability of online platforms but does not modify their liability regime consolidated in the Directive on Electronic Commerce and by the CJEU case law.

Over the years, the CJEU has settled that the condition to establish exemption of liability to Internet Service Providers for third-party wrongdoings depends on whether the role played by them is neutral.[1561] The Court construed

---

[1555]   *See* chapter 1.

[1556]   Article 14, 1 (a), Directive on Electronic Commerce.

[1557]   Article 14, 1 (b), Directive on Electronic Commerce.

[1558]   Vassilis Hatzopoulos, *The Collaborative Economy and the EU Law, op. cit.*, p 47..

[1559]   Aleksandra Kuczerawy, "The Power of Positive Thinking: Intermediary Liability and the Effective Enjoyment of the Right to Freedom of Expression" (2017), *op. cit.*, p 227;

[1560]   Proposal for a Regulation of the European Parliament and of the Council on a Single Market for Digital Services (Digital Services Act) and amending Directive 2000/31/EC. COM/2020/825 final.

[1561]   *See* C-18/18 *Glawischnig-Piesczek v Facebook*, ECLI:EU:C:2019:821; C-236/08 *Google France v Louis Vuitton* EU:C:2010:159, §114.

that neutrality means that the internet provider merely conducts the content in a technical, automatic, and passive manner and lacks knowledge or control over the content stored.[1562] Internet Service Providers are not neutral when they somehow assist in promoting third-party content by optimizing the presentation of the offers, for instance.[1563]

Concerning the liability of online platforms for their users' discrimination against other users, platforms, in their capacity of Internet Service Providers, only hold liability for their users' discriminatory misconduct once they acknowledge it and do not take any expeditious action to address it. Not taking expeditious action to remove third-party illegal content/wrongdoings makes platforms liable for the damages caused by the third-party illegal content/wrongdoings.

This system is more balanced and differs from the American liability regime, because Internet Service Providers in the United States are not liable for third-party illegal wrongdoings in general even when they acknowledge it and do not take any expeditiously measure to remove it, except in cases related to copyrighted content, trademark infringement, and criminal and electronic communications privacy law breaches.[1564] However, the liability of online platforms is still conditioned to their knowledge and lack of action about their users' wrongdoings in the EU.

The approach of comparing online platforms to traditional businesses to attribute vicarious liability in case of their users' discriminatory conduct against other users is also not free of obstacles in EU countries. While cases have been reported of discrimination involving real estate agents against potential home seekers, whether they were required to do so or not by the house owner, a company's vicarious liability often requires a link of subordination with their agents.[1565]

The issue of whether companies face vicarious liability in the cases their agents perpetrate direct discrimination against prospective tenants and clients is regulated by the laws of the member states.[1566] Overall, companies/employers are vicariously responsible for the illegal behavior of their employees. This context is particularly clear in legal statutes in Austria, Belgium, Denmark, Ireland, and the UK (for the UK, until January 2020).[1567] Some convergence is found about the conditions by which the company/employer might be responsible for its employees' actions, including the fact that the illegal conduct is committed

---

[1562] Case C-236/08 *Google France v Louis Vuitton* EU:C:2010:159, §114.
[1563] Case C-324/09 *L'Oreal v eBay* EU:C:2011:474, §123.
[1564] CDA, section 230 (e) (1)-(4).
[1565] *See* chapter 1.
[1566] Helmut Werner, Eugenia Caracciolo di Torella, Bridgette McLellan, *Gender Equal Access to Goods and Services Directive 2004/113/EC: European Implementation Assessment* (January 2017), *op. cit.*, p 69 (1-29).
[1567] *Ibid*, p 69 (1-29).

during the time and under the subordination of the employment chore, and the company was negligent in preventing the employee to act unlawfully. Cases of non-employment vicarious liability are considerably limited among the member states[1568] and mainly concern the responsibility of schools over their students' actions.[1569]

The matter of whether online platforms shall be vicariously liable for the illegal actions conducted by their users in their contractual relationships with other users was argued in contexts different from discrimination in the member states.[1570] For instance, in France, Airbnb was held liable for negligently allowing users to illegally rent their apartment through the platform without the proper consent of the apartment owner, which is forbidden in France.[1571]

Regarding the liability of online platforms for discrimination perpetrated by users against users, Daft, a real estate online platform focused on matching property seekers with homeowners, was held liable for publishing third-party discriminatory housing advertisements on its platform in Ireland.[1572] Several third-party advertisements for rental properties were visible on Daft with conditions such as "suit family only,"[1573] which excluded persons who were not under the meaning of family provided by the Equal Act; "would suit young professionals," which excluded older tenants[1574]; "rent allowance not accepted" and "work letter of reference needed,"[1575] which excluded persons who received public rent supplement. The Irish Human Rights and Equality Commission decided that the advertisements discriminated against prospective tenants on the grounds of age, family status, and social economic status. Moreover, the Equal Status Act expressly provides that "a person shall not publish or display or cause to be published or displayed" advertisements that indicate an intention to discriminate or "might reasonably be understood as indicating such an intention."[1576]

[1568] See Phillip Morgan, "Certainty in Vicarious Liability: A Quest for a Chimaera?" (2016), *op. cit.*.
[1569] Aileen Mc Colgan, *National Protection Beyond the Two EU Anti-Discrimination Directives: The Grounds of Religion and Belief, Disability, Age and Sexual Orientation Beyond Employment* (September 2013), *op. cit.*, p 45.
[1570] Vassilis Hatzopoulos, *The Collaborative Economy and the EU Law, op. cit.*, p 22.
[1571] Airbnb was notified a few times about the illegal rental. Tribunal d'Instance, Paris, Jugement du 6 février 2018, RG 11-17-000190. There was a reported case in the Netherlands. Rosalie Koolhoven, *Impulse Paper on Specific Liability Issues Raised by the Collaborative Economy in the Accommodation Sector, Paris-Amsterdam-Barcelona* (May 2016), *op. cit.*, p 12. Referring to *Duinzigt* Hoge Raad 16 October 2015, NL:HR:2015:3099, Prejudiciele beslissing op vraag van NL:RBDHA:2015:1437.
[1572] *Irish Human Rights and Equality Commission v Daft Media Limited t/a Daft/ie*, ADJ-00005960, WRC, August 2019.
[1573] Section 2, (c), Equal Status Act 2000–2015. (Family status).
[1574] Section 3, (f), Equal Status Act 2000–2015. (Age status).
[1575] Section 3, (3B), Equal Status Act 2000–2015. (Housing assistance status).
[1576] Section 12, I, Equal Status Act 2000–2015.

The Irish Human Rights and Equality Commission compromised to withdraw the complaint if Daft agreed to write a statement refraining itself from publishing discriminatory offers.[1577] Daft refused to make such a commitment by arguing that it was not the advertiser nor the publisher of the illegal content, but alternatively an Internet Service Provider that gave neutral access for users to publish their offers in the terms provided by the Directive on Electronic Commerce and the transposed Irish statute.[1578] These statutes do not impose any legal responsibility on Internet Service Providers to monitor the content published by third-parties – users – and, in addition, make Internet Service Providers immune for liability on such illegal content when they are not aware of their existence. Daft argued that it had voluntarily offered several measures to help advertisers in complying with the Equal Status Act, including the implementation of a tool that put on hold advertisements containing terms previously reported as discriminatory. Daft also implemented a "notice-and-take-down" policy. All users were able to report discriminatory content with a flag system. Finally, Daft implemented a section dedicated to educating users about the illegal discriminatory language that shall not appear in housing offers.

When the case was referred to adjudication, the Workplace Relation Commission ruled Daft was vicariously liable for the illegal discriminatory housing offers published by third-parties. The Commission refused to recognize that the Directive on Electronic Commerce safeguarded Daft from liability imposed by the Equal Status Act, because according to the Commission Daft was not an Internet Service Provider, but instead a company that provides services related to accommodation, equivalent to real estate agencies. The Equal Status Act, in particular, forbids companies to discriminate against protected classes when they provide services related to accommodation.[1579] In addition, the Commission imposed Daft to "refrain from publishing or, displaying, or permitting to be published or displayed on its website advertisements" that discriminate against protected classes.[1580] In practice, the Commission required from Daft the responsibility to monitor third-party housing advertisements prior to their publication.

In my view, the decision is problematic because it imposed on Daft the duty to monitor several thousands of third-party contents published daily on its server. This inverts the logic settled by the Directive on Electronic Commerce that services such as Daft should not be imposed to monitor illegal content, but instead should be compelled to take it down once they are aware of it. This decision shows how fine the line is to distinguish Internet Service Providers that

---

[1577] *Irish Human Rights and Equality Commission v Daft Media Limited t/a Daft/ie*, ADJ-00005960, WRC, 2019.
[1578] Article 14, Directive on Electronic Commerce and Regulation 2003, (S.I. 68 of 2003) (Ireland).
[1579] Article 6 (1)(c), Equal Status Act 2000–2015.
[1580] *Irish Human Rights and Equality Commission v Daft Media Limited t/a Daft/ie*, ADJ-00005960, WRC, 2019.

intermediate the relation of users from companies that provide other kinds of services.

Regarding the liability of online intermediaries, however, the design of matching tools does not benefit from the same set of immunities enshrined in the Communications Decency Act and the Directive on Electronic Commerce.

3.2. MATCHING TOOLS: PLATFORMS AS CONTENT PROVIDERS

Both the Directive on Electronic Commerce and the Communications Decency Act exempt Internet Service Providers from tort liability for illegal third-party wrongdoings and content under certain circumstances. Matching tools are not third-party content, but, alternatively, they are developed, designed, and provided by online platform businesses. Neither the Directive on Electronic Commerce nor the Communications Decency Act exempt Internet Service Providers for discriminating by design when they provide matching tools that will necessarily cause their users to discriminate against protected classes. When an online platform's matching tools mandatorily make property owners, employers, and business in general exclude protected classes from their search or from receiving their offer, these online platforms breach antidiscrimination laws for developing such tools.[1581]

In the United States, an example of how online platforms are not exempted from liability when they provide matching tools that are discriminatory is found in the *Fair Housing Council of the San Fernando Valley v Roommates* case. Roommates was held liable for designing a drop-down menu that matched individuals looking for a shared place to live based on protected grounds.[1582] In this case, the matching tool gave the possibility for landlords to exclude or include potential tenants based on their gender, sexual orientation, and family status. On the one hand, landlords had to mandatorily fill these categories, on the other hand, potential tenants had to provide their gender, sexual orientation, and family status to use the services provided by the platform. In the case, the Fair Housing Act and the California Fair Employment and Housing Act outlawed discrimination against house seekers based on these criteria.[1583] When the platform actively created the drop-down menu with questions and choices for answers that were illegal under the terms of the Fair Housing Act and California Fair Employment and Housing Act, the platform was not only the carrier of the

---

[1581] *Fair Housing Council of San Fernando Valley v Roommates, LLC*, 2012 WL 310849 (9th Cir. February 2, 2012) and *Irish Human Rights and Equality Commission v Daft Media Limited t/a Daft/ie*, ADJ-00005960, WRC, August 2019.

[1582] *Fair Housing Council of San Fernando Valley v Roommates, LLC*, 521, F.3d 1157 (9th Cir. 2008).

[1583] The FHA 42 U.S.C. §3601 et seq. and Section 804 [42 U.S.C. 3604], FEHA, §12955 (a).

illegal questions but also the author. Roommates was the "information content provider" in addition to acting as the Internet Service Provider.[1584] A real estate agent, for instance, when intermediating a housing transaction, cannot ask about the sexual orientation and the family status of a prospective tenant in California.[1585]

The Court of Appeals ruled that Roommates was not protected by Section 230 of the Communications Decency Act from tort liability for implementing a questionnaire that required potential tenants to disclose their sex, sexual orientation, and familial status. Moreover, Roommates was liable for limiting the scope of searches according to the users' preferences based on the potential tenants' sex, sexual orientation, and familial status, and it was also liable for implementing a matching system that paired landlords and tenants based on those preferences. The Court of Appeals confirmed that the CDA only grants immunity for publishing third-party illegal content, as long as the illegal content is wholly created by third-parties and not by the provider itself.[1586] In short, inducing landlords to express illegal preferences is not shielded by the CDA.[1587] The case was vastly commented on because of the discussions held in the ruling around design and immunity provided by the CDA.[1588] Roommates' discriminatory design was not protected by the CDA and was considered to breach the terms of the Fair Housing Act and FEHA.[1589]

However, less explicit forms of matching users and content exist, such as the case of targeted advertising. Online platforms may deliver advertisements with offers to users with specific demographic details, including their geographic location, gender, ethnic origin, and sexual orientation, among several others. Advertisements may contain housing, employment, and credit offers, for instance. The practice poses risks to the principle of equality by excluding protected classes from receiving offers concerning services, goods, and employment. Is it legal to send housing advertisements only to white internet users? Or is it legal to exclude women from an employment offer advertisement?

In the United States, even though no specific federal law explicitly addresses discrimination in targeted advertising practices, throughout the past decades, enforcement agencies and federal courts have construed that Title VII of the Civil Rights of 1964 (employment-related discrimination), the Fair Housing

---

[1584] *Fair Housing Council of San Fernando Valley v Roommates, LLC*, CV 03–9386 PA (RZx) (C.D. Cal. Nov. 7, 2008), §3455.

[1585] FEHA, §12955 (a).

[1586] CDA, 47 U.S.C. §230, (c)(2).

[1587] *Fair Housing Council of San Fernando Valley v Roommates, LLC*, CV 03–9386 PA (RZx) (C.D. Cal. Nov. 7, 2008), §3456.

[1588] *See* Varty Defterderian, "Fair Housing Council v Roommates.com: A New Path for Section 230 Immunity" (2009), *op. cit.*; Bradley M Smyer, "Interactive Computer Service Liability for User-Generated Content After Roommtes.com" (2009), *op. cit.*.

[1589] *Fair Housing Council of San Fernando Valley v Roommates, LLC*, 2012 WL 310849 (9th Cir. 2012).

Act (housing-related discrimination), and the Equal Credit Opportunity Act (credit-related discrimination) provide a cause of litigation against businesses that have invested in discriminatory advertising, not only when the content of the advertisement is discriminatory against a particular protected class but also in the cases in which certain individuals or communities with the majority of individuals with a protected class are targeted to receive the advertisements or are excluded from receiving them, regardless of the discriminatory content of the materials.[1590]

In the case of employment, for instance, when employers use targeted advertisements with employment offers, in practice they exclude individuals from receiving them. The exclusion of individuals is circumvented by Title VII of the Civil Rights Act of 1964[1591], the Age Discrimination in Employment Act of 1967[1592], and the Americans with Disabilities Act of 1990[1593], which prohibit, with some exceptions, employers from refusing to hire any qualified individual because of their "race, color, religion, sex, national origin," "age," and "disability" or from implementing any apparent neutral measure that has a disparate impact on individuals having one of these protected classes.[1594] In the context of employment offers, direct discrimination involves intentionally excluding employment applicants because of their protected aspects. Alternatively, indirect discrimination (disparate impact) involves the implementation of apparent neutral policies that disproportionately affect protected classes in a negative way.[1595] In this case, employers are liable for discrimination even when they did not have the intention to discriminate. Deciding to exclude users from certain neighborhoods or areas of the city might have a disparate impact in some minorities in spatially segregated cities.

The offer of goods and services, particularly, housing, places of public accommodation, and credit, are also protected against targeted advertising at the federal level. Regarding housing, precedents have established that targeting practices in advertisement content are not legal under the Fair Housing Act.[1596] When a particular newspaper constantly published real estate advertisements only with white models, the court considered that the offers were targeting white prospective tenants and excluding prospective Black American tenants. In this

---

[1590] Willy E Rice, "Race, Gender, 'Redlining' and the Discriminatory Access to Loans, Credit, and Insurance: A Historical and Empirical Analysis of Consumers Who Sued Lenders and Insurers in Federal and State Courts, 1950–1995", *op. cit.*.
[1591] Title VII, 42 U.S.C. §2000e-2(a)(1).
[1592] 29 U.S.C. §621 et seq., ADEA
[1593] 42 U.S.C. §12112 (a), ADA.
[1594] Title VII, 42 U.S.C. §2000e-2(k).
[1595] *Griggs v Duke Power Co.*, 401 U.S. 424, 91 S. Ct. 849, 28 L. Ed. 2d 158 (1971).
[1596] Ross D Petty, Anne-Marie G Harris, Toni Broaddus, "Regulating Target Marketing and Other Race-Based Advertising Practices", *op. cit.*, p 375.

case, the newspaper in its capacity of a publisher of the illegal content was held liable under the terms of the Fair Housing Act.[1597]

Concerning credit, targeted credit offers have not been tolerated by public authorities because of their potential to disparately impact protected groups[1598], even if the Equal Credit Opportunity Act does not mention discrimination related to advertising.[1599] The Act prohibits credit institutions and intermediaries (credit brokers) from discriminating against applicants, with respect to any aspect of a credit transaction, on the grounds of their race, color, religion, national origin, sex, marital status, and age.[1600] Precedents have settled that the practice of excluding protected classes from receiving credit offers breaches the Act.[1601] For instance, Chevy Chase Federal Saving Bank was sued by the United States Department of Justice for having refused to advertise its credit services in neighborhoods predominantly populated by Black American individuals.[1602] When the case was settled, the bank consented to advertise its credit services and make sales calls to real estate professionals in neighborhoods where Black Americans were overrepresented. Recently, the credit institution GE Capital was condemned for excluding credit to customers who have admitted speaking Spanish as their main language.[1603] A credit institution may target protected classes to receive their credit advertisements online, but they may not lawfully exclude these classes from receiving them.[1604] The Equal Credit Opportunity Act was enacted with the precise aim to prevent credit institutions from excluding some classes from credit opportunities. At the time, credit institutions often redlined minority neighborhoods and refused loans based on the property location.[1605] By analogy, this same rule applies to advertisements with credit offers online.

Credit institutions have direct tort liability when they exclude protected classes from their online credit offers.[1606] The question of whether other players

---

[1597] *Ragin v New York Times Company*, 923 F.2d 995 (2d Cir. 1991), §997. It is worth noting that, contrarily to other antidiscrimination statutes, the FHA provides liability to the publishers of discriminatory advertisements. FHA, 42 U.S.C. §3604(c).

[1598] Linda E Fisher, "Target Marketing of Subprime Loans: Racialized Consumer Fraud & Reverse Redlining" (2010), *op. cit.*.

[1599] 15 U.S.C. §1691 et seq., ECOA.

[1600] 15 U.S.C., §1691a (e), ECOA and 15 U.S.C., §1961(a)(1), ECOA.

[1601] Peter Swire, "Lessons from Fair Lending Law for Fair Marketing and Big Data", *op. cit.*, p 8; Carol Evans, Westra Miller, "From Catalogs to Clicks: The Fair Lending Implications of Targeted, Internet Marketing" (2019), *op. cit.*.

[1602] *United States v Chevy Chase Federal Saving Bank*, civil action n. CV94–1824JG (D.D.C. 1994).

[1603] Press Release, *CFPB Orders GE Capital to Pay $225 Million in Consumer Relief for Deceptive and Discriminatory Credit Card Practices* (June 2014), *op. cit.*.

[1604] Peter Swire, "Lessons from Fair Lending Law for Fair Marketing and Big Data", *op. cit.*, p 8.

[1605] Willy E Rice, "Race, Gender, 'Redlining' and the Discriminatory Access to Loans, Credit, and Insurance: A Historical and Empirical Analysis of Consumers Who Sued Lenders and Insurers in Federal and State Courts, 1950–1995", *op. cit.*.

[1606] 15. U.S.C., §1961(a)(1), ECOA. Contrarily to the FHA, the ECOA does not provide liability for publishers of such offers.

involved in advertising credit offers, such as online platforms, would also be liable for illegal targeting in these cases remains open. The liability of Internet Service Providers comes into play again.

The exclusion of protected classes from receiving employment, housing, and credit offers through targeted advertisements has served as a basis for several class actions against Facebook.[1607] The liability of the platform for third-party targeting was at stake. Facebook had implemented tools that allowed companies to target the users who received their advertisements with great demographic precision. Between 2016 and 2018, class actions were filed against Facebook seeking declaratory and injunctive relief, penalties, and monetary damages to redress racial, sex, and age discrimination, based on what the lawyers then called Facebook's "exclude people" button.[1608] Plaintiffs alleged that the platform and its third-party advertisers had breached Title VII of the Civil Rights Act, the Fair Housing Act, and the Equal Credit Opportunity Act, among other statutes, by excluding protected classes from receiving their advertisements with housing, credit, and employment offers.

In the first case, *Onuoha v Facebook,* Facebook was charged for racial discrimination for providing tools to companies that allowed them to exclude Black Americans, Latinos, and Asian Americans from receiving advertisements with housing, employment, and credit opportunities. At the time, Facebook had 26 million users who identified as "African Americans," eight million who identified as "Asian Americans," and 32 million who identified as "Hispanic." These people did not receive several advertisements with employment vacancies and credit and housing opportunities. Similarly, in the second case, *Bradley et al. v T-Mobile US,* Facebook was charged for illegally excluding older users from receiving third-party employment advertisement offers.[1609] The class action advocated for the rights of older workers to be free of age discrimination in employment advertising, recruitment, and hiring practices through Facebook. Finally, in *Spees et al. v Facebook,* female class representatives accused Facebook of targeting and sending employment advertisements and related recruitment and hiring opportunities to male Facebook users "while excluding female prospective job applicants from receiving the job advertisements and opportunities."[1610]

In these cases, the protected classes argued that Facebook was not a passive player in its advertising business. Instead, the tools provided by Facebook

---

[1607] See chapter 4.
[1608] *Onuoha v Facebook, Inc.,* No. 5: 16-cv-06440-EJD (N.D. Cal. Apr. 7, 2017); *Bradley v T-Mobile US, INC.,* No. 17-cv-07232-BLF (N.D. Cal. June 4, 2019); *National Fair Housing Alliance v Facebook, Inc.,* No. 1:18-cv-02689-JGK (S.D. N.Y. Aug. 08, 2018); *Riddick v Facebook, Inc.,* No. 3:18-cv-04429 (N.D. Cal. Mar. 19, 2019); *Spees et al v Facebook, Inc.* (EEOC, September 2018).
[1609] *Bradley et al v T-Mobile US, Inc. et al,* (cv 07232, United States California Northern District Court, 2017), amended complaint, p 8. Breaching the ADEA.
[1610] *Spees et al v Facebook, Inc.* (EEOC, September 2018).

constituted a central element for companies to selectively advertise in a discriminatory manner. While Facebook decided that it was desirable to limit which users would be able to see advertisements based on their race, national origin, location, age, and sex, federal and state statutes prohibit racial, age, and sex discrimination in advertising employment, housing, and credit opportunities.

Plaintiffs compared Facebook to a traditional publisher, employer, employment agency, credit institution, and housing agency to seek tort liability from the platform. The liability of publishers, employers, employment agencies, creditors, and housing agencies for discrimination in the offer of credit, housing, and employment are explicitly provided by several civil rights acts. However, Facebook claimed that as an Internet Service Provider it could not be liable for the acts of its users.[1611] In the context, the Communication Decency Act would exempt it from tort responsibility for the third-party content and third-party targeted advertisements.[1612] Advertisers should be the only ones responsible for the targets they chose. Ultimately, the platform only provided neutral matching tools to them. In the case, third-party advertisers, and not the platform, had the power to select the criteria used to target their audience.[1613] Moreover, Facebook alleged that it had antidiscrimination policies forbidding discrimination in advertising.[1614] The difference between these cases and Roommates is that, on Facebook, advertisers had the freedom to target users or not, while in Roommates, users mandatorily had to select categories on the drop-down menu. Finally, the cases against Facebook were privately settled and the platform's liability was not assessed.

However, over the years, Facebook's tort and criminal liability for publishing illegal third-party content have been consistently denied by district courts and courts of appeals.[1615] Recently, the Supreme Court rejected hearing a case against Facebook claiming it provides material support to terrorists when it hosts their content.[1616] The case concerned the family of Americans who were injured or killed during attacks in Israel. The parties had claimed that Facebook's algorithm promoted terrorist content to users who liked similar pages and posts and, therefore, should not be protected under the Communications Decency Act, which generally exempts Internet Service Providers from liability for illegal third-party content. The Court of Appeals had dismissed the case before by ruling that Facebook's recommendation system was fundamental for the proper functioning of the platform.

[1611] Particularly in *Onuoha v Facebook* and *Bradley v T-Mobile US* cases.
[1612] CDA 47 U.S.C. §230 (c)(1).
[1613] *Bradley v T-Mobile US*, motion to dismiss first amended complaint, p 12.
[1614] *See* chapter 4, section II.
[1615] *See* chapter 4, section II.
[1616] *Facebook, Inc., et al v. Superior Court of CA, et al* (Super. Ct. n 13035658, March 2020).

Even though the Communication Decency Act does not exempt online platform businesses for designing illegal content that lead to discrimination, such as matching tools, courts have been stringent when deciding the role of such instruments in the perpetration of discrimination by third-parties. In Roommates, users had to mandatorily choose a protected class in the matching tool, therefore, the platform was held liable for such a design.[1617] In the class actions against Facebook, advertisers had the option to exclude or include protected classes from receiving their targeted offers on the matching tool offered by the platform. Even though the case was not decided by the district court, other precedents regarding Facebook's liability for its algorithms tools promoting illegal third-party content suggest that it would be unlikely liable in the cases it provided matching tools that allowed advertisers to exclude or include protected classes from receiving their offers.

The practice of targeted advertising also encompasses monitoring internet users' activities; the collection of their data; and the creation of their digital profiles to ensure the delivery of the advertisement to the user with the required demographic aspects. Given that targeted advertising fully depends on the collection and processing of data, discrimination within the practice has been addressed by data protection and antidiscrimination laws together. Targeted advertisements are part of the concern of data legal experts and are often subjected to the scrutiny of data authorities in Europe and in the United States.[1618]

In the United States, privacy laws do not provide enough protection to internet users from being tracked and having their personal and demographic information collected and processed for online targeting purposes. No federal statute directly regulates data collection or misuse of data in the context of targeted advertising.[1619] The collection of personal data to online targeted advertising purposes is currently addressed in the light of the Federal Trade Commission Act[1620], even though the Act itself does not specifically mention privacy and was enacted more than 100 years ago. The Act forbids unfair and deceptive practices towards consumers.[1621]

The Federal Trade Commission understands that online targeted advertising is an allowed practice in the light of the Federal Trade Commission Act.[1622] However, the Federal Trade Commission has construed over the years that practices that are likely to mislead a reasonable consumer are deceptive and

---

[1617] *Fair Housing Council v Roommate.Com, LLC*, 666 F.3d 1216 (9th Cir. 2012).

[1618] *See* chapter 3.

[1619] *See* Hayes Hagan, "How to Protect Consumer Data? Leave It to the Consumer Protection Agency: FTC Rulemaking as a Path to Federal Cybersecurity Regulation" (2019), *op. cit.*.

[1620] FTC Act, 15 U.S.C., §§41–58.

[1621] FTC Act, 15 U.S.C., §§45.

[1622] Federal Trade Commission, *FTC Staff Report: Self-Regulatory Principles for Online Behavioral Advertising* (February 2009), *op. cit.*, p 4–5.

unfair under the Federal Trade Commission Act.[1623] Therefore, when companies have privacy policies and breach them, they are committing unfair and deceptive acts. It is worth noting that the Federal Trade Commission Act is only enforced by the Federal Trade Commission when companies have voluntary self-regulatory privacy policies and when they somehow breach them, because the Federal Trade Commission Act itself does not bind companies to have privacy policies informing their users how their personal data is used. The Commission considers that, when companies have self-regulatory privacy policies and do not respect them, they deceive consumers' expectations.

Even though the Federal Trade Commission has released guidelines with principles for targeting practices, they are not mandatory.[1624] These principles include the recommendation that companies may obtain expressed consent before collecting and using sensitive personal data described as financial data, data about children, health information, precise geographic location information, and social security numbers. Therefore, consumers' consent is not required for collecting and processing data such as gender, race, nationality, age, political beliefs, and most data used for targeted advertisement purposes. Given that consent for the collection of individuals' personal data is not mandatory in the context of targeted advertising, even though recommended by the Federal Trade Commission, consumers are not required in general to provide their consent to allow tracking cookies. Companies are only advised to request consent for tracking cookies that collect sensitive personally identifiable information, being financial data, data about children, health information, precise geographic location information, and social security numbers. The Federal Trade Commission has engaged in regulatory enforcement and private class action lawsuits against companies that have failed to disclose or have misrepresented their use of tracking cookies when they promised to do so in their private policies.[1625]

The commission feared that online companies could "webline" users notably in the real estate and financial markets.[1626] Scholars have argued that self-regulation is not the most effective way to protect consumers against the misuse of their data and against discrimination.[1627] Online platforms might legally collect their users' demographic data – without their knowledge and consent – to deliver specific goods, services, and employment offers.

[1623] Daniel J Solove, Woodrow Hartzog, "The FTC and the New Common Law of Privacy", *op. cit.*, p 628–629.

[1624] Federal Trade Commission, *FTC Staff Report: Self-Regulatory Principles for Online Behavioral Advertising* (February 2009), *op. cit.*.

[1625] *See* chapter 4, section I.

[1626] Steven C Bennett, "Regulating Online Behavioral Advertising", *op. cit.*, p 906.

[1627] Gordon Hull, "Successful Failure: What Foucault Can Teach Us About Privacy Self-Management in a World of Facebook and Bid Data" (2015), *op. cit.*.

In the European Union, antidiscrimination lawyers have barely addressed the issue of discriminatory online targeted advertising. However the practice is also widespread among online platform across EU countries[1628], and, the European Equality Directives and their transposed national laws could be used in the fight against discrimination in online targeted advertisement, especially in the employment sector. This legal framework protects individuals from being excluded from employment offers and from the provision of goods and services because of their protected characteristics, including their gender, ethnic origin, religion or belief, disability, age, or sexual orientation.[1629] Given that online targeted advertising takes into account personal characteristics – that can be a protected ground or not – to include or exclude individuals from receiving such offers, the European equality legal framework provides guidance on whether certain targeting practices are legal or not.

The Gender Equality Directive, Racial Equality Directive, and Employment Equality Directive aim to implement the principle of equality in the context of employment and occupation. The prohibition of direct or indirect discrimination against the aspects of race, ethnic origin, sex, religion, belief, age, sexual orientation, and disability might guide work conditions as well as the access to employment, including recruitment practices.[1630] In particular, employment applicants are under the personal scope of the directives and their transposed laws. In *Feryn*, the CJEU interpreted access to employment as included in both recruitment circumstances and selection requirements. In this case, the CJEU ruled that the exclusion of protected classes from employment recruitment was illegal.[1631] Even though no applicant for the job position was concretely identified, the CJEU construed that deliberated exclusion of a protected class from the employment offer was a sufficient reason to constitute direct discrimination.[1632]

The Court's reasoning in *Feryn* can be applied to online targeted employment offers. An employer might directly discriminate against employment applicants with one or more protected aspects by excluding them from receiving the online advertisement with the employment offer. In this instance, direct discrimination occurs even if no victim is identified. It is enough to identify that the advertiser has excluded a protected class from its targeting options to configure direct

---

[1628] *See* chapter 3.

[1629] Race Equality Directive; Employment Equality Directive; Gender Equality Directive; Gender Equal Access to Goods and Services Directive.

[1630] Gender Equality Directive, Article 14 (1)(a); Racial Equality Directive, Article 3(1)(a); Employment Equality Directive, Article 3 (1)(a).

[1631] C-54/07, *Centrum voor gelijkheid van kansen en voor racismebestrijding v Firma Feryn NV*, ECLI:EU:C:2008:397. *Also*, C-507/18, *N.H. c. Associazione Avvocatura per i diritti LGBTI – Rete Lenford*, ECLI:EU:C:2020:289 and C-81/12, *Asociaţia Accept v Consiliul Naţional pentru Combaterea Discriminării*, ECLI:EU:C:2013:275.

[1632] Case C-54/07, *Centrum voor gelijkheid van kansen en voor racismebestrijding v Firma Feryn NV*, ECLI:EU:C:2008:397.

discrimination. In this regard, if an online employment campaign is created and excludes female internet users, for instance, direct discrimination is a fact regardless of whether the victims of discrimination are identified or not.

Indirect discrimination might also occur in the context of targeted advertising of employment offers. Given that indirect discrimination materializes under European law when a facially neutral practice puts individuals with protected aspects at a disadvantage compared with other individuals in a similar position[1633], when employers target a specific IP address to advertise employment offers to certain groups in cities that have neighborhoods with spatial ethnic concentration, they indirectly discriminate against this group.[1634]

Concerning targeted advertisements with goods and services offers, the Race Equality Directive and Gender Equal Access to Goods and Services Directive protect the grounds of race, ethnic origin, and gender against discrimination in the access to goods and services. However, the Gender Equal Access to Goods and Services Directive explicitly excludes media content and advertisement from its material scope.[1635] The European Union left the member states free to regulate and set the boundaries of how goods and services shall be advertised.[1636] Most member states did not transpose the exclusion of media content into their equality laws when they transposed the directive into their national laws.[1637]

However, the protection against discrimination in advertising services and goods is related to the content of the ads. It is established that advertisements may not have discriminatory terms against protected classes. Less obvious is whether businesses may exclude protected classes when they deliver their advertisements either online or offline. With this respect, the *Association Belge des Consomateurs Test-Achats v Conseil des Ministres* case provides an example of how targeted advertisements involving the offer of insurance services is understood in the EU.[1638] In this case, the CJEU established that insurance institutions are not allowed to consider the gender of the insurance holder to determine their premiums. Despite this obligation, the European Commission guidelines on the application of the directive in light of this case made it clear that the directive does not apply to advertising. The guidelines determined that insurers may still use marketing strategies to captivate new clients by targeting

---

[1633] Gender Equality Directive, art 2(1)(b); Race Equality Directive, art 2(2)(b); Employment Equality Directive, art 2(2)(b).

[1634] Moreover, statistical data is not required to prove indirect discrimination in Europe. Even if statistics might be helpful in charges of indirect discrimination, the only requirement is that the neutral policy put the person in a disadvantageous position. C-237/94, *O'Flynn*, ECLI:EU:C:1996:206; and Sandra Fredman, *Discrimination Law, op. cit.*, p 187.

[1635] Article 3(3), Gender Equal Access to Goods and Services.

[1636] Evelyn Ellis, Philippa Watson, "EU Anti-Discrimination Law", *op. cit.*, p 368.

[1637] *See* chapter 3.

[1638] C-236/09 *Association Belge des Consomateurs Test-Achats v Conseil des Ministres*, ECLI:EU:C:2011:100.

either women or men to see their advertisements.[1639] In summary, the guidelines indicate that insurance companies may target their offers based on sex, even if they cannot differentiate the amount of premiums based on that same ground. However, further clarification about this issue might be necessary for the context of online targeting for goods and services in general.

The liability of online intermediaries when providing targeting tools that may or may not allow third-party users to discriminate when targeting their advertisements also comes into play in the context of the EU. Even though the CJEU has not assessed the liability of Internet Service Providers in the context of discrimination, it has ruled several times that Internet Service Providers are liable when implementing policies or tools that somehow helped users to commit wrongdoings. In this regard, it is precedential that Internet Service Providers are only exempted from liability under the terms of the Directive on Electronic Commerce for third-party wrongdoings when they play a neutral role.[1640] The CJEU has construed that neutrality means that the service provider merely conducts the content in a technical, automatic, and passive manner and lacks knowledge or control over the content stored.[1641] Additionally, Internet Service Providers are not neutral when they somehow assist in promoting the illegal content by optimizing the presentation of the offers.[1642] If Internet Service Providers offer targeting or matching tools that help users to illegally exclude protected classes from offers, they are not playing a passive role, according to the CJEU rationale.

The CJEU has more strict criteria to exempt Internet Service Providers from third-party liability than courts in the United States. Moreover, the CJEU has interpreted that the equality directives also protect employment applicants against discrimination. Therefore, the practice of excluding protected classes from receiving at least employment offers through online platforms is clearly illegal. Even if this possibility currently exists in Europe, on platforms such as Facebook, the practice has been overlooked by antidiscrimination scholars and researchers through the angle of antidiscrimination law.

Moreover, in the European Union, data protection laws provide a comprehensive framework to protect personal data from being collected, processed, and used in a discriminatory manner by automated systems in targeted advertising.[1643] The General Data Protection Regulation provides that

---

[1639] Guidelines on the application of Council Directive 2004/113/EC to insurance, in light of the judgement of the court of Justice of the European Union in case C-236/09.

[1640] See C-18/18 *Glawischnig-Piesczek v Facebook*, ECLI:EU:C:2019:821 and Case C-236/08 *Google France v Louis Vuitton* EU:C:2010:159, §114. Also, the Digital Services Act will have special rules for targeted advertising.

[1641] C-236/08 *Google France v Louis Vuitton* EU:C:2010:159, §114.

[1642] C-324/09 *L'Oreal v eBay* EU:C:2011:474, §123.

[1643] See European Union Agency for Fundamental Rights, *Handbook on European Data Protection Law, op. cit.*.

discrimination is a risk to the rights and freedoms of natural persons that may result from personal data processing.[1644]

The GDPR defines personal data as "any information relating to an identified or identifiable natural person."[1645] In this context, personal data comprise names, identification numbers, location data, online identifiers, or aspects related to the physical, physiological, genetic, mental, economic, cultural, or social identity of a natural person. Furthermore, IP addresses and tracking cookies have also been defined as personal data.[1646] The GDPR also specifies that processing special categories of personal data is *a priori* prohibited and should only be processed after explicit consent from the data subject.[1647] Special categories of personal data are usually named as sensitive data, and include data revealing racial or ethnic origin, political opinions, religious beliefs, philosophical beliefs, trade union membership, genetic data, biometric data with the aim of uniquely identifying a natural person, data concerning health, and data concerning a natural person's sex life or sexual orientation.[1648] The data defined as personal in the GDPR is collected and processed for targeted advertising.[1649]

The European Union approach to targeted advertising differs from that in the United States.[1650] In the EU, targeted advertising is legal as long as companies meet all the GDPR principles and have legal grounds for processing personal data. In the near future, the Digital Services Act will also provide further regulatory obligations on targeted advertising practices.

The GDPR is based on six sets of principles that must guide any targeted advertising practice. These principles include lawfulness, fairness, and transparency; legitimacy of purposes; data minimization; accuracy; time storage limitation; and integrity and confidentiality.[1651] The principles of lawfulness, fairness, and transparency that companies should meet when collecting and processing data for targeted advertising are essential in the fight against discrimination for multiple reasons. First, the requirement of lawfulness obliges businesses to comply with antidiscrimination laws when processing any personal data. Second, transparency requires businesses to make individuals/consumers aware of what kind of data are collected about them and for which purpose. If businesses respect the principle of transparency, consumers/individuals will be given a chance to learn which kind of personal data were used

---

[1644] Recital 75, GDPR.

[1645] Art 4 (1), GDPR.

[1646] *See* chapter 3.

[1647] Art 9 (2), GDPR.

[1648] Art 9 (1), GDPR.

[1649] Frederik Zuiderveen Borgesius, "Singling Out People Without Knowing Their Names: Behavioural Targeting, Pseudonymous Data, and the New Data Protection Regulation", (2016) *op. cit.*, p 257.

[1650] Philip Yannella, "The Differing US and EU Regulatory Responses to Rise in Algorithmic Profiling" (2018), *op. cit.*.

[1651] Art 5 (1) (a), (b), (c), (d), (e), (f), GDPR.

and were decisive to deliver a particular targeted advertisement to them. Third, the principle of fairness relates to the avoidance of discrimination. Fourth, legitimate purpose compels businesses to only collect and process personal data for precise purposes. These reasons cannot be vague, and therefore, businesses must be clear that are collecting personal data for targeted advertisements. Fifth, according to the principle of minimization, businesses shall only collect data that are useful for legitimate purposes, and not because this data might be useful in the future. Sixth, accuracy means that businesses must ensure that all data used to make a decision impacting individuals, or targeted advertising, is not flawed.[1652] Inaccurate data may lead to incorrect predictions about the data subject. In this case, businesses must proactively ensure that data subjects have the possibility to correct their data in case it is not accurate. In addition to the above six principles that must be met by businesses when processing personal data for targeted advertising, the GDPR ultimately requires valid consent from data subjects.

Even though data protection laws in the EU offer tools to avoid that the processing of personal data results in discrimination, these overarching rules do not provide any strong definition of discrimination – which implies practical obstacles to address concrete cases of discrimination. Similarly, the Digital Services Act does not offer a substantial legal definition of discrimination. Furthermore, antidiscrimination laws must be mobilized, which has not been done so far.

3.3. EVALUATION TOOLS: BUSINESS NECESSITY

Similarly to matching tools, evaluation tools are developed and provided by online platforms. Neither the Directive on Electronic Commerce nor the Communications Decency Act exempt Internet Service Providers *a priori* from tort liability for developing tools that will directly or indirectly discriminate against protected classes. However, in the United States, contrarily to the European Union, courts have held considerably restricted interpretations of whether the content/tools developed and provided by online platforms are not neutral and lead to discrimination. In cases against Facebook, courts of appeals have ruled that the platform had no liability over illegal third-party content even when it promoted it through algorithms and recommendation systems.[1653]

Several online platforms manage the permanence of their users through evaluation tools, which reflect the aggregated satisfaction of the demand about the experience on the service provided. Given that poor evaluations generally result in the unilateral termination of users' contract with the platform, scholars

---

[1652] Art 5(1) d, GDPR.
[1653] *Facebook, Inc., et al v. Superior Court of CA, et al* (Super. Ct. n 13035658, March 2020).

have argued that biased evaluations might result in the discriminatory exclusion of protected classes from online platforms.[1654] The main reason for this is that evaluation systems have had biased decisions that have mainly impacted the grounds of race and gender, particularly in online labor platforms.[1655] However, nothing prevents other protected grounds from also being affected.

Regarding platforms dedicated to labor, the risk of biased ratings is increased on on-demand platforms in which workers provide their service locally and have direct contact with clients.[1656]

In the United States, the liability of online platforms relies on their business identity, considering that courts have construed that they are not liable for the wrongdoings of their users even when users employ tools developed by them.[1657] Under the rationale that Section 230 of the Communications Decency Act exempts Internet Service Providers from third-party liability, the manner to hold online platforms liable for discriminating against users through their evaluation system is by framing them as employers or places of public accommodation. When employers and businesses considered as places of public accommodation have policies that discriminate against consumers and employees, they must be held liable under the Public Accommodation Act and antidiscrimination provisions of Title VII, the Age Discrimination in Employment Act, and the Americans with Disabilities Act.[1658]

Are online platforms places of public accommodation? Case law addressing the issue of whether online platforms are places of public accommodation is scant. Nevertheless, courts have already construed whether other sorts of online business shall be considered places of public accommodation. In a case concerning the liability of an online chat room and third-party harassing comments that blasphemed and defamed Islamic religion[1659], the referred district court ruled that the chat room should not be considered a place of public accommodation, because Title II makes it clear that "places of public accommodation" are limited to actual, physical places and structures. Since online businesses are not actual, physical facilities, they are considered virtual forums for communication provided by an Internet Service Provider.[1660] Moreover, in a case against Southwest Airlines[1661], the company was charged for violating Title III of the Americans with Disabilities Act[1662], given that its

---

[1654] Solon Barocas, Andrew D Selbst, "Big Data's Disparate Impact" (2016), *op. cit.*, p 732; Devin G Pope, Justin R Syndor, "Implementing Anti-Discrimination Policies in Statistical Profiling Models" (2011), *op. cit.*.

[1655] *See* chapter 5.

[1656] Such as the case of *TaskRabbit, Uber, Lyft*, and *Foodora*.

[1657] *See* Roommates case.

[1658] Title VII, 42 U.S.C., §2000e(b); ADEA, 29 U.S.C., §630 (b) and ADA, 42 U.S.C., §12112 5(A).

[1659] *Noah v AOL Time Warner, Inc*, 261 F. Supp. 2d 532 (E.D. Va. 2003).

[1660] *Welsh v Boy Scouts of America*, 993 F.2d 1267 (7ᵗʰ Circuit, 1993).

[1661] *Access Now, Inc. v Southwest Airlines, Co.*, 227 F. sup. 2d 1312, 1316 (S.D. Fla. 2002).

[1662] 42 U.S.C. §12182, Title III.

website was not compatible with "screen reader" programs, and, consequently, was inaccessible to blind persons. The issue of whether the airline's website should fit into the concept of a place of public accommodation under the Americans with Disabilities Act was pertinent, because if the website was considered a place of public accommodation, it should have then provided reasonable accommodation for blind users. The district court ruled that places of public accommodation under the Americans with Disabilities Act are restricted to physical, concrete structures, and the website was not a physical structure.[1663] In a more recent precedent, a district court ruled that Scribd[1664], a website/ service that allows subscribers to read eBooks from its library for a small fee, was a place of public accommodation under the category of library and should accommodate blind users by being accessible through a special screen reader software. However, this precedent would hardly hold online platforms as "places of public accommodation," because contrarily to Scribd, online platforms do not provide *a priori* services of accommodation, such as hotels, restaurants, and public transportation. Alternatively, online platforms provide services for networking.

Another possibility would be to frame certain platforms as employers of their service providers. Federal statutes provide significant legal protections against discrimination in the sphere of employment on the grounds of the employee's race, color, religion, sex, national origin, age, and disability.[1665] The personal scope of those rules relates to the worker's employment status. Self-employed workers are out of this scope.[1666]

Platforms' biased evaluation systems based on clients' ratings are comparable to cases where employers discriminated against their employees based on clients' discriminatory preferences. When employers implement customer feedback to guide their decisions about employees' work conditions, including sanctions or termination, they might meet antidiscrimination law requirements or otherwise face liability when protected classes are discriminated against due to the implementation of an evaluation policy. This outcome might happen when feedback is biased and employees suffer the termination of their contract due to their protected aspect. In this regard, Title VII of the Civil Rights Act, the Age Discrimination in Employment Act, and the Americans with Disabilities Act are partially equipped to hold employers liable for terminating their employees based on customers' discriminatory preferences.

Defining platforms workers' employment status has not been straightforward in the United States, mainly because of arbitration clauses and the difficulty

---

[1663]   *Access Now, Inc. v Southwest Airlines, Co.*, 227 F. sup. 2d 1312, 1316 (S.D. Fla. 2002).
[1664]   *National Federation of the Blind v Scribd, Inc.*, case 2:14-cv-162 (United States District Court for the District of Vermont 2015).
[1665]   Title VII 42 U.S.C., §2000e-2(a)(1); ADA, 42 U.S.C., §12112 (a), ADEA, 29 U.S.C., §623 (a)(1).
[1666]   Title VII, 42 U.S.C., §2000e(b); ADEA, 29 U.S.C., §630 (b) and ADA, 42 U.S.C., §12112 5(A).

to prove the level of control the platforms exert over their users.[1667] The disparate impact of some of on-demand platforms' organizational practices, including rating systems, risks never being assessed by District Courts because of the pervasiveness of arbitration clauses that waive trial rights imposed on most platform workers in the United States.[1668] Litigation related to the misclassification of Uber drivers and cases of discrimination concerning these same drivers were entirely rejected by district courts because the drivers consented to arbitration clauses when they started working for the platform.[1669]

However, even in cases where online platforms might be considered as employers, their liability for discrimination when they terminate the contract of their protected class employees based on biased clients' ratings is not considered direct, because courts have been accepting policies created to accommodate customers' preferences as a business necessity that justifies disparate impact against protected classes.[1670] Quantitative methods, such as evaluation systems that use rating scores, that potentially evaluate employees' performance in a biased-discriminatory fashion will most likely fit a charge of indirect discrimination, because in disparate impact charges the victims might only prove that the implemented "neutral" policy had a disproportional effect on protected classes, instead of having to demonstrate that the policy was implemented to discriminate against the protected class.[1671]

In the European Union, regarding the protection against discrimination in working conditions and termination of contracts, the personal scope of the Employment Equality Directive is less limited than Title VII of the Civil Rights Act, the Age Discrimination in Employment Act, and the Americans with Disabilities Act, but it still establishes outer limits. The directive applies to employment and to self-employment contracts[1672] to circumstances that include working conditions, dismissals, and payment.[1673] Scholars sustain that even though the directive clearly indicates that it applies to employees and self-employment contracts, given it expressly relates to employment and

---

[1667] Case *Uber*, chapter 5 and 6.

[1668] Jill Gross, "The Uberization of Arbitration Clauses" (2017), *op. cit.*, p 45.

[1669] For instance, in *O'Connor v Uber Technologies*, Inc, 82 F. Supp. 3d 1133 (N.D. Cal. 2015); *Kendall Reese v Uber Technologies, Inc.* (2:18-cv-03300, United District Court for The Eastern District of Pennsylvania, Aug 2018); and *Mohamed v Uber Technologies, Inc.*, 848 F.3d 1201 (9th Circuit 2016).

[1670] *EEOC v Sephora USA, LLC* 419 F.Supp.2ed 408 (United States District Court New York 2005). *See* chapter 5.

[1671] 42 U.S.C. §2000e-2(k)(1)(A)(i).

[1672] Art 3(1)(a) of the Race Equality Directive and Employment Equality Directive; Art 14(a) of the Gender Equality Directive. *See* Sandra Fredman, "Pasts and Futures: EU Equality Law", *op. cit.*, p 391.

[1673] Art 3(1)(c) of the Race Equality Directive and Employment Equality Directive; Art 14(c) of the Gender Equality Directive.

occupation[1674], a sort of subordination must be existent in the relationship between the hiring party and the individual.[1675] Therefore, the personal scope of the Employment Equality Directive might be limited to employees and dependent self-employed persons and would not comprise genuine self-employed workers.

However, the contractual status of platform workers is not relevant to the protection against discrimination on the grounds of race, ethnic origin, and sex, provided that the Race Equality Directive and the Gender Equal Access to Goods and Services Directive apply not only to work-related situations, but also in occasions concerning the access to goods and services. Therefore, rating systems that adversely impact individuals with a particular "race," ethnic origin, and sex are illegal, no matter if workers are employees, self-employed, or customers. Alternatively, the grounds provided by the Employment Equality Directive relies on the contractual status of workers. This distinction is important, because most online platforms do not employ their workforces but instead have services provided by self-employed persons or independent contractors. Cases concerning the reclassification of platform workers into employees have emerged in countries of the European Union.[1676] Moreover, discriminatory employment termination due to biased ratings was challenged in the UK. On this occasion, a woman driver argued that Uber's rating system placed women in a disadvantageous position compared to men.[1677]

The relevant issue remains of whether online platforms, either as an employer or service provider, are liable for direct or indirect discrimination in cases in which they terminate the contract of protected classes of workers based on discriminatory clients' ratings. So far, the CJEU has been scantly confronted with litigation involving employers' discrimination against employees to cater to customer preferences.[1678] In one precedent, the CJEU established that discriminatory treatment against employees due to organizational policies are acceptable when the purpose of the related policy is to maintain an image

---

[1674] Art 1 of the Race Equality Directive, Employment Equality Directive and Gender Equality Directive.

[1675] Catherine Barnard, *EU Employment Law, op. cit.*, p 347; Nicola Countouris, *The Changing Law of the Employment Relationship, op. cit.*, chapter 5.

[1676] Notably in the UK and in France, *O'Connor v Uber Technology Inc.*, 82 F Supp 3d 1133, 1135–38 (ND Cal 2015); *Yucesoy et al v Uber Technology Inc et al*, Civil Action No 1:14-cv-13938-IT (US District Court for the District of Massachusetts); *Uber BV v Aslam* [2018] EWCA civ 2748; Cour d'Appel de Paris, pôle 6, chamber 2, arrêt du 10 janvier 2019, sn rg 18/08357, n portalis 35L7-V-B7C-B6AZK.

[1677] Leigh Day, *British Female Driver Launches Sex Discrimination Claim Against Uber Over Practices* (September 2017).

[1678] Clients' evaluations might be comparable to an expression of their preference regarding employees. C-157/15 *Achbita v G4S Solutions NV* ECLI:EU:C:2017:203 and C-54/07 *Centrum voor gelijkheid van kansen en voor racismebestrijding v Firma Feryn NV*, ECLI:EU:C:2008:397.

of neutrality towards clients.[1679] In the case, a Muslim employee was fired because she wanted to wear a headscarf during her working hours.[1680] The company rejected her request and approved a written workplace regulation expressly prohibiting employees from wearing any visible signs of their political, philosophical, or religious beliefs due to the company's neutrality policies towards the clients. The company alleged that Ms. Achbita's behavior violated the neutrality policy in force. The CJEU ruled that the company did not directly discriminate against the employee, given the neutrality policy treated all workers of the company in the same way.[1681] Moreover, even if the neutrality policy had put individuals of a certain religion in a disadvantageous position, the policy did not result in indirect discrimination because it was objectively justified by a legitimate aim, and the means of achieving that aim were appropriate and necessary. In the case, the Court held that the business' interest to project an image of neutrality towards customers is legitimate under its freedom to conduct business[1682], and requiring employees not to wear a headscarf was a necessary and proportionate means to project the company's image of neutrality.

Considering that ratings might be considered as an expression of customers' preference, it has been argued that the *Achbita* and *Bougnaoui* cases might clarify how the CJEU would address the use of biased-customer ratings to base employment-related decisions.[1683] In *Bougnaoui*, the court ruled that clients' preference does not serve as a genuine occupational requirement that justifies discrimination against employees on the ground of religion.[1684] However, the Court ruled that the implementation of an organizational policy, such as the prohibition to wear headscarves in the presence of clients, to project the company's image of neutrality to the clients was a legitimate aim aligned with the freedom to conduct business in *Achbita*.[1685] Therefore, even though catering to clients' preferences does not justify direct discrimination against employees, a policy that prevents employees from expressing their religious conviction to project the image of neutrality is legitimate according to the freedom to conduct business.

Based on these cases, scholars support that the CJEU would likely assess the eventual negative impact on protected classes (termination of their contract)

[1679] For neutrality policies, *see* C-157/15 *Achbita v G4S Solutions NV* ECLI:EU:C:2017:203. Also, chapter 5, section II, 3.

[1680] C-157/15 *Achbita v G4S Solutions NV* ECLI:EU:C:2017:203, §12.

[1681] This position was vastly criticized. *See* chapter 5, section II, 2.2.2.

[1682] Article 16, Charter of Fundamental Rights of the European Union, OJ C 326, 26.10.2012, p 391–407.

[1683] Rossana Ducato, Miriam Kullmann, Marco Rocca, "European Legal Perspectives on Customer Ratings and Discrimination", in Tindara Addabbo, Ylenia Curzi, Olga Rymkevich, *Performance Appraisal in Modern Employment Relations: An Interdisciplinary Approach, op. cit.*, p 255.

[1684] *Asma Bougnaoui and ADDH v Micropole SA*, Case C-188/15, ECLI:EU:C:2017:204.

[1685] *Achbita v G4S Solutions NV* case-157/15 ECLI:EU:C:2017:203, §38.

by the implementation of a rating system as justifiable under the freedom to conduct business.[1686] Since the Court reasoned in *Achbita* that an organizational policy implemented to project the image of neutrality was legitimate under the freedom to conduct business, the Court would likely accept rating systems that put certain classes of employees in a disadvantageous position as legitimate aims to project an image of quality under the company's freedom to conduct business. In my view, this reasoning needs further verification in an eventual CJEU ruling. It is an extrapolation to consider that the image of neutrality would justify discrimination on other grounds, such as sexual orientation or disability, as a possibility allowed by the principle of freedom to conduct business.

4. TRANSPARENCY, FAIRNESS, AND BUSINESSES COOPERATION: AN ALTERNATIVE PATH

User-generated online content and activities have mushroomed in the past two decades. To a great extent, online platforms have intermediated, facilitated, and optimized participation online by creating specialized markets in which users can easily publish and exchange their assets with interested parties. As the number of user-generated activities and content have increased, more inquiries about whether or how online platforms should be liable for intermediating their users' illegal activities have been posed. On the one hand, the federal statute Communication Decency Act in the United States and its construed meaning by district courts and courts of appeals have set a precedent for strong intermediary immunity, in which intermediaries are only liable for any illegal content when they have actively contributed to its creation.[1687] Courts have been resistant to broaden the CDA meaning, even in cases where intermediaries help to promote third-party illegal content with algorithmic technology.[1688] Platforms are free to self-regulate their intermediation spaces at their convenience and on a voluntary basis. On the other hand, in the European Union the Directive on Electronic Commerce has provided a more balanced regime, in which intermediaries might hold liability for their users' illegal wrongdoings and content once they are notified. This co-regulatory regime imposes on online intermediaries the duty to be responsive to notifications, to assess their interest, and to act when necessary. These duties are not voluntary but are imposed by the Directive's regime.[1689]

I argue that the European regime of co-regulation offers more remedies for victims of discrimination in these online spaces without imposing an

---

[1686] Rossana Ducato, Miriam Kullmann, Marco Rocca, "European Legal Perspectives on Customer Ratings and Discrimination", *op. cit.*, p 261.
[1687] *Fair Housing Council of San Fernando Valley v. Roommates, LLC*, 2012 WL 310849 (9th Cir. February 2, 2012).
[1688] *See* chapter 1.
[1689] Art 14, Directive on Electronic Commerce.

inadequate burden on businesses. Online platforms, in cases of reported discrimination, for instance, must expeditiously act and remove the content posted by a user in the case of illegal activity. Alternatively, in cases where the platform does not expeditiously act, the victim can seek reparations from the platform business. This system creates incentives for platform businesses to be proactive against illegal activities occurring on their online spaces and through their intermediation. It also prevents victims, such as Cecilia Barnes who had her intimate photographs exposed along with her telephone number and address on fake profiles on Yahoo!, from being redressed for the defamatory content in the United States.[1690] Cecilia asked Yahoo! several times, for more than three months, to take the content down, without any results. The Court of Appeals for the Ninth Circuit ultimately held that the platform had, first, no liability for the defamatory content and, second, no legal duty to take it down.[1691]

Even though the EU framework provides more guarantees of remediation to victims of discrimination in online platforms, I also argue that both American and EU liability regimes do not consider several aspects embedded into these platforms' designs and algorithmic tools that might lead to discrimination. First, over-emphasizing users' protected markers is not illegal in any of the regimes. Second, even if courts in Europe and in the United States (under more stringent conditions) have held platforms liable for developing matching tools that have led users to necessarily discriminate against other users, most matching activities are undertaken outside the view and awareness of users.[1692] Third, final evaluations in scored systems do not provide any clear evidence that users were discriminated against because they represent an aggregated score without written opinions. In short, both the opacity of the criteria used by matching tools and the lack of clarity in rating systems hinder the awareness of potential discrimination engaged by these systems.

Against this backdrop, I suggest that the fight against discrimination in online platforms might produce the best results when also oriented by a model of regulation that incites online platforms to implement the principle of transparency and fairness in their interactions with users. The model of self-regulation to promote transparency and fairness in online platform markets has proven to fail, because businesses only acted after great civil society pressure and heavy-burdened lawsuits. In this sense, it is true that Facebook and Airbnb have acted to create tools to increase transparency and address discriminatory outcomes in their online markets, but they only did so after the formidable mobilization of the media and antidiscrimination activists.[1693] Accountability and regulatory incentives are necessary to address the issue of transparency in

---

[1690]   *Barnes v Yahoo Inc,* no 05–36189 (9th Circuit, 2009). Also, chapter 1.
[1691]   *Ibid.*
[1692]   Cases of targeted advertisement, for instance.
[1693]   *See* chapter 2 and 4.

online platforms that are less in the spotlight of the media in comparison to the big players.[1694]

With this in mind, the model provided by Regulation 2019/1150, which entered into force in July 2020 in the European Union, promotes fairness and transparency for business users of online intermediation services and may serve as an aspirational model for offering useful tools in the fight against discrimination by design.[1695] Even though the Regulation only applies to online intermediation services and online search engines that provide services to business users and corporate users and does not apply to online advertising tools[1696], it does provide some clues to address certain design aspects that might result in discrimination, such as opaque matching and evaluation tools.

The initiative for undertaking Regulation 2019/1150 that aims to ensure a fair, predictable, and trusted environment for users of online intermediation was the result of efforts to meet the goals of the Digital Single Market Strategy.[1697] These strategies included the objective to enable all actors of the digital market to be exposed to a fair and balanced environment with an adequate degree of transparency.[1698] In this regard, Regulation 2019/1150 empowers providers of services and goods in platform marketplaces, which are marked by great asymmetry of power. If, on the one hand, businesses operating online platforms possess great market strength and unilaterally dictate the contractual terms and structure of the marketplaces they intermediate, on the other hand, the provider/user side is highly fragmented and has weak power to determine the conditions of the market they operate in. Regulation 2019/1150 empowers providers against potentially harmful platform practices such as the "delisting of goods or services and the suspension of accounts without a clear statement of reasons; lack of transparency related to the ranking of goods and services and of undertakings offering them; unclear conditions for access to, and use of, data collected by providers."[1699]

Regulation 2019/1150 imposes on online platform businesses the duty to provide a clear statement with the reasons why they suspended or terminated users from their intermediation services.[1700] Moreover, it

---

[1694] These suggestions were made before substantial discussions around the Digital Services Act have occurred. Some of them are contemplated in the act to a certain extent. *See* chapter 3.
[1695] Regulation (EU) 2019/1150 of the European Parliament and of the Council of 20 June 2019 on Promoting Fairness and Transparency for Business Users of Online Intermediation Services, OJ L 186, 11.7.2019, p 57–79.
[1696] Art 1 (1) and (2), Regulation (EU) 2019/1150. The Digital Services Act foresees accountability measures to targeted advertising practices.
[1697] Brussels, 26.4.2018 COM(2018) 238 final. Proposal for a Regulation on the European Parliament and of the Council on Promoting Fairness and Transparency for Business Users of Online Intermediation Services, p 3.
[1698] *Ibid.*
[1699] *Ibid*, p 2.
[1700] Art 4, Regulation (EU) 2019/1150. Also, *see* Vassilis Hatzopoulos, "Vers un Cadre de la Régulation des Plateformes? (2019) 3 Revue Internationale de Droit Économique 399.

requires a description of the main criteria used to determine the ranking of users in search results.[1701] This description must be available by means of an easily available and public explanation. The users must also be able to understand the design traits of matching tools (called search engines in the text). Ultimately, online platform businesses intermediating the provision of services and goods must also include a detailed description of the access to personal or other data that users provide or that are inferred.[1702] This last obligation complements the requirements of the General Data Protection Regulation.

These high-level disclosure duties promote more transparency regarding the actions and structures of online platform businesses. They might shed some light on the opacity of the criteria used by matching tools and the lack of clarity of rating systems that prevent awareness to potential discriminatory outcomes engaged by these systems. First, alleged discriminatory termination of platform users due to evaluation scored systems might be clarified by the provision that requires online intermediation services to give the concerned user a clear statement of reasons for the decision.[1703] The aim is to improve transparency in the process of terminating users' contract with the platform. Second, platforms shall be required in cases of termination to give users the opportunity to clarify the facts and circumstances in the framework of an internal complaint process.[1704] Third, the transparency principle formulated for ranking systems should be positively transposed to matching systems.[1705] In this case, platform businesses shall set out in their terms and conditions the main parameters determining matching and the reasons for the relative importance of those main parameters as opposed to others.[1706] Ultimately, online platforms should provide an accessible and public description, drafted in plain and intelligible language about those parameters.[1707] These mechanisms altogether improve the fairness and transparency related to platform design and shall, therefore, help users to understand the precise conditions related to their termination and their matching parameters.

What the rules on transparency and disclosure in the terms set by Regulation 2019/1150 do not resolve is third-party discrimination as a side effect of aesthetic

---

[1701] Art 5, Regulation (EU) 2019/1150.

[1702] Art 7, Regulation (EU) 2019/1150.

[1703] Art 4 (1), Regulation (EU) 2019/1150.

[1704] Art 4 (2), Regulation (EU) 2019/1150.

[1705] Art 5 (1), Regulation (EU) 2019/1150.

[1706] This possibility is provided for targeted advertising in the proposal for the Digital Services Act. *See* Amendment 335 to art 30, paragraph 2, point d, European Parliament, *Amendments Adopted by the European Parliament on 20 January 2022 on the Proposal for a Regulation of the European Parliament and of the Council on a Single Market for Digital Services (Digital Services Act) and Amending Directive 2000/31/EC* (2022), online: European Parliament <https://www.europarl.europa.eu/doceo/document/TA-9-2022-0014_EN.html>.

[1707] Art 5 (2), Regulation (EU) 2019/1150.

choices that over-highlight users' protected markers before transactions are concluded. Moreover, neither antidiscrimination laws of the federal statutes in the United States nor the Equality Directives in the EU address this issue. These provisions never aimed to hide protected classes to avoid discrimination. Furthermore, vicarious liability rules hardly apply to online platforms both in the United States and in the member states of the EU, because they heavily depend on agency theories that do not guide most relationships between users and online platform businesses.

One possible alternative to address third-party discrimination as a side effect of highlighting protected markers would be simply to suggest that platforms change their design. However, online platforms have persistently claimed that this aspect enhances trustworthiness within their markets, which is fundamental for transactions to be concluded.[1708] In this case, I suggest that the principle of transparency coupled with cooperation between antidiscrimination bodies and private businesses could also help without imposing on platforms the burden of changing their design. Often, evidence of discrimination in these cases is subtle and involves the refusal of the service based on lack of availability.[1709] Moreover, evidence is scant because the transaction involves only two private parties. In this context, online platforms could facilitate or even promote the realization of situation tests, which are already mobilized in some offline markets. Nevertheless, in opposition to offline markets, online platforms have technology to prevent these tests from happening. Airbnb, for instance, has consistently blocked fake profiles created by researchers to ask hosts about housing opportunities.[1710] Non-verifiable or fake profiles are against the platform's policy. Furthermore, external auditing might provide a comprehensive understanding of ongoing discrimination, in addition to evidence against perpetrators.[1711] Running situation tests in online platforms demands much fewer human resources than in offline markets and offers more transparency on the level of unjustified refusals in these markets.

All in all, the fight against discrimination in online platforms, in my view, might be oriented by 1) a balanced co-regulatory liability regime that involves online intermediaries in some circumstances, 2) a regulatory model that incites companies operating as online intermediaries to implement

---

[1708] *See* chapter 1 and 2.
[1709] *See* chapter 2.
[1710] *See* chapter 2.
[1711] External audit is contemplated for very large online platforms in the proposal for the Digital Services Act. This measure aims to give interested stakeholders the possibility to assess whether online platforms have complied with certain requirements implemented by the Act. Art 28, proposal for a Regulation of the European Parliament and of the Council on a Single Market for Digital Services (Digital Services Act) and amending Directive 2000/31/EC. COM/2020/825 final.

the principle of transparency and fairness in their interactions with users, and 3) permanent cooperation between these private companies and antidiscrimination agents interested in implementing the equality principle in online spaces.

BIBLIOGRAPHY

1. ARTICLES AND BOOKS

Adrian G Carpusor, Willian E Loges, "Rental Discrimination and Ethnicity in Names" (2006) 36 Journal of Applied Social Psychology 934.

Adrian J Hawley, "Should Europe Regulate Labor Platforms in the Sharing Economy?" in Russell W Belk, Giana M Eckhardt, Fleura Bardhi, *Handbook of the Sharing Economy* (Edward Elgar Publishing, 2019).

Agnieszka A McPeak, "Sharing Tort Liability in the New Sharing Economy" (2016) 49:1 Connecticut Law Review 171.

Ajay Agrawal, John Horton, Nicola Lacetera, Elizabeth Lyons and others, "Digitization and the Contract Labor Market: A Research Agenda" in Avi Goldfarb, Shane M Greenstein, Catherine E Tucker (eds), *Economic Analysis of the Digital Economy* (Chicago: University of Chicago Press, 2015).

Alan L Bogg, "Sham Self-Employment in the Supreme Court" (2012) 41:3 Industrial Law Journal 328;

Alberto de Franceschi, "Uber Spain and the Identity Crisis of Online Platforms" (2018) 7:1 Journal of European Consumer and Market Law 1.

Alek Felstiner, "Working the Crowd: Employment and Labor Law in the Crowdsourcing Industry" (2011) 32 Berkeley Journal of Employment & Labor Law 143.

Aleksandra Kuczerawy, "Intermediary Liability & Freedom of Expression: Recent Developments in the EU Notice & Action Initiative" (2015) 31 Computer Law & Security Review 46.

Aleksandra Kuczerawy, "The Power of Positive Thinking: Intermediary Liability and the Effective Enjoyment of the Right to Freedom of Expression" (2017) 8:3 Journal of Intellectual Property, Information, Technology and Electronic Commerce Law 226.

Aleksandra Kuczerawy, *Intermediary Liability and Freedom of Expression in the EU: From Concepts to Safeguards* (Intersentia, 2018).

Alex Rosenblat, Karen E C Levy, Solon Barocas, Tim Hwang, "Discriminating Tastes: Uber's Customer Ratings as Vehicles for Workplace Discrimination" (2017) 9:3 Policy & Internet 256.

Alex Rosenblat, Uberland: *How Algorithms Are Rewriting the Rules of Work* (University of California Press, 2018).

Alex Veen, David Oliver, Caleb Goods, Tom Barrat, "The 'Gigification' of Work" in Russell D Lansbury, Anya Johnson, Diane Van de Broek, *Contemporary Issues in Work and Organisations: Actors and Institutions* (Routledge, 2019).

Alexander Bleier, Maik Eisenbeiss, "Personalized Online Advertising Effectiveness: The Interplay of What, When, and Where" (2015) 34 Marketing Science 669.

Alexander J S Colvin, "Mandatory Arbitration and Inequality of Justice in Employment" (2014) 25 Berkeley Journal of Employment & Labor Law 71.

Alexandra Chouldechova, "Fair Prediction with Disparate Impact: A Study of Bias in Recidivism Prediction Instruments" (2017) 5 Big Data 153.

Alexandra Harwin, "Title VII Challenges to Employment Discrimination against Minority Men with Criminal Records" (2012) 14:1 Berkeley Journal of African-American Law & Policy 1.

Alysia Blackham, Catherine Barnard, "The Self-Employed and the Welfare State in the EU: Insights from Gender and Race Equality Law", in Mies Westerveld, Marius Olivier (eds), *Social Security Outside the Realm of Employment Contract* (Edward Elgar Publishing, 2019).

Amanda Agan, Sonja Starr, "Ban the Box, Criminal Records, and Racial Discrimination: A Field Experiment" (2018) 133:1 The Quarterly Journal of Economics 191.

Amit Datta, Michael Carl Tschantz, Anupam Datta, "Automated Experiments on Ad Privacy Settings: A Tale of Opacity, Choice and Discrimination" (2015) 1 Proceedings on Privacy Enhancing Technologies 92.

Amnesty International, ENAR, *Wearing the Headscarf in the Workplace: Observation on Discrimination Based on Religion in the Achbita and Bougnaoui Cases* (October 2016), online: Amnesty <https://www.amnesty.org/en/documents/eur01/5077/2016/en/>.

Ana Maria Corrêa, "Regulatory Risks Faced by the Transportation Sharing Economy: Workforces at Stake" (2018) 9:4 European Journal of Risk Regulation 641.

Andrea Doneff, "Arbitration Clauses in Contracts of Adhesion Trap 'Sophisticated Parties' Too" (2010) Journal of Dispute Resolution 235.

Andrei Hagiu, Julian Wright, "The Status of Workers and Platforms in the Sharing Economy" (2019) 28:1 Journal of Economics & Management Strategy 97.

Andrene N Plummer, "A Few New Solutions to a Very Old Problem: How the Fair Housing Act Can Be Improved to Deter Discriminatory Conduct by Real Estate Brokers" (2003) Howard Law Journal 163.

Andrew Geddes, Virginie Guiraudon, "Britain, France, and EU Anti-Discrimination Policy: The Emergence of an EU policy Paradigm" (2004) 27:2 West European Politics 334.

Andrew Hanson, Michael Santas, "Field Experiment Tests for Discrimination Against Hispanics in the US Rental Housing Market" (2014) 81:1 Southern Economic Journal 135.

Andrew Hanson, Zackary Hawley, "Do Landlords Discriminate in the Rental of Housing Market? Evidence from an Internet Field in US Cities (2011) 70:2 Journal of Urban Economics 99.

Andrew J Robinson, "Language, National Origin, and Employment Discrimination: The Importance of the EEOC Guidelines" (2009) 157 University of Pennsylvania Law Review 1513.

Andrew Koppelman, "Signs of the Times: Dale v Boy Scouts of America and the Changing Meaning of Nondiscrimination" (2002) 23 Cardozo Law Review 1819.

Andrew Selbst, Solon Barocas, "Big Data's Disparate Impact" (2016) 104 California Law Review 671.

Andrew Serwin, "The Federal Trade Commission and Privacy: Defining Enforcement and Encouraging the Adoption of Best Practices" (2011) 48 San Diego Law Review 809.

Andrey Fradkin, "Search Frictions and the Design of Online Marketplaces" (2015) Working Paper Massachusetts Institute of Technology.

Aniket Kittur, Jeffrey V Nickerson, Michael Bernstein, Elizabeth Gerber, Aaron Shaw, John Zimmerman, Matt Lease, John Horton, "The Future of Crowd Work" (2013) Proceedings of the 2013 Conference on Computer Supported Cooperative Work (ACM) 1301.

Ánikó Hannák, Claudia Wagner, David Garcia, Alan Mislove, Markus Strohmaier, Christo Wilson, "Bias in Online Freelance Marketplaces: Evidence from TaskRabbit and Fiverr" (2017) Proceedings of the 2017 ACM Conference on Computer Supported Cooperative Work and Social Computing 1914.

Anja Lambrecht, Catherine Tucker, "Algorithmic Bias? An Empirical Study of Apparent Gender-Based Discrimination in the Display of STEM Career Ads" (2019) Management Science 1.

Anja Lambrecht, Catherine Tucker, "When Does Retargeting Work? Information Specificity in Online Advertising" (2013) 50 Journal of Marketing Research 561.

Annabelle Gawer, *Online Platforms: Contrasting Perceptions of European Stakeholders. A Qualitative Analysis of the European Commission's Public Consultation on the Regulatory Environment for Platforms. A Study Prepared for the European Commission DG Communications Networks, Content & Technology* (May 2016), online: European Commission <https://ec.europa.eu/newsroom/dae/document.cfm?doc_id=15932>.

Annarosa Pesole, Maria Cesira Urzi Brancati, Enrique Fernandez Macias, Federico Biagi, Ignacio Gonzalez Vasquez, Platform Workers in Europe Evidence from the COLLEEM Survey (December 2018), online: EUR Scientific and Technical Research Reports <https://publications.jrc.ec.europa.eu/repository/handle/JRC112157>.

Annick Masselot, "The State of Gender Equality Law in the European Union" (2007) 13 European Law Journal 152.

Antonio Aloisi, "Commoditized Workers: Case Study Research on Labor Law Issues Arising from a Set of on-Demand/Gig Economy Platforms" (2016) 37 Comparative Labor Law & Policy Journal 653.

Article 29 Data Protection Working Party, *Guideline on Transparency Under Regulation 2016/679 WP260*, (November 2017), online: European commission <http://ec.europa.eu/newsroom/just/document.cfm?doc_id=48850>.

Article 29 Working Party, *Opinion 03/2013 on purpose limitation, WP 203 (April 2013), online: EC* <https://ec.europa.eu/justice/article-29/documentation/opinion-recommendation/files/2013/wp203_en.pdf> p 46.

Arun Sundararajan, *The Sharing Economy: The End of Employment and The Rise of Crowd-Based Capitalism* (Cambridge: MIT Press, 2017).

Asma AI Vranaki, "Regulating Social Networking Sites: Facebook, Online Behavioral Advertising, Data Protection Laws and Power" (2017) 43 Rutgers Computers and Technology Law Journal 168.

Atul Parvatiyar, Jagdish N Sheth, "Customer Relationship Management: Emerging Practice, Process, and Discipline" (2001) 3:2 Journal of Economic & Social Research 1.

Aude Bernheim, Flora Vincent, *L'Intelligence Artificielle, Pas Sans Elles! Faire de l'IA un Levier pour l'Égalité* (Paris: Belin, 2019).

Avi Goldfarb, "What Is Different About Online Advertising?" (2014) 44 Review of Industrial Organization 115.

Avi Goldfarb, Catherine E Tucker, "Privacy Regulation and Online Advertising" (2011) 57:1 Management Science 57.

Avi Golfarb, Catherine Tucker, "Implications of Online Display Advertising and Obtrusiveness" (2011) 30:3 Marketing Science 389.

Barbara K Kaye, Norman Medoff, *Just a Click Away: Advertising on the Internet* (Massachusetts: Allyn and Bacon, 2011).

Barbara Y Welke, "Beyond Plessy: Space, Status, and Race in the Era of Jim Crow" (2000) Utah Law Review 267.

Ben L Martin, "From Negro to Black to African American: The Power of Names and Naming" (1991) 106 Political Science Quarterly 83.

Benjamin Edelman, Michael Luca, Dan Svirsky, "Racial Discrimination in the Sharing Economy: Evidence from a Field Experiment" (2017) 9 American Economic Journal: Applied Economics 1.

Benjamin G Edelman, Michael Luca, *Digital Discrimination: The Case of Airbnb.com* (January 2014), online: Harvard Business School <https://www.hbs.edu/faculty/Publication%20Files/Airbnb_92dd6086-6e46-4eaf-9cea-60fe5ba3c596.pdf>.

Benjamin Howell, "Exploiting Race and Space: Concentrated Subprime Lending as Housing Discrimination" (2006) 94: 1 California Law Review 101.

Benjamin Means, Joseph A Seiner, "Navigating the Uber Economy" (2016) 49 University of California Davis Law Review 1511.

Benoît Frydman, "Les Défis du Droit Global", in Caroline Bricteux, Benoît Frydman, Grands Défis du Droit Global (Brussels: Bruylant, 2018).

Benoit Frydman, Ludovic Hennebel, Gregory Lewkowicz, "Public Strategies for Internet Co-Regulation in the United States, Europe and China" in E. Brousseau, M Marzouki, C. Méadel, Governance, Regulations and Powers on the Internet (Cambridge: Cambridge University Press, 2008).

Benoit Frydman, Isabelle Rorive, "Regulating Internet Content through Intermediaries in Europe and the USA" (2002) 23:1 Zeitschrift Für Rechtssoziologie 41.

Bernard J Jansen, Amanda Spink, "How Are We Searching the World Wide Web? A Comparison of Nine Search Engine Transaction Logs" (2006) 42:1 Information Processing & Management 248.

Bernd Waas, "The Legal Definition of the Employment Relationship" (2010) 1:1 European Labour Law Journal 45.

Birgitta Bergvall-Kareborn, Debra Howcroft, "Amazon Mechanical Turk and the Commodification of Labour" (2014) 29:3 New Technology, Work and Employment 213.

Bob Rietjens, "Trust and Reputation on eBay: Towards a Legal Framework for Feedback Intermediaries" (2006) 15:01 Information & Communications Technology Law 55.

Bradley M Smyer, "Interactive Computer Service Liability for User-Generated Content After Roommtes.com" (2009) 43 University of Michigan of Law Reform 811.

Brenna R McLaughlin, "#Airbnbwhileblack Repealing the Fair Housing Act's Mrs. Murphy Exemption to Combat Racism on Airbnb" (2018) Wisconsin Law Review 149.

Brishen Rogers, "The social costs of Uber" (2016) 82 University of Chicago Law Review Dialogue 85.

Brishen Rogers, "Employment Rights in the Platform Economy: Getting Back to Basics" (2016) 10 Harvard Law & Policy Review 479.

Bruno de Witte, "News Institutions for Promoting Equality in Europe: Legal Transfers, National Bricolage and European Governance (2012) 60:1 The American Journal of Comparative Law 49.

Caitlin Toto, "Sharing Economy Inequality: How the Adoption of Class Action Waivers in the Sharing Economy Presents a Threat to Racial Discrimination Claims" (2017) 58 BCL Review 1355.

Carol Evans, Westra Miller, "From Catalogs to Clicks: The Fair Lending Implications of Targeted, Internet Marketing" (2019) 3 Consumer Compliance Outlook 9.

Caroline Vallet, *La Réglementation des Contenus Illicites Circulant sur Internet: Étude en Droit Comparé* (Éditions Universitaires Européennes, 2012).

Cassandra Jones Harvard, "'On the Take': The Black Box of Credit Scoring and Mortgage Discrimination" (2011) 20 Boston University Public Interest Law Journal 241.

Catherine Barnard, "Discrimination, Self-Employment and the Liberal Professions" (2011) 12 European Anti-Discrimination Law Review 21.

Catherine Barnard, Alysia Blackham, Self-Employed: The Implementation of Directive 2010/41 on the Application of the Principle of Equal Treatment Between Men and Women Engaged in an Activity in a Self-Employed Capacity (March 2015), online: European Commission Directorate-General for Justice and Consumers <https://www.equalitylaw.eu/component/edocman/self-employed-en>.

Catherine Barnard, *EU Employment Law* 4th Edition (Oxford: Oxford University Press, 2012).

Catherine E Tucker, "Social Networks, Personalized Advertising, and Privacy Controls" (2014) 51:5 Journal of Marketing Research 546.

Catherine Barnard, Steve Peers, *European Union Law* (New York: Oxford University Press, 2017).

Cesira Urzi Brancati, Annarosa Pesole, Enrique Fernandez-Macías, Digital Labour Platforms in Europe: Numbers, Profiles, and Employment Status of Platform Workers (January 2019), online: Publications Office of the European Union <https://publications.jrc.ec.europa.eu/repository/bitstream/JRC117330/jrc117330_jrc117330_dlp_counting_profiling.pdf>.

Chang-Dae Ham, Michelle R Nelson, "The Role of Persuasion Knowledge, Assessment of Benefit and Harm, and Third-Person Perception in Coping with Online Behavioral Advertising" (2016) 62 Computer in Human Behavior 689.

Charlotte O'Brien, Eleanor Spaventa, Joyce De Coninck, Comparative Report 2015: The Concept of Worker Under Article 45 TFEU and Certain Non-Standard Forms of Employment (April 2016), online European Commission <http://dro.dur.ac.uk/18690/1/18690.pdf?DDC72+DDC71+DDD19+dla0es+d700tmt>.

Chris J Hoofnagle, Ashkan Soltani, Nathaniel Good, Dietrich J Wambach, Mika Ayenson, "Behavioral Advertising: The Offer You Cannot Refuse", (2012) 6:1 Harvard Law & Policy Review 673.

Chris Jay Hoofnagle, *Federal Trade Commission Privacy Law and Policy* (Cambridge University Press 2016).

Chris Warhusrt, Wil Hunt, "The Digitalisation of Future Work and Employment: Possible Impact and Policy Responses (2019) European Commission JRC117404 1.

Christa Tobler, "Case C-236/09, Association Belge Des Consommateurs Test-Achats ABSL, Yann Van Vurgt, Charles Basselier v Conseil Des Ministres" (2011) 48 Common Market Law Review 2041.

Christina Angelopoulos, Stijn Smet, "Notice-and-Fair Balance: How to Reach a Compromise Between Fundamental Rights in European Intermediary Liability" (2016) 8:2 Journal of Media Law 266.

Christine Barwick, "Patterns of Discrimination Against Blacks and Hispanics in the US Mortgage Market" (2010) 25 Journal of Housing and the Built Environment 117.

Christoph Busch, "The Sharing Economy at the CJEU: Does Airbnb pass the Uber test? Some observations on the pending case c-390/18 Airbnb Ireland" (2018) 7:4 Journal of European Consumer and Market Law 172.

Christopher McCrudden, "Two Views of Subordination: The Scope of Employment Discrimination Law in Jivraj v Hashwani" (2012) 41 Industrial Law Journal 30.

Corey Omer, "Intermediary Liability for Harmful Speech: Lessons From Abroad" (2014) 28 Harvard Journal Law & Technology 289.

Council of Europe, Comparative Study on Blocking, Filtering and Take-Down of Illegal Internet Content (January 2017), online: CoE <https://edoc.coe.int/fr/internet/7289-pdf-comparative-study-on-blocking-filtering-and-take-down-of-illegal-internet-content-.html>.

Craig Smith, Eric V Moyé, "Outsourcing American Civil Justice: Mandatory Arbitration Clauses in Consumer and Employment Contracts" (2012) 44 Texas Tech Law Review 281.

Cristiano Codagnone, Federico Biagi, Fabienne Abadie, The Passions and the Interests: Unpacking the Sharing Economy (Luxembourg: European Commission, 2016), JRC Science for Policy Report.

Dallan F Flake, "When Should Employers Be Liable for Factoring Customer Feedback into Employment Decisions" (2018) 102:5 Minnesota Law Review 2169.

Daniel Castro, "Benefits and Limitations of Industry Self-Regulation for Online Behavioral Advertising" (2011) The Information Technology & Innovation Foundation 1.

Daniel E Rauch, David Schleicher, "Like Uber, But for Local Government Law: The Future of Local Regulation of The Sharing Economy (2015) 76 Ohio St Law Journal 901.

Daniel Guttentag, "Airbnb: Disruptive Innovation and the Rise of an Informal Tourism Accommodation Sector" (2015) 18 Current Issues in Tourism 1192.

Daniel J Solove and Woodrow Hartzog, "The FTC and the New Common Law of Privacy" (2014) 114:3 Columbia Law Review 583.

Danielle Keats Citron, Frank Pasquale, "The Scored Society: Due Process for Automated Predictions" (2014) 89 Washington Law Review 1.

Danielle Keats Citron, Frank Pasquale, "The Scored Society" (2014) 89:1 Washington Law Review 1.

David A Vise, Mark Malseed, The Google Story: Inside the Hottest Business, Media and Technology Success of Our Time (New York: Bantam Books, 2018).

David B Oppenheimer, "Sources of United States Equality Law: The View from 10000 Meters" (2010) 10 European Anti-Discrimination Law Review 19;

David Horton, "Arbitration About Arbitration" (2018) 70 Stanford Law Review 363, p 363.

David Horton, "Arbitration as Delegation" (2011) 86 New York Law Review 437.

David J Garrow, "Toward a Definitive History of Griggs v Duke Power" (2014) 67 Vanderbilt Law Review 197.

David Jacobus Dalenberg, "Preventing Discrimination in the Automated Targeting of Job Advertisements" (2018) 34 Computer Law & Security Review 615.

David Kirkpatrick, The Facebook Effect: The Real Inside Story of Mark Zuckerberg and the World's Fastest Growing Company (Croydon: Ebury Publishing, 2011).

David Lehr and Paul Ohm, "Playing with the Data: What Legal Scholars Should Learn About Machine Learning" (2017) 51 U C Davis Law Review 653.

David M Forman, "A Room for 'Adam and Steve' at Mrs. Murphy's Bed and Breakfast: Avoiding the Sin of Inhospitality in Places of Public Accommodation" (2012) 23 Columbia Journal of Gender and Law 326.

David Oppenheimmer, "Sources of United States Equality Law: The View from 10000 Meters" (2010) European Antidiscrimination Law Review" 19.

David Restrepo Amariles, Gregory Lewkowicz, "Global Contract Governance: Selden V Airbnb", in: Horatia Muir Watt, Lucia Biziková, Agatha Brandao de Oliveira, Diego P Fernandez Arroyo, Global Private International Law (Edward Elgar Publishing, 2019).

David S Ardia, "Free Speech Savior or Shield for Scoundrels: An Empirical Study of Intermediary Immunity Under Section 230 of the Communication Decency Act" (2009) 43 Loyola of Los Angeles Law Review 373.

David S Evans, "The Online Advertising Industry: Economics, Evolution and Privacy" (2009) 23:3 Journal of Economic Perspectives 37.

David S Evans, Richard Schmalensee, The Antitrust Analysis of Multi-Sided Platform Businesses, in: Roger Blair, Daniel Sokol (eds), Oxford Handbook on International Antitrust Economics (New York: Oxford University Press, 2014).

Dawn Woodard, "Dynamic Pricing and Matching in Ride-Hailing Platforms" (2019) NRL Journal.

Deanna N Conn, "When Contract Should Preempt Tort Remedies: Limits on Vicarious Liability for Acts of Independent Contractors" (2010) 15 Fordham Journal of Corporate and Financial Law 179.

Debra Howcroft, Birgitta Bergvall-Kareborn, "A Typology of Crowdwork Platforms" (2019) 33:1 Work, Employment and Society 21.

Debra Howcroft, Tony Dundon, Cristina Inversi, "Fragmented Demands and Gig-Working in the UK", in: M Sullivan (ed), Zero Hours and On-Call Work in Anglo-Saxon Countries: Work, Organization, and Employment (Springer, 2019).

Desiree de Lima, Adam Legge, "The European Union's Approach to Online Behavioural Advertising: Protecting Individuals or Restricting Business? (2014) 30:1 Computer Law & Security Review 67.

Devin G Pope, Justin R Sydnor, "What's in a Picture? Evidence of Discrimination from Prosper.com" (2011) 46:1 Journal of Human Resources 53.

Devin G Pope, Justin R Syndor, "Implementing Anti-Discrimination Policies in Statistical Profiling Models" (2011) 3:3 American Economic Journal 206.

Donald N Anderson, "Not Just a Taxi? For Profit Ridesharing, Driver Strategies, and VMT" (2014) 41:5 Transportation 1099.

Dongyu Chen, Xialin Li, Fujun Lai, "Gender Discrimination in Online Peer-to-Peer Credit Lending: Evidence from a Lending Platform in China" (2017) 17:4 Electronic Commerce Research 553.

Douglas B Luftman, "Defamation Liability for Online Services: The Sky is Not Falling" (1997) 65 George Washington Review 1071.

Douglas S Massey, Jacob S Rugh, Justin P Steil, Len Albright, "Riding the Stagecoach to Hell: A Qualitative Analysis of Racial Discrimination in Mortgage Lending" (2016) 15:2 City and Community 118.

Edith G Smit, Guda Van Noort, Hilde A Voorveld, "Understanding Online Behavioural Advertising: User Knowledge, Privacy Concerns, and Online Coping Behaviour in Europe" (2014) 32 Computers in Human Behavior 15.

Einat Albin, "A Worker Employer Customer Triangle: The Case of Tips" (2011) 40 Industrial Law Journal 181.

Elaine W Shoben, "Disparate Impact Theory in Employment Discrimination: What's Griggs Still Good For? What Not?" (2004) 42 Brandeis Law Journal 597.

Eleanor Spaventa, What is the Point of Minimum Harmonization of Fundamental Rights? Some Further Reflection on the Achbita Case (March 2017), online: EU Law Analysis <http://eulawanalysis.blogspot.com/2017/03/what-is-point-of-minimum-harmonization.html>.

Elena Gil González, Paul de Hert, "Understanding the Legal Provisions That Allow Processing and Profiling of Personal Data – an Analysis of GDPR Provisions and Principles" (2019) 19 ERA Forum 597.

Elizabeth A Deitch, Adam Barksy, Rebecca M Butz, Suzanne Chan, Arthur P Brief, Jill C Bradley, "Subtle Yet Significant: The Existence and Impact of Everyday Racial Discrimination in the Workplace" (2003) 56:11 Human Relations 1299.

Elizabeth Aguirre et al, "Unraveling the Personalization Paradox: The Effect of Information Collection and Trust-Building Strategies on Online Advertisement Effectiveness" (2015) 91 Journal of Retailing 34.

Elke Cloots, "Safe Harbour or Open Sea for Corporate Headscarf Ban? Achbita and Bougnaoui" (2018) 55:2 Common Market Law Review 589.

Emilio J Castilla, "Bringing Managers Back In: Managerial Influences on Workplace Inequality" (2011) 76:5 American Sociological Review 667.

Emilio J Castilla, "Merit and Discrimination within Organizations: Gender and Racial Differences in the Evaluation and Compensation of Employees" (2010) 129 Revista Espanola de Investigaciones Sociologicas 61.

Emma Parry, Shaun Tyson, "An Analysis of the Use and Success of Online Recruitment Methods in the UK" (2008) 18 Cranfield School of Management Human Resource Management Journal 257.

Emmanuella Plakoyiannaki, Yorgos Zotos, "Female Role Stereotypes in Print Advertising: Identifying Associations with Magazine and Product Categories" (2009) 43 European Journal of Marketing 1411.

Emmanuelle Bribosia, Isabelle Rorive, *In Search of a Balance Between the Right to Equality and Other Fundamental Rights* (February 2010), online: European Commission Directorate General for Employment, Social Affairs and Equal Opportunities <https://tandis.odihr.pl/bitstream/20.500.12389/21232/1/07052.pdf>.

Emmanuelle Bribosia, Isabelle Rorive, "Equality and Non-Discrimination: Column" (2014) 2 European Journal of Human Rights 205.

Emmanuelle Bribosia, Isabelle Rorive, "Anti-Discrimination Law in the Global Age" (2015) 3 European Journal of Human Rights 3.

Emmanuelle Bribosia, Isabelle Rorive, "Equality and Non-Discrimination: Column" (2016) 2 European Journal of Human Rights 254.

Emmanuelle Bribosia, Isabelle Rorive, "Equality and Non-Discrimination: Column" (2017) 2 European Journal of Human Rights 191.

Emmanuelle Bribosia, Isabelle Rorive, "Affaires Achbita et Bougnaoui: Entre Neutralité et Préjugés" (2017) 112:3 Revue Trimestrielle des Droits de L'Homme 1018.

Emmanuelle Bribosia, Isabelle Rorive, "Equality and Non-Discrimination: Column" (2018) 2 European Journal of Human Rights 126.

Emmanuelle Bribosia, Isabelle Rorive, "Les Paroles Ont des Ailes et Peuvent Discriminer: Regard sur l'Arrêt N.H. c. Association Avvocatura per I diritti LGBTI – Rete Lenford, rendu en Grand Chambre par la CJUE le 23 avril 2020, C-507/18", (2020) Journal Européen des Droits de l'Homme.

Engin Bozdag, "Bias in Algorithmic Filtering and Personalization" (2013) 15 Ethics Information Technology 209.

Enrique Estellés-Arolas, Fernando González, "Towards an Integrated Crowdsourcing Definition" (2012) 38:2 Journal of Information Science 189.

Eric C Bosset and others, "Private Actions Challenging Online Data Collection Practices Are Increasing: Assessing the Legal Landscape" (2011) 23 Intellectual Property & Technology Law Journal 3.

Eric Schmidt, Jonathan Rosenberg, *How Google Works* (London: John Murray, 2015).

Eric V Moyé, "Outsourcing American Civil Justice: Mandatory Arbitration Clauses in Consumer and Employment Contracts" (2012) 44 Texas Tech Law Review 281 p 287.

Erica Howard, "Islamic Headscarves and the CJEU: Achbita and Bougnaoui" (2017) 24:3 Maastricht Journal of European and Comparative Law 348.

Erica Howard, *Religious Clothing and Symbols in Employment: A Legal Analysis of the Situation in the EU Member States* (November 2017), online: European Commission European Network of Legal Experts in Gender Equality and Non-Discrimination <https://www.equalitylaw.eu/downloads/4493-religious-clothing-and-symbols-in-employment-pdf-928-kb>.

Esteve Asunción, "The Business of Personal Data: Google, Facebook, and Privacy Issues in the EU and the USA" (2017) 7 International Data Privacy Law 36.

Ethem Alpaydin, Machine Learning: The New AI (New Haven: MIT Press 2016).

Etienne Montero, Quentin Van Enis, "Enabling Freedom of Expression in Light of Filtering Measures Imposed on Internet Intermediaries: Squaring the Circle? (2011) 27:1 Computer Law & Security Review 21.

Eugenia Caracciolo di Torella, "Gender Equality after Test Achats" (2012) 12 ERA Forum 59.

European Group on Ethics in Science and New Technologies, Future of Work, Future of Society (December 2018), online: European Commission Directorate-General for Research and Innovation <https://ec.europa.eu/info/sites/info/files/research_and_innovation/ege/ege_future-of-work_opinion_122018.pdf>.

European Union Agency for Fundamental Rights, Handbook on European Data Protection Law (Luxembourg: European Union Agency for Fundamental Rights and Council of Europe, 2018).

Eva Brems, European Court of Justice Allows Bans on Religious Dress in the Workplace (March 2017), online: IACL-AIDC <https://blog-iacl-aidc.org/test-3/2018/5/26/analysis-european-court-of-justice-allows-bans-on-religious-dress-in-the-workplace>.

Evelyn Ellis, Philippa Watson, "EU Anti-Discrimination Law" 2ed (Oxford University Press, 2012).

Ewan McGaughey, "Could Brexit Be Void?" (2018) 29 King's Law Journal 331.

Ewan McGaughey, "Uber, the Taylor Review, Mutuality and the Duty Not to Misrepresent Employment Status" (2019) 48:2 Industrial Law Journal 180.

Eyal Ert, Aliza Fleischer, Nathan Magen, "Trust and Reputation in the Sharing Economy: The Role of Personal Photos in Airbnb" (2016) 55 Tourism Management 62.

Frances L Edwards, Grayson Bennet Thomson, "The Legal Creation of Raced Space: The Subtle and Ongoing Discrimination Created Through Jim Crow Laws" (2010) 12 Berkeley Journal of African-American Law & Policy 145.

Frans Pennings, "The European Union and the Issue of the Employment Relationship" in Frans Pennings, Claire Bosse, The Protection of Working Relationships (Wolters Kluwer, 2011).

Frederik Zuiderveen Borgesius and Joost Poort, "Online Price Discrimination and EU Data Privacy Law" (2017) 40 Journal of Consumer Policy 347.

Frederik Zuiderveen Borgesius and others, "Tracking Walls, Take-It-or-Leave-It Choices, the GDPR, and the ePrivacy Regulation" (2017) 3 European Data Protection Law Review 353.

Frederik Zuiderveen Borgesius, "Singling Out People Without Knowing Their Names: Behavioural Targeting, Pseudonymous Data, and the New Data Protection Regulation", (2016) 32 Computer Law & Security Review 256.

Frederik Zuiderveen Borgesius, Discrimination, Artificial Intelligence, and Algorithmic Decision-Making. Council of Europe Study (December 2018), online: Council of Europe <https://rm.coe.int/discrimination-artificial-intelligence-and-algorithmic-decision-making/1680925d73>.

Frederik Zuiderveen Borgesius, Improving Privacy Protection in the Area of Behavioral Targeting (Alphen aan den Rijn: Kluwer Law International 2015).

Frederik Zuiderveen Borgesius, J Van Hoboken, K Irion, M Rozendaal, "An Assessment of the Commission's Proposal on Privacy and Electronic Communications" (June 2017), online: Directorate-General for Internal Policies, Policy Department Citizen's Rights and Constitutional Affairs <https://ssrn.com/abstract=2982290>.

Fundamental Rights Agency (FRA), Handbook on European Non-Discrimination Law (Luxembourg: Publications Office of the European Union, 2018).

Future of Work Commission, *Future of Work* (August 2019), online: Labor & Workforce Development Agency <https://labor.ca.gov/fowc/>.

Gary W Loveman, "Employee Satisfaction, Customer Loyalty, and Financial Performance: An Empirical Examination of the Service Profit Chain in Retail Banking" (1998) Journal of Service Research 18.

Gautam Hans, "Privacy Policies, Terms of Service, and FTC Enforcement: Broadening Unfairness Regulation for a New Era" (2012) 19 Michigan Telecommunications and Technology Law Review 163.

Gavin Sutter, "Don't Shoot the Messenger? The UK and Online Intermediary Liability" (2003) 17:1 International Review of Law 73.

Geoffrey Dudley, David Banister, Tim Schwanen, "The Rise of Uber and Regulating the Disruptive Innovator" (2017) 88:3 The Political Quarterly 493;

Geoffrey G Parker, Marshall W Van Alstyne, Sangeet Paul Choudary, Platform Revolution: How Networked Markets Are Transforming the Economy and How to Make Them Work for You (Norton & Company, 2016).

George C Thornton III, Deborah E Rupp, Alyssa M Gibbons, Adam J Vanhove, "Same-Gender and Same-Race Bias in Assessment Center Ratings: A Rating Error Approach to Understanding Subgroup Differences" (2019) 27:1 International Journal of Selection and Assessment 54.

George Galster, Erin Godfrey, "By Words and Deeds: Racial Steering by Real Estate Agents in the US in 2000" (2005) 71:3 Journal of the American Planning Association 251.

Georgios Zervas, Davide Proserpio, John W Byers, "The Rise of the Sharing Economy: Estimating the Impact of Airbnb on the Hotel Industry" (2017) 54 Journal of Marketing Research 687.

Gerard Quinn, Eilionóir Flynn, "Transatlantic Borrowings: The Past and Future of EU Non-Discrimination Law and Policy on the Ground of Disability" (2012) 60:1 The American Journal of Comparative Law 23.

Giancarlo F Frosio, "Reforming Intermediary Liability in the Platform Economy: A European Digital Single Market Strategy" (2018) 112 Northwestern University Law Review 18.

Global Commission on the Future of Work, *Work for a Brighter Future* (January 2019), online: ILO <https://www.ilo.org/global/publications/books/WCMS_662410/lang--en/index.htm>;

Gloria Boone, Jane Secci, Linda Gallant, "Emerging Trends in Online Advertising" (2010) 5 Doxa Comunicación 244.

Gordon Hull, "Successful Failure: What Foucault Can Teach Us About Privacy Self-Management in a World of Facebook and Bid Data" (2015) 17 Ethics and Information Technology 89.

Graham Pearce, Nicholas Platten, "Promoting the Information Society: The EU Directive on Electronic Commerce" (2000) 6:4 European Law Journal 363.

Gráinne de Búrca, "Evolutions in Antidiscrimination Law in Europe and North America" (2012) 60:1 The American Journal of Comparative Law 1.

Gregory C Keating, "The Idea of Fairness in the Law of Enterprise Liability" (1997) 95 Michigan Law Review 1266.

Gregory C Keating, "The Theory of Enterprise Liability and Common Law Strict Liability" (2001) 54 Vanderbilt Law Review 1285.

Gregory Voss, Kimberly A Houser, "GDPR: The End of Google and Facebook or a New Paradigm in Data Privacy?" (2018) 25 Richmond Journal of Law & Technology 1.

Gunnar Bender, "Bavaria v Felix Somm: The Pornography Conviction of the Former CompuServe Manager" (1998) International Journal of Communication Law and Policy 1.

Guy Davidov, "The Three Axes of Employment Relationships: A Characterization of Workers in Need of Protection" (2002) 52 The University of Toronto Law Journal 357.

Harold Davis, *Google Advertising Tools: Cashing in With AdSense, AdWords, and the Google APIS* (Sebastopol: O'Reilly Media, 2006).

Hayes Hagan, "How to Protect Consumer Data? Leave It to the Consumer Protection Agency: FTC Rulemaking as a Path to Federal Cybersecurity Regulation" (2019) 2019 Columbia Business Law Review 735.

Hazel Oliver, "Sexual Orientation: Perceptions, Definitions and Genuine Occupational Requirements" (2004) 33 Industrial Law Journal 1.

Helen Katz, The Media Handbook: A Complete Guide to Advertising Media Selection, Planning, Research, and Buying 3rd ed (Lawrence Erlbaum Associates 2009).

Hiro N Aragaki, "Equal Opportunity for Arbitration" (2011) 58 UCLA Law Review 1189;

Howard Beales, "The Value of Behavioral Targeting" (2010) 1 Network Advertising Initiative 1.

Hubert S Field, William H Holley, "The Relationship of Performance Appraisal System Characteristics to Verdicts in Selected Employment Discrimination Cases" (1982) 25:2 Academy of Management Journal 392.

Hugh J Cunningham, "Fair Housing Act: Newspaper Liability for Discriminatory Advertisements (1992) 37 Loyola Law Review 981.

Hunton & Williams LLO, Centre for Information Policy Leadership GDPR Implementation Project, Recommendations for Implementing Transparency, Consent and Legitimate Interest under the GDPR (May 2017), online: IOP <https://www.informationpolicycentre.com/uploads/5/7/1/0/57104281/cipl_recommendations_on_transparency_consent_and_legitimate_interest_under_the_gdpr_-19_may_2017-c.pdf>.

Ian Ayres, Frederick E Vars, Nasser Zakariya, "To Insure Prejudice: Racial Disparities in Taxicab Tipping" (2005) 114: The Yale Law Journal 1613.

Ibrahim Altaweel, Nathaniel Good, Chris Jay Hoofnagle, Web Privacy Census (December 2015), online: Technology Science <https://techscience.org/a/2015121502/>.

Ifeoma Ajunwa, "Age Discrimination by Platforms" (2019) 40 Berkeley Journal of Employment & Labor Law 1.

Ilaria Buri, Joris van Hoboken, The Digital Services Act (DSA) Proposal: A Critical Overview (October 2021), online: DSA Observatory, Institute for Information Law <https://dsa-observatory.eu/wp-content/uploads/2021/11/Buri-Van-Hoboken-DSA-discussion-paper-Version-28_10_21.pdf>.

Isabelle Rorive, "Lutter contre les Discriminations", in Caroline Bricteux, Benoit Frydman, *Grands Défis du Droit Global* (Brussels: Bruylant, 2018).

Jaani Riordan, *The Liability of Internet Intermediaries* (Oxford: OUP 2016).

Jackelyn Hwang, Michael Hankinson, Kreg Seven Bown, "Racial and Spatial Targeting: Segregation and Subprime Lending within and Across Metropolitan Areas" (2015) 93:3 Social Forces 1081.

James A Kushner, "Fair Housing Amendments Act of 1988: The Second Generation of Fair Housing" (1989) 42 Venderbilt Law Review 1049.

James D Shanahan, "Rethinking the Communications Decency Act: Eliminating Statutory Protection of Discriminatory Housing Advertisements on the Internet" (2007) 60 Federal Communications Law Journal 135.

James D Walsh, "Reaching Mrs. Murphy: A Call for Repeal of the Mrs. Murphy Exemption to the Fair Housing Act" (1999) 34 Harvard Civil Rights-Civil Liberties Law Review 605.

James W Fox Jr, "Intimations of Citizenship: Repressions and Expressions of Equal Citizenship in the Era of Jim Crow" (2006) 50 Howard Law Journal 113.

Jan Ahrens, James R Coyle, "A Content Analysis of Registration Processes on Websites: How Advertisers Gather Information to Customize Marketing Communications" (2011) 11 Journal of Interactive Advertising 12.

Jan Ondrich, Stephen Ross, Jon Yinger, "Geography of Housing Discrimination" (2001) 12 Journal of Housing Research 217.

Janine Berg, Marianne Furrer, Ellie Harmon, Uma Rani, Six Silberman, *Digital Labour Platforms and the Future of Work Towards Decent Work in the Online World* (September 2018), online: International Labour Organisation <https://www.ilo.org/wcmsp5/groups/public/---dgreports/---dcomm/---publ/documents/publication/wcms_645337.pdf >.

Janine Berg, Valerio de Stefano, *Regulating Work in the Gig Economy* (July 2015) online: ILO <https://iloblog.org/2015/07/10/regulating-work-in-the-gig-economy/>.

Jaqueline May Tom, "A Simple Compromise: The Need for a Federal Data Breach Notification Law" (2010) 84 St. John's Law Review 1569.

Jean Eberhart Dubofsky, "Fair Housing: A Legislative History and a Perspective" (1969) 8 Washburn Law Journal 149.

Jean R Sternlight, "Disarming Employees: How American Employers are Using Mandatory Arbitration to Deprive Workers of Legal Protection" (2015) 80 Brook. Law Review 1309.

Jean-Victor Maublanc, *Uberpop Est un Service de Transport Avant d'Etre un Service de Mise en Relation par Voie Électronique* (March 2018), online: Journal d'Actualité des Droits Européens <https://revue-jade.eu/article/view/2184>.

Jeff Kenner, "Uber Drivers Are Workers: The Expanding Scope of the Worker Concept in the UKs Gig Economy", in Jeff Kenner, Izabela Florczak, Marta Otto, *The Challenge of Labour Law in Europe* (Edward Elgar Publishing, 2019).

Jeff Kosseff, "Defending Section 230: The Value of Intermediary Immunity" (2010) 15:2 Journal of Technology Law & Policy 123.

Jeff Kosseff, "The Gradual Erosion of the Law that Shaped the Internet: Section 230's Evolution Over the Two Decades" (2016) 18:1 The Columbia Science & Technology Law Review 1.

Jefferson Duarte, Stephan Siegel, Lance Young, "Trust and Credit: The Role of Appearance in Peer-to-Peer Lending" (2012) 25:8 Review of Financial Studies 2455.

Jenny Van Doorn, Janny C Hoekstra, "Customization of Online Advertising: The Role of Intrusiveness" (2013) 24 Marketing Letters 339.

Jerian Oskam, Albert Boswijk, "Airbnb: The Future of Networked Hospitality Businesses" (2016) 2:1 Journal of Tourism Futures 22.

Jessica k Sink, Richard Bales, "Born in the Bandwidth: Digital Native as Pretext for Age Discrimination in Hiring" (2016) 31 ABA Journal of Labor & Employment Law 521.

Jessica Reingold Katz, "Finding Fault: Implications of Importing the Title VII Standard for Vicarious Punitive Liability to the Fair Housing Act" (2008) 29 Cardozo Law Review 2749.

Jianqing Chen, Jan Stallaert, "An Economic Analysis of Online Advertising Using Behavioral Targeting" (2014) 38 MIS Quarterly 429.

Jill Gross, "The Uberization of Arbitration Clauses" (2017) 9 Arbitration Law Review 43.

Jillian Kaltner, "Employment Status of Uber and Lyft Drivers: Unsettlingly Settled" (2018) 29 Hastings Women's Law Journal 29.

Jim Isaak and Mina J Hanna, "User Data Privacy: Facebook, Cambridge Analytica, and Privacy Protection" (2018) 51 Computer 56.

Joachim Brüb, "Experiences of Discrimination Reported by Turkish, Moroccan and Bangladeshi in Three European Cities" (2008) 34:6 Journal of Ethnic and Migration Studies 875l.

Joe R Feagin, "Excluding Blacks and Others from Housing: The Foundation of White Racism" (1999) 4:3 Cityscape 79.

John C P Goldberg, *Torts* (New York: OUP, 2010).

John D Inazu, "The Unsettling 'Well-Settled' Law of Freedom of Association" (2010) 43: 1 Connecticut Law Review 149.

John Purcell, *Individual Disputes at the Workplace: Alternative Dispute Resolution* (April 2010), online: Eurofound <https://www.eurofound.europa.eu/publications/report/2010/individual-disputes-at-the-workplace-alternative-disputes-resolution>.

John S Heywood, Patrick L O'Halloran, "Racial Earnings Differentials and Performance Pay" (2005) 40:2 The Journal of Human Resources 435.

Jon Messenger, Oscar Vargas Llave, Lutz Gschwind, Simon Boehmer, Greet Vermeylen, Mathijn Wilkens, *Working Anytime, Anywhere: The Effects on the World of Work* (February 2017) online: Eurofond <https://www.eurofound.europa.eu/publications/report/2017/working-anytime-anywhere-the-effects-on-the-world-of-work>.

Jonathan R Mayer and John C Mitchell, "Third-Party Web Tracking: Policy and Technology" (2012) IEEE Symposium on Security and Privacy 413.

Jonathan Zasloff, "The Secret History of the Fair Housing Act" (2016) 53 Harvard Journal of Legislation 247.

José González Cabañas, Ángel Cuevas, Rubén Cuevas, "Facebook Use of Sensitive Data for Advertising in Europe" (2018) Social and Information Networks Cornell University 1.

Joseph Stauffer, Ronald Buckley, "The Existence and Nature of Racial Bias in Supervisory Ratings" (2005) 90:3 Journal of Applied Psychology 586.

Joseph Turow, *The Daily You: How the New Advertising Industry Is Defining Your Identity and Your Worth* (Yale University Press 2011).

Joshua A Fairfield, "The God Paradox" (2009) 89:3 Boston University Law Review 1017.

Joy S Kimbrough, "The Federal Housing Act: No More Absolute Owner Liability When Employees Discriminate" (2003) 31 Southern University Law Review 109.

Juan Miguel Carrascosa, Jakub Mikians, Ruben Cuevas, Vijay Erramily, and Nikolaos Laoutaris, "I Always Feel Like Somebody's Watching Me: Measuring Online Behavioural Advertising" (2015) Proceedings of the 11th ACM Conference on Emerging Networking Experiments and Technologies 13.

Judith J Johnson, "Reasonable Factors Other than Age: The Emerging Specter of Ageist Stereotypes" (2009) 33 Seattle University Law Review 49.

Julie Adler, "The Public's Burden in a Digital Age: Pressures on Intermediaries and the Privatization of Internet Censorship" (2011) Journal Law & Policy 231.

Julie E Cohen, "Law for the Platform Economy" (2017) 51 UCDL Rev 133.

Julie Le Gallo, Yannick l'Horty, *Loic Du Parquet, Pasquale Petit, Les Discriminations dans L'Accès au Logement en France: un Testing de Couverture Nationale* (September 2018) online: HAL <https://halshs.archives-ouvertes.fr/halshs-01878188/document>.

Julie Ringelheim, "The Prohibition of Racial and Ethnic Discrimination in Access to Services under EU Law" (2010) 10 European Anti-Discrimination Law Review 11.

Jun Wand, Weinan Zhang, Shuai Yuan, "Display Advertising with Real-Time Bidding (RTB) and Behavioural Targeting" (2017) 11:5 Foundations and Trends in Information Retrieval 297.

Karen Alexander Horowitz, "When Is §230 Immunity Lost? The Transformation from Website Owner to Information Content Provider" (2007) 3:4 Washington Journal of Law, Technology & Arts 14.

Karine Perset, "The Economic and Social Role of Internet Intermediaries" (2010) 171 OECD Digital Economy Papers 1.

Kate Klonick, "The New Governs: The People, Rules, and Processes Governing Online Speech" (2017) 131 Harvard Law Review 1598.

Katherine Van Wezel Stone, "Mandatory Arbitration of Individual Employment Rights: The Yellow Dog Contract of the 1990's" (1996) 73 Denver University Law Review 1017.

Keith Cunningham-Parmeter, "From Amazon to Uber: Defining Employment in the Modern Economy" (2016) 96 Boston University Law Review 1673.

Keshab Nath, Sourish Dhar, Subhash Basishtha, "Web 1.0 to Web 3.0: The Evolution of the Web and Its Various Challenges" (2014) International Conference on Reliability Optimization and Information Technology 86.

Kit Burden, "Case Report: Liability of ISPs for Third Party Postings to Newsgroups Godfrey v Demon" (1999) 15:4 Computer Law & Security 260.

Koen Van der Bracht, "The Not-in-My-Property Syndrome: The Occurrence of Ethnic Discrimination in the Rental Housing Market in Belgium" (2015) 41:1 Journal of Ethnic and Migration Studies 158.

Kristof Heylen, Katleen Van den Broeck, "Discrimination and Selection in the Belgian Private Rental Market" (2015) 31:2 Housing Studies 223.

Larry D Kelly, Donald W Jugenheimer, Kim Bartel Sheehan, *Advertising Media Planning: A Brand Management Approach* (Routledge 2011).

Latanya Sweeney, "Discrimination in Online Ad Delivery" (2013) 56 ACM 44.

Laura Abramovsky, Rachel Griffith, "Outsourcing and Offshoring of Business Services: How Important Is ICT?" (2006) 4 Journal of the European Economic Association 594.

Lauren Guth Barnes, "How Mandatory Arbitration Agreements and Class Action Waivers Undermine Consumer Rights and Why We Need Congress to Act" (2015) 9:2 Harvard Law & policy Review 329.

Lauren M Weinstein, "The Role of Labor Law in Challenging English-Only Policies" (2012) 47 Harvard Civil Rights-Civil Liberties Law Review 219.

Laurie McCann, "The Age Discrimination in Employment Act at 50: When Will It Become a "Real" Civil Rights Statute" (2018) 33 ABA Journal of Labor & Employment Law 89.

Lawrence Rosenthal, "Saving Disparate Impact" (2012) 34 Cardozo Law Review 2157.

Leigh Gallagher, *Airbnb Story: How Three Ordinary Guys Disrupted an Industry, Made Billions, and Created Plenty of Controversy* (New York: Houghton Mifflin Harcourt, 2017).

Lilla Farkas, The Meaning of Racial or Ethnic Origin in EU Law: Between Stereotypes and Identities (January 2017), online: European Commission Directorate General for Justice and Consumers <https://op.europa.eu/en/publication-detail/-/publication/c1cf6b78–094c-11e7–8a35–01aa75ed71a1>.

Lincoln Quillian and others, "Meta-Analysis of Field Experiments Shows No Change in Racial Discrimination in Hiring Over Time" (2017) 114 Proceedings of the National Academy of Sciences 10870.

Linda E Fisher, "Target Marketing of Subprime Loans: Racialized Consumer Fraud & Reverse Redlining" (2010) 18 Journal of Law and Policy 121.

Linda Lye, "Title VII's Tangled Tale: The Erosion and Confusion of Disparate Impact and the Business Necessity Defense" (1998) 19 Berkeley Journal of Employment & Labor Law 315.

Linda L Schlueter, *Punitive Damages* (LexisNexis, 2015).

Lisa B Bingham, "Employment Arbitration: The Repeat Player Effect (1997) 1 Employment Rights & Employment Policy Journal 189.

Lisa Webley, "Qualitative Approaches to Empirical Legal Research", in Peter Cane, Herbert Kritzer (eds), Oxford Handbook of Empirical Legal Research (OUP, 2010).

Lisl Brunner, "The Liability of an Online Intermediary for Third-Party Content: The Watchdog Becomes the Monitor: Internet Liability after Delfi v Estonia" (2016) Human Rights Law Review 163.

Liza Estino Daoanis, "Performance Appraisal System: its Implication to Employee Performance" (2012) 2:3 International Journal of Economics and Management Sciences 55.

Lothar Determann, "Case Update: German CompuServe Director Acquitted on Appeal" (1999) 23:1 Hastings International and Comparative Law Review 109.

Lynn Frewer, Hans Van Trijp, *Understanding Consumers of Food Products* (Woodhead Publishing, 2006).

Lu-in Wang, "When the Customer is King: Employment Discrimination as Customer Service (2016) 23 Virginia Journal of Social Policy & the Law 249.

Lucy Vickers, "Achbita and Bougnaoui: One Step Forward and Two Steps Back for Religious Diversity in the Workplace" (2017) 8:3 European Labour Law Journal 232.

Magnus Carlsson, Stefan Eriksson, "Discrimination in the Rental Market for Apartments" (2014) 23 Journal of Housing Economics 41.

Manson Ameri, Sean Rogers, Lisa Schur, Douglas Kruse, "No Room at the Inn? Disability Access in the New Sharing Economy" (2019) Academy of Management 1.

Marc Bendick Jr, *Discrimination Against Racial and Ethnic Minorities in Access to Employment in the United States: Empirical Findings from Situation Testing* (Employment Department International Labor Office, 1996).

Marc Galanter, "The Vanishing Trial: An Examination of Trials and Related Matters in Federal and State Courts (2004) 1 Journal of Empirical Legal Studies 459.

Marcel Gommans, Krish S Krishman, Katrin B Scheffold, "From Brand Loyalty to e-Loyalty: A Conceptual Framework (2001) 3:1 Journal of Economic & Social Research 43.

Mareike Glöss, Moira McGregor, Barry Brown, "Designing for Labour: Uber and the On-Demand Mobile Workforce" (2016) Proceedings of the 2016 CHI conference on Human Factors in Computing Systems 1632.

Margot S Rubin, "Advertising and Title VIII: The Discriminatory Use of Models in Real Estate Advertisements" (1988) 98 Yale Law Journal 165, 178.

Marisa Salanova, Sonia Agut, José Maria Peiró, "Linking Organizational Resources and Work Engagement to Employee Performance and Customer Loyalty: The Mediation of Service Climate" (2005) 90:6 Journal of Applied Psychology 1217.

Mark A Lemley, "Rationalizing Internet Safe Harbors" (2007) 6 Journal on Telecommunication & High Technology Law 101.

Mark Bell, "Beyond European Labour Law? Reflections on the EU Racial Equality Directive" (2002) 8:3 European Law Journal 384.

Mark Bell, "The Principle of Equal Treatment, Widening and Deepening", in Paul Craig, Grainne de Búrca (eds) The Evolution of EU Law (New York: Oxford University Press, 2011).

Lisa Waddington, Mark Bell, "Exploring the Boundaries of Positive Action under EU Law: a Search for Conceptual Clarity" (2011) 48 Common Market Law Review 5.

Mark Freedland, Jeremias Adams-Prassl, "Employees, Workers, and the 'Sharing Economy" (2017) Oxford Legal Studies Research Paper No.19 1.

Mark N Wexler, "Reconfiguring the Sociology of the Crowd: Exploring Crowdsourcing" (2010) 31:1 International Journal of Sociology and Social Policy 6.

Marta Elvira, Robert Town, "The Effects of Race and Worker Productivity on Performance Evaluations" (2001) 40:4 Industrial Relations a Journal of Economy and Society 571.

Martien Y Shaub, "Why Uber Is an Information Society Service?" (2018) 7:3 Journal of European Consumer and Market Law 109.

Massimiliano Delfino, "Work in the Age of Collaborative Platforms Between Innovation and Tradition" (2018) 9:4 European Labour Law Journal 346.

Mathieu Brunel, Yannick l'Horty, Loic du Parquet, Pascale Petit, Les Discriminations dans l'Accès au Logement à Paris: Une Expérience Contrôlée (March 2017) online: HAL <https://ideas.repec.org/p/tep/tepprr/rr17–01.html>.

Matthew A Stowe, "Interpreting Place of Public Accommodation Under Title III of the ADA: A Technical Determination with Potentially Broad Civil Rights Implications" (2000) 50:1 Duke Law Journal 297.

Mattew Desmond, Monica Bell, "Housing, Poverty and the Law" (2015) 11 Annual Review of Law and Social Science 15.

Maurice Crul, Liesbeth Heering, The Position of the Turkish and Moroccan Second Generation in Amsterdam and Rotterdam: The TIES Studies in the Netherlands (Amsterdam: Amsterdam University Press, 2008).

Micah Jost, "Independent Contractors, Employees, and Entrepreneurialism Under National Labor Relations Act: A Worker-by-Worker Approach" (2011) 68 Washington & Lee Law Review 311.

Michael Ewens, Bryan Tomlin, Liang Choon Wang, "Statistical Discrimination or Prejudice? A Large Sample Field Experiment" (2014) 96 The Review of Economics and Statistics 119.

Michael J Klarman, "The Plessy Era" (1998) The Supreme Court Review 303.

Michael JA Berry, Gordon S Linoff, Data Mining Techniques: For Marketing, Sales, and Customer Relationship Management (Indianapolis: John Wiley & Sons, 2004).

Michael Luca, "Designing Online Marketplaces: Trust and Reputation Mechanisms" (2017) 17 Innovation Policy and the Economy 77.

Michael Lynn, Michael C Sturman, "Is the Customer Always Right? The Potential for Racial Bias in Customer Evaluations of Employee Performance" (2011) 41:9 Journal of Applied Social Psychology 2312.

Michael R Siebecker, "Cookies and the Common Law: Are Internet Advertisers Trespassing on Our Computers?" (2003) 76 Southern California Law Review 893.

Michael Todisco, "Share and Share Alike: Considering Racial Discrimination in the Nascent Room-Sharing Economy" (2014) 67 Stanford Law Review 121.

Michael Veale, Lilian Edwards, "Clarity, Surprises, and Further Questions in the Article 29 Working Party Draft Guidance on Automated Decision-Making and Profiling" (2018) 34 Computer Law & Security Review 398.

Michael Selma, "Was the Disparate Impact Theory a Mistake?" (2006) 53 UCLA Law Review 701.

Michèle Finck, "Distinguishing Internet Platforms from Transport Services: Elite Taxi v Uber Spain" (2018) 55:5 Common Market Law Review 1619.

Mike Bourne, Pippa Bourne, Handbook of Corporate Performance Management (Cornwall: John Wiley & Sons, 2011).

Mike Eisner, Christian Welz, Collective Dispute in an Enlarged European Union (November 2008) online: Eurofound <https://www.eurofound.europa.eu/publications/report/2006/industrial-relations-law-and-regulation/eiro-thematic-feature-collective-dispute-resolution-in-an-enlarged-european-union>.

Min Kyung Lee, Daniel Kusbit, Evan Metsky, Laura Dabbish, "Working with Machines: The Impact of Algorithmic and Data-Driven Management on Human Workers" (2015) Proceedings of the 33rd Annual ACM Conference on Human Factors in Computing Systems 1603.

Mireille Hildebrandt, "Criminal Law and Technology in a Data-Driven Society" in M Dubber and T Hörnle (eds), *The Oxford Handbook of Criminal Law* (Oxford: OUP 2014), p 174–176.

Mireille Hildebrandt, "Defining Profiling: A New Type of Knowledge?" in Mireille Hildebrandt and Serge Gutwirth (eds), *Profiling the European Citizen* (Spinger 2008).

Miriam A Cherry, "Beyond Misclassification: The Digital Transformation of Work" (2016) 37 Comparative Labor Law & Policy Journal 577.

Miriam Kullmann, "Platform Work: Algorithmic Decision-Making, and EU Gender Equality Law (2018) 34:1 International Journal of Comparative Labour Law and Industrial Relations 1.

Mitchell H Rubenstein, "Our Nation's Forgotten Workers: The Unprotected Volunteers" (2006) 9 Journal of Labor and Employment Law 147.

Molly Cohen, Arun Sundararajan, "Self-Regulation and Innovation in the Peer-to-Peer Sharing Economy" (2015) 82 University of Chicago Law Review 116.

Morgane Laouenan, Roland Rathelot, *Ethnic Discrimination on an Online Marketplace of Vacation Rental* (April 2017), online: HAL Working Paper Series <https://hal.archives-ouvertes.fr/hal-01514713/document>.

Myra B Young Armstead, "Revisiting Hotels and Other Lodgings: American Tourist Spaces Through the Lens of Black Pleasure Travelers 1850, 1950" (2005) 25 The Journal of Decorative and Propaganda 136.

Nancy Leong, "The First Amendment and Fair Housing in the Economy Platform" (2017) 78 Ohio State Law Journal 1001.

Nancy Leong, Aaron Belzer, "The New Public Accommodations: Race Discrimination in the Platform Economy" (2017) 105 The Georgetown Law Journal 1271.

Nancy S Kim, "Web Site Proprietorship and Online Harassment" (2009) 3 Utah Law Review 993.

Natalie Boccadoro, "Housing Rights and Racial Discrimination" (2009) 9 European Anti-Discrimination Law Review 21.

Natasha Simmons, "Facebook and the Privacy Frontier" (2012) 33:3 Business Law Review 58.

Nathaniel Decker, "Housing Discrimination and Craigslist" (2010) 14.1 The Public Policy Journal of the Cornell Institute for Public Affairs 43.

Nathaniel Persily, "The 2016 US Election: Can Democracy Survive the Internet?" (2017) 28 Journal of Democracy 63.

Neil Richards, Andrew Serwin and Tyler Blake, "Understanding American Privacy" in Gloria González Fuster, Rosamunde Van Brakel and Paul De Hert (eds), *Research Handbook on Privacy and Data Protection Law: Values, Norms and Global Politics* (Edward Elgar Publishing 2018).

Nick Kotz, *Judgement Days: Lyndon Baines Johnson, Martin Luther King Jr, and the Laws that Changed America* (Mariner Books 2006).

Nicola Countouris, "The Concept of 'Worker' in European Labour Law: Fragmentation, Autonomy, and Scope" (2018) 47:2 Industrial Law Journal 192.

Nicola Countouris, Mark Freedland, *The Personal Scope of the EU Sex Equality Directives* (April 2012), online: European Commission European Network of Legal Experts in the Field of Gender Equality <https://op.europa.eu/en/publication-detail/-/publication/d6139fa9-b67b-4bfb-99c6-526d016f7a7d>.

Nicola Countouris, *The Changing Law of the Employment Relationship* (Aldershot: Ashgate, 2007).

Nicolas Bernard, "Les Femmes, la Précarité et le Mal-Logement: un Lien Fatal à Dénouer" (2007) 1970 Courrier Hebdomadaire du Crisp 5.

Nicolas Bernard, "Les Lois Anti-Discrimination et le Secteur du Logement (Privé et Social)" in Sébastien Van Drooghenbroeck et al, *De Nieuwe Federale Antidiscriminatiewetten – Les Nouvelles Lois Luttant Contre la Discrimination* (Bruxelles: La Charte, 2008).

Nicole Gurran, "Global Home-Sharing, Local Communities and the Airbnb Debate: A Planning Research Agenda (2018) 19:2 Planning Theory & Practice 298.

Nicole J DeSario, "Re-conceptualizing Meritocracy: The Decline of Disparate Impact Discrimination Law" (2003) 38 Harvard Civil Rights Civil Liberties Law Review 479.

Nigel Hill, Greg Roche, Rachel Allen, *Customer Satisfaction: The Customer Experience Through the Customer's Eyes* (Cogent Publishing, 2007).

Noah D Zatz, "Managing the Macaw: Third-Party Harassers, Accommodation, and the Disaggregation of Discriminatory Intent" (2009) 109 Columbia Law Review 1357.

Noah Zatz, "Working Beyond the Reach or Grasp of Employment Law" in Anette Bernhardt, Heather Boushey, Laura Dresser, Chris Tilly, *The Gloves-Off Economy: Workplace Standards at the Bottom of America's Labor Market* (Champaign: Labor and Employment Relations Association, 2008).

Nupur Choudhury, "World Wide Web and Its Journey from Web 1.0 to Web 4.0" (2014) 5:6 International Journal of Computer Science and Information Technologies 8096.

OECD, *An Introduction to Online Platforms and their Role in the Digital Transformation* (Paris: OECD Publishing, 2019).

OECD, *New Forms of Work in the Digital Economy (June 2016) online: OECD Digital Economy Papers* <https://www.oecd-ilibrary.org/science-and-technology/new-forms-of-work-in-the-digital-economy_5jlwnklt820x-en>.

OECD, *Policy Responses to New Forms of Work* (Paris: OECD Publishing, 2019).

OECD, *The Role of Internet Intermediaries in Advancing Public Policy Objectives*, DSTI/ICCP (2010)11/FINAL (June 2011), online: OECD Directorate for Science, Technology and Industry <www.oecd.org/internet/ieconomy/48685066.pdf>.

Olivier De Schutter, Julie Ringelheim, "Ethnic Profiling: A Rising Challenge for European Human Rights Law" (2008) 71 Modern Law Review 358.

Olivier De Schutter, *Links Between Migration and Discrimination: A Legal Analysis of the Situation in EU Member States, European Network of Legal Experts in Gender Equality and Non-Discrimination* (July 2016) online: European Commission Directorate General for Justice and Consumers <https://www.equalitylaw.eu/downloads/3917-links-between-migration-and-discrimination>.

Olivier De Schutter, Natalie Boccadoro, *Le Droit au Logement Dans l'Union Européenne* (February 2005) online: CRIHO Working Paper Series <https://cridho.uclouvain.be/documents/Working.Papers/CridhoWPs022005.PDF>.

Omer Tene, Jules Polenetsky, "To Track or Do Not Track: Advancing Transparency and Individual Control in Online Behavioral Advertising" (2012) 13 Minnesota Journal of Law 281.

Open Society Justice Initiative, *Employer's Bar on Religious Clothing and European Union Discrimination Law* (2016), online: Justice Initiative <https://www.justiceinitiative.org/uploads/3ee205fb-ad07-4ef2-9d45-2af0ec8101dc/briefing-cjeu-headscarves-20160712.pdf>.

Orin S Kerr, "Norms of Computer Trespass" (2016) 116 Columbia Law Review 1143.

Orly Lobel, "The Gig Economy & the Future of Employment and Labor Law" (2017) 51 University of San Francisco Law Review 51.

Orly Lobel, "The Law of The Platform" (2016) 101 Minnesota Law Review 87.

Patrick F McKay, Michael A McDaniel, "A Reexamination of Black-White Mean Differences in Work Performance: More Data, More Moderators" (2006) 91:3 Journal of Applied Psychology 538.

Patrick Van Eecke, "Online service providers and liability: A plea for a balanced approach" (2011) 48:5 Common Market Law Review 1455.

Paul Barford, "Adscape: Harvesting and Analyzing Online Display Ads" (2014) Proceedings of the 23rd International Conference on World Wide Web 597.

Paul Conway, "Preservation in the Age of Google, Digitization, Digital Preservation, and Dilemmas" (2010) 80:1 The Library Quarterly 61.

Paul M Schwartz, Daniel Solove, "The PII Problem: Privacy and a New Concept of Personally Identifiable Information" (2011) 86 New York University Law Review 1814.

Pauline T Kim and Sharion Scott, "Discrimination in Online Employment Recruiting" (2019) 63 St. Louis University Law Journal 1.

Peter C Evans, Annabelle Gawer, "The Rise of the Platform Enterprise: A Global Survey" (2016) The Emerging Platform Economy Series 1.

Peter Swire, *Lessons from Fair Lending Law for Fair Marketing and Big Data* (September 2014), online: Federal Trade Commission <https://www.ftc.gov/system/files/documents/public_comments/2014/09/00042-92638.pdf>.

Philip Yannella, "The Differing US and EU Regulatory Responses to Rise in Algorithmic Profiling" (2018) 33 Forum Committee on Communications Law American Bar Association 19.

Philipe Aigran, *Sharing: Culture and the Economy in the Internet Age* (Amsterdam: Amsterdam University Press, 2012).

Philipp Hacker, "Uber Pop, UberBlack, and the Regulation of Digital Platforms after the Asociación Profesional Elite Taxi Judgement of the CJEU" (2018) 14:1 European Review of Contract Law 80.

Philippa Watson, "Equality, Fundamental Rights and the Limits of Legislative Discretion: Comment on Test Achats" (2011) 36 European Law Review 896.

Phillip Morgan, "Certainty in Vicarious Liability: A Quest for a Chimaera?" (2016) 75:2 The Cambridge Law Journal 202.

R Hayes Johnson Jr, "Defamation in Cyberspace: A Court Takes a Wrong Turn on the Information Superhighway in Stratton Oakmont, Inc. v Prodigy Services Co" (1996) Arkansas Law Review 589.

Rachel Botsman, Roo Rogers, *What's Mine is Yours: The Rise of Collaborative Consumption* (New York: HarperCollins, 2010).

Ramesh Neupane, "Relationship Between Customer Satisfaction and Business Performance: A Case Study of Lloyds Bank UK" (2014) 1:2 International Journal of Social Sciences and Management 74.

Ray Fisman, Michael Luca, "Fixing Discrimination in Online Marketplaces" (2016) 94:2 Harvard Business Review 2.

René Böheim, Ilrike Muehlberger, "Dependent Forms of Self-Employment in the UK: Identifying Workers on the Border between Employment and Self-Employment" (2009) 42:2 Journal of Labour Market Research 182.

Richard A Epstein, "Public Accommodations Under the Civil Rights Act of 1964: Why Freedom of Association Counts as a Human Right" (2014) 66 Stanford Law Review 1241.

Richard A Primus, "Equal Protection and Disparate Impact: Round Three" (2003) 117 Harvard Law Review 493.

Richard Painter, Ann Holmes, Cases and Materials on Employment Law 10th ed (Oxford University Press, 2015).

Richard Rothstein, The Color of Law: A Forgotten History of How Our Government Segregated America (New York: Liveright Publishing, 2017).

Rigel C Oliveri, "Discriminatory Housing Advertisements Online: Lessons from Craigslist" (2010) 43 Indiana Law Review 1125.

Rishi Ahuja, Ronan C Lyons, "The Silent Treatment: LGBT Discrimination in the Sharing Economy" (2017) Trinity Economics Papers, Trinity College Dublin, Department of Economics 1.

Rob Jagtenberg, Annie de Roo, "Employment Disputes and Arbitration: An Account of Irreconcilability With Reference to the EU and the USA" (2018) 68 Zbornik PFZ 17.

Robert L Redfearn III, "Sharing Economy Misclassification: Employees and Independent Contractors in Transportation Network Companies" (2016) 31 Berkeley Technology Law Journal 1023.

Robert Sprague, "Worker (Mis)Classification in the Sharing Economy: Trying to Fit Square Pegs into Round Holes" (2015) 31:1 ABA Journal of Labor & Employment Law 53.

Roberto J Gonzalez, "Hacking the Citizenry? Personality Profiling, Big Data and the Election of Donald Trump" (2017) 33 Anthropology Today 9.

Robin L Snipes, Neal F Thomson, Sharon L Oswald, "Gender Bias in Customer Evaluations of Service Quality: An Empirical Investigation" (2006) 20:4 Journal of Services Marketing 274.

Rosa Julia-Barcelo, Kamiel J Koelman, "Intermediary Liability: Intermediary Liability in the E-Commerce Directive, So Far, So Good, But It's Not Enough" (2000) 16:4 Computer Law & Security Review 231.

Rosalie Koolhoven, *Impulse Paper on Specific Liability Issues Raised by the Collaborative Economy in the Accommodation Sector*, Paris-Amsterdam-Barcelona (May 2016), online: <https://sharingcitiesalliance.knowledgeowl.com/help/impulse-

paper-on-specific-liability-issues-raised-by-the-collaborative-economy-in-the-accommodation-sector>.

Rosamunde Van Brakel, Paul De Hert, "Policing, Surveillance and Law in a Pre-Crime Society: Understanding the Consequences of Technology Based Strategies" (2011) 20 Technology-Led Policing 165.

Ross D Petty, Anne-Marie G Harris, Toni Broaddus, "Regulating Target Marketing and Other Race-Based Advertising Practices" (2003) 8:2 Michigan Journal of Race & Law 335.

Rossana Ducato, Miriam Kullmann, Marco Rocca, "European Legal Perspectives on Customer Ratings and Discrimination", in Tindara Addabbo, Ylenia Curzi, Olga Rymkevich, *Performance Appraisal in Modern Employment Relations: An Interdisciplinary Approach* (Palgrave Macmillan, 2019).

Ruomeng Cui, Jun Li, Dennis Zhang, "Reducing Discrimination with Reviews in the Sharing Economy: Evidence from Field Experiments on Airbnb" (2019) Management Science 1.

Russel Belk, "You Are What You Can Access: Sharing and Collaborative Consumption Online" (2014) 67:8 Journal of Business Research 1595.

Ryan Calo, Alex Rosenblat, "The Taking Economy: Uber, Information and Power" (2017) 117 Columbia Law Review 1623.

Sako Musterd, "Social and Ethnic Segregation in Europe: Levels, Causes and Effects" (2005) 27:3 Journal of Urban Affairs 331.

Samuel R Bagenstos, "The Unrelenting Libertarian Challenge to Public Accommodations Law" (2014) 66 Stanford Law Review 1205.

Sandra F Sperino, "Disparate Impact or Negative Impact? The Future of Non-Intentional Discrimination Claims Brought by the Elderly" (2005) 13 Elder Law Journal 339.

Sandra Fredman, "Equality: A New Generation?" (2001) 2:1 Industrial Law Journal 145.

Sandra Fredman, *Discrimination Law* 2ed (Oxford University Press, 2012).

Sandra Fredman, "Pasts and Futures: EU Equality Law", in Alan Bogg, Cathryn Costello, CLA Davies (eds), Research Handbook on EU Labour Law (Edward Elgar Publishing, 2016).

Sandra Fredman, Darcy Du Toit, "One Small Step Towards Decent Work: Uber v Aslam in the Court of Appeal" (2019) 48:2 Industrial Law Journal 260.

Sandra Wachter, "Affinity Profiling and Discrimination by Association in Online Behavioral Advertising" (2020) 35:2 Berkeley Technology Law Journal 367.

Sandra Wachter, "Normative Challenge of Identification in the Internet of Things: Privacy, Profiling, Discrimination, and the GDPR" (2018) 34 Computer Law & Security Review 436.

Schona Jolly, "Islamic Headscarves and the Workplace Reach the CJEU: The Battle for Substantive Equality" (2016) 6 European Human Rights Law Review 622.

Scott Galloway, *The Four: The Hidden DNA of Amazon, Apple, Facebook, and Google* (New York: Portfolio, 2017).

Shahrzad T Radbod, "Craigslist: A Case for Criminal Liability for Online Service Providers?" (2010) 25 Berkeley Technology Law Journal 597.

Shawn Marie Boyne, "Data Protection in the United States" (2018) 66 The American Journal of Comparative Law 299.

Simon Deakin, "Interpreting Employment Contracts: Judges, Employers and Workers" (2004) 20:2 International Journal of Comparative Labour Law and Industrial Relations 201.

Siona Listokin, "Does Industry Self-Regulation of Consumer Data Privacy Work?" (2017) 15 IEEE Security & Privacy 92.

Sofia Ranchordás, "Does Sharing Mean Caring? Regulating Innovation in the Sharing Economy" (2015) 16:1 Minnesota Journal of Law, Science & Technology 413.

Sofia Ranchordás, "Public Values, Private Regulators: Between Regulation and Reputation in the Sharing Economy" (2019) 13:2 The Law & Ethics of Human Rights 203.

Solon Barocas, Andrew D Selbst, "Big Data's Disparate Impact" (2016) 104:3 California Law Review 671.

Sonia Arbaci, "(Re)Viewing Ethnic Residential Segregation in Southern European Cities: Housing and Urban Regimes as Mechanisms of Marginalisation (2008) 23 Housing Studies 589.

Soontae An, Hannah Kang, Hyun Seug Jin, "Self-Regulation for Online Behavioral Advertising (OBA): Analysis of OBA Notices" (2018) 24 Journal of Promotion Management 270.

Sophie C Boerman, Sanne Kruikemeier, Frederik Zuiderveen Borgesius, "Online Behavioral Advertising: A Literature Review and Research Agenda" (2017) 46 Journal of Advertising 363.

Sophie Robin-Olivier, "The Evolution of Direct Effect in the EU: Stocktaking, Problems, Projections" (2014) 12:1 International Journal of Constitutional Law 165.

Sophie Robin-Olivier, "French Labour Law: Testing the Possibility of a Legal Transplant", in Reasonable Accommodation for Religion, and Other Motives, Bulletin of Comparative Labour Relations, Vol 93, 2016, p 145.

Sophie Stalla-Bourdillon, "Chilling ISPs... When Private Regulators Act Without Adequate Public Framework" (2010) 26:3 Computer Law & Security Review 290.

Sophie Stalla-Bourdillon, "Internet Intermediaries as Responsible Actors? Why It Is Time to Rethink the e-Commerce Directive as Well", in: Luciano Floridi, Mariarosaria Taddeo, The Responsibilities of Online Service Providers (Springer, 2017).

Sophie Stalla-Bourdillon, "Sometimes One Is Not Enough! Securing Freedom of Expression, Encouraging Private Regulation, or Subsidizing Internet Intermediaries or All Three at the Same Time: The Dilemma of Internet Intermediaries' Liability (2012) 7:2 Journal of International Commercial Law and Technology 154.

Stacy E Seischnaydre, "Is Disparate Impact Having Any Impact: An Appellate Analysis of Forty Years of Disparate Impact Claims under the Fair Housing Act" (2013) 63 American University Law Review 357.

Stan Malos, "Overt Stereotype Biases and Discrimination in the Workplace: Why haven't We fixed this by now?" (2015) 27:4 Employee Responsibilities and Rights Journal 271.

Stephen Collins, "Saving Fair Housing on the Internet: The Case for Amending the Communication Decency Act" (2008) 102:3 Northwestern University Law Review 1471.

Stephen F Befort, "An Empirical Examination of Case Outcomes Under the ADA Amendments Act" (2013) 70: Washington & Lee Law Review 2027.

Stephen L Ross, Margery Austin Turner, "Housing Discrimination in Metropolitan America: Explaining Changes Between 1989 and 2000" (2005) 52:2 Social Problems 152.

Stephen R Miller, "First Principles for Regulating the Sharing Economy" (2016) 53 Harvard Journal on Legislation 147.

Steven C Bennett, "Regulating Online Behavioral Advertising" (2011) 44:4 The John Marshall Law Review 889.

Susan D Carle, "A Social Movement History of Title VII Disparate Impact Analysis" (2011) 63 Florida Law Review 251.

Susan Freiwald, "Comparative Institutional Analysis in Cyberspace: The Case of Intermediary Liability for Defamation" (2000) 14 Harvard Journal Law & Technology 569.

Susan M Freese, Craigslist: *The Company and Its Founder* (ABDO, 2011).

Susan Rose-Ackerman, "Regulation and the Law of Torts (1991) 81 American Economic Review 54.

Taco Van Peijpe, "EU Limits for the Personal Scope of Employment Law" (2012) 3:1 European Labour Law Journal 35.

Tae H Baek and Mariko Morimoto, "Stay Away from Me: Examining the Determinants of Consumers Avoidance of Personalized Advertising" (2012) 41 Journal of Advertising 59.

Tal Z Zarsky, "Understanding Discrimination in the Scored Society" (2014) 89 Washington Law Review 1375.

Thomas J Stipanowich, J Ryan Lamare, "Living with ADR: Evolving Perceptions and Use of Mediation, Arbitration and Conflict Management in Fortune 1000 Corporations" (2014) 19 Harvard Negotiation Law Review 1;

Till Speicher, "Potential for Discrimination in Online Targeted Advertising" (2018) 81 Proceedings of Machine Learning Research 1.

Tim Iglesias, "Does Fair Housing Law Apply to 'Shared Living Situations'? Or, the Trouble with Roommates" (2014) 22:2 Journal of Affordable Housing & Community Development Law 111.

Tim O'Reilly, "What is Web 2.0? Design Patterns and Business Models for the Next Generation of Software", in Helen Margaret Donelan, Karen Lesley Kear, Magnus Ramage, *Online Communication and Collaboration* (New York: Routledge, 2010).

Tindara Addabbo, "Wage Discrimination by Gender and Performance Evaluation", in Tindara Addabbo, Edoardo Ales, Ylenia Curzi, Tommaso Fabbri, Olga Rymkecivh, Iacopo Senatori (eds) *Performance Appraisal in Modern Employment* Relations (Palgrave Macmillan, 2019).

Tobias Kollmann, Carina Lomberg, Anika Peschl, "Web 1.0, Web 2.0 and Web 3.0: The Development of E-Business", in *Encyclopedia of E-Commerce Development, Implementation and Management* (IGI Global, 2010).

Tony Cole, Ilias Bantekas, Frederico Ferretti, Christine Riefa, Barbara Warwas, Pietro Ortolani, *Legal Instruments and Practice of Arbitration in the EU* (November 2014), online: European Parliament <https://www.europarl.europa.eu/RegData/etudes/STUD/2015/509988/IPOL_STU%282015%29509988_EN.pdf>.

Usama Fayyad, "The Digital Physics of Data Mining" (2001) 44 Communication of the ACM.

V Kumar, Gupta Shaphali, "Conceptualizing the Evolution and Future of Advertising" (2016) 45:3 Journal of Advertising 302.

Valerio de Stefano, Antonio Aloisi, *European Legal Framework for Digital Labour Platforms* (October 2018) online: European Commission <jrc112243_legal_framework_digital_labour_platforms_final.pdf>.

Valerio de Stephano, "The Rise of the Just-in-Time Workforce: On-Demand Work, Crowdwork, and Labor Protection in the Gig-Economy" (2016) 37 Comparative Labor Law & Policy Journal 471.

Vanessa Katz, "Regulating the Sharing Economy" (2015) 30:4 Berkeley Technology Law Journal 1067.

Varty Defterderian, "Fair Housing Council v Roommates.com: A New Path for Section 230 Immunity" (2009) 24 Berkeley Technology Law Journal 563.

Vassilis Hatzopoulos, "Vers un Cadre de la Régulation des Plateformes? (2019) 3 Revue Internationale de Droit Économique 399.

Vassilis Hatzopoulos, Sofia Roma, "Caring for Sharing? The Collaborative Economy under EU law (2017) 54:1 Common Market Law Review 81.

Vassilis Hatzopoulos, *The Collaborative Economy and the EU Law* (Oregon: Hart Publishing, 2018).

Veena B Dubal, "Winning the Battle, Losing the War: Assessing the Impact of Misclassification Litigation on Workers in the Gig Economy (2017) Wiscosin Law Review 739.

Veena Dubal, "The Drive to Precarity: A Political History of Work, Regulation, & Labor Advocacy in San Francisco's Taxi & Uber Economies" (2017) 38:1 Berkeley Journal of Employment & Labor Law 73.

Venoo Kakar, Joel Voelz, Julia Wu, Julisa Franco, "The Visible Host: Does Race Guide Airbnb Rental Rates in San Francisco? (2018) 40 Journal of Housing Economics 25.

Veronica M Reed, "Civil Rights Legislation and the Housing Status of Black Americans: Evidence from Fair Housing Audits and Segregation Indices" (1991) 19 The Review of Black Political Economy 29.

Victor S Maas, Raquel Torres-González, "Subjective Performance Evaluation and Gender Discrimination" (2011) 101 Journal of Business and Ethics 687.

Viktor Mayer-Schönberger, Kenneth Cukier, Big Data: A Revolution That Will Transform How We Live, Work and Think (Houghton Mifflin Harcourt 2013).

Will Qiu, Palo Parigi, Bruno Abrahao, "More Stars or More Reviews? Differential Effects of Reputation on Trust in the Sharing Economy" (2018) Proceedings of the CHI 20.

Willem Pieter De Groen, Ilaria Maselli, Brian Fabo, The Digital Market for Local Services: A One-Night Stand for Workers? (April 2016), online: CEPS European Commission <https://publications.jrc.ec.europa.eu/repository/handle/JRC100678>.

Willem Pieter De Groen, Ilaria Maselli, The Impact of the Collaborative Economy on the Labour Market (June 2016), online CEPS European Commission <https://www.ceps.eu/system/files/SR138CollaborativeEconomy_0.pdf>.

Willy E Rice, "Race, Gender, 'Redlining' and the Discriminatory Access to Loans, Credit, and Insurance: A Historical and Empirical Analysis of Consumers Who Sued

Lenders and Insurers in Federal and State Courts, 1950–1995" (1996) 33 San Diego Law Review 583.

Wilma B Liebman, Andrew Lyubarsky, "Crowdwork, the Law, and the Future of Work" (2016) 1 Perspectives on Work 22.

Winnie F Taylor, "The ECOA and Disparate Impact Theory: A Historical Perspective" (2018) 26:2 Journal of Law and Policy 576.

Winnie F Taylor, "Proving Racial Discrimination and Monitoring Fair Lending Compliance: The Missing Data Problem in Nonmortgage Credit" (2011) 31:1 Review of Banking and Financial Law 199.

Woodrow Hartzog, Daniel J Solove, "The Scope and Potential of FTC Data Protection" (2015) 83 The George Washington Law Review 2230.

World Summit on the Information Society (WSIS), Declaration of Principles: Building the Information Society: A Global Challenge in the New Millennium. Document WSIS-03/Geneva/Doc/4-E/2003 (December 2003) online: ITU <www.itu.int/net/wsis/docs/geneva/official/dop.html >.

WP25, Guidelines on Automated Individual Decision Making and Profiling for the Purposes of Regulation 2016/679 (February 2018), online: European Commission <https://ec.europa.eu/newsroom/article29/item-detail.cfm?item_id=612053>   p 5–6.

Yasmine Taraseviwicz, Niki Borofsky, "International Labor and Employment Arbitration: A French and European Perspective" (2013) 28 ABA Journal of Labor and Employment Law 349.

Yioula Melanthiou, Fotis Pavlou and Eleni Constantinou, "The Use of Social Network Sites as an E-Recruitment Tool" (2015) 20 Journal of Transnational Management 31.

Yulia A Timofeeva, "Hate Speech Online: Restricted or Protected. Comparison of Regulations in the United States and Germany (2003) 12 Transatlantic Law & Policy 253.

2.   REPORTS

Adrijana Martinovic, *Country Report Gender Equality Croatia* (January 2019), online: European Commission Directorate General for Justice and Consumers <https://www.equalitylaw.eu/downloads/4995-croatia-country-report-gender-equality-2019-pdf-1-20-mb>.

Aileen Mc Colgan, *National Protection Beyond the Two EU Anti-Discrimination Directives: The Grounds of Religion and Belief, Disability, Age and Sexual Orientation Beyond Employment* (September 2013), online: European Commission Directorate for Consumers and Justice <https://tandis.odihr.pl/handle/20.500.12389/21745>.

Alexandra Timmer, Linda Senden, *A Comparative Analysis of Gender Equality Law in Europe 2018* (January 2019), online: European Commission Directorate-General for Justice and Consumers <https://www.equalitylaw.eu/downloads/4829-a-comparative-analysis-of-gender-equality-law-in-europe-2018-pdf-807-kb>.

Alexandra Timmer, Linda Senden, *How Are EU Rules Transposed into National Law in 2018? Thematic Report of the European Network of Legal Experts in the Non-Discrimination Field* (January 2019), online: European Commission Directorate-General for Justice and Consumers <https://www.equalitylaw.eu/downloads/4830-gender-equality-law-in-europe-2018-pdf-554-kb>.

Amparo Ballester, *Country Report Gender Equality Spain* (January 2019), online: European Commission Directorate General for Justice and Consumers <https://www.equalitylaw.eu/downloads/4994-spain-country-report-gender-equality-2019-pdf-1-19-mb>.

Andras Kadar, *Report on Measures to Combat Discrimination Directives 2000/43/EC and 2000/78/EC Country Report Hungary* (January 2013), online: European Commission European Network of Legal Experts in the Non-Discrimination Field <https://www.equalitylaw.eu/downloads/4177-hungary-country-report-non-discrimination-2013-1-23-mb>.

Andras Kadar, *Transposition and Implementation at National Level of Council Directives 2000/43 and 2000/78 Country Report Hungary* (January 2019), online: European Commission Directorate for Justice and Consumers <https://www.equalitylaw.eu/downloads/5001-hungary-country-report-non-discrimination-2019-pdf-1-80-mb>.

Anu Iaas, *Country Report Gender Estonia (January 2019), online: European Commission Directorate General for Justice and Consumers* <https://www.equalitylaw.eu/downloads/5060-estonia-country-report-gender-equality-2019-pdf-1-18-mb>.

Article 19, *Self-Regulation and "Hate Speech" on Social Media Platforms* (March 2018), *online: article 19* <https://www.article19.org/wp-content/uploads/2018/03/Self-regulation-and-'hate-speech'-on-social-media-platforms_March2018.pdf>.

Athanasios Theodoris, *Country Report Non-Discrimination: Transposition and Implementation at National Level of Council Directives 2000/43 and 2000/78 Greece* (January 2019), online: European Commission Directorate-General for Justice and Consumers <https://www.equalitylaw.eu/downloads/4962-greece-country-report-non-discrimination-2019-pdf-1-28-mb>.

Bill Edgar, *Policy Measures to Ensure Access to Decent Housing for Migrants and Ethnic Minorities* (December 2004), online: European Commission <https://ec.europa.eu/employment_social/social_inclusion/docs/decenthousing_en.pdf>.

Biruté Sabatauskaité, *Country Report Non-Discrimination: Transposition and Implementation at National Level of Council Directives 2000/43 and 2000/78 Lithuania* (January 2019), online: European Commission Directorate-General for Justice and Consumers <https://www.equalitylaw.eu/downloads/5015-lithuania-country-report-non-discrimination-2019-pdf-1-77-mb>.

Chiara Faille, *Country Report Non-Discrimination: Transposition and Implementation at National Level of Council Directives 2000/43 and 2000/78 Italy* (January 2019), online: European Commission Directorate-General for Justice and Consumers <https://www.equalitylaw.eu/downloads/5014-italy-country-report-non-discrimination-2019-pdf-1-36-mb>.

Compact, *Report on Current Policies and Regulatory Frameworks* (February 2019), online: European Commission <http://compact-media.eu/wp-content/uploads/2019/11/D2.1-Report-on-current-policies-and-regulatory-frameworks.pdf>.

Corina Demetriou, *Country Report Non-Discrimination: Transposition and Implementation at National Level of Council Directives 2000/43 and 2000/78 Cyprus* (January 2019), online: European Commission Directorate-General for Justice and Consumers <https://www.equalitylaw.eu/downloads/5067-cyprus-country-report-non-discrimination-2019-pdf-2–07-mb>.

David S Pedulla, *Pathways the Poverty and Inequality Report – Gender* (November 2018), online: Stanford <https://inequality.stanford.edu/sites/default/files/Pathways_SOTU_2018.pdf>.

Dieter Schindlauer, *Country Report Non-Discrimination: Transposition and Implementation at National Level of Council Directives 2000/43 and 2000/78* (January 2019), online: European Commission Directorate General for Justice and Consumers <https://www.equalitylaw.eu/downloads/4984-austria-country-report-non-discrimination-2019-pdf-1–49-mb>.

Emmanuelle Bribosia, Isabelle Rorive, with the collaboration of Areg Navasartian, Assal Sharifrazi, *Country Report Non-Discrimination: Transposition and Implementation at National Level of Council Directives 2000/43 and 2000/78 Belgium* (January 2019), online: European Commission Directorate-General for Justice and Consumers <https://www.equalitylaw.eu/downloads/5034-belgium-country-report-non-discrimination-2019-pdf-2–09-mb>.

Equal Employment Opportunity Commission, *Age Discrimination in Employment Act Charges Filed with EEOC* (December 2018), online: EEOC <https://www.eeoc.gov/eeoc/statistics/enforcement/adea.cfm>.

Equality and Human Rights Commission, *How Fair is Britain? Equality, Human Rights and Good Relations in 2010* (October 2010) online: Equality Human Rights <https://www.equalityhumanrights.com/sites/default/files/how-fair-is-britain.pdf>.

Eugenia Caracciolo di Torella, *Directive 2004/113/EC on Gender Equality in Goods and Services – In Search of the Potential of a Forgotten Directive* (2021) online: European Commission Directorate General for Justice and Consumers <https://www.equalitylaw.eu/downloads/5614-directive-2004–113-ec-on-gender-equality-in-goods-and-services-in-search-of-the-potential-of-a-forgotten-directive-1–38-mb>.

Eugenia Caracciolo di Torella, Bridgette McLellan, *Gender Equality and the Collaborative Economy* (March 2018), online: European Commission <https://www.equalitylaw.eu/downloads/4573-gender-equality-and-the-collaborative-economy-pdf-721-kb>.

European Commission, *2018 Report on Equality Between Women and Men in the EU* (March 2018), online: Publication Office of the EU <https://op.europa.eu/en/publication-detail/-/publication/950dce57–6222–11e8-ab9c-01aa75ed71a1>.

European *Commission, The Use of Collaborative Platforms: Flash Eurobarometer 438* (July 2016) online: EU Open Data Portal <ec.europa.eu/ COMMFrontOffice/PublicOpinion/index.cfm/ResultDoc/download/DocumentKy/72885 >.

European Network Against Racism (ENAR), *Racism & Discrimination in Employment in Europe 2013–2017* (March 2017), online: European Website on Integration <https://ec.europa.eu/migrant-integration/librarydoc/enar-shadow-report-racism-discrimination-in-employment-in-europe-2013–2017>.

European Network of Legal Experts in Gender Equality and Non-Discrimination, *Girls Only" Housing Illegal* (April 2015), online: Equality Law <https://www.equalitylaw.eu/downloads/2743–13-be-ge-girls-only-housing-illegal>.

Federal Trade Commission, *FTC Staff Report: Self-Regulatory Principles for Online Behavioral Advertising* (February 2009), online: FTC <https://www.ftc.gov/sites/default/files/documents/reports/federal-trade-commission-staff-report-self-regulatory-principles-online-behavioral-advertising/p085400behavadreport.pdf >.

Federal Trade Commission, Protecting Consumer Privacy in an Era of Rapid Change (December 2010), online: FTC <https://www.ftc.gov/sites/default/files/documents/reports/federal-trade-commission-bureau-consumer-protection-preliminary-ftc-staff-report-protecting-consumer/101201privacyreport.pdf>.

Federal Trade Commission, Protecting Consumer Privacy in an Era of Rapid Change: Recommendations for Businesses and Policymakers (March 2012), online: Federal Trade Commission <https://www.ftc.gov/reports/protecting-consumer-privacy-era-rapid-change-recommendations-businesses-policymakers>.

Federal Trade Commission, How to Make Effective Disclosures in Digital Advertising (March 2013), online: FTC <https://www.ftc.gov/system/files/documents/plain-language/bus41-dot-com-disclosures-information-about-online-advertising.pdf>.

Frances Meenan, *Country Report Gender Equality Ireland* (January 2019), online: European Commission Directorate General for Justice and Consumers <https://www.equalitylaw.eu/downloads/5047-ireland-country-report-gender-equality-2019-pdf-1-14-mb>.

Genoveva Tisheva, *Country Report Gender Equality Bulgaria* (January 2019), online: European Commission Directorate General for Justice and Consumers <https://www.equalitylaw.eu/downloads/5068-bulgaria-country-report-gender-equality-2019-pdf-1-21-kb>.

Grace James, *Country Report Gender Equality the United Kingdom* (January 2019), online: European Commission Directorate General for Justice and Consumers <https://www.equalitylaw.eu/downloads/5064-united-kingdom-country-report-gender-equality-2019-pdf-1-39-mb>.

Helmut Werner, Eugenia Caracciolo di Torella, Bridgette McLellan, *Gender Equal Access to Goods and Services Directive 2004/113/EC: European Implementation Assessment* (January 2017), online: EPRS European Parliamentary Research Service Ex-Post Impact Assessment Unit <https://www.europarl.europa.eu/RegData/etudes/STUD/2017/593787/EPRS_STU(2017)593787_EN.pdf>.

House of Commons, *Older People and Employment Fourth Report of Session 2017–19* (May2019), online: Age UK <https://www.ageuk.org.uk/globalassets/age-uk/documents/reports-and-publications/later_life_uk_factsheet.pdf>.

House of Lords, *Revised Transcript of Evidence Taken Before the Select Committee on the European Union Inquiry on Online Platforms and the EU Digital Single Market Session 15* (December 2015), online: UK Parliament <http://data.parliament.uk/writtenevidence/committeeevidence.svc/evidencedocument/eu-internal-market-subcommittee/online-platforms-and-the-eu-digital-single-market/oral/25770.html>.

HUD, *An Estimate of Housing Discrimination Against Same-Sex Couple* (June 2013), online: US Department of Housing <https://www.huduser.gov/portal/publications/fairhsg/discrim_samesex.html>.

HUD, *Housing Discrimination Against Racial and Ethnic Minorities* (June 2013), online: US Department of Housing <https://www.huduser.gov/portal/publications/fairhsg/hsg_discrimination_2012.html>.

HUD, *Housing Discrimination in the Rental Housing Market Against People Who Are Deaf and People Who Use Wheelchairs: National Study Findings* (June 2015), online: US Department of Housing <https://www.huduser.gov/portal/publications/fairhsg/hds_disability.html>.

Ines Bojic, *Country Report Non-Discrimination: Transposition and Implementation at National Level of Council Directives 2000/43 and 2000/78 Croatia* (January 2019), online: European Commission Directorate-General for Justice and Consumers <https://www.equalitylaw.eu/downloads/4965-croatia-country-report-non-discrimination-2019-pdf-1-18-mb>.

Isabelle Chopin, Carmine Conte, Edith Chambrier, *A Comparative Analysis of Non-Discrimination Law in Europe 2018, European Network of Legal Experts in Gender Equality and Non-Discrimination* (November 2018), online: European Commission Directorate-General for Justice and Consumers <https://www.equalitylaw.eu/downloads/4804-a-comparative-analysis-of-non-discrimination-law-in-europe-2018-pdf-1-02-mb>.

Jakub Tomsej, *Country Report Non-Discrimination: Transposition and Implementation at National Level of Council Directives 2000/43 and 2000/78 Czech Republic* (January 2019), online: European Commission Directorate-General for Justice and Consumers <https://www.equalitylaw.eu/downloads/4959-czech-republic-country-report-non-discrimination-2019-pdf-1-21-mb>.

Julie Ringelheim, Nicolas Bernard, *Discrimination in Housing: Thematic Report of the European Network of Legal Experts in the Non-Discrimination Field* (February 2013), online: European Commission Directorate General for Justice and Consumers <https://op.europa.eu/en/publication-detail/-/publication/c8cf0ff7-8676-4751-8d36-59eeffe379ee/language-en>.

Joris Van Hoboken, João Pedro Quintais, Joost Poort, Nico van Eijk, Hosting Intermediary Services and Illegal Content Online: An Analysis of the Scope of Article 14 ECD in Light of Developments in the Online Service Landscape (2018), online: European Commission <https://op.europa.eu/en/publication-detail/-/publication/7779caca-2537-11e9-8d04-01aa75ed71a1/language-en>.

Karin de Vries, *Country Report Non-Discrimination: Transposition and Implementation at National Level of Council Directives 2000/43 and 2000/78 Netherlands* (January 2019), online: European Commission Directorate-General for Justice and Consumers <https://www.equalitylaw.eu/downloads/4970-the-netherlands-country-report-non-discrimination-2019-pdf-1-92-mb>.

Kristina Koldinska, *Country Report Gender Equality Czech Republic* (January 2019), online: European Commission Directorate General for Justice and Consumers <https://www.equalitylaw.eu/downloads/5030-czech-republic-country-report-gender-equality-2019-pdf-825-kb>.

Kristine Dupate, *Country Report Gender Equality Latvia* (January 2019), online: European Commission Directorate General for Justice and Consumers <https://www.equalitylaw.eu/downloads/5049-latvia-country-report-gender-equality-2019-pdf-1-1-mb>.

Laura W Murphy, Airbnb's to Fight Discrimination and Build Inclusion: A Report Submitted to Airbnb (September 2016), online: Airbnb <https://blog.atairbnb.com/

wp-content/uploads/2016/09/REPORT_Airbnbs-Work-to-Fight-Discrimination-and-Build-Inclusion_09292016.pdf>.

Laura Murphy, Three Year Review – Airbnb's Work to Fight Discrimination and Build Inclusion (September 2019), online: Airbnb <https://news.airbnb.com/wp-content/uploads/sites/4/2019/09/Airbnb_Work-to-Fight-Discrimination_0909_3.pdf>.

Les Défenseur des Droits, *Enquête sur les Discriminations dans L'Accès au Logement* (October 2012) online: le Défenseur des Droits <https://juridique.defenseurdesdroits.fr/doc_num.php?explnum_id=10627>.

Lidia Hermina Balogh, *Country Report Gender Equality Hungary* (January 2019), online: European Commission Directorate General for Justice and Consumers <https://www.equalitylaw.eu/downloads/5044-hungary-country-report-gender-equality-2019-pdf-1-26-mb>.

Lorenzo Cachón, *Country Report Non-Discrimination: Transposition and Implementation at National Level of Council Directives 2000/43 and 2000/78 Spain* (January 2019), online: European Commission Directorate-General for Justice and Consumers <https://www.equalitylaw.eu/downloads/4963-spain-country-report-non-discrimination-2019-pdf-1-32-mb>.

Lucy Vickers, *Country Report Non-Discrimination: Transposition and Implementation at National Level of Council Directives 2000/43 and 2000/78 United Kingdom* (January 2019), online: European Commission Directorate-General for Justice and Consumers <https://www.equalitylaw.eu/downloads/4976-united-kingdom-country-report-non-discrimination-2019-pdf-1-39-mb>.

Lukasz Bojarski, *Country Report Non-Discrimination: Transposition and Implementation at National Level of Council Directives 2000/43 and 2000/78 Poland* (January 2019), online: European Commission Directorate-General for Justice and Consumers <https://www.equalitylaw.eu/downloads/4801-poland-country-report-non-discrimination-2018-pdf-2-79-mb>.

Malcolm Harrison, Ian Law, Deborah Phillips, *Migrants, Minorities and Housing: Exclusion, Discrimination and Anti-Discrimination in 15 Member States of the European Union* (December 2005), online: European Monitoring Center on Racism and Xenophobia <https://fra.europa.eu/sites/default/files/fra_uploads/188-CS-Housing-en.pdf>.

Margery Austin Turner, Rob Santos, Diane K Levy, Doug Wissoker, Claudia Aranda, Rob Pitingolo, *Housing Discrimination Against Racial and Ethnic Minorities 2012* (June 2013) online: US Department of Housing and Urban Development <www.huduser.gov/portal/Publications/pdf/HUD-514_HDS2012.pdf>.

Maria do Rosário Palma Ramalho, *Country Report Gender Equality Portugal* (January 2019), online: European Commission Directorate General for Justice and Consumers <https://www.equalitylaw.eu/downloads/4998-portugal-country-report-gender-equality-2019-pdf-976-kb>.

Marie Mercat-Bruns, *Country Report Gender Equality France* (January 2019), online: European Commission Directorate General for Justice and Consumers <https://www.equalitylaw.eu/downloads/5043-france-country-report-gender-equality-2019-pdf-1-6-mb>.

Marlies Vegter, *Country Report Gender Equality the Netherlands* (January 2019), online: European Commission Directorate General for Justice and Consumers <https://

www.equalitylaw.eu/downloads/5050-the-netherlands-country-report-gender-equality-2019-pdf-1-25-mb>.

Nathalie Wuiame, *Country Report Gender Equality Belgium* (January 2019), online: European Commission Directorate General for Justice and Consumers <https://www.equalitylaw.eu/downloads/4992-belgium-country-report-gender-equality-2019-pdf-1-0-mb>.

Nathalie Wuiame, *How are EU Rules Transposed into National Law? Country Report Gender Equality, Belgium* (February 2019) online: European Commission Directorate-General for Justice and Consumers <https://www.equalitylaw.eu/downloads/4992-belgium-country-report-gender-equality-2019-pdf-1-0-mb>.

National Fair Housing Alliance, *2010 Fair Housing Trends Report* (May 2010), online: National Fair Housing <https://nationalfairhousing.org/wp-content/uploads/2017/04/fair_housing_trends_report_2010.pdf>.

Neza Kogovsek Salamon, *Country Report Non-Discrimination: Transposition and Implementation at National Level of Council Directives 2000/43 and 2000/78 Slovenia* (January 2019), online: European Commission Directorate-General for Justice and Consumers <https://www.equalitylaw.eu/downloads/4974-slovenia-country-report-non-discrimination-2019-pdf-1-31-mb>.

Nicole Kerschen, *Country Report Gender Equality Luxembourg* (January 2019), online: European Commission Directorate General for Justice and Consumers <https://www.equalitylaw.eu/downloads/5074-luxembourg-country-report-gender-equality-2019-pdf-860-kb>.

Patricia Hornich, *Country Report Non-Discrimination: Transposition and Implementation at National Level of Council Directives 2000/43 and 2000/78 Liechtenstein* (January 2019), online: European Commission Directorate-General for Justice and Consumers <https://www.equalitylaw.eu/downloads/4966-liechtenstein-country-report-non-discrimination-2019-pdf-1-09-mb>.

Paul Hitlin, Lee Raine, *Facebook Algorithms and Personal Data Complete Report* (January 2019), online: Pew Research Center <https://www.pewinternet.org/2019/01/16/facebook-algorithms-and-personal-data/>.

Paul Lappalainen, *Country Report Non-Discrimination: Transposition and Implementation at National Level of Council Directives 2000/43 and 2000/78 Sweden* (January 2019), online: European Commission Directorate-General for Justice and Consumers <https://www.equalitylaw.eu/downloads/4973-sweden-country-report-non-discrimination-2019-pdf-1-44-mb>.

Peter Swire, *Lessons from Fair Lending Law for Fair Marketing and Big Data* (September 2014), online: Federal Trade Commission <https://www.ftc.gov/system/files/documents/public_comments/2014/09/00042-92638.pdf>.

Pia Justesen, *Country Report Non-Discrimination: Transposition and Implementation at National Level of Council Directives 2000/43 and 2000/78 Denmark* (January 2019), online: European Commission Directorate-General for Justice and Consumers <https://www.equalitylaw.eu/downloads/4985-denmark-country-report-non-discrimination-2019-pdf-1-51-mb>.

Rainer Hiltunen, *Country Report Non-Discrimination: Transposition and Implementation at National Level of Council Directives 2000/43 and 2000/78 Finland* (January 2019), online: European Commission Directorate-General for Justice and Consumers

<https://www.equalitylaw.eu/downloads/4964-finland-country-report-non-discrimination-2019-pdf-1-27-mb>.

Romanita Iordache, *Country Report Non-Discrimination: Transposition and Implementation at National Level of Council Directives 2000/43 and 2000/78 Romania* (January 2019), online: European Commission Directorate-General for Justice and Consumers <https://www.equalitylaw.eu/downloads/4971-romania-country-report-non-discrimination-2019-pdf-1-27-mb>.

Sophie Latraverse, *Country Report on Measures to Combat Discrimination Directives 2000/43/EC and 2000/78/EC France* (January 2012), online: European Network of Legal Experts in the Non-Discrimination Field <https://www.refworld.org/pdfid/525534b70.pdf>.

Sophie Latraverse, *Transposition and Implementation at National Level of Council Directives 2000/43 and 2000/78, Country Report Non-Discrimination, France* (January 2019), online: Equality Law <https://www.equalitylaw.eu/downloads/5000-france-country-report-non-discrimination-2019-pdf-1-94-mb>.

Stacy Seicshnaydre, Robert Collins Cashuana Hill, Maxwell Ciardullo, *Rigging the Real Estate Market: Segregation, Inequality, and Disaster Risk* (April 2018) online: The New Orleans Prosperity Index: Tricentennial Collection <https://s3.amazonaws.com/gnocdc/reports/TDC-prosperity-brief-stacy-seicshnaydre-et-al-FINAL.pdf>.

Stine Jorgensen, *Country Report Gender Equality Denmark* (January 2019), online: European Commission Directorate General for Justice and Consumers <https://www.equalitylaw.eu/downloads/5031-denmark-country-report-gender-equality-2019-pdf-828-kb>.

Tania Hoffmann, *Country Report Non-Discrimination: Transposition and Implementation at National Level of Council Directives 2000/43 and 2000/78 Luxembourg* (January 2019), online: European Commission Directorate-General for Justice and Consumers <https://www.equalitylaw.eu/downloads/4967-luxembourg-country-report-non-discrimination-2019-pdf-781-kb>.

The Interactive Advertising Bureau, *IAB Internet Advertising Revenue Report* (November 2018), online: IAB <https://www.iab.com/wp-content/uploads/2018/11/IAB-WEBINAR-HY18-Internet-Ad-Revenue-Report1.pdf>.

United States Securities and Exchange Commission, *Annual Report Pursuant to Section 13 15 (d) of the Securities Exchange Act* (December 2018), online: Facebook Commission File <https://www.sec.gov/Archives/edgar/data/1326801/000132680119000009/fb-12312018x10k.htm#s7598225E01E95F77950D4736C39C55F1>.

United States Securities and Exchange Commission, *Annual Report Pursuant to Section 13 15 (d) of the Securities Exchange Act* (December 2018), online: Alphabet Inc. Commission File <https://www.sec.gov/Archives/edgar/data/1652044/000165204419000004/goog10-kq42018.htm>.

United States Securities and Exchange Commission Washington, *Annual Report Pursuant to Section 13 or 15(d) of The Securities Exchange Act of 1934 for the Fiscal Year Ended December 31, 2017* (2017), online: <https://www.sec.gov/Archives/edgar/data/1326801/000132680118000009/fb-12312017x10k.htm>.

Vanda Durbakova, *Country Report Non-Discrimination: Transposition and Implementation at National Level of Council Directives 2000/43 and 2000/78*

Slovakia (January 2019), online: European Commission Directorate-General for Justice and Consumers <https://www.equalitylaw.eu/downloads/4975-slovakia-country-report-non-discrimination-2019-pdf-1-40-mb>.

Zuzana Magurová, *Country Report Gender Equality Slovakia* (January 2019), online: European Commission Directorate General for Justice and Consumers <https://www.equalitylaw.eu/downloads/5076-slovakia-country-report-gender-equality-2019-pdf-1-1-mb>.

3. EUROPEAN COMMISSION COMMUNICATIONS, RECOMMENDATIONS, GUIDELINES

Brussels, 9.12.2021 COM (2021) 777 final, Communication from the Commission to the European Parliament and the Council, A More Inclusive and Protective Europe: Extending the List of EU Crimes to Hate Speech and Hate Crimes.

Brussels, 15.12.2020 COM (2020) 825 final. Proposal for a Regulation of the European Parliament and of the Council on a Single Market for Digital Services (Digital Services Act) and amending Directive 2000/31/EC.

Brussels, 8.4.2019 COM(2019)168 final. Communication from the Commission to the European Parliament, the Council, the European Economic and Social Committee and the Committee of the Regions: Building Trust in Human Centric Artificial Intelligence.

Brussels, 26.4.2018 COM(2018) 238 final. Proposal for a Regulation on the European Parliament and of the Council on Promoting Fairness and Transparency for Business Users of Online Intermediation Services.

Brussels, 25.4.2018 COM (2018)237 final. Communication from the Commission to the European Parliament, the European Council, the European Economic and Social Committee and the Committee of the Regions: Artificial Intelligence for Europe.

Brussels, 2.6.2016 COM(2016) 356 final. Communication from the Commission to the European Parliament, the Council, the European Economic and Social Committee and the Committee of the Regions: A European Agenda for the Collaborative Economy.

Brussels, 25.5.2016 COM(2016) 288 final. Communication from the Commission to the European Parliament, the Council, the European Economic and Social Committee and the Committee of the Regions: Online Platforms and the Digital Single Market: Opportunities and Challenges for Europe.

Brussels, 5.5.2015 COM(2015) 190 final. Report from the Commission to the European Parliament, the Council and the European Economic and Social Committee: Report on the Application of Council Directive 2004/113/EC Implementing the Principle of Equal Treatment Between Men and Women in the Access to and Supply of Goods and Services.

Brussels, 17.1.2014 COM(2014) 2 final. Report from the Commission to the European Parliament and the Council: Joint Report on the Application of Council Directive 2000/43/EC of 29 June 2000 Implementing the Principle of Equal Treatment Between Persons Irrespective of Racial or Ethnic Origin (Racial Equality Directive) and of

Council Directive 2000/78/EC of 27 November 2000 establishing a general framework for equal treatment in employment and occupation (Employment Equality Directive).

Brussels, 2.7.2008, COM (2008) 426 final. Proposal for a Council Directive on Implementing the Principle of Equal Treatment between Persons Irrespective of Religion or Belief, Disability, Age or Sexual Orientation.

Brussels, 15.12.2006 COM (2006)643 final/2. Report from the Commission to the Council and the European Parliament: The Application of Directive 2000/43/EC of 29 June 2000 implementing the principle of equal treatment between persons irrespective of racial or ethnic origin.

Commission Recommendation (EU) 2018/334 of 1 March 2018 on Measures to Effectively Tackle Illegal Content Online c/2018/1177, OJ L 63, 6.3.2018.

European Commission, Guidelines on Automated Individual Decision Making and Profiling for the Purposes of Regulation 2016/679, (wp251rev.01), revised in August 2018.

Guidelines on the application of Council Directive 2004/113/EC to insurance, in the light of the judgement of the court of Justice of the European Union in case C-236/09.

4. STATUTES

4.1. EUROPEAN UNION

Charter of Fundamental Rights of the European Union, OJ C 326, 26.10.2012, p 391–407.

Council Directive 2000/31 of 8 June 2000 on certain legal aspects of information society services, in particular electronic commerce, in the Internal Market (Directive on electronic commerce), OJ L 178, 17.07.2000, p 1–16.

Council Directive 2000/43/EC of 29 June 2000 implementing the principle of equal treatment between persons irrespective of racial or ethnic origin, OJ L 180, 19.7.2000, p 22–26.

Council Directive 2000/78/EC of 27 November 2000 establishing a general framework for equal treatment in employment and occupation, OJ L 303, 2.12.2000, p 16–22.

Council Directive 2003/109/EC of 25 November 2003 concerning the status of third-country nationals who are long-term residents, OJ L 16, 23.1.2004, p 44–53.

Council Directive 2004/113/EC of 13 December 2004 implementing the principle of equal treatment between men and women in the access to and supply of goods and services OJ L 373, 21.12.2004, p 37–43.

Directive (EU) 2015/1535 of the European Parliament and of the Council of 9 September 2015 laying down a procedure for the provision of information in the field of technical regulations and of rules on information society services, OJ L 241, 17.9.2015, p 1–15.

Directive (EU) 2019/790 of the European Parliament and of the Council of 17 April 2019 on Copyright and Related Rights in the Digital Single Market and Amending Directives 96/9/EC and 2001/29/EC, OJ L 130, 157.5.2019, p 92–125.

Directive (EU) 2019/790 of the European Parliament and of the Council of 17 April 2019 on Copyright and Related Rights in the Digital Single Markets and Amending Directives 96/9/EC and 2001/29/EC, OJ L 130, 17.5.2019, p 92–125.

Directive 2000/31/EC of the European Parliament and of the Council of 8 June 2000 on certain legal aspects of information society services, in particular electronic commerce, in the Internal Market (Directive on electronic commerce), OJ L 178, 17.7.2000, p 1–16.

Directive 2003/33/EC of the European Parliament and of the Council of 26 May 2003 on the approximation of laws, regulations and administrative provisions of the Member States relating to the advertising and sponsorship of tobacco products, OJ L 152, 20.6.2003, p 16–19.

Directive 2004/27/EC of the European Parliament and of the Council of 31 March 2004 Amending Directive 2001/83/EC on the Community Code Relating to Medicinal Products for Human Use, OJ L 136/34, 30.04.2004, p 34–57.

Directive 2005/29/EC of the European Parliament and of the Council of 11 May 2005 concerning unfair business to consumer commercial practices in the internal market, and amending Council Directive 84/450/ECC, Directives 97/7/EC, 98/27/EC and 2002/65/EC of the European Parliament and of the Council and Regulation (EC) No 2006/2004 of the European Parliament and of the Council, OJ L 149/22, 11.6.2005, p 22–39.

Directive 2005/29/EC of the European Parliament of the Council of 11 May 2005 concerning unfair business-to-consumer commercial practices in the internal market and amending Council Directive 84/450/ECC, Directives 97/7/EC, 98/27/EC and 2002/65/EC of the European Parliament and of the Council and Regulation (EC) No 2006/2004 of the European Parliament and of the Council (Unfair Commercial Practices Directive), OJ L 149, 11.6.2005, p 22–39.

Directive 2006/123/EC of the European Parliament and of the Council of 12 December 2006 on services in the internal Market, OJ L 367, p 36, 27.12.2006, p 36–68.

Directive 2006/123/EC of the European Parliament and of the Council of 12 December 2006 on Services in the Internal Market, OJ L 376, 27.12.2006, p 36–68.

Directive 2006/54/EC of the European Parliament and of the Council of 5 July 2006 on the implementation of the principle of equal opportunities and equal treatment of men and women in matters of employment and occupation (recast) OJ L 204, 26.7.2006, p 23–36.

Directive 2010/41/EU of the European Parliament and of the Council of 7 July 2010 on the application of the principle of equal treatment between men and women engaged in an activity in a self-employed capacity and repealing Council Directive 86/613/EEC, OJ L 180, 15.7.2010, p 1–6.

Directive 2010/41/EU of the European Parliament and of the Council of 7 July 2010 on the application of the principle of equal treatment between men and women engaged in an activity in a self-employed capacity and repealing Council Directive 86/631/EEC, OJ L 180/1, 15.7.2010, p 1–16.

Directive 2002/58/EC of the European Parliament and of the Council of 12 July 2002 concerning the processing of personal data and the protection of privacy in the electronic communications sector (Directive on privacy and electronic communications), OJ L 201, 31.7.2002, p 37–47.

Directive 95/46/EC of the European Parliament and of the Council of 24 October 1995 on the protection of individuals with regard to the processing of personal data and the free movement of such data, OJ L 281, 23.11.1995, p 31–50.

Regulation (EU) 2021/784 of the European Parliament and of the Council of 29 April 2021 on addressing the dissemination of terrorist content online, OJ L 172, 17.4.2021.

Proposal for a Regulation of the European Parliament and of the Council on a Single Market for Digital Services (Digital Services Act) and amending Directive 2000/31/EC. COM/2020/825 final.

Regulation (EU) 2016/679 of the European Parliament and of the Council of 27 April 2016 on the protection of natural persons with regard to the processing of personal data on the free movement of such data, and repealing Directive 95/46/EC (General Data Protection Regulation), OJ L 119, 4.5.2016, p 1–88.

Regulation (EU) 2019/1150 of the European Parliament and of the Council of 20 June 2019 on Promoting Fairness and Transparency for Business Users of Online Intermediation Services, OJ L 186, 11.7.2019, p 57–79.

Regulation (EU) No 492/2011 of the European Parliament and of the Council of 5 April 2011 on Freedom of Movement for Workers Within the Union, OJ L 141, 27.5.2011, p 1–12.

Treaty on the Functioning of the European Union, OJ C 326, 26.10.2012, p 47–390.

4.2. INTERNATIONAL

Protocol amending the Convention for the Protection of Individuals with regard to Automatic Processing of Personal Data, Strasbourg, 10.10.2018, Council of Europe (Protocol CETS No 233).

Convention 108+ for the Protection of Individuals with Regard to the Processing of Personal Data.

Convention for the Protection of Individuals with regard to Automatic Processing of Personal Data, ETS No. 108, Strasbourg, 1981.

European Convention on Human Rights (1950).

International Convention on the Elimination of All Forms of Racial Discrimination imposes the prevention, prohibition and eradication of racial segregation.

The International Covenant on Economic Social and Cultural Rights, G.A. res. 2200A (XXI) (1966).

Universal Declaration of Human Rights, G.A. res. 217A (III), U.N. Doc A/810 at 71 (1948).

4.3. UNITED STATES

15 U.S.C. §6809 (4)(A) (2006), Gramm-Leach-Bliley Act of 1999.

15 U.S.C. §§6801–6827, Financial Services Modernization Act (GLB Act).

15 U.S.C. §§6501–6506, Children's Online Privacy Protection Act (COPPA).

15 U.S.C. §§7701–7713 and 18 U.S.C., §1037, Controlling the Assault of Non-Solicited Pornography and Marketing Act (CAN-SPAN Act).

15 U.S.C., §1681, Fair Credit Reporting Act.

15 U.S.C. Federal Trade Commission Act

15 U.S.C. §§41–58, The Federal Trade Commission Act (FCT Act).

18 U.S.C. §2710, Video Privacy Protection Act of 1988.

18 U.S.C., §1030, the Computer Fraud and Abuse Act.

18 U.S.C., §2510, Electronic Communications Privacy Act.

21 U.S.C. §301, Federal Food, Drug, and Cosmetic Act.

21 U.S.C., Family Smoking Prevention Tobacco Control Act.

27 U.S.C., Federal Alcohol Administration Act.

29 U.S.C. §§621–634(2006) The Age Discrimination in Employment Act (ADEA).

29 U.S.C. §791 Rehabilitation Act of 1973.

42 U.S.C. §2000a(a)-(b) (2006) (Title II). Public Accommodations.

42 U.S.C. §3604 (2006). Fair Housing Act (FHA).

42 U.S.C. §§12101–12213. American with Disability Act (ADA).

42 U.S.C. §§1301, Health Insurance Portability and Accountability Act (HIPAA).

47 U.S.C., §230, (1) (1996), Communications Decency Act (CDA).

9 U.S.C., Federal Arbitration Act (FAA).

Restatement, Second of Torts §578 (1977).

Assembly Bill No 5, Chapter 296, §2, 2750.3 (a)(1) (A) (California).

California Labor Code §2802.

Unruh Civil Rights Act (Unruh Act) (Civ. Code, §51) (California).

4.4. THE UNITED KINGDOM

Defamation Act 1996 (UK).

Employment Equality Acts 1998–2011 (IE)s 15(1) and (3).

Employment Rights Act 1996 (ERA);

Equality Act 2010 (UK) s109,

National Minimum Wage Act 1998 (NMWA)

Working Time Regulations 1998 (WTR).

4.5. IRELAND

Equal Status Act 2000–2015.

4.6. FRANCE

Code du Tourisme, modifié para la loi du 7 Octobre 2016.

Loi Hoguet, loi n 70–9 du 2 janvier 1970 réglement les conditions d'exercice des activités relatives à certaines opérations portant sur les immeubles et les fonds du commerce.

Ordonnance n° 2018–1125 du 12 décembre 2018 prise en application de l'article 32 de la loi n° 2018–493 du 20 juin 2018 relative à la protection des données personnelles et portant modification de la loi n° 78–17 du 6 janvier 1978 relative à l'informatique, aux fichiers et aux libertés et diverses dispositions concernant la protection des données à caractère personnel.

5. LEGAL CASES

5.1. EUROPE

5.1.1. Court of Justice of the European Union

C-507/18 N.H. c. Associazione Avvocatura per i diritti LGBTI – Rete Lenford, ECLI:EU:C:2020:289.

C-311/18 Data Protection Commissioner v Facebook Ireland and Maximillian Schrems, ECLI:EU:C:2020:559.

C-390/18 Airbnb Ireland, ECLI:EU:C:2019:1112.

C-18/18 Glawischnig-Piesczek v Facebook, ECLI:EU:C:2019:821.

C-804/18, IX v Wabe eV and MH Müller Handels GmbH v MJ, ECLI:EU:C:2021:594.

C-414/16 Egenberger v Evangelisches Werk Für Diakonies un Entwicklung eV, ECLI:EU:C:2018:257.

C-434/15 Asociación Profesional Elite Taxi v Uber Systems Spain, ECLI, EU:C:2017:981.

C-188/15 Asma Bougnaoui and ADDH v Micropole SA, ECLI:EU:C:2017:204.

C-157/15 Achbita v G4S Solutions NV ECLI:EU:C:2017:203.

C-317/14 European Commission v Kingdom of Belgium, ECLI:EU:C:2015:63.

C-416/13 Mario Vital Pérez v Ayuntamiento de Oviedo, ECLI:EU:2014:2371.

C-276/12, Jiří Sabou v Finanční ředitelství pro hlavní město Prahu, ECLI:EU:C:2013:678.

C-81/12 Asociaţia Accept v Consiliul Naţional pentru Combaterea Discriminării, ECLI:EU:C:2013:275.

C-415/10 Galina Meister v Speech Design Carrier Systems GmbH, ECLI:EU:C:2012:217.

C-324/09 L'Oreal v eBay, ECLI:EU:C:2011:474.

C-232/09 Danosa v LKB Līzings SIA ECLI:EU:C:2010:674.

C-236/09 Association Belge des Consomateurs Test-Achats v Conseil des Ministres, ECLI:EU:C:2011:100.

C-236/08 Google France v Louis Vuitton, ECLI:EU:C:2010:159.

C-54/07 Centrum voor gelijkheid van kansen en voor racismebestrijding v Firma Feryn NV, ECLI:EU:C:2008:397.

C-555/07, Seda Kücükdeveci v Swedex GmbH & Co. KG, ECLI:EU:C:2010:21.

C-303/06 Coleman v Attridge Law, ECLI:EU:C:2008:415.

C-506/06 Mayr v Flöckner OHG, ECLI:EU:C:2008:119.

C-10/05 Mattern v Ministre du Travail et de l'Emploi, ECLI:EU:C:2006:220.

C-109/04 Kranemann v Land Nordrhein-Westfalen, ECLI:EU:C:2005:187.

C-456/02 Trojani v Centre public d'aide sociale de Bruxelles, ECLI:EU:C:2004:488.

C-256/01 Allonby v Accrington & Rossendale College, ECLI:EU:C:2004:18.

C-256/01 Debra Allonby v Accrington & Rossendale College ECLI:EU:C:2004:18.

C-188/00 Kurz, née Yüce v Land Baden-Württemberg, ECLI:EU:C:2002:694.

C-268/99 Aldona Malgorzata Jany and others v Staatssecretaris van Justitie ECLI:EU:C:2001:616.

C-180/95 Draehmpaehl v Urania Immobilienservice OHG, ECLI, EU:C:1997:208.

C-116/94 Meyers v Chief Adjudication Officer, ECLI:EU:C:1995:247.

C-237/94 O'Flynn v Adjudication Officer, ECLI:EU:C:1996:206.

C-3/87 Agegate ECLI:EU:C:1989:650.

C-196/87 Steymann Staatssecretaris van Justitie, ECLI:EU:C:1988:475.

C-344/87 Bettray v Staatssecretaris Van Justitie, ECLI:EU:C:1989:226.

C-66/85 Lawrie-Blum v Land Baden-Württemberg ECLI:EU:C:1986:284.

C-170/84 Bilka – Kaufhaus GmbH v Karin Weber von Hartz, ECLI:EU:C:1986:204.

C-165/82 Commission v UK, ECLI:EU:C:1983:311.

C-96/80 JP Jenkins v Kingsgate, ECLI:EU:C:1981:80.

C-6/64 Costa v ENEL, ECLI:EU:C:1964:66.

C-75/63 Hoekstra v Bestuur der Bedrijfsvereniging voor Detailhandel en Ambachten ECLI:EU:C:1964:19.

5.1.2. France

Conseil Constitutionnel, Décision n 2015–484 QPC, 22.09.2015.

Cour d'Appel de Paris, pôle 6, chamber 2, arrêt du 10 janvier 2019, sn rg 18/08357, n portalis 35L7-V-B7C-B6AZK.

Cour d'Appel de Toulouse [Toulouse Court of Appeal], 3rd Criminal Chamber, 5 Oct. 2004, decision n. 03/00593, Juris-Data, no 2004–254288, confirmed by the Cour de Cassation [Supreme Court of Appeal], Criminal Chamber, 7 June 2005, n 04–87354.

Cour d'Appel Grenoble [Grenoble Court of Appeal], no 06/0053, 08/11/2006, Dezempt, Boyer c. Ghezzal.

J'accuse c. AFA et autres, TGI Paris, ord. réf., 30 octobre 2001, Comm. comm. électr. Janvier 2002. n°1, 30, n°8.

Tribunal Correctionnel de Paris [Paris Regional Criminal Court], 20 Sept. 2007, no 0308500058.

Tribunal d'Instance, Paris, Jugement du 6 février 2018, RG 11–17–000190.

Tribunal de Grande Instance de Paris [Paris Regional Court], 16 Nov. 2006, n. 0527808770.

Tribunal de Grande Instance de Paris [Paris Regional Court], no 0527808779, 16/11/2006, MRAP, ADIB c. TESSIAU.

UEJF et LICRA c/ Yahoo! Inc. et Yahoo France, TGI Paris (22 mai 2000).

5.1.3. Ireland

Irish Human Rights and Equality Commission v Daft Media Limited t/a Daft/ie, ADJ-00005960, WRC, August 2019.

5.1.4. United Kingdom

Aslam v Uber BV [2016] EW Misc B68 (ET), 28 October 2016.
Uber BV v Aslam [2021] UKSC.
Autoclenz Ltd v Belcher [2011] UKSC 41.
Cox v Ministry Justice [2016] UKSC 10.
Jivraj v Hashwani [2011] UKSC 40.
Mohamud v Wm Morrison Supermarkets plc (2016) UKSC 1.
Uber BV v Aslam [2017] UKEAT 0056171011, 10 November 2017.
Uber BV v Aslam [2018] EWCA civ 2748.

5.2. UNITED STATES

5.2.1. District Courts

Access Now, Inc. v Southwest Airlines, Co., 227 F. sup. 2d 1312, 1316 (S.D. Fla. 2002).
Bradley v T-Mobile US, Inc., No. 17-cv-07232-BLF (N.D. Cal., 2019).
Cotter v Lyft, Inc., 60 F. Supp. 3d 1067 (N.D. Cal. 2015).
Cubby, Inc. v CompuServe Inc., 776 F. Supp. 135 (S.D.N.Y. 1991).
EEOC v Sephora USA, 419 F. Supp. 2d 408 (S.D.N.Y. 2005).
Freeman v Dal-Tile Corp., 750 F.3d 413 (4th Cir. 2014).
Kendall Reese v Uber Technologies, Inc. 2:18-cv-03300 (E.D. Pen., 2018).
Kercado-Clymer v City of Amsterdam, 608 F. Supp. 2d 303 (N.D.N.Y. 2009).
Merritt v WellPoint, Inc., 615 F. Supp. 2d 440 (E.D. Va. 2009).
National Fair Housing Alliance v Facebook, Inc., No. 1:18-cv-02689-JGK (S.D. N.Y. Aug. 08, 2018).
National Federation of the Blind v Scribd Inc., 97 F. Supp. 3d 565 (D. Vt. 2015).
Noah v AOL Time Warner, Inc., 261 F. Supp. 2d 532 (E.D. Va. 2003).
O'Connor v Uber Technologies, Inc., 82 F. Supp. 3d 1133 (N.D. Cal. 2015).
Onuoha v Facebook, Inc., No. 5: 16-cv-06440-EJD (N.D. Cal., 2017).
Riddick v Facebook, Inc., No. 3:18-cv-04429 (N.D. Cal. 2019).
Selden v Airbnb, Inc., No. 16-cv-00933 (CRC) (D.C. Col., 2016).
Stratton Oakmont, Inc. v Prodigy Services Company, (S. Ct. N.Y. 1995).
Yucesoy v Uber Technologies, Inc., 109 F. Supp. 3d 1259 (N.D. Cal. 2015).

5.2.2. Circuit Courts

Alexander v FedEx Ground Package System, Inc., 765 F.3d 981 (9th Cir. 2014).
Barnes v Yahoo Inc., no 05–36189 (9th Cir., 2009).
Beckford v Department of Corrections, 605 F.3d 951 (11th Cir. 2010).
Breaux v City of Garland, 205 F.3d 150 (5th Cir. 2000).
Chaney v Plainfield Healthcare Center, 612 F.3d 908 (7th Cir. 2010).
Chicago Lawyers' for Civil Rights v Craigslist, 519 F.3d 666 (7th Cir. 2008).
Davis v Time Warner Cable of Southeastern Wis., 651 F.3d 664 (7th Cir. 2011).

Diaz v Pan Am. World Airways, Inc., 442 F.2d 385 (5th Cir. 1971).

Doe v MySpace Inc., 528, F.3d 413 (5th Cir., 2008).

Dunn v Washington County Hosp., 429 F.3d 689 (7th Cir. 2005).

Fair Housing Council v Roommate.Com, LLC, 666 F.3d 1216 (9th Cir. 2012).

Flowers v Carville, 210 F.3d 1118 (9th Cir., 2002).

Mohamed v Uber Technologies, Inc., 848 F.3d 1201 (9th Circuit 2016).

Ragin v New York Times Company, 923 F.2d 995 (2d Cir. 1991).

Richardson v Monitronics Intern., Inc., 434 F.3d 327 (5th Cir. 2005).

Tibbs v Calvary United Methodist Church, No. 11–5238 (6th Cir. 2012).

Tiffany (NJ) Inc. v eBay Inc., 600 F. 3d 93 (2d Cir. 2010).

US v Space Hunters, Inc., 429 F.3d 416 (2d Circ. 2005).

Welsh v Boy Scouts of America, 993 F.2d 1267 (7th Cir. 1993).

Yahoo! Inc. v La Ligue Contre le Racisme, 433 F.3d 1199 (9th Cir. 2006).

5.2.3. Supreme Court of the United States

Bostock v Clayton County, Georgia., 139 S. Ct. 1599 (2019).

Masterpiece Cakeshop v Colorado Civil Rights, 138 S. Ct. 1719, 584 U.S., 201 L. Ed. 2d 35 (2018).

Griggs v Duke Power Co., 401 U.S. 424, 91 S. Ct. 849, 28 L. Ed. 2d 158 (1971).

Boy Scouts of America v. Dale, 530 U.S. 640, 120 S. Ct. 2446, 147 L. Ed. 2d 554 (2000).

Meyer v Holley, 537 U.S. 280, 123 S. Ct. 824, 154 L. Ed. 2d 753 (2003).

Epic Systems Corp. v Lewis, 138 S. Ct. 1612, 584 U.S., 200 L. Ed. 2d 889 (2018).

Raytheon Co. v Hernandez, 540 U.S. 44, 124 S. Ct. 513, 157 L. Ed. 2d 357 (2003).

Smith v City of Jackson, 544 U.S. 228, 125 S. Ct. 1536, 161 L. Ed. 2d 410 (2005).

Wards Cove Packing Co. v Atonio, 490 U.S. 642, 109 S. Ct. 2115, 104 L. Ed. 2d 733 (1989).

Watson v Fort Worth Bank & Trust, 487 U.S. 977, 108 S. Ct. 2777, 101 L. Ed. 2d 827 (1988).

AT&T Mobility LLC v Concepcion, 563 U.S. 333, 131 S. Ct. 1740, 179 L. Ed. 2d 742 (2011).

Rent-A-Center, West, Inc. v Jackson, 561 U.S. 63, 130 S. Ct. 2772, 177 L. Ed. 2d 403 (2010).

5.2.4. Supreme Court of California

SG Borello & Sons, Inc. v Department of Industries Relations, Case No S003956 (SC Cal 1989).

5.3. EUROPEAN COURT OF HUMAN RIGHTS

Delfi AS v Estonia (2015) ECtHR 64669/09.

Eweida and others v United Kingdom (2013) ECtHR 48420/10.

6. PRESS

Ariana Tobin and Jeremy B Merril, *Facebook Is Letting Job Advertisers Target Only Men* (2018), online: ProPublica <https://www.propublica.org/article/facebook-is-letting-job-advertisers-target-only-men>.

Alexia Fernández Campbell, *The Worldwide Uber Strike is a Key Test for the Gig Economy* (May 2019) online: Vox <https://www.vox.com/2019/5/8/18535367/uber-drivers-strike-2019-cities>.

Henri Seckel, *Pour Réserver sur Airbnb, Mieux Vaut S'Appeler Isabelle que Djamila* (August 2018), online: LeMonde <https://www.lemonde.fr/societe/article/2018/08/24/airbnb-abritel-discriminations-en-ligne_5345587_3224.html>.

Julia Angwin and Terry Parris, *Facebook Lets Advertisers Exclude Users by Race ProPublica* (2016), online: Propublica <https://www.propublica.org/article/facebook-lets-advertisers-exclude-users-by-race>.

Julia Angwin, Ariana Tobin, Madeleine Varner, *Facebook (Still) Letting Housing Advertisers Exclude Users by Race* (2017), online: Propublica <https://www.propublica.org/article/facebook-advertising-discrimination-housing-race-sex-national-origin>.

Julia Angwin, Noam Scheiber and Ariana Tobin, *Dozens of Companies Are Using Facebook to Exclude Older Workers from Job Ads* (2017), online: Propublica <https://www.propublica.org/article/facebook-ads-age-discrimination-targeting>.

Melissa Heikkilä, *Uber Drivers Wage Battle to Obtain their Data (October 2019), online: Politico* <https://www.politico.eu/article/uber-drivers-wage-battle-to-obtain-their-data/>.

Nellie Bowles, *Airbnb Faces Outcry After Transgender Guest Was Denied Stay by a Host* (June 2016), online: The Guardian <https://www.theguardian.com/technology/2016/jun/06/airbnb-criticism-transgender-guest-denied-super-host>.

Olivia Solon, *Airbnb Host Who Canceled Reservation Using Racist Comment Must $5,000* (July 2017), online: The Guardian <https://www.theguardian.com/technology/2017/jul/13/airbnb-california-racist-comment-penalty-asian-american>.

Rob Price, *Facebook Has Appointed the Privacy Committee on Its Board Designed to Prevent Another Cambridge Analytica Scandal* (May 2020), online: Business Insider <https://www.businessinsider.com/facebook-announces-privacy-committee-board-of-directors-2020–5?r=US&IR=T>.

Ryan Singel, *Oct. 27, 1994: Web Gives Birth to Banner Ads* (October 2010), online: Wired <https://www.wired.com/2010/10/1027hotwired-banner-ads/>;

Sarah Phillips, *A Brief History of Facebook* (July 2007), online: The Guardian <https://www.theguardian.com/technology/2007/jul/25/media.newmedia>.

Stephen Engelberg, *HUD Has 'Serious Concerns' About Facebook's Ethnic Targeting* (2016), online: Propublica <https://www.propublica.org/article/hud-has-serious-concerns-about-facebooks-ethnic-targeting>.

7. WEBSITES AND PRESS RELEASES

Abritel, *Publie Votre Annonce sur Arbitrel.fr et Dites Bonjour à de Nouveaux Revenues* (December 2019), online: Arbitrel <https://abitrel.fr>.

ACLU, *Facebook Settles Civil Rights Cases by Making Sweeping Changes to its Online Ad Platform* (March 2019), online: ACLU <https://www.aclu.org/blog/womens-rights/womens-rights-workplace/facebook-settles-civil-rights-cases-making-sweeping>.

AddThis, *About us* (June 2019), online: AddThis <www.addthis.com/about>.

AdWeek, *Survey: 92% of Recruiters Use Social Media to Find High-Quality Candidates* (September 2015), online: AdWeek <www.adweek.com/socialtimes/survey-96-of-recruiters-use-social-media-to-findhigh-qualitycandidates/627040>.

Agencia Española de Datos, *Procedimiento no. PS/00219/2017 – Resolución: R/00259/2018* <https://www.aepd.es/media/resoluciones/PS-00219–2017_Resolucion-de-fecha-02–03–2018_Art-ii-culo-11–6-LOPD.pdf>.

Airbnb, *An Update on Airbnb's Work to Fight Discrimination* (September 2019), online: Airbnb <https://news.airbnb.com/an-update-on-airbnbs-work-to-fight-discrimination/>.

Airbnb, *Homepage* (November 2019), online: Airbnb <https://www.airbnb.com>.

Airbnb, *La Communauté Airbnb en France en 2016* (November 2016), online: Airbnb <http://hr-infos.fr/wp-content/uploads/2017/04/EIS-France.pdf>.

Airbnb, *Politique de Non-Discrimination d'Airbnb: Notre Engagement en Matière d'Inclusivité et de Respect* (March 2018), online: Airbnb <https://www.airbnb.fr/help/article/1405/airbnb-s-nondiscrimination-policy--our-commitment-to-inclusion-and-respect>.

Airbnb, *Toolkit* (May 2018), online: Airbnb <https://www.airbnb-toolkits.com/outline/8y7bu00k/cover>.

Airbnb, *What is Instant Book?* (March 2018), online: Airbnb <https://www.airbnb.com/help/article/523/what-is-instant-book>.

Amazon Mechanical Turk, *Overview* (November 2019), online: mturk <https://www.mturk.com>, and Clickworker, Our Solutions at a Glance (November 2019), online: clickworker <https://www.clickworker.com>.

Amnesty International, *Position on the Proposals for a Digital Services Act and a Digital Markets Act* (March 2021), online: Amnesty International <https://www.amnesty.eu/wp-content/uploads/2021/04/Amnesty-International-Position-Paper-Digital-Services-Act-Package_March2021_Updated.pdf>.

Autoriteit Persoonsgegevens, *Common Statement by the Contact Group of the Data Protection Authorities of the Netherlands, France, Spain, Hamburg and Belgium* (May 2017), online: DPA <https://autoriteitpersoonsgegevens.nl/sites/default/files/atoms/files/common_statement_16_may_2017.pdf>.

Autoriteit Persoonsgegevens, *Common Statement by the Contact Group of the Data Protection Authorities of the Netherlands, France, Spain, Hamburg and Belgium* (May 2017), online: DPA <https://autoriteitpersoonsgegevens.nl/sites/default/files/atoms/files/common_statement_16_may_2017.pdf>.

Autoriteit Persoonsgegevens, *Informal English Translation of the Conclusions of the Dutch Data Protection Authority in its Final Report of Findings About Its Investigation Into the Processing of Personal Data by Facebook Group* (February 2017), online: DPA

<https://autoriteitpersoonsgegevens.nl/sites/default/files/atoms/files/conclusions_
facebook_february_23_2017.pdf>.

BEUC, *The Digital Services Act Proposal BEUC Position Paper* (April 2021), online: BEUC
<https://www.beuc.eu/publications/beuc-x-2021–032_the_digital_services_act_
proposal.pdf>.

Burson-Marsteller, *The On-Demand Economy Survey* (2015), online: The Aspen Institute
<https://www.aspeninstitute.org/publications/demand-economy-survey/>.

Clickworker, *Our Solutions at a Glance* (November 2019), online: clickworker <https://
www.clickworker.com>.

Communications Workers of America, *about* (June 2019), online: CWA <https://cwa-
union.org>.

Congress of the United States, *Letter to Zuckerberg about "Ethnic Affinities" filters*
(November 2016), online: cbc house <https://cbc.house.gov/uploadedfiles/
facebook_housing_letter.pdf>.

Couchsurfing, *About Us* (December 2019), online: <https://www.couchsurfing.com/
about/about-us/>.

Craig Smith, *Airbnb Statistics and Facts* (September 2019), online: Business Statistics
<https://expandedramblings.com/index.php/airbnb-statistics/>.

Craig Smith, *Craigslist Statistics and Facts* (May 2019), online: Business Statistics
<https://expandedramblings.com/index.php/craigslist-statistics/>.

Craigslist, *Fair Housing is Everyone's Right! Stating a Discriminatory Preference in a
Housing Post is Illegal* (March 2018), online: Craigslist <https://www.craigslist.org/
about/FHA>.

Craigslist, *Forum* (May 2018), online: Craigslist <https://forums.craigslist.
org/?forumID=3604>.

Daft.ie, *About Us* (December 2019), online <https://www.daft.ie/about/>.

Daft.ie., *Instant Access to Ireland's Largest Property Audience List Your Place Today*
(December 2019), online: Daft.ie <https://www.daft.ie/ad-entry/sharing>.

Dan Adams, *Boston-Based Attorney Argues Uber's Star Ratings Are Racially Biased*
(October 2016) online: Lichten & Liss-Riordan, P.C. <https://www.llrlaw.com/
wp-content/uploads/2015/04/Boston-based-Attorney-Argues-Uber's-Star-Ratings-
are-Racially-Biased.pdf>.

Didi, *About Us* (November 2019) online: Didi <https://www.didiglobal.com>.

Digital Advertising Alliance, *About* (June 2019), online: DAA <https://
digitaladvertisingalliance.org>.

EASA, *Best Practice Recommendation on Online Bahavioural Advertising* (October
2016), online: EASA <www.easa-alliance.org/sites/default/files/EASA%20
Best%20Practice%20Recommendation%20on%20Online%20Behavioural%20
Advertising_0.pdf>.

EDAA, *European Interactive Digital Advertising Alliance* (June 2019), online: edaa
<https://www.edaa.eu/about/>.

EEOC, *Hurley Medical Center Agrees to Settle EEOC Race Discrimination* Case
(November 2019), online: EEOC <https://www.eeoc.gov/eeoc/newsroom/
release/9–26–13e.cfm>.

Ellen McGirt, *Facebook's Mark Zuckerberg: Hacker. Dropout. CEO* (May 2007), online: Fast Company <https://www.fastcompany.com/59441/facebooks-mark-zuckerberg-hacker-dropout-ceo>.

Equal Employment Opportunity Commission, *Adoption of Question and Answers to Clarify and Provide a Common Interpretation of the Uniform Guidelines on Employee Selection Procedures*, online: EEOC <https://www.eeoc.gov/policy/docs/qanda_clarify_procedures.html>.

Equality and Human Rights Commission, *Advertising What Equality Law Means for Advertisers and Publishers* (February 2016), online: Equality and Human Rights <https://www.equalityhumanrights.com/sites/default/files/ehrc_advertising_-_equality_law_12.pdf>.

European Commission, *The Digital Services Act Package* (April 2022), online: European Commission <https://digital-strategy.ec.europa.eu/en/policies/digital-services-act-package>.

European Commission, *Joint Press Statement from European Commissioner for Justice Didier Reynders and US Secretary of Commerce Wilbur Ross* (August 2020), online: Press Release <https://ec.europa.eu/info/news/joint-press-statement-european-commissioner-justice-didier-reynders-and-us-secretary-commerce-wilbur-ross-7-august-2020–2020-aug-07_en>.

European Commission, *EU consumer rules: Airbnb commits to complying with European Commission and EU consumer authorities' demands* (September 2018), online: European Commission <http://europa.eu/rapid/press-release_IP-18–5809_en.htm>.

European Commission, *EU consumer rules: the European Commission and EU consumer authorities push Airbnb to Comply* (July 2018), online: European Commission <http://europa.eu/rapid/press-release_IP-18–4453_en.htm>.

European Commission, *European Commission and United States Joint Statement on Trans-Atlantic Data Privacy Framework* (March 2022), online: Press Release <https://ec.europa.eu/commission/presscorner/detail/en/ip_22_2087>.

European Commission, *Public Consultation on the Regulatory Environment for Platforms, Online Intermediaries, Data and Cloud Computing and the Collaborative Economy* (September 2015), online: European Commission <https://ec.europa.eu/information_society/newsroom/image/document/2016–7/efads_13917.pdf>.

European Group on Ethics in Science and New Technologies, Future of Work, Future of Society (December 2018), online: European Commission Directorate-General for Research and Innovation <https://ec.europa.eu/info/sites/info/files/research_and_innovation/ege/ege_future-of-work_opinion_122018.pdf>.

European Institute for Gender Equality, Gender Statistics Database (January 2019), online: EIGE <https://eige.europa.eu/gender-statistics/dgs>.

European Parliament, *Amendments Adopted by the European Parliament on 20 January 2022 on the Proposal for a Regulation of the European Parliament and of the Council on a Single Market for Digital Services (Digital Services Act) and Amending Directive 2000/31/EC* (2022), online: European Parliament <https://www.europarl.europa.eu/doceo/document/TA-9–2022–0014_EN.html>.

European Parliament, *Digital Services Act: Agreement for a Transparent and Safe Online Environment* (23 April 2022), online: European Parliament Press Release <https://

www.europarl.europa.eu/news/en/press-room/20220412IPR27111/digital-services-act-agreement-for-a-transparent-and-safe-online-environment>.

European Parliament, *Legislative Train Schedule: Anti-Discrimination Directive* (December 2019), online: European Parliament <https://www.europarl.europa.eu/legislative-train/theme-area-of-justice-and-fundamental-rights/file-anti-discrimination-directive>.

European Parliament Committee on Civil Liberties, Justice and Home Affairs, *Opinion on the Proposal for a Regulation of the European Parliament and of the Council on a Single Market for Digital Services* (Digital Services Act) and Amending Directive 2000/31/EC (June 2021), online: European Parliament <https://www.europarl.europa.eu/doceo/document/LIBE-AD-692898_EN.pdf>.

Facebook, *Data Policy* (June 2019), online: Facebook <https://www.facebook.com/full_data_use_policy>.

Facebook, *Improving Enforcement and Promoting Diversity: Updates to Ads Policies and Tools* (February 2017), online: Facebook <https://newsroom.fb.com/news/2017/02/improving-enforcement-and-promoting-diversity-updates-to-ads-policies-and-tools/>

Facebook, *Improving Enforcement and Promoting Diversity: Updates to Ethnic Affinity Market* (November 2016), online: Facebook <https://newsroom.fb.com/news/2016/11/updates-to-ethnic-affinity-marketing/>.

Federal Reserve Bank of Chicago, *Banker's Guide to Risk-Based Fair Lending Examinations* (January 1999), online: Federal Reserve Bank of Chicago <https://www.chicagofed.org/digital_assets/others/utilities/about_us/cca/bankers_guide_to_risk_based_fair_lending_examinations.pdf>.

Federal Trade Commission, *Google and YouTube Will Pay Record $ 170 Million Alleged Violations of Children's Privacy Law* (September 2019), online: Federal Trade Commission <https://www.ftc.gov/news-events/press-releases/2019/09/google-youtube-will-pay-record-170-million-alleged-violations>.

Federal Trade Commission, *40 Years of Experience with the Fair Credit Reporting Act: An FTC Staff Report with Summary of Interpretations* (July 2011) online: FTC <https://www.ftc.gov/sites/default/files/documents/reports/40-years-experience-fair-credit-reporting-act-ftc-staff-report-summary-interpretations/110720fcrareport.pdf>.

Fizber, *Free Real Estate Listing by Fizber* (December 2019), online: Fizber <https://www.fizber.com/>.

ForSalebyOwner, *Free Listing* (December 2019), online: ForSalebyOwner <https://www.forsalebyowner.com>.

Future of Work Commission, *Future of Work* (August 2019), online: Labor & Workforce Development Agency <https://labor.ca.gov/fowc/>.

Global Commission on the Future of Work, *Work for a Brighter Future* (January 2019), online: ILO <https://www.ilo.org/global/publications/books/WCMS_662410/lang--en/index.htm>.

Google AI, *Google Brain Team* (June 2019), online: Google <https://ai.google/research/teams/brain/> AI is currently used in all sectors of the company from photos identification to advertising.

Google Waymo, *Introducing Waymo One* (June 2019), online: Google <https://waymo.com>

Google Wing, *Transforming the Way Goods Are Transported* (June 2019), online: Google <https://x.company/projects/wing/>

Google, *Google Privacy Policy* (June 2019), online: Google <https://policies.google.com>.

HomeAway, *List Your Property* (December 2019), online: HomeAway <https://homeaway.com>

IAB Europe, *IAB Europe recording: European Digital Advertising Spend 2017* (December 2017), online: IAB <https://iabeurope.eu/iab-europe-webinar-recording-european-digital-advertising-spend-2017/>.

IAB, *IAB Europe EU Framework for Online Behavioural Advertising* (April 2011), online: IAB <https://www.edaa.eu/wp-content/uploads/2012/10/2013–11–11-IAB-Europe-OBA-Framework_.pdf>.

Immoweb, *hostpage* (December 2019), online: Immoweb <https://www.immoweb.be/fr>.

JD*Supra*, *California Assembly Bill Five Excepts Certain Categories of Workers From Independent Contractor Classification Overhaul* (September 2019), online: JD*Supra* <https://www.jdsupra.com/legalnews/california-assembly-bill-five-excepts-58372/>.

Jennifer Luty, *Number of Airbnb Listings in Selected European Cities as of 2019* (August 2019), online: Statista <https://www.statista.com/statistics/815145/airbnb-listings-in-europe-by-city/>.

Jon Messenger, Oscar Vargas Llave, Lutz Gschwind, Simon Boehmer, Greet Vermeylen, Mathijn Wilkens, *Working Anytime, Anywhere: the Effects on the World of Work* (February 2017) online: Eurofond <https://www.eurofound.europa.eu/publications/report/2017/working-anytime-anywhere-the-effects-on-the-world-of-work>.

Leboncoin, *Annonces Location Immobilières* (December 2019), online: leboncoin <https://www.leboncoin.fr/locations/offres/>.

Leigh Day, *British Female Driver Launches Sex Discrimination Claim Against Uber Over Practices* (September 2017), online: Leigh Day Office <https://www.leighday.co.uk/News/News-2017/September-2017/British-female-driver-launches-sex-discrimination>.

Ligue des Droits Humains, *communiqué de presse* (June 2019), online: LDH <http://2ur2r.r.ca.d.sendibm2.com/mk/mr/UrbaMII0WjtmxReLSprj_R7V06S93d_CzxiYS6on0Hc0KrHFTpgYjto0M6OpQwMaxuSsWJfJASPqf2MraSfdwjBjnYydK ivSTy6hgUaq5_rVmvht>.

Lyft, *About us* (November 2019) online: Lyft <www.lyft.com>.

Lyft, *Driver and Passenger Ratings* (November 2019), online: Lyft <https://help.lyft.com/hc/en-us/articles/115013079948-Driver-and-passenger-ratings>.

Motion by Amicus Parties, Brief of Amici Amazon.com, Inc., AOL llc, eBay Inc., Google Inc., Yahoo! Inc., Electronic Frontier Foundation, Internet Commerce Coalition, NetChoice, NetCoalition, and United States Internet Service Provider Association in support of Craigslist's Motion for Judgement on the Pleadings (June 2017), online: Justia <https://docs.justia.com/cases/federal/district-courts/illinois/ilndce/1:2006cv00657/195440/24/1.html>.

NAI, *Nai Members* (June 2019), online: NAI <https://www.networkadvertising.org/participating-networks/?page=1>.

National Conference of State Legislatures, State Public Accommodation Laws (December 2019), online: NCSL <https://www.ncsl.org/research/civil-and-criminal-justice/state-public-accommodation-laws.aspx#_ftn8>.

Network Advertising Initiative, *NAI Code of Conduct: Enforcement* (May 2018), online: NAI <https://www.networkadvertising.org/sites/default/files/nai_code2018.pdf>

Niels Brügger, *A Brief History of Facebook as a Media Text: The Development of an Empty Structure* (2015) online: First Monday <https://s21.q4cdn.com/399680738/files/doc_financials/2018/Q2/Q218-earnings-call-transcript.pdf >.

OlaCabs, *About Us* (November 2019) online: OlaCabs <www.olacabs.com>.

Press Release, *CFPB Orders GE Capital to Pay $225 Million in Consumer Relief for Deceptive and Discriminatory Credit Card Practices* (June 2014), online: Consumer Finance <www.consumerfinance.gov/newsroom/cfpb-orders-ge-capital-to-pay-225-million-in-consumer-relief-for-deceptive-and-discriminatory-credit-card-practices/>.

Research and Markets, *Global Online Accommodation Booking Market* 2019 Report (yStats GmbH, 2020).

Roommates, *Find Your Perfect Match* (June 2019), online: Roommates <https://www.roommates.com>.

Sara E Rix, *The Employment Situation, May 2011: Average Duration of Unemployment for Older Jobseekers Continues to Rise* (May 2011), online: AARP Public Policy Institute <https://assets.aarp.org/rgcenter/ppi/econ-sec/fs226-employment.pdf>.

Senator Amy Klobuchar, *S.2728 Social Media Privacy and Consumer Protection Act of 2018* (April 2018), online: US Congress <https://www.congress.gov/bill/115th-congress/senate-bill/2728>.

Senator Edward Markey, *S.2639 Consent Act* (October 2018), online: US Congress <https://www.congress.gov/bill/115th-congress/senate-bill/2639>.

Sheryl Sandberg, *Letter to Chairman Richmond* (November 2017), online <https://www.documentcloud.org/documents/4312370-Facebook-Sheryl-Sandberg-Letter-2017-11–29.html>

SHRM, *Survey Findings: Using Social Media for Talent Acquisition. Recruitment and Screening* (January 2016), online: SHRM <https://www.shrm.org/hr-today/trends-and-forecasting/research-andsurveys/Documents/SHRM-Social-Media-Recruiting-Screening-2015.pdf>.

Smith, *Craigslist Statistics and Facts* (May 2019), online: Business Statistics <https://expandedramblings.com/index.php/craigslist-statistics/>.

Social Media Stats Worldwide, *Statcounter* (July 2019), online: GlobalStats <http://gs.statcounter.com/social-media-stats/all/united-states-of-america/2018>.

Spareroom, *Find Home Together* (December 2019), online: spareroom, <https://www.spareroom.co.uk>.

Stefan Des, *The History of Facebook Ads: How Facebook Advertising Evolved in the Last 13 Years* (2017) online: <https://leadsbridge.com/infographic-history-facebook-ads/>.

Summary of Settlements Between Civil Rights Advocates and Facebook, https://www.aclu.org/sites/default/files/field_document/3.18.2019_joint_statement_final_0.pdf

T-PD(2019)01, *Consultative Committee of the Convention for the Protection of Individuals with Regard to Automatic Processing of Personal Data, Convention 108, Guideline on Artificial Intelligence and Data Protection, Guidance for Developers,*

Manufacturers and Service Providers (January 2019), online: COE <https://rm.coe. int/guidelines-on-artificial-intelligence-and-data-protection/168091f9d8>.

TaskRabbit, *The Convenient & Affordable Way to Get Things Done Around the Home* (November 2019), online: TaskRabbit <https://www.taskrabbit.com>.

Twitter, *#airbnbwhileblack* (November 2019), online: twitter <https://twitter.com/ hashtag/airbnbwhileblack?lang=fr>.

Uber, *2020 Investor Presentation* (February 2020), online: Uber <https://s23.q4cdn. com/407969754/files/doc_financials/2019/sr/InvestorPresentation_2020_Feb6. pdf>.

Uber, *Country List* (October 2019) online: Uber <https://www.uber.com/en-BE/country-list/>; and Uber, Uber Works (October 2019) online: Uber <https://www.works. co>.

United Kingdom Government, *Good Work: A Response to the Taylor Review of Modern Working Practices* (February 2018) online: Government UK <assets.publishing. service.gov.uk/government/uploads/system/uploads/attachment_data/file/679767/ 180206_BEIS_Good_Work_Report Accessible_A4_pdf >.

Urteil des Landgerichts Berlin vom 16.01.2018, Az. 16 O 341/15 <https://www.vzbv.de/ sites/default/files/downloads/2018/02/12/facebook_lg_berlin.pdf>.

Villeurbanne, *Testing (tests de discrimination) sur l'accès au prêt immobilier et au prêt à la création d'entreprise réalisé par la ville de Villeurbanne* (July 2017), online: Défenseur des Droits <https://www.defenseurdesdroits.fr/sites/default/files/atoms/ files/170921_synthese_testing_credit_villeurbanne.pdf>.

Vrbo, *List Your Property on Vrbo and Open Your Door to Rental Income* (December 2019), online: VRBO <https://www.vrbo.com>.

Zillow, *Post a For Sale by Owner Listing* (December 2019), online: Zillow <https://www. zillow.com/for-sale-by-owner/>.

ANNEXES

ANNEX 1. AIRBNB EDIT PROFILE PAGE

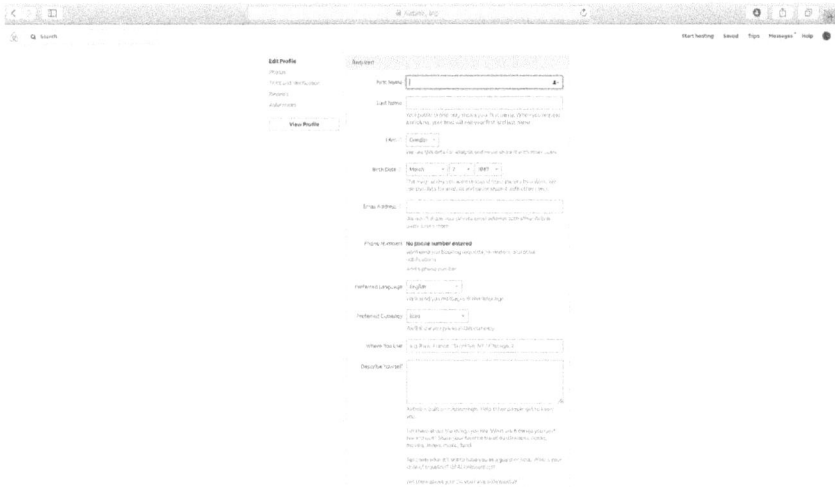

ANNEX 2. AIRBNB PROFILE PHOTO REQUIREMENT PAGE

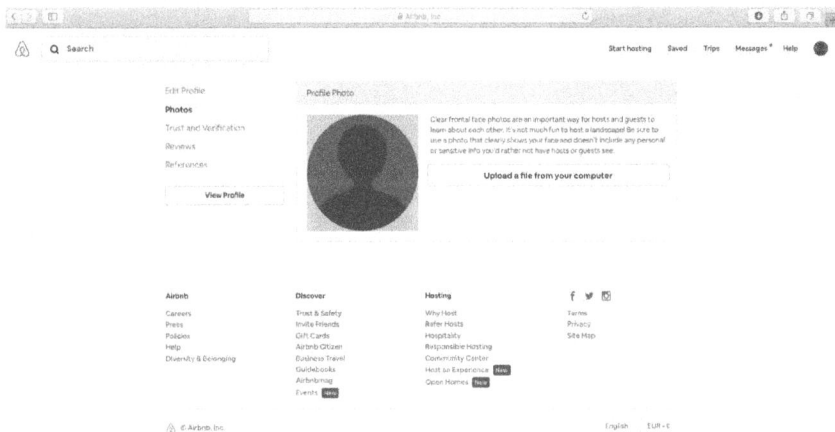

ANNEX 3. AIRBNB TRUST AND VERIFICATION PAGE

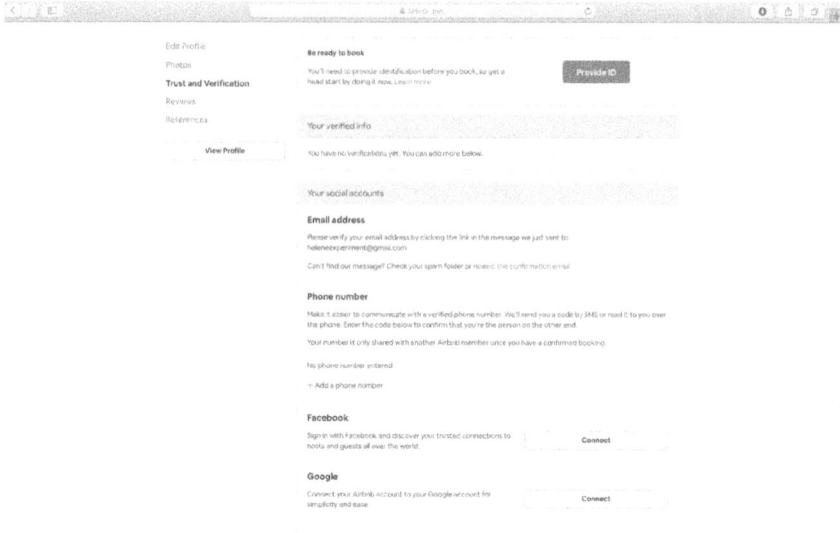

ANNEX 4. AIRBNB FLAGGING PAGE

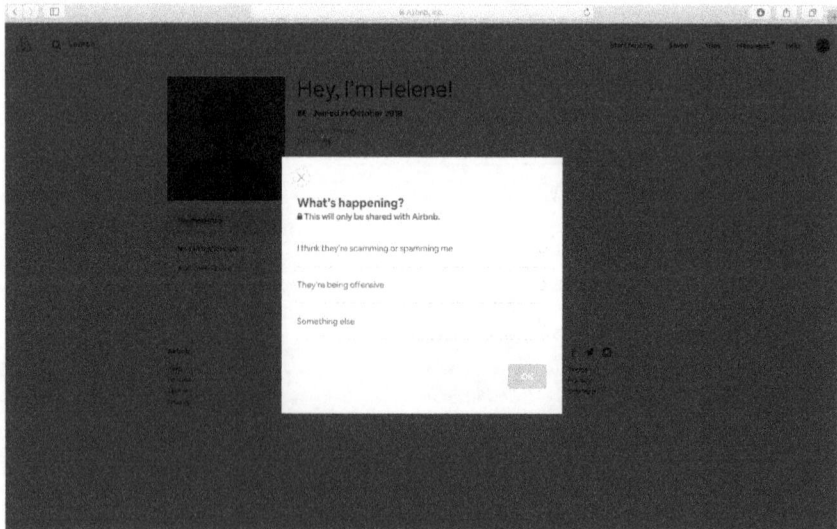

ANNEX 5. AIRBNB REVIEWS PAGE

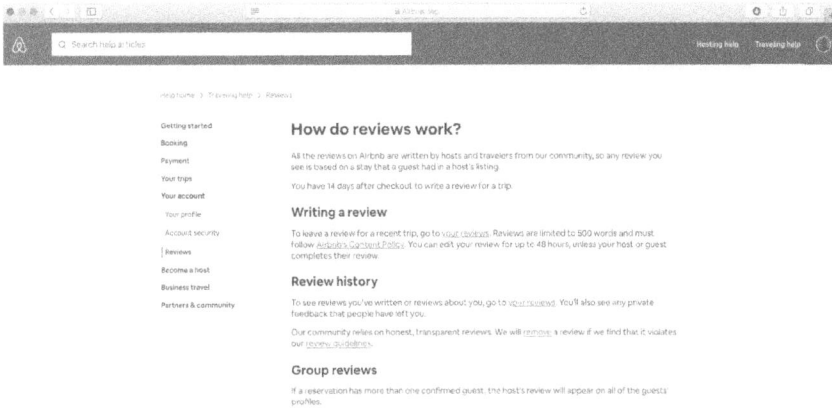

ANNEX 6. AIRBNB COMMUNITY COMMITMENT PAGE

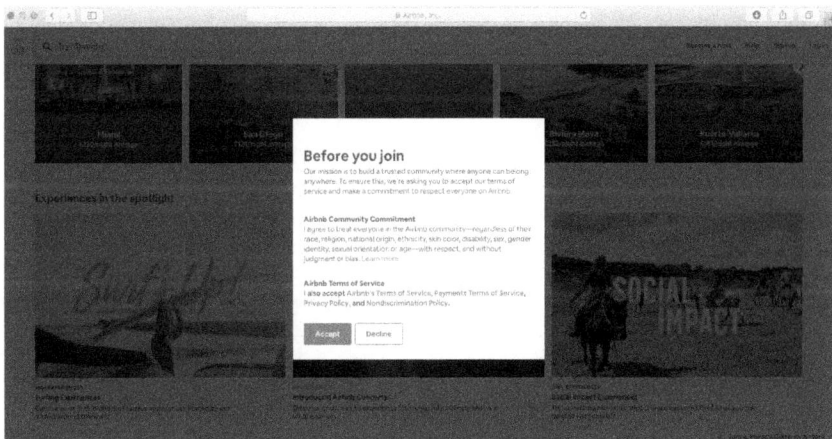

ANNEX 7. AIRBNB PREAPPROVED BOOKING PAGE

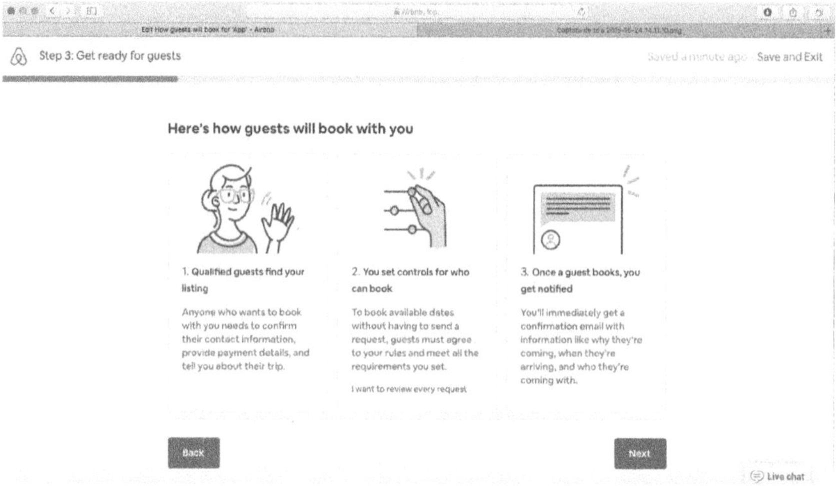

ANNEX 8. AIRBNB ANTIDISCRIMINATION POLICY PAGE

Getting started

Finding a place to stay

Understanding experiences

| Traveling safely

Booking

Payment

Your trips

Your account

Become a host

Business travel

Partners & community

Airbnb's Nondiscrimination Policy: Our Commitment to Inclusion and Respect

Airbnb is, at its core, an open community dedicated to bringing the world closer together by fostering meaningful, shared experiences among people from all parts of the world. Our community includes millions of people from virtually every country on the globe. It is an incredibly diverse community, drawing together individuals of different cultures, values, and norms.

The Airbnb community is committed to building a world where people from every background feel welcome and respected, no matter how far they have traveled from home. This commitment rests on two foundational principles that apply both to Airbnb's hosts and guests: **inclusion and respect**. Our shared commitment to these principles enables every member of our community to feel welcome on the Airbnb platform no matter who they are, where they come from, how they worship, or whom they love. Airbnb recognizes that some jurisdictions permit, or require, distinctions among individuals based on factors such as national origin, gender, marital status or sexual orientation, and it does not require hosts to violate local laws or take actions that may subject them to legal liability. Airbnb will provide additional guidance and adjust this nondiscrimination policy to reflect such permissions and requirements in the jurisdictions where they exist.

- **Inclusion** – We welcome guests of all backgrounds with authentic hospitality and open minds. Joining Airbnb, as a host or guest, means becoming part of a community of inclusion. Bias, prejudice, racism, and hatred have no place on our platform or in our community. While hosts are required to follow all applicable laws that prohibit discrimination based on such factors as race, religion, national origin, and others listed below, we commit to do more than comply with the minimum requirements established by law.
- **Respect** – We are respectful of each other in our interactions and encounters. Airbnb appreciates that local laws and cultural norms vary around the world and expects hosts and guests to abide by local laws, and to engage with each other respectfully, even when views may not reflect their beliefs or upbringings. Airbnb's members bring to our community an incredible diversity of background experiences, beliefs, and customs. By connecting people from different backgrounds, Airbnb fosters greater understanding and appreciation for the common characteristics shared by all human beings and undermines prejudice rooted in misconception, misinformation, or misunderstanding.

Specific Guidance for Hosts in the United States and European Union

As a general matter, we will familiarize ourselves with all applicable federal, state, and local laws that apply to housing and places of public accommodation. Hosts should contact Airbnb customer service if they have any questions about their obligations to comply with this Airbnb Nondiscrimination Policy. Airbnb will release further discrimination policy guidance for jurisdictions outside the United States in the near future. Guided by these principles, our U.S. and EU host community will follow these rules when considering potential guests and hosting guests:

Race, Color, Ethnicity, National Origin, Religion, Sexual Orientation, Gender Identity, or Marital Status

- Airbnb hosts **may not**
  - Decline a guest based on race, color, ethnicity, national origin, religion, sexual orientation, gender identity, or marital status.
  - Impose any different terms or conditions based on race, color, ethnicity, national origin, religion, sexual orientation, gender identity, or marital status.
  - Post any listing or make any statement that discourages or indicates a preference for or against any guest on account of race, color, ethnicity, national origin, religion, sexual orientation, gender identity, or marital status.

Gender Identity

Airbnb does not assign a gender identity to our users. We consider the gender of an individual to be what they identify and/or designate on their user profile.

- Airbnb hosts **may not**:
  - Decline to rent to a guest based on gender <u>unless</u> the host shares living spaces (for example, bathroom, kitchen, or common areas) with the guest.
  - Impose any different terms or conditions based on gender unless the host shares living spaces with the guest.
  - Post any listing or make any statement that discourages or indicates a preference for or against any guest on account of gender, unless the host shares living spaces with the guest.

- Airbnb hosts **may**:
  - Make a unit available to guests of the host's gender and not the other, where the host shares living spaces with the guest.

Age and Familial Status

- Airbnb hosts **may not**:
  - Impose any different terms or conditions or decline a reservation based on the guest's age or familial status, where prohibited by law.
- Airbnb hosts **may**:
  - Provide factually accurate information about their listing's features (or lack of them) that could make the listing unsafe or unsuitable for guests of a certain age or families with children or infants.
  - Note in their listing applicable community restrictions (e.g. senior housing) that prohibit guests under a particular age or families with children or infants.

Disability

- Airbnb hosts **may not**:
  - Decline a guest based on any actual or perceived disability.
  - Impose any different terms or conditions based on the fact that the guest has a disability.
  - Substitute their own judgment about whether a unit meets the needs of a guest with a disability for that of the prospective guest.
  - Inquire about the existence or severity of a guest's disability, or the means used to accommodate any disability. If, however, a potential guest raises his or her disability, a host may, and should, discuss with the potential guest whether the listing meets the potential guest's needs.
  - Prohibit or limit the use of mobility devices.
  - Charge more in rent or other fees for guests with disabilities, including pet fees when the guest has an assistance animal (such as a service or emotional support animal) because of the disability

---

  - Charge more in rent or other fees for guests with disabilities, including pet fees when the guest has an assistance animal (such as a service or emotional support animal) because of the disability.
  - Post any listing or make any statement that discourages or indicates a preference for or against any guest on account of the fact that the guest has a disability.
  - Refuse to communicate with guests through accessible means that are available, including relay operators (for people with hearing impairments) and e-mail (for people with vision impairments using screen readers).
  - Refuse to provide reasonable accommodations, including flexibility when guests with disabilities request modest changes in your house rules, such as bringing an assistance animal that is necessary because of the disability, or using an available parking space near the unit. When a guest requests such an accommodation, the host and the guest should engage in a dialogue to explore mutually agreeable ways to ensure the unit meets the guest's needs.

- Airbnb hosts **may**:
  - Provide factually accurate information about the unit's accessibility features (or lack of them), allowing guests with disabilities to assess for themselves whether the unit is appropriate to their individual needs.

Personal Preferences

- Airbnb hosts **may**:
  - Except as noted above, Airbnb hosts may decline to rent based on factors that are not prohibited by law. For example, except where prohibited by law, Airbnb hosts may decline to rent guests with pets, or to guests who smoke.
  - Require guests to respect restrictions on foods consumed in the listing (e.g., a host who maintains a kosher or vegetarian kitchen may require guests to respect those restrictions). These restrictions should be stated clearly in your house rules.
  - Nothing in this policy prevents a host from turning down a guest on the basis of a characteristic that is not protected under the civil rights laws or closely associated with a protected class. For example, an Airbnb host may turn down a guest who wants to smoke in a unit, or place limits on the number of guests in a unit.

When guests are turned down. Hosts should keep in mind that no one likes to be turned down. While a host may have, and articulate, lawful and legitimate reasons for turning down a potential guest, it may cause that member of our community to feel unwelcome or excluded. Hosts should make every effort to be welcoming to guests of all backgrounds. Hosts who demonstrate a pattern of rejecting guests from a protected class (even while articulating legitimate reasons) undermine the strength of our community by making potential guests feel unwelcome, and Airbnb may suspend hosts who have demonstrated such a pattern from the Airbnb platform.

Specific Guidance for Hosts Outside the United States and European Union

Outside of the United States and the European Union, some countries or communities may allow or even require people to make accommodation distinctions based on, for example, marital status, national origin, gender or sexual orientation, in violation of our general nondiscrimination philosophy. In these cases, we do not require hosts to violate local laws, nor to accept guests that could expose the hosts to a real and demonstrable risk of arrest, or physical harm to their persons or property. Hosts who live in such areas should set out any such restriction on their ability to host particular guests in their listing, so that prospective guests are aware of the issue and Airbnb can confirm the necessity for such an action. In communicating any such restrictions, we expect hosts to use clear, factual, non-derogatory terms. Slurs and insults have no place on our platform or in our community.

ANNEX 9. FACEBOOK FIRST HOMEPAGE

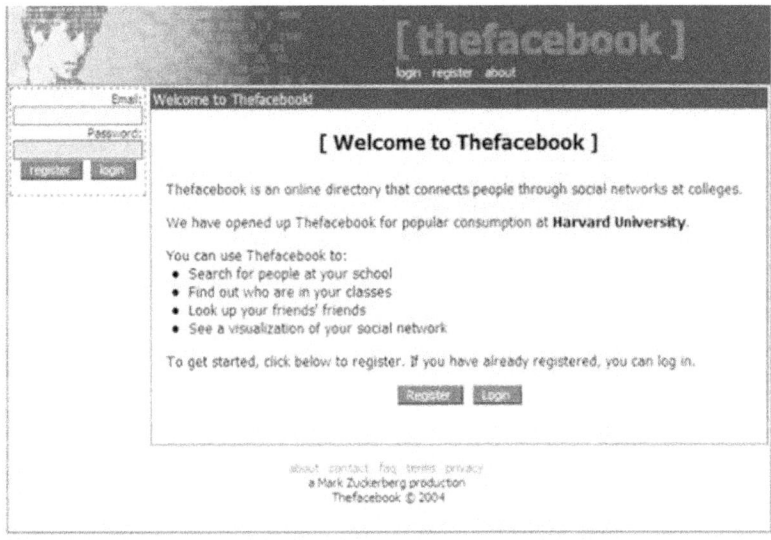

Source: https://www.businessinsider.com/what-facebook-used-to-look-like-2014–2?r=US&IR=T#
          remember-when-facebook-was-called-thefacebook-it-started-at-harvard-and-slowly-opened-
          up-to-other-colleges-1

ANNEX 10. FACEBOOK FIRST PROFILE PAGE

Source: https://www.businessinsider.com/what-facebook-used-to-look-like-2014–2?
r=US&IR=T#back-in-2005-before-the-news-feed-launched-facebook-was-
essentially-just-a-collection-of-disconnected-profiles-4

KU Leuven Centre for IT & IP Law

The KU Leuven Centre for IT & IP Law Series brings together the results of research activities of the Centre for IT & IP Law. The central research themes of the series concern the legal and ethical aspects of information technology, innovation and intellectual property.

Each book in the series focuses on the essential developments in the current legal framework, necessitated by the rapid evolution of technology in various fields, such as government, media, health care, informatics, digital economy, banking, transport and culture. The research is characterised by an interdisciplinary approach, constantly cross-fertilising legal, technical, economic, ethical and socio-cultural perspectives.

Books are published in English, Dutch and/or French.

Recently published in this series:

1. Rán Trygvadóttir, *European Libraries and the Internet: Copyright and Extended Collective Licences*, 2018.
2. Niels Vandezande, *Virtual Currencies*, 2018.
3. Aleksandra Kuczerawy, *Intermediary Liability and Freedom of Expression in the EU: From Concepts to Safeguards*, 2018.
4. Letizia Paoli, Jonas Visschers Cedric Verstraete, Elke van Hellemont, *The Impact of Cybercrime on Belgian Businesses*, 2019.
5. Niels Vandezande, *When An Original Is Not Original. The Originality Requirement in Belgian Law*, 2019.
6. Brendan Van Alsenoy, *Data Protection Law in the EU: Roles, Responsibilities and Liability*, 2019.
7. A. Vedder, J. Schroers, C. Ducuing and P. Valcke (eds.), *Security and Law. Legal and Ethical Aspects of Public Security, Cyber Security and Critical Infrastructure Security*, 2019.
8. M-C. Janssens, *Handboek Merkenrecht*, tweede editie, 2022.
9. KU Leuven Centre for IT & IP Law (ed.), *Rethinking IT and IP Law. Celebrating 30 Years CiTiP*, 2019.
10. Valerie Verdoodt, *Children's Rights and Commercial Communication in the Digital Era*, 2020.
11. Pieter-Jan Aerts, Frank Hoogendijk, Niels Vandezande, *Smart contracts. Een overzicht vanuit juridisch perspectief*, 2020.
12. Griet Verhenneman, *The Patient, Data Protection and Changing Healthcare Models. The impact of e-health on informed consent, anonymisation and purpose limitation*, 2021.
13. Jan De Bruyne en Cedric Vanleenhove, *AI and the Law*, second edition, 2022 (forthcoming).

Lightning Source UK Ltd.
Milton Keynes UK
UKHW051502080223
416688UK00008B/103